Czech Yearbook
of International Law®

Czech Yearbook
of International Law®

Volume V

2014

The Role of Governmental and Non-governmental
Organizations in the 21st Century

Editors

Alexander J. Bělohlávek   **Naděžda Rozehnalová**   **Filip Černý**

Professor
at the VŠB TU
in Ostrava
Czech Republic

Professor
at the Masaryk University
in Brno
Czech Republic

Dr. Iur.
Charles University
in Prague
Czech Republic

JURIS

Questions About This Publication

For assistance with shipments, billing or other customer service matters, please call our Customer Services Department at:
1-631-350-2100

To obtain a copy of this book, call our Sales Department:
1-631-351-5430
Fax: 1-631-351-5712

Toll Free Order Line:
1-800-887-4064 (United States & Canada)
See our web page about this book:
www.jurispub.com

Printed in the United States of America.
ISBN 978-1-57823-344-1
ISSN 2157-2976

Juris Publishing, Inc.
71 New Street
Huntington, New York 11743 U.S.A.
www.jurispub.com

The title *Czech Yearbook of International Law*® as well as the logo
appearing on the cover are protected by EU trademark law.

Typeset in the U.S.A. by Juris Publishing, Inc.

Address for correspondence & manuscripts

Czech Yearbook of International Law®
Jana Zajíce 32, Praha 7, 170 00, Czech Republic

www.czechyearbook.org

Editorial support:
František Halfar, Jan Halfar, Lenka Němečková, Karel Nohava

Impressum

Institutions Participating in the CYIL Project

Academic Institutions within the Czech Republic

Masaryk University (Brno), Faculty of Law,
Department of International and European Law
> [*Masarykova univerzita v Brně, Právnická fakulta,
> Katedra mezinárodního a evropského práva*]

University of West Bohemia in Pilsen, Faculty of Law,
Department of Constitutional Law & Department of International Law
> [*Západočeská univerzita v Plzni, Právnická fakulta,
> Katedra ústavního práva & Katedra mezinárodního práva*]

VŠB – TU Ostrava, Faculty of Economics,
Department of Law
> [*VŠB – TU Ostrava, Ekonomická fakulta, Katedra práva*]

Charles University in Prague, Faculty of Law,
Department of Commercial Law, Department of European Law & Centre for
Comparative Law
> [*Univerzita Karlova v Praze, Právnická fakulta,
> Katedra obchodního práva, katedra evropského práva & Centrum právní
> komparatistiky, PrF UK*]

University College of International and Public Relations Prague
> [*Vysoká škola mezinárodních a veřejných vztahů Praha*]

**Institute of State and Law of the Academy of Sciences of the Czech
Republic, v.v.i.**
> [*Ústav státu a práva Akademie věd ČR, v.v.i.*]

Non-academic Institutions in the Czech Republic

Office of the Government of the Czech Republic,
Department of Legislation, Prague
[*Úřad vlády ČR, Legislativní odbor, Praha*]

Arbitration Court attached to the Economic Chamber of the Czech Republic and Agricultural Chamber of the Czech Republic, Prague
[*Rozhodčí soud při Hospodářské komoře České republiky a Agrární komoře České republiky*]

ICC National Committee Czech Republic, Prague
[*ICC Národní výbor Česká republika, Praha*]

Institutions outside the Czech Republic Participating in the CYIL Project

Austria

University of Vienna [*Universität Wien*],
Department of European, International and Comparative Law,
Section for International Law and International Relations

Poland

Jagiellonian University in Krakow [*Uniwersytet Jagielloński v Krakowie*],
Faculty of Law and Administration,
Department of Private International Law

Slovak Republic

Slovak Academy of Sciences, Institute of State and Law
[*Slovenská akadémia vied, Ústav štátu a práva*], Bratislava

University of Matej Bel in Banská Bystrica
[*Univerzita Mateja Bela v Banskej Bystrici*],
Faculty of Political Sciences and International Relations,
Department of International Affairs and Diplomacy

Trnava University in Trnava [*Trnavská Univerzita v Trnave*],
Faculty of Law, Department of Labour Law and Social Security Law

| | |

Proofreading and translation support provided by: Agentura SPĚVÁČEK, s.r.o., Prague, Czech Republic, and Pamela Lewis, USA.

Contents

Contents

All contributions in this book are subject to academic review.

List of Abbreviations

AML	Anti-Money Laundering
BSA	Bank Secrecy Act
CAHDE	Ad hoc Committee on E-democracy
CAS	Court of Arbitration for Sport
CAT	Committee against Torture
CED	Committee on Enforced Disappearances
CEDAW	Committee on the Elimination of Discrimination against Women
CERD	Committee on the Elimination of Racial Discrimination
CESCR	Committee on Economic, Social and Cultural Rights
CICC	Coalition for the International Criminal Court
CISG	UN Convention on Contracts for the International Sale of Goods
CMW	Committee on Migrant Workers
CRC	Committee on the Rights of the Child
CRPD	Committee on the Rights of Persons with Disabilities
DBO	Conditions of Contract for Design, Build and Operate Projects Gold Book
ECB	European Central Bank
ECOSOC	Economic and Social Council
ECT	Energy Charter Treaty
ECtHR	European Court of Human Rights
ESM	European Stability Mechanism
EU	European Union
Europol	European Police Office
FATF	Financial Action Task Force on Money Laundering
FAU	Financial Analytical Unit of the Ministry of Finance of the Czech Republic

Czech Yearbook of International Law

FBI	Federal Bureau of Investigation
FIDIC	Fédération Internationale des Ingénieurs-Conseils
FIFA	International Football Federation
FIU	Financial Intelligence Unit
FIUs	Financial Intelligence Units
FIUs	Financial Intelligence Units
ICAS	International Council of Arbitration for Sport
ICC	International Criminal Court
ICCPR	International Covenant on Civil and Political Rights
ICESCR	International Covenant on Economic, Social and Cultural Rights
ICM	Inter-Committee Meetings
IFs	International Sports Federations
ILO	International Labour Organisation
INGOs	international non-governmental organizations
IOC	International Olympic Committee
MFN	most-favoured nation treatment clause
NGOs	non-governmental organizations
NHRI	national human rights institutions
NOCs	National Olympic Committees
QUANGOs	quasi non-governmental organizations
SPT	Subcommittee on Prevention of Torture and Other Cruel, Inhuman or Degrading Treatment or Punishment
TB	Treaty bodies
TEU	Treaty on European Union
TFEU	Treaty on the Functioning of the European Union
UN	United Nations
UNIDROIT	International Institute for the Unification of Private Law
UPICC	UNIDROIT Principles for International Commercial Contracts

Articles

Aslan Abashidze

The Process of Strengthening the Human Rights Treaty Body System

Key words:
Treaty Body System | the core international human rights treaties | the intergovernmental process on strengthening of the TB | reporting procedure | calendars of reporting | common core documents | concluding observations | general comments | communications | independence of experts

Abstract | *The human rights treaty bodies, which now number ten, have developed as a system (TB) and occupy a rightful place in the framework of universal human rights. The activities of TBs and their significance are highly appreciated by groups and individuals. Various initiatives which have been undertaken from 1997 to strengthen the Treaty Body System are analyzed in this article. Since the late 1990s, various initiatives have been undertaken to strengthen the TBs. In 2012, the United Nations High Commissioner for Human Rights presented the Report on the strengthening of the human rights treaty bodies. On February 23, 2012, the General Assembly adopted resolution 66/254, entitled the 'Intergovernmental process of the General Assembly on strengthening and enhancing the affective functioning of the human rights treaty body system'. The resolution requests the President of the General Assembly to launch an open-ended intergovernmental process within the framework of the General Assembly, to conduct open, transparent and inclusive negotiations on how to strengthen and enhance the effective functioning of the human rights treaty body system, and to appoint two co-facilitators to assist him in this process. In this article the progress report of the co-facilitators which deals with the key issues of TB's activities is analyzed.*

Prof. Aslan Abashidze
is Doctor of legal sciences programme, Professor of International Law; Head of the Department of International Law, Law Faculty, Peoples' Friendship University of Russia; Professor, International Law Department, Moscow State Institute of International Relations (University) under the Ministry of Foreign Affairs of Russia; Member of the United Nations Committee on Economic, Social and Cultural Rights; Author of more than 350 papers in international law, published in Russia, Belgium, Georgia, Greece, Kazakhstan, Azerbaijan, Italy, Serbia, Switzerland, UK, USA, Uzbekistan, Armenia, etc.
e-mail: abashidze.rudn@gmail.com

| | |

1.01. The human rights treaty bodies, which now number ten,[1] have developed as a system, the human rights treaty body system (TB) and occupy a rightful place in frameworks of universal human rights.

1.02. The TB is based on the core international human rights treaties,[2] which create legal obligations for the States Parties to promote and protect human rights at the national level. Each core international human rights treaty sets up an international body of independent experts to monitor the implementation of its provisions by the States Parties. However, there is one exception: the Committee on economic, Social and Cultural Rights (CESCR) was established by Economic and Social Council (ECOSOC) resolution. Each TB is composed of independent experts with recognized competence in human rights, who are nominated and elected by the States Parties.

1.03. The activities of TBs and their significance are highly appreciated both by academics and at an institutional or governmental level. For example, Professor Christof Heyns and Professor Frans Vijoen both regard TBs as 'custodians of the legal norms established by the human rights treaties'.[3]

1.04. In the foreword to the Report of the United Nations High Commissioner for Human Rights on the strengthening of the human rights treaty bodies, the Secretary-General Ban Ki-moon noted:

> The United Nations human rights treaty body system, which combines noble ideals with practical measures to realize them, is one of the greatest achievements in the history of the global struggle for human rights. The treaty bodies stand at the heart of the international human rights protection system as engines translating universal norms into social justice and individual well being. Using a

---

[1] Human Rights Committee (HR Committee); Committee on Economic, Social and Cultural Rights (CESCR); Committee on the Elimination of Racial Discrimination (CERD); Committee on the Elimination of Discrimination against Women (CEDAW); Committee against Torture (CAT); Committee on the Rights of the Child (CRC); Committee on Migrant Workers (CMW); Committee on the Rights of Persons with Disabilities (CRPD); Committee on Enforced Disappearances (CED); The Subcommittee on Prevention of Torture and other Cruel, Inhuman or Degrading Treatment or Punishment (SPT).

[2] International Convention on the Elimination of All Forms of Racial Discrimination (1965); International Covenant on Civil and Political Rights (1966); International Covenant on Economic, Social and Cultural Rights (1966); Convention on the Elimination of All Forms of Discrimination against Women (1979); Convention against Torture and Other Cruel, Inhuman or Degrading Treatment (1984); Convention on the Rights of the Child (1989); International Convention on the Protection of the Rights of All Migrant Workers and Members of Their Families (1990); International Convention on the Rights of Persons with Disabilities (2006); International Convention for the Protection of All Persons from Enforced Disappearance (2006).

[3] CHRISTOR HEYNS & FRANS VIJOEN, THE IMPACT OF THE UNITED NATIONS HUMAN RIGHTS TREATIES ON THE DOMESTIC LEVEL, Hague: Kluwer Law International (2002).

growing set of tools, this system provides authoritative guidance on human rights standards, advises on how treaties apply in specific cases, and informs States parties of what they must do to ensure that all people enjoy their human rights.[4]

1.05. The Secretary-General also noted the benefits gained by all parties from the work of TBs.

Victims reach out to treaty bodies for redress and reparation through the individual complaints system. Governments depend on them for a greater understanding of their obligations under international human rights law. And the involvement of experts, civil society groups and government representatives in reporting and other processes generates a genuine dialogue at the national level that empowers individuals and improves laws, policies, programmes and institutions.[5]

1.06. Finally, it is appropriate to include an additional quote by the Secretary-General, who said on 2 April 2012:

The treaty bodies constitute a unique framework for dialogue and debate on changes in policy and law that are necessary to improve social justice and equitable development. They guide and assist States to achieve those goals through greater human rights protection.[6]

1.07. The first TB, namely Committee on the Elimination of Racial Discrimination (CERD) was set up on the basis of International Convention on the Elimination of All Forms of Racial Discrimination in 1965. Other TBs have been added since that time. Until 2000, only three TBs were competent to address individual complaints. Now all ten of the TBs have the possibility of receiving individual communications.

1.08. There have been increases in membership in some TBs, bringing the total number of TB experts to 172 in 2013 (versus 97 in 2000). The time allotted for the meetings has also increased – from 51 weeks in 2000 to 74 weeks in 2012.

1.09. States have increased ratification under international human rights treaty bodies. The six core international human rights treaties in force in 2000 attracted 927 ratifications. In 2012, this total increased by over 50% and amounted to 1586 ratifications.

1.10. By the end of the 2011-12 biennium, the TBs reviewed 246 States Parties' reports and over 250 individual complaints.

---

4   UN Doc. A/66/860, 26 June 2012, at 7.
5   Ibid.
6   Ibid., at 16.

1.11. Since the late 1990s, various initiatives have been undertaken to strengthen the TBs. The relevant provisions were reflected in the writings of independent expert Philip Alston's final report of 1997 on enhancing the long-term effectiveness of the United Nations human rights treaty system.[7] They were also outlined in the Secretary-General's report of 2002 on the strengthening of the United Nations 'An Agenda for Further Change' and in two meetings on reform of the human rights treaty bodies in 2003 and 2006 (Malbun I and II).

1.12. The former High Commissioner, Louise Arbour, in her 2005 Plan of Action put forward a proposal for a unified standing treaty body.[8] Although this proposal was not adopted, it stimulated sustained movement among TB membership to harmonize the working methods and procedures of the TBs, mainly through Inter-Committee Meetings (ICM) and Chairpersons Meetings between 2006 and 2009.

1.13. The new process was initiated by High Commissioner Navanethem Pillay in 2009. This initiative was based on the mandate given to her by the GA Res. 48/141 to 'rationalize, adapt, strengthen and streamline the UN machinery in the field of human rights with a view to improving its efficiency and effectiveness',[9] and to enhance the visibility, accessibility and impact of the TB system.

1.14. The treaty body strengthening process benefited from many consultations that took place among different actors, including TB experts, States, national human rights institutions (NHRI), non-governmental organizations (NGO), civil society and United Nations entities. Main consultations of stakeholders on TB strengthening include the following:

- Dublin consultation for treaty body members organized by the University of Nottingham (November 2009);
- Marrakesh consultation for National Human Rights Institutions organized by the National Human Rights Commission of Morocco (June 2010);
- Poznan consultation for treaty body members organized by the Adam Mickiewicz University (October 2010);
- Seoul consultation for civil society organizations organized by the National Human Rights Commission of Korea (April 2011);
- Dublin II consultation organized by the University of Nottingham (November 2011);
- consultation with UN entities and specialized agencies organized by OHCHR in Geneva and New York (November 2011);

---

[7] UN Doc. E/CN.4/1997/74.

[8] UN Doc. HRI/MC/2006/2, 22 March 2006.

[9] UN Doc. A/RES/48/141, 20 December 1993, para. 4 (j)

- second consultation with States Parties in Geneva organized by OHCHR (7-8 February 2012)
- and others.

1.15. The main challenges confronting the TB system are as follows. First of all there is the issue of non-compliance with reporting obligations. Along with the nine core international human rights treaties, there are two Optional Protocols known as the Optional Protocol to the Convention on the Rights of the Child on the involvement of children in armed conflict or CRC-OPAC, and the Optional Protocol to the Convention on the Rights of the Child on the sale of Children, child prostitution and child pornography or CRC-OPSC. All of these establish a reporting obligation for the States Parties. The average reporting period under the nine core international human rights treaties is between four and five years. If a State ratifies all nine treaties and two optional protocols it is bound to submit approximately 20 reports to the TB in the time frame of 10 years, i.e. two a year.

1.16. The increase in ratifications has not been matched by a proportionate increase in the number of reports submitted by the States Parties. There were 102 in 2000, when there were 927 States Parties in total, and 136 in 2011, when there were 1508 States Parties in total .

1.17. The reporting includes a national process followed by a meeting between the State Party and the experts of the TB in Geneva during a constructive dialogue. Today, very few of the States Parties to the core international human rights treaties are called upon to strictly adhere to the timeline established under each treaty. Only 16% of the reports due in 2010 and 2011 were submitted in strict accordance with the due dates established in the treaties or by TBs.

1.18. With such a high level of non-compliance with reporting obligations, TBs have established an ad hoc schedule of work based on the submission of reports by States as they come in. As a consequence, a State that complies with its reporting obligations faithfully will be reviewed more frequently by the concerned TB compared to a State that adheres less faithfully to its obligations. Therefore, non-compliance generates differential treatment of States.

1.19. Under some treaties such as International Covenant on Economic, Social and Cultural Rights of 1966 (ICESCR), Convention against Torture and Other Cruel, Inhuman or Degrading Treatment or Punishment (CAT) and International Covenant on Civil and Political Rights (ICCPR), around 20% of the States Parties have never submitted an initial report. For others such as the ICRMW, CRPD and the two Optional Protocols to the CRC, the figure is even higher. In other words, a significant proportion of ratifications have never resulted in a report or a review.

1.20. As of April 2012, 626 State Party reports were overdue. If the trend of ratification growth or the establishment of new treaty bodies continues, this figure will increase.

1.21. Even at this level of non-compliance TBs face backlogs amounting to a total of 281 State Party reports pending consideration (as of March 2012). As a result, as it presently operates, the States Parties that invest the time to prepare their reports are made to wait for the holding of a constructive dialogue for years after their submissions.

1.22. We should also take into consideration the issue of more general reporting obligations. There are also other reporting obligations of States in a large variety of other areas of work of the United Nations, such as Universal Periodic Review, the Millennium Development Goals (MDGs), environment, labour rights, and sustainable development. In addition to their expanding reporting duties at the regional level, these obligations leave most States acutely challenged to keep pace.

1.23. The next challenge confronting the TB system deals with the considerations of individual communications and the increasing number of petitions (an average of 480 individual communications pending in 2011) which has led to significant delays in this procedure. For instance, for the HR Committee, with 333 pending cases, the average time lag between registration and final decision on a case is around three and a half years. This has a negative impact on petitioners who face a long wait before their case is decided upon, and on the States Parties who are often faced with a Committee's request for implementation of interim measures over a long period of time.

1.24. It should also be noted that some States do not cooperate with TBs despite frequent reminders to submit their comments on the individual communications, thereby further delaying the consideration of the complaint.[10]

1.25. The next challenge confronting TBs deals with resources. Support provided by Office of the High Commissioner for Human Rights to TBs is currently drawn from two sources: the United Nations regular budget and voluntary contributions. Thus, in 2010-2011, the regular budget provided 76% of the total $39.3 million in resources. From the regular budget allocations, some $12.1 million was used to fund the travel of members to TB sessions, and $17.6 million went to OHCHR, mainly for the staff to support the work of TBs. In addition, $9.6 million was made available from voluntary contributions, to increase the level of support provided to TBs.

---

[10] UN Doc. A/66/860, 26 June 2012, at 23.

1.26. While TB members do not receive a salary for their work, the United Nations covers the cost of their travel and stay to participate in the sessions of TBs. This accounts for a large percentage of the overall costs of TBs. The budget increased from $4.3 million for the biennium 2000-2001 to $12.1 million for the biennium 2010-2011, due to the increase from 74 experts in 2000 to 172 experts in 2011. Those numbers increased further for 2012-2013, reflecting the creation of new TBs. Meanwhile, the actual costs have outpaced this increase in the approved budget leading to revised appropriations. At this stage the Human Rights Treaties Division has 61 Professionals and 22 General Service posts, including 40 Professional posts.

1.27. A workload analysis conducted in 2010 found a 30% gap between the number of Human Rights Officers required and the number in place supporting TB sessions. The reasons for this shortfall can be attributed to the fact that the TBs have not received full and adequate resources from the outset and only in a few cases was this situation re-evaluated. To clearly establish the appropriate number of posts to provide an adequate level of support today, an updated review of the current and projected workload should be undertaken once decisions are made on this report. In principal, the resources allocated to TBs should be commensurate with the task they have been mandated to fulfil and drawn from the regular budget of the United Nations, given that TB functions are core mandated activities.

1.28. The consistent under-resourcing of the TB system over many years has reached a stage where the status quo can no longer be sustained; failure to confront the issue poses a threat to the future of the system. When a treaty mechanism must function despite an 84 % rate of non-compliance in reporting, serious measures are in order.

1.29. The United Nations High Commissioner for Human Rights presented the Report on the strengthening of the human rights treaty bodies[11] pursuant to GA Resolution 66/254. The Report is based on proposals made by a variety of actors.

1.30. In the Introduction of the Report, the UN High Commissioner for Human Rights mentioned the key principles dealing with this process:

- The ultimate objective of this process was to take stock of the challenges and improve the impact of TBs on the States Parties and individuals or groups of individuals at the national level by strengthening their work while fully respecting their independence.
- The process sought to heighten awareness among all stakeholders of the challenges facing the system and to stimulate the formulation of concrete suggestions on how to address these challenges.

---

[11] UN Doc. A/66/860, 26 June 2012.

- The process sought to bring about gradual improvements and harmonization of working methods of TBs and OHCHR in its support for their work.
- The process aimed at 'strengthening' rather than 'reforming' the TB system.
- The process is based on the promise that the legal parameters of core international human rights treaties should not be altered. The proposals must respect these treaties and not require treaty amendments.

1.31. This Report contains several proposals. These include:

- establishing a comprehensive reporting calendar ensuring strict compliance with human rights treaties and equal treatment of all the States Parties;
- enhancing independence and impartiality of members, and strengthening the election process;
- establishing a structured and sustained approach to capacity building for State Parties for their reporting duties;
- ensuring continued consistency of TB jurisprudence in individual communications,
- increasing coordination among TBs in their work on individual communications and their adoption of common guidelines on procedural questions;
- increasing accessibility and visibility of the TB system, through web-casting of public meetings and the use of other new technologies;
- establishing a simplified focused reporting procedure to assist State Parties in meeting their reporting obligations with cost savings both for them and the UN while maintaining the quality of the process;
- aligning other working methods to the maximum extent without contradicting the normative specificities of the treaties and
- limiting the length of documentation.

1.32. The Report of the UN High Commissioner for Human Rights reminds that States' primary responsibility is to ensure the implementation of the principles of the universality and the indivisibility of human rights. This requires that States ratify treaties, but, more importantly, implement them. It also requires a strong TB system conducting regularly periodic, non-politicized, non-discriminatory and expert-led independent reviews of all State Parties, without selectivity or double standards, in line with their legally binding obligations to realize human rights for all, and enhancing the protection of individuals and groups from alleged violations of their rights. The UN High Commissioner for Human Rights underlined the above mentioned vision with the aim to put an end to ad hoc solutions and to introduce a sustainable system, once and for all.

1.33.   On February 23, 2012, the General Assembly adopted resolution 66/254, entitled 'Intergovernmental process of the General Assembly on strengthening and enhancing the affective functioning of the human rights treaty body system'.

1.34.   The resolution requests the President of the General Assembly to launch an open-ended intergovernmental process within the framework of the General Assembly. The aim of the process is to conduct open, transparent and inclusive negotiations on how to strengthen and enhance the effective functioning of the human rights treaty body system. Under the resolution the President appoints two co-facilitators to assist him in this process. The President of the General Assembly appointed Permanent Representatives of Iceland and Tunisia in the UN, in New York to co-facilitate the process.

1.35.   The General Assembly extended the intergovernmental process three times. It was last extended to the first half of February 2014, in order to finalize the elaboration of an outcome of the intergovernmental process.

1.36.   The co-facilitators have had numerous consultations, including informal meetings with Member States, informal briefings and meetings with delegations, human rights treaty bodies, civil society, meetings with the Chairs of TBs and others.

1.37.   The co-facilitators introduced the draft resolution and presented their progress report containing the elements for a substantive resolution. Surinam, on behalf of the Caribbean Community and Common Market (CARICOM), expressed regret that an agreement on a substantive outcome had not been reached at the 67th session and expressed hope that the process would be finalized at the 68th session. The group requested that the cost-assessment include the new provisions on capacity building in the substantive resolution. Switzerland, Liechtenstein, New Zealand, the USA, Australia, the EU and El Salvador, on behalf of the like-minded Latin American group, jointly praised the work of the co-facilitators and noted with regret that the process could not be completed, emphasizing the importance of finalizing the process in February 2014 to enable the treaty bodies to carry out their work in an effective and efficient manner and with the necessary resources. Several delegates underscored the importance of the cost assessment to achieve a comprehensive outcome. The Russian Federation (on behalf of the Cross Regional Group) emphasized that the root causes of the challenges faced by the TBs were not solely linked to resources. Expressing doubts on the February deadline, the

Russian Federation noted that the main goal was not a quick outcome, but a meaningful and holistic one.

1.38. The progress report of the co-facilitators dealt with 32 issues most of which correlate with the proposals put forward in the High Commissioner's report. The issues are put forward in no particular order and without prejudice to their importance.[12]

1.39. The main suggestions of the co-facilitators for a resolution are that it:

- encourages the human rights treaty bodies to continue enhancing their efforts towards achieving greater efficiency, transparency, effectiveness and harmonization through their working methods;

- encourages the treaty bodies to continue to review good practices regarding the application of rules of procedure and methods of work in their on-going efforts towards strengthening and enhancing their effective functioning;

- encourages the human rights treaty bodies to offer a simplified reporting procedure and to set a limit to the number of the questions;

- encourages State Parties to consider submitting a Common Core Document and update it as required through a comprehensive update;

- decides that the annual reports of treaty bodies will not reproduce documents published separately and referenced therein;

- encourages the treaty bodies to adopt an aligned methodology for the constructive dialogue between State Parties and the treaty bodies, bearing in mind the specificity of the respective committees and their specific mandates, with a view to making the dialogue more effective, maximizing the use of the time available and allowing for a more interactive and productive dialogue with State Parties;

- encourages the treaty bodies to adopt short, focused and concrete concluding observations and to this end, further encourages them to develop common guidelines for the elaboration of such concluding observations, bearing in mind the specificity of the respective committees and their specific mandates as well as the views of the State Parties;

- encourages State Parties to continue their efforts to nominate experts of recognized competence and experience in the field covered by the relevant treaty;

- encourages State Parties to consider equitable geographical distribution, representation of the different forms of civilization and

---

12   See UN Doc. A/67/995, 16 September 2013, Annex II.

of the principal legal systems, balanced gender representation and participation of experts with disabilities as stipulated in the relevant human rights instruments, during the election of treaty body experts;

- encourages the treaty bodies to develop an aligned consultation process for the elaboration of general comments that provides for consultations with all stakeholders on new general comments;
- decides to establish page limits for all documentation produced by the treaty bodies, in line with the established practice for other United Nations documentation, such as for individual communications, list of issues, concluding observations, annual reports, general comments, decisions and views;
- decides to establish page limits for all State Party documentation submitted to the treaty body system, including the State Party reports, for initial reports (60 pages), and subsequent periodic reports (40 pages) and common core documents (80 pages), as endorsed by the treaty bodies;
- requests the Secretary-General to strengthen the capacity of the Office of the High Commissioner for Human Rights to support State Parties to increase compliance with reporting obligations, including through providing the necessary staff for the coordination of capacity building and the necessary technical support assistance to State Parties, funded from the regular budget;
- decides in principle, with the aim to enhance the accessibility and visibility of treaty bodies and in line with the report of the Committee on Information, to establish webcasting, as soon as feasible, of the public meetings of the treaty bodies and requests the Department of Public Information to report on the feasibility of providing in all official languages of the United Nations provided in the respective Committee, live webcasts and video archives of relevant meetings of the human rights treaty bodies;
- decides that the treaty bodies can meet in dual chambers as an exceptional and temporary measure when necessitated by the work load of the Committee, within the resources allocated by the General Assembly and reaffirms its view that it is the responsibility of the chairpersons of each committee to ensure the balance between the chambers with regard to geographical and gender balance, as well as the professional background of the experts;
- decides that the allocation of meeting time and correspondent services will be guided by the number of ratifications to the respective human rights instruments in a way that provides for a full review of reporting obligations of States Parties under the

treaties over a period of 6 years and allows for the consideration of individual communications within a reasonable delay, under the assumption that each committee will consider at least 2.5 reports per week;

- decides, based on the above principle, starting from 2014 to authorize:
  a) 9 weeks of total meeting time for the Committee on the Rights of Persons with Disabilities;
  b) 11 weeks of total meeting time for the Committee against Torture;
  c) 12 weeks of total meeting time for the Committee for the Elimination of Racial Discrimination;
  d) 11 weeks of total meeting time for the Committee for Economic, Social and Cultural Rights;
  e) 15 weeks of total meeting time for the Committee for the Rights of the Child;
  f) 14 weeks of total meeting time for the Committee on the Elimination against Women;
  g) 13 weeks of total meeting time for the Human Rights Committee;
- decides to allocate a maximum of three working languages for the work of the treaty bodies, while on an exceptional basis a fourth official language could be provided, as determined by the committee concerned, taking into account that these measures will not be seen as a precedent, given the special nature of the treaty bodies;
- decides, as an exceptional measure and with a view to achieving greater compliance with reporting obligations by the States Parties and eliminating the current backlog of reports, that States Parties should, as applicable and with the agreement of the relevant treaty body, submit one combined report which shall be deemed to satisfy the reporting obligations of that State Party to the relevant treaty body for the entire time period for which reports to that treaty body are currently outstanding at the time of adoption of this resolution;
- further decides, as an exceptional measure and with a view to achieving greater compliance with reporting obligations by the States Parties and eliminating the current backlog of reports, that, without prejudice to the existing practices of the human rights treaty bodies or to the right of a State Party to provide, or a treaty body to request, a short addendum for the purpose of reflecting significant and relevant recent national developments, all State Party reports which, as of the date of this resolution, have been submitted and are awaiting consideration by a treaty body shall be

deemed to satisfy the reporting obligation of the State Party concerned to the relevant treaty body in respect of their next due report as of the date of this resolution and will be subsumed under the next scheduled review;

• decides to consider the status of the treaty body system no later than six years from the date of adoption of this resolution, to ensure the sustainability of measures taken.

1.40. Among key suggestions of the co-facilitators for a resolution, was a recommendation that the Economic and Social Council consider replacing the existing procedure for the election of experts to the Committee on Economic, Social and Cultural rights, set forward in ECOSOC Resolution 17/1985, by a meeting of State Parties to the Covenant on Economic, Social and Cultural Rights.

1.41. On the one hand, this proposal is consistent with the general rule according to which members of other treaty bodies, i.e., experts from other committees, are elected by the State Parties to respective international conventions. Thus, members of the Committee on economic, social and cultural rights must also be elected by the States Parties to the International Covenant on Economic, Social and Cultural Rights.

1.42. On the other hand, the above-mentioned proposal does not take into consideration the fact that human rights issues gradually prove to be under control of the UN General Assembly. Moreover, the Human Rights Council, subordinated to the UN General Assembly, claims to be one of the main bodies of the UN which in practice could weaken the authority of ECOSOC which focuses on the similar issues, regulated by the International Covenant on Economic, Social and Cultural Rights. All things considered, the above-mentioned proposal seems premature.

| | |

Summaries

DEU [*Prozess zur Stärkung des Systems der Menschenrechtsvertragsorgane*]
Die bisher auf der Grundlage von internationalen Menschenrechtsabkommen geschaffenen zehn Menschenrechtsvertragsorgane bilden ein System (UN Treaty Bodies) und nehmen eine vollgültige Stellung innerhalb des Systems des globalen Schutzes der Menschenrechte ein. Die Aktivitäten der Menschenrechtsvertragsorgane und deren Bedeutung kommen vielen Gruppierungen, aber auch konkreten Einzelpersonen zugute. Der vorliegende Artikel befasst sich mit einer Reihe von Initiativen, die seit 1997 in Angriff genommen wurden, um das System der

Menschenrechtsvertragsorgane zu stärken. Seit dem Ende der 1990er ist eine Reihe derartiger Initiativen auf den Weg gebracht worden und im Jahre 2012 veröffentlichte die UN-Hochkommissarin für Menschenrechte ihren Bericht über die Stärkung der Menschenrechtsvertragsorgane. Am 23. Februar 2012 verabschiedete die Generalversammlung die Resolution Nr. 66/254 unter der Bezeichnung Zwischenstaatlicher Prozess der Generalversammlung zur Stärkung und Verbesserung der wirksamen Arbeitsweise des Systems der Menschenrechtsvertragsorgane. In dieser wird dem Vorsitzenden der Generalversammlung auferlegt, offene, transparente und alle Seiten einbeziehende Verhandlungen über die Möglichkeiten zur Stärkung und Verbesserung der wirksamen Arbeitsweise des Systems der Menschenrechtsvertragsorgane zu führen. Die Resolution erlaubt ihm außerdem die Beiziehung zweier weiterer Personen ("Ko-Moderatoren"), die ihm bei der Umsetzung dieser Aufgaben behilflich sein sollen. Der vorliegende Beitrag befasst sich mit den Ergebnissen der Arbeit dieser Personen an den Schlüsselfragen des institutionalisierten Systems zum Schutz der Menschenrechte.

CZE **[Proces posilování systému institucí vytvořených mezinárodními smlouvami na ochranu lidských práv]**
Instituce existující na základě smluv na ochranu lidských práv, kterých je doposud deset, tvoří systém (TB) a zaujímají právoplatné místo v systému globální ochrany lidských práv. Aktivity TB a jejich význam oceňují jak mnohá uskupení, tak konkrétní fyzické osoby. Tento článek se zabývá řadou iniciativ realizovaných za účelem podpory systému institucí vytvořených mezinárodními smlouvami od roku 1997. Právě od konce 90. let minulého století byla realizována řada takových iniciativ. V roce 2012 pak Vysoký komisař OSN pro lidská práva zveřejnil zprávu o posilování systému institucích vytvořených mezinárodními smlouvami za účelem podpory lidských práv. Dne 23. února 2012 přijalo Valné shromáždění rezoluci 66/254 označenou jako "Mezivládní postupy realizované Valným shromážděním při zlepšování institucionálního systému vytvořeného úmluvami na ochranu lidských práv". Tato rezoluce ukládá Předsedovi Valného shromáždění vést otevřená, transparentní a široká jednání o možnostech posílení a rozšíření efektivního fungování tohoto systému. Současně mu tato rezoluce umožňuje přibrání dvou osob, které mají být nápomocny při plnění těchto úloh Předsedy Valného shromáždění. Tento příspěvek se zabývá právě výsledky činnosti těchto osob ve vztahu ke klíčovým otázkám institucionálního systému zaměřeného na ochranu lidských práv.

POL [*Proces wzmacniania systemu instytucji utworzonych na mocy międzynarodowych umów dotyczących ochrony praw człowieka*] *Niniejszy artykuł poświęcono rożnym inicjatywom realizowanym od 1997 roku w celu wspierania zinstytucjonalizowanej ochrony praw człowieka. Szczególna uwaga poświęcona jest raportowi Wysokiej Komisarz NZ ds. Praw Człowieka, opublikowanemu w 2012 roku i dotyczącemu zinstytucjonalizowanego systemu ochrony praw człowieka utworzonego na mocy konwencji międzynarodowych oraz kwestii trwającego procesu międzyrządowego na platformie Zgromadzenia Ogólnego. Artykuł zawiera szczegółową analizę kluczowych wyników tego procesu, zgodnie z treścią raportów m.in. osób działających z upoważnienia przewodniczącego Zgromadzenia Ogólnego do realizacji zadań w tym zakresie, nałożonych przez Rezolucję Zgromadzenia Ogólnego.*

FRA [*Le renforcement du système des organes créés au nom des traités internationaux des droits de l'homme*] *On s'intéresse ici aux différentes initiatives prises depuis 1997 visant à apporter un soutien aux organes de traités sur les droits de l'homme. On a apporté la plus grande attention au rapport publié en 2012 par le Haut-Commissariat aux droits de l'homme des Nations Unies sur le système des organes de traités sur les droits de l'homme et aux questions du processus intergouvernemental mise en place par l'Assemblée générale de l'ONU sur le renforcement de ces organes. On a analysé ici avec le plus grand soin les principaux résultats de ce processus tels qu'ils sont présentés dans les rapports des personnes chargées d'aider le président de l'Assemblée générale de l'ONU à remplir les missions fixées dans ce domaine par les résolutions de l'Assemblée générale.*

RUS [*Процесс укрепления системы договорных органов по правам человека*] *В статье анализируются различные инициативы, которые предпринимаются с 1997 г., по укреплению системы договорных органов по правам человека. Особое внимание уделено рассмотрению Доклада об усилении договорных органов по правам человека, подготовленного Верховным комиссаром по правам человека ООН в 2012 г., и открытого межправительственного процесса, запущенного в рамках ГА ООН. Детально проанализированы основные аспекты прогрессивного доклада, представленного сопредседателями межправительственного процесса, а также основные элементы предполагаемого итогового документа этого неправительственного процесса.*

ESP [*El proceso de refuerzo del sistema de instituciones creadas mediante acuerdos internacionales para la protección de los derechos humanos*]

El artículo examina las diferentes iniciativas llevadas a cabo desde 1997 a fin de apoyar la protección institucionalizada de los derechos humanos. Se dedica una atención especial al informe de la Alta Comisionada de Naciones Unidas para los Derechos Humanos publicado en 2012 sobre el sistema institucional de protección de los derechos humanos, creado mediante tratados internacionales, así como a las cuestiones del proceso intergubernamental en curso en la plataforma de la Asamblea General. El artículo incluye un minucioso análisis de los resultados más relevantes de este proceso tal y como aparecen contenidos en los informes de las personas provistas del apoyo del Presidente de la Asamblea General para hacer cumplir los cometidos impuestos por la Resolución de la Asamblea General en este ámbito.

|||

Jaroslav Valerievich Antonov

Legal Instruments of E-democracy for the Development of Civil Society in International Practice

Key words:
e-democracy | civil society
| practices of e-democracy
| instruments of
e-democracy | tools of
e-democracy | private
interests | e-voting
| e-governance
e-participation |
information and legal
environment

Abstract | The historical development of civil society is accompanied by the ever-increasing need to improve the participation of citizens. The structures of civil society pursue the private interests of citizens and their ability to express their opinions. The greatest development of civil society is not just establishing democratic regimes, but also providing real opportunities for citizens to express their opinions, interact with public authorities to realise their subjective rights and legal interests and establish mechanisms for a productive and systematic cooperation between the state, society, individual citizens and organisations to solve current and prospective issues. E-democracy is a fairly well-known notion, but because of its multidimensional nature, it is generally insufficiently studied. The Council of Europe in 2009 defined the basic legal parameters of e-democracy, including improving people's participation in democratic processes, transparency and public accountability, remote communication and electronic workflow. Different practices of e-democracy after 2009 were increased and transformed substantially, covering many different areas of private interests, which suggest the direct influence of e-democracy on the development of civil society.

Jaroslav Valerievich Antonov is a practicing lawyer. He is also a lecturer in the Department of Constitutional Law of the North-west Institute of the Russian Presidential Academy of National Economy and Public Administration.
e-mail: reoverclock@gmail.com

I. Introduction

2.01. Currently, almost every politician believes that the core value of democracy is to ensure majority rule.[1] E-democracy concepts do not dispute this position; they actively expand and refine it. There are several major issues that confront modern democracy. How have major errors affected modern democratic procedures? Does it provide a real power of the majority and in what ways? E-democracy provides responses to these questions that arise from implementing democracy in each state. There are two extreme positions on the issue. According to the first position, e-democracy is a new remote method of interaction between citizens and public authorities on the provision of public services. In the framework of the concept, the notion of 'e-democracy' has some similarities with the notion of 'e-government'. In this case, the legal position of the state is not subject to change.

2.02. According to the second position, e-democracy is a direct method of power by the people, 'direct democracy', by means of remote electronic voting. The state, in this case, is the executor of decisions of the people. Therefore, its legal standing, legal status, constitutional and legal principles of separation of powers and other fundamental constitutional ideas are put in doubt.

2.03. Depending on the chosen approach, there are various legal issues relating to the non-compliance with the requirements of current law. For example, the constitutional legislative procedure can change as it would introduce the people or a group of people as a dominate subject in this procedure. It can also involve a redistribution of the main power to legislate to the people.

2.04. One issue is the constitutionality of certain provisions of the concept of e-democracy or its indirect inconsistencies, specifically those where the performance of a legal act cannot fully comply with its meaning. There are differences between the legal act and the procedure for its application. There are for example, legal uncertainties in its regulation, the procedure for implementing certain provisions, the technological impossibility of complying with all legal requirements, information security problems and social problems.

2.05. The development of civil society can be directly related to the development of e-democracy, and in this sense it is particularly important to consider the content and prospects of e-democracy in international practice.

---

[1]　See http://usinfo.org/enus/government/overview/docs/ang.pdf (accessed on 10 October 2013).

2.06.   The development of democracy has led to the need to implement a more direct participation and ensure the legitimacy of decisions made to the formation of the 'system of deliberative democracy'. Basically, the idea of deliberative democracy laid the foundations of modern concepts of e-democracy.

II. Legal Practices and E-democracy Instruments: Definitions

2.07.   The practices of e-democracy after 2009 have increased substantially and there are some common characteristic that will sum up each aspect of the electronic environment.

2.08.   E-government ensures effective remote interaction between the executive bodies of the state on the one hand and all interested parties on the other hand. This is about the organization of transparent, understandable and accessible work of the executive power.

2.09.   E-mediation ensures effective remote interaction between stakeholders about a qualified pre-trial settlement of conflicts and disputes.[2]

2.10.   E-environment ensures effective remote interaction between the government and all stakeholders in civil society about the effective and efficient use of natural resources and control in this area.

2.11.   E-referendum ensures effective remote interaction between the state and municipalities and citizens about the organization and conduct of the referendum.

2.12.   E-election ensures effective remote interaction between the state and municipalities and citizens on the other hand about the organization and conduct of elections.

2.13.   E-voting ensures effective remote and other interaction between the state and municipalities and citizens about a vote by using electronic tools.

2.14.   E-parliament ensures effective remote interaction between the legislative bodies of the state and all interested parties about the organization of transparent, understandable and accessible work of the legislative power.

2.15.   E-legislation ensures effective remote interaction between the state and all interested parties about the participation of all stakeholders in the legislative process in one form or another.

2.16.   E-justice electronic environment that ensures effective remote interaction between the judicial authorities of the state and all interested parties about the organization of a transparent, understandable and accessible judicial power.

---

[2]   See https://e-justice.europa.eu/content_mediation-62-en.do (accessed on 10 October 2013).

2.17. E-initiative ensures effective remote interaction between the state and municipalities and citizens and other interested parties about the submission and consideration of civil initiatives for some socially important issues.

2.18. E-consultation ensures effective remote interaction between the state and municipalities and citizens about the identification of public opinion, and discusses ways to address socially important issues.

2.19. E-petitioning ensures effective remote interaction between the state and municipalities and citizens about the submission and consideration of collective complaints of some socially important issues.[3]

2.20. E-campaigning ensures effective remote interaction between all stakeholders about the mass of information or about a campaign to draw attention to something, such as. Elections issues.

2.21. E-polling ensures effective remote interaction between state municipalities and all interested parties about the identification of the views of interested parties who have voted on any matter.

2.22. E-surveying[4] ensures effective remote interaction between all stakeholders about the reviews and surveys on any subject using a variety of methods.

2.23. E-Municipalities[5] ensure effective remote interaction between municipalities and all interested parties about the organization of transparent, understandable and accessible work of municipal authorities.

2.24. E-mobilization[6] ensures effective remote interaction between all interested parties about the awareness of the existence of any of the features, as well as the need to use them, such as information about a petition.[7]

2.25. E-business ensures effective remote interaction between government and business representatives about the effective implementation of economic activity, including international trade and investment in the private sector.

---

[3] See http://www.change.org/petition (accessed on 10 October 2013); http://www.ipetitions.com/ (accessed on 10 October 2013).

[4] Recommendation CM/Rec (2009)1 of the Committee of Ministers to Member States on electronic democracy (e-democracy), available at: http://www.coe.int/t/dgap/democracy/Activities/GGIS/CAHDE/2009/RecCM2009_1_and_Accomp_Docs/Recommendation%20CM_Rec_2009_1E_FINAL_PDF.pdf (accessed on 10 October 2013).

[5] See http://www.abmindia.com/projects/mainet_replication.html (accessed on 10 October 2013); http://fr.slideshare.net/MASITMacedonia/zoran-aleksov-emunicipality (accessed on 10 October 2013).

[6] ANDREW CHADWICK, INTERNET POLITICS: STATES, CITIZENS, AND NEW COMMUNICATION TECHNOLOGIES, Oxford: Oxford Univ. Press (2006).

[7] See https://blogs.law.harvard.edu/idblog/2008/06/26/id-budapest-session-3-e-mobilization-and-participation/ (accessed on 10 October 2013).

2.26. E-learning ensures effective remote interaction between all interested parties about effective distance education in various branches of knowledge.

2.27. E-health ensures effective remote interaction between all stakeholders about the management and control of health and education in this area, including the remote transmission of data on human health.

2.28. E-employment ensures effective remote interaction between all stakeholders about the rights and duties of 'electronic' workers and 'electronic' employers in view of the specificity of labour relations in this sphere.

2.29. E-agriculture ensures effective remote interaction between all stakeholders about the sphere of agriculture and free information in the field of agriculture.

2.30. E-science[8] ensures effective remote interaction between all stakeholders about data sharing and collaboration between research institutions at national and international levels.

2.31. E-care ensures effective remote interaction between all stakeholders about the provision of aid and assistance in a variety of situations.[9]

2.32. E-identification ensures effective remote interaction between all stakeholders about the setting and fixing of data about the user and assigning a unique identifier required to participate in projects of e-democracy.[10]

2.33. E-authentication ensures effective remote interaction between all stakeholders about the authentication of a unique user ID.[11]

2.34. E-procurement[12] ensures effective remote interaction between all stakeholders about the supply of goods and the provision of works and services.[13]

2.35. E-commerce ensures effective remote interaction between all stakeholders about distance buying and selling of goods and services.

2.36. The tools of implementing the practices of e-democracy are:

- E-participation is electronic public participation in projects of e-democracy.
- E-deliberation is electronic public debate in e-democracy projects in order to achieve consensus on some socially important issues. As a rule, it requires a complete identification of the parties.

---

[8] See http://www.itu.int/wsis/docs/geneva/official/poa.html#c7-20 (accessed on 10 October 2013).

[9] See http://www.ecare.com/index.html (accessed on 10 October 2013).

[10] See http://monetcom.eu/joomla/webcontent/courses/ISTU/IS/IS_Lec11_ru.pdf (accessed on 10 October 2013).

[11] Ibid.

[12] See http://www.epractice.eu/en/library?page=1 (accessed on 10 October 2013).

[13] See http://www.epractice.eu/community/eprocurement (accessed on 10 October 2013).

2.37. E-forum is the discussion in e-democracy projects of any socially significant issues to achieve consensus. As a rule, it does not require full identification of the parties and in some cases may be anonymous.[14]

2.38. Thus, we believe that legal instruments of e-democracy should be understood as a combination of e-democracy practices and e-tools of implementation.

III. History of the Development of E-democracy in International Legal Practice

2.39. There is a well-founded belief that the internet can play an important role in strengthening representative democracy,[15] because it allows the introduction of elements of a deliberative democratic system.

2.40. The Council of Europe Committee of Ministers notes the need to promote the active participation of the public in the use of the internet and free communication.[16]

2.41. In 2009, a special committee on e-democracy 'Ad hoc Committee on e-democracy' (CAHDE), summarised the existing international legal experience in the field of e-democracy and developed recommendations such as CM / Rec (2009) 1.[17] They can be considered as the first international legal document aimed at setting standards in the field of e-democracy. Some of the standards that they identified were:

1) The principles of individual freedom, political freedom, human rights and the rule of law are the basis of all genuine democracies.[18]

2) Effective integration of citizens and civil society in democratic values, their involvement and attraction for participation in democratic processes and good governance are essential to

---

[14] Recommendation CM/Rec(2009)1 of the Committee of Ministers to Member States on electronic democracy (e-democracy), available at: http://www.coe.int/t/dgap/democracy/Activities/GGIS/CAHDE/2009/RecCM2009_1_and_Accomp_Docs/Recommendation%20CM_Rec_2009_1E_FINAL_PDF.pdf (accessed on 10 October 2013).

[15] ARMIN GRUNWALD, NETZÖFFENTLICHKEIT UND DIGITALE DEMOKRATIE. TENDENZEN POLITISCHER KOMMUNIKATION IM INTERNET, Berlin: Ed. Sigma 9-15 (2006).

[16] Recommendation of the Committee of Ministers to Member States on measures to promote the public service value of the internet CM/Rec(2007)16, available at: https://wcd.coe.int/ViewDoc.jsp?id=1207291 (accessed on 10 October 2013).

[17] Recommendation CM/Rec (2009)1 of the Committee of Ministers to Member States on electronic democracy (e-democracy) available at: http://www.coe.int/t/dgap/democracy/Activities/GGIS/CAHDE/2009/RecCM2009_1_and_Accomp_Docs/Recommendation%20CM_Rec_2009_1E_FINAL_PDF.pdf (accessed on 10 October 2013).

[18] Declaration of the Committee of Ministers on human rights and the rule of law in the Information Society. CM (2005)56 final 13 May 2005, available at: https://wcd.coe.int/ViewDoc.jsp?id=849061 (accessed on 10 October 2013).

preventing conflicts in society, enhancing stability. It can promote economic and social progress and cohesion at all levels.[19]

3) The democratic regime is the only way of control that provides a systemic solution of political, economic, social and cultural problems facing European societies. This can take different forms in different countries, depending on the political and constitutional traditions, and the political and legal culture of each Member State.[20]

4) It is necessary to maintain and improve democratic institutions and processes in the context of new opportunities and challenges of the information society, given that the information and communication technology (ICT) gradually promotes the flow of political information and discussion of political issues.[21]

5) Wide democratic participation of individuals and groups is necessary for greater transparency and accountability of democratic institutions and processes, and benefits society by allowing citizens to participate in other democratic forums.[22]

2.42. The Recommendations of the Council of Europe state that it is important to ensure that e-democracy is a complement to the traditional democratic processes and does not exclude officials in order to expand the opportunities for citizens to participate in political processes and contribute to the realization of each of the rights guaranteed by Article 10 of the European Convention on the Protection of Human Rights. It is for the good of every person and the democratic culture of each society.[23]

---

[19] Political message from the Committee of Ministers to the World Summit on the Information Society (WSIS). (Geneva, 10-12 December 2003). CM(2003)87 final 24 June 2003.

[20] Recommendation Rec (2004)15 of the Committee of Ministers to Member States on electronic governance (e-governance), available at: http://www.coe.int/t/dgap/democracy/activities/ggis/e-governance/Key_documents/Rec(04)15_en.pdf (accessed on 10 October 2013).

[21] Recommendation Rec (2003)9 of the Committee of Ministers to Member States on measures to promote the democratic and social contribution of digital broadcasting, available at: https://wcd.coe.int/ViewDoc.jsp?id=38043&Site=CM (accessed on 10 October 2013).

[22] DANIEL MEDIMOREC, PETER PARYCEK & JUDITH SCHOSSBÖCK, VITALIZING DEMOCRACY THROUGH E-PARTICIPATION AND OPEN GOVERNMENT: AN AUSTRIAN AND EASTERN EUROPEAN PERSPECTIVE, Bertelsmann Stiftung 14 (2011).

[23] Recommendation CM/Rec(2007)11 of the Committee of Ministers to Member States on promoting freedom of expression and information in the new information and communications environment, available at: https://wcd.coe.int/ViewDoc.jsp?id=1188541 (accessed on 10 October 2013).

2.43. It should be noted that e-democracy, provided the proper implementation, helps to ensure greater transparency and accountability, and it improves the levels of participation, accessibility and social orientation, the principle of subsidiarity (good governance), and increasing social cohesion. Proper implementation in this case means stability, regular implementation in various practices and projects, reproducibility, an ability to implement a variety of practices and projects and institutional support, creating legal and infrastructural bases.[24]

2.44. The Council of Europe also notes in the Recommendations following the principles:

1) E-democracy in itself does not affect the constitutional duties and other duties and responsibilities of decision-makers, although it may provide them with additional benefits.

2) E-democracy requires information, dialogue, communication, discussion and regular creation of open virtual public spaces where citizens can come together to maintain their civil interests.

3) E-democracy is an integral part of the information society, which presumes the existence of traditional and innovative tools and instruments that can be usefully applied in the democratic process such as the ability to simultaneously communicate with the general public.

2.45. The Recommendations of the Council of Europe are highlighted in subsections on e-democracy, which are also referred to as forms of implementation of e-democracy or species or practices of e-democracy. These include: e-voting, e-parliament, e-legislation, e-justice and electronic mediation.[25]

IV. Current State and Problems of E-democracy

2.46. As part of modern democracy at present there are three problems affecting the development of civil society:

1) The problem of participation.[26] Currently, there is a clear shortage of real opportunities for citizen participation in the political life of society. In fact, participation is usually limited to elections.

---

[24] Recommendation CM/Rec(2009)1 of the Committee of Ministers to Member States on electronic democracy (e-democracy) available at: http://www.coe.int/t/dgap/democracy/Activities/GGIS/CAHDE/2009/RecCM2009_1_and_Accomp_Docs/Recommendation%20CM_Rec_2009_1E_FINAL_PDF.pdf.

[25] Ibid.

[26] RICHARD SENNETT, THE FALL OF PUBLIC MAN, NY: W.W. Norton (1996); Baruch Fischhoff, *Risk Perception and Communication Unplugged: Twenty Years of Process*, 15(2) RISK ANALYSIS 137–145 (1995); Simon French, David R. Insua, Fabrizio Ruggerie, *Participation and Decision Analyses*, 4(4) DECISION ANALYSIS 211–226 (2007).

2) The problem of representation.[27] There are existing 'democratic expenses' and election 'thresholds' in the electoral system to limit the level of representation. In addition, the voter votes in the election at a time, usually every five years, which does not take into account the dynamics of public opinion.

3) The problem of accountability.[28] There is a lack of real opportunities to influence the performance of the electoral programs of political parties and the elected candidates.

2.47. In principle, e-democracy is designed to increase the level of participation, transparency, accountability and representation of public opinion. E-democracy attempts to deal with these problems.

2.48. The basis of e-democracy defines such a fundamental concept as e-governance, as all the electronic democratic processes that are intended for democratic governance, that are, directly or indirectly through public authorities an exercise by the people of their power.[29]

2.49. Researcher Benjamin Barber called this trend the demand for a 'strong democracy' or the transition from a passive to active voting system - participation by voting for a concrete proposal.[30] The implementation of such a system, of course, requires from voters sustainable civic and political activism on socially significant issues.

2.50. At the same time, public discussion of topical issues on which voters should be educated and competent must have a certain legal culture, skills, political discussion and the ability to make reasonable conclusions.[31]

2.51. The concept of deliberative democracy is for voters even more demanding. They must actively discuss the problem and come to a consensus with opponents. In addition, they have to make decisions and therefore understand the principles of how the final solution was obtained.

---

[27] Ibid.

[28] Allan Gibbard, *Manipulation of Voting Schemes: A General Result*, 41(4) ECONOMETRICA 587–601 (1973); JONATHAN K. HODGE, RICHARD E. KLIMA, THE MATHEMATICS OF VOTING AND ELECTIONS: A HANDS-ON APPROACH, American Mathematical Society 226 (2005).

[29] Stephen Clift, E-Governance to E-Democracy: Progress in Australia and New Zealand toward Information-Age Democracy (2003) available at: http://www.publicus.net/articles/edempublicnetwork.html (accessed on 10 October 2013).

[30] BENJAMIN R. BARBER, STRONG DEMOCRACY: PARTICIPATORY POLITICS FOR A NEW AGE, Berkeley: University of California Press (1984).

[31] Council of Europe Resolution 76 (1999) on local and regional information society; The Parliamentary Assembly of the Council of Europe Recommendation 1379 (1998) Basic education in science and technology; The Parliamentary Assembly of the Council of Europe Recommendation 1586 (2002) The digital divide and education.

2.52. Jürgen Habermas offered that 'deliberative discourse' should mean that all citizens have an equal opportunity to participate in a public exchange of information and no one can be excluded (free choice of the topic discussion, the discussion may be delayed; the debate takes place without external pressure or any other influence, and allows communication with all participants). [32] This position was mentioned separately in the Committee of Ministers of the Council of Europe's recommendations. [33]

2.53. It should be noted that such common forms as participation in online debates and public consultations are quite unpopular in relative terms, although these forums are important to inform interested citizens about decisions. [34] But the citizens don't see the influence in real as a result of applying of these forms and because of that it can to be unpopular and ineffective.

2.54. The development of civil society is directly due to the possibility of participating in the political life of the society, so the importance of the new concepts of democracy, a gradual transition from the 'representative' of democracy to the 'deliberative', and e-democracy lies in the fact that it promotes the participation of citizens in public life and it is difficult to overestimate.

2.55. Under civil society, it is generally understood that a set of non-governmental organizations and institutions show the particular interests and the will of the citizens. In general, all individuals and organizations in a society do not depend on the government[35]. These organizations and institutions pursue the goal of the realization of the rights and freedoms of citizens. [36]

---

[32] JÜRGEN HABERMAS, DER PHILOSOPHISCHE DISKURS DER MODERNE: ZWÖLF VORLESUNGEN, Frankfurt am Main: Suhrkamp (1986).

[33] Recommendation of the Committee of Ministers to member states on electronic governance ('e-governance') Rec(2004)15, available at: http://www.coe.int/t/dgap/democracy/activities/ggis/e-governance/Key_documents/Rec(04)15_en.pdf (accessed on 10 October 2013).

[34] RALF LINDNER & BERND BECKERT, E-DEMOCRACY IN EUROPE – PROSPECTS OF INTERNET-BASED POLITICAL PARTICIPATION, Theoretical Framework and Overview, European Technology Assessment Group, Karlsruhe Institute of Technology 21-22 (2010), available at: http://www.isi.fraunhofer.de/isi-media/docs/t/de/veranstaltungen/STOA_E-Democracy_Deliverable2_final-version_02-2011.pdf?WSESSIONID=uirkmuzx (accessed on 10 October 2013).

[35] Available at: http://dictionary.reference.com/browse/civil+society (accessed on 10 October 2013).

[36] Available at: http://www.macmillandictionary.com/dictionary/british/civil-society (accessed on 10 October 2013).

IV. 1. The Problem of Creating the Public Sphere of E-democracy

2.56. According to Habermas, the public sphere has played an indispensable role in the political legitimacy of democratic politics.[37] Thus, the public sphere is the foundation of deliberative democracy, an intermediate level between the parties, political decision makers, and politically active citizens. From this point of view, the public sphere is not an institution, an organization or a special form of the collective. The public sphere should be regarded rather as an open area of communicative exchange. It consists of communication flows and public discourse that contributes to understanding and harmony in society[38]and the development of national and cultural identity.[39]

2.57. The public sphere, in essence, sums up the legal aspects of – the environment in which real social relationships are formed between government, society and individuals. The public sphere is also responsible for the functioning of democracy in general and e-democracy in particular. There must be a place for public discussion, to establish a real connection between the population of the electoral district and its representatives. The communication of the results should really depend on the adoption of concrete policy decisions.

2.58. Thus, the 'public sphere' is not just some form of public communication; it always presumes the existence of certain deliberative qualities that ensure the adoption of legitimate decisions.[40]

---

[37] JÜRGEN HABERMAS, BETWEEN FACTS AND NORMS: CONTRIBUTIONS TO A DISCOURSE THEORY OF LAW AND DEMOCRACY, Cambridge, MA (1996).

[38] Hans-Jörg Trenz, *In Search of the European Public Sphere. Between Normative Overstretch and Empirical Disenchantment*, RECON ONLINE WORKING PAPER 2008/07 (2008), available at: http://www.reconproject.eu/main.php/RECON_wp_0807.pdf?fileitem =16662548 (accessed on 10 October 2013).

[39] JÜRGEN HABERMAS, SO, WHY DOES EUROPE NEED A CONSTITUTION? Florence: European University Institute, Robert Schuman Centre of Advanced Studies 18 (2001).

[40] Nancy Fraser, *Transnationalising The Public Sphere: On the Legitimacy and Efficacy of Public Opinion in a Post-Westphalian World*, 24(4) THEORY, CULTURE AND SOCIETY 7-30 (2007); Hans-Jörg Trenz, *supra* note 38; Nancy Fraser, *Rethinking the Public Sphere: A Contribution to the Critique of Actually Existing Democracy, in* HABERMAS AND THE PUBLIC SPHERE, Cambridge, Mass.: MIT Press (Craig J Calhoun ed., 1992); JOHN ERIK FOSSUM & PHILIP SCHLESINGER, THE EUROPEAN UNION AND THE PUBLIC SPHERE: A COMMUNICATIVE SPACE IN THE MAKING? London; New York: Routledge 1-20 (2007).

IV. 2. The Basic Concepts of Legal Regulation of E-democracy

2.59.   In general, in the analysis of the international legal development of e-democracy there are three fundamental concepts that define the extent and level of legal regulation, including the definitions and changes to the constitutional obligations and the power of officers:

1)   Electronic democratic awareness. It is a system of emerging social relations about the education and dissemination of information regarding the democratic processes of public authorities, citizens and all interested parties regarding the search and retrieval of this information with the other party.

2)   Electronic democratic consultation. It is a system of emerging social relations about the interaction between public authorities on the one hand, and citizens and other interested parties on the other hand, to identify and approve the will of the population, the result of which is not a legally significant consequence.

3)   Electronic democratic cooperation. It is a system of emerging social relations about the interaction between public authorities on the one hand, and citizens and other interested parties on the other hand, to identify and approve the will of the population, the result of which is a legally significant consequence and, as a rule, is binding on the parties involved.

2.60.   An example is the Estonian internet portal 'Osale', which provides search capabilities, the ability of legally non-binding consultations between the government and all stakeholders, opportunities for suggestions and ideas and initiatives to reach nationals, subject to collecting the required number of signatures.[41]

V. The Future of E-democracy

2.61.   In electronic governance,[42] some scholars determine how the use of ICT at various levels of government, the public sector and beyond, increases the effectiveness of governance.[43] Other scholars define it as a

---

[41]   See http://osale.ee (accessed on 10 October 2013).

[42]   Shailendra C. Jain Palvia, Sushil S. Sharma, *E-Government and E-Governance: Definitions/Domain Framework and Status around the World*, available at: http://www.csi-sigegov.org/1/1_369.pdf (accessed on 10 October 2013).

[43]   KIRAN BEDI, PARMINDER JEET SINGH & SANDEEP SRIVASTAVA, GOVERNMENT@NET: NEW GOVERNANCE OPPORTUNITIES FOR INDIA, New Delhi: Sage (2001); DOUGLAS HOLMES, EGOV: EBUSINESS STRATEGIES FOR GOVERNMENT, London: Nicholas Brealey (2001); Rogers W. Okot-Uma, *Electronic Governance: Re-Inventing Good Governance*, Commonwealth Secretariat London (2000), available at: http://tulcingodevalle.gob.mx/work/sites/ELOCAL/resources/LocalContent/1192/9/Okot-Uma.pdf (accessed on 10 October 2013).

set of processes and institutions, both formal and informal. Governance does not have to be carried out exclusively by the government. Private firms or organizations, associations of companies, non-governmental organizations and associations are also involved in the governance process. They form it, for the most part, in cooperation with public authorities and sometimes without them.[44] Thus, the concept of e-governance includes, in particular, such a thing as e-participation of citizens and organizations.

2.62.   Considering that e-governance is a way of ensuring the equal participation of citizens in the democratic process, we once again see the concept of continuous democratic evolution. When in the early nineties of the twentieth century there was a dramatic expansion of the internet most researchers in the field of democracy considered the internet as an information and communication environment potentially suitable for the realization of the idea of plebiscitary democracy.[45] Such an approach, using elements of direct democracy and ICT in elections and referendums in the system of e-democracy, is called electronic voting. It should be noted that this approach is a more expansive view of electronic voting than the approach of electronic voting in usual elections by electronic means. This expanded definition allows more accurate determinations of public opinion on various issues in the democratic process.[46]

V.1. The Electronic Voting System in E-democracy

2.63.   A special role in the implementation of e-democracy is a democratic procedure of electronic voting. Electronic voting in the broadest sense can be defined as complex information due to the direction of the development of e-democracy, which reflects its true content, in the sense in which democracy depends on citizens' opinions. E-voting in the process of technological and conceptual development acquires context not only as a form of realization of e-democracy, but also as the main method of its implementation. Democracy cannot be limited to

---

[44]   Robert O. Keohane & Joseph S. Nye Jr., *Introduction, in* GOVERNANCE IN A GLOBALIZING WORLD, Washington, D.C.: Brookings Institution Press 1-41 (Joseph S Nye & John D Donahue eds., 2000).

[45]   Stephen Coleman, *The Future of the Internet and Democracy: Beyond Metaphors, Towards Policy, in* PROMISE AND PROBLEMS OF E-DEMOCRACY: CHALLENGES OF ONLINE CITIZEN ENGAGEMENT, Paris: OECD 148 (2003).

[46]   Andrew Korac-Kakabadse & Nada Korac-Kakabadse, *Information Technology's Impact on the Quality of Democracy: Reinventing the Democratic Vessel, in* REINVENTING GOVERNMENT IN THE INFORMATION AGE, New York: Routledge 214 (Richard Heeks ed., 1999).

discussion and debate, democracy in the original sense of the term is the power of the people, and the power is exercised by the choice of a particular variant of conduct approved by a majority of the population. In such a culture, electronic voting has new prospects for 'material', or the real, expression of the population. It's not a formal opinion, through the use of a much more complex mixed electoral systems, the use of which in the framework of the 'traditional' vote is technically and economically disadvantageous.

2.64.   In the opinion of the Committee of Ministers of the Council of Europe, the framework of the electronic voting system must respect the principles of democratic elections and referendums ensuring reliability and safety in the same way as in the 'traditional' voting system. Notably, this idea includes all the basic electoral issues related to e-voting systems.[47] It should also provide the requirements of transparency, accountability and verifiability of the electronic voting system, complying with international standards and recommendations.[48]

2.65.   These are the main areas which should be considered in an electronic voting system:

1)   It should increase of initiative and participation in national, regional and local public life. It should introduce genuine public participation, including through direct forms of democracy, promoting the formation of a more dynamic system of relations between the individual, society and state.

2)   It should increase the transparency of democratic decision-making and accountability of democratic institutions.

3)   It should improve efficiency and effectiveness, including cost-effectiveness in the activities of public authorities such as elections. It should also increase the accessibility of communicating with government agencies and elected representatives by e-initiatives and petitions, as well as improve the relationship between public authorities and .voters[49]

4)   It should promote public debate and control in decision-making.[50]

---

[47]   Recommendation Rec (2004)11 of the Committee of Ministers to Member States on legal, operational and technical standards for e-voting (Adopted by the Committee of Ministers on 30 September 2004 at the 898th meeting of the Ministers' Deputies), available at: https://wcd.coe.int/ViewDoc.jsp?id=778189 (accessed on 10 October 2013).

[48]   CM(2003)87 final 24 June 2003. Political message from the Committee of Ministers to the World Summit on the Information Society (WSIS) (Geneva, 10-12 December 2003).

[49]   Recommendation Rec (2004)15 of the Committee of Ministers to Member States on electronic governance (e-governance), available at: http://www.coe.int/t/dgap/democracy/activities/ggis/e-governance/Key documents/Rec(04)15 en.pdf (accessed on 10 October 2013).

[50]   Ibid.

5) The rights of all citizens to participate in political life must be expanded. In particular, attention should be given to the introduction of elements of direct democracy, such as a referendum or a citizens' legislative initiative. They should be carefully designed in order to make democracy more representative and ensure better social integration and the implementation capacity of the state and society.[51]

V.2. The Legal Foundations of E-democracy

2.66. E-democracy usually consists of two main parts; the most common are e-government and e-voting.[52] In this case, the basic element of real democracy in the full sense of the word is electronic voting.

2.67. E-democracy presumes an open and free access to expression, open communication, freedom of speech and freedom of expression on the internet, access to a global communication system from any place, effective legal support, information security, electronic voting and internet voting, transparency in the electronic environment, 'a system of electronic citizenship' and the creation of a special electronic and information environment.[53]

2.68. The analysis of a number of foreign sources[54] can highlight specific principles on which, electronic governance, should be built. These principles of e-governance include:

---

[51] Resolution 1547 (2007) State of human rights and democracy in Europe adopted by the Assembly on 18 April 2007 (15th Sitting), available at: http://assembly.coe.int/ ASP/XRef/X2H-DW-XSL.asp?fileid=17531&lang=en (accessed on 10 October 2013).

[52] T. G. Roessler, *Electronic Voting over the Internet – An E-Government Speciality*, Online, DISSERTATION – UNIVERSITY OF TECHNOLOGY GRAZ, AUSTRIA 3-4 (2007), available at: https://online.tugraz.at/tug_online/voe_main2.getvolltext?pCurrPk=34776 (accessed on 10 October 2013); John D. Gregory, *Solving Legal Issues in Electronic Government: Jurisdiction, Regulation, Governance* (2002), available at: http://cjlt.dal.ca/ vol1_no3/pdfarticles/gregory.pdf (accessed on 10 October 2013); Lilian Mitrou, Dimitris Gritzalis, Pelopidas Donos & Georgia Georgaroudi, *Legal and regulatory issues on e-voting and data protection in Europe*, available at: http://www.instore.gr/evote/ evote_end/htm/3public/doc3/public/public_deliverables/d_3_4/e_vote_D_3_4_v22_20_02 _02.doc (accessed on 10 October 2013); INDEPENDENT COMMISSION ON ALTERNATIVE VOTING METHODS, ELECTIONS IN THE 21ST CENTURY: FROM PAPER BALLOT TO E-VOTING, London : Electoral Reform Society, 2002.

[53] http://www.iaria.org/conferences2012/CYBERLAWS12.html (accessed on 10 October 2013).

[54] Michiel Backus, *E-Governance and Developing Countries, Introduction and Examples*, THE INTERNATIONAL INSTITUTE FOR COMMUNICATION AND DEVELOPMENT – Research Report (2001), available at: http://www.iicd.org/about/publications/egovernance-and-developing-countries-introduction-and-examples/report3.pdf (accessed on 10 October

2.69. A) Freedom and quality of information: the information must be significant, and have the selectivity, reliability and verifiability of information. There should be the opportunity to check that the information is current and accurate. The information must have an adequate form of presentation so as to prevent distortion or ambiguous information.

2.70. B) Redistribution of power: it must be the redistribution of powers between the state and citizens, between the state and organizations or businesses in the framework of forms of electronic democracy.

2.71. C) Co-ordination and harmonisation of private and public interests: e-governance should coordinate the interests by matching positions, and as a consequence the adoption of constructive solutions. Private and public interests are harmonized by comparison and combination of decision-making in a constructive, meaningful dialogue between citizens, organizations or businesses and the state.

2.72. D) Information and legal support: special attention should be made to information in the context of modern conditions of the media. Currently, the media have all the capabilities to realise its rights of freedom of information and freedom of expression. Although there are still no developed effective mechanisms for filtering low-quality information and approaches to the definition of abuse of the right to freedom of information. There are no uniform requirements for the content, security of information and form of presenting it. At present, the information directly determines the need for decision-making and legal assessment of the concrete situation. In this regard, there is a need for qualitative changes in the field to enable the adoption of informed decisions.

2.73. To implement an effective public sphere and a single information environment of e-democracy, it is necessary to examine the concept of information and legal space. Information and legal space is a system of legal norms regulating social relations in the field of education and dissemination of information. The purpose of legal regulation is to improve the quality of information. It is proposed that a special system of legal regulation be developed, providing the implementation of these principles and a comprehensive legal review of e-democracy and technological solutions for compliance with these legal requirements.

2.74. E) The electronic part and a special identification system: it must be a system of individual electronic IDs or passports.

2013); DONALD F. KETTL, THE TRANSFORMATION OF GOVERNANCE, Baltimore: Johns Hopkins University Press (2002).

2.75. F) Accessibility: it is the improvement of the legal and information culture to create a sustainable relationship between citizens, organisations and the state, based on an understanding of the need to cooperate with each other in political processes. It is necessary to create a simple technique to avoid potential or actual infringement of opportunities, control and belittlement of anyone's political rights.

2.76. G) Information security in the legal aspect: it should be quality legal support and the introduction of new measures of legal responsibility, including limiting access to participate in decision-making in the e-democracy.

2.77. H) Civic participation: this includes the full involvement of civil society in the process of e-democracy.

2.78. Competent participation: this would include the creation of a special system of qualifications in order to exclude the incompetent from participation in the processes of e-democracy such as qualifications for persons who do not have the minimum required amount of subject matter knowledge. It seems that this would help avoid making incompetent management decisions.[55]

2.79. From a legal point of view, e-governance is a special system of legal relations between citizens, government and business about collaboration, coordinated implementation of government functions, operating under a special information and communication environment and , in this case within the legal and information space.

2.80. E-governance, as a political and legal notion and at the same time a doctrinal concept, reflects the specifics of e-democracy as an expression of the people's power in electronic form.

2.81. Thus, the concept of 'e-governance' should be interpreted very broadly, to the extent that it is considered as content of the concept of 'e-democracy'. E-governance, on the basis of the above, can be understood as a system of relations between the government, citizens and organizations on the basis of information and communication links about the implementation of e-democracy.[56]

2.82. E-democracy in this case is a comprehensive view of all democratic processes using information and communication technologies based on the principles of e-governance.

2.83. E-democracy is a concept composite that is multi-faceted. In general, as a political phenomenon, e-democracy determines how the electronic

---

[55] Jaroslav V. Antonov, *E-Democracy as the Instrument of Development of the Civil Society in Russia*, (3) Journal 'CIVIL SOCIETY IN RUSSIA AND ABROAD' 2-4 (2012).

[56] Valentin A. Ovchinnikov & Jaroslav V. Antonov, *Theoretical and Practical Aspects of E-Democracy and E-Voting*, (4) All-Russian scientific-practical journal 'JURIDICAL WORLD' 18-21 (2013).

submission of the democratic process should be made. From a legal point of view, the electronic submission of the democratic process should be carried out within the framework of the legal requirements and principles which form the legal regulation of public institutions such as elections and the government. The existence and functioning of these institutions or some parts of it in an electronic environment should not be a reason to ignore the legal matter in which they exist at the present time.[57]

VI. Conclusion

2.84. E-democracy, just as e-participation, is an interdisciplinary and multi-dimensional direction, which combines legal, political and many other aspects. .[58] At the same time, e-democracy, even though it consists of many different practices implemented in various projects and subprojects, is a system of democratic development. Thus, all the practices of e-democracy have substantial legal characteristics. E-democracy supports democratic processes, and therefore it should not replace or alter the nature of existing democratic processes. It is designed to enhance civic participation and implementation of private interests, which are the foundation of civil society.

2.85. The development of e-democracy after 2009 has given rise to many new practices and projects, each of which contributes to the implementation of various groups of private interests and the overall formation of a qualitatively new civil society. This suggests that e-democracy, provided with the proper implementation, effectively contributes to the development of civil society.

| | |

Summaries

DEU [*Die rechtlichen Instrumente der E-Demokratie beim Aufbau der Zivilgesellschaft in der internationalen Praxis*]
Die historische Entwicklung der Zivilgesellschaft geht mit einem unaufhaltsam zunehmenden Bedürfnis nach der Verbesserung der Teilhabe der Bürger einher. Die Strukturen der Zivilgesellschaft wahren die privaten Interessen der Bürger und deren Fähigkeit, ihre Meinungen

---

[57] Ibid.

[58] Ann Macintosh, Stephen Coleman, *Multidisciplinary Roadmap and Report on E-Participation Research*, Demo-Net (2006); Ø. Sæbø, J. Rose, *The shape of eParticipation: Characterizing an emerging research area*, (25) GOVERNMENT INFORMATION QUARTERLY 400-428 (2008).

kundzutun. Der bisher größte Entwicklungsschub der Zivilgesellschaft schafft nicht nur demokratische Staatswesen, sondern bietet den Bürgern außerdem reale Möglichkeiten, ihre Meinung zu äußern und interaktiv mit Stellen der öffentlichen Gewalt zu kommunizieren, wenn es darum geht, ihre subjektiven Rechte und Rechtsinteressen durchzusetzen und Mechanismen für eine produktive und systematische Zusammenarbeit zwischen Staat, Gesellschaft. konkreten Bürgern und Organisationen zu schaffen, um gegenwärtige und potenzielle künftige Probleme zu lösen. Der Begriff der E-Demokratie ist in aller Munde; angesichts seines multidimensionalen Charakters ist er aber nur unzulänglich erforscht. Im Jahre 2009 definierte der Europarat die rechtliche Grundlage für die Maßstäbe der E-Demokratie, auch was solche Fragen anbelangt wie die Vervollkommnung der Teilhabe der Bürger am demokratischen Prozess, Transparenz und öffentliche Verantwortung, Fernkommunikation und elektronische Prozesse. Nach 2009 wurden die verschiedenen Ansätze für die praktische Umsetzung der E-Demokratie erweitert und durchliefen eine wesentliche Wandlung; heute decken sie die verschiedensten Gebiete von Privatinteressen ab, womit zugleich der direkte Einfluss der E-Demokratie auf die Entwicklung der Zivilgesellschaft gefördert wird.

CZE *[Právní nástroje e-demokracie při budování civilní společnosti v mezinárodní praxi]*

Historický vývoj civilní společnosti doprovází neustále rostoucí potřeba zlepšování účasti občanů. Struktury civilní společnosti hájí soukromé zájmy občanů a jejich schopnost vyjadřovat své názory. Největší vývoj civilní společnosti nejen vytváří demokratické režimy, nýbrž poskytuje také reálné možnosti občanům vyjadřovat své názory, interaktivně komunikovat s orgány veřejné moci při prosazování jejich subjektivních práv a právních zájmů a při vytváření mechanismů pro produktivní a systematickou spolupráci mezi státem, společností, konkrétními občany a organizacemi za účelem řešení současných a možných budoucích problémů. E-demokracie je obecně známým pojmem, s ohledem na její mnohadimenzionální charakter je však nedostatečně prostudována. Rada Evropy definovala v roce 2009 právní základ měřítek e-demokracie, včetně otázek týkajících se zdokonalování účasti občanů v procesu demokracie, transparentnosti a veřejné odpovědnosti, distanční komunikace a elektronických procesů. Po roce 2009 došlo k rozšíření různých postupů při praktikování e-demokracie, k jejich podstatné transformaci tak, že tyto postupy pokrývají nejrůznější odlišné oblasti soukromých zájmů a došlo tedy i k podpoře přímého vlivu e-demokracie na vývoj civilní společnosti.

| | |

POL [*Instrumenty prawne e-demokracji a budowanie społeczeństwa obywatelskiego w praktyce międzynarodowej*]
Wraz z rozwojem społeczeństwa obywatelskiego następuje bieżący wzrost udziału obywateli w życiu politycznym państwa. E-demokracja daje szereg istniejących i potencjalnych możliwości korzystania z procedur zdalnych i elektronicznych w kwestiach prawnych, a także ze środków i narzędzi umożliwiających realizację prywatnych interesów obywateli. Dlatego e-demokracja bezpośrednio stymuluje i wspiera rozwój społeczeństwa obywatelskiego oraz jego rozmaitych instytucji.

FRA [*Les instruments juridiques de la cyberdémocratie dans la construction d'une société civile sans frontières*]
Le développement de la société civile est indissociable d'une participation croissante des personnes privées à la vie politique des États. La cyberdémocratie met à leur disposition toutes les opportunités existantes offertes par les procédures électroniques et à distance dans le domaine du droit ainsi que des moyens et des outils pour faire aboutir leurs intérêts privés. La cyberdémocratie stimule donc et apporte une contribution décisive au développement de la société civile et de ses différentes institutions.

RUS [*Правовые инструменты электронной демократии в процессе создания гражданского общества в международной практике*]
Развитие гражданского общества непрерывно связано с повышением участия граждан в политической жизни государства. Электронная демократия предоставляет возможности использования множества существующих и потенциальных дистанционных электронных правовых практик и инструментов для реализации своих частных интересов. Тем самым непосредственно стимулируется и поддерживается развитие гражданского общества и его отдельных структур.

ESP [*Instrumentos jurídicos de la democracia electrónica en la construcción de la sociedad civil en la práctica internacional*]
El desarrollo de la sociedad civil suele ir acompañado de una creciente participación de los ciudadanos en la vida política del Estado. La democracia electrónica permite aprovechar toda una serie de posibilidades, tanto existentes como potenciales, relativas a procedimientos remotos y electrónicos de materia jurídica, a la vez que posibilita el uso de medios e instrumentos para alcanzar sus intereses privados. La democracia electrónica, por tanto, estimula directamente y fomenta el desarrollo de la sociedad civil y de sus diferentes instituciones.

Czech Yearbook of International Law

Gabriela Augustínyová |
Aiste Dumbryte

The Indispensable Role of Non-governmental Organizations in the Creation and Functioning of the International Criminal Court

Key words:
NGOs | International
Criminal Court | Rome
Statute | Coalition for
the International
Criminal Court | Rome
Conference

Abstract | *This article discusses the role of non-governmental organizations (NGOs) in the creation and functioning of the International Criminal Court (ICC or the Court). The creation of the Court is referred to as the 'civil society achievement' by numerous scholars. NGOs advocating for an effective, just and independent international criminal court joined their efforts in a unique form of cooperation – the Coalition for the ICC, a loose network of NGOs, based on several common principles. During the Rome Conference, the Coalition actively engaged with State representatives and managed to influence numerous provisions of the final Statute, such as the Prosecutor's power to initiate investigations on their own initiative, and the prohibition of a wide range of sexual and gender-based crimes.*

The active involvement of NGOs in the work of the ICC continues today. The Rome Statute contains explicit references to the NGOs, which provide a basis for a potentially important contribution of the NGOs to the proceedings of the Court, as well as the work of the Assembly of States Parties. In addition, local presence and knowledge makes the NGOs a natural partner of the Court in a number of its functional areas, such as outreach, victims' issues or complementarity.

Gabriela Augustínyová holds an LL.B. in European, International and Comparative Law from University of Sheffield, United Kingdom, and LL.M. *cum laude* in Public International Law from Leiden University, Netherlands. The author currently works as a lecturer at the Faculty of Law, Comenius University in Bratislava, Slovakia. Previously the author worked at the International Criminal Court in The Hague and the Organisation for Security and Cooperation in Europe, Mission to Serbia. e-mail: augustinyova.g @gmail.com

Aiste Dumbryte holds a MA in International and European Law from Vilnius University, Lithuania, and Advanced LL.M. *cum laude* in

The continuous engagement of NGOs with the ICC, from the Rome Conference to the present, makes them indispensable to the Court.

| | |

I. Introduction

3.01. The International Criminal Court (ICC or the Court), the first permanent international criminal judicial body, was established in 1998 by a multi-lateral treaty known as the Rome Statute. The drafting process of the Statute was heavily shaped by the involvement and the advocacy work of non-governmental organizations (NGOs), loosely grouped in a novel form of cooperation called the Coalition for the International Criminal Court (CICC or the Coalition). The creation of the ICC is often referred to by scholars as the 'civil society achievement'[1] and it is an outstanding example for assessing the general role of NGOs in current international affairs.

International Criminal Law from Leiden University, Netherlands. The author currently works at the Secretariat of the Organization for Security and Cooperation in Europe. Previously the author worked at the Victims' Participation and Reparations Section of the International Criminal Court, the legal section of the Coalition for the ICC (internship) and the Department of Refugee Affairs of the Lithuanian Red Cross Society.
e-mail: aiste_dumbryte @yahoo.com.

3.02. The first part of the article will discuss the role of NGOs in the creation of the ICC. It will outline the creation of the Coalition for the ICC as a distinct entity, its involvement in the drafting process of the Rome Statute, and some of the main successes and failures of NGOs at the Rome Conference. The second part will cover the role of NGOs in the functioning of the Court. The Coalition and its member NGOs have continued in their active advocacy work after the conclusion of the Rome Conference, focusing mainly on the ratification and implementation of the Statute. The Rome Statute and its subsidiary documents contain some explicit references to NGOs and they play an important role in some other areas of the Court's work as well. The remarkable cooperation of the NGOs in the Coalition and their continued active and coordinated involvement with the Court's issues has nowadays transpired into an indispensable role for the NGOs in the functioning of the Court.

---

[1]   MARLIES GLASIUS, THE INTERNATIONAL CRIMINAL COURT: A GLOBAL CIVIL SOCIETY ACHIEVEMENT, Oxford: Routledge xiii-xiv (2006); Cenap Çakmak, *Transnational Activism in World Politics and Effectiveness of a Loosely Organised Principled Global Network: The Case of the NGO Coalition for an International Criminal Court,* 12(3) INT'L J. OF HUMAN RIGHTS 373-374 (2011).

II. The Creation of the International Criminal Court

II.1. Coalition for the ICC

3.03. The idea of a permanent international criminal court had been on the agenda of global civil society at least since the late 1980s.[2] In 1995, when the UN General Assembly created the Ad Hoc Committee on the Establishment of an International Criminal Court, it seemed that the international community was finally determined to bring this idea to life.[3] At this point, the world's NGOs realized that they could play an important role in ensuring that this determination did not fade – and that in order to maximize their impact, they had to coordinate their efforts.[4]

3.04. With this goal in mind, the World Federalist Movement, an organization working to advance access to justice and transparent governance, called a meeting of several NGOs in New York in early 1995. The attendees included Amnesty International, Human Rights Watch, the International Commission of Jurists and Parliamentarians for Global Action, among others.[5] All the participating NGOs agreed on the importance of coordinating their action in support of the ICC, as well as the need to reach out to more civil society actors worldwide,[6] and the achievement of these goals necessitated some type of organization. Thus, on 25 February 1995 the Coalition for the ICC was born.[7]

3.05. The CICC was intended as a loose network of NGOs, united by their support for an effective, just and independent International Criminal Court.[8] Any NGO subscribing to this idea was able to join. Although the steering committee of the Coalition adopted a list of Basic Principles (including universal jurisdiction of the Court, rights of victims to participate in the proceedings, and adequate attention to the

---

[2]   Insight on the International Criminal Court: Newsletter of the NGO Coalition for the ICC: Tenth Anniversary Special Edition, available at: http://www.iccnow.org/documents/insight_anniv_en.pdf (accessed on 9 October 2013).

[3]   Claude E. Welch Jr. & Ashley F. Watkins, *Extending Enforcement: The Coalition for the International Criminal Court*, 33(4) HUMAN RIGHTS QUARTERLY 927, 959 (2011).

[4]   Cenap Çakmak, *supra* note 1, at 375.

[5]   Claude E. Welch Jr. & Ashley F. Watkins, *supra* note 3, at 963-964, 966.

[6]   Cenap Çakmak, *supra* note 1, at 375-376.

[7]   William R. Pace & Mark Thieroff, *Participation of Non-Governmental Organizations, in* THE INTERNATIONAL CRIMINAL COURT: THE MAKING OF THE ROME STATUTE: ISSUES, NEGOTIATIONS, RESULTS, The Hague: Kluwer Law International 391, 391 (Roy S. Lee ed., 1999).

[8]   Claude E. Welch Jr. & Ashley F. Watkins, *supra* note 3, at 967.

needs of women and children),[9] its members did not have a common position on many substantive issues and, disagreements within the CICC were not uncommon.

3.06.   From 25 founding members,[10] to over 800 by the time of the Rome Conference,[11] the Coalition now unites more than 2,500 NGOs in 150 countries.[12]

II.2. NGO Participation in the Rome Conference

3.07.   The Rome Conference saw the participation of 236 NGOs.[13] While the number in itself was not outstanding in comparison with other international conferences, what made this event unprecedented was the civil society's systematic and fully accepted presence.[14]

3.08.   The participants ranged from big global NGOs, such as Amnesty International and Human Rights Watch, to small local organizations,[15] including human rights NGOs, bar associations, women's organizations, national coalitions for the ICC and organizations focused on peace and conflict resolution, among others.[16]

3.09.   Even though nearly all of the NGOs accredited to participate in the Rome Conference were gathered under the umbrella of the Coalition,[17] they did not always share homogenous views. One notable divide emerged between women's rights groups and religious or 'pro-family' organizations regarding sexual and gender crimes.[18] Nonetheless, the Coalition managed to coordinate the actions of its members effectively. They split into three types of groups: the first group consisted of regional caucuses, which lobbied state representatives from their own regions; the second group included thematic caucuses on various issues, such as gender justice, victims' rights, protection of children,

---

[9]   MARLIES GLASIUS, *supra* note 1, at 70, 80.

[10]   Cenap Çakmak, *supra* note 1, at 376.

[11]   William R. Pace & Mark Thieroff, *supra* note 7, at 392.

[12]   Coalition for the International Criminal Court: About the Coalition, available at: http://www.iccnow.org/?mod=coalition (accessed on 9 October 2013).

[13]   William R. Pace & Mark Thieroff, *supra* note 7, at 392.

[14]   Marie Törnquist-Chesnier, *How the International Criminal Court Came to Life: The Role of Non-Governmental Organisations,* 21(3) GLOBAL SOCIETY 449, 460 (2007).

[15]   Zoe Pearson, *Non-Governmental Organizations and the International Criminal Court: Changing Landscapes of International Law,* 39 CORNELL INT'L L.J. 243, 260 (2006).

[16]   Marlies Glasius, *Expertise in the Cause of Justice: Global Civil Society Influence on the Statute for an International Criminal Court,* 2 GLOBAL CIVIL SOCIETY 137, 141 (2002).

[17]   William R. Pace & Mark Thieroff, *supra* note 7, at 392.

[18]   Johan D. Van den Vyver, *Civil Society and the International Criminal Court,* 2(3) J. OF HUMAN RIGHTS 425, 429 (2003).

etc.; and the third group encompassed 12 working groups, each focusing on a different part of the draft statute.[19]

3.10. The work of the Coalition and its member NGOs before and during the Rome Conference took a variety of forms. Firstly, they worked hard to ignite a global debate about the ICC among states, actors of civil society, legal practitioners and academics. In order to do that, NGOs attended intergovernmental conferences, lobbied state representatives and organized numerous national and international seminars, expert meetings and public debates.[20] Secondly, they sought to inform the specialist public and wider audiences about the developments at the Rome Conference, as well as to promote certain proposals by presenting arguments in their support.[21] Thirdly, the Coalition assisted the smaller delegations of states by providing them with legal experts and interns and thus enabling them to participate in more working groups.[22] It also raised funds from various donors to support the participation of NGOs and experts from lesser-developed and transitional countries.[23] Finally, various NGOs organized demonstrations to attract the attention of the general public.[24]

3.11. Several participants of the Rome Conference noted the good relationship between NGOs and state representatives.[25] In the words of the distinguished legal scholar Cherif Bassiouni, who was the Chairman of the Drafting Committee of the Rome Conference, 'unlike other multilateral negotiation processes, where governmental delegates and NGO representatives are frequently in opposition, the cooperation between the two groups at the Conference was optimal'.[26]

II.3. Successes

3.12. NGOs attempted to influence nearly all areas of the Rome Statute – from the Court's jurisdiction, to definitions of crimes and procedural rules, to the financing of the Court and its relations with states.[27] They

---

[19] William R. Pace & Mark Thieroff, *supra* note 7, at 392.

[20] Marlies Glasius, *supra* note 16, at 147-150.

[21] MARLIES GLASIUS, *supra* note 1, at 38, 41-42; Zoe Pearson, *supra* note 15, at 272-278.

[22] William R. Pace & Mark Thieroff, *supra* note 7, at 394.

[23] Ibid., at 393.

[24] Marlies Glasius, *supra* note 16, at 152.

[25] John Washburn, *The Negotiations of the Rome Statute for the International Criminal Court and International Lawmaking in the 21st Century*, 11(2) PACE INT'L L. REV. 361, 367-368 (1999); Cenap Çakmak, *supra* note 1, at 385-387.

[26] M. Cherif Bassiouni, *Negotiating the Treaty of Rome on the Establishment of an International Criminal Court*, 32 CORNELL INT'L L.J. 443, 455 (1999).

[27] Marlies Glasius, *supra* note 16, at 153.

succeeded in ensuring that the ICC would have jurisdiction over non-international armed conflicts,[28] and that the Statute would grant victims the right to participate in proceedings and to receive reparations.[29] However, the most significant achievements of NGO advocacy were giving the ICC prosecutor the power to initiate investigations on their own initiative and including a broad list of sexual and gender-based crimes in the Rome Statute.

II.3.1.   Prosecutor's Power to Initiate Investigations

3.13. The draft statute of the ICC, prepared by the International Law Commission (ILC), envisaged two ways of triggering the Court's jurisdiction: a complaint by a state party and a referral by the UN Security Council.[30] This drew criticism from the civil society. In one of the earliest NGO reports on the ICC, Amnesty International argued that few cases were likely to come before the Court through these trigger mechanisms – it pointed out that existing state complaint procedures under human rights treaties were rarely, if ever, used.[31] Such concerns were expressed by the International Commission of Jurists as well.[32] Additionally, the report by Amnesty International warned that complaints by states and the UN Security Council risked being politicized.[33] As an alternative, it proposed granting the prosecutor the power to initiate investigations on their own initiative.[34]

3.14. Such a power of the prosecutor became 'a collective bottom line' of the CICC members in the Rome Conference – NGOs saw the prosecutor's ability to initiate investigations as an essential feature of an independent ICC.[35] Meanwhile the positions of states on this issue at the start of the Conference were divided. Argentina and Germany had submitted a formal proposal to grant the prosecutor *proprio motu* powers, subject to review by a pre-trial chamber. This proposal was

---

[28]   Philippe Kirsch & John T. Holmes, *The Rome Conference on an International Criminal Court: The Negotiating Process*, 93(2) AM. J. INT'L L. 1, 5 (1999).

[29]   Mahnoush H. Arsanjani, *The Rome Statute of the International Criminal Court*, 93(2) AM. J. INT'L L. 22, 39 (1999); Håkon Friman, *The International Criminal Court: Negotiations and Key Issues*, 8(6) AFRICAN SECURITY R. 3, 10 (1999).

[30]   Draft Statute for an International Criminal Court with commentaries, II(part 2) YEARBOOK OF THE INTERNATIONAL LAW COMMISSION Art. 21, 23 (1994).

[31]   AMNESTY INTERNATIONAL, ESTABLISHING A JUST, FAIR AND EFFECTIVE INTERNATIONAL CRIMINAL COURT, London: Amnesty International 25-26 (1994).

[32]   INTERNATIONAL COMMISSION OF JURISTS, THE INTERNATIONAL CRIMINAL COURT: THIRD ICJ POSITION PAPER, Geneva: International Commission of Jurists 36-37 (1995).

[33]   AMNESTY INTERNATIONAL, *supra* note 31, at 25.

[34]   Ibid., at 24.

[35]   Marlies Glasius, *supra* note 16, at 153; Mahnoush H. Arsanjani, *supra* note 29, at 27.

supported by France but opposed by the USA, China and Russia, and many other states were undecided.[36]

3.15. NGOs of the Coalition attempted to foster support for the idea of an independent prosecutor mainly in the three following ways:

3.16. Firstly, they proposed an even more radical idea for triggering the Court's jurisdiction: complaints by individuals and/or NGOs, a common practice in regional human rights courts. The aim of this strategy was to make the independent prosecutor seem like a more acceptable and less threatening alternative.[37]

3.17. Secondly, NGOs engaged with states' arguments against the *proprio motu* powers, presenting strong rebuttals. For example, the USA, one of the most adamant opponents to this idea, submitted a position paper, arguing that 'allowing the prosecutor to initiate investigations based on information from non-state entities would inundate the prosecutor with frivolous complaints'.[38] In response, the Lawyers Committee for Human Rights, while recognizing that prosecutorial discretion must be accompanied by appropriate safeguards, pointed out that states and the UN Security Council may not always have the resources to monitor and react to all cases of grave crimes, and thus a broader power of the prosecutor was essential to ensure that these cases are brought before the ICC.[39]

3.18. Thirdly, the Coalition disseminated information about the positions of states on the issue of the independent prosecutor, aiming to demonstrate that the realization of this idea was politically possible. It presented regular reports on the shifting positions for and against the prosecutor's *proprio motu* powers, showing the increasing support of states and thereby encouraging other like-minded states to stay in favour.[40]

3.19. These efforts materialized in Article 15 of the Rome Statute, which grants the Prosecutor the power to initiate investigations on their own initiative.[41] While this could not have happened without the approval of states, it is commonly agreed that NGOs played a crucial role in

---

[36] MARLIES GLASIUS, *supra* note 1, at 52.

[37] Marlies Glasius, *supra* note 16, at 153-154.

[38] Allison Marston Danner, *Enhancing the Legitimacy and Accountability of Prosecutorial Discretion at the International Criminal Court*, 97 AM. J. OF INT'L L. 510, 514 (2003).

[39] Lawyers Committee for Human Rights, *The International Criminal Court: Trigger Mechanism and the Need for an Independent Prosecutor*, New York: Lawyers Committee for Human Rights 6-7 (1997).

[40] Marlies Glasius, *supra* note 16, at 154-155.

[41] Rome Statute of the International Criminal Court (adopted 17 July 1998, entered into force 1 July 2002) 2187 UNTS 90, Art. 15.

convincing state representatives that an independent prosecutor with investigative powers was both necessary and possible.[42]

II.3.2. Inclusion of Sexual and Gender-based Crimes in the Statute

3.20.   In the original ILC draft, the Court's jurisdiction did not explicitly cover sexual and gender-based crimes.[43] The first proposal to include these crimes in the Rome Statute was submitted by New Zealand and Switzerland in early 1997. However, it solely concerned the crime of rape.[44]

3.21.   The Women's Caucus for Gender Justice, a coalition of several hundreds of women's rights groups from all over the world, argued that when sexual and gender-based crimes are not explicitly mentioned in legal instruments, they are very often ignored by courts and their particular impact on victims is not captured.[45] Thus, in its paper of 1997, the Women's Caucus proposed adding a separate sub-paragraph to the provision on war crimes that would include rape, sexual slavery, forced prostitution, forced pregnancy, forced sterilization and other sexual or gender violence or abuse.[46] This became one of the main lobbying issues of the Women's Caucus in the Rome Conference.

3.22.   However, it must not be forgotten that NGOs focusing on women's issues did not hold uniform positions. The so-called right-to-life or pro-family groups opposed the use of the term 'gender', arguing that it implies endorsement of homosexuality.[47] They were also strongly against the inclusion of the crime of forced pregnancy into the Statute, fearing that this would oblige states to guarantee access to abortion.[48] In the Rome Conference, the latter issue became especially controversial due to vehement opposition to the crime of forced pregnancy by Arab states and the Vatican.[49] Nonetheless, the proposal of the Women's Caucus on the inclusion of sexual and gender-based crimes was ultimately supported and the pro-family groups had hardly any influence. This can be explained by several factors.

---

[42]   MARLIES GLASIUS, *supra* note 1, at 59-60.

[43]   Draft Statute for an International Criminal Court, *supra* note 30, Art. 20.

[44]   Marlies Glasius, *supra* note 16, at 156.

[45]   Women's Caucus for Gender Justice in the International Criminal Court, *Recommendations and Commentary for December 1997 PrepCom on the Establishment of an International Criminal Court*, The Hague: Women's Caucus for Gender Justice 43 (1997).

[46]   Ibid., at 26.

[47]   Marlies Glasius, *supra* note 16, at 156.

[48]   Johan D. Van den Vyver, *supra* note 18, at 429.

[49]   Marlies Glasius, *supra* note 16, at 156.

3.23. Firstly, the Women's Caucus had numerous delegates in the Rome Conference, including legal experts and women from conflict areas, which allowed it to actively participate in meetings and engage with state representatives.[50] Moreover, its membership consisted of NGOs from nearly all the regions of the world, which made the Caucus look representative of women's voices worldwide.[51] In contrast, the pro-family movement consisted of much fewer NGOs, mainly coming from North America, which undermined their ability to present a globally supported position on women's issues.[52]

3.24. Secondly, the fears of conservative and religious governments concerning forced pregnancy and right to abortion were addressed by the Bosnian delegation. Its testimony of numerous cases of women who were raped and forcibly kept pregnant during the conflict, in order to change the ethnical composition of the population, emphasised that laws regulating access to abortion had little to do with the crime of forced pregnancy.[53] In addition, the Women's Caucus proposed an additional safeguard to address the concerns of states: a statement in the relevant provision that the prohibition of forced pregnancy shall not affect national abortion laws.[54] This further helped states to reach an agreement on the inclusion of forced pregnancy in the Statute.

3.25. As a result, the Rome Statute became the first international treaty to recognize sexual and gender-based crimes among the most serious crimes under international law. Its provisions on crimes against humanity and war crimes include the crimes of rape, sexual slavery, enforced prostitution, forced pregnancy, enforced sterilization and other sexual violence[55] – taken almost verbatim from the proposal of the Women's Caucus.

II.4. Failures

3.26. Not all the ideas of NGOs were welcomed in the Rome Conference, and many of their proposals did not make it to the Statute.

3.27. One such example was universal jurisdiction of the ICC, i.e. its power to investigate and prosecute crimes listed in the Statute without

---

[50] Ibid., at 156-157.

[51] MARLIES GLASIUS, *supra* note 1, at 80-81.

[52] Ibid., at 83.

[53] Valerie L. Oosterveld, *The Making of a Gender-Sensitive International Criminal Court*, 1(1) INT'L L. FORUM DU DROIT INT'L 38, 39 (1999).

[54] Cate Steains, *Gender Issues, in* THE INTERNATIONAL CRIMINAL COURT: THE MAKING OF THE ROME STATUTE: ISSUES, NEGOTIATIONS, RESULTS, The Hague: Kluwer Law International 357, 366-368 (Roy S. Lee ed., 1999).

[55] Rome Statute, *supra* note 41, Art. 7(1)(g), 8(2)(b)(xxii), 8(2)(e)(vi).

requesting additional consent of the states concerned. Universal jurisdiction was one of basic principles of the CICC, vocally supported by Amnesty International, Human Rights Watch and the Lawyers Committee for Human Rights.[56] However, states adopted a more restricted approach: they only allowed the Court to exercise jurisdiction over crimes which are committed in the territory or by nationals of State Parties.[57]

3.28. Another failed attempt of the civil society concerned the prohibition of all indiscriminate weapons. A group of NGOs called the Peace Caucus argued for a general prohibition of weapons that cause superfluous injury or unnecessary suffering, or are inherently indiscriminate, as well as for a specific list of prohibited weapons that would include chemical, biological and nuclear weapons.[58] However, this initiative was almost entirely unsuccessful. Many states were opposed to prohibiting nuclear weapons, and this accordingly led other states to protest the inclusion of chemical and biological weapons (regarded as 'poor man's weapons') in the Statute.[59] Thus, the adopted Statute explicitly prohibits only certain types of weapons (poison or poisoned weapons; asphyxiating, poisonous or other gases; expanding bullets).[60] Meanwhile any broader prohibition of indiscriminate weapons is subject to the adoption of an annex to the Rome Statute which would list these weapons.[61] However, to date such an annex has not been adopted.

3.29. Several reasons stand behind these failures. On the one hand, members of the Coalition were fragmented in their position towards banning indiscriminate weapons. Many of them chose to remain silent on this issue and instead to direct their efforts elsewhere, where they expected more success.[62] On the other hand, the abovementioned proposals may have been seen by states as threatening to limit their sovereignty more than they were ready to accept.

II.5. Concluding Observations

3.30. Numerous NGOs from all over the world united under the umbrella of the Coalition to advocate for an effective, just and independent ICC. Looking back to the Rome Conference, it is evident that they managed to achieve this goal. Due to their active presence in the Conference,

---

[56] MARLIES GLASIUS, *supra* note 1, at 70-73.
[57] Rome Statute, *supra* note 41, Art. 12(2).
[58] Marlies Glasius, *supra* note 16, at 157.
[59] Ibid., at 158.
[60] Rome Statute, *supra* note 41, Art. 8(2)(b)(xvii)-(xix).
[61] Ibid., Art. 8(2)(b)(xx).
[62] MARLIES GLASIUS, *supra* note 1, at 109-110.

diverse and efficient working methods and good cooperation with state representatives, NGOs were able to make their voices heard and ensure widespread support for their position. Although not all the demands of NGOs are reflected in the final version of the Rome Statute, it can be argued that the majority of essential provisions were influenced by NGOs. The examples discussed above show that the Court was made more independent by empowering the Prosecutor to initiate investigations *proprio motu*, and that it was made more just by prohibiting a wide range of sexual and gender-based crimes. Thus, the role of NGOs in the creation of the ICC was undoubtedly indispensable.

III. Explicit References to NGOs in the Rome Statute and Its Subsidiary Documents

III.1 Rome Statute and the Rules of Procedure and Evidence

3.31.   The involvement of NGOs in the drafting process of the Rome Statute resulted in a number of explicit references to NGOs in the Statute and its subsidiary documents.[63]

3.32.   One example is Article 15(2) of the Rome Statute, which states that when deciding whether to initiate investigation *proprio motu*, the Prosecutor may also seek additional information from non-governmental organizations. This provision provides for a potentially important contribution of NGOs to the early stages of the proceedings at the Court.[64] This includes the possibility for NGOs to bring suspected crimes to the attention of the Prosecutor and encourage investigation into these crimes by the ICC. NGOs are often the first to respond to a humanitarian crisis and are present on the scene long before peacekeeping forces or criminal investigators.[65] As a result, humanitarian organizations are in a privileged position to observe what happens in war. Thus, it is not surprising that the international criminal tribunals and the ICC, which are set up to try these atrocities,

---

[63]   Francesca Trombetta-Panigadi, *NGOs and the Activities of the International Criminal Court, in* CIVIL SOCIETY, INTERNATIONAL COURTS AND COMPLIANCE BODIES, The Hague: T.M.C. Asser Press 121 (Tullio Treves et al., eds., 2005).

[64]   Ibid., at 121.

[65]   Andrea E. K. Thomas, *Nongovernmental Organizations and the International Criminal Court: Implications of Hobbes' Theories of Human Nature and the development of Social Institutions for their Evolving Relationship,* 20 EMORY INTERNATIONAL LAW REVIEW 435, 436 (2006).

turn to these organizations to see what evidence they can offer.[66] NGOs are very active in this area and are nowadays a major source of information for the Prosecutor and the Court in the preliminary stages of the proceedings.[67]

3.33. NGOs are also mentioned in Article 44(4) of the Rome Statute, which allows the Court, in exceptional circumstances, to employ the expertise of gratis personnel offered by States Parties, intergovernmental organizations or non-governmental organizations to assist with the work of any of the organs of the Court. This provision clearly recognizes the value of the expertise of the NGO personnel for the work of the Court. The long-serving members of the NGO community have often been involved with the ICC project since its early stages. As a result, NGOs have become repositories of a great amount of institutional historical knowledge about the ICC[68] and have long-lasting and detailed expertise in many areas of the Court's functioning.

3.34. Another important role for NGOs is envisaged in Rule 103(1) of the Rules of Procedure and Evidence. This provides a legal basis for NGOs to act as *amici curiae* and submit to a Chamber, upon invitation, written or oral observations on any issue that the Chamber deems appropriate at any stage of the proceedings. Even though the rule does not specifically mention non-governmental organization but speaks solely about 'organization', it has been confirmed in the judicial practice of the Court that NGOs can and do act as *amici curiae* in the proceedings of the Court.[69]

III.2. Assembly of States Parties to the Rome Statute

3.35. As regards the Assembly of States Parties (ASP or the Assembly), NGOs are explicitly mentioned in Rules 92, 93 and 95 of the Rules of Procedure of the ASP. Rule 92 provides for representatives of intergovernmental organizations with standing invitation from the UN General Assembly to attend the meetings of the ASP as observers. Rule 93 provides for authorised NGOs to attend the meetings of the Assembly and its subsidiary bodies, receive copies of official documents and make

---

[66] Kate Mackintosh, *Note for humanitarian organizations on cooperation with international tribunals*, 86(853) INTERNATIONAL REVIEW OF THE RED CROSS 131 (2004).

[67] BENJAMIN N. SCHIFF, BUILDING THE INTERNATIONAL CRIMINAL COURT, New York: Cambridge University Press 156 (2008).

[68] Ibid., at 156.

[69] See for example: The Lubanga Case (Observations of the Women's Initiatives for Gender Justice on Reparations) ICC-01/04-01/06 (10 May 2012) or the Bemba Case (Amicus Curiae Observations on Superior responsibility Submitted pursuant to Rule 103 of the Rules of Procedure and Evidence) ICC-01/05-01/08 (20 April 2009).

oral statements under certain conditions. Rule 95 further authorises NGOs to submit written statements on a subject related to the work of the Assembly, in which the organization has a special competence.

3.36. NGOs are traditionally very active in the meetings of the Assembly. Apart from submitting oral and written statements, every year they organize a number of high-level side-events to the meetings of the Assembly, drawing the attention of the delegates and other participants to the various issues related to the functioning of the ICC. In the period building up to and during the meetings of the Assembly, as well as during the meetings of its subsidiary bodies, the NGOs and the CICC continue their active advocacy work, which started in the context of the Rome Conference. The CICC is traditionally invited to attend meetings of The Hague Working Group and is granted the right to participate as an observer and make a presentation to the Committee on Budget and Finance. The CICC and its members undoubtedly continue to exercise influence on the decisions of the Assembly on certain matters.

3.37. One area of vocal involvement of the NGOs in the meetings of the Assembly has been the process of the elections of the Court officials. Court officials are elected by the Assembly upon nominations of candidates by the States Parties. Even though the Rome Statute specifies the conditions to be fulfilled by the candidates for each position, there has been strong criticism of the quality of some of the elected officials, and the CICC and other observers have continuously pledged with the States Parties to elect only the most qualified candidates. During the judicial elections of six judges at the tenth session of the ASP in 2011, the CICC decided to take its involvement to a brand new level. In the absence of an Advisory Committee on nominations, which may be established by the Assembly pursuant to Article 36(4)(c) of the Rome Statute, the CICC decided to establish the Independent Panel on International Criminal Court Judicial Elections (the Panel) in December 2010. The purpose of the Panel was to raise awareness of the qualifications for judicial candidates required by the Rome Statute and to encourage States Parties to nominate the most qualified candidates to be judges on the International Criminal Court.[70] The Panel was presented as an independent assessment body and consisted of former and present distinguished judges with strong relationships to international criminal law. The Panel conducted an assessment of the candidates and subsequently made public both the

---

[70] Independent Panel on Judicial Nominations: Report on International Criminal Court Judicial Nominations 2011, available at: http://www.iccnow.org/?mod=elections (accessed on 11 October 2013).

assessment process, as well as its assessments of individual candidates. Pursuant to its Terms of Reference, the Panel made an assessment of individual candidates as 'Qualified' or 'Not Qualified'. The Panel provided reasons only if it found a candidate 'Not Qualified'.[71]

3.38. In the statement to the Assembly, the Coalition proclaimed that the purpose of the Panel was to help fill a significant gap in the procedures – the lack of a competent, fair, independent assessment of whether the nominees actually fulfilled the qualifications prescribed by the Rome Statute.[72] The activities of the Coalition in the sphere of the elections of the Court officials have become an important part of the advocacy work of the Coalition in the post-Rome period. The Coalition proved once again to be prepared to step in to fill a lacuna in the functioning of the Court and other bodies, as well as the Assembly. The work of the Panel was acknowledged by The Hague Working Group[73] and the newly established Advisory Committee on nominations of Judges held a discussion with two members of the Panel regarding the experience and the lessons which it had learned.[74] The work of the Coalition and its members once again proved to be the basis for progressive and improved functioning of the ICC.

IV. Some Other Areas of NGOs' Involvement in the Functioning of the International Criminal Court

IV.1. Outreach and Victims' Issues

3.39. Apart from the activities undertaken by NGOs pursuant to explicit references to non-governmental organizations in the Rome Statute and its subsidiary documents, NGOs have also been particularly active in a number of other areas. One such area has been the outreach of the Court, mainly in the situation countries.[75]. Despite the creation of field offices, the ICC continues to have very little presence in situation

---

[71] Ibid.

[72] Coalition for the International Criminal Court: Announcement to the Assembly of States Parties on The Independent Panel on International Criminal Court Judicial Elections December 2010, available at http://www.coalitionfortheicc.org/documents/ Judicial_Panel_Announcement.pdf (accessed on 11 October 2013).

[73] Report of the Bureau on the Study Group on Governance, ICC-ASP/10/30 (22 November 2011), para. 13.

[74] Report of the Advisory Committee on Nominations of Judges on the work of its first meeting, ICC-ASP/12/23 (31 May 2013), paras. 6 and 7.

[75] In the context of the ICC, the situation countries are those countries where active investigation by the Court is ongoing. At the moment, the Court is conducting investigations in 8 situation countries.

areas[76] and NGOs have stepped in to at least partially rectify this shortcoming. As stated by the Court in its Report on the public information strategy 2011-2013, 'while the Court has a central role to play in making information available, it seeks to coordinate efforts with partners such as international organizations, non-governmental organizations (NGOs), legal associations, media, external experts, academic foundations and victims' associations, and in particular States Parties, to maximize the Court's own impact and to prioritize the use of limited resources.'[77]

3.40. In the absence of sufficient outreach by the Court itself, various international and local NGOs have taken upon themselves to do their own outreach, informing local populations about the investigations of the Court and more particularly about the legal possibility of participating in the Court procedure in an independent capacity as victims.[78] The NGOs have been undoubtedly instrumental in the substantial increase in the number of applications for victims' participation in the proceedings of the Court. The NGOs not only spread information in affected communities about the possibility to participate in the proceedings, but also help the applicants to fill in the applications, collect them and send them to the Court for further assessment. Especially in remote areas and areas with ongoing armed conflict, the Court depends upon local NGOs, community organizations and local leadership for contact with local populations.[79] However, the reliance on NGOs in situation areas is not without great controversies and the Court has to approach it with caution and due consideration.

3.41. In the *Lubanga* case which arose from the situation in the Democratic Republic of the Congo, the Trial Chamber at one point ordered a stay of the proceedings and the release of the defendant in light of the expressed inability of the Chamber to ensure a fair trial.[80] The Chamber's decision constituted a reaction to the Prosecutor's investigative methods, notably the fact that the Office of the Prosecutor (OTP) had primarily relied on documents obtained from the UN and NGOs and had accepted that persons working for NGOs had been the exclusive intermediaries between the OTP and the victims and

[76] BENJAMIN N. SCHIFF, *supra* note 67, at 156.
[77] Report of the Court on the public information strategy 2011-2013, ICC-ASP/9/29 (22 November 2010).
[78] Marlies Glasius, *What is Global Justice and Who Decides? Civil Society and Victim Responses to the International Criminal Court's First Investigations*, 31 HUMAN RIGHTS QUARTERLY 496, 511 (2009).
[79] BENJAMIN N. SCHIFF, *supra* note 67, at 156.
[80] Lubanga Case (Decision on the release of Thomas Lubanga Dyilo) ICC-01/04-01/06 (2 July 2008).

witnesses.[81] Since then, the Court has paid increased attention to the issue of intermediaries and their use has become much more limited and strictly controlled. The issue of intermediaries was one of the priorities of the Working Group on Strategic Planning of the Court.[82] The new Draft Guidelines governing the Relations between the Court and Intermediaries developed by the Court were subject to discussions between the Court, the States Parties and NGOs in the context of The Hague Working Group.[83]

3.42. It is without question that the work of local and international NGOs in situation areas plays an indispensable role for the proper functioning of the Court. At the same time, the NGOs differ in their opinions on ICC matters and can pursue their own interests in their dealings with the Court. In general, the Court faces challenges in picking trustworthy and credible local intermediaries and information sources.[84] As a result, it is of crucial importance that the relationship and working methods of the collaboration between the Court and NGOs in the field are governed by specific, well-defined rules and are subject to strict system of checks and balances in order to avoid any doubt cast on the process of judicial proceedings, perception of fair trial, the rights of the accused and the credibility of the Court.

IV.2. Complementarity

3.43. Following the end of the Rome Conference and the adoption of the Rome Statute, the NGOs which were involved in the process of the drafting of the Statute shifted their focus towards ensuring that the Statute came into force as soon as possible and was subsequently implemented properly. The CICC engaged in a widespread ratification campaign, involving arranging informational seminars and national and regional meetings of parliamentarians, other NGOs, legal experts and local leaders.[85] The Rome Statute came into force on 1 July 2002, after obtaining 60 ratifications, pursuant to its Article 126.

3.44. However, ratification is only the first step in a long process, and the NGOs devoted considerable attention towards bringing the Statute fully into effect. Pursuant to the Preamble, Articles 1 and 17 of the Statute, the jurisdiction of the ICC is complementary to national

---

[81] Heikelina Verrijn Stuart, *The ICC in Trouble*, 6 JOURNAL OF INTERNATIONAL CRIMINAL JUSTICE 409 (2008).

[82] Report of the Bureau on the Strategic planning process of the International Criminal Court, ICC-ASP/11/30 (6 November 2012).

[83] Ibid., paras. 11-18.

[84] BENJAMIN N. SCHIFF, *supra* note 67, at 156.

[85] Ibid., at 152.

jurisdictions, which retain the primary duty to exercise their criminal jurisdiction over those responsible for international crimes.[86] Since the adoption of the Statute, international, national and local NGOs have been working at the state level to support the development and drafting of implementing legislation allowing for cooperation with the ICC and the exercise of complementarity.[87] Via this activity, the NGOs not only ensure a strong output, but as a result also understand the legislation and are in a position to play an invaluable role in the application of that law in national investigations and prosecutions.[88]

3.45.   Another important role for NGOs and civil society is also visible within the concept of 'positive complementarity', which has become predominant in the complementarity discussion in the last couple of years. Based on this principle, the Court should not only step in when a state fails to prosecute the Rome Statute crimes but should actively encourage prosecutions by national governments of crimes within the Court's jurisdiction. In the report of the Bureau on complementarity, which was the basis for the discussions on the topic at the Kampala Review Conference in June 2010, the States Parties endorsed the concept of positive complementarity as an integral part of the Rome Statute system, while highlighting the judicial nature of the Court's mandate and function and stressing that activities aimed at strengthening national jurisdictions should be carried out by states, together with international and regional organizations and civil societies.[89] It was acknowledged that other actors, rather than the Court itself, were better placed to support the strengthening of national jurisdictions, the ability to conduct genuine national investigations and trials of crimes included in the Rome Statute, and other activities such as in capacity building, financial support and technical assistance.[90]

3.46.   Apart from activities more inherently linked to the judicial activities of the Court, the NGOs' activities in support of positive complementarity are aimed at enabling national jurisdictions to conduct genuine investigations and prosecutions of the core crimes and therefore support the system of international criminal justice as a whole. In this respect, the limited resources and capabilities of the ICC enable it to only conduct a limited number of trials. Therefore, for achieving the main aim of the ICC - to put an end to impunity for the most serious

---

[86]   Rome Statute, *supra* note 41, Preamble, para. 6.
[87]   Francesca Trombetta-Panigadi, *supra* note 63, at 125.
[88]   Ibid., at 126.
[89]   Report of the Bureau on Stocktaking: Complementarity, ICC-ASP/8/51 (18 March 2010) para. 4.
[90]   Ibid., para. 16.

crimes - it is crucial that the whole system of international criminal justice functions well, starting with national prosecutions and ending with effective deterrence. In this framework, the ICC acts as the court of last resort if other levels of the system fail to fulfil their respective roles. As stated by the first Chief Prosecutor of the ICC Luis Moreno-Ocampo upon taking office on 16 June 2003, '[a]s a consequence of complementarity, the number of cases that reach the Court should not be a measure of its efficiency. On the contrary, the absence of trials before this Court, as a consequence of the regular functioning of national institutions, would be a major success.'[91] The NGOs with their knowledge and understanding of the national proceedings and local customs, as well as the specific needs and expectations of the people are particularly well-placed to be an indispensable part of this process, and consequently of the functioning of the ICC in particular, as well as the whole international criminal justice system in general.

V. Conclusion

3.47. The ICC is a unique institution not only because it is the first permanent international criminal court but also because it owes its existence and efficiency in large part to NGOs. From the drafting of the Rome Statute in 1998 to this day, NGOs continue to play a significant role in many aspects of the Court's work.

3.48. The Rome Conference witnessed a well-coordinated and fully accepted presence of more than 200 NGOs. In their quest for an effective, just and independent Court, the NGOs of the Coalition for the ICC were instrumental in assisting the debates among states parties, as well as promoting their own position on what the Court should be. NGOs have left their mark in the Rome Statute, most notably by ensuring an independent power for the Prosecutor to initiate investigations on their own initiative and by achieving a comprehensive prohibition of sexual and gender-based crimes. These significant achievements can be explained by several factors: an active participation of NGO representatives, good communication between NGOs and states' officials, and numerous different forms of NGO involvement – from lobbying, to disseminating information, to staging public demonstrations.

3.49. While not all the proposals of NGOs were equally welcomed in Rome – for example, the ban of all indiscriminate weapons did not make it to the Statute – this is better explained by the reluctance of States Parties

---

[91] ICC Office of the Prosecutor: Statement made at the ceremony for the solemn undertaking of the Chief Prosecutor of the ICC, 16 June 2003, at 2.

to limit their sovereignty too much, rather than by the lack of NGO efforts. Nonetheless, despite a few failures, it is universally recognized that the role of NGOs in ensuring that the newly-created ICC is indeed independent, effective and just was indispensable.

3.50. The adoption of the Rome Statute did not mark an end of NGOs' involvement with the Court's issues. The Coalition and its member NGOs have continued in their active advocacy work and added to these activities an important role on the ground in situation countries, where the Court carries out its investigations. The local presence and knowledge makes the NGOs a natural partner of the Court in a number of its functional areas, such as outreach, victims' issues or complementarity. The Rome Statute and its subsidiary documents contain explicit references to the NGOs, which provide a basis for a potentially important contribution of the NGOs to the proceedings of the Court, as well as the work of the Assembly of States Parties. In a little more than ten years of the Court's existence, NGOs have proved to be an important partner of the Court, making an instrumental and indispensable contribution to its proper functioning and helping the Court to achieve its main aim to put an end to impunity for the most serious crimes.

| | |

Summaries

FRA [*Le rôle essentiel des organisations non-gouvernementales dans la constitution et le fonctionnement de la Cour pénale internationale*]
On s'intéresse ici au rôle des organisations non-gouvernementales (ONG) dans la constitution et le fonctionnement de la Cour pénale internationale (ci-après CPI ou Cour).
Un certain nombre de théoriciens considèrent la constitution de la Cour comme un "succès de la société civile". Des ONG désireuses de créer un tribunal pénal international efficace, rapide et indépendant, ont joint leurs efforts en constituant la Coalition internationale pour la Cour pénale internationale, forme unique de fédération libre d'ONG unies par des grands principes généraux. Durant la Conférence de Rome, cette Coalition a activement collaboré avec les représentants des États et a eu une influence sur un grand nombre de dispositions du Statut, comme par exemple sur celles qui s'intéressent aux compétences des enquêteurs ouvrant une enquête de leur propre initiative ou sur celles qui se consacrent à la criminalité dans le domaine des violences sexuelles ou de la discrimination fondée sur le sexe.

L'engagement actif des ONG dans les activités de la CPI n'a pas cessé. Le Statut de Rome comporte des références explicites aux ONG constituant un socle pour leurs éventuelles contributions aux procédures engagées devant la Cour et auxquelles peut également se référer l'Assemblée des États parties dans ces procédures. De plus, la présence des ONG dans les procédures et leur connaissance de ces procédures en font des partenaires naturels de la Cour dans de nombreux domaines de son fonctionnement, comme par exemple dans ses relations publiques, dans les questions se rapportant aux victimes ou dans la corrélation avec des affaires qui ne sont pas directement l'objet des procédures instruites.

CZE **[Nezastupitelná úloha nevládních organizací při konstituování a fungování Mezinárodního trestního tribunálu]**

Tento článek se zabývá úlohou nevládních organizací (NGOs) při konstituování a fungování Mezinárodního trestního tribunálu (ICC nebo Soud).

Konstituování Soudu označuje řada teoretiků za „úspěch civilní společnosti". NGOs snažící se o vytvoření efektivního, rychlého a nezávislého mezinárodní trestního tribunálu se v tomto úsilí spojily v rámci unikátní formy spolupráce představované Koalicí za ICC jako volného sdružení NGOs provázaných několika obecnými principy. V průběhu Římské konference Koalice aktivně spolupracovala se zástupci států a řídila ovlivňování mnoha ustanovení Statutu, jako například těch, které se zabývají pravomocemi vyšetřovatelů při zahajování vyšetřování z jejich vlastní inciativy, stejně jako kriminalitou širokého spektra trestných činů v oblasti sexuální nebo diskriminace pohlaví.

Aktivní angažovanost NGOs týkající se činnosti ICC však pokračuje dodnes. Římský statut obsahuje výslovné odkazy na NGOs, přičemž tato ustanovení poskytují základ pro případný významný přínos NGOs v řízeních vedených u Soudu, jakož i pro Shromáždění států, které jsou stranami v těchto řízení. Navíc přítomnost NGOs při řízeních a jejich informovanost o řízeních z nich činí přirozeného partnera Soudu v mnoha oblastech jeho fungování, například ve vztazích s veřejností, otázkách týkajících se poškozených nebo v oblasti provázanosti se záležitostmi, které nejsou bezprostředně předmětem projednávání v řízeních.

| | |

POL [*Niezastąpiona rola organizacji pozarządowych w ukonstytuowaniu i funkcjonowaniu Międzynarodowego Trybunału Karnego*]

Niniejszy artykuł poświęcono roli organizacji pozarządowych (NGOs) w konstytuowaniu i funkcjonowaniu Międzynarodowego Trybunału Karnego. Ukonstytuowanie Trybunału określa się często jako „sukces społeczeństwa obywatelskiego" i stanowi on nową formę współpracy między NGOs. Współpraca ta oraz aktywne zaangażowanie NGOs trwa do dziś, przy czym pełnią one niezastąpioną rolę w funkcjonowaniu Trybunału.

DEU [*Zur unverzichtbaren Rolle von Nichtregierungsorganisationen bei der Konstituierung und Arbeitsweise des Internationalen Strafgerichtshofs*]

Dieser Beitrag befasst sich mit der Rolle, welche Nichtregierungsorganisationen (NRO bzw. NGOs - non-governmental organizations) bei der Konstituierung des Internationalen Strafgerichtshof gespielt haben und für dessen Arbeit bis heute spielen. Die Einrichtung dieses Gerichtshofs wird oft als „Erfolg der Zivilgesellschaft" bezeichnet und stellt eine neue Form der Zusammenarbeit zwischen nichtstaatlichen Organisationen dar. Diese Zusammenarbeit und das aktive Engagement der NGOs setzen sich bis heute fort, wobei die NGOs für die Tätigkeit des Gerichts eine unverzichtbare Rolle spielen.

RUS [*Незаменимая роль неправительственных организаций в формировании и функционировании Международного уголовного трибунала*]

В данной статье рассматривается роль неправительственных организаций (НПО) в формировании и функционировании Международного уголовного трибунала. Формирование Трибунала часто считается «успехом гражданского общества» и представляет собой новую форму сотрудничества между НПО. Это сотрудничество и активное участие НПО продолжается до сих пор, причем НПО играют незаменимую роль в функционировании Трибунала.

ESP [*El papel irremplazable de las organizaciones no gubernamentales en la constitución y el funcionamiento de la Corte Penal Internacional*]

Este artículo examina el papel que desempeñan las organizaciones no gubernamentales (ONG) en la constitución y el funcionamiento de la Corte Penal Internacional. A menudo se hace referencia a la constitución de la Corte como un "éxito de la sociedad civil" que, además, representa una nueva forma de colaboración entre las ONG. Esta colaboración y la participación activa de las ONG continúan siendo actuales, a la vez que las ONG ejercen una función irremplazable en la actividad de la Corte.

| | |

Czech Yearbook of International Law

Helena Barancová

Current Lawmaking of the International Labour Organization with regard to EU Law

Key words:
International Labour Organization |
Recommendations of ILO | *working time* | *discrimination in employment* | *atypical employment* | *agency work* | *part-time employment relationship* | *telework* | *compulsory and forced labour* | *employment relationship* | *child labour*

Abstract | *In the development of the systems of international labour law and EU labour law the author focuses on the field of employment relationship, working time, antidiscrimination law, atypical employment, decent work, termination of employment relationship by employer as well as elimination of the worst forms of child labour including prohibition of slavery, forced and compulsory work. The author deduces from a comparison of the examined systems some common law characteristics. One of them is the convergence of the development of both legal systems particularly in the field of atypical employment and working time. This is evident even if the substantive scope of atypical employment in the ILO legislation is significantly narrower than in comparison with EU law.*

The level of EU anti-discrimination law, its substantive and personal range, is in comparison with ILO Conventions significantly higher. The termination of employment relationship from employer initiation is in ILO standardization on a substantially wider and more social level. In conclusion it can be said that among differentiating characteristics of the actual ILO standardisation and development of EU labour law, the areas of considerably wider material and personal scope belong to the ILO Conventions.

Prof. JUDr. Helena Barancová, DrSc., is the Dean of the Law Faculty of Trnava University, Head of the Department of Labour Law and Social Security Law, Slovak Republic. She has penned 38 academic monographs and over 370 academic and expert studies and articles. Of these, approximately one third have been published abroad. She is known in the broader academic and professional community for her numerous books and expert articles on international and European labour law. She was awarded the Order of the Deputy Prime Minister of the Slovak Republic in November 2008 for her scholarship on European and international labour law. e-mail: dekan.prf@truni.sk

| | |

I. Introduction

4.01. The Slovak Republic has ratified 18 conventions of the International Labour Organisation (hereinafter ILO) over the past two decades, thereby increasing substantially the rate of conformity of Slovak labour law with international labour law. Concurrently with this process of ratification of ILO conventions, the Slovak Republic since its formation in 1993 has been preparing responsibly for accession to the European Union and it has harmonised its labour law with the EU law.

4.02. Apart from the legal system of international labour law, developing through numerous conventions and recommendations of ILO and supranational law of the EU, the legal system of the Council of Europe law was also developing. This bears legal significance for the development of national labour law, mainly regarding the Council of Europe's European Convention on Human Rights, the European Social Charter and the Revised European Social Charter.

4.03. The current relevance of the ILO legislation and EU law can be understood from a time perspective and also with regard to specific issues with which the EU Member States are concerned today, in an age affected by world economic and financial crises.

4.04. The significance of ILO legislation for labour law lies in its versatility and in a relatively detailed regulation of all essential aspects of labour law of the International Labour Organisation's member states. Its complexity and relatively detailed regulations, the international labour law, represented by conventions and recommendations of ILO, is significantly ahead of the labour law of the EU. Apart from conventions and recommendations, the ILO Constitution itself is extremely important to ILO member states, incorporating certain human rights such as freedom of association. The right to form coalitions, freedom of assembly and collective bargaining, prohibition of forced and compulsory labour and prohibition of discrimination are among human rights of this type.

4.05. Compared to ILO legislation, the labour law of the European Union began to develop only some time after the EEC was founded. The labour law played a marginal role from the beginning because the Community's objective was to implement the harmonisation of economic conditions.[1]

---

[1] Articles 30-36 of the EURATOM Treaty contained regulation for protection of employees' health. The EEC Treaty of 1957 incorporated the right of workers to free movement as a fundamental condition of free economic competition in Article 48. Article 119 incorporated the principle of equal treatment in remuneration of men and women.

4.06. The second phase of development of the EU labour law took place in the 1970s, when important directives in the field of social protection of workers,[2] technical protection of workers[3] and first directives on equal treatment were adopted.[4]

4.07. The Maastricht Treaty (the Treaty on European Union of 2 February 1992) and the Social Policy Agreement between Member States and the Community, with the exception of the United Kingdom and Northern Ireland, as well as the Amsterdam Treaty of 1997, through which the EC acquired new jurisdiction in the field of labour law, had significant impact on the further development of EU labour law at the beginning of the 1990s.

4.08. The greatest advancement of EU labour law took place in the 1990s, when numerous directives were adopted at the EU level, part of which was the result of the European social dialogue.[5] In this period, a fundamental step mainly in the field of anti-discrimination law was made at the EU level. Also in the first decade of this century, important directives in the field of collective labour law were adopted. Also adopted were Directive 2003/88/EC of the European Parliament and of

---

[2] Council Directive 75/129/EEC, later the Council Directive 98/59/EC on the approximation of the laws of the Member States relating to collective redundancies, codified form, in the Council Directive 77/187/EEC on the approximation of the laws of the Member States. This related to the safeguarding of employees' rights in the event of transfers of undertakings, businesses or parts of undertakings or businesses, to protect employees in the event of insolvency of their employer, as amended by the Council Directive 2002/74/EC and the Council Directive 2008/94/EC on the protection of employees in the event of insolvency of their employer.

[3] The framework of Council Directive 89/391/EEC and another more than 20 partial Directives is the introduction of measures to encourage improvements in the safety and health of workers at work.

[4] Council Directive 75/117/EEC is on the approximation of the laws of the Member States relating to the application of the principle of equal pay for men and women. Council Directive 76/207/EEC is on the implementation of the principle of equal treatment for men and women as regards access to employment, vocational training and promotion, and working conditions. Council Directive 97/80/EC is on the burden of proof in cases of discrimination based on sex.

[5] Council Directive 96/34/EC on the framework agreement on parental leave, Directive 96/71/EC of the European Parliament and of the Council concerning the posting of workers in the framework of the provision of services, Council Directive 97/81/EC concerning the Framework Agreement on part-time work, Council Directive 1999/70/EC of concerning the framework agreement on fixed-term work, Council Directive 2000/78/EC establishing a general framework for equal treatment in employment and occupation, Council Directive 2000/43/EC implementing the principle of equal treatment between persons irrespective of racial or ethnic origin, Council Directive 2001/23/EC on the approximation of the laws of the Member States relating to the safeguarding of employees' rights in the event of transfers of undertakings, businesses or parts of undertakings or businesses.

the Council concerning certain aspects of the organisation of working time and Directive 2008/104/EC of the European Parliament and of the Council on temporary agency work.[6]

4.09. The international labour law of ILO has been developing since 1919; therefore, it has, contrary to the EU law, a quite significant time advance. The international labour law, represented by conventions and recommendations of ILO, is not only more complex, compared to the EU law, but also in case of certain conventions is even more social. From time to time it inspires liberal-oriented politicians of the Slovak Republic to toy with the idea of the Slovak Republic leaving the ILO.

4.10. Given the number of legal sources of international labour law and EU law, as well as the extent of the issue in question, the system of international labour law and EU law can be examined from various aspects. Mainly it is worth comparing questions related to the prohibition of discrimination, issues of forced labour and issues of atypical employments, which are especially relevant at times of economic and financial crisis. There are also new challenges in the development of international labour law and EU law related to rising levels of unemployment in the EU and in the world and to unfavourable demographics in Europe.

II. Prohibition of Discrimination in Employment Relationships

4.11. The questions of the prohibition of discrimination are one of the most important for the whole field of labour law. Similarly to the ILO Constitution, the European Union law also considers the principle of equal treatment as a fundamental human right that is demonstrated in numerous cases from the Court of Justice of the European Union.[7]

4.12. The legal regulation of the prohibition of discrimination in the development of the international labour law began when ILO Convention No. 100/1951 on equal remuneration for men and women was adopted in 1951, ahead of the EU law. In 1958 ILO Convention No.

---

[6]   It concerns mainly Council Directive 94/45/EC on the establishment of a European Works Council or a procedure in Community-scale undertakings and Community-scale groups of undertakings for the purposes of informing and consulting employees, Council Directive 2001/86/EC of supplementing the statute for a European company with regard to the involvement of employees, Directive 2002/14/EC of the European Parliament and of the Council establishing a general framework for informing and consulting employees in the European Community and Council Directive 2003/72/EC supplementing the Statute for a European Cooperative Society with regard to the involvement of employees.

[7]   ECJ Judgment (Grand Chamber) of 22 November 2005, C-144/04, *Werner Mangold v Rüdiger Helm* [2005] I-09981.

111/1958 on discrimination concerning employment and occupation was adopted. Both of these conventions were ratified by the Slovak Republic.

4.13. Already the ILO Declaration of Philadelphia, which is part of the ILO Constitution, incorporated in Article II that all human beings, irrespective of race, creed or sex, have the right to pursue both their material well-being and their spiritual development in conditions of freedom and dignity, economic security and equal opportunity. Achieving these conditions must constitute the main objective of national and international policy.

4.14. ILO Convention No. 100/1951 on equal remuneration for men and women constitutes a part of the ILO Constitution similar to ILO Convention No. 111/1957, which in Article I incorporates the definition of remuneration for work and guarantees legal safeguards for employees. Even though this ILO Convention is very positively regarded with the passage of time, because it guarantees new international legal standards in remuneration for work of men and women, the actual practical execution of equality in remuneration of men and women still falls significantly behind the written international legal standards.

4.15. ILO Convention No. 111/1958 on discrimination concerning employment and occupation comprises a relatively broad legal framework. With regard to its personal scope, it applies to wage and self-employed persons, as well as persons preparing for an occupation. Article I, section 1 of the convention defines discrimination as any distinction, exclusion or preference made in employment or occupation on the basis of one of the seven discrimination characteristics of race, colour, sex, religion, political opinion, national or social origin.

4.16. The Convention guarantees not only equality in performance of employment or occupation, but in Article II it also binds the member states with the obligation to support equality of opportunities to ensure real equality in practice.[8] With regard to the current development of EU anti-discrimination law, this Convention is undergoing a tough test at present. The current case law of the Court of Justice of the EU admits, under certain conditions, a possibility for an employer to dismiss an employee upon reaching the retirement age. This follows from a relatively broadly conceived exception from the equal treatment principle based on age, as regulated by Council Directive 2000/78/EC establishing a general framework for equal treatment in employment and occupation. This Directive indeed extended the discrimination

---

[8]   The Convention was ratified in 1990.

characteristics, but at the same time, it conceives exceptions from the prohibition of discrimination based on age (which is an unfavourable situation on the labour market) in a relatively broad way. The current development of case law of the Court of Justice of the EU is construing these exceptions rather extensively.[9] Maybe because of that it can be expected with a high degree of probability in EU Member States that in the following period the existing labour law legislation of EU Member States will also allow an employee's dismissal due to reaching the retirement age. It can be likewise expected that certain ILO member states will withdraw from Convention No. 111/1958.

4.17. Convention No. 156/1981 concerning equal opportunities and equal treatment for men and women workers and workers with family responsibilities, which was ratified by the Slovak Republic in 2003 and published in the Collection of Laws under No. 205/2003 Coll., has specific significance in the development of labour law of ILO member states and in its humanisation.

4.18. The primary anti-discrimination legislation of the European Union has begun to incorporate Article 119 of the EEC Treaty on equal treatment in remuneration of men and women. It is now also incorporating Council Directive 75/117/EEC, which unlike Article 119 of the EEC Treaty, incorporated the prohibition of discrimination in remuneration of men and women with regard to both the same and equal work. Compared to the ILO Conventions, the regulation of the issue of equal treatment and prohibition of discrimination in employment relationships is broader and elaborated on a higher level in the EU law.

4.19. The most important directive in the field of EU anti-discrimination legislation in the twentieth century is Council Directive 1976/207/EEC on the implementation of the principle of equal treatment for men and women concerning access to employment, vocational training and promotion and working conditions. It was amended by Directive 2002/73/EC of the European Parliament and of the Council and Council Directive 97/80/EC on the burden of proof in cases of discrimination based on sex.

---

[9]   ECJ Judgment (Grand Chamber) of 22 November 2005, *supra* note 7; ECJ Judgment (Grand Chamber) of 03 October 2006, C-17/05, *B. F. Cadman v Health & Safety Executive* [2006] I-09583; ECJ Judgment (Grand Chamber) of 16 October 2007, C-411/05, *Félix Palacios de la Villa v Cortefiel Servicios SA* [2007] I-08531; ECJ Judgment (Third Chamber) of 18 June 2009, C-88/08, *David Hütter v Technische Universität Graz* [2009] I-05325; ECJ Judgment (Grand Chamber) of 12 October 2010, C-45/09, *Gisela Rosenbladt v Oellerking Gebäudereinigungsges. mbH* [2010] I-09391; ECJ Judgment (Grand Chamber) of 13 September 2011, C-447/09, *Reinhard Prigge and Others v Deutsche Lufthansa AG* [2011] I-08003; ECJ Judgment (Second Chamber) of 05 July 2012, C-141/11, *Torsten Hörnfeldt v Posten Meddelande AB* [Not yet published].

4.20. The boom of EU anti-discrimination legislation is connected mainly with the adoption of Council Directive 2000/78/EC establishing a general framework for equal treatment in employment and occupation (hereinafter Directive 2000/78/EC) and Council Directive 2000/43/EC implementing the principle of equal treatment between persons irrespective of racial or ethnic origin. Directive 2000/78/EC extended, in compliance with the Amsterdam Treaty, the discrimination characteristics of age, disability and sexual orientation.

4.21. The EU incorporates, outside the scope of ILO international labour law, the prohibition of discrimination on the grounds of disability and sexual orientation. The Court of Justice has adopted very important supportive case law.[10]

4.22. Apart from the prohibition of direct and indirect discrimination, the EU law explicitly also prohibits unlawful instructions of superiors, incitement to discrimination and the prohibition of harassment of an employee in the workplace including sexual harassment.

---

[10] ECJ Judgment (Grand Chamber) of 11 July 2006, C-13/05, *Sonia Chacón Navas v Eurest Colectividades SA* [2006] I-06467; ECJ Judgment (Grand Chamber) of 17 July 2008, C-303/06, *S. Coleman v Attridge Law and Steve Law,* [2008] I-05603; ECJ Judgment (Grand Chamber) of 01 April 2008, C-267/06, *Tadao Maruko v Versorgungsanstalt der deutschen Bühnen* [2008] I-01757; ECJ Judgment (Grand Chamber) of 10 May 2011, C-147/08, *Jürgen Römer v Freie und Hansestadt Hamburg* [2011] I-03591; ECJ Judgment (Grand Chamber) of 22 November 2005, *supra* note 7; ECJ Judgment (Grand Chamber) of 03 October 2006, *supra* note 9; ECJ Judgment (Grand Chamber) of 16 October 2007, *supra* note 9; ECJ Judgment (Grand Chamber) of 23 September 2008, C-427/06, *Birgit Bartsch v Bosch und Siemens Hausgeräte (BSH) Altersfürsorge GmbH* [2008] I-07245; ECJ Judgment (Third Chamber) of 5 March 2009, C-388/07, *The Queen, on the application of The Incorporated Trustees of the National Council for Ageing (Age Concern England) v Secretary of State for Business, Enterprise and Regulatory Reform* [2009] I-01569; ECJ Judgment (Grand Chamber) of 19 January 2010, C-555/07, *Seda Kücükdeveci v Swedex GmbH & Co. KG* [2010] I-00365; ECJ Judgment (Third Chamber) of 18 June 2009, *supra* note 9; ECJ Judgment (Grand Chamber) of 12 January 2010, C-229/08, *Colin Wolf v Stadt Frankfurt am Main* [2010] I-00001; ECJ Judgment (Grand Chamber) of 12 January 2010, C-341/08, *Domnica Petersen v Berufungsausschuss für Zahnärzte für den Bezirk Westfalen-Lippe* [2010] I-00047; Judgment (Grand Chamber) of 12 October 2010, *supra* note 9; ECJ Judgment (Second Chamber) of 18 November 2010, C-250/09, *Vasil Ivanov Georgiev v Tehnicheski universitet - Sofia, filial Plovdiv* [2010] I-11869; ECJ Judgment (Grand Chamber) of 13 September 2011, *supra* note 9; ECJ Judgment (Second Chamber) of 21 July 2011, joined cases C-159/10 and C-160/10, *Gerhard Fuchs (C-159/10) and Peter Köhler (C-160/10) v Land Hessen* [2011] I-06919; ECJ Judgment (Second Chamber) of 8 September 2011, joined cases C-297/10 and C-298/10, *Sabine Hennigs (C-297/10) v Eisenbahn-Bundesamt and Land Berlin (C-298/10) v Alexander Mai* [2011] I-07965; ECJ Judgment (Second Chamber) of 19 April 2012, C-415/10, *Galina Meister v Speech Design Carrier Systems GmbH* [Not yet published]; ECJ Judgment (Second Chamber) of 05 July 2012, *supra* note 9.

4.23. After adopting the Treaty of Lisbon, equality between men and women has also been incorporated in Article 23 of the Charter of Fundamental Rights of the European Union, under which equality between men and women should be ensured in all areas, including employment, work and pay. The principle of equality does not prevent maintaining or adopting measures providing for specific advantages in favour of the under-represented sex. Therefore, the Charter of Fundamental Rights of the European Union allows for 'positive' discrimination (e.g. affirmative action) in favour of the under-represented sex, which includes mostly women. Procedures for European lawmakers with regard to positive measures has its foundation in the primary EU law itself. It is incorporated in Article 157(4) of the Treaty on the Functioning of the European Union.[11]

III. Prohibition of Slavery, Compulsory and Forced Labour

4.24. The prohibition of slavery, as a fundamental human right, as well as the prohibition of compulsory and forced labour is a subject of international law and the European Convention on Human Rights, the basic source of law of the Council of Europe. With regard to regulation of this fundamental human right, international law is significantly ahead of the legal regulation of the Council of Europe. Apart from the Universal Declaration of Human Rights, as well as the International Covenant on Civil and Political Rights, the prohibition of slavery, compulsory and forced labour is the subject of two ILO Conventions, ILO Convention No. 29 of 1930 on forced or compulsory labour and Convention No. 105 of 1957 on the abolition of forced labour. The Slovak Republic ratified both conventions. [12]

4.25. Even today, the prohibition of slavery, compulsory and forced labour is relevant. The prohibition of slavery and forced labour are closely

---

[11] ECJ Judgment of 17 October 1995, C- 450/93, *Eckhard Kalanke v Freie Hansestadt Bremen* [1995] I-03051; ECJ Judgment of 11 November 1997, C-409/95, *Hellmut Marschall v Land Nordrhein-Westfalen* [1997] I-06363; ECJ Judgment (Fifth Chamber) of 6 July 2000, C-407/98, *Katarina Abrahamsson and Leif Anderson v Elisabet Fogelqvist* [2000] I-05539; ECJ Judgment of 19 March 2002, C-476/99, *H. Lommers v Minister van Landbouw, Natuurbeheer en Visserij* [2002] I-02891; ECJ Judgment (Second Chamber) of 30 September 2004, C- 319/03, *Serge Briheche v Ministre de l'Intérieur, Ministre de l'Éducation nationale and Ministre de la Justice* [2004] I-08807.

[12] The ILO Convention No. 105/1957 on abolition of forced labour was ratified in 1990 (announcement No. 340/1998). ILO Convention No. 29/1930 on forced and compulsory labour was ratified in 1990 (announcement No. 506/1990 and item 14 of the announcement No. 110/1997).

Czech Yearbook of International Law

connected with the right to human dignity. Any person cannot be degraded to an object of state or private act. The person must not be treated as a thing. It is the fundamental human right which has its purpose also in the third millennium. However, forms of slavery and forced labour are changing.

4.26. Although the prohibition of slavery has the legal nature of an absolute right, new forms of slavery, mainly trafficking in women and child prostitution, are occurring. Prohibitions of slavery and 'modern' slavery practices have the nature of ius cogens according to both international and European law. According to current literature, slavery and forced labour is threatening more than 27 million people in the world even in the twenty-first century.[13]

4.27. A source for modern slavery is the corrupt conduct of states, state officials, the economic collapse of states and social and economic crises. Methods and practices of worldwide economic globalisation lead to new slavery. They are more delicate and refined than in the past, compared to classical historical methods of forced labour. The up-to-date methods of modern slavery are often used against employees who have to be constantly available to their employer, who are handled by their employer as a commodity, such as employees working in slave-like conditions in Bangladesh, and for whom the employee works under humiliating and demeaning salary and work conditions 7 days a week, 16 hours a day.

4.28. The existence and number of slave practices in the twenty-first century require thinking about revising the ILO Conventions, so that people that grossly breach these rights could not hide behind requirements of flexibility and liberalisation of employment relationships.

4.29. ILO Convention No. 182/1999 concerning the prohibition and immediate action for the elimination of the worst forms of child labour is connected with the prohibition of slavery and forced labour.[14] It was adopted by the General Conference of ILO in Geneva at its 87th session on 17 June 1999. The Convention became effective on 19 November 2000 and was ratified by the Slovak Republic on 20 December 1999.[15] The Convention is related to ILO Convention No. 23/1030 and ILO Convention No. 105 on abolition of forced and compulsory labour, as well as to the 1989 UN Convention on the Rights of the Child. It

---

[13] Miłosz Borowski, *Verbot Volter und unmenschlicher oder erniedriger Strafe oder Behandlung, in* CHARTA DER GRUNDRECHTE DER EUROPÄISCHEN UNION, Baden-Baden: Nomos 187 (N. Bernsdorff & J. Meyer, eds., 2011).

[14] The Convention became effective on 19 November 2000 and was announced in the Collection of Laws under No. 38/2001.

[15] Announcement No. 38/2001 Coll.

considers the sale and trafficking of children, forced and compulsory labour including forced or compulsory recruitment of children for use in armed conflicts, use of children for prostitution, production of pornography and other illicit activities (e.g. trafficking of drugs) to be the worst form of child labour. Such labour is also considered work that could harm the health, safety or morals of children. The ILO member states that have ratified the Convention ILO have rather broad obligations. Apart from the obligation to legally incorporate the types of works prohibited by Article 3 of the Convention, they are also obliged to monitor whether such types of works, which are the worst forms of child labour, occur on their territory. The developed list of types of works must be reviewed on a regular basis by the member state and adequate mechanisms for inspection and control of the Convention's application concerning the prohibition and immediate action for the elimination of the worst forms of child labour must be introduced.

4.30. Compared to the ILO legislation, the EU law protects children and minors up to the age of 18 with Council Directive 94/33/EC on the protection of young people at work. Unlike ILO Convention No. 182/1992, it focuses on the protection of children carrying out easier work, a list of which it incorporates as an example, as well as on protection of favourable work conditions for young workers ages 15 to 18.

IV. Atypical Employment

4.31. Over the last few years, the European Union has implemented various initiatives supporting work in flexible employment relationships as one of the options to enter the labour market. The EU law supports employment of natural persons in atypical employment relationships, such as part-time employment, agency work or fixed-term employment relationships. On the other hand, it lays down certain limits for laws of member states to ensure the social and legal protection of the employee. The European Economic and Social Committee stresses in its Opinion of 1 October 2009, item 1.9, that 'the reform of the labour markets in the Member States should ensure that the number of insecure jobs offering more flexibility than security, which has steadily increased over the last few years, does not increase further' because 'a weighting of the balance towards external flexibility might allow for extensive deregulation of normal working conditions so as to increase precarious employment'.[16] The Committee regards internal, not

---

[16] A similar opinion was adopted on 7 February 2008 by the Committee of the Regions, published in the Official Journal of the European Union, No. C 105, of 25 April 2008, page

external flexibility as an efficient combat against unemployment in a period of economic crisis, which should not be regarded as a set of measures to facilitate dismissal of employees or to undermine and endanger general social protections of employees.

4.32. Especially in times of world economic crisis, EU bodies are appealing to business entities – employers – not to dismiss their employees and instead to prefer flexible forms of employment that are, unlike unemployment, a better alternative for employees providing options to maintain work-related habits and skills. Even for employers, the substitution of typical full-time employment with atypical employment relationships is better than collective redundancies and subsequent recruitment of new employees without work-related habits and skills.

4.33. All not full-time employment relationships and those for an indefinite period can be considered as atypical forms of employment. ILO Recommendation No. 197 of 1998 follows from the principle that the full-time an employment relationship for an indefinite period still remains the basic type of employment relationship. Parties choose atypical forms of employment in a situation when it is not possible to establish a full-time employment relationship for an indefinite period or if they choose these forms freely.

4.34. The fixed-term employment relationship, part-time employment relationship and agency work are regulated by the EU directives. The equal treatment principle is their common legal characteristic. From this point of view, we also consider these flexible forms of employment to be a systematic part of anti-discrimination law in EU legislation.

IV.1. Agency Work

4.35. If we follow the development of international labour law with regard to agency work, the material scope of the regulation of atypical employments in ILO conventions is narrower than EU law. The ILO conventions do not regulate fixed-term employment relationships or telework. On the other hand, home work is regulated today only in the ILO Convention concerning home work.

4.36. The ILO regulation on agency work is quite ahead of the EU law. Already in 1933, the ILO adopted Convention No. 34 on fee-charging employment agencies, which was replaced by Convention No. 96/1949 in 1949. This Convention was revised in 1997 by ILO Convention No. 181 on private employment agencies. The Slovak Republic withdrew

16, item 22. See also Green Paper: "Modernising labour law to meet the challenges of the 21st century." (COM 2006 708).

from Convention No. 34/1933 in 2008 and subsequently ratified Convention No. 181/1997 on private employment agencies on 22 February 2011. The Convention applies to legal entities and natural persons providing placement services.

4.37. The Convention's objective is to ensure the equal treatment principle in the legal position of agency workers. The Convention formulates the prohibition of discrimination of agency workers also with regard to age, disability or any other form of discrimination. For example, sexual orientation does not appear in the Convention as an independent discriminatory feature, but the Convention incorporates the prohibition of discrimination in any other form of discrimination. The Convention is an expression of efforts of the ILO to protect the employee from agency work abuse and, at the same time, it enables ILO member states to exclude certain work categories from the personal scope of this Convention, assuming that their protection has been ensured otherwise.

4.38. Under Article 2 of the Convention, the member state may, after consulting the most representative organizations of employers and employees concerned, prohibit, under specific circumstances, private employment agencies from representing certain categories of workers, branches of economic activity or types of provided services. Equally under the above mentioned conditions, a member state is authorized to exclude employees from certain branches of economic activity, or parts thereof, from the scope of the Convention or from certain provisions, provided that adequate protection is otherwise assured for the employees concerned.

4.39. Even though the Convention follows the principle that employment agencies shall not charge any costs or any other fees to employees (Article 7(1) of the Convention), the Convention does allow a member state to authorize an exception for certain categories of employees and types of services.

4.40. Only after 11 years, in 2008, the EU regulation followed the international legal regulation of agency employees in ILO Convention No. 181 with Directive 2008/104/EC of the European Parliament and of the Council on temporary agency work. Similarly to ILO Convention No. 181 of 1997, Directive 2008/104/EC regulates the performance of agency work. On the one hand, it significantly liberalizes the performance of agency work; on the other hand, it requires compliance with the equal treatment principle more consistently compared to ILO Convention No. 181/1997. Directive 2008/104/EC incorporates the prohibition of agency employees' discrimination in comparison to employees working in standard employment relationships. Directive

2008/104/EC incorporates, apart from the prohibition of discrimination in Article 5, the possibility for a member state to adopt necessary measures against the abuse of agency work.

4.41. The current labour law regulation of agency work in the Slovak Republic is one of the most liberal in the whole European Union. So far, it has no required legal tools against the abuse of agency work. The amendment to Act No. 5/2004 Coll., on the services of employment, as amended, became effective on 1 May 2013 (Act No. 96/2013 Coll.). It brought certain legal restrictions to agency work concerning chaining fixed-term employment contracts.[17] The sanction for chaining fixed-term employment contracts is the irrefutable presumption of the termination of an employment relationship with the temporary employment agency and the establishment of an employment relationship for an indefinite period with the user employer. According to Section 29(2) of Act No. 5/2004 Coll., as amended, it is not a temporary assignment if the user employer has repeatedly agreed with the temporary employment agency that the same employee will be assigned more than 5 times in a row during 24 consecutive months. In such cases, the employment relationship between the employee and the temporary employment agency is terminated and the employment relationship for an indefinite period is established between the user employer and the employee.

IV.2. Part-time Work

4.42. Of atypical forms of employment, the EU law noticeably favours part-time employment relationships. Regulation of part-time work in Council Directive 97/81/EC is formulated as a type of flexible employment that should be supported in every possible way without obstacles. The newest case law of the Court of Justice of the EU speaks in support of it.[18] The part-time employment relationship has great significance for increasing the employment rate over the whole European Union. Extending the possibility to enter the labour market is nowadays connected with requirements for a minimum level of employee protection. Under Council Directive 97/81/EC, the EU Member States have the obligation, on the one hand, to expand their part-time work, and on the other hand, to meet the Directive's objective by complying with the principle of equal treatment of part-time employees with full-time employees.

---

[17] Fixed term employment relationship, Job aharing, Part-time.
[18] Ibid.

4.43. In 1994, the ILO adopted Convention No. 175 in advance of the EC legislation. Only three years later, Council Directive 97/81/EC concerning the Framework Agreement on part-time work concluded by UNICE, CEEP and the ETUC (European Trade Union Confederation) (hereinafter Directive 97/81/EC) was adopted at the EU level.

4.44. The ILO Convention concerning part-time work now has certain higher standards of legal status for part-time employees and it is approximating the legal status of full-time employees in many aspects. According to Article 4 of the Convention, part-time employees should be provided with the same legal protection as is provided to full-time employees with respect to rights to organize and bargain collectively, occupational health and safety, as well as discrimination in employment and occupation. Through this, the Convention concerning part-time work has approximated the part-time employee's status to the full-time employee's status although not in all aspects of the employment relationship. The Convention in Article 3 allows the member states to exclude partially or fully individual categories of employees from the scope of the Convention. ILO Convention No. 175 of 1994 on part-time work presented a substantive step towards the equal treatment principle at the time of its adoption, even though it did not fully develop this central legal principle. The Convention became effective on 28 February 1998, during the time when the preparations for adoption of the Council Directive concerning the Framework Agreement on part-time work were finishing in the EC and as a result of the agreement of social partners on the European level.

4.45. Council Directive 97/81/EC concerning the Framework Agreement on part-time work follows from the principle of equal treatment of full-time and part-time employees, including equal labour law protection against a one-sided termination of the employment relationship by an employer.

4.46. Even though Clause 2 of Directive 97/81/EC allows the member state to exclude from the Directive's personal scope, partially or fully, employees who work on a casual basis, Slovak lawmakers did not use this opportunity. Therefore, according to the current state of the law, the equal treatment principle incorporated in Section 49(5) of the Slovak Labour Code applies to occasional work as well. Compared to ILO Convention 175/1994 on part-time work, Council Directive 97/81/EC concerning the Framework Agreement on part-time work incorporated the equal treatment principle as a central principle and offered to EU member states a substantially higher standard of employee protection compared to ILO Convention 175/1994. This fact is the substantial reason why the Slovak Republic like other EU Member States, has not ratified the ILO Convention on part-time work, yet.

IV.3. Fixed-term Employment Relationships

4.47. The fixed-term relationship is a subject of constant concern of business entities as one form of increasing the flexibility of existing employment relationships. Its regulation within labour law has its limits mainly in the EU law that puts quite essential legal restrictions on successive conclusion of fixed-term employment contracts in order to prevent the abuse of fixed-term employment relationships against the social and legal protection of employees.

4.48. A fixed-term employment relationship in a member state's national legislation must be in compliance with Council Directive 1999/70/EC concerning the framework agreement on fixed-term work, which presents considerable demands on national lawmakers of member states. The relatively rich case law of the Court of Justice of the European Union also speaks for it.[19] Article 4 of the Directive, expressing the equal treatment principle, has a horizontal direct legal effect.

4.49. Clause 5(1) of the Directive is concerned with adoption of measures by EU member states against the abuse of successive fixed-term employment relationship

4.50. International labour law does not specifically regulate the issue of a fixed-term employment relationship, even though ILO Recommendation No. 166/1985 concerning termination of employment incorporates in Article 3 that the protection of employees working on fixed-term employment contracts can be done in one of the following ways:
1) fixed-term employment relationships will be limited only to cases where given the nature of the work or circumstances or interests of the employee an employment relationship for an indefinite period cannot be concluded,
2) to consider fixed-term employment contracts concluded in other cases as an employment relationship for an indefinite period (irrefutable legal presumption) or
3) to consider fixed-term employment contracts, if concluded successively in other cases than stipulated in item 1, as employment contracts for an indefinite period.

---

[19] For example, ECJ Judgment (Second Chamber) of 7 September 2006, C-180/04, *Andrea Vassallo v Azienda Ospedaliera Ospedale San Martino di Genova e Cliniche Universitarie Convenzionate* [2006] I-07251; ECJ Judgment (Grand Chamber) of 4 July 2006, C- 212/04, *Konstantinos Adeneler and Others v Ellinikos Organismos Galaktos (ELOG)* [2006] I-06057; ECJ Judgment (Second Chamber) of 7 September 2006, C-53/04, *Cristiano Marrosu and Gianluca Sardino v Azienda Ospedaliera Ospedale San Martino di Genova e Cliniche Universitarie Convenzionate* [2006] I-07213; ECJ Judgment (Grand Chamber) of 15 April 2008, C-268/06, *Impact v Minister for Agriculture and Food and Others* [2008] I-02483.

4.51. The ILO Recommendation in question became good legal grounds for adoption of Council Directive 1999/70/EC concerning fixed-term work, which was adopted by social partners at the European level on the basis of the Framework Agreement. ILO Recommendation No. 166/1982 concerning termination of employment was partially used by the Slovak labour law that follows from the irrefutable legal presumption of the existence of an employment relationship for an indefinite period, should legal conditions for a conclusion of fixed-term employment not be met.

IV.4. Home Work

4.52. ILO Convention No. 177 concerning home work was adopted in 1996. It has not been ratified by the Slovak Republic so far, and neither was ILO Recommendation No. 184/1996 concerning home work.

4.53. According to ILO Convention No. 177, home work includes not only work at home, but also work carried out anywhere at a place different from the workplace resulting in a product or a service.

4.54. Convention No. 177 requires that homeworkers are provided with basic social rights, such as the right to freely associate, to protection from discrimination at work, to occupational health and safety, to remuneration, to social security, to access to education and to maternity protection (Article 4). Under Article 4(1) of the Convention, the national policy on home work shall promote, as far as possible, the equality of treatment between homeworkers and other wage earners, taking into account the special characteristics of home work.

4.55. Based on the facts above, Convention No. 177/1996 does not require unconditional compliance with the equal treatment principle to the full extent, as is legally guaranteed by the Slovak labour law regulation in the Labour Code.

4.56. At the same time, the Convention on home work incorporates in Article 7 that certain types of work and use of certain materials should be prohibited due to occupational health and safety reasons. It concurrently allows using intermediaries (agencies) to intermediate home work, while the member state is obliged in these cases to define the responsibilities of employers and intermediaries.

4.57. ILO Convention No. 177/1996 on home work is followed by ILO Recommendation 184/1996 on home work, under which the registration of employers of homeworkers and intermediaries should be provided at a national level and where appropriate, at the regional, sectoral or local levels. Under the Recommendation in question, the employer should keep a register of all homeworkers, classified according to sex, and labour inspectors should be allowed to enter parts of a home or other private premises to perform an inspection. In cases of serious violations of the laws concerning home work, appropriate measures should be taken by national law, including the possible prohibition of carrying out home work. The Slovak Republic has not ratified the Convention yet. Home work has not been the subject of EU law regulation so far.

IV.5. Convention concerning Decent Work for Domestic Workers

4.58. In 2011, the ILO's General Conference adopted Convention No. 189/2011 concerning decent work for domestic workers, supplemented with a Recommendation on domestic workers. The Convention was adopted as a response to consequences of a world economic crisis and a high unemployment rate both inside and outside the EU.

4.59. ILO Convention No. 189/2011 concerns decent work for domestic workers. It is one of the newest legal regulations of atypical employment in international labour law. It concerns mainly home work that is carried out in the employee's household, which often provides the employer with an opportunity to abuse and break elementary labour law standards with regard to hours of work, daily and weekly rest and provision of wages.

The main objective of the Convention is to ensure a more efficient protection of human rights for all homeworkers. It is formulated by the Convention in Article 3(2) as fundamental obligations of ILO member states to respect the freedom to associate, eliminate all forms of forced and compulsory labour, effectively abolish child labour and eliminate discrimination.

4.60. The Slovak Republic has not ratified the ILO Convention yet. In case of ratification, the existing would require numerous fundamental legislative changes to the Labour Code and the Act on employment services. Preparation for ratification of this Convention by the Slovak Republic would still require a relatively long time before the labour law regulation reaches a higher level of compliance with the basic requirements of the Convention on home work.

4.61. Because the Convention requires ensuring the same quality of legal status between homeworkers and other employees, the labour law regulation of employees' rights would be important should an employee live in his employer's household. Cases of home work of this type are not numerous in the Slovak Republic. Therefore, I believe that Slovak lawmakers will not hurry with ratification of this Convention, which also is consistent with the Opinion of the Ministry of Labour, Social Affair and Family of the Slovak Republic on the ability to ratify ILO Convention No. 189 of 2011.[20] OK!!!

IV.6. Telework

4.62. Telework is regulated by the Framework Agreement on Telework, concluded at the European level by social partners (UNICE, UEAPME, CEEP, ETUC) on 16 July 2002 (hereinafter Framework Agreement on Telework). Telework at the EU level is carried out as a modern form of the employment relationship.

4.63. Telework is considered to be work carried out by a natural person usually at a place that is outside the employer's premises that is different from the traditional place of work, for the employer or a client, using telecommunication and information technologies as essential elements of the work. The Agreement's objective is to provide teleworking employees with social security and the same rights and benefits as other employees. In the first place, the equal treatment principle must be guaranteed. The employer has to provide teleworking employees with equal pay, equal access to education and career development as to the employees working on the employer's premises.

4.64. The European Union and the Slovak labour law regulation both follow from the voluntary character of telework and guarantee the same working conditions to teleworking employees as to employees within a typical employment relationship.

4.65. The European Union has incorporated basic working conditions for telework in the telework agreement. The employer should be responsible for the protection of an employee's life and health at work. The employer is obliged to ensure and maintain necessary workplace equipment and to cover additional work-related costs of an employee's household. The employer should use these less usual forms of employment for trusted employees whose type of work allows it. On the other hand, the employer should pay close attention that no violation of the Act on personal data protection occurs especially in telework.[21]

---

[20] The opinion of the Department of Employment Relations of the MoLSAaF of the SR on the ability to ratify the ILO Convention concerning decent work for homeworkers, 2012.

[21] Andrea Olšovská, *Atypické zamestnania,(Atypical Employments) in* PRACOVNÉ PRÁVO V EURÓPSKEJ PERSPEKTÍVE (*European Law in European Perspective*), Plzeň: Vydavatelství a nakladatelství Aleš Čeněk (Helena Barancová ed., 2009).

V. Termination of Employment at the Initiative of the Employer

4.66. ILO Convention No. 158 of 1982 concerning termination of employment at the initiative of the employer is the most significant of the numerous ILO Conventions that have influenced the development of labour law in the Slovak Republic for essential conditions of employees. The Slovak Republic ratified this Convention in 2010. Apart from Convention No. 158, the International Labour Organisation adopted a Recommendation to ILO Convention No. 166 concerning termination of employment at the initiative of the employer, as well.

4.67. Also under the influence of ratification of this Convention, the labour law in the Slovak Republic succeeded in maintaining a socially acceptable level of labour law protection of employees upon a unilateral termination of the employment relationship at the employer's initiative. During every proposed legislative change to the Labour Code, Slovak employers request lowering the protection of employees upon unilateral terminations of employment relationships by employers. For example, there are proposals concerning the removal or substantial decrease of notice periods and to lower employee protections in other situations.

4.68. There is no universal protection of an employee from termination of employment at the initiative of the employer in the EU labour law. Specific protection of employees in the case of a transfer of a business or parts of a business is subject to regulation of Council Directive 2001/23/EC on the approximation of laws of the member states relating to the safeguarding of employees' rights in the event of transfers of undertakings, businesses or parts of undertakings or businesses. Council Directive 2001/23/EC, transposed to the Labour Code, ensures that employees will not fall victim to an employer's on-going restructuring changes and it guarantees them continuation of the employment relationship by the new, assuming employer. Transfers of businesses or parts of a business may not be a reason by itself for a unilateral termination of the employment relationship by the employer. On the other hand, in compliance with the principle of contractual freedom it ensures that the employee can freely decide whether to work for the new employer.

4.69. Council Directive 98/59/EC on the approximation of the laws of the member states relating to collective redundancies, incorporates the legal model that imposes on the employer a complex set of obligations to provide information to the social partner at the workplace as well as to the respective Labour Office. It also has consultation procedures with the social partner with whom the employer carries out the 'social selection' of employees, if collective redundancy cannot be avoided.

VI. ILO Recommendation No. 198 of 2006 concerning the Employment Relationship

4.70. Even though Recommendations of the International Labour Organisation are not legally binding, Recommendation No. 198 concerning the employment relationship was the most significant ILO Recommendation of the past decades that affected the direction of labour law of the Slovak Republic, the Czech Republic and other ILO member states.

4.71. The Recommendation responds to the particularly urgent situation of the beginning of the twenty-first century when commercial and civil law relationships in wage employment began to displace the labour law relationships. This still unfavourably developing situation is not only in the EU countries, but also worldwide, which has forced the ILO to pay serious attention to these issues. The Recommendation encourages member states to adopt necessary legal regulations to protect wage employment with employment contracts and the employment relationship. It recommends that states define the term wage employment or the term employment relationship as substantial legal indicators in their legislation. The Recommendation asks the member states, on the basis of thorough global comparative analysis, to incorporate the presumption of an employment relationship in cases of certain standard occupations in order to protect employees. It has to be stated that the ILO Recommendation has significantly appealed to Slovak lawmakers when solving issues of illegal work and in incorporating the current employer's obligation to carry out wage employment only in its legal forms. At the same time, the Labour Code in Section 1 lays down the prohibition to perform wage employment through contractual forms of civil or commercial law.

VII. The Latest Challenges in Legislation of the International Labour Organisation and EU Law

4.72. The International Labour Organisation is currently concerned with the legal implications of an ageing population globally and new challenges arising from this irreversible process. It is expected that the number of citizens older than 65 will triple by 2050.[22] This new demographic context has important impacts on employment and social protection policies. The global economic crisis aggravated the situation in labour

---

[22] Decision No 940/2011/EU of the European Parliament and of the Council of 14 September 2011 on the European Year for Active Ageing and Solidarity between Generations.

markets and increased the unemployment rates for all groups of citizens. This is causing financial pressure on social security systems.

4.73. Based on long-term trends, the key social and economic challenges caused by demographic changes are being analysed within the ILO today. The need for an integrated framework of decent work, widening through the life cycle and accepting intergenerational solidarity, is being emphasized.

4.74. To provide access to decent work for all has proven to be the most important challenge of the current century. While the continuing global economic crisis deteriorated the environment and social protection, recognition of the key role of decent work for sustainable development is still on the rise. This is reflected in the number of recent national political initiatives. The necessity to build on interaction between ecologically sustainable development and decent work to overcome the crisis and eradicate poverty was explicitly formulated in June 2012 at the United Nations conference on sustainable development (Rio+20).

4.75. The International Labour Conference in its 97th session (in 2008) adopted the ILO Declaration on social justice for fair globalisation. The Declaration expresses the universality of the Decent Work Programme. According to this Declaration, all members of the International Labour Organisation must carry out policies on the basis of ILO strategic objectives - employment, social protection, social dialogue and rights at work.

4.76. The need for cohesive environmental, economic and social policies in compliance with the ILO Declaration on social justice for fair globalisation of 2008 is emphasized. An emphasis is put on the need to adopt necessary policies and apply strategies that maximise opportunities for decent work and strengthen social inclusion on the way to environmentally sustainable development.

4.77. The issue of the ageing population and the substantive results of the current demographic development in the whole EU are of long-term interest to the EU bodies, resulting in the EU Programme on intergenerational solidarity. The expected consequences of the decade-long unfavourable demographic development in the whole European Union present huge risks for Europe. The labour market in the European Union will inevitably require a massive engagement of employees from outside the European Union.

4.78. The age pyramid to date is gaining more dramatic shapes every year due to a decline in the birth rate in the European Union countries and a rising life expectancy. Today, there are no jobs for young people.

Already there are many suggestions for changes to present traditional business employment and human resources policies for the near future.

4.79. Council Decision 20/707/EU of 21 October 2010 on guidelines for the employment policies of the Member States invites the Member States to a greater engagement in the labour market through policies to increase the employment rate of older workers through innovations in companies' work organisations and to increase their level of employment through life-long learning.

4.80. Far-reaching measures and improvements by the Member States are necessary to allow older people to remain in working life longer.[23]

4.81. Also, current EU legal documents point out the issue of active ageing, mainly the decision of the European Parliament and Council 940/2011/EU of 14 September 2011 on the European Year for Active Ageing and Solidarity between generations. The current demographic development poses a threat to fulfilment of the EU's basic objectives in economic, social and geographic cohesion.

4.82. As a direct negative impact of Europe's demographic development, the need for employing older employees will rise. The European Union has resolved to honour and protect fundamental human rights in this regard.

4.83. On the other hand, the rate of youth unemployment has risen radically during the economic and financial crisis, which is a serious risk for social unrest in the upcoming years. It mainly concerns highly educated young people without the required professional life perspective. This category of society should deserve primary attention within the European Union. However, improvement in the employment rate of young people can hardly be expected without increasing economic growth. As administrative measures alone are not capable of solving this problem, the tools of the free market also do not present sufficient solutions. Adoption of a complex set of economic and legal tools to improve the situation of young people in the European labour market can be expected in the near future.

VIII. Conclusion

4.84. The ILO legislation is, compared to the EU law, more complex and historically older. Convergence between numerous ILO Conventions and Recommendations and the EU labour law has happened over the last two decades. A gradual increase in this development is quite

---

[23] Opinion of the European Economic and Social Committee on the Proposal for a decision of the European Parliament and of the Council on the European Year for Active Ageing COM (2010) 462, 2011/C/51/11 of 7 September 2010.

evident, mainly in the fields of anti-discrimination law and other fundamental human rights, protection of employees during restructuring of businesses and in the field of atypical employments.

4.85. The issue of atypical employment is regulated by the EU law in a broader material scope with an emphasis on the prohibition of discrimination that applies not only to agency work, but also to fixed-term employment relationships, part-time work and to telework.

4.86. On the other hand, the protection of employees from dismissal at the initiative of the employer is significantly better ensured by ILO Convention No. 158/1982, as opposed to the EU law, which is limited only to issues of collective redundancies, regulation of employees' rights during transfers of businesses or parts of a business and maintaining the rights of employees in the event of the insolvency of their employer. This regulation at the level of EU law is directly connected with the still dynamic process of business restructuring.

4.87. Very dynamic development has occurred in the field of collective labour law over the past decades not only in international labour law, but also in the law of the European Union. The Slovak Republic has ratified all-important ILO Conventions concerning collective labour law and reflected them in its own labour laws. A similar process of a high level of compliance is also shown in the approximation of numerous EU directives concerning collective labour law. However, the remaining differences in labour law regulations concerning collective labour law and different traditions of internal laws of the EU Member States will be the basic limiting factor of achieving a significantly higher level of unification of collective labour law of the EU member states with the EU collective labour law in the future.

| | |

Summaries

FRA   [*La réglementation actuelle de l'Organisation internationale du travail et le droit de l'UE*]

Le présent article s'intéresse dans le système du droit international du travail et du droit de l'UE qui se développe au domaine des relations de travail, du temps de travail, du droit anti-discriminatoire, des métiers atypiques, de la notion de travail décent, de la résiliation du contrat de travail par l'employeur, tout comme à l'élimination des pires formes de travail des enfants, à l'interdiction de l'esclavage, du travail forcé et obligatoire. Quelques caractéristiques juridiques communes aux systèmes examinés apparaissent dans leur comparaison. L'une d'entre elles est la convergence de l'évolution des deux systèmes dans les domaines des métiers atypiques et du temps de travail. Cette convergence apparaît clairement, quoique l'éventail des métiers atypiques soit bien plus réduit dans la législation de l'Organisation internationale du travail que dans le droit de l'UE.

D'un autre côté, le niveau des mesures anti-discriminatoires est bien plus grand dans le droit de l'UE que dans les conventions de l'Organisation internationale du travail. La résiliation du contrat de travail à l'initiative de l'employeur est envisagée pour une palette plus large de niveaux matériels et sociaux dans la normalisation de l'Organisation internationale du travail. On constate pour conclure que ce qui différencie la normalisation actuelle de l'Organisation internationale du travail du droit du travail de l'Union européenne en train de se développer, c'est entre autres le caractère plus large, sur un plan matériel comme sur un plan humain, des conventions de l'Organisation internationale du travail.

CZE *[**Aktuální legislativa Mezinárodní organizace práce s ohledem na právo EU**]*

Ve vývoji systému mezinárodního pracovního práva a práva EU se autorka zaměřuje na oblast pracovního poměru, pracovní doby, antidiskriminačního práva, atypických zaměstnání, důstojné práce, skončení pracovního poměru ze strany zaměstnavatele, jakož i na odstraňování nejhorších forem dětské práce, včetně zákazu otroctví, povinné a nucené práce. Z porovnání zkoumaných systémů autorka vyvozuje některé společné právní charakteristiky. Jednou z nich je konvergence vývoje obou právních systémů v oblasti atypických zaměstnání a pracovní doby. Tato je zřejmá, ačkoliv věcný rozsah atypických zaměstnání je v právní úpravě Mezinárodní organizace práce, ve srovnání s právem EU, podstatně užší.

Na druhé straně úroveň antidiskriminačního práva EU, jeho věcný a osobní rozsah, je ve srovnání s úmluvami Mezinárodní organizace práce podstatně vyšší. Skončení pracovního poměru z iniciativy zaměstnavatele je v normotvorbě Mezinárodní organizace práce na věcně širší a více sociální úrovni. Na závěr lze konstatovat, že mezi diferenciační charakteristiky současné normotvorby Mezinárodní organizace práce a vývoje pracovního práva EU patří podstatně širší věcný a osobní rozsah úmluv Mezinárodní organizace práce.

| | |

POL [*Aktualne rozwiązania prawne Międzynarodowej Organizacji Pracy w świetle prawa UE*]

Autorka bada aktualne prawodawstwo Międzynarodowej Organizacji Pracy w nawiązaniu do zmian w prawie pracy UE. Przedmiotem porównania systemu międzynarodowego prawa pracy i prawa UE jest przede wszystkim prawo zapobiegające dyskryminacji, zakaz niewolnictwa, pracy obowiązkowej i przymusowej, nietypowe formy zatrudnienia, zwalczanie najgorszych form pracy dzieci, problematyka godnej pracy i prawne uregulowania w zakresie zwalniania pracowników.

DEU [*Aktuelle Gesetzgebung der Internationalen Arbeitsorganisation unter Berücksichtigung des EU-Rechts*]

Die Autorin verfolgt die aktuelle Normgebung der Internationalen Arbeitsorganisation im Gefolge der Entwicklung, die das Arbeitsrecht in der EU genommen hat. Gegenstand dieses Vergleichs zwischen dem System des internationalen Arbeitsrechts und dem EU-Recht sind v. a. das Recht zur Bekämpfung von Diskriminierung, das Verbot von Sklaverei, Pflicht- und Zwangsarbeit, Formen atypischer Beschäftigung, die Beseitigung der schlimmsten Formen von Kinderarbeit, der Problemkreis würdige Arbeit und die rechtliche Regelung der Entlassung von Arbeitskräften.

RUS [*Действующее законодательство Международной организации труда с учетом права ЕС*]

Автор рассматривает действующий процесс принятия норм в Международной организации труда с учетом развития трудового законодательства ЕС. Предметом сравнения системы международного трудового права и права ЕС, в первую очередь, является закон о недискриминации, запрещение рабства, принудительного и обязательного труда, форм нетипичной занятости, искоренение наихудших форм детского труда, вопросы достойного труда и правовое регулирование в области увольнения работников.

ESP [*La legislación vigente de la Organización Internacional del Trabajo con respecto a la legislación de la UE*]

La autora explora la actual creación de las normas de la Organización Internacional del Trabajo en relación con el desarrollo de la legislación laboral comunitaria. El objeto de la comparación del sistema del derecho laboral internacional y de la legislación comunitaria es, sobre todo, la ley contra la discriminación, la prohibición de la esclavitud, los trabajos forzados, las formas de empleo atípico, la eliminación de las peores formas de trabajo infantil, la cuestión del trabajo digno y la reglamentación sobre despidos de los trabajadores.

|||

Milan Bakeš | Michael Kohajda

Legal Regulation of and Influence of International Institutions on Financial Markets

Key words:
Basel Committee on Banking Supervision | Czech National Bank | Czech Republic | Financial Market | Financial Market Regulation | Financial Market Supervision

Abstract | *This paper attempts to offer a theoretical view on the regulation of the financial market. It focuses on the influence that international institutions, especially the Basel Committee on Banking Supervision, have on the regulation of the financial market.*

As we presume readers of the paper are unaware of Czech financial market regulations and theoretical points of view on legal regulation of the financial market, the opening portion of the paper will bring to their attention several fundamental pieces of information to introduce to them these topics.

The next part of the paper concentrates on the supervision of the financial market in general, its branches and its aims and will address the situation concerning financial market supervision in the Czech Republic.

The last part of the paper will be briefly dedicated to the influence of international organisations on financial market regulation, especially in the Czech Republic. The authors will focus on the Basel Committee on Banking Supervision and its influence on European Union legislation and on Czech legal rules on the financial market.

| | |

Prof. JUDr. Milan Bakeš, DrSc., is a professor at Charles University in Prague, School of Law, Department of Financial Law and Financial Science and an attorney at Bakeš & partneři Attorneys at Law office, Prague.
e-mail: bakes@ prf.cuni.cz

JUDr. Michael Kohajda, Ph.D., is an assistant professor at Charles University in Prague, School of Law, Department of Financial Law and Financial Science and an attorney at Diligentis Legal, Prague.
e-mail: kohajda@ prf.cuni.cz

Both authors focus their professional interest on issues related to financial law, especially on financial market regulation, banking law and financial marker supervision law.

I. Legal Regulation

5.01. Although the term 'legal regulation' can be widely found in oral and written professional practice, the definition of the term is rarely found in Czech professional print. The reason is that it is a term of deep science about the legal theory[1].

5.02. The great Czech legal theorist of the twentieth century Prof. Viktor Knapp says that the term *regulativnost* ('regulativeness') is similar in meaning to the term *normativnost* ('normativeness') and that the term *regulativnost* ('regulativeness') is similar in meaning to the term 'rule of law', stating that the boundary between the term 'regulativeness' and the term 'rule of law' is not explicit.[2] Elsewhere he writes[3] that the second side of 'normativeness' (as well as 'regulativeness') consists of the fact that the rule of law sets up a regulatory effect on concrete legal relations. Both of them arrange concrete social relationships, meaning they have a regulative character.

5.03. Ass. Prof. Zdenek Šín also finds[4] the substance of legal regulation through the effect of legal rule on social relationships, usually a system of legal relationships in the society. Therefore legal regulation creates a system of legal rules in a social order, social relationships and even becomes their legal guarantees.

5.04. From the economic point of view, which is not less important in the field of regulation and supervision on the financial market, the regulation is considered[5] as an instrument that provides supervision and control of private sector economic activities with the aim of efficient and normative economics.

5.05. In the field of financial market supervision Prof. Zdenek Revenda defines[6] banking regulations as the creation of rules, conditions and guidelines for banking institution activity and their enforcement in a real economy.

5.06. In contemporary Czech legislation related to the financial market there are only a few uses of the terms 'regulation' or 'regulated'. In law there

---

[1] This paper has been elaborated under the program 'PRVOUK P06 - Public Law in the context of Europeanization and globalization' realized at the School of Law of Charles University in Prague in the year of 2013.

[2] VIKTOR KNAPP, TEORIE PRÁVA, Prague: C.H.Beck Int. 148 (1995).

[3] VIKTOR KNAPP and col.: TVORBA PRÁVA A JEJÍ SOUČASNÉ PROBLÉMY, Prague: Linde Praha Int. 32 (1998).

[4] ZDENĚK ŠÍN, TVORBA PRÁVA A JEJÍ PRAVIDLA, Olomouc: VUP Int. 51 (2000).

[5] MILAN ŽÁK and col., VELKÁ EKONOMICKÁ ENCYKLOPEDIE, Prague: Linde Praha Int. 654 (the term *regulace*) (2nd ed. 2002).

[6] ZDENĚK REVENDA, CENTRÁLNÍ BANKOVNICTVÍ, Prague: Management Press Int. 119 (1999).

is the term 'regulated person'.[7] There is not a legal definition of the term but only an enumeration of kinds of subjects who are considered as regulated persons. There is a term 'regulated market'[8] which can be found in the legal definitions. In practice the definition of a regulated market is a market with investment instruments. The fundamental aspects of legal regulation according to this legal definition include: i) the existence of rules binding the market; ii) the performance of regular and systematic activities on the market; and iii) the existence of public authority supervision over these activities.

5.07. From the point of view of financial market regulation the definition of the term 'banking regulation' appears in the most widely known Czech financial law textbook[9] where banking regulation entails the concrete sum of restrictive and directive rules that must be respected by banks in their activities.

5.08. We can conclude that legal regulation of the financial market creates formulas and rules of behaviour of the financial market that are boosted by the authority of rules of law.

5.09. With regard to the Czech Republic, legal rules relating to the financial market are created not only by the Czech Parliament, but also by the Czech National Bank as the author of by-law rules. The Ministry of Finance then prepares drafts of bills for the Government, which is empowered to propose them to the Parliament.

II. Arguments for Regulation of the Financial Market

5.10. The law regulates most aspects of our society, but if we compare the scope of legal regulation in different spheres the degree of regulation differs substantially. The financial market, involving subjects' activities in the market and investment instruments, can be considered one of the spheres which is very highly regulated. This statement may be surprising, and for this reason it is appropriate to explain in a theoretical manner why the legal regulation of the financial market is so broad.

5.11. Usually the 'the invisible hand' is used as the one of the fundamental arguments for minimizing the scope of legal regulation of the financial market. But even in countries that can be considered very liberal and that agree with the idea of the invisible hand, the financial market is still highly regulated.

---

[7] Provision § 2 let. g) Act No. 377/2005 Coll., on Financial Conglomerates.

[8] Provision § 37 and following Act No. 256/2004 Coll., Capital Market Undertakings Act.

[9] See MILAN BAKEŠ, MARIE KARFÍKOVÁ, PETR KOTÁB & HANA MARKOVÁ, FINANČNÍ PRÁVO, Prague: C.H.Beck Int. 482 (6th ed. 2012).

II.1. Reasons in Favour of Regulation

5.12. The most relevant concrete reason and most important aim of legal regulation is the stability of the financial system of a state or international grouping. Very large financial institutions in the market (such as banks, insurance companies, regulated stock exchanges, investment companies and funds) strongly influence the functionality of the financial system as a whole.

5.13. A properly functioning and non-problematic financial system is the foundation of every state economy. It is in every state's economic and legal interest to protect the financial systems and its function; this can be best accomplished through legal regulation. It is in the interest of society as a whole to create legal rules for financial markets that would protect the markets themselves and all subjects acting in them.

5.14. When writing about large financial institutions, especially banks, we must mention that the majority of payment operations are realised through the financial market, specifically financial institutions, mainly by way of non-cash transactions. Money is the blood of every economy so that when the circulation of money is interrupted, it can have significant consequences for an economy. Non-cash money transfers can lead to issues for people, companies and even the state itself when not done correctly. This presents so great a risk for economies that it is fundamentally in the state's interest to legally regulate the financial market very broadly. In recent events in Cyprus, after a period of several days during which banks were closed, cash started to be expended and people were not able to fulfil basic needs because although they had money in the banks they had no cash in their hands.

5.15. The next reason for greater legal regulation of the financial market is the high potential of profit in this branch of business. In this kind of business they work directly with money on the financial market and money is easily transferable or is subject to 'disappearing' perhaps to an offshore location. This high potential of profit potentially high profitability, especially if perceived as a way to obtain a large profit quickly, can attract those who wish to attain such financial gains in a short period, without concerning themselves with the long term sustainability of their business activity. Consequently, where proper and strict legal regulation of the financial market is lacking it is possible that some subjects will abuse the confidence of creditors or investors and they would not return the credited assets.

5.16. But even 'well thinking' subjects can get to a situation where, with the aim of producing high profits for shareholders or to overwhelm competitors, they would overstep acceptable risk and perform such business that would be unprofitable, whereby the subjects would jeopardize the payback of creditors assets. Because of this risk legal regulations must enforce conditions of business that will prevent detrimental results.

5.17.   The next reason to regulate the financial market is also related to the protection of creditors and investors. It is called information asymmetry. If retail creditors or investors give money to a financial institution, they may be put into a disadvantageous position regarding accessible information, possibilities of consideration of this information and the making of qualified decisions. One party may have more or better information than another. Unfortunately even with quite careful legislation on the informational duties of financial institutions, a client is not often able to consider all relevant aspects of intended activities and there may be an imbalance of power in the transactions.

5.18.   Some possible trades on the financial market are so complicated that it is not possible to expect the ordinary lay client to understand them without help. Financial market regulations push financial institutions to provide clients all required information to reach an informed decision.

5.19.   Further issues favouring the financial market regulations are also related to knowledge on the subject. It is about available information about the institution offering its services on the market. This information is very important for the decision-making processes of clients. Legal regulations state that institutions must provide equal access to this information for all clients. It mainly concerns information about the financial health of institutions (especially banks or other credit institutions). This information is very much related to the trust of clients that is required when a client decides if he wishes to credit his available assets to the institution or not.

5.20.   Finally, it is necessary for supervisory authorities to have all relevant information to perform proper supervision of financial institutions and financial markets, even if the information is not in favour of the obligated institution. This crucial reason is why there must be broad legal regulation of the financial market.

II.2. Arguments against Regulation

5.21.   It is not difficult to discover arguments against broad regulation of the financial market, subjects who perform their activity there and financial instruments.

5.22.   There are several fundamental economic reasons that oppose market regulation. If the market is regulated it provides a high grade of protection for existing subjects against the access of new subjects, which reduces competition in the market, which otherwise could be beneficial for all related parties.

5.23. Legal regulation is expensive to enforce, although it is the supervision that makes it so. The regulations are printed words, whereas physical supervision requires substantial funding. These expenses must be covered by someone. If these expenses are covered by the regulated subjects, it is likely that these expenses would result in worse competitive positions for these subjects than those who are not liable to regulation (or are liable to regulation of a lesser degree). If the expenses are transferred to clients it is a disadvantage for such financial products, and the clients would probably seek other products where similar expenses do not occur.

5.24. Furthermore, it is evident that the stricter the regulation, the more incentive there is for institutions to discover a way to avoid them. This behaviour causes a need for greater regulation to oppose this avoidance. Therefore it is very important to find equilibrium – to have as low a degree of legal regulation as is possible while still maintaining a well-functioning financial market.

5.25. The negatives of legal regulation of the financial market can be identified even from the legal point of view. Some of the concrete instruments of regulation, for example the deposit insurance scheme, can cause clients (whose protection it was originally designed for) to behave in a risky manner, because they feel protected and do not realize the real risk of their activity. This client behaviour increases the risk for the whole financial system.

III. Theoretical Classification of the Legal Regulation

5.26. In legal theory there are several methods for how to classify legal regulation of the financial market. The function, the object of regulation or the institutional organization are three such methods.

5.27. The functional criterion can be considered such when the characteristic of the activity of the regulated subject is decisive, not the characteristic of the regulated subject itself. The classification related to the object of regulation can be considered concerning the aim of the regulation. Again this classification exists without respect to the characteristic of the regulated subject itself. On the contrary the characteristics, quality of the regulated subject itself are important for the institutional organization criterion

5.28. David T. Llewellyn[10] went further in classifying the object of regulation. He distinguishes four kinds of regulation:

- prudential regulation;
- systemic regulation;
- regulation protecting the consumer (client);
- regulation protecting competition in the market.

5.29. The aim of prudential regulation is the creation of conditions for safe existence, functioning and general solidity of subjects enacting business activities on the financial market such as financial institutions. The main aim of systemic regulation is the achievement and preservation of the stability of the whole financial sector including primarily the banking industry, payment systems, a capital market and the insurance industry. The aim of regulation focused on the protection of clients is the behaviour of financial institutions towards clients. This regulation protects clients in their unequal position concerning information access with regard to financial institutions. Finally, the aim of regulations protecting competition on the market is the regulation of a competitive environment in business activities of subjects in the financial market. The market enables free and fair competition of the subjects and all unfair behaviour is banned.

IV. Financial Market Supervision

5.30. Legal regulation of financial market supervision follows legal regulation of the financial market itself. Legal regulation without supervision would be pointless. Who would follow regulations in the absence of enforcement?

5.31. The Czech legal dictionary defines the term 'financial market supervision' as follows: '...it is the special kind of administrative supervision that is performed by a public authority different from the state in its own force.'[11]

5.32. The organisation of financial market supervision follows the same classification as that of financial market regulation. Consequently the above mentioned classification of financial market regulations also applies to classification of types of supervision. Financial market supervision can be divided into prudential supervision, the supervision of financial stability, business activity supervision and market competition supervision.

---

[10] DAVID T. LLEWELLYN, INSTITUTIONAL STRUCTURE OF FINANCIAL REGULATION AND SUPERVISION: THE BASIC ISSUES, Int. 14. Paper presented at a World Bank seminar Aligning Supervisory Structures with Country Needs, Washington DC, 6th and 7th June 2006, available at: http://siteresources.worldbank.org/INTTOPCONF6/Resources/2057292-1162909660809/F2FlemmingLlewellyn.pdf (accessed on 31 July 2013).

[11] See Michael Kohajda, the term *'dohled nad finančním trhem'*, in DUŠEN HENDRYCH and col., PRÁVNICKÝ SLOVNÍK, Prague: C. H. Beck Int. 154 (3rd ed. 2009).

V. Financial Market Supervision in the Czech Republic

5.33. This section will briefly discuss some basic issues in Czech financial market supervision for readers who are not familiar with it.

5.34. The most relevant change in the organisation of financial market supervision occurred on 1 April 2006 when the previously existing supervision organised pursuant to sectors of the financial market in several authorities was integrated into supervision performed by only one authority, the Czech National Bank, following the integration process in other European countries.

5.35. The Czech National Bank (the central bank of the state) performs supervision in all sectors of the financial market and on activities that occur in the market. Therefore the Czech National Bank performs both prudential supervision and supervision of business activity. This supervision is not only integrated, but even unified.

5.36. There are some theoretical issues with this model of supervisory organisation which analyse the fact that the Czech National Bank performs its monetary policy role as well as its supervision activities. In theory these aims could conflict in some critical situation.[12]

5.37. Although the new organisation of the financial market supervision in the Czech Republic takes inspiration from Great Britain (and its former Financial Services Authority) and Germany (and its Bundesanstalt für Finanzdienstleistungsaufsicht), the Czech Republic ultimately did much more than just follow these international examples.

5.38. In the Czech Republic, before integration more than two-thirds of the financial market (the share of the banks in the financial market according to the amount of credited assets) was supervised by the Czech National Bank. This can be considered the main reason for integration. Even today it can be strongly felt that the Czech National Bank still persists in its previous orientation and cares mainly about banks and slightly ignores other parts of financial market.

VI. Influence of International Institutions

5.39. Although the Czech Republic was inspired in how to change the organisation of financial market supervision from examples abroad, the decision itself was made completely freely. The Czech Republic must however respect the rules of the European Union within the creation of

---

[12] See Michael Kohajda, *Česká národní banka – Teoretické aspekty jejího postavení po 1. dubnu 2006, in* NADĚJE PRÁVNÍ VĚDY, BÝKOV, 2006, Pilsen: Vydavatelství a nakladatelství Aleš Čeněk Int. 279 et seq. (VILEM KNOLL & VÁCLAV BEDNÁŘ eds., 2006).

the aims and objects of the financial market regulation. The European Union focuses mostly on the prudential supervision and the supervision of the banking industry.

5.40. With regard to regulation of the banking industry, the influence of international institutions on financial market regulation can be found in an informal influence, namely the Basel Committee on Banking Supervision. A formal influence can be seen in legal regulation from the European Union by means of legal rules or decision making activities of the EU authorities. Both influences are closely related.

5.41. The Basel Committee on Banking Supervision is a highly respected international association of professionals in which the Czech Republic does not have a representative. The Committee adopts recommendations for fundamental standards of banking supervision performance; these standards are mostly concerned with prudential rules. These recommendations arise on the basis of wide professional discussion and are generally well adopted by professionals, although there are some problematic issues as well. One was the determination of the concrete risk ratio of state bonds that, as seen recently in Greece, can be dangerous and can create important problems with the assessment of the capital adequacy of banks.

5.42. The standards of the Committee (the Basel III) are so highly respected that the European Union assume them more or less indiscriminately and incorporate them into the EU legislation on financial markets. Subsequently the legislation is transferred into legislation of the EU member states.

VII. Conclusion

5.43. In this paper we focused on the issue of legal regulation of the financial market. The view of Czech legal science on these issues was elaborated on and relevant information was provided about the theoretical definitions of legal regulation. Financial market supervision, its classification and the supervision organization was explored. Actual details about the financial market supervision in the Czech Republic and its influence of international instructions, namely the Basel Committee on Banking Supervision, was also discussed. Legal regulation of financial market can be theoretically classified into: i) prudential regulation, ii) systemic regulation, iii) regulation protecting the clients, and iv) regulation protecting competition in the market as the most suitable classification of the market regulation.

5.44. Most national, as well as international legal regulation of the financial market aims at the prudential and systemic regulation. The regulation protecting the clients however stands outside of the interest of regulatory authorities. Even the Basel Committee on Banking Supervision as one of the most respected international organization concentrates on prudential regulation and does not deal with the protection of clients. We conclude that the clients' protection is important for a well-functioning financial market because the trust of clients is one of the market's essential elements. Therefore the authorities should concentrate more on clients' protection.

5.45. In conclusion, there are several strong arguments in favour of the strict legal regulation of financial markets and all the activities which are carried out in the market. It is mainly the protection of the financial stability in a state's economy and the protection of creditors and investors that asks for broad and complex legal regulation of this environment. Even the arguments as to the reduction of competition on the financial market or the costs of such regulation and supervision do not overbalance the above mentioned reasons. The well-functioning financial market of recent time is so important for modern society that it is one of the most important issues that must be legally well regulated by state authority.

|||

Summaries

FRA   [*La réglementation des institutions internationales et l'impact sur les marchés financiers*]

On propose ici aux lecteurs un aperçu théorique de la régulation juridique des marchés financiers et l'on s'intéresse ensuite à l'influence toute particulière exercée sur la régulation des marchés financiers dans l'Union européenne et en particulier en République tchèque par le Comité de Bâle sur le contrôle bancaire.

Étant donné que la majorité des lecteurs qui liront cette contribution ne sera pas particulièrement familiarisée avec la théorie juridicofinancière tchèque et avec la science du droit financier, on offre dans un premier temps un bref aperçu théorique des questions générales de surveillance et de régulation juridique.

Une partie est ensuite consacrée à la surveillance des marchés financiers, au partage et à l'objectif de cette surveillance, en se référant de nouveau à la situation actuelle en République tchèque.

La dernière partie est brièvement consacrée aux éléments influant sur les organismes de surveillance des marchés financiers en République tchèque et ailleurs, et s'intéresse en particulier à la transposition dans les normes communautaires et nationales des exigences de régulation émises par des organisations internationales indépendantes comme le Comité de Bâle sur la surveillance bancaire.

CZE [*Právní úprava mezinárodních institucí a vliv na finanční trhy*]
V tomto příspěvku autoři zamýšlí čtenářům nabídnout teoretický pohled na právní regulaci finančního trhu a následně se zaměřit na zvláštní vliv Basilejského výboru pro bankovní dohled na regulaci finančního trhu v Evropské unii a zejména v České republice.

Vzhledem k tomu, že tento příspěvek budou číst v převážné většině čtenáři, kteří nejsou podrobněji seznámeni s českou finančněprávní teorií a vědou o finančním právu, nabídnou autoři nejprve krátký a zcela teoretický pohled na obecné otázky právní regulace a dohledu.

V další části se pak zaměří na dohled nad finančním trhem, jeho rozdělení a jeho cíle, a to opět také s poukazem na současnou situaci v České republice.

Poslední část tohoto článku je pak krátce věnována vlivům, které ovlivňují organizaci dohledu nad finančním trhem nejen v České republice, zejména se pak článek zaměřuje na přenášení regulatorních požadavků z mezinárodní nezávislé organizace jakou je Bazilejský výbor pro bankovní dohled, do unijních a vnitrostátních právních norem.

| | |

POL [*Uregulowania prawne instytucji międzynarodowych i wpływ na rynki finansowe*]
Niniejszy artykuł dotyczy definicji regulacji prawnych ze szczególnym uwzględnieniem rynków finansowych. Czytelnik ma okazję poznać tę problematykę w perspektywie czeskiej nauki o prawie. Artykuł przybliża teoretyczną definicję pojęcia nadzoru nad rynkami finansowymi, jego podział, a także sam nadzór nad rynkami finansowymi, wykonywany na podstawie regulacji. Wreszcie zarysowano tu aktualny sposób organizacji nadzoru nad rynkami finansowymi w Czechach oraz wpływ, jaki mają na nie instytucje międzynarodowe, takie jak Bazylejski Komitet Nadzoru Bankowego.

DEU [*Rechtliche Regelung internationaler Institutionen und Einfluss auf die Finanzmärkte*]
Dieser Beitrag befasst sich mit dem Begriff der rechtlichen Regulierung mit dem Schwerpunkt Finanzmarkt. Dem Leser wird vermittelt, wie die tschechische Rechtswissenschaft diesen Problemkreis wahrnimmt. Dabei wird ihm das theoretische Verständnis des Begriffs der Finanzmarktaufsicht und dessen Gliederung nahegebracht, sowie die

eigentliche Aufsicht über den Finanzmarkt selbst, die auf der Grundlage der Regulierung wahrgenommen wird. Abschließend enthält der Beitrag auch einen Abriss der aktuellen Ausgestaltung der Finanzmarktaufsicht in der Tschechischen Republik und des Einflusses, der von internationalen Institutionen auf diese Aufsicht ausgeübt wird, d. h. insbesondere vom Basler Ausschuss für Bankenaufsicht.

RUS [*Правовое регулирование международных институтов и влияние на финансовые рынки*]

Настоящая статья посвящена понятию правовое регулирование с акцентом на финансовый рынок. Читатели ознакомятся с точкой зрения чешской юриспруденции по данному вопросу. В статье изложено теоретическое толкование понятия надзор за финансовым рынком, его структура, а также непосредственно надзор за финансовым рынком, который реализуется на основе регулирования. В заключение представлен актуальный способ организации надзора за финансовым рынком в Чешской Республике, а также описано влияние, которое на него оказывают международные организации, а именно Базельский комитет по банковскому надзору.

ESP [*La regulación legislativa de las instituciones internacionales y su impacto sobre los mercados financieros*]

El artículo está dedicado al concepto de la regulación legislativa, centrándose en el mercado financiero. Proporciona a los lectores el enfoque de la jurisprudencia checa sobre el tema. Aclara el concepto teórico del término de la supervisión sobre el mercado financiero y su estructura, así como la propia supervisión del mercado financiero, que se efectúa en virtud de esta regulación. Por último, describe la forma actual de la organización de la supervisión del mercado financiero en la República Checa y el impacto de las instituciones internacionales, en particular, del Comité de Supervisión Bancaria de Basilea, sobre dicho mercado.

| | |

Alexander J. Bělohlávek

Institutionalized Promotion and Protection of Investments in the Energy Sector

Czech Yearbook of International Law

Key words:
energy sector | Energy Charter Treaty (ECT) | Energy Charter | foreign direct investment | investment protection | non-discrimination | environment | dispute resolution | arbitration | energy efficiency | investor | host state | political cooperation | scientific cooperation | exchange of information | emissions | intellectual property rights | national treatment | most-favoured nation treatment (MFN) clause | umbrella clause | denial of advantages | tax filter | appointing authority | cooling-off period | fork-in-the-road

Alexander J. Bělohlávek, Univ. Professor, Dr.iur., Mgr., Dipl. Ing. oec/MB, Dr.h.c. Lawyer admitted and practising in Prague/CZE (Branch N.J./US), Senior Partner of the Law Offices Bělohlávek, Dept. of Law, Faculty of Economics, Ostrava, CZE, Dept. of Int. and European Law, Faculty of Law, Masaryk University, Brno, CZE (visiting), Chairman of the Commission on Arbitration ICC National Committee CZE, Arbitrator in Prague, Vienna, Kiev etc. Member of ASA, DIS, Austrian Arb. Association. The President of the WJA – the World Jurist Association, Washington D.C./USA. e-mail: office@ablegal.cz

Abstract | The "energy sector" is generally interpreted as referring to industries focused on the (•) extraction, (•) refining, (•) transport, (•) use of various forms of energy, and (•) related research and associated infrastructure. Despite the fact that no law or regulation contains any general definition of the energy sector, the Energy Charter Treaty contains at least the fundamental guidelines and identification of terms. The ECT provides a multilateral framework for energy cooperation that is unique under international law. In its Preamble, the ECT refers to the Charter of Paris for a New Europe as a declaration of the new era of peaceful cooperation of countries following the end of the Cold War. The ECT thereby creates a binding legal basis for permanent economic cooperation in the energy sector. It is the first multilateral treaty for the protection of investments, i.e. a binding source of international law. The Charter and the ensuing ECT are not the only multilateral initiatives in the energy sector; however, it is the only multilateral treaty providing a substantive-law international basis from the perspective of energy investments protection. Other important general treaties and conventions in the energy sector include the Convention on Long-Range Transboundary Air Pollution, the Charter of Paris for a New Europe – OSCE, and the United Nations Framework Convention on Climate Change.

| 99

I. Energy Sector and International Organizations

I.1. Concept of "Energy Sector" in International and European Structures

6.01. The "energy sector" is generally interpreted as referring to industries focused on the (•) extraction, (•) refining, (•) transport, (•) use of various forms of energy, and (•) related research and associated infrastructure. We speak of all kinds of energy. As concerns the order of importance,[1] the most significant fields include the (•) production of electricity in power stations and the distribution of electricity by way of transmission grids, but also the extraction, distribution and use of coal, oil, natural gas, atomic fuel and wood, and to some extent also the production and processing of propane-butane or the use of water, wind, tidal or geothermal energy. Broadly speaking, the energy sector also includes the construction and manufacture of energy facilities.[2]

I.2. European Energy Charter (Charter) and Energy Charter Treaty (ECT)

I.2.1. Definition of Energy Sector under Charter and ECT

6.02. The abovementioned general delimitation of the *"energy sector"* is also related to the individual areas of legal regulation of the energy industries and the structure thereof, meaning the use of all different forms of energy. The fundamental act in the domain of "energy law", in terms of the intended regulation of energy activities, is the **Energy Charter Treaty** (ECT).

6.03. Despite the fact that no law or regulation contains any general definition of the *energy sector*, the ECT contains at least the fundamental guidelines and identification of terms. The reason is that the Treaty (ECT) lays down the following definition: *"'Economic Activity in the Energy Sector' means an economic activity concerning the exploration, extraction, refining, production, storage, land transport,*

---

[1] Such *importance*, however, is impossible to express in the potential priorities, in terms of legal rules, or legal protection, as applicable, including the legal protection of investments. In this respect, the applicable legal rules usually make no differences, at least at the general level.

[2] Basic resources include: LADISLAV VOŽENÍLEK; FRANTIŠEK LSTIBŮREK, ZÁKLADY ELEKTROTECHNIKY II [*Electrical Engineering Basics*], Prague: Státní nakladatelství technické literatury (1989); ZBYNĚK IBLER (SEN)., ZBYNĚK IBLER (JUN), JAN KARTÁK & JIŘINA MERTLOVÁ, TECHNICKÝ PRŮVODCE ENERGETIKA [*Technical Guide for Power Engineers*]. Prague: Nakladatelství BEN – technická literatura (2002); ZBYNĚK IBLER (SEN)., ZBYNĚK IBLER (JUN), JAN KARTÁK & JIŘINA MERTLOVÁ, ENERGETIKA V PŘÍKLADECH [*Energy Sector: Examples*], Prague: Nakladatelství BEN – technická literatura (2003).

transmission, distribution, trade, marketing, or sale of Energy Materials and Products, except those included in Annex NI, or concerning the distribution of heat to multiple premises. 'Energy Materials and Products', based on the Harmonized System of the Customs Co-operation Council and the Combined Nomenclature of the European Communities, means the items included in Annex EM.'[3]

6.04.   No other area of economic activity is exposed to such fluctuations as the energy sector. An area where finances, politics, national security, privatisation and environmental protection collide, the contracting partners easily get into legal disputes. The *Energy Charter Treaty* ("ECT") was adopted on 17 December 1994 in Lisbon for the purpose of protecting international investments in this particular area. The first decisions that resolved disputes between investors and ECT member states and that were rendered under the ECT indicate new and fundamental developments.[4]

I.2.2. European Energy Charter (Charter)

6.05.   The Energy Charter (*Charter*) of 1991, also known as the European Energy Charter,[5] provides the policy basis for the Charter process. **The Charter is a concise expression of principles meant to promote international cooperation in the energy sector**, based on the common interest of securing the supply of energy and sustainable economic development. The initiation and articulation of the Energy Charter (*Charter*) was an expression of the political process launched in the early 1990s, i.e. at a time when the end of the Cold War provided and justified a legitimate need to ensure that a generally acceptable basis would be established for developing energy cooperation between states on the European continent.

6.06.   The first step leading to the adoption of the Charter, and subsequently the ECT, can be associated with the initiative organised by the Dutch Prime Minister, *Ruud Lubbers*, who submitted a proposal to set up the **European Energy Community** at a European Council meeting in Dublin in June 1990. The charter was signed in The Hague on 17

---

[3]   See primarily the NI and EM Annexes to the ECT.

[4]   Richard Kreindler, *Rechtsschutz für ausländische Direktinvestitionen im Energiesektor: Neue Möglichkeiten in der Investitionsschiedsgerichtsbarkeit – Der Vertrag über die Energiecharta, in* ENERGIE UND KLIMAWANDEL : TAGUNGSBAND ZUM 14. MÜNSTERANER AUSSENWIRTSCHAFTSRECHTSTAG 2009, Frankfurt am Main: Verlag Recht und Wirtschaft 49 (Dirk Ehlers; Hans-Michael Wolffgang; Ulrich Jan Schröder & Stefan Altenschmidt eds., 2010)

[5]   The official title is the *"Concluding Document of the Hague Conference on European Energy Charter".*

December **1991**. Three years later, on **17 December 1994**, the following instruments were signed in Lisbon: (•) **Energy Charter Treaty (ECT)** and (•) **Energy Charter Protocol on Energy Efficiency and Related Environmental Aspects.** The ECT entered into force on **16 April 1998** following ratification by the first thirty members. On such occasion, the trade provisions of the ECT were amended, bringing them in line with the WTO rules.

6.07.   Counting Indonesia, this political declaration is currently signed by 58 states (including the U.S. and Canada), as well as the European Communities (currently binding on the EU, following the Lisbon Treaty). All signatories of the Charter are observers in the *Charter* process. Signature is the first and indispensable step on the way to accession to the Energy Charter Treaty (ECT) of 1994.[6]

I.2.3.   Energy Charter Treaty (ECT)

6.08.   The Energy Charter Treaty (ECT) was developed on the basis of the European Energy Charter (Charter) of 1991. Whereas the Charter was drawn up as a declaration of political intent to promote *East-West* energy cooperation, the ECT is an international treaty, i.e. a legally binding multilateral contractual instrument (treaty) of international law,[7] dealing specifically with inter-governmental cooperation in the energy sector. Hence, the ECT builds on the European Energy Charter (*Charter*) of 1991.

6.09.   The ECT provides a multilateral framework for energy cooperation that is unique under international law. Its primary objective is to promote energy security by operating more open and competitive energy markets, while honouring the principles of sustainable development and their sovereignty over energy resources.

6.10.   Whereas the *Charter* is a declaration of a political nature and an expression of the political will to strengthen international energy relations, the ECT is a binding act of international law, a multilateral international treaty. It is the only treaty of its kind dealing with inter-governmental cooperation in the energy sector, covering the entire energy chain (from prospecting of sites to final use), as well as any and all energy products and related facilities. In its Preamble, the ECT

---

[6]   1991 Charter, available at: http://www.encharter.org/index.php?id=29&L=1%2F (accesed on 15 June 2010).

[7]   Concerning the issue of resources, see also VLADIMIR BALAŠ & PAVEL STURMA, KURS MEZINÁRODNÍHO EKONOMICKÉHO PRÁVA, [*Lectures in International Economic Law*], Prague: C. H. Beck (1997); Pavel Sturma, *Režim a ochrana investic na základě mnohostranných instrumentů* [*Investments Regime and Protection under Multilateral Instruments*], (1) NOTITIAE EX ACADEMIA BRATISLAVENSI IURISPRUDENTIAE 67-79 (2008).

refers to the *Charter of Paris for a New Europe* as a declaration of the new era of peaceful cooperation of countries following the end of the Cold War.

6.11. The ECT thereby creates a binding legal basis for permanent economic cooperation in the energy sector. It is the first multilateral treaty for the protection of investments, i.e. a binding source of international law. The fundamental aim of the ECT is to support foreign investment and provide protection against political risks, such as expropriation or discrimination. But the ECT also contains a wide range of rules, which concern energy transmission, energy efficiency and environmental protection. Last, but not least, the ECT sets forth generally binding rules for the resolution of disputes under international law.

6.12. The Energy Charter Treaty and the Energy Charter Protocol on Energy Efficiency and Related Environmental Aspects (Protocol) were adopted on 17 December 1994 in Lisbon.[8]

---

[8]   *Czech Republic:* The ECT and the Protocol were signed on behalf of the Czech Republic in Lisbon on 8 June 1995. The ECT and the Protocol entered into force on 16 April 1998; this is also the date on which both instruments entered into force for the Czech Republic (see Ministry of Foreign Affairs Notice No. 372/1999 Coll. and 373/1999 Coll., book No. 112). The text of the ECT has never been published in the Czech Republic; the Collection of Laws only provides that *"the text can be studied at the Czech Ministry of Foreign Affairs and at the Czech Ministry of Industry and Trade".* The method of publication complied with the then applicable rules incorporated in Section 3(2) of Act No. 545/1992 Coll., on the Collection of Laws of the Czech Republic, as amended on the day on which the Notice was published (Notice regarding the ECT of 30 December 1999). However, it appears somewhat questionable that the ECT has not been attributed greater significance, in terms of the evaluation of the importance of an international treaty, and its text has not been published in full. It would probably be too daring to believe that the state was aware of its importance, and the very reason why it refrained from publishing the text was that the state wished to hinder the disclosure of this international treaty's contents. We must bear in mind that, at that time, broad accessibility of international sources (sources of international origin) through a global electronic network was not so widespread as to enable such access at any time and from any place. Paradoxically, despite the Notice published in the Collection of Laws (see above), the Czech Ministry of Industry and Trade does not possess the original text of the ECT or any other authorised copy. The Ministry has at its disposal only the printed English version in the form of the published source and electronic references to its version according to the www-eur-lex.eu database. Neither text is, however, binding. The only binding text in the Czech Republic is available at the Czech Ministry of Foreign Affairs. Access is granted on the basis of a special request – the text is available for studying in the archives study room of the Czech Ministry of Foreign Affairs (the author of this publication gained access to the ECT at the Czech Ministry of Foreign Affairs by submitting a request). The Ministry's archives contain a certified copy of the ECT and an unauthorised translation to Czech. Consequently, the ECT has been properly *published* in the Czech Republic in terms of the then valid laws, but it has not been published in the material sense of the word.

6.13. As of March 2011, the ECT was signed or acceded to by fifty-one states, plus the European Communities (now it is binding on the EU). All states that signed or acceded to the ECT are members of the Energy Charter Conference as an inter-governmental organisation and a governing and decision-making body for the Energy Charter process.

6.14. The fundamental aim of the Treaty is to strengthen the rule of law on energy issues, by creating a level playing field of rules to be observed by all participating states (governments), thus minimising the risks associated with energy-related investments and trade.

The ECT's provisions focus on **five fundamental, relatively broad areas:**[9]

6.15. ► Protection of foreign investments based on the extension of the national treatment principle, or the afforded most-favoured nation treatment clauses (whichever is more favourable), and protection against key non-commercial risks. These issues are the main topic of this publication, together with issues relating to the resolution of *Investor-to-State* disputes.

6.16. ► Non-discriminatory conditions for trade in energy materials, products and energy-related equipment based on WTO rules and rules securing the reliable (free) cross-border transit of energy through pipelines, electricity grids and other energy transit facilities.

6.17. ► Reduction of the environmental impact of the energy cycle through improving energy efficiency.

6.18. ► Resolution of *State-to-State* disputes and, **in the case of investments,** *Investor-to-State* disputes (**disputes between investors and host states**).

6.19. ► Supporting energy efficiency and efforts to minimise the environmental impact of the production and use of energy.[10]

Cf. also Petr Mlsna, *K nepublikování předpisů práva ES/EU v českém jazyce v Úředním věstníku EU* [*Regarding Non-Publication of EC/EU Laws in Czech in Official Journal of EU*], (9) PRÁVNÍ ZPRAVODAJ 6-9 (2004).

Poland: In Poland, the ECT (*Traktat Karty Energetycznej oraz Protokół Karty Energetycznej dotyczący efektywności energetycznej i odnośnych aspektów ochrony środowiska, sporządzone w Lizbonie dnia 17 grudnia 1994 r.*) was published in: Dz.U. 2003 Nr 105 note 985.

Slovakia: The Cabinet of the *Slovak Republic* gave its consent with the treaty in its Resolution No. 1190 of 12 December 1994, and the President of the Slovak Republic ratified the treaty on 7 September 1995; it entered into force on 16 April 1998.

[9] Some sources refer to *four* areas, arguing that the theory and practice of the ECT have only gradually and partially spun off the *reduction of the environmental impact of energy cycle* into a specific category.

[10] Available at: http://www.encharter.org/index.php?id=28&L=1 (accessed on 24 March 2011).

I.2.4. Protection of Investments under Energy Charter Treaty

6.20. The Energy Charter Treaty provides a level playing field for the access of investors to energy resources. On the one hand, there is the issue of national sovereignty over energy resources. Each Member State may freely decide how and to what extent its national and state energy resources ought to develop, and to what extent the individual energy sectors will be open to foreign investment. On the other hand, the Treaty articulates the requirement that the rules for prospecting, developing and extracting energy resources are to be publicly accessible, non-discriminatory and transparent.

6.21. If the foreign investment complies with the domestic legal rules of the country, the ECT is proposed as an instrument for securing a reliable and stable mutual relationship between the investor and the host state. The ECT protects foreign investors against non-commercial risks, such as discrimination, direct or indirect expropriation, or violation of the individual investment treaties. The need for stable relations between investors and host states (governments and the *public sector* of the host states) is especially acute in the energy sector. The reason is that projects implemented in this particular sector are intended to last for a longer period of time and often involve huge capital investments.[11]

I.2.5. Structure of Charter and ECT

I.2.5.1. Energy Charter Conference

6.22. The **Energy Charter Conference** is the supreme body of the ECT and its powers are specifically enumerated in the ECT. The Conference is an **inter-governmental organisation**, the governing and decision-making body for the Charter process. All states who have signed or acceded to the ECT are members of the Conference. The Conference meets on a regular basis (usually twice a year) to discuss policy issues affecting energy cooperation among the ECT's signatories, to review implementation of the provisions of the Treaty and the Protocol, and to discuss new instruments and projects on energy issues.[12]

---

[11] Available at: http://www.encharter.org.

[12] Members of the Charter Conference: (•) Albania, (•) Armenia, (•) Austria, (•) Australia, (•) Azerbaijan, (•) Belarus, (•) Belgium, (•) Bosnia and (•) Herzegovina, (•) Bulgaria, (•) Croatia, (•) Czech Republic, (•) Cyprus, (•) Denmark, (•) Estonia, (•) European Communities (EU), (•) Finland, (•) France, (•) Georgia, (•) Germany, (•) Greece, (•) Hungary, (•) Iceland, (•) Ireland, (•) Italy, (•) Japan, (•) Kazakhstan, (•) Kyrgyzstan, (•) Latvia, (•) Liechtenstein, (•) Lithuania, (•) Luxembourg, (•) Malta, (•) Moldova, (•) Mongolia, (•) Netherlands, (•) Norway, (•) Poland, (•) Portugal, (•) Romania, (•) Russian Federation,[12] (•) Slovakia, (•) Slovenia, (•) Spain, (•) Sweden, (•) Switzerland, (•)

I.2.5.2. Subsidiary Bodies

6.23. **The Charter Conference has the following subsidiary bodies:** (•) Investment Group, (•) Trade Group, (•) Energy Efficiency Group, (•) Transit Group, (•) Budget Committee, and (•) Legal Advisory Committee. The Charter Conference is served by a permanent Secretariat based in Brussels. The Secretariat is staffed by energy sector experts from member states of the Charter Conference and headed by a Secretary General. Cooperation with the Energy Charter Secretariat is secured by a particular body in each individual country.[13] In compliance with Article 20(3) of the ECT, the individual member states have also set up *enquiry points* for inquiries concerning the Charter and the ECT.[14]

I.2.6. Selected Advantages and Risks Connected with Interpretation and Application of ECT

6.24. The Energy Charter Treaty, as a relatively recent international treaty in connection with the rules regulating the most-favoured nation treatment and direct enforceability of the rights arising from the treaty, has adopted certain established legal mechanisms already employed in bilateral investment treaties. On the other hand, the ECT stipulates benchmarks that significantly exceed BITs in several respects: the broad territorial and temporal application of the treaty comprising more than 50 member states, the extensively interpreted term "investments", and the ample choice between various methods of dispute settlement, both judicial and extrajudicial.[15] The ECT offers not only a high degree of protection, which can stand up to comparison with modern BITs, but also a higher degree of legal certainty. The ECT is used in relations between the individual member states; consequently, the awards rendered by arbitral tribunals are no longer

---

Tajikistan, (•) The former Yugoslav Republic of Macedonia, (•) Turkey, (•) Turkmenistan, (•) Ukraine, (•) Uzbekistan, (•) United Kingdom of Great Britain and Northern Ireland. Observers to the Charter Conference are the following states: (•) Algeria, (•) Bahrain, (•) People's Republic of China, (•) Canada, (•) Indonesia, (•) Islamic Republic of Iran, (•) Republic of Korea, (•) Kuwait, (•) Morocco, (•) Oman, (•) Qatar, (•) Saudi Arabia, (•) Tunisia, (•) United Arab Emirates, (•) USA (United States of America), (•) Venezuela, (•) Federal Republic Yugoslavia. Other observers include the following international organisations: (•) EBRD, (•) IEA, (•) OECD, (•) UN- ECE, (•) World Bank, (•) WTO, (•) CIS Electric Power Council, (•) BSEC, (•) BASREC.

[13] Meaning various state agencies in the individual countries, such as the Czech Ministry of Industry and Trade in the Czech Republic.

[14] Such as the Energy Policy Department of the Czech Ministry of Industry and Trade in the Czech Republic.

[15] Richard Kreindler, *supra* note 4, at 11.

based on similarity, but on one and the same text (although there are many differences compared to the official versions, and even more inconsistencies among translations into national languages).[16] The first decisions have demonstrated that, based on the publication of the proceedings through the Secretariat of the ECT Conference, the arbitral tribunals have attempted to arrive at a uniform interpretation of the treaty. Based on these decisions, the results of legal disputes in the future relating to the ECT charter will be much more foreseeable than they have been up to now.[17]

6.25. International energy enterprises, primarily those that have experienced *problems* in certain countries (especially in connection with their participation in privatisation projects), have already availed themselves of the new possibilities offered by the ECT charter. The value of the subject matter of disputes handled in proceedings regarding claims under the ECT is usually above average, which causes the governments of the countries involved to proceed with utmost caution. Consequently, it is advisable to invest in a diligent individual analysis whenever a particular dispute arises.[18] Indeed, such analysis and comparison with the international practice, primarily case law, are the most commonly employed methods for resolving (international) legal disputes at the international level; nonetheless, the author believes that the specific features of each individual case should not be neglected. Moreover, investments in the energy sector feature major specifics. If the parties *overlook* these specific elements and rely on the frequently *misleading* international practice, they can end up facing *fatal consequences*. The author also uses the method of comparison with the available case law as the *prevalent method* in this publication, but considers it necessary to take this opportunity (introduction to the publication) to point out the associated risks. Another reason is that decisions concerning the ECT are scarce, and the ECT is an instrument of international law that differs from other instruments for the protection of foreign direct investments in a number of respects: in its concept, the broadness of issues covered by its rules, and certain mechanisms. Naturally, it also extensively employs institutions that are considered a stable basis of *investment law*, i.e. an area featuring many

---

[16] The author's publication is based primarily on the English version; however, inconsistencies have also been resolved with the use of the Russian version. The translation of selected provisions in Annex IV is new, but many parts of it are, naturally, identical to the text that is also published in a translation to Czech on the EU website (see the notes to Annex IV to the core part of the publication).

[17] Richard Kreindler, *supra* note 4, at 11.

[18] Ibid.

specifics, which have been undergoing a gradual separation from the main stream of international legal practice, and have been evolving into a *sui generis* domain of international law ever since the 1950s, and on top of that, is an area that is fundamentally closer to *private law* practice than other international law sectors.

I.2.7. Future of ECT and Approach Adopted by Russia

6.26. The opportunity for the Charter and for the ECT opened up with the change in the political and economic system in the countries of Central and Eastern Europe in the late 1980s and early 1990s. The Charter and the ECT (especially the latter) have openly and from the outset endeavoured to create a mutual system of security and safety in the energy sector, including investments; the countries of Central and Eastern Europe would open their energy sector, and the countries of "the then" *"Western World"* would, in return, open their markets for energy commodities. It is only logical that the point of main interest inhered especially in the energy raw materials available in the countries of the former Soviet Union, primarily Russia (currently the Russian Federation).

6.27. However, Russia substantially *undermined* the countries' expectations regarding the future development of the cooperation under the Charter and the application of the ECT. The preliminary application of the ECT in relation to Russia was terminated in accordance with a notification of the Russian Federation of 20 August 2009 pursuant to Article 45(3)(a) of the ECT, in which the **Russian Federation announced that it did not intend to become a Contracting Party to the ECT.** Article 45(3)(a) reads as follows (cit.): "Termination of provisional application for any signatory shall take effect upon the expiration of 60 days from the date on which such signatory's written notification is received by the Depository." Hence, the 60-day period with respect to Russia expired on 19 October 2009. Article 45(3)(b) of the ECT stipulates that the obligations with respect to any investments, including the obligation to submit investment disputes to arbitration pursuant to Part V of the ECT, remain in effect for 20 years following the effective date of termination of the provisional application. This means, with respect to the Russian Federation, that any investments made in Russia before 19 October 2009 will continue to enjoy the protection afforded by the Charter for a period of 20 years – i.e. until 19 October 2029.[19] According to the decision in *Yukos* v. *Russia*, disputes in the said period fall within the jurisdiction of arbitral panels constituted for the

---

[19] See *Yukos Universal Limited* (Isle of Man) v *Russian Federation*, PCA Proceedings No. AA227, Interim AA of 30 November 2009, paragraph (339). Emphasis added by author.

resolution of disputes arising from the ECT (continuing provisional application[20] of Article 26 of the ECT). Despite this adjudicated legal opinion and a number of other, similar professional opinions presented in various forums, it is obvious that Russia's decision not to ratify the ECT means a fundamental historical landmark with respect to this important international initiative. Russia's approach has, naturally, prompted the Charter (and ECT) structures to focus on the future of these instruments. The result of this initiative was the presentation and adoption of a *new strategy* at a Charter Conference meeting on 24 November 2010, entitled "Road Map for the Modernisation of the Energy Charter Process".[21]

I.3. Other International Initiatives and EU Initiatives in Energy Sector

6.28. The Charter and its successor, the ECT, are not the only multilateral initiatives in the energy sector. However, the scope of (especially the material scope and purpose, as well as the established mechanisms) and the support enjoyed by the said instruments elevate both the *political* Charter and the ECT to the level of the most important initiatives. But it would be wrong to dismiss the other multilateral (global) projects expressed in various forms.

I.3.1. Convention on Long-Range Transboundary Air Pollution

I.3.1.1. Purpose and Principles of Convention

6.29. The Convention on Long-Range Transboundary Air Pollution[22] of 1979 (Convention)[23] establishes a framework for intergovernmental cooperation with the aim of protecting health and the environment from air pollution that is liable to affect several countries. This cooperation covers the development of appropriate policies, the exchange of information, research, and the introduction and development of a monitoring system.

---

[20] Concerning the issue of the provisional application of the ECT, though partly before the decision in *Yukos* v *Russia*, see also a number of authors. See also Matthew Belz, *Provisional Application of the Energy Charter Treaty:* Kardassopoulos v Georgia *and Improving Provisional Application in Multilateral Treaties.* 22 EMORY INT'L. L. REV 727-760 (2008).

[21] Road Map for the Modernisation of the Energy Charter Process. See also: http://www.encharter.org/index.php?id=344&L=0 (accessed on 25 March 2011).

[22] 1979 Convention on Long-Range Transboundary Air Pollution. See Council Decision No 81/462/EEC of 11 June 1981 on the conclusion of the Convention on long-range transboundary air pollution, published in: *OJ* L 171 of 27 June 1981; CELEX:31981D0462.

[23] The abbreviated term *Convention* as defined above is only used in this part of the *Introduction* to the publication.

6.30. In this Convention, the Contracting Parties (i.e. the States or the European Community, which are signatories to the Convention) have committed themselves to limiting, and to gradually preventing and reducing their discharges of air pollutants, and thus to combating the resulting transboundary pollution.

6.31. Long-range transboundary air pollution is defined as the introduction by man of substances or energy into the air that have deleterious effects on human health, the environment or material property in another country, and for which the contribution of individual emissions sources or groups of sources cannot be distinguished.

I.3.1.2. Policy Cooperation

6.32. The Convention provides that states will develop and implement appropriate policies and strategies, particularly systems of air quality management. It also provides for the possibility of an emergency measure in the case of pollution or a serious risk of pollution in the territory of a Contracting Party.

6.33. The Contracting Parties have agreed to meet regularly (at least annually) to assess the progress achieved in matters relating to the Convention.

I.3.1.3. Scientific Cooperation

6.34. The states will initiate negotiations regarding research and development, particularly to reduce emissions of major air pollutants, for monitoring and measuring emissions rates and concentrations of these pollutants, as well as to gain an understanding of the effects of these pollutants on health and the environment.

I.3.1.4. Exchange of Information

6.35. The Contracting Parties to the Convention have agreed to exchange information. Such information should include, in particular, (•) data regarding emissions of major air pollutants (starting with sulphur dioxide) and the effects thereof, (•) aspects likely to cause significant changes in long-range transboundary air pollution (particularly in national policies and industrial development), (•) control technologies for reducing air pollution, and (•) national policies and strategies to combat the major air pollutants.

I.3.1.5. Cooperation in Field of Training

6.36.   The Contracting Parties will participate in *"the Cooperative Programme for Monitoring and Evaluation of Long-range Transmission of Air Pollutants in Europe"* (EMEP). This programme is governed by a separate protocol. It aims to provide parties to the Convention with scientific information regarding the monitoring of the atmosphere, the provision of IT models, the assessment of emissions, and the development of projections.

6.37.   In order for this cooperation to succeed, the parties provide for the following **principles and procedures**:

6.38.   ▶ The application of this programme, initially focused on monitoring sulphur dioxide and similar substances, to other major air pollutants;

6.39.   ▶ The monitoring of the composition of media susceptible to contamination by these pollutants (water, soil and vegetation), as well as the effects on health and the environment;

6.40.   ▶ The provision of meteorological and physicochemical data relating to processes during transmission;

6.41.   ▶ The use, whenever possible, of comparable or standardised monitoring and modelling methods;

6.42.   ▶ The integration of EMEP into relevant national and international programmes; and

6.43.   ▶ The regular exchange of data obtained by monitoring.[24]

I.3.1.6. Context of Convention

6.44.   The Convention was signed in 1979 in Geneva, within the framework of the European Economic Commission of the United Nations (for Europe), and entered into force in 1983.

It has been extended by eight specific protocols for the following areas:

6.45.   ▶ Long-term financing of the Cooperative Programme for Monitoring and Evaluation of Long-range Transmission of Air Pollutants in Europe (EMEP) – The protocol was signed in 1984, and entered into force in 1988.

6.46.   ▶ Reduction of sulphur emissions by at least 30 per cent- The protocol was signed in 1985, and entered into force in 1987.

6.47.   ▶ Nitrogen oxides - The protocol was signed in 1988, and entered into force in 1991.

---

[24] Convention on Long-Range Transboundary Air Pollution; available at: http://europa.eu/legislation_summaries/environment/air_pollution/l28162_en.htm (accessed on 25 March 2011). See also: http://eur-lex.europa.eu/smartapi/cgi/sga_doc?smartapi !celexplus!prod!DocNumber&lg=en&type_doc=Decision&an_doc=1981&nu_doc=462 [last accessed on 25 March 2011]; CELEX:31981D0462.

6.48. ▶ Volatile organic compounds (VOC) – The protocol was signed in 1991, and entered into force in 1997.

6.49. ▶ Further reduction of sulphur emissions – The protocol was signed in 1994, and entered into force in 1998.

6.50. ▶ Persistent organic pollutants (POPs) – The protocol was signed in 1998, and entered into force in 2003.

6.51. ▶ Heavy metals – The protocol was signed in 1998, and entered into force in 2003.

6.52. ▶ Acidification, eutrophication and ground-level ozone – The protocol was signed in 1999, and entered into force in 2005.

I.3.2. Charter of Paris for New Europe – OSCE[25]

6.53. Thirty-four states, members of the Conference for Security and Cooperation in Europe (CSCE), which ended the finalisation of the division of Europe and the end of the Cold War, signed the Charter of Paris on 21 November 1990. The signatories committed to apply democracy and legality and to respect human rights. At present, the organisation has more than 40 member states. In 1995, the CSCE was transformed into the Organisation for Security and Cooperation in Europe.

6.54. The Charter of Paris was established on the foundation of the Final Act of the Conference for Security and Cooperation in Europe (CSCE) of 1975, and was further amended in 1999 by the Charter for European Security. All of these documents together form the basis for the *Organisation for Security and Cooperation in Europe* (OSCE).

6.55. The Charter of Paris established the Office for Free Elections (later renamed the Office for Democratic Institutions and Human Rights) in Warsaw, a Conflict Prevention Centre in Vienna, and a secretariat. Later, in 1992, a Secretary General was also appointed. It was agreed that the Foreign Ministers are to convene regularly for political consultations.

6.56. The Charter of Paris and its principles are also referenced in the Preamble to the ECT.

I.3.3. United Nations Framework Convention on Climate Change

6.57. The energy sector is closely connected with the protection of the environment. The *United Nations Framework Convention on Climate Change*, which was agreed upon and adopted by the Intergovernmental Committee for a Framework Convention (Convention) during its session held in New York from 30 April to 9 May 1992, and

---

[25] Charter of Paris for a New Europe.

subsequently signed in June 1992 (hereinafter referred to as the *Convention* in this part of the Introduction)[26] at the United Nations Conference on Environment and Development (UNCED) in Rio de Janeiro; it entered into force on 21 March 1994.[27]

6.58.   The fundamental aim of the Convention is to create **conditions for the expeditious stabilisation of greenhouse gas concentration in the atmosphere at a level that would prevent dangerous anthropogenic interference with the climate system**. Its introduction in practice is meant to facilitate a process by which ecosystems would adapt naturally and as fast as possible to the potential risks of climate change. The Convention is based on **five main principles**:

6.59.   ▶ *Intergenerational equity and differentiated responsibility,* which are based on the efforts to protect the climate system of the Earth for the benefit of present, but also future generations. It is a reaction to the fact that, contrary to local or transboundary pollution, this issue cannot be solved by the mere application of general rules (laws) within a single state or smaller regions. The climate change solution requires global approaches. States that accede to the Convention must tackle the risks endangering the atmosphere together, and their efforts must be differentiated according to their share in the causes of our status quo. Economically developed countries ought to assume special liability.

6.60.   ▶ *Special needs of developing countries*, with an emphasis placed on the increased needs of developing states, especially those which are more sensitive to the consequences of the effects of climate change and which would have to pay disproportionately high costs to eliminate such consequences (primarily African states and states situated in South and Southeast Asia, as well as small island states in the Pacific).

6.61.   ▶ *Precaution.* Measures must be adopted sufficiently in advance. The fact that we are currently facing a lack of strong and scientifically well-supported arguments cannot justify postponement of the solution of subsequent problems.[28]

---

[26]   The abbreviated term *Convention* as defined above is only used in this part of the *Introduction* to the publication.

[27]   See http://unfccc.int/2860.php (accessed on 25 March 2011). This website also allows access to the *status chart* and the text of the Convention in the UN languages.

[28]   Although the causes of certain long-term weather effects have not yet been fully proven, the nexus between the increased concentration of the emissions of greenhouse gases in the atmosphere and the changes in the global climate system has been physically supported. Postponing a solution to the future and waiting for "sufficient evincible evidence" could have the result that the Earth's ecosystems could be irreversibly altered. This is the underlying premise of the Convention. The author needs to emphasize that he feels by no means competent to judge the accuracy of these conclusions. After all, a treatise on these issues would undesirably depart from the main purpose and focus

6.62. ▶ *Right of all countries to support and protect the interests in the permanently sustainable development of society.* Approaches and measures adopted in order to protect the climate system must correspond to the specific conditions of the individual states, and must comply with the programmes for their economic and social development.

6.63. ▶ *The contracting states must cooperate* and secure relationships that would not hinder the implementation of the Convention and that would support further development of Third World countries, while honouring the principles of the Convention.

6.64. The Framework Convention contains a number of general commitments and rules that the contracting states must observe, such as: (•) to formulate and regularly update national programmes containing measures to mitigate adverse effects of climate change; (•) to process adaptation strategies; (•) to promote permanently sustainable economy management systems and systems of nature protection; (•) to regularly monitor national volumes of greenhouse gases emitted into the atmosphere and to monitor their sinks; (•) to pay regard to the risks of the consequences of climate change when adopting social and economic measures and environmental measures, and the minimisation thereof; (•) and to promote international scientific and technical cooperation and to promote educational and information exchange programmes.

6.65. The Convention contains **two Annexes (Protocols). Protocol I** contains a list of economically developed countries (OECD countries, except South Korea and Mexico) and countries with economies in transition to market economies (most countries of Central and Eastern Europe). **Protocol II** represents a special category of states / a subcategory of the states under Annex I (only OECD countries, except the **Czech Republic, Poland,** Hungary, South Korea and Mexico). The Convention stipulates that the states listed in both Annexes are under the obligation to adopt significantly stronger measures compared to other states; in the interest of the successful completion of economic reforms, countries with economies in transition to market economies have a "certain degree of flexibility".[29]

6.66. The UN Framework Convention on Climate Change has been ratified or acceded to by 191 nations of the world.

---

thereof. Hence, the overview of the individual principles in this part must be understood as a mere *statement*, in terms of an *outline* of the existence of the relevant circumstances at the international level, especially from the legal perspective, not in terms of any evaluation of the underlying principles.

[29] Secretariat of the UN Framework Convention on Climate Change. Available at: http://unfccc.int/secretariat/items/1629.php (accesed on 6 December 2013).

II. Specific Features of Investment Protection under the ECT Compared to Bilateral Investment Treaties and Other Instruments for Promotion and Protection of Foreign Direct Investments

6.67. It is certainly appropriate to open this chapter with an overview of the basic differences between the investment protection under the Energy Charter Treaty (ECT) and the protection afforded by *standard*, or *typical*, bilateral treaties on the promotion and mutual protection of investments (BITs).

6.68. The ECT aims to provide, on a multilateral basis and specifically in relation to the energy sector, the same kind of investment protection as the protection offered under BITs.[30] Consequently, the standards incorporated in most BITs are, to a major extent, reflected in the aspects of investment protection enshrined in the ECT. Despite the fact that similarities significantly prevail over differences, there are certain features that distinguish the ECT from BITs. The differences inhere in **(i)** the member states and the subject matter of the ECT; **(ii)** the scope of the ECT; **(iii)** selected aspects of investment protection standards, as well as **(iv)** selected issues relating to the resolution of disputes under the ECT. The above differences will be the focus of our analysis in the following paragraphs of this publication.

II.1. ECT Parties (Subjective Dimension of Investment Protection) and Subject Matter of the ECT

6.69. One of the obvious differences consists in the broad *membership* of the ECT (more than 50 contracting parties) and in the subject matter of the ECT. The subject matter is delimited as *investments connected with economic activities in the energy sector.*[31]

II.1.1. Definition of Investment

6.70. The definition of *investment* under the ECT is probably broader than under most BITs. The ECT defines *investment* in Article 1(6) [of the ECT] as follows:

---

[30] The ECT procedures regulating transit, competition and environment are unique and innovative features of the ECT; however, they are not covered in the following parts of this chapter, which is focused on the protection of investors under the ECT.

[31] Article 1(6) of the ECT. However, the ECT and the arbitral awards rendered in disputes under the ECT do not precisely specify what is meant by *related* with an economic activity in the energy sector.

6.71. *"[...] every kind of asset, owned or controlled directly or indirectly by an Investor [and includes]:*[32] *tangible and intangible, and movable and immovable, property, and any property rights, such as leases, mortgages, liens, and pledges;*[33]

6.72. *a company or business enterprise, or shares, stock, or other forms of equity participation in a company or business enterprise, and bonds and other debt of a company or business enterprise;*[34]

6.73. *claims to money and claims to performance pursuant to contract having an economic value and associated with an Investment;*[35]

6.74. *intellectual property;*[36]

6.75. *returns;*[37]

6.76. *any right conferred by law or contract or by virtue of any licences and permits granted pursuant to law to undertake any Economic Activity in the Energy Sector."*[38]/[39]

6.77. According to the interpretation adopted by a certain arbitral tribunal, the definition also includes **cross-border sales of energy,** which most BITs would not necessarily consider investments. In *Petrobart* v. *Kyrgyzstan,*[40] the claimant and a state entity entered into a purchase contract for the purchase and sale of gas condensates implemented in the form of several partial deliveries supplied over the period of one year. Several deliveries were made. However, the claimant's claims under three invoices remained due and outstanding. Consequently, the

---

[32] Cf. also: OECD draft: Article 2 [...] every kind of asset owned or controlled, directly or indirectly, by an investor, including: [...]

[33] OECD draft: Article 2 [...] (viii) any other tangible and intangible, movable and immovable property, and any related property rights, such as leases, mortgages, liens and pledges [note: also retention] rights; [...]

[34] OECD draft: Article 2 [...] (ii) enterprises (whether as a legal person or any other entity constituted and organised under the applicable law of a Contracting Party, whether or not [established] for profit, and whether private or government owned or controlled, and includes a corporation, trust, partnership, sole proprietorship, [branch], joint venture, association or organisation); [...]

[35] OECD draft: Article 2 [...] (v) claims to money and claims to performance; [...]

[36] OECD draft: Article 2 [...] (vi) intellectual property rights; [...]

[37] OECD draft: Article 2 [...] (ii) shares, stocks or other forms of equity participation in an enterprise, and rights derived therefrom; (iii) bonds, debentures, loans and other forms of debt, and rights derived therefrom; (iv) rights under contracts, including turnkey, construction, management, production or revenue-sharing contracts; [...]

[38] OECD draft: Article 2 [...] (vii) rights conferred pursuant to law or contract, such as concessions, licenses, authorisations, and permits; [...]
BIT: Czech Republic-Hungary. Article 1(1)(e) – [...] rights conferred pursuant to law or contract, licenses or permits issued under the law, including concessions to explore, extract, cultivate or use natural resources.

[39] Article 1(6) of the ECT.

[40] *Petrobart* v *Kyrgyzstan*, arbitral award, 29 March 2005, SCC Case No. 126/2003.

claimant ceased further deliveries. One of the issues that had to be resolved in the arbitration that followed was whether the claim constituted an investment.

6.78. Consequently, in the said case, the appointed arbitral tribunal had to establish, according to the ECT, whether the claimant's right to receive payment for goods provided under a contract constituted an asset that represented an investment under the ECT. The tribunal held that it did. When making a decision on the said issue, the arbitral tribunal took into consideration that the investment consisted of a purchase contract (contract for purchase and sale), which falls within the scope of Article 1(6)(f) of the ECT, which stipulates that an investment is (cit.) [...] *any right conferred by law or contract or by virtue of any licences and permits granted pursuant to law to undertake any Economic Activity in the Energy Sector.*

6.79. This conclusion is in direct conflict with the conclusion that could probably be drawn on the basis of the [usual] wording of a number of other investment protection treaties (usually bilateral, i.e. BITs) that lack such a broad definition of investment. The claimant in *Petrobart* v. *Kyrgyzstan* filed a request for arbitration pursuant to the Kyrgyz Act on Foreign Investments,[41] in compliance with the UNCITRAL Rules,[42] and

---

41   National law of the Kyrgyz Republic:
Act on Foreign Investments in the Kyrgyz Republic, June 1991, published in: *Vedomosti* of the Supreme Soviet of the Republic of Kyrgyzstan, 1991, Law No. 13, at 449 et seq. The 1991 Act regulated the establishment and status of enterprises with foreign property participation, including those owned exclusively by foreigners. The law is meant to guarantee the transferability of revenues and allow foreign investments in all areas of the economy, except production for military purposes and certain areas of agricultural production. The Law was substantially amended in 1995, especially with respect to refining the rights of investors. The law guarantees national treatment.
The 1991 Act was replaced with the Act on Foreign Investments in the Kyrgyz Republic of 16 September 1997, published in: *Vedomosti* of the Supreme Soviet of the Republic of Kyrgyzstan, 1997, issued on 24 September 1997, Law No. 66. The English version of the Law is available online at: http://www.angelfire.com/ar/researchkyrgyzstan/laws/forinv.htm (accessed on 30 October 2010).
42   Act on Foreign Investments in the Republic of Kyrgyzstan of 16 September 1997, published in: *Vedomosti* of the Supreme Soviet of the Republic of Kyrgyzstan, 1997, issued on 24 September 1997, Law No. 66, Article 23 (approximate translation, cit.): Article 23- Settlement of Investment Disputes – 1. *Without limiting other means of legal protection that could be used by a foreign investor in accordance with the legislation of the Kyrgyz Republic, an investment dispute shall be settled in accordance with any applicable rule that is previously [before the dispute arises] agreed upon between the foreign investor and the authorized governmental organs of the Kyrgyz Republic. 2. In the absence of such an agreement, an investment dispute between the authorized governmental organs of the Kyrgyz Republic and a foreign investor shall be settled, if possible, through consultations between the parties thereto. If the parties thereto cannot come to an amicable settlement of*

the arbitral tribunal in the given case held that the purchase contract did not constitute an investment, because an investment (approximate translation, cit.) *requires a relationship between the foreign investor and the host state, which is more permanent than a relationship established under a transitional international sales transaction.*[43] Hence, the narrower definition that is incorporated in the ICSID Convention (and other instruments) and that corresponds to the relatively broad case law does not define a foreign investment as an asset, but rather as a permanent investment of a managing component of a capital and active nature in a project intended to generate profit.

6.80. The definition of investment in the ECT basically comprises any right that has any financial value (which can be evaluated in money),[44] including claims for financial and non-financial performance established under a contract. The ECT is a unique instrument in this respect, because it explicitly employs a broad concept of investment, which comprises property rights of any kind. But it is necessary to point out that if the claimants opt for the jurisdiction of the *ICSID Centre*, as opposed to the SCC or *ad hoc* arbitration pursuant to the UNCITRAL Rules, the claimant must meet not only the less rigorous requirements regarding *investments* under Article 1(6) of the ECT, but also the more rigorous requirements under Article 25 of the ICSID Convention.

---

the dispute within three months from the day of the first written request for such consultations, the dispute shall be settled through arbitration in accordance with one of the following procedures: (●) Regulations of the Third Party Arbitration Court under the Chamber of Industry and Commerce of the Kyrgyz Republic; (●) The ICSID Convention (the "Convention ICSID" signed in Washington DC on 19 March 1965), if applicable; (●) Arbitration (Auxiliary) regulations of the International Centre for the Settlement of the Investment Disputes (ICSID), if applicable; (●) Arbitration regulations of the Commission of the United Nations Organizations on International Trade Law (UNCITRAL Regulation); in this case, the appointing body [appointing authority] shall be the Secretary-General of the ICSID. 3. The Kyrgyz Republic, through its authorized governmental body, shall consent to the transfer of the investment dispute for arbitration by virtue of this law. A foreign investor's agreement may be given at any time through a written notification to the State Body effectuating the attraction of investments or at the moment of resorting to arbitration. 4. Disputes between foreign investors and individuals or legal entities of the Kyrgyz Republic are resolved upon the agreement of the parties through a Third Party Arbitration Court located inside or outside the Kyrgyz Republic. In the event that there is no such agreement, the disputes are decided in accordance with the procedure established by legislation of the Kyrgyz Republic. A decision of the Court shall be binding and final.

43 Petrobart Ltd. v Kyrgyzstan, supra note 40, paragraph (41).

44 Cf. also Alexander J. Bělohlávek & Renáta Hótová, Pojem investice z pohledu jejich mezinárodněprávní ochrany [Concept of Investment from Perspective of Protection Thereof under International Law], (4) PRÁVO PRO PODNIKÁNÍ A ZAMĚSTNÁNÍ 3–12 (2006).

II.1.2. Definition of Investor

6.81. Investor under the ECT can also include a natural person who is not considered to be an investor of a Contracting Party to the ECT by way of being a citizen or national of the ECT Contracting Party, provided that he or she at least has his/her permanent residence in the [contracting] state. This is a significant difference compared to the ICSID Convention, which stipulates that only a natural person who is a citizen or national of a contracting state is an investor.

II.1.3. Provisional Application

6.82. Another difference distinguishing the ECT from most BITs or other instruments is the fact that the ECT mandates that every contracting state must apply the ECT *provisionally, until* [the ECT] *enters into force*,[45] i.e. after signing, but before ratification of the ECT.

II.2. Specific Features of Substantive Rules on Investment Protection

II.2.1. National Treatment

6.83. Most BITs secure the most-favoured nation treatment ("MFN" or "MFN clause") for investors and their investments, **both before the investment is made and in relation to already existing investments.** Conversely, most BITs do not stipulate commitments of the host states that would guarantee **national treatment**. Conversely, the ECT accords treatment to existing investments in the host state in compliance with the MFN clause and, simultaneously, national treatment,[46] but the ECT provisions regulating the period **before the investment is made** guarantee a regime with a limited standard. Article 10(2) of the ECT stipulates that each Contracting Party (cit.) *shall endeavour to accord to Investors of other Contracting Parties, as regards the Making of Investments in its Area*, national treatment or treatment in compliance with the MFN clause, whichever is the most favourable in the given case.[47] This provision is a *maximum effort clause*, rather than the strict commitment that can be found in most BITs.

---

[45] Article 45(1) of the ECT.
[46] Article 10(7) of the ECT reads as follows (cit.): Each Contracting Party shall accord to Investments in its Area of Investors of other Contracting Parties, and their related activities, including management, maintenance, use, enjoyment or disposal, treatment no less favourable than that which it accords to Investments of its own Investors or of the Investors of any other Contracting Party or any third state and their related activities, including management, maintenance, use, enjoyment or disposal, whichever is the most favourable.
[47] Article 10(2) of the ECT.

6.84. Despite the fact that Article 10(4) of the ECT anticipates that supplementary arrangements will enter into force, which will extend the obligation of national treatment and MFN treatment to the stage preceding the making of the investment, no such treaty has been concluded yet.

II.2.2. Minimum Standard of Treatment

6.85. The ECT contracting parties are obliged to refrain from any treatment of the FDI that would be less favourable than the treatment required by international law. This is a regular rule, which is also contained in most BITs, but the ECT continues with another provision that distinguishes the ECT from most BITs, namely Article 10(1) [of the ECT], which stipulates that investments shall not be *accorded treatment less favourable than that required by international law, **including** [international] **treaty obligations**.*[48]

6.86. This addition could probably be interpreted as meaning that a breach of an obligation arising from any other treaty concluded by the contracting party could constitute a breach of the ECT and be subject to the procedural mechanisms of dispute resolution incorporated in the ECT. In this respect, the ECT would differ from other treaties, which explicitly limit the obligations concerning the [standard of] treatment to obligations arising from customary international law – not international treaty law.

II.2.3. Umbrella Clause

6.87. Article 10(1) of the ECT reads as follows (cit.): *Each Contracting Party shall observe any obligations it has entered into with an Investor or an Investment of an Investor of any other Contracting Party.* Such clauses, commonly referred to as *umbrella clauses* (the English expression is commonly used in other languages too), are known to a number of BITs. But the ECT, contrary to other instruments of international law for the promotion and protection of investments, stipulates that the contracting parties may, when signing the ECT, refuse to give their consent with the resolution of disputes arising from the umbrella clause by way of international arbitration.[49]

---

[48] Emphasis in bold added by author. Here in the sense of commitments arising from international treaties.

[49] See Article 26(3) of the ECT. Only four states refused to give their consent: Australia and Norway (the status as of September 2004 is: ratification of the ECT), Canada (has not signed the ECT) and Hungary (see the special status according to Annex IA to the ECT). The Russian Federation announced in August 2009 that it would not ratify the ECT.

6.88. Authors of certain commentaries and treatises regarding the ECT also argue that the reference to [...] *any obligations* [...] *it has entered into* [...], as articulated in Article 10(1) of the ECT, limits the applicability of this *umbrella clause* to treaty commitments, whereas umbrella clauses incorporated in BITs usually contain more general references to any and all obligations *assumed* by the state, and may also apply to unilateral commitments, such as obligations arising from foreign laws [of national origin] concerning foreign direct investments.[50] However, the arbitral tribunal in *SGS* v. *Pakistan*[51] interpreted similar words as (cit.) [...] *obligations* [...] that Pakistan and Switzerland *have entered into* under their BIT (BIT of 1995) as sufficiently broad to include unilateral administrative acts.[52] Hence, the wording of Article 10(1) of the ECT need not necessarily limit the obligations of the state to obligations arising from treaties (treaty obligations).

II.2.4. Denial of Advantages Clause

6.89. Similarly to certain BITs, the ECT also contains a *denial of advantages* clause, which stipulates that the host states may deny the advantages required under the ECT for the benefit of an investor of another contracting party if the investor is an enterprise (entity, company etc.) of the party, provided that the entity has no substantial business activity in the area of the party in which the enterprise was incorporated, and provided that the persons who own or control the enterprise are citizens or nationals of a third state or citizens or nationals of the host state. However, contrary to Article 17(1) of the ECT, most BITs make the denial of advantages afforded by the BIT contingent on the fulfilment of a condition that stipulates that the denying party must first announce and discuss the denial with the other party or parties involved; such condition is another obstacle to the exercise of the right to deny advantages. The requirement of prior announcement (notification) that is usually incorporated in BITs is logical if the instrument is a bilateral international treaty; it would, however, be somewhat difficult to apply under multilateral treaties.

---

[50] Emmanuel Gaillard & Mark McNeill, *The Energy Charter Treaty*, in ARBITRATION UNDER INTERNATIONAL INVESTMENT AGREEMENTS, Oxford: OUP 37, 48 (Katia Yannaca-Small ed., 2010).

[51] *SGS* v *Pakistan*, decision on jurisdictional objections.

[52] *SGS* v *Pakistan*, decision on jurisdictional objections, paragraphs (97) through (101).

II.2.5. Tax Filter

6.90. Many BITs contain a *tax filter* that limits the type of complaints against taxation measures that can be submitted to arbitration. The regular practice is that, before a complaint is submitted challenging a taxation measure as a measure constituting expropriation, the claimant must first submit the matter to the tax authorities of both parties (for resolution, or at least for discussion). Only if the authorities fail to agree that the respective taxation measure does not constitute expropriation may the claimant submit his or her claims to arbitration.

6.91. The ECT also has a tax filter, but it is different and more complicated. As is the case under a number of BITs, claimants who wish to challenge a taxation measure as a measure constituting expropriation under the ECT must first submit their complaints to the competent tax authorities of both parties. However, the arbitral tribunal is not bound by the conclusion reached by the tax authorities: the arbitral tribunal may take into account the conclusions arrived at by the competent tax authorities.[53] But if the claimant argues that the tax that allegedly constitutes expropriation is also discriminatory, the arbitral tribunal must take into account the decision of the tax authorities.[54]

6.92. The ECT rules are also substantially longer than the rules incorporated in most BITs, and distinguish between several categories of taxes.

II.3. Dispute Settlement Rules

II.3.1. Forum and Applicable Procedural Rules

6.93. Article 26(4) of the ECT stipulates that the investor may submit the dispute[55] to **arbitration** conducted by:

6.94. ▶ The International Centre for Settlement of Investment Disputes [ICSID] [...] if the Contracting Party of the Investor and the Contracting Party that is party to the dispute are both parties to the ICSID Convention; or

6.95. ▶ The International Centre for Settlement of Investment Disputes [ICSID] [...] under the rules governing the Additional Facility for the Administration of Proceedings by the Secretariat of the Centre (hereinafter referred to as the "Additional Facility Rules"), if the Contracting Party of the Investor or the Contracting Party that is party to the dispute, but not both, is a party to the ICSID Convention;

---

[53] Article 21(5)(iii) of the ECT.
[54] Article 21(5)(iii) of the ECT.
[55] Considering the wording of Article 26, which stipulates that the dispute must concern a breach of the investment protection under Part III, the provision is probably narrower than arbitration agreements in BITs, which cover, for instance, *"any and all disputes arising from the investment"*.

6.96. ▶ A sole arbitrator or *ad hoc* arbitration tribunal [panel] established under the Arbitration Rules of the United Nations Commission on International Trade Law (UNCITRAL Rules); or

6.97. ▶ An arbitral proceeding under the Arbitration Institute of the Stockholm Chamber of Commerce (SCC).

6.98. Both arbitration within the framework of the ICSID and arbitration conducted pursuant to the UNCITRAL Rules are possibilities envisaged in a number of, if not most, BITs. Arbitration under the SCC and jurisdiction of the SCC is less common in BITs, but not exceptional.[56]

II.3.2. *Authority for Appointing the Arbitrator or the Chairman of the Arbitral Panel (Appointing Authority)*

6.99. Another *procedural aspect* that distinguishes the ECT from most BITs is the absence of any provision (arrangement) regarding the authority for appointing an arbitrator or the chairman of the arbitral panel (*appointing authority*) directly in the ECT. Some BITs stipulate that the *appointing authority* is, for instance, the ICSID Secretary-General. As concerns arbitration under the UNCITRAL Rules, the BITs stipulate that the ICSID Secretary-General appoints an arbitrator if any of the parties fails to do so. The entity (*appointing authority*) also resolves arbitrator challenges. Conversely, in arbitration under the ECT conducted pursuant to the UNCITRAL Rules, the appointing authority for the given arbitral proceedings must be selected by the Secretary-General of the Permanent Court of Arbitration (PCA).[57]

II.3.3. *Forum Selection (Choice of Forum)*

6.100. If a dispute arises between an investor of one contracting party and another contracting party, the investor has the right to choose between two basic alternatives: (i) resolution of the dispute at an international forum, or (ii) submission of the dispute to the courts of the host state. A number of BITs contain a *fork-in-the-road* provision, which usually stipulates that as soon as the investor opts for a national court, he or she cannot subsequently demand that the same claims be submitted to and resolved by an international forum – and vice versa.[58]

---

[56] See also: BIT: Czech Republic-Cyprus (Article 8(2d)), BIT: Czech Republic-UK (Article 8(2)(b)); moreover, subparagraph (c) of the same provision envisages the jurisdiction of the VIAC, which is even less common than the jurisdiction of the SCC), BIT: Czech Republic-Poland (Article 7(2); here together with the ICC as another alternative).

[57] See Article 6(2) of the UNCITRAL Rules and Article 7(2) of the UNCITRAL Rules.

[58] GRAHAM COOP & CLARISSE C RIBEIRO, INVESTMENT PROTECTION AND THE ENERGY CHARTER TREATY, Huntington (NY): JurisNet 316 (2008).

6.101. The ECT stipulates that any contracting party may, when signing the Treaty, refuse to give its consent with arbitration if the investor has previously submitted the given dispute to local courts or administrative authorities.[59] Twenty-four member states, as well as the United States and Canada (who are not signatories to the ECT),[60] have essentially created such a *fork-in-the-road* provision in the ECT by making such a declaration.

II.3.4. Cooling-off Period

6.102. Article 26(1) of the ECT and Article 26(2) of the ECT provide for a three-month period to settle the disputes between the investor and the host state amicably before any proceedings are commenced. A number of BITs commonly provide for a period of three or six months.[61] However, whereas investors in certain investment arbitration proceedings commenced on the basis of BITs initiated arbitration under the MFN clauses before the expiration of the cooling-off period, the three-month period stipulated for arbitration under the ECT is usually honoured.[62]

III. Interpretation of International Law Instruments in Relation to the ECT

III.1. Investment Protection Regimes under International Law

6.103. The primary focus of this chapter is on two areas, namely **(i)** the extent to which the case law concerning BITs can be applied to interpret the ECT, and **(ii)** the differences in the interpretation of international treaties and, in the broader context, the issues of investment protection under BITs, the ICSID and under the ECT.

6.104. **The BIT regime** means the system of bilateral investment (protection) treaties, which usually contain a clause regarding the settlement of investor-to-state disputes that offers both investors and states multiple forums for the purpose of settling their disputes; in the overwhelming majority of cases, the disputes are resolved in arbitration. The first option is institutional arbitration under the ICSID Centre or under selected permanent international arbitral institutions, such as the ICC

---

[59]   Article 26(3)(b)(i) of the ECT.
[60]   ECT, Annex ID.
[61]   In this respect, BITs concluded by the United Kingdom are exceptional, in that they often contain a four-month period.
[62]   GRAHAM COOP & CLARISSE C RIBEIRO, *supra* note 58, at 24.

International Court of Arbitration, the SCC, exceptionally the Vienna International Arbitral Centre at the Austrian Economic Chamber [VIAC], etc. Another option is to employ arbitral proceedings different from any institutionalised arbitration, i.e. *ad hoc* arbitration, for instance, arbitration pursuant to the UNCITRAL Rules. The individual BITs very often offer the alternative of proceedings before the courts of the host state. It is necessary to point out that the parties only avail themselves of this last-mentioned possibility (if an equal alternative to arbitration) exceptionally, and the sources offer no case law in this respect.[63]

6.105. **The ECT regime** means the regime of a multilateral international treaty, which also contains provisions on the settlement of *investor-to-state* disputes that offers investors and states the possibility of proceedings according to the ICSID Convention, in *ad hoc* arbitration pursuant to the UNCITRAL Rules, or in arbitration under the Arbitration Institute of the Stockholm SCC.

6.106. **The ICSID regime** represents a dispute resolution system based on a multilateral treaty – the ICSID Convention – which offers a forum to investors and states in which they can settle their disputes. The ICSID Centre is only vested with jurisdiction over a dispute (i) if the parties to the dispute agreed in the individual (particular) case to submit the dispute to the Centre, or (ii) if the jurisdiction to hear the case has been established by an international treaty. The ICSID Centre offers signatories of the ICSID Convention a set of rules regulating the arbitral proceedings. Apart from that, the ICSID Centre has also implemented the Additional Facility for cases in which only one of the parties (or an entity of one party only, as applicable) is a signatory to the ICSID Convention. References to the ICSID Centre are incorporated in bilateral investment (promotion and mutual protection) treaties (BITs), as well as in multilateral treaties, such as the NAFTA or the ECT.

6.107. The dispute resolution regime within the jurisdiction of the ICSID Centre can also be described as an all-embracing mechanism, which represents a platform for mechanisms envisaged under both multilateral and bilateral treaties. **Investors are therefore forced to meet the criteria of a double jurisdiction test**, both the criteria under the applicable BIT (or the ECT, considering the context of the main focus of this publication), and the criteria of the ICSID regime. This means that if the respective dispute is a dispute under a BIT or under

---

[63] One of the national reporters from the international protection of investments section *laconically* commented on this issue at the July 2010 congress of the International Academy of Comparative Law held in Washington D.C. (cit.): *it is hard to conceive that anybody would address the courts of the host state*, meaning that there is de facto no equal alternative to arbitration.

the ECT that ought to be resolved under the ICSID Centre, it is necessary to pay regard to two levels of interpretation, i.e. interpretation under the applicable investment protection treaty [BIT] (ECT), and interpretation under the ICSID Convention.

III.2. Differences in Interpretation Methods under BIT/ICSID/ECT Regimes

III.2.1. Interpretation Pursuant to the Vienna Convention on the Law of Treaties (1969; VCLT)

6.108. Forums dealing with the interpretation of any of the three abovementioned regimes consistently start with the VCLT. Alternatively, they also apply the available case law.

6.109. The VCLT is currently the crucial source for the interpretation of [international] treaties. References to the VCLT in the case law of tribunals are more and more frequent, even though the tribunals do not employ the consecutive method. Interestingly, despite the fact that certain countries (such as the U.S.) have not ratified the VCLT, the Convention is still considered a broad international standard that codifies customary international law; moreover, the Convention itself is able to serve as a unified platform in relation to third countries (countries that are not signatories to the Convention).

6.110. At the ECT adoption session, the Chairman to the final Plenary Session of the European Energy Charter Conference held on 17 December 1994 made the following statement (cit.): "[t]he Treaty shall be applied and interpreted in accordance with generally recognized rules and principles of observance, application and interpretation of treaties as reflected in Part III of the Vienna Convention on the Law of Treaties of 25 May 1969. [...] The Treaty shall be interpreted in good faith in accordance with the ordinary meaning to be given to the terms of treaty in their context and in light of its object and purpose."

6.111. There are two different approaches to the application of the VCLT. English law emphasizes the *ordinary meaning* of the text of the treaty, whereas Continental law accentuates the teleological approach focused on the *object and purpose* of the treaty.

III.2.2. Article 31 of the Vienna Convention on the Law of Treaties

6.112. Article 31(1) of the VCLT can be applied in a consecutive fashion, beginning with the ordinary or regular meaning, the overall context, and ending with the purpose of the treaty; alternatively, the provision can be applied as a single integrated rule.

6.113. Article 31(1) of the VCLT and Article 31(2) of the VCLT refer to the overall context within the framework of which the interpretation must focus on the overall textual, grammatical and functional context of the treaty. When determining the overall context of the ECT, the text of the Treaty itself would not suffice; it is necessary to analyse and factor in the ECT's Preamble and its numerous Annexes, a number of Decisions, interpretation clauses (*Understandings*) and Declarations, including the Final Act, and the Protocol on Energy Efficiency.

6.114. The **object and purpose of the ECT** are not so easy to identify; they can be associated with the aims of the treaty stipulated in the Preamble, with the provision itself regarding the Purpose, with the Preamble to the European Energy Charter of 1991, as well as with Article 2 of the ECT of 1994. Interpretation of the ECT requires us to tackle a difficult task, namely the determination of the correct sequence of more than 50 provisions or paragraphs that could be, both individually and in their mutual context, designated as *object* and/or *purpose*. However, tribunals should not, as a rule, give precedence to any meaning that is more closely related to the *object* and *purpose* of a treaty over the text of the treaty itself, or they should do so only very cautiously.

6.115. We should determine the overall purpose of the treaty, but also examine the specific purpose of the given particular mechanism and concept. For instance, the purpose of Article 17(1) of the ECT is to provide states that are not signatories to the ECT with the motivation to become signatories to the ECT – the instrument employed by the ECT in order to do so inheres in the denial of advantages to "free riders". This purpose is more specific than the general purpose of "investment promotion", which can be found in most investment treaties.

6.116. For the purposes of interpreting the meaning of the provisions of a given treaty, the tribunals may refer to any subsequent agreements regarding interpretation and practice (see Article 31(3)(a) and (b) of the VCLT). The VCLT does not proclaim such tools adopted after the execution of the treaty as binding on the tribunal; it merely provides that the tribunals may take them into account.

6.117. Parties to the ECT may issue declarations regarding interpretation through the medium of the Energy Charter Conference and Article 34(3)(i) of the ECT, specifically in the form of Declarations. Indeed, such opportunity is also provided to BIT contracting parties.

6.118. When interpreting a BIT that is the subject matter of the dispute, the tribunals often pay regard to the practice of the respondent [host] state with respect to other BITs entered into by the same state.[64] Such

---

[64] See the following decisions: *Maffezini v Spain*, arbitral award; and *Parkerings-Compagniet AS v Lithuania*, award on jurisdiction and arbitral award on the merits.

practice can only be considered an implied agreement if it is accepted by other contracting states as well. The current case law to the ECT does not suggest that, when interpreting the ECT, the tribunals will pay regard to the practice of the respondent state under other (international) treaties.

III.2.3. Article 32 of the VCLT

6.119. Article 32 of the VCLT stipulates that recourse may be had to supplementary information in order to confirm the meaning of the treaty resulting from the application of Article 31 of the VCLT, or if the application of Article 31 of the VCLT would leave the meaning of the treaty *ambiguous or obscure*, or *lead to a result that is manifestly absurd or unreasonable*.

6.120. Supplementary means of interpretation envisaged under Article 32 of the VCLT include preparatory work of the treaty (*travaux preparatoires*) and the circumstances of the conclusion thereof.

6.121. There are usually no reliable and available *travaux preparatoires* with respect to BITs, because the text of a BIT is usually adopted from its earlier version, or it is contained in a model BIT. Moreover, it is relatively common for the preparatory works with respect to multilateral international treaties to often involve a broad discussion attended by professionals. Conversely, the preparation of bilateral treaties is often an administrative matter, and the course of the preparatory works is frequently almost unknown, even to specialized professionals. As concerns the ICSID Convention, there are numerous proposals, formulation concepts and preparatory materials available to the general public. With respect to the ECT, however, the public does not have access to any such materials; this is somewhat exceptional in the practice of multilateral international treaties, and even if the ECT Secretariat allows access to these materials, it is subject to very restrictive conditions.

III.2.4. The VCLT in Decisions Rendered under the ECT

6.122. In *Plama* v. *Bulgaria*, the arbitral tribunal, when substantiating its conclusions regarding the applicable law, provided the following reasoning concerning the VCLT and invoked the applicable BIT, ECT and the ICSID Convention (cit.): *All three instruments are treaties under international law; and their interpretation is governed by rules of international law, expressed in Articles 31 and 32 of the Vienna Convention on the Law of Treaties of 1969* [VCLT] [...]. *Under Article 31(1), the general rule requires a treaty to be interpreted in good faith in accordance with the ordinary meaning to be given to the terms of the* *treaty in their "context" and in light of the treaty's "object" and "purpose"; Article 31(2) [VCLT] defines "context"; and the remaining provisions of Articles 31 and 32 [VCLT] provide further means of interpretation as applicable.*[65]

6.123. When making a decision on the merits in *Plama* v. *Bulgaria*, the tribunal again emphasized the necessity of using the VCLT; the tribunal held that a treaty must be interpreted in good faith in accordance with the ordinary meaning to be given to the terms of the treaty in their context and in light of its object and purpose.[66]

6.124. In *Petrobart Ltd.* v. *Kyrgyzstan*, the tribunal reiterated the arguments proposed by the tribunal in *Plama* v. *Bulgaria*; the tribunal held that since the dispute arose in connection with the Treaty, the interpretation of any of its provisions should be ascertained in accordance with the generally accepted rules of (international) treaty interpretation. The general principles of (international) treaty interpretation are set out in Articles 31 through 33 of the Vienna Convention on the Law of Treaties of 1969 [VCLT]. Article 31 [of the VCLT] indicates as follows (cit.): *"Since this dispute has arisen in connection with the Treaty, the interpretation of any of its provisions should be ascertained in accordance with the generally accepted rules of treaty interpretation. The general principles of treaty interpretation are set out in Articles 31– 33 of the Vienna Convention on the Law of Treaties of 1969 [VCLT]. It follows from Article 31 that the determination of the common intention of the parties to the treaty in their choice of certain terms must be undertaken "in accordance with the ordinary meaning to be given to the terms of the treaty in their context and in light of its object and purpose". It is to be noted that one of the **central objectives of the Treaty is to provide a high level of protection to the investments of investors in the energy sector.*"[67]

6.125. In *Yukos Universal Ltd.* v. *Russia*,[68] *Hulley Enterprises Ltd.* v. *Russia*[69] and *Veteran Petroleum Ltd.* v. *Russia*,[70] the tribunal employed the VCLT in order to ascertain the meaning of Article 45 of the ECT in the reasoning for its ruling, which also outlined the relationship between Article 31 of the VCLT and Article 32 of the VCLT.[71]

---

[65] *Plama* v *Bulgaria*, award on jurisdiction, paragraph (117).

[66] Ibid., paragraph (138).

[67] *Petrobart* v *Kyrgyzstan*, *supra* note 40, paragraph (98). Emphasis in the text cited above added by author.

[68] *Yukos* v *Russia*, *supra* note 19.

[69] *Hulley* v *Russia*, interim award on jurisdiction.

[70] *Veteran* v *Russia*, interim award on jurisdiction.

[71] *Yukos* v *Russia*, *supra* note 19.

6.126. It appears that tribunals that make decisions under the ECT apply the VCLT systematically and persuasively. Considering the small number of available cases, it is difficult to predict whether tribunals will always invoke the VCLT whenever they are confronted with interpretation issues. But it is most likely that whenever issues arise that are connected with treaty interpretation, the tribunal will employ the VCLT. The fact that the VCLT is a crucial interpretation tool is corroborated by the above-cited case law, as well as the case law concerning the protection of FDI as such.

III.3. Prior Rulings (Importance of Case Law)

III.3.1. Approach Adopted by Tribunals (Arbitral Tribunals)

6.127. General international law knows no system of precedents. Hence, the interpretation of the ECT, BITs and the ICSID Convention rendered by tribunals in previous cases can only be endowed with the power of persuasion, and thereby influence the decision-making of the tribunals that are interpreting the text of any of these instruments at a later moment.

6.128. But arbitral tribunals dealing with investment disputes commonly invoke the decisions of other tribunals when interpreting any particular treaty. This can be illustrated by the practice of proceedings under the ICSID Centre and, indeed, also outside the jurisdiction of the ICSID; this practice consists of the use of the *Salini* test (criterion) to determine whether or not the particular case concerns FDI covered by protection under international law. However, despite the fact that tribunals frequently invoke prior rulings, they are not bound by them. The nonbinding nature of prior case law has been confirmed by tribunals in several cases concerning the protection of investments.[72]

6.129. The voluminous case law available in disputes arising from alleged violations of BITs provides us with a large quantity of materials that the tribunals dealing with the interpretation of a BIT may use, even if the rulings of the tribunals do not concern the interpretation of any particular provision of the same BIT. Areas that are substantially based on prior arbitral awards include: the definition of investor and investment, the extension of the applicability of MFN clauses (*umbrella clause*) to dispute resolution, the meaning of indirect expropriation, and the standard of fair and equal treatment.

---

[72] See also the following decisions: *Enron* v *Argentina*, decision on jurisdiction, paragraph (25); *LETCO* v *Liberia*, arbitral award, 2 ICSID REPORTS 346, 352; *AES* v *Argentina*, decision on jurisdiction, paragraph (25); and *SGS* v *The Philippines*, decision on jurisdiction, paragraph (97).

6.130. Similarly under the ICSID Convention, tribunals have been frequently called upon to construe the meaning of particular provisions of a given treaty, and tribunals in later cases invoke such interpretation in their own decisions. Interpretation of the ICSID Convention also benefits from the very well-documented and available *travaux preparatoires*; this does not hold true for most BITs. Moreover, tribunals may also employ a number of excellent commentaries to the ICSID Convention.[73]

6.131. Considering the fact that the number of disputes arising from the ECT is still rather small, the tribunals that render decisions under the ECT have only a limited number of rulings to draw on. But the tribunals nonetheless invoke prior rulings (case law).[74]

III.3.2. BIT and ECT Case Law

6.132. This section is devoted to the most important disputes resolved under the ECT, in which the tribunals invoked the case law relating to the interpretation and use of BITs. The author would first like to mention specific cases in which the tribunal, dealing with an ECT case, invoked case law relating to a BIT; second, the author provides an analysis of the broader implications that such references have for the ECT case law.

6.133. In *Petrobart Ltd.* v. *Kyrgyzstan*,[75] the tribunal invoked the ruling in (●) *Fedax* v. *Venezuela*, (●) *Salini* v. *Morocco*, (●) *SGS* v. *Pakistan* when resolving the issue of whether an investment was made that meets the criteria of the applicable definition.[76]

6.134. In *Amto LLC* v. *Ukraine*,[77] the tribunal invoked (●) *Banco International, Inc.* v. *Argentina* in the part of its ruling that concerned the state's consent with arbitration in a dispute concerning the protection of investments.[78] The tribunal also mentioned (●) *Ethyl Corporation* v. *Canada (regarding an arbitral award on jurisdiction),* (●) *SGS Societe*

---

[73]   See also CHRISTOPH SCHREUER, ICSID CONVENTION: COMMENTARY ON CONVENTION ON SETTLEMENT OF INVESTMENT DISPUTES BETWEEN STATES AND NATIONALS OF OTHER STATES, Cambridge: CUP (2009). This commentary is considered a most valuable source of information, offering a specific interpretation of the individual provisions of the ICSID Convention. See also decisions that refer to the commentary provided by Prof. Schreuer: *ADF Group Inc.* v *U.S.A*, arbitral award, 6 January 2003, ICSID Case No. ARB(AF)/00/1, footnote 151; *Bayindir Insaat Turizm Ticaret ve Sanayi A Ş* v *Pakistan*, decision on jurisdiction, 14 November 2005, ICSID Case No. ARB/03/29.

[74]   See also reference to *Kardassopoulos* v *Georgia*, decision on jurisdiction, 6 July 2007, ICSID Case No. ARB/05/18; in *Yukos* v *Russia*, *supra* note 19, paragraph 269, 442 and reference to *Plama* v *Bulgaria*, *supra* note 65.

[75]   *Petrobart* v *Kyrgyzstan*, *supra* note 40.

[76]   Ibid., paragraphs (393) through (395).

[77]   *Amto* v *Ukraine*, final award.

[78]   Ibid., paragraph (45).

Generale de Surveillance S. A. v. *Pakistan*; in the reasons for the decision, the tribunal analysed provisions regulating consultations, or settlement negotiations in investment protection treaties. The tribunal has noted that each settlement and every case must be assessed separately. The same issue was the subject matter of the tribunal's reference to the ruling in (●) *Generation Ukraine, Inc.* v. *Ukraine.* Finally, as concerns the denial of justice, the tribunal invoked the ruling in (●) *Mondev International Ltd.* v. *U.S.A.*

6.135. In connection with an analysis of the MFN clause, the arbitral tribunal in *Plama* v. *Bulgaria*[79] invoked in its arbitral award on jurisdiction the rulings rendered in (●) *Mafezzini* v. *Spain* and (●) *Salini* v. *Jordan.*[80] In the award on the merits,[81] the same arbitral tribunal invoked (●) *Inceysa* v. *El Salvador* when making a decision on whether the respective investment violated legal principles.[82] The tribunal also invoked (●) *World Duty Free* v. *Kenya*, i.e. a case in which the arbitral tribunal held that international public policy had been breached.[83] When interpreting the standard of fair and equal treatment under the ECT, the arbitral tribunal in *Plama* v. *Bulgaria* invoked (●) *MTD* v. *Chile*[84] and (●) *CMS* v. *Argentina.*[85] Further, when interpreting the concept of permanent protection and security, the tribunal referred to (●) *AMT* v. *Zaire*, (●) *Wena* v. *Egypt,* and (●) *Saluka* v. *Czech Republic.*[86] And finally, when ruling on the obligations assumed by states vis-à-vis investors, the tribunal in *Plama* v. *Bulgaria* invoked the decision on annulment of the arbitral award in (●) *CMS* v. *Argentina.*[87]

6.136. In *Cementownia* v. *Turkey*, the tribunal invoked (●) *Phoenix Action Ltd.* v. *Czech Republic* when ruling on the requirement of making the investment in good faith as a condition for classifying the investment as eligible for international protection. The tribunal also invoked the following cases when making a decision on the penalty that could be imposed on the investor for abusing the proceedings, or the mechanisms protecting investors, as applicable: (●) *Benvenuti & Bonfant* v. *Congo*, (●) *MINE* v. *Guinea*, (●) *American Manufacturing Trading* v. *Zaire*, and (●) *LETCO* v. *Liberia.*[88]

---

[79] *Plama* v *Bulgaria,supra* note 65.
[80] Ibid., paragraph (119).
[81] Ibid.
[82] Ibid., paragraph (141).
[83] Ibid., paragraph (142).
[84] Ibid., paragraph (175).
[85] Ibid., paragraph (177).
[86] Ibid., paragraph (179).
[87] Ibid., paragraph (186).
[88] *Cementownia* v *Turkey*, arbitral award, paragraph (158).

6.137. Finally, in *Europe Cement Investment & Trade S. A.* v. *Turkey*,[89] the tribunal referred to (●) *Inceysa* v. *El Salvador*[90] when analysing the fraud committed by the investor while implementing the investment, and to (●) *Phoenix* v. *Czech Republic*[91] when analysing investments made in good faith.

6.138. Analysis of these cases does not reveal any settled procedure according to which the tribunals that resolve disputes arising from the ECT would invoke BITs, or the case law in investment protection matters under BITs.

6.139. The tribunals rendering decisions under the ECT invoked the BIT case law to a differing extent, if at all. Sometimes they only mentioned a particular case rendered under a BIT in the references used in the reasoning for the decision, while sometimes they incorporated in their decision an extensive citation from the relevant [different] case rendered under the BIT. In none of the cases, however, did the tribunals explain the basis on which they employed references to BIT case law, nor did they analyse the relationship between the regime of the BIT and the ECT regime.

6.140. In some of those cases, the BIT case law was presented to the arbitral tribunals by the parties; in other cases, the initiative regarding such reasoning originated with the arbitrators themselves. It is also impossible to trace any specific moment when the tribunals hearing disputes concerning the ECT started to invoke the BIT case law.

6.141. The practice of using prior rulings, whether rulings concerning BITs or rulings concerning the ECT, was already mentioned above in Chapter II. In this connection, it is appropriate to point out that when tribunals are called upon to resolve disputes arising from the ECT under the ICSID regime, they need to apply the abovementioned double level of treaty interpretation; hence, if the tribunal invokes a related case under a BIT, which simultaneously falls within the ICSID Convention, it does not necessarily imply that the tribunal uses the interpretation of the given provision of the BIT for the purpose of interpreting the ECT. It is possible for the tribunal in such a case (when the employed dispute resolution mechanism requires the application of the ICSID Convention[92] both for the ECT and for the

---

[89]   *Europe Cement Investment* v *Turkey*, arbitral award.

[90]   Ibid., paragraph (172).

[91]   Ibid., paragraph (173).

[92]   VLADIMIR KOSTKA, WASHINGTONSKÁ ÚMLUVA O ŘEŠENÍ INVESTIČNÍCH SPORŮ MEZI STÁTY A PŘÍSLUŠNÍKY Z DRUHÝCH STÁTŮ Z 18. 3. 1965 [*Washington Convention on Settlement of Investment Disputes between States and Nationals of Other States of 18 March 1965*], Acta Universitatis Carolinae – Iuridica 3-18 (1991).

BIT) to simply invoke the ICSID Convention and its interpretation practice, not the BIT (or the ECT, as applicable). Arbitral tribunals do not usually draw such strict distinctions in the reasoning for their decisions. The cumulative application of the ICSID Convention and the relevant instrument underlying the regime of the particular investment may have the result that the reference to prior rulings in cases resolved within the jurisdiction of the ICSID Centre appears somewhat misleading.

| | |

Summaries

FRA [*Soutien institutionnel et protection des investissements dans le domaine énergétique*]

Par « énergétique », on comprend généralement une branche de l'industrie s'intéressant à (•) l'obtention, (•) la transformation, (•) le transport, (•) l'utilisation de différentes formes d'énergie, (•) la recherche et les infrastructures qui lui sont afférentes. Bien que la définition générale de l'énergétique ne comprenne aucune réglementation, on peut trouver au moins des directives de base et des définitions de concepts dans le Traité sur la Charte de l'énergie. Le Traité sur la Charte de l'énergie offre un cadre de collaboration mutipartite dans le domaine de l'énergétique unique dans le monde du droit international. Le Traité sur la Charte de l'énergie se réfère dans son préambule à la Charte de Paris pour une nouvelle Europe comme déclaration de l'ouverture d'une nouvelle ère de collaboration pacifique commençant après la fin de la guerre froide. Le Traité sur la Charte de l'énergie constitue également une base juridique contraignante pour une collaboration économique à long terme dans le secteur énergétique. Il s'agit du premier traité multipartite sur la protection des investissements au sens d'une source contraignante du droit international. La Charte et le Traité sur la Charte de l'énergie qui lui est associé ne constituent pas l'unique initiative multipartite dans le domaine de l'énergétique, mais il s'agit de l'unique accord multipartite fournissant une base juridique internationale sur le plan de la protection des investissements énergétiques. Les autres accords importants sur un plan général dans le domaine de l'énergétique sont par exemple la Convention sur la pollution atmosphérique transfrontière à longue distance (CPATLD), la Charte de Paris pour une nouvelle Europe – l'OSCE, la Convention-cadre des Nations Unies sur les changements climatiques.

CZE [*Institucionalizovaná podpora a ochrana investic v energetice*]
Pod pojmem „energetika" se obecně rozumí průmyslová odvětví
zabývající se (•) získáváním, (•) přeměnou, (•) dopravou, (•) využitím
různých forem energie a (•) související výzkum a navazují
infrastruktura. Ačkoliv obecnou definici energetiky neobsahuje žádný
předpis, lze alespoň základní vodítka a identifikaci pojmů nalézt právě
v Energy Charter Treaty. ECT poskytuje mnohostranný rámec pro
spolupráci v oblasti energetiky, který je jedinečný v rámci
mezinárodního práva. Ve své preambuli ECT odkazuje na Pařížskou
Chartu pro Novou Evropu jako deklaraci nové éry mírové spolupráce
krajin po skončení Studené války. ECT tak vytváří závazný právní
základ pro trvalou hospodářskou spolupráci v energetickém sektoru. Jde
o první mnohostrannou smlouvou o ochraně investic ve smyslu
závazného pramene mezinárodního práva. Charta a na ni navazující
ECT není jedinou mnohostrannou iniciativou v oblasti energetiky, byť
jde o jedinou mnohostrannou úmluvu poskytující hmotněprávní
mezinárodní základ z pohledu ochrany energetických investic. Dalšími
významnými úmluvami v oblasti energetiky z obecného hlediska jsou
například Úmluva o dálkovém znečišťování ovzduší přesahujícím
hranice států, Pařížská charta pro novou Evropu – OBSE, United
Nations Framework Convention on Climate Change.

| | |

POL [*Zinstytucjonalizowane wsparcie i ochrona inwestycji w energetyce*]
Energy Charter Treaty stanowi wielostronne ramy współpracy w branży
energetycznej, wyjątkowe na płaszczyźnie prawa międzynarodowego.
ECT tworzy wiążące podstawy prawne dla trwałej współpracy
gospodarczej w sektorze energetycznym. Jest to pierwsza wielostronna
umowa o ochronie inwestycji w sensie wiążącego źródła
międzynarodowego prawa.

DEU [*Institutionelle Förderung und Schutz von Investitionen in der
Energiewirtschaft*]
Der Vertrag über die Energiecharta (Energy Charter Treaty) stellt einen
multilateralen Rahmen für die Zusammenarbeit im Bereich
Energiewirtschaft dar, der im internationalen Recht seinesgleichen sucht.
Der ECT schafft eine verbindliche rechtliche Grundlage für die
nachhaltige wirtschaftliche Zusammenarbeit im Energiesektor. Er war
das erste multilaterale Abkommen zum Schutz von Investitionen im
Sinne einer verbindlichen Quelle des internationalen Rechts.

RUS [*Институционализированная поддержка и защита инвестиций в энергетическом секторе*]

Договор к Энергетической Хартии (ДЭХ) является многосторонней основой для сотрудничества в сфере энергетики, который является уникальным в международном праве. ДЭХ создает обязательную юридическую основу для постоянного экономического сотрудничества в энергетическом секторе. Это первый многосторонний договор о защите инвестиций с точки зрения обязательного источника международного права.

ESP [*El apoyo institucionalizado y la protección de inversiones en el sector energético*]

El Tratado sobre la Carta de la Energía proporciona un marco multilateral de cooperación en el ámbito de la eficacia energética, que es el único en el ámbito del derecho internacional. El Tratado crea un fundamento jurídico vinculante para la continua cooperación económica en el sector energético. Es el primer tratado multilateral sobre la protección de las inversiones en condición de fuente vinculante en el derecho internacional.

| | |

Czech Yearbook of International Law

Pavel Hamerník

The Non-state Adjudication of Disputes by the Court of Arbitration for Sport as an Inspiring Alternative for Effective Dispute Resolution

Key words:
Court of Arbitration for Sport | International Olympic Committee | Sport | The Swiss Federal Tribunal | Stare decisis

Abstract | *This article introduces the Court of Arbitration for Sport as performing the role of a private global "sports judiciary". The International Olympic Committee established the CAS to provide the sport sector with an independent and specialized dispute resolution organ. This article provides an evaluation of this alternative in the light of the specifics of sport, and compared to ordinary courts. It first explores concerns about the independence and credibility of the CAS. After this institutional background, the article demonstrates the procedures that the CAS offers, especially the so-called Appeal procedures. This procedure makes the CAS special in comparison with other arbitration tribunals and closer in function to state courts. From there, the article explores the issue of precedent (Stare decisis) in arbitration. In light of the judicial review by the Swiss Federal Tribunal in the Matuzalem case, the CAS is often seen as uneasily straddling the border between sports regulation and general law. A Czech football case described in this article may point the way to a resolution of this dilemma, since it has a similar controversy to the Matuzalem case. An exploration of this case by CAS will allow us to see what remains of the scope of review of the CAS and its reflections in the sports world. The article concludes*

JUDr. Pavel Hamerník Ph.D. works at the Institute of State and the Law at the Czech Academy of Sciences, Prague, researching specializing in Sports Law and EU Law. He is the author of the Czech book Sports Law with International Elements and the Czech e-book Sports Law: In search of the balance between specific sports regulation and general law. He cooperates with the T.M.C. Asser Instituut's International Sports Law Centre projects, has worked as Director of the Legal department of Czech FA, has teaching experience of EU Law and Sports Law and sits on the Czech Ice-hockey Association's Arbitration Commission. e-mail: pavel.hamernik @ilaw.cas.cz

that this very detailed private dispute resolution is indeed similar to state courts and provides a functioning and effective "Highest court of sports".

| | |

I. Introduction to the CAS

7.01.   The Court of Arbitration for Sport (CAS) was created by the International Olympic Committee (IOC) in 1983 as an independent arbitral institution to resolve sport-related cases. Its seat has been in Lausanne and its first statute came into force on June 30th 1984. While sport-legal disputes can always be settled by ordinary courts, an international court like the CAS, which can offer specialist knowledge, low cost and rapid action, provides a means of resolving sport disputes adapted to the specific needs of the international sporting community.[1] The CAS offers to resolve disputes in an Appeals Arbitration Procedure, if the Appellant has exhausted the legal remedies available prior to the appeal.[2] It also offers an Ordinary Arbitration Procedure for resolving any commercial cases related to sport.[3] The CAS has been a living dispute resolution organ since it not only resolves disputes in sport but also pushes for improvements and more progressive resolutions of sport cases. Within this objective the CAS also organizes fruitful discussions on various topics concerning this type of arbitration, with one recent example being the 4th Conference on International Sports Law and Jurisprudence of the CAS.[4] Amendments to the CAS Code are made based on the practical experiences that

---

[1]   Mathieu Reeb, *The Role and Functions of the Court of Arbitration for Sport (CAS),* 2 (2) ISLJ 21, 21 (2002). The CAS has become a popular venue for dispute resolution. The workload of the CAS has grown since its beginning in 1984 which is apparent in statistics published by CAS available at http://www.tas-cas.org/d2wfiles/document/437/5048/0/stat2012.pdf (accessed on 9 July 2013).

[2]   Art. R 47 of the Code of Sports-related Arbitration (CAS Code).

[3]   The CAS also provides for a Mediation procedure. The CAS is likewise known for its Ad-hoc tribunals for Olympic Games, designed to resolve disputes within 24 hours, and within a maximum of 72 hours in total. These were created first time for the 1996 Olympic Games in Atlanta to cover the games and later other major sport events. The CAS Ad-hoc division rules are derived from a variety of statutory frameworks, including the Olympic Charter, the applicable regulations, and the general principles of law and the rules of law, the application of which it deems appropriate.

[4]   Organized by the CAS and Swiss Bar Association (FSA/SAV) in Lausanne on the 7th and 8th of September 2012. More than 300 participants, consisting of legal experts from all over the world, were present. The CAS also publishes a Bulletin on current issues of sport arbitration available at http://www.tas-cas.org/bulletins (accessed on 9 July 2013).

emerge from its decision making. The aim is that the CAS is 'a court independent of the judicial structures of the federations themselves, so as to ensure an objective, swift, independent, confidential and specialist means of resolving disputes arising directly or indirectly from sport, whether at national or international level'.[5]

II. The Independence of the CAS

7.02.   Initially the CAS was established without legal personality. This was not ideal mainly in cases where its founder, the IOC, was a party to the dispute. In its judgement of *Gundel*[6], the Swiss Federal Tribunal drew attention to the numerous links which existed between the CAS and the IOC. These included the fact that the CAS was financed almost exclusively by IOC, the fact that the IOC was competent to modify the CAS statute, and the considerable power given to the IOC and its President to appoint the members of the CAS.[7] In response, the International Council of Arbitration for Sport (ICAS) was created. This private law foundation was subject to Swiss law, and was set up as the supreme organ to manage and finance the CAS, adopt its Code, draw up the list of arbitrators, and safeguard the independence of the CAS and the rights of the parties.[8] These changes were approved on the 22nd of June 1994 by the IOC President and by the Association of Summer Olympic IFs, the Association of International Winter Sports Federations and the Association of National Olympic Committees in Paris. The new Code of Sport Related Arbitration came to force on the 22nd of November in the

---

[5]   ALEXANDRE MIGUEL MESTRE, THE LAW OF THE OLYMPIC GAMES, Hague: T.M.C. Asser Press 56 (2009).

[6]   Gundel was the horse rider who appealed a sanction concerning a doping offence. Since he did not succeed to his satisfaction in front of the CAS tribunal, he brought his case to the Swiss Federal Tribunal (Judgement of 15 March 1993, *G. v Fédération Equestre Internationale and CAS (TAS)*, Official Digest of Federal Tribunal Judgments 119 II 271) disputing among other issues the impartiality and independence of CAS.

[7]   Mathieu Reeb, *supra* note 1, at 23.

[8]   The ICAS is composed of twenty members. All are experienced jurists, but are appointed from different sources. Four members are appointed by the International Sports Federations (IFs), 3 of which come from the Association of Summer Olympic IFs and 1 by the Association of Winter Olympic Sports Federations, chosen from within or outside their membership. Four members are appointed by the Association of the National Olympic Committees (ANOC), chosen from within or outside its membership. Four members are appointed by the International Olympic Committee (IOC), chosen from within or outside its membership. Four members are appointed by the twelve members of ICAS listed above, after appropriate consultation with a view to safeguarding the interests of the athletes. Four members are appointed by the sixteen members of ICAS listed above, chosen from among personalities independent of the bodies designating the other members of the ICAS (Art. S4 of the CAS Code).

same year. It was not until the *Lazutina* ruling of the Swiss Federal Tribunal[9] that its sufficient independence from the IOC was definitively acknowledged and accepted, even when the latter is a party.[10]

7.03. Regarding funding, the CAS acknowledged its dependence on television revenue from the Olympic Games – reflected in the (then) Rule 11 of the Olympic Charter – but pointed out that this amounted to only one third of its revenue. Since 1994 another third was sourced from the International Sports Federations (IFs) and another third from National Olympic Committees (NOCs), and so its independence from the IOC was not at risk.[11] By way of contrast, at the time of the aforementioned *Lazutina* case, the IOC was financing 31,5% of the ICAS budget whereas the International Football Federation (FIFA) is 'only' financing 10,5% of the present ICAS budget.[12] The CAS aims to be an independent and credible institution and this was emphasized again by the CAS representatives during the opening of the previously mentioned 4th CAS conference in Lausanne.

III. Swift Resolution of Disputes

7.04. Above all the sport sector has always sought a speedy dispute resolution system, since 'the normal slow pace of justice is not compatible with the timetable of sports competitions'.[13] The process in the CAS takes the form of an Appeal Procedure, which begins when a brief Statement of Appeal is submitted to the CAS.[14] The CAS Court Office may grant a one-time-only short deadline to the Appellant to complete its Statement of Appeal in case some information is missing. However in keeping with the objective of speedy proceedings, this new deadline for completion of the Statement of Appeal does not suspend the pre-existing deadline outlined in Art. R 51 of the CAS Code. This article brings another step in the appeal proceedings. Within ten days

---

9   SFT, Judgment of 23 May 2003, *Lazutina at al. v IOC, FIS and CAS (TAS)*, ATF 129 III 425.

10   ALEXANDRE MIGUEL MESTRE, *supra* note 5, at 58. The author asserts that everybody finally recognizes its impartiality, the quality of its decisions and its equivalence to court of law (despite the fact that the court noticed the literature which disputes the independence of CAS in *para* 3.3.3 of the *Lazutina* judgment).

11   Ibid., at 59.

12   CAS Arbitral Award, January 31st 2012, 2011/O/2574 *UEFA v Olympique des Alpes SA/FC Sion, para*.120.

13   ALEXANDRE MIGUEL MESTRE, *supra* note 10, at 56.

14   'In the absence of a time limit set in the statutes or regulations of the federation, association or sport-related body concerned, or in a previous agreement, the time limit for appeal shall be twenty-one days from the receipt of the decision appealed against.' (Art. R 49 of CAS Code).

following the expiry of the time limit for submission of Statement of Appeal, the Appellant shall file an Appeal Brief with the CAS Court Office which includes the facts and legal arguments giving rise to the appeal, together with all exhibits and specification of other evidence upon which Appellant intends to rely.[15] Thus a detailed submission of Appeal Brief goes on when the machinery of the case is already moving, since the Statement of Appeal was already submitted before the detailed Appeal Brief.[16] The proceedings are flexible since Counsel of CAS remains available for any further information to help to fulfil any procedural requirements of the CAS by the parties to the dispute. Flexibility will soon be even greater since the amended 2013 version of the CAS Code provides that filing of the submissions by electronic mail is permitted under the conditions set out in the CAS Guidelines on Electronic Filing.[17] Another element that helps a speedy trial is the amended provision R 37 of the CAS Code on provisional and

---

[15] Alternatively, the Appellant shall inform the CAS Court Office in writing within the same time limit that the Statement of Appeal shall be considered as the Appeal Brief.

[16] The Statement of Appeal includes only the name and full address of the Respondent(s); a copy of the decision appealed against; the Appellant's request for relief; the nomination of the arbitrator chosen by the Appellant from the CAS list, unless the Appellant requests the appointment of a sole arbitrator; if applicable, an application to stay the execution of the decision appealed against, together with reasons; and a copy of the provisions of the statutes or regulations or the specific agreement providing for appeal to CAS. In some countries it could be a problem to find someone familiar with the CAS proceedings to fulfill all the requirements of the CAS Code when applying to start the proceedings. The CAS Office repeatedly advises in its communications when some procedural steps are to be taken by the parties according to CAS Code, 'failing which appeal shall be deemed withdrawn'. Therefore in some jurisdictions the 21 days for the submission of the Statement of Appeal (plus ten days for the Appeal Brief) might seem short to find an expert and collect evidence in comparison with the time-limits related to ordinary court proceedings, see for example Ulrich Haas, *The "Time Limit for Appeal" in Arbitration Proceedings before the Court of Arbitration for Sport (CAS)*, (2) CAS BULLETIN 3 (2011), available at http://www.tas-cas.org/d2wfiles/document/5940/5048/0/Bulletin 202 2011.pdf (accessed on 15 July 2013).

[17] Art. R 31, para 4 of CAS Code. At the time of submission of this article to the publisher, the CAS guidelines on electronic filing were not yet released. Currently the practice is that the Brief of Appellant is sent by courier as mentioned in the Appeal Procedure pursuant to Art. R 31, para 4 of CAS Code the Appeal. The exhibits to the appeal brief can be filed on CD-ROM and sent likewise by courier or by email to the address of CAS, which is info@tas-cas.org. If the exhibits are sent by email by the Appellant, the Appellant shall provide an email address for the Respondent and the CAS office shall forward the exhibits by email to the Respondent. On other communication experiences in practice see some comments on CAS Code amendments at: http://www.lawinsport.com/blog/roy-levy/item/the-new-cas-rules-what-you-need-to-know (accessed on 9 July 2013).

conservatory measures.[18] Further contributing to the speedy proceedings may also be the new scope of the CAS panel's review at hearing as will be seen below in part VI.

IV. Precedent in CAS Arbitration

7.05. The CAS arbitrators are individuals with appropriate legal training, recognized competence with regards to sport law and/or international arbitration, a good knowledge of sport in general and a good command of at least one working language used by the CAS. To be chosen as arbitrators, their names and qualifications are brought to the attention of ICAS, from the IOC, the IFs and the NOCs.[19] It has been stated in the *Lazutina* ruling that the list of arbitrators created by CAS enables consistency in the decisions of the CAS.[20] Arbitrators not in the list cannot be selected by parties to resolve their dispute. Parties who choose to select an arbitrator from outside the CAS list obtain in return

---

[18] In previous practice before the amendments 'the parties had to file the request for arbitration or the statement of appeal prior to or at least at the same time with the application for provisional measures. This did not help in receiving a speedy decision regarding the provisional measures. The previous rule could cause delays which the parties were not willing to accept and in some cases even chose to lodge their claims for interim measures with the state courts rather than the CAS'. See http://www.lawinsport. com/blog/roy-levy/item/the-new-cas-rules-what-you-need-to-know (Accessed on 9 July 2013). According to Art. 31 of the CAS Code, when deciding whether to award preliminary relief, there are criteria for examining if the relief is necessary to protect the applicant from irreparable harm, the likelihood of success on the merits of the claim, and whether the interests of the Applicant outweigh those of the Respondent(s). These were described in detail in light of the previous practice by Antonio Rigozzi, *Provisional Measures in CAS Arbitrations, in* THE COURT OF ARBITRATION FOR SPORT 1984-2004, The Hague: T.M.C. Asser Press 216 (Ian Stewart Blackshaw, Robert C R Siekmann & Janwillem Soek eds., 2006).

[19] According to the CAS Code in force in 2011, the arbitrators were selected by ICAS in an equal number from the recommendations of International Olympic Committee (IOC), IFs, National Olympic Committees (NOCs), including the number of arbitrators which were selected by ICAS with a view to safeguard the interests of the athletes and also ICAS selected determined number of arbitrators independent of the aforementioned bodies. In this respect the CAS Secretary General, Mathieu Reeb, admitted in the CAS Arbitral Award, 31 January 2012, 2011/O/2574 *UEFA* v *Olympique des Alpes SA/FC Sion, para.* 209 that the above proportionality rule referred to in Article S14 of the CAS Code was not always followed and that Article S14 of the CAS Code would be amended soon. This has indeed happened, as the above is no more in the CAS Code and now at least when appointing arbitrators and mediators, the ICAS considers continental representation and differing juridical cultures (Article S16 of CAS Code).

[20] SFT, Judgment of 23 May 2003, *Lazutina at al.* v *IOC, FIS and CAS (TAS)*, ATF 129 III 425, *para* 3.3.3.2. Since 1 March 2013 ICAS may identify the arbitrators with a specific expertise to deal with certain types of disputes.

from the CAS Court office an invitation to consult the CAS website to select an arbitrator from the CAS list.[21] It is true on one hand that in the jurisprudence of the CAS there is no principle of binding precedent, or *Stare decisis*. However according to Gabrielle Kaufmann-Kohler, the year 2003 brought drastic changes and after that date, nearly every award contained one or more references to earlier awards by the CAS.[22] Some panels were pioneers of importing the principle of *Stare decisis* and ironically these were not published, as Erbsen notes. He referred to the case where the panel stated:

7.06.   '[T]he Panel feels that CAS rulings form a valuable body of case law and can contribute to strengthen legal predictability in international sports law. Therefore, although not binding, previous decisions can and should be taken into consideration by subsequent CAS panels, in order to help [in] developing legitimate expectations among sports bodies and athletes.'[23]

7.07.   It is true that we may now find in CAS case law phrases like 'In light of the above CAS precedents' referring to particular CAS cases or the CAS using such cases in support of its reasoning.

7.08.   The problem of deploying precedent is the nature of the CAS proceedings which are still based on private arbitration. Awards in the Ordinary Arbitration procedure are not to be made public unless all parties agree or the Division President decides that they should be.[24] On the other hand in the Appeal Procedure the award, a summary and/or a press release setting forth the results of the proceedings is to be made public by the CAS, unless both parties agree that they should remain confidential. In any event, the other elements of the case record remain confidential.[25] There are, however, arbitration cases where the public interest and the right to information are stronger than the obligation of confidentiality.[26]

---

[21]   Available at http://www.tas-cas.org/arbitrators-genlist (accessed on 9 July 2013).

[22]   Gabrielle Kaufmann-Kohler, *Arbitral Precedent: Dream, Necessity or Excuse?* 23(3) AI 357, 365 (2006).

[23]   Allan Erbsen, *The Substance and Illusion of Lex Sportiva, in* THE COURT OF ARBITRATION FOR SPORT 1984-2004, The Hague: T.M.C. Asser Press 441, 451 (Ian Stewart Blackshaw, Robert C R Siekmann & Janwillem Soek eds., 2006).

[24]   Article R43 of CAS Code.

[25]   Art. R 59 of CAS Code.

[26]   Mathieu Reeb, *supra* note 1, at 25.

| 143

V. The CAS at the Border between General Law and Sport Regulation

7.09. The award of the CAS can be challenged at the Swiss Federal Tribunal on very restricted grounds. These are specified in Art. 190 para 2 of the Swiss Private International Law Act. Among other issues, these grounds include the improper constitution of the arbitral tribunal, jurisdiction wrongfully accepted or declined, the arbitral tribunal having dealt with issues which were not submitted to it or did not deal with issues it should have, the violation of the principle of equal treatment or the right to be heard and finally any incompatibility with public policy. A CAS award was recently successfully challenged by Appellant Francelino Matuzelem da Silva where the Swiss Federal Tribunal held that:

7.10. The threat of an unlimited occupational ban based on Art. 64 (4) of the FIFA Disciplinary Code constitutes an obvious and grave encroachment in the Appellant's privacy rights and disregards the fundamental limits of legal commitments as embodied in Art. 27 (2) ZGB [Swiss Civil Code]. Should payment fail to take place, the award under appeal would lead not only to the Appellant being subjected to his previous employer's arbitrariness but also to an encroachment in his economic freedom of such gravity that the foundations of his economic existence are jeopardized without any possible justification by some prevailing interest of the world football federation or its members. In view of the penalty it entails, the CAS arbitral award of June 29, 2011 contains an obvious and grave violation of privacy and is contrary to public policy.[27]

7.11. The player was unilaterally sanctioned for breach of contract with his employer without just cause.[28] The Football sector provided private enforcement which comes into operation when some subject of the football sector owes a duty towards a creditor, in this case the player's former club. The Swiss Federal Tribunal noted that:

7.12. Upon a simple request by the creditor the Appellant should undergo a ban from all professional activities in connection with football

---

[27] Available at: http://www.swissarbitrationdecisions.com/sites/default/files/27%20mars %202012%204A%20558%202011.pdf (accessed on 15 July 2013), Judgement of March 27 2012, *Francelino da Silva Matuzalem* v *Fédération Internationale de Football Association (FIFA)*, 4A_558/2011.

[28] For a discussion of how the rules apply concerning contractual stability in football see FRANS DE WEGER, THE JURISPRUDENCE OF THE FIFA DISPUTE RESOLUTION CHAMBER, The Hague: T.M.C. Asser Press, (2008) or The FIFA Regulations on Status and Transfer of Players, available at: http://www.fifa.com/mm/document/affederation/administration/ 01/95/83/85//regulationsstatusandtransfer_e.pdf (accessed 15 July 2013).

until a claim in excess of € 11 million with interest at 5% from the middle of 2007 (i. e. € 550'000 yearly) is paid. This is supposed to uphold the interest of a member of FIFA to the payment of damages by the employee in breach and indirectly the interest of the sport federation to contractual compliance by football players. The infringement in the Appellant's economic freedom would be suitable to promote the willingness to pay and to find the funds for the amount due; however if the Appellant rightly says that he cannot pay the whole amount anyway, the adequacy of the sanction to achieve its direct purpose – namely the payment of the damages – is questionable. Indeed the prohibition to continue his previous economic and other activities will deprive the Appellant from the possibility to achieve an income in his traditional activity which would enable him to pay his debt.[29]

7.13. A very similar case has emerged in Czech football and is on its way to the CAS at the time of this writing. In 2006, a player named Zbynek Pospech signed a Mandate Contract with his football agent. In 2008, the player made negotiations about his future contract with a new club without the Agent and finally transferred to this new club. According to the player, his agent only had a contract available for the player with another club which offered worse terms and conditions for playing than the club in which the player transferred himself without the agent's assistance. The provisions set out in FIFA Regulations on Players' Agents are without prejudice to the player's right to conclude an employment contract or to rendering a transfer agreement without the assistance of the agent.[30] Nevertheless Pospech's agent called for a sanction in the amount of EUR 100 000 from the Mandate Contract with the player in the case where the player choose to act without the Agent. The agent applied to the Arbitration Commission of the Czech FA to enforce this sanction and the Arbitration Commission decided in the agents' favor. The Arbitration Commission did not consider the FIFA Players' Agents Regulations at all. This is a typical case which would be appropriately resolved in front of the CAS since the FIFA Players' Agents Regulations had a substantial influence on a player's career. However, the decision of the Arbitration Commission was not the end of the story as the decision was imposed with finality only within first instance proceedings. The Czech FA's rules in force at that time and the Arbitration Commission did not provide for the possibility

---

[29] *Supra* note 27.
[30] Art. 19/7 of The FIFA Regulations on Players' Football Agents, edition 2008, which are available at http://www.fifa.com/mm/document/affederation/administration/51/55/18/players_agents_regulations_2008.pdf (accessed on 15 July 2013).

of appeal. In 2009, the decision was enforced by the Disciplinary Commission and when the player did not pay EUR 100 000 to the agent, the commission imposed a ban on the player's football activity. The player's ban and the failure of Czech FA to provide a regular appeal to the player resulted in the player's insolvency.[31] It would be interesting to see if the CAS is able to resolve this difficult case. Apparently in this post-*Matuzalem* time, a new chapter is being written in CAS history since, due to the Swiss Federal Tribunal, the CAS will now scrutinize more closely what rules are enforced. The Pospech case could be another test.

VI. The Scope of Review

7.14. The CAS has already passed an interesting stage in its history when dealing with the pure rules of games (field of play). According to the case-law of the CAS, these are immune from challenges in sport arbitration:

7.15. 'The "Game Rules" are the rules intended to ensure the correct course of the game and competition respectively. The application of such rules cannot, save in very exceptional circumstances, lead to any judicial review. On the contrary, the "Rules of Law" are proper statutory sanctions that can affect the judicial interests of the person upon whom a sanction has been imposed other than in the course of the game or competition. For this reason, they have to be subject to judicial review.'[32]

7.16. Concerning the rules of game, a review is possible if a referee has acted in bad faith,[33] or if the rules of the game are so strict that they do not provide any discretion.[34] A similar transition also occurred in the Court

---

[31] The case was covered by the Czech media, for example at http://sport.lidovky.cz/zbynek-pospech-v-brne-konci-nemohl-plnit-fotbalove-povinnosti-p7p-/fotbal.aspx?=A100 428 094637 ln-sport-fotbal vrb (accessed on 15 July 2013).

[32] Arbitration CAS 2003/A/461 & 471 & 473 WCM-GP Limited v Fédération Internationale Motocycliste (FIM), Award of 19 August 2003. Abstention in regards to the rules of the game is explained in ADAM LEWIS & JONATHAN TAYLOR, SPORT: LAW AND PRACTICE, Tottel Publishing Ltd. 346 (2nd ed., reprint, 2010). Several issues can lead to abstention, such as the arbitrator's lack of expertise in the technical side of sport, the inevitable element of subjectivity of judging resulting in part from different physical perspectives in judging, the fear of constant interruption to the course of play, the opening of floodgates and the problems of rewriting a result after the event.

[33] CAS OG 96/006 M. v/ AIBA, in CAS Digest I, at 413, CAS OG 00/013, Segura v/ IAAF, in CAS Awards – Sydney 2000, at 131 and CAS OG 02/007 Korean Olympic Committee v/ ISU, award of 23 Feb. 2002. Arbitration CAS ad hoc Division (OG Turin) 06/006 Canadian Olympic Committee (COC) v International Skating Union (ISU), award of 17 February 2006.

[34] Arbitration CAS 2001/A/354 Irish Hockey Association (IHA)/Lithuanian Hockey Federation (LHF) and International Hockey Federation (FIH) and Arbitration CAS

of Justice of EU, which in the famous *Bosman* case had 'the difficulty of severing the economic aspects from the sporting aspects of football'.[35]

7.17. Concerning the process of review in the procedures of the CAS, in the Appeal Procedure, the Panel has full power to review the facts and the law.[36] It may issue a new decision which replaces the decision challenged, or it may annul the decision and refer the case back to the previous instance. A hearing *de novo* applies here. As Antonio Rigozzi explained generally during his contribution 'Evidentiary Questions before CAS' in the 4th Conference of CAS & Swiss Bar Association (FSA/SAV) in Lausanne, the more serious the allegations, especially in doping, the larger the space for acceptance of evidence is necessary.[37] Since amendments made to the CAS Code beginning March 2013, the Panel has had discretion to exclude evidence presented by the parties if it was available to them or could reasonably have been discovered by them before the challenged decision was rendered. Hilary Findlay, in the 2004 book dedicated to 20th anniversary of the CAS, brought up the issue as well, asking: 'is the arbitration system intended to be a review for errors that may have been made within the internal appeal process, or a whole new review of the situation, such as in a hearing de novo?'[38] Antonio Rigozzi's example of doping or the unhappy case of Zbyněk Pospěch discussed previously suggest a preference towards the direction of *de novo*. On the other hand, arbitrators seem to be limited by written texts of the sport associations and cannot be 'legal idealists

---

2001/A/355 Lithuanian Hockey Federation (LHF)/International Hockey Federation (FIH), award of 15 April 2002: 'A deviation by a referee or umpire from a mandatory game rule undermines the utility of the rule and, moreover, may affect the outcome of the game or the tournament' (referring to CAS 93/103 *SC Langnau v/ Ligue Suisse de Hockey sur Glace*, in CAS Digest I, at 307). For an overview of this topic see ADAM LEWIS & JONATHAN TAYLOR, Ibid., Frank Oschutz, *The Arbitrability of Sport Disputes and the Rules of the Game*, in THE COURT OF ARBITRATION FOR SPORT 1984-2004 200, 205 (I. Blackshaw, R. Siekmann, J. Soek eds., 2006).

[35] Noted by STEPHEN WEATHERILL, EUROPEAN SPORTS LAW, The Hague: T.M.C. Asser Press 263 (2007).

[36] Article R 57 of CAS Code.

[37] See for example in the CAS Award of February 2nd 2006, Ad hoc Division (OG Turin) 06/001 *World Anti-Doping Agency (WADA) v United States Anti-Doping Agency (USADA), United States Bobsled & Skeleton Federation (USBSF) and Zachery Lund, para* 20: 'Mr. Lund would have to establish either that he did not know or suspect or that he could not reasonably have known or suspected even with the exercise of utmost caution that he was not using a Prohibited Substance.'

[38] Hilary Findlay, *Form Follows Function: Crafting Rules for a Sport Specific Arbitration Process – 'The Canadian CAS'*, in THE COURT OF ARBITRATION FOR SPORT 1984-2004 280, 282 (I. Blackshaw, R. Siekmann, J. Soek eds., 2006).

creating a new form of substantive law'.[39] They can fill gaps, or ensure fair trial principles are followed. However they cannot invent some 'novel sport-specific legal regime'[40]: 'any judicial body subsequently examining...should be reluctant to impose on the sports body a materially different standard....than that which the parties accepted though their membership of the sports body'.[41]

VII. Applicable Law and Standing to Be Sued

7.18. The Panel will decide a dispute in the Appeal Procedure according to several considerations. They will take into account the applicable regulations and the subsidiary rules of law chosen by the parties. In the absence of such a choice, they will consider the law of the country in which the federation, association or sport-related body which has issued the challenged decision is domiciled or according to the rules of law that the Panel deems appropriate. In the latter case, the Panel must give reasons for its decision.[42] The Panel will decide the dispute in the Ordinary Procedure according to the rules of law chosen by the parties or, in the absence of such a choice, according to Swiss law. The parties may authorize the Panel to decide *ex aequo et bono*.[43] The CAS Court Office assigns the submitted case to the appropriate Division. Such assignment may not be contested by the parties nor may it be raised by them as a cause of irregularity.[44] The standard practice seems to be to limit the application of the Appeal Procedure to disputes arising out of last instance decisions of sport bodies which are of a disciplinary nature.[45] All others go to the Ordinary arbitration. This has been criticized in the literature since the procedure for handling an appeal or a first instance case is not the same. This explains why many rules in the Appeal procedure are different than in the Ordinary procedure.[46]

---

[39]   Allan Erbsen, *supra* note 23, at 442.

[40]   Ibid., at 451.

[41]   CAS 98/209 *Spanish Basketball Federation (FEB) v International Basketball Federation*, noted by Ken Foster, *Lex Sportiva and Lex Ludica: The Court of Arbitration for Sport's Jurisprudence, in* THE COURT OF ARBITRATION FOR SPORT 1984-2004 420, 429 (I. Blackshaw, R. Siekmann, J. Soek eds., 2006).

[42]   Art. R 58 of CAS Code.

[43]   Art. R 45 of CAS Code.

[44]   Art. S 20 of CAS Code.

[45]   Gabrielle Kaufmann-Kohler, Philippe Bartsch, *The Ordinary Arbitration Procedure of the Court of Arbitration for Sport, in* THE COURT OF ARBITRATION FOR SPORT 1984-2004 69, 73 (I. Blackshaw, R. Siekmann, J. Soek eds., 2006).

[46]   Some authors refer to the above described differences between art. R 45 and R 58 of the CAS Code about the choice of applicable law or differences concerning the above described confidentiality of the proceedings.

The CAS Panels have also consistently noted that neither the CAS Code nor for example the FIFA Regulations contain any specific rule regarding the issue of standing to be sued. This is connected to the problem of whether the case goes to the Appeal or the Ordinary procedure. The approach of the CAS is influenced by Swiss law, namely art. 75 of Swiss Civil Code:

7.19.   If, for example, there is a dispute between two association members (e.g. regarding the payment for the transfer of a football player) and the association decides that a club (member) has to pay the other a certain sum, this is not a decision which can be subject to an appeal within the meaning of Art. 75 Swiss Civil Code. The sports association taking a decision is not doing so in a matter of its own, i.e. in a matter which concerns its relationship to one of its members, rather it is acting as a kind of first decision-making instance, as desired and accepted by the parties.[47]

7.20.   The other opinion to the contrary says that:

7.21.   In particular the term 'resolution' in Art. 75 CC does not only refer to resolutions passed by the assembly of an association but, instead, encompasses any other (final and binding) decision of any other organ of the association, irrespective of the nature of such decision (disciplinary, administrative, etc.) and the composition of said organ (one or several persons). Hence, contrary to the reasoning in CAS2009/A/1828 and 1829 (cf. supra), in CAS 2008/A/1639, the Panel considered that the issuance of a provisional registration for a player with a national federation touches upon the relationship between FIFA and its members.[48]

7.22.   There have indeed been some examples which have the flavor of an Appeal procedure but were nevertheless put into the Ordinary procedure.[49] It seems this is an issue decided on a case-by-case basis.

---

[47]   Estelle de La Rochefoucauld, *Standing to be sued, a procedural issue before the Court of Arbitration for Sport (CAS)*, (1) CAS BULLETIN (2010) available at http://www.tas-cas.org/d2wfiles/document/4761/5048/0/Bulletin01112010.pdf (accessed on 15 July 2013), referring to Swiss literature listed there (at p. 52) including the text of Art. 75 of CC according to which: 'Any member who has not consented to a resolution which infringes the law or the articles of association is entitled by law to challenge such resolution in court within one month from the day on which he became cognizant of such resolution'.

[48]   CAS Awards referred to by Estelle de La Rochefoucauld, Ibid., at 53.

[49]   For example, the CAS Award 2008/A/1468, 9 February 2009 (unreported). The dispute concerned a player transferred between two Czech clubs. When the transferee further undertook to pay to the transferor the amount of money in case the player from the transferee's club was transferred or plays as a guest in another club, the clubs did not agree on interpretation of this clause. The losing party of this dispute challenged the Czech FA's decisions of the Arbitration Commission. The CAS stated (despite the Czech FA not

VIII. Conclusion

7.23.   In general it has to be admitted, as stated by the Swiss Federal Tribunal about the CAS that 'there appears to be no viable alternative to this institution, which can resolve international sport-related disputes quickly and inexpensively...and remains one of the principal mainstays of organized sport'.[50] It provides specialized, independent and speedy resolution for disputes related to sport. When we consider how many years cases take to work across the state court systems (with a possible detour in European law enroute to the Court of Justice of the EU), it is an incomparable advantage to resolve disputes at the level of the CAS. Perhaps small claims concerning provincial clubs or players are not worth the travel to Swiss jurisdiction and might better remain within state local courts with actions on the legality of the acts of sport associations in the light of their statutes and the law. Also for Olympic disputes the CAS gets huge credit as an alternative to sending the Olympics cases to some local court.[51] According to Ulrich Haas, in the Appeal procedure the CAS is comparable to the state courts.[52] Thus, the awards pronounced by the CAS have the same force as judgments pronounced by ordinary courts.[53] The New York Convention on the Recognition and Enforcement of Foreign Arbitral Awards is also applicable to enforce the CAS decisions abroad. Nevertheless since all Olympic IFs have recognized the jurisdiction of the CAS, a more effective means of enforcement in the sport world is the threat of disciplinary proceedings which may result in exclusion from competitions and other sanctions like deductions of obtained points in

---

being party to the proceedings) that the fundamental principle of procedural fairness was breached, which on many occasions the CAS had recognized and protected.

[50]   SFT, Judgment of May 23rd 2003, *Lazutina at al. v IOC, FIS and CAS (TAS)*, ATF 129 III 425, *para* 3.3.3.3. Although for some Appellant CAS might seem initially expensive, for example in situation if Appellant is banned to perform professional activity of sport, deprived of an income and if the Respondent refuses to pay advance costs of CAS proceedings, CAS invites the Appellant to substitute for the Respondent to pay Respondent's share of the advance costs of the proceedings according to the Article R 64.2 of CAS Code (in other words Appellant pays advance costs of both parties to the dispute otherwise the appeal will be deemed withdrawn).

[51]   If there is any at all since in Greece during Olympics there were court holidays, see ELENI TROVA, VANGELIS ALEXANDRAKIS, PANAGIOTIS SKOURIS, THE OLYMPIC GAMES OF THE EUROPEAN UNION, Baden-Baden: Nomos 102 (2011), referring to M. Beloff as well.

[52]   Ulrich Haas, *supra* note 16.

[53]   Foreword by former CAS President Kéba Mbaye to the Guide to arbitration of CAS (at that time 2004 edition), still available at http://www.sportrecht.org/EU-Recht/CASguideArbitration.pdf (accessed on 15 July 2013).

sport competitions.[54] The enforcement claim under the New York Convention at the level of ordinary courts may take considerable time and effort since it has to be filed at the jurisdiction of the domestic court of the person or entity refusing to follow the CAS decision. Nevertheless, after the *Matuzalem* case the CAS may be more careful which sanctions it is enforcing. It should also be noted that according to the New York Convention, enforcement could be refused if the competent authority in the country where enforcement is sought finds that sport-related disputes are not capable of settlement by arbitration under the laws of that country.[55]

7.24.   Cassini has made an observation that sport judicial mechanisms like the CAS 'display many more similarities with public international law regimes than with private ones. This is a further confirmation of the theory that the more complex private regimes become, the more they will come to resemble public law regimes'.[56] The CAS is a venue with a very high number of disputes as was demonstrated by the statistics listed in the introduction to this article, proving popularity of this institution. Some authors claim that the CAS works more effectively than other international courts like ICJ[57]: 'through creativity and cooperation sports officials have created a working, functional international tribunal that can serve as example for future efforts at transnational dispute resolution'.[58] The CAS is also the final appeal organ in doping disputes according to World Anti-Doping Code. Activities of public institutions like UNESCO follow up on the principles to which the CAS has contributed while interpreting the World Anti-Doping Code: 'the provisions of the Code build on the principles established by earlier decisions of CAS and seek to address areas of uncertainty in the approach to the interpretation and application of earlier anti-doping regimes, particularly in relation to the imposition of sanctions, which are reflected in the decisions of various

---

[54]   For example see the FIFA Statutes, edition 2012, art 13 (1) a]: 'Members have the following obligation to comply fully with the Statutes, regulations, directives and decisions of FIFA bodies at any time as well as the decisions of the Court of Arbitration for Sport (CAS) passed on appeal on the basis of art. 66 par. 1 of the FIFA Statutes'. http://www.fifa.com/mm/document/affederation/generic/01/66/54/21/fifastatutes2012e.pdf

[55]   Mathieu Reeb, *supra* note 1, at 25.

[56]   Lorenzo Cassini, *The Making of a Lex Sportiva by the Court of Arbitration for Sport,* 12 (5) GLJ 1317, 1340 (2011).

[57]   Which indeed is a special comparison since the former president of the CAS K. Mbaye was also a judge of the ICJ.

[58]   Daniel H. Yi, *Turning Medals into Metal: Evaluating the Court of Arbitration for Sport as an International Tribunal,* 6 ARIBTL 289, 316 (2006).

CAS Panels'.[59] This also adds value to the CAS.[60] The CAS is a very inspiring jurisdiction and perhaps other subjects will try to create a similar working body in fields other than sport.

|||

Summaries

FRA [*Le Tribunal arbitral du sport, exemple inspirant d'une résolution efficace et différente des litiges par une structure non-gouvernementale*]
Présentation est faite du Tribunal arbitral du sport, institution internationale chargée de rendre la justice dans le monde du sport. Le mouvement olympique a créé ce tribunal afin de doter le secteur sportif d'un organisme spécialisé et indépendant pour résoudre ses litiges. Les voies alternatives de résolution des litiges sont ici évaluées à la lumière des spécificités du sport. On s'est appliqué à mettre en place une justice sportive fiable et avant tout indépendante. Une fois passées ces questions institutionnelles, on s'intéresse aux procédures du TAS et en particulier à ladite Procédure arbitrale d'appel, tout à fait unique pour un tribunal arbitral, qui rapproche le TAS d'un tribunal ordinaire, ce à quoi contribue également la création d'une base de règles stare decisis dans les jugements rendus. Le TAS apparaît dans cet esprit à l'interface entre une réglementation spécifique sportive et le droit commun, ce que montre l'intervention du Tribunal fédéral suisse dans l'affaire Matuzalem, préfigurant la direction qu'il suivra à l'avenir lorsqu'il s'agira de réexaminer des actes venant d'associations sportives. On présente également ici un cas tchèque comparable à l'affaire Matuzalem que le TAS va devoir résoudre. On estime pour conclure que la réglementation détaillée du TAS en fait un tribunal comparable à n'importe quel autre tribunal ordinaire et permet de résoudre réellement efficacement les litiges.

CZE [*Nestátní rozhodování sporů Rozhodčím soudem pro sport jako inspirující alternativa pro efektivní způsoby rozhodování sporů*]
Článek představuje Rozhodčí soud pro sport jako instituci vykonávající funkci soudnictví v privátní sféře globálního sportovního odvětví. Olympijské hnutí založilo tento soud s cílem zajistit pro sportovní sektor

---

[59] PAUL DAVID, A GUIDE TO THE WORLD ANTI-DOPING CODE, A FIGHT FOR THE SPIRIT OF SPORT, Cambridge: Cambridge University Press 18 (2009).

[60] I have described the topic already in my previous article *On the Specifics of Doping Regulation in Sport*, 3(1) TLQ 43 (2013).

nezávislý a specializovaný orgán pro řešení sporů. Článek nabízí hodnocení této alternativní cesty řešení sporů ve světle specifik sportu. Vysvětluje snahu docílit důvěryhodné a především nezávislé sportovní justice. Po představení této institucionální otázky se článek zaměřuje na procedury CAS, zejména na tzv. Odvolací řízení, které je ojedinělé v porovnání s ostatními rozhodčími tribunály a přibližuje CAS k tomu, že skutečně připomíná řádný soud, mj. i ve světle snahy založit základ precedentu Stare decisis v rozhodování CAS. V tomto duchu pak článek představuje CAS na rozhraní mezi specifickou sportovní úpravou a obecným platným právem, pokud jde o soudní kontrolu Švýcarského federálního Tribunálu ve světle kauzy Matuzalem a jeho budoucího nasměrování při přezkumu aktů sportovních asociací. V článku je představen i český případ, který je kauze Matuzalem podobný a CAS jej bude muset řešit. Článek následně v závěru vyhodnocuje statut CAS tak, že jeho detailní úprava jej činí podobným soudem jako je kterýkoliv jiný řádný soud a poskytuje skutečně efektivní řešení sporů.

| | |

POL [*Niepaństwowe rozstrzyganie sporów przez Sportowy Sąd Arbitrażowy jako inspirująca alternatywa efektywnej metody rozstrzygania sporów*]
Niniejszy artykuł prezentuje Sportowy Sąd Arbitrażowy (CAS) będący niezależnym, wiarygodnym organem rozstrzygającym spory, który jest zbliżony charakterem do zwykłych sądów. W artykule wysunięto taki wniosek w świetle szczegółowej i licznej regulacji, stworzonej najpierw przez Międzynarodowy Komitet Olimpijski, a później Międzynarodową Radę ds. Arbitrażu Sportowego, która jest zbliżona raczej do uregulowań w prawie publicznym, nie zaś do wcześniejszych podstaw wynikających z prawa prywatnego.

DEU [*Die nichtstaatliche Streitschlichtung des Sportsgerichtshofs als inspirierende Alternative für effektive Streitbeilegungsmethoden*]
Der Artikel stellt den Internationalen Sportsgerichtshof (CAS) als unabhängige und vertrauenswürdige Schiedsstelle vor, die ihrem Charakter nach den gängigen allgemeinen Gerichten nahesteht. Dieser Schluss wird vom Artikel im Lichte der überaus detaillierten und umfänglichen Regulierung gezogen, die ursprünglich vom Internationalen Olympischen Komitee und späterhin vom International Council of Arbitration for Sport entwickelt wurde, und die sich von ihrer ursprünglich privatrechtlichen Basis auf eine eher öffentlich-rechtliche Regulierung hin zubewegt hat.

RUS [*Негосударственное рассмотрение и разрешение споров в Спортивном арбитражном суде как вдохновляющая альтернатива для эффективных способов разрешения споров*] *В данной статье Спортивный арбитражный суд (CAS) рассматривается как независимый и авторитетный орган по урегулированию споров, который по своему характеру аналогичен обычным судам общей юрисдикции. Этот вывод сделан в статье с учетом ряда подробных и многочисленных правовых норм, первоначально принятых Международным олимпийским комитетом, а затем – Международным комитетом по спортивному арбитражу, которые соответствуют скорее публичному регулированию, чем первоначальной частноправовой базе.*

ESP [*Resoluciones de litigios no públicas pronunciadas por el Tribunal de Arbitraje del Deporte como una alternativa inspirativa para resoluciones dictadas con eficacia*] *El artículo presenta al Tribunal de Arbitraje del Deporte (TAS) como una autoridad independiente y fidedigna para resolver litigios, que por su carácter es similar a cualquier tribunal común y corriente. Esta conclusión se hace a la luz de una regulación muy detallada y usual originalmente creada por el Comité Olímpico Internacional y, consecutivamente, por el Consejo Internacional de Arbitraje Deportivo. Se aproxima más a la regulación pública que a la base privada original.*

| | |

Czech Yearbook of International Law

Marie Karfíková | Zdeněk Karfík

The Role of Foundations at the Beginning of the 21ˢᵗ Century[1]

Key words:
foundation | endowment fund | foundation fund | endowment deed | foundation statute and the Foundation 'Nadání Josefa, Marie a Zdeňky Hlávkových'

Abstract | *The authors have prepared their paper to present, to the extent allowed by its scope, a comprehensive view of the legal regulation of foundations. Such branch of law is often referred to as foundation law. The first part represents a short excursion into history, describing the status of foundation law after the establishment of the independent Czechoslovak Republic following the disintegration of Austro-Hungarian monarchy. In the following part, the paper deals with the new legal (statutory) regulation of the establishment and operation of foundations and endowment funds. With regard to the new Civil Code, which is now in force and is to become effective as of 1 January 2014, the authors make a brief excursion into the new legislation. The final part of the paper presents an overview of the oldest foundation existing in the Czech Republic, the Foundation Nadání Josefa, Marie a Zdeňky Hlávkových, which was founded in 1904 and which has preserved its legal continuity to the present.*

| | |

Prof. JUDr. Marie Karfíková, CSc. is a professor of financial law and financial science at the School of Law, Charles University in Prague. Since 2012 she has headed the Department of Financial Law and Financial Science. Her scientific work deals with issues of financial law, with a special focus on tax and insurance law. She has been regularly publishing articles on these issues in legal journals. She is a co-author of a number of textbooks and monographs. In 1999-2006, she was a member of the Legislative Council of the Government of the Czech Republic. At present, she is a member of the recourse commission of the Czech National Bank and the recourse commission for review of decisions issued by the Ministry of Education, Youth and Sports under the Act on Universities. Since

---

[1] This paper was elaborated through a financial grant and within the project 'PRVOUK– Public law in the context of Europeanisation and globalisation' at the School of Law of Charles University in Prague in 2013.

I. Introduction

8.01. It is generally said that the present crisis in society is no longer an economic crisis but affects also professed ethical and philosophical values. The time has come for a common reflection whether foundations and endowment activities may also have a positive impact on social relations, probably because foundations are among the few legal entities that are not business entities as their activity is not based on generating profit and is not dependent on state subsidies. After a short historic introduction about the legal regulation of foundations, we will discuss the development and role of foundations at the beginning of this century.

II. Definition of the Term 'Foundation'

8.02. A foundation (endowment-the Czech term used is 'nadání') is an arrangement designated for permanent donation of specific assets for a social, namely universal beneficial purpose. Independent foundations are considered as special legal entities existing alongside corporations, from which they differ by the fact that their tangible basis, 'substrate', is a set of assets (hence the term endowment = *universitas bonorum*). The tangible basis of a corporation is an association of persons (hence the term corporation = *universitas personarum*). Foundations are fully equal to corporations with regard to the capacity of possessing rights and a capacity to act. Like corporations, foundations are capable of assuming rights and property obligations. State supervision over foundations is exercised by political (land) authorities, who are competent to control whether the foundations are established in accordance with the law, their assets are duly identified, deposited and managed and their obligations are properly fulfilled. To be valid, the land authority must approve foundation deeds.[2]

2009, she has been a member of the Presidium of the Council for Public Supervision of Audit. She is also an arbitrator at the Arbitration Court attached to the Economic Chamber of the Czech Republic and the Agrarian Chamber of the Czech Republic. Since 2005, she has been a member of the board of trustees of the Foundation *Nadání Josefa, Marie a Zdeňky Hlávkových* (*Foundation of Josef, Marie and Zdeňka Hlávka*). e-mail: karfikov@ prf.cuni.cz

JUDr. Zdeněk Karfík, CSc. is an attorney-at-law, an arbitrator at the Arbitration Court attached to the Economic Chamber of the Czech Republic and the Agrarian Chamber of the Czech Republic, a member of the recourse commission of the Minister of Finance of the Czech Republic and has been a long-term external lecturer at the School of Law, Charles University in Prague. In his legal practice, he focuses on issues of financial, civil and commercial law. He publishes legal articles in this field and is also a co-author of a number of monographs. e-mail: karfik@volny.cz

---

[2] 17 OTTŮV SLOVNÍK NAUČNÝ (*Otto's encyclopedia*), Prague: J.Otto 968 (1901).

8.03. A total of 933 foundations existed in Bohemia at the end of 1891, 536 of them administered by the Emperor and King Governor's Office and 397 by other authorities. By the end of 1893, their number exceeded 1,000.[3]

8.04. The term 'foundation' meant a special-purpose estate, with assets devoted to a special, particularly charitable or religious purpose. Foundations were considered as independent legal entities capable of having rights and obligations. At present, their original form of a special purpose estate has become obsolete and no longer legally exists.[4] The foregoing was the legal position arising from the existing laws and opinions on foundations in the political and economic conditions existing before 1989.

III. Historical Overview of the Legislative Development

8.05. The idea behind foundations is as old as mankind. Offering help to fellow human beings and mutual solidarity among people have long been among generally recognized values. On the other hand, founders of endowments have been often led, in addition to the desire to do something for general welfare, by less noble motives such as an attempt to redeem their sins and the donation of property to a specific purpose to influence developments after their death.

8.06. Until the establishment of an independent Czechoslovak state in 1918, today's Czech Republic and Slovak Republic had been parts of the Austro-Hungarian monarchy. The Austrian concept is an example of the approach under which the foundation law was regulated primarily by public law. The Austrian Universal Civil Code of 1811 ignored foundations and mentioned them only marginally in Section 646, where it referred to a special law. Even in the mid-nineteenth century, there were no uniform rules for the establishment and administration of foundations in the territory of the Austrian monarchy. The regulation of this issue was left to each state. In his efforts to gain control over the constituent foundation sector, the emperor in 1841 issued a royal decree,[5] which institutionalized state supervision over foundations. Under this decree, the establishment of a foundation required a

---

[3]   The collection *Studijní nadání v král. Českém* (*Study Foundations in the Czech Kingdom*), which was published in 1894 by the Office of the Governor of the Czech Kingdom.

[4]   ZDENĚK MADAR, PRÁVNICKÝ SLOVNÍK, Prague: Orbis, Panorama 473 (1978).

[5]   Das Hofkanzleidekret vom 21. Mai 1841, politische Gesetzssammlung, Band 69, nr. 60. This decree was not annulled until the Federal Act on Foundations and Funds of 1974, effective from 1 January 1975.

manifestation of the founder's will to donate property for a permanent purpose and the state's consent with its establishment. The authorities exercising supervision over foundations were either central or land authorities.

8.07. The romanticism of the second half of the nineteenth century, as well as relative political stability and economic growth, revived an interest in endowment activities. However, the activities in this sphere were dampened by subsequent historical events-World War I, the disintegration of the Austria-Hungarian monarchy and a great economic crisis. A number of foundations lost a significant part of their assets due to inflation, and World War II created a hostile and inappropriate environment for those activities.

8.08. Following the establishment of Czechoslovakia (28 October 1918), the regulation of legal entities and foundations in their undeveloped form was adopted by a reception act.[6] This arrangement ultimately resulted in the constitution of an independent endowment sector in the territory of the Czechoslovakia. However, an economic crisis and the arrival of fascism did not leave room for issuing new foundation laws.[7] The situation in the field of foundation law was adversely affected by the events in 1948 and later, which led to the abolishment of the foundation as a legal form and of the existing foundations.

8.09. The reconstruction of the essentially non-existent foundation sector (with certain exceptions), which required the establishment of a legal framework, started only at the beginning of the 1990s in connection with the political and economic changes in society. The non-transparent situation, where domestic and foreign foundations and other non-profit organizations began to operate spontaneously in the federal territory, required an immediate solution to overcome the absence of the law of foundations and associations. Mandatory regulation of individual forms of legal entities and an absence of the institute of foundation in our legal system gave rise to a number of problems. These were to be at least generally and expediently resolved by an amendment to Act No. 103/1990 Coll., the then Economic Code, effective from 1 May 1990. The institute of foundation was re-established in a single provision (Section 389b), which granted to foundations the status of a separate type of legal entity.

8.10. The foundation was conceived as a special-purpose fund with a separate legal personality, which could be established 'for the purpose

---

[6]   See JAN HURDÍK & IVO TELEC, ZÁKON O NADACÍCH A NADAČNÍCH FONDECH, Prague: C. H. Beck XXVI (1998).

[7]   A certain tendency in this respect could be perceived, see EMANUEL HERMANN-OTAVSKY, NÁVRH NA ZÁKONNOU ÚPRAVU NADAČNÍHO PRÁVA, Prague (1938).

of developing spiritual values, protection of human rights or other humanitarian objectives, environmental protection and preservation of natural values'.[8] The essential importance of this legislation consisted in the creation of a legal framework for a restored type of legal entity, allowing the composition of a number of legal subjects. However, its brevity had a negative effect, which resulted in the deformation of the real legal life of the endowment sphere. Another problem was the systematic inconsistency in the inclusion of the endowment-related provisions in the Economic Code and a lack of understanding of principal differences between foundations and corporations.

IV. Post-1989 Legislation

8.11. The unsatisfactory legislation contained in Section 389b of the then Economic Code was to be improved by the major amendment to the Civil Code No. 509/1991 Coll. (Sections 18, 20b to 20e and 477(2)), effective as of 1 January 1992, and by a new law.[9] Partial success was achieved. The possibility of establishing a foundation by testament was expressly stipulated and the basic particulars of the foundation statute were specified. Section 20e(2) of the Civil Code also included a reference to a detailed regulation, which was to be made by a separate law. It is true that Act No. 248/1991 Coll. on public benefit societies, which was adopted in the interim period, set a legal framework for legal entities of a special endowment (constitutional) type-public benefit societies, which are the most similar to foundations providing public benefit services (operating foundations) existing in other European countries. Rather than stabilizing the situation, however, this law resulted in a fragmentation of the understanding of foundation as a legal institute and confusion of terminology. Despite the criticism by foundations and the legal public, this torso of the foundation law survived in the Czech Republic, with all its deficiencies and without a detailed legislation, until the end of 1997 with the adoption of Act No. 227/1997 Coll. on foundations and endowment funds and on the amendment to certain related laws. This undesirable situation was due to legal reasons and particularly to the absence of the political will to adopt an appropriate regulation. Despite several draft regulations of foundations prepared in compliance with the ideas of jurisprudence and legal practice, the situation in the field of foundation law changed

---

[8]   Section 1(1) Act No. 227/1997 Coll. on foundations and endowment funds and on the amendment to certain related laws.

[9]   Act No. 102/1992 Coll. regulating certain issues related to the promulgation of Act No. 509/1991 Coll., which modifies and amends the Civil Code.

Czech Yearbook of International Law

only upon the adoption of the Act on Foundations and Endowment Funds, and the existing situation had to be understood as transitory. However, due to its long-term existence, this situation had far-reaching negative consequences.

8.12. The excessive liberalism of this legal regulation led to frequent abuse of the institute of foundation and to the loss of public trust in the honesty of foundations and in the implementation of their public benefit mission. It has to be noted that this scepticism survives to the present. It was also reflected during the preparation of a proposed amendment to the Act on Foundations and Endowment Funds in 2010 in the unwillingness of some politicians to make any changes to the strict legal regime.

8.13. Even after the split of the Czechoslovak state, the Slovak Republic took over the legal regulation contained in Sections 20e et seq. of the Civil Code, which was subsequently replaced, like in the Czech Republic, first by the separate Act No. 207/1996 Coll. on foundations and later on by Act No. 34/2002 Coll. on foundations. This currently constitutes the legal framework governing the operation of foundations in the Slovak Republic.

V. Legal Regulation in the New Civil Code

8.14. The provisions of the new Civil Code concerning legal entities[10] are divided into four chapters. The first one regulates general issues concerning all types of legal entities (Sections 118-209); each of the other three chapters focuses on specific types of legal entities (Sections 210-302 deal with corporations, Sections 303-401 with foundations[11] and Sections 402-418 with institutes). The legal entities of the fund type are collectively referred to as foundation funds (in Czech *fundace*). This term has not had any meaning in the Czech normative language and is not used in the general language, but has long been known to literary Czechs. Its general meaning does not represent only a term synonymous to foundations, but also a general name of the asset base dedicated to a social purpose.[12] Hence, it may be used functionally for joint naming of foundations and funds, because the term *fundace*

---

[10] Act No. 89/2012 Coll., the Civil Code.
[11] When the term 'fundace' appeared in the outline of the Civil Code, it was encountered with some resistance; even the press considered it as a strange neologism. The word 'fundace' is a correct Czech word, which has existed in the Czech vocabulary for some 100 years and designates either property (assets) that are to serve a specific purpose or a legal entity managing such assets. Moreover, the acoustic perception of this term sounds like both funds and foundations.
[12] 1 SLOVNÍK SPISOVNÉHO JAZYKA ČESKÉHO, Prague: Academia 527 (1989).

resembles the names of both categories of legal entities and seems also as a proper antonym to the term 'corporation'.[13]

8.15. A foundation fund (*fundace*) (Section 303 et seq.) is a legal entity created by certain property (assets) designated for a specific purpose. The foundation fund's activities are linked to the purpose for which it has been established. Its internal arrangements are regulated by a statute. Two legal entities of this type are subsumed under the term 'foundation fund' in the new Civil Code-the foundation and the endowment fund.

8.16. Under Section 306-393 a foundation is a legal entity established to permanently serve a socially or economically beneficial purpose. A foundation may have both a public benefit purpose such as support of public welfare and a charitable purpose which include provisions of support to a specific group of persons designated individually or otherwise.

8.17. The possibility of a foundation to carry out business activities is restricted to a similar extent as in the case of an association, society or club. A foundation may carry out business activities only if such activities represent its ancillary activities and the proceeds from them solely serve to support the purpose of the foundation. However, the creator of a foundation may exclude the performance of any business activities in its deed of establishment. Such foundation may not carry out any business activities.

8.18. The assets (estate) of a foundation consist of the foundation's principal and other assets. The foundation principal is the sum of objects of contributions to the foundation and of endowment donations, if applicable. Its total value must be at least CZK 500,000. The foundation principal expressed in money is the foundation capital. A number of restrictions have been set with regard to the disposal of the foundation principal (cf. Section 339 et seq.). Such restrictions are justified by the required permanent nature of the foundation.

8.19. The provisions of the new Civil Code concerning foundations also include provisions concerning associated funds (trusts), or 'non-independent foundations' (Sections 349-352) These are property that can constitute a contribution to a foundation but are not deposited in it and are only entrusted to its management under a contract. In such a contract, the foundation is authorized to use that entrusted property for the agreed purpose relating to its mission. The property in the associated fund is recorded separately from the foundation's property. The disposal of the associated fund constitutes solely the rights and obligations of the foundation that manages the fund. The associated

---

[13] Explanatory report to Act No. 89/2012 Coll., the Civil Code.

fund is not a legal entity because it consists only of assets managed by the foundation.

8.20. An endowment fund (Sections 394-401) is a legal entity established for a socially or economically beneficial purpose. Unlike a foundation, the endowment fund need not permanently serve such a purpose. Hence, the property of an endowment fund may also consist of contributions and donations whose purpose need not fulfil the prerequisite of a permanent generation of revenue. No foundation principal or foundation capital is created in an endowment fund. All property of an endowment fund may be disposed of if it complies with the purpose of the endowment fund. An umbrella term for entities other than corporations is introduced, i.e. a name for entities created by allocation of property for a specific purpose. Foundation funds include foundations, endowment funds and funds under public law. As of its effective date, the new Civil Code will supersede Act No. 227/1997 Coll. on foundations and endowment funds.

8.21. Acts adopted on behalf of legal entities must be adopted by individuals authorised for such purpose. Such action is designated systematically by the new Civil Code as 'representation' (cf. particularly Sections 161, 162 and 164 of the Civil Code), despite the fact that such term is ascribed in this respect a more extensive meaning than the institute of representation regulated in Section 436 et seq. Section 161 stipulates that anyone who represents a legal entity shall manifest what grants him the power to do so. This concept of acting on behalf of a legal entity represents a change of the current approach to this issue (cf. Section 20 of the Civil Code of 1964 and particularly Section 13(1) of the Commercial Code, which indicates that the acts taken by the statutory body are the acts of the legal entity itself).

8.22. One of the basic prerequisites for changes in society is the cooperation among people and creation of such communities that will seek common programmes. The objectives of such programmes should mainly consist of open naming of problems and crises and of the offer of alternative solutions for such problems. We stand at the beginning of the twenty-first century and do not naturally know and cannot foresee the development of society in the upcoming decades. A certain revival of the foundation law did not occur by mere adoption of legislation in the field of foundation law; we are convinced that the adoption of this legislation was induced by a change of societal relations and essentially by a spontaneous renovation of foundation traditions. There are currently a large number of foundations and endowment funds, which carry out activities similar to the *Foundation Nadání Josefa, Marie a Zdeňky Hlávkových*, which is, however, the only foundation that has been in existence since its establishment.[14] With regard to its almost 110 years of existence, we would like to provide some details about this foundation.

VI. The Foundation *Nadání Josefa, Marie a Zdeňky Hlávkových*

8.23. The Foundation *Nadání Josefa, Marie a Zdeňky Hlávkových* (hereinafter the Foundation) was established by Josef Hlávka[15] in 1904 and constituted it as the universal heir of all his estate amounting to several million Czech crowns. He ordered this legal entity to support in accordance with its Statute all scientific, literary and artistic activities of the Czech nation and to make available the results of such activities, as well as the results of all scientific activities in the world, to the cultural life of the nation so that the nation may draw from them in all aspects of its executive activities.

8.24. Another part of the huge estate left by Josef Hlávka to the Foundation was to be used for support of

'diligent and eligible students of Prague universities so as to allow them to devote all their efforts, based on the provision of partial or (if possible) full subsistence, solely to their full education, which constitutes the basis of their own and of the entire nation's future. [...] Entrusting this Foundation of Josef, Marie and Zdeňka Hlávka with all sincere devotion and with all good will for the sake of

---

14 Marie Karfíková, *Hlávkova nadace a další nadační fondy v ČR (Hlávka's Foundation and the Other Endowment Funds in Czech Republic)*, (1) FORUM-JOURNAL OF CHARLES UNIVERSITY IN PRAGUE 27 (2008).

15 PhDr. Josef Hlávka (1831-1908), an architect and senior construction counsellor, was a renowned benefactor of the last decades of the nineteenth century and beginning of the twentieth century. He spent significant sums for the establishment and direct support of various institutions and events, which contributed to scientific, cultural, artistic and economic activities of the Czech people. Hundreds of scientists, artists, writers, musicians and students owed thanks to Josef Hlávka for his financial support and scholarships, which provided them the necessary social basis for their work, creation and study or a possibility to create and study abroad.

In his eulogy to Josef Hlávka, Prof. Dr. Antonín Chevalier Randa stated on 15 March 1908 'Josef Hlávka, this hero of spirit and work, originating from the people, was almost alone in providing to the Czech people everything what is provided in other countries for cultural purposes by the state or by the country or partly by a higher rich circles of the society. Until his last breath, he worked for his nation to which he devoted boundless love.' He also expressed his hope that the Czech people would not forget Hlávka's merits and his efforts would be taken up by others.

The architectonic compound of the architect and building engineer Josef Hlávka in Černovce, Ukraine, was registered in 2011 in UNESCO's list of world cultural heritage sites.

elevation and strengthening of the Czech nation, with all its assets, tasks and purposes, to the God's will-which is the sole ground for its desirable success and achievable beneficial result-I conclude, full of trust in God's Providence and in the strength of my nation, with an impassioned plea: that the Supreme Ruler of all people and nations takes this 'Foundation', its tasks and objectives, with utmost mercy, under His most powerful protection, protects it from all evil and did not let it be doomed.'[16]

8.25. These are the words of the last will and testament of Josef Hlávka, where he constituted The Foundation *Nadání Josefa, Marie a Zdeňky Hlávkových* his universal heir.

8.26. The execution of the orders included in the last will and testament of Josef Hlávka fell upon his successor in office of the president of the Czech Academy who also became, according to the Foundation's Statute, the first president of the Foundation,–Prof JUDr. Antonín Chevalier Randa, an excellent lawyer and professor of civil law. Prof. Randa also held the post of a minister in the Austrian government and maintained a close personal relationship with Josef Hlávka.[17]

8.27. The concept and activities of the Foundation were profoundly affected by social changes, particularly by those occurring after 1939 and 1948. Following the establishment of the independent Czechoslovak Republic in 1918, the Foundation succeeded in following the concept and actual activities specified by Josef Hlávka in his last will and testament and in the foundation deed. The Foundation was supposed to serve the education of the Czech nation and to support the Czech Franz Joseph's Academy for Science Literature and Arts in Prague, Student hostels of Czech universities in Prague and the Institute of National Economy. Despite the financial and economic shock connected with the course of World War I, which devalued the assets of the Foundation's estate, the activities carried out by the Foundation from 1904 until 1939 represented a benefit for Czech society and its level of education. The support of three and a half thousand university students accommodated free of charge in Hlávka's Hostel opened a way for the development of Czech intelligentsia and for the establishment of its position in our society.

8.28. During World War II, the Foundation and its estate were seized by German authorities, like the rest of Czech educational institutions. A

---

[16] Last will and testament of Josef Hlávka. Archives of the Lužany Castle.

[17] Václav Pavlíček, *Prof. JUDr. Antonín Randa a odkaz Josefa Hlávky*, in PROF. DR. ANTONÍN RANDA : ZAKLADATELSKÁ OSOBNOST PRAŽSKÉ CIVILISTIKY : SBORNÍK PRACÍ K 175. VÝROČÍ NAROZENÍ A 95. VÝROČÍ ÚMRTÍ, Prague: Charles University (Vladimír Kindl (ed.), 2006).

receivership was imposed on the Lužany Castle and a significant part of the archives was destroyed. However, the interior of the castle was preserved and, thanks to the constitutional decree of the President of the Republic on renovation of legal order issued after the end of the war and to other post-war legal acts, the Foundation could renew its activities under the principles of legal continuity. Renewed attention and respect began to be paid to Josef Hlávka's legacy.

8.29.   However, the communist party soon interfered with the Foundation's estate in connection with the assumption of political power in 1948. At that time, the Foundation lost its agricultural and forest lands, ponds and agricultural facilities. It kept its buildings in Prague and the castle in Lužany, which served, in accordance with the then cultural policy, as a monument and a natural reserve and as an institution for support of scientific research. Remarkable attention was paid at that time to the personality and works of Antonín Dvořák, as indicated by the memorial desk in the chapel of the Lužany Castle.

8.30.   After World War II, the Foundation was presided over by Prof. Zdeněk Nejedlý by virtue of his position of President of the Academy, an expert on music and a historian, who was at that time also a politician. However, the Foundation Board still included outstanding scientists and university professors of various political affiliations, including Prof. Dr. Bohumil Němec. According to preserved documents, Prof. Němec since 1945 had exercised a substantial influence on the activities of the Foundation. After his election as President in 1952, he succeeded, by his wisdom, energy and political foresight, to protect the Foundation from dissolution. Prof. Dr. Bohumil Němec held this office to the benefit of the Foundation until his death in 1966. Due to previous interventions, however, not much was left then from the original estate of the Foundation.

8.31.   A new danger for the very existence of the Foundation was represented by the decision of its Board to hand over the assets, due to economic difficulties, to the socialist ownership of the state, which was issued in 1987. A more qualified description of the merits of the then management of the Czech Technical university (ČVUT) in the preservation of the Foundation's existence could be provided by the participants or contemporary witnesses of such negotiations.

8.32.   Only little of the Foundation's estate was left after 1989. Even ČVUT's management had to prove its courage and dedication to a good cause when it adopted Josef Hlávka's legacy shortly before this social upturn, when the Foundation was threatened with dissolution due to economic difficulties. The Foundation's bodies were faced with a task of renewing the Foundation's activities in the new conditions. The new legal environment did not allow the return of the original estate to the Foundation, which was the source of revenues that could be used at the time of its founder for support of Czech science, literature and arts, and young students and scientists. On the other hand, the new conditions made room for economic use of rental buildings, which were retained by the Foundation and which had been rather a burden in the past.

8.33. It appeared soon that certain fields of education were not considered by the state as its practical priority. Therefore, following Hlávka's ideas, the Foundation, which was headed at that time by Doc. PhDr. Jaroslav Nedvěd, focused primarily on support of students and young scientists.

8.34. The ideas and conclusions contained in the last will and testament of Josef Hlávka have been also followed by the current President of the Board of Trustees of the Foundation, Prof. JUDr. Václav Pavlíček, CSc. Josef Hlávka Prize has been awarded since 1993 to the best students and graduates of universities, the Technical University in Brno and young talented scientists of the Academy of Science of the Czech Republic.

8.35. Upon the proposal of universities, the Academy of Science of the Czech Republic or upon the initiative of the Foundation's Board of Trustees, Josef Hlávka medal has been awarded since 1996 to founding personalities of Czech science and culture, who were ignored in the past, as a follow-up of the tradition established by the Academy of Science of the Czech Republic.

8.36. Since 1993, the Foundation has been participating, together with the Foundation of the Czech Literary Fund, in the award of Josef Hlávka Literary Prizes in the field of scientific literature. This prize is designated to authors of the best selected scientific publications.

8.37. As one of the forms of its independent Foundation activities, the Board of Trustees established, by its decision adopted in 1994, the Institute of National Economy with Josef Hlávka's name complemented to it (Institute). Acting in the spirit of Josef Hlávka's legacy and with regard to the objectives of the original Institute of National Economy, which was founded by Josef Hlávka in 1907, the restored Institute contributes its activities to the economic elevation of the Czech people. The Institute's mission is to support independent research activities and studies of the issues of the Czech national economy and its development in the context of broader social connections in the spirit of the legacy of the Foundation's founder. The Institute does not carry out its own scientific research but supports research activities in the form of scholarships and editing activities. Since 2010, the Institute has been awarding, in cooperation with the University of Economics and

Management, Milan Sojka Prize in honour and commemoration of Prof. Ing. Milan Sojka, CSc., an excellent economist and university lecturer, member of the Board of Trustees of the Foundation and of the Board of the Institution, who prematurely died in 2009.

8.38. In 1999, the Foundation succeeded in the revival of the Hlávka's Hostel concept, which offers accommodation subsidized by the Foundation to post-graduate students who achieve excellent study results, are impecunious, have no flat in Prague and are not businessmen.[18]

8.39. The Josef Hlávka Architect Prize has also been awarded since 2007 in the competition 'Young Architect Award ABF'. This award is designated to students of bachelor, master or doctoral studies or to graduates of architecture up to 33 years of age.

8.40. The legal basis and form of *Nadání Josefa, Marie a Zdeňky Hlávkových* was so perfect that it has been able to implement Hlávka's legacy until the present time. It is a foundation which has survived more than 100 years and was not dissolved upon a decision of its bodies, of the state authorities or by the law (*ex lege*).

8.41. At present, the *Foundation Nadání Josefa, Marie a Zdeňky Hlávkových* administers its estate, primarily real properties, particularly Josef Hlávka's castle in Lužany u Přeštic and the foundation buildings in Prague. Revenues from rent are used to cover all necessary expenses incurred in connection with the foundation activities, with the administration and improvement of the property. The foundation property has been increased by a contribution provided by the state from a foundation investment fund, whose proceeds are used in support of scientific life, particularly Josef Hlávka's Institute of National Economy. The revenues provide independent funds to the foundation programme, which is based on the intellectual legacy of the Foundation's founder. Each foundation contribution is approved by the Board of Trustees of the Foundation. Contributions paid by the Foundation are granted to anyone who has met the required criteria and has been recommended by prominent personalities of Czech science and culture.

VII. Conclusion

8.42. With regard to the scope available to us, we tried to refer concisely to the specific tradition of foundation law in the Czech Republic, from the establishment of Czechoslovakia in 1918, which followed the legislation of the Austro-Hungarian monarchy after its dissolution to the current status. Historical experience indicates that the boom of foundations has

---

[18] Marie Karfíková, *100.výročí úmrtí Josefa Hlávky*, (6) PRÁVNÍK 695-701 (2008).

Czech Yearbook of International Law

been always affected by crises in the society and logically also by wars. Social relations established in 1948 also hindered any foundation activities and it is really a miracle that, despite the loss of property, but not of its legal continuity, the *Foundation Nadání Josefa, Marie a Zdeňky Hlávkových* has survived since its founding. We believe that the existence and activities of this foundation represent certain guidance for other foundations. This is represented primarily by thorough de-politicization of activities and massive support to the education of the nation. Due to the foregoing, we believe that foundation activities inevitably require the involvement of educated people. The benefits of such involvement in this activity should consist, in particular, in its contribution to the establishment in the Czech environment of a tradition of independent institutions that are capable not only of naming urgent social problems but also of presenting, after discussion, proposals for solutions to such problems. This should be a contribution to the improvement of the quality of life of the entire society and of the quality of public discussion. Such issues have a principal impact on our lives and our future.

| | |

Summaries

FRA [*Rôle des fondations au début du XXIe siècle*]
C'est un aperçu exhaustif de la réglementation des fondations – partie du droit souvent présentée comme droit des fondations - qu'on a tenté ici d'apporter. La première partie, qui constitue un bref rappel historique, décrit la situation dans le domaine du droit des fondations après l'indépendance de la Tchécoslovaquie au moment de l'écroulement de l'empire austro-hongrois. Suit une discussion sur la législation réglementant la création et les activités des fondations et des fonds de dotation. Il était également impossible de passer sous silence les nouvelles réglementations en rapport avec le nouveau Code civil entrant en application le 1er janvier 2014. Pour ne pas en rester uniquement à de la théorie, on présente pour conclure la plus ancienne fondation tchèque, la fondation Hlávka (Nadaci Nadání Josefa, Marie a Zdeňky Hlávkových) qui a conservé la même structure juridique depuis sa création en 1904.

CZE [*Úloha nadací na počátku 21. století*]
Autoři připravili příspěvek tak, aby byl podán, pokud to rozsah příspěvku umožňuje, komplexní pohled na právní úpravu nadací, kdy se mnohdy uvádí tato část práva jako právo nadační. V prvé části, která je

krátkým historickým exkursem, je popsán stav na úseku nadačního práva po vzniku samostatné Československé republiky po rozpadu Rakousko-Uherska. Dále je pojednání o nové právní, a to zákonné, úpravě vzniku a působení nadací a nadačních fondů. S ohledem na dnes již platný nový občanský zákoník, který má nabýt účinnosti dnem 1. ledna 2014, nebylo možné se vyhnout i krátkému exkursu do nové právní úpravy. Aby celý příspěvek nebyl pouhým pokusem o teoretizování v dané oblasti, byl na závěr příspěvku zařazen pohled na nejstarší nadaci v České republice, a to Nadaci Nadání Josefa, Marie a Zdeňky Hlávkových založenou v roce 1904, jež si udržela právní kontinuitu do dnešních dnů.

| | |

POL   [*Rola fundacji na początku XXI wieku*]
Prezentowany artykuł dotyczy na pozór marginalnej strefy życia społecznego, jednak autorzy dostrzegają wielką wagę regulacji prawnych w zakresie fundacji, i to nie tylko ze względu na niedawno przyjętą odrębną ustawę o fundacjach, ale również w świetle nowej i stosunkowo obszernej regulacji prawnej zawartej w kodeksie cywilnym, wchodzącym w życie 1 stycznia 2014 roku.

DEU   [*Sinn und Zweck der Stiftung zu Beginn des 21. Jahrhunderts*]
Der vorliegende Beitrag betrifft ein vermeintlich randständiges Gebiet des gesellschaftlichen Lebens; die Autoren erachten aber den rechtlichen Rahmen, in dem sich Stiftungen bewegen, für wichtig, und zwar nicht nur im Hinblick auf das kürzlich verabschiedete eigenständige Stiftungsgesetz, sondern auch im Hinblick auf die neue und relativ weitreichende Regelung, wie sie im zum 1. Januar 2014 in Kraft tretenden neuen Bürgerlichen Gesetzbuch enthalten ist.

RUS   [*Роль фондов в начале XXI века*]
На первый взгляд, настоящая статья посвящена не столь значимым областям общественной жизни. Однако ее авторы видят важность правового регулирования в области фондов не только с учетом недавно принятого отдельного закона о фондах, но и с учетом нового и довольно обширного правового регулирования, закрепленного в Гражданском кодексе, который вступит в законную силу 1 января 2014 года.

ESP [*El papel de las fundaciones a comienzos del siglo XXI*]

El presente artículo se refiere a un tema aparentemente periférico de la vida de la sociedad, pero los autores consideran importante la regulación legislativa de las fundaciones con respecto a la recientemente aprobada Ley de fundaciones, así como a la nueva y bastante extensa regulación legislativa implementada por el Código civil, que entrará en vigor el 1 de enero de 2014.

| | |

Lukáš Klee | Ondřej Ručka

FIDIC: Significance in the Construction Industry

Key words:
FIDIC | Fédération Internationale des Ingénieurs-Conseils | International Federation of Consulting Engineers | Red Book | Yellow Book | Silver Book | CONS | P&DB | EPC | DBO

Abstract | *From its beginnings, the Fédération Internationale des Ingénieurs-Conseils (FIDIC) has led the industry by providing commentary, explanations and sample forms to its users. This article pays particular attention to the FIDIC forms, FIDIC influence in the construction industry, networking activities, membership and further connected matters. FIDIC forms provide the user with a complete toolbox of documents. Their popularity and reliability has been proven by their world-wide application in construction projects. FIDIC is often perceived as only an organisation which provides sample forms of construction contracts. This article however, explores FIDIC as a much broader joining force in the contemporary construction world.*

| | |

Lukáš Klee is an expert on International Construction Law and FIDIC sample forms of contract, Lukáš Klee currently works for a large construction company in central Europe. When away from the office, he lectures on International Construction Law at the Charles University Faculty of Law in Prague. As an extension of his teaching duties, Mr. Klee also trains lawyers at the Judicial Academy of the Czech Republic. He regularly publishes articles in the Czech Republic and abroad and is the author of three books related to International Construction Law.
e-mail: klee@email.cz

Ondřej Ručka is in-house legal counsel in a large, Czech industrial group, Ondřej Ručka's main task is to provide legal support for the international business dealings of the group.

I. FIDIC

9.01. Based in Lausanne, Switzerland, the *Fédération Internationale des Ingénieurs-Conseils* (FIDIC) in English, *The International Federation of Consulting Engineers*, was founded in France in 1913 and has been expanding by new membership all over the world. It is a non-governmental organization recognized by the United Nations, major global banks, the European Commission, and other international institutions. The FIDIC was set up to support and promote the overall interests of its member associations. But the FIDIC did not become a major significant organization until the post-WWII era when it started expanding at such a rate that it now unites the associations from more than ninety countries on all the continents.[1]

In particular, he provides support concerning large investments and engineering projects outside the Czech Republic. He is a graduate of the Masaryk University Faculty of Law in Brno. e-mail: ondrej.rucka@gmail.com

9.02. After a meeting of expert consultants at the World Fair Exhibitions (EXPO) in 1913, held in Ghent, Belgium, a large number of participating consulting engineers discussed the possibility of forming an international federation of consulting engineers. Discussions and preparations led to the successful acceptance of the organization's constitution on 22 July 1913, by which the *Fédération Internationale des Ingénieurs Conseils* was established. Although there were representatives of 59 countries participating during preparations of the constitution, only 3 of them became founding members - Belgium, France and Switzerland. Other countries maintained more informal relations with the organization. The number of members increased slowly but steadily, despite obvious complications resulting from two world wars. Until 1959, all of the FIDIC members were from European countries. Australia, Canada, South Africa, and the USA joined during that year and FIDIC became a global organization. Later FIDIC spread its influence and member base to the developing world and now includes all parts of the world.[2]

9.03. Formally, according to its constitution, the organization of FIDIC is compromised of the General Assembly, the Executive Committee, the Auditor(s) and the Secretariat.

9.04. The General Assembly, held at least once every year, consists of the duly appointed delegates of the Member Associations. Its major activities are the election of the members of the Executive Committee and the Auditor(s), and decision making of membership issues.

---

[1] See LUKÁŠ KLEE, SMLUVNÍ PODMÍNKY FIDIC, Praha: Wolters Kluwer 2 (2011).

[2] See FIDIC: History, available at: http://fidic.org/about-fidic/fidic-history (accessed on 28 August 2013).

9.05. The Executive Committee is responsible for daily management and administration of the organization, namely for all aspects of FIDIC activity outside direct competence of the General Assembly. It is led by a President and Vice-President or President Elect, voted from the Executive Committee members by the General Assembly.

9.06. The Secretariat is lead by a Managing Director who is appointed by the Executive Committee and responsible to it. The General Assembly votes for one or two Auditors every 4 years, in order to duly audit accounts and finances of the organization.[3]

9.07. Other FIDIC activities are organized and managed by standing committees, appointed Task Force groups and forums.[4]

9.08. The FIDIC's objectives are to:[5]

1) represent the consulting engineering industry globally;
2) enhance the image of consulting engineers;
3) be the authority on issues relating to business practice;
4) promote the development of a global and viable consulting engineering industry;
5) promote quality;
6) actively promote conformance to a code of ethics and to business integrity;
7) promote commitment to sustainable development.

9.09. The first edition of the *Conditions of Contract for Works of Civil Engineering Construction* was released in 1957, giving rise to a tradition of the *FIDIC Conditions of Contract for Construction* commonly referred to as '*The Red Book*'. Due to the ever-advancing technological development in the construction industry it became obvious to FIDIC and users that the contractual conditions in their original version would have to be revised. In 1999, the latest and the most widely used First Editions[6] came into existence with its *Red Book, Yellow Book* and *Silver Book* as the forms are called.

I.1. FIDIC Forms of Contract

9.10. The conditions of contracts prepared by the FIDIC are the most widely used sample conditions of contract for construction projects. These sample documents are perceived as the 'International best practise

---

[3] See FIDIC: Statutes and By-Laws (October 2011), available at: http://fidic.org/node/769 (accessed on 28 August 2013).

[4] See FIDIC: Committees, available at: http://fidic.org/node/771 (accessed on 28 August 2013).

[5] See Ibid., at 3.

[6] The most recent 1999 version of FIDIC documents was almost written from scratch, and was therefore considered to be a first edition..

documents', enjoying ever growing popularity. This is mainly due to significant international lenders who want to have generally accepted and proven 'rules of game' within their construction projects. One of the advantages of FIDIC forms is that a user is not dealing with only the conditions of a contract, but with a complete set of documents without which successful realization of a project could hardly be possible. These mainly consist of a variety of sample documents, from tendering forms up to dispute adjudication issues. Each of these individual forms also contains the comments, explanations and user instructions.[7]

9.11. At present, the most popular FIDIC sample conditions of contract are the *Red Book, Yellow Book* and *Silver Book* published in the 1999 First Edition.

I.1.1. Conditions of Contract for Construction (First Ed. 1999) Red Book (CONS)

9.12. CONS is for the conditions with well-balanced risk allocation and is assumed to be used for projects where the risks associated with the design are to be largely borne by the Employer. They are the contractual conditions for General Contracting delivery method. It is common in such arrangements that the Employer (his designer) prepares a detailed design including bill of quantities, specifications and drawings for the purpose of the tender (terms of reference). The contractor evaluates the rates and prices of the tender bill of quantities. The works are measured on the basis of actual completed works, using the mentioned unit and item prices that are fixed. Contract administration is done by the Engineer.[8]

I.1.2. Conditions of Contract for Plant and Design-Build (First Ed, 1999) Yellow Book (P&DB)

9.13. P&DB is for the conditions with well-balanced risk allocation and assumed to be used for Design-Build projects where the risks associated with the design are to be largely borne by the Contractor. Unlike CONS, the P&DB do not use the Employer's detailed design for the purpose of the tender (terms of reference). Instead they come from the 'Employer's Requirements' that define, above all, the purpose, scope,

---

[7] For further details see the official guides prepared by FIDIC; INTERNATIONAL FEDERATION OF CONSULTING ENGINEERS, THE FIDIC CONTRACTS GUIDE, Lausanne: FIDIC (1st ed. 2000) and INTERNATIONAL FEDERATION OF CONSULTING ENGINEERS, FIDIC PROCUREMENT PROCEDURES GUIDE, Geneva: FIDIC (1st ed. 2011).

[8] INTERNATIONAL FEDERATION OF CONSULTING ENGINEERS, CONDITIONS OF CONTRACT FOR CONSTRUCTION, Lausanne: FIDIC (1st ed. 1999).

standard, performance and other criteria, depending on the Employer's expectations and priorities. The Employer's requirements are not assumed to contain excessive details. The Contractor shall prepare his proposal based on the Employer's requirements which become a part of the contract. Even though the contract price is conceived as a lump price, it may become subject to modifications mainly through variations and due to the claims raised for additional payments and extensions of time. Contract administration is done by the Engineer.[9]

I.1.3. Conditions of Contract for Engineer, Procure and Construct (EPC)/Turnkey Projects (First Ed. 1999) Silver Book (EPC or EPCT)

9.14. EPC is for the conditions that are typical for Design-Build projects where the risks, mainly those associated with the design, site conditions and the complications having an effect on time and price, are allocated to the Contractor. This form is recommended where the entire investment (such as nuclear power plants) is to be contracted and where there is a requirement to secure a more reliable total price and a definite time frame. EPC also applies where the price is conceived as a lump sum, the works are not measured, but they can become subject to modifications, mainly through variations and due to a limited number of claims raised for additional payments and extensions of time. Contract administration is done by the Employer or his representative.[10]

9.15. In order to distinguish between the P&DB and EPC conditions, FIDIC clarifies the cases when it is recommended to use the P&DB conditions. They are the situations where any of the following circumstances are encountered:
- There is insufficient time or information for tenderers to scrutinise and check the Employer's requirements or for them to carry out their designs, risk assessment studies and estimating.
- Construction will involve substantial work underground or work in other areas which tenderers cannot inspect.
- The Employer intends to supervise closely or control the Contractor's work, or to review most of the construction drawings.
- The amount of each interim payment is to be determined by an official or other intermediary.

---

[9]   INTERNATIONAL FEDERATION OF CONSULTING ENGINEERS, CONDITIONS OF CONTRACT FOR PLANT AND DESIGN-BUILD, Lausanne: FIDIC (1st ed. 1999).
[10]   See INTERNATIONAL FEDERATION OF CONSULTING ENGINEERS, CONDITIONS OF CONTRACT FOR EPC/TURNKEY PROJECTS, Lausanne: FIDIC (1st ed. 1999).

9.16. FIDIC recommends that the P&DB be used in the above circumstances for works designed by or on behalf of the Contractor.[11] FIDIC publishes many other forms of contracts and documents including *The Short Form of Contract* (First Ed. 1999) *Green Book* which is the contractual conditions intended for construction works of small value. Furthermore, there is the *Conditions of Subcontract for Construction* (First Ed. 2011) for use with construction subcontracts and originally issued by FIDIC in 2009. It is intended for use in combination with CONS.

9.17. For Design-Build (DB) projects where an operation period is needed, FIDIC prepared *Conditions of Contract for Design, Build and Operate Projects* (First Ed. 2008) *Gold Book* (DBO). This publication reflects the trend that contractors not only construct but also maintain and operate the facility.

9.18. FIDIC published also *The Client/Consultant Model Services Agreement* (Fourth Ed. 2006) *White Book* and *The Model Representative Agreement* (First Ed. 2013) *Purple Book*.

9.19. Due to the needs and demands of its partners, FIDIC is constantly updating existing contract forms and developing new ones. For example, the aforementioned *Model Representative Agreement* (First Ed. 2013) *Purple Book* was introduced recently[12] into the collection of contract conditions. This will assist consultants enter into contracts with a representative or agent for the provision of representative or specialist services. *The Purple Book* was developed in close cooperation with multi-lateral development banks in order to mitigate the ever present risks of corruption and bribery. These risks threaten large investment projects worldwide.

9.20. Another ongoing activity is the preparation, translation and issuing of the most popular contract forms and documents in various languages such as Arabic, Chinese, Vietnamese, Polish, Hungarian and Estonian.[13] Other language translations are issued unofficially by local FIDIC members and national consulting associations.[14]

---

[11] See Axel-Volkmar Jaeger & Götz-Sebastian Hök, Fidic – A Guide for Practitioners, Berlin: Springer Verlag 135 (2010).

[12] See FIDIC: July 2013 Newsletter, available at: http://fidic.org/node/2751#business3 (accessed on 28 August 2013).

[13] See FIDIC: Bookshop, available at: http://fidic.org/bookshop (accessed on 28 August 2013).

[14] Fidic: An Analysis of International Construction Contracts, London: Kluwer Law International, page 18 (Robert Knutson ed., 2005).

II. FIDIC Influence on the Construction Industry

9.21. In recent years, FIDIC has experienced growth in its influence on the construction industry worldwide. With the spread of globalisation, internationally active organisations are looking for a uniform set of construction project standards independent of countries and governments. Such organisations include The World Bank, European Bank for Reconstruction and Development, the Inter-American Development Bank, the African Development Bank and the Islamic Development Bank. Various other organisations are cooperating with FIDIC to develop broad, worldwide standards of business practice, ranging from the International Standards Organization, International Labour Organization and others such as Transparency International or the United Nations Environment Program. Close cooperation with the above mentioned organisations and others is helping the development of widely used best practice standards. This is not only for consulting engineers, but for the wider construction industry and business in general. Clearly defined, well-known and globally recognised standards are helping to reduce various costs and to develop a predictable legal and business environment. This applies not only to countries in the developing world, but to countries of the developed world. FIDIC promotes its objectives through annual meetings and conferences. The first conference was held in London in 1988 with cities in South East Asia, Middle America and North America hosting annual programs in recent years. Moreover, about 100 training events are held annually worldwide.[15]

II.1. FIDIC Membership

9.22. The nature and type of organisations who are FIDIC members are diverse. They range from individual members from independent countries to regional federations and broader member associations.[16] For example, the African members of FIDIC associate themselves with the Group of Africa Member Associations (GAMA) with its FIDIC Regional Office in Dar-es- Salaam, Tanzania. Members from the Asia Pacific region are associated with the Asia-Pacific Group (ASPAC). The most important and influential members of FIDIC are regional federations such the Pan American Federation of Consultants (FEPAC)

---

[15] See FRANCOIS BAILLON, THE USE OF FIDIC CONTRACTS WORLDWIDE, presented at FIDIC – ICC Conference – Paris – 25 June 2013 (2013).

[16] See FIDIC: Regional Groups, available at: http://fidic.org/node/834 (accessed on 28 August 2013).

and the European Federation of Engineering Consultancy Associations (EFCA). The latter is closely cooperating with FIDIC in various areas such as the coordination of EU/EEC policy and with international governmental and non-governmental organisations and individual states.

II.2. Other FIDIC Activities

9.23. Aware of the growing popularity and support for its activities, FIDIC organises a number of training events to help local businesses expand globally and to spread FIDIC values. These activities have culminated in the development of the *Business Practice Training Manual* which is applicable in both the developed and developing world. Moreover, the organisation of International Training Programmes (in cooperation with member associations) is ongoing. FIDIC also accredits trainers and training suppliers through its *Accredited Trainer and Development Programme*.[17] Online training courses are available directly from FIDIC.

9.24. The scope of FIDIC training is focused on hard skills, such as the mastering of contract conditions and their use. It also focuses on soft skills such as the development of managerial skills required for successful project implementation. The former includes courses on Professional Services Agreements, Practical Use of FIDIC Contracts, Claims and Dispute Resolution, Dispute Adjudication Boards and Contract Management. The latter is comprised of courses such as Business Development, Business Administration, Risk Management, Quality Management, Business Integrity Management and Project Sustainability Management.[18]

II.3. Networking Activities

9.25. FIDIC influence goes beyond the formalities of international best business practice and commercial relationships. FIDIC's informal, but significant, influence on the opinions of global leaders and decision makers is, arguably, even more important. Numerous meetings and events help FIDIC participants from across the globe to build specific professional communities, spread ideas and exchange valuable contacts. Networking and gatherings of consulting engineers, clients, contractors and other professionals are crucial to promoting FIDIC values. Therefore, these events are strongly supported by the organisation.

---

[17] See FRANCOIS BAILLON, *supra* note 14, at 15.
[18] See Ibid., at 15.

II.4. Dispute Resolution

9.26.   FIDIC is fully aware of the rising importance of alternative dispute resolution (ADR) in business. Not only is ADR becoming the best business practice generally, the use of ADR has become important in cases when the local legal environment substantially differs from internationally recognised legal standards. That is why a Dispute Adjudication Board (DAB) was developed and must be included in all FIDIC contract forms. It sets precise rules for solving disputes in a way most beneficial to the parties (within contractual limits). In order to guarantee the quality of its DAB proceedings, an official FIDIC President's List of Approved Dispute Adjudicators is managed by the organisation. Training and assistance is provided to member associations to help establish reliable DAB proceedings, even without direct involvement of FIDIC.[19] It is not always possible to solve all disputes amicably or even through the use of well defined and conducted DAB proceedings. In such cases, arbitration under the rules of the International Chamber of Commerce remains the recommended option for dispute resolution in every FIDIC contract form.

III. Conclusion

9.27.   FIDIC currently presents the most common form of contract used in large construction projects. These include monumental nation building efforts such as the re-building of Libya after the Arab Spring revolution, development of an independent Timor-Leste and the building of infrastructure for the FIFA World Cup in Qatar in 2022.[20]

9.28.   FIDIC is involved in a vast field of global activity as well. Such a worldwide presence and influence also brings with it substantial responsibility and related commitments. Therefore, FIDIC representatives and members decided to use their organisational capabilities to promote the values of sustainable development. Consultants participating in development and infrastructure projects could network their experience and knowledge directly in cooperation with project investors and clients. The use of valuable know-how from the beginning of every project to realisation helps make it more effective and sustainable in every aspect.[21]

|||

---

[19]   See FRANCOIS BAILLON, *supra* note 14, at 15.
[20]   See Ibid., at 15.
[21]   See FIDIC: 2011/2012 Annual Report, available at: http://fidic.org/node/813 (accessed on 29 August 2013).

Summaries

FRA [*La FIDIC et son importance dans l'industrie du bâtiment*]

La Fédération Internationale des Ingénieurs Conseils (FIDIC) a constitué dès le départ pour ses utilisateurs une référence pour ses commentaires, ses interprétations et ses contrats types. On s'intéresse ici principalement aux contrats FIDIC, à l'influence de la FIDIC dans l'industrie du bâtiment, au networking, à l'adhésion à la FIDIC et à d'autres thèmes en lien. Les contrats FIDIC ouvrent l'utilisation d'une documentation très large à leurs utilisateurs. Leur application internationale dans des projets de construction montre combien ils sont appréciés et fiables. La FIDIC est souvent perçue comme une organisation dont l'unique activité serait de délivrer des modèles élaborés de contrats de construction. On verra ici que la FIDIC est un élément fédérateur dans le monde actuel de l'industrie du bâtiment dont les activités sont bien plus étendues.

CZE [*FIDIC a jeho význam ve stavebnictví*]

Již od svých počátků je Mezinárodní federace konzultačních inženýrů (FIDIC) pro své uživatele vedoucím poskytovatelem komentářů, výkladů a smluvních vzorů. Tento článek se zabývá zejména smluvními vzory FIDIC, vlivem FIDICU na stavební průmysl, networkingem, členstvím a dalšími souvisejícími tématy. Smluvní vzory FIDIC poskytují svým uživatelům komplexní sadu dokumentace. Jejich oblíbenost a spolehlivost je prokázána celosvětovým využitím při stavebních projektech. FIDIC je často vnímána pouze jako organizace poskytující vypracované vzory stavebních smluv. Tento článek se ovšem zabývá FIDICEM coby mnohem rozsáhlejším sjednocujícím aktérem ve světě současného stavebnictví.

| | |

POL [*FIDIC i jego znaczenie w budownictwie*]

Międzynarodowa Federacja Inżynierów Konsultantów (FIDIC) to jedna z czołowych organizacji budowlanych, oferująca istotne wsparcie swoim klientom. Niniejszy artykuł przedstawia bogatą działalność FIDIC. FIDIC często postrzegana jest wyłącznie jako organizacja dostarczająca gotowe wzory umów budowlanych, jednak zakres jej działalności jest znacznie szerszy.

DEU [*FIDIC und seine Bedeutung im Bauwesen*]

Der internationale Dachverband beratender Ingenieure im Bauwesen (FIDIC) nimmt in der Bauindustrie dank seiner wichtigen Hilfestellung für Ratsuchende eine führende Stellung ein. Der vorliegende Beitrag befasst sich mit den mannigfaltigen Aktivitäten von FIDIC – einer Organisation, die oft nur als Quelle für Musterbauverträge wahrgenommen wird, die aber auf viel breiterer Basis tätig ist.

RUS [*FIDIC (ФИДИК) и ее значение в области строительства*]

Международная федерация инженеров-консультантов (FIDIC) является одной из ведущих организаций в области строительства, которая предоставляет важную поддержку своим пользователям. В этой статье рассматриваются различные направления деятельности FIDIC. FIDIC часто воспринимается только как организация, предоставляющая составленные образцы строительных контрактов, однако, ее деятельность гораздо шире.

ESP [*FIDIC y su importancia en la industria de la construcción*]

La Federación Internacional de Ingenieros Consultores (FIDIC) es una de las organizaciones líderes en la industria de la construcción gracias al esencial apoyo que prestan a sus usuarios. Este artículo se refiere a las diversas actividades de la FIDIC. A menudo, la FIDIC se percibe solamente como una organización que facilita formularios normalizados de contratos de construcción, pero sus actividades son mucho más amplias.

||||

Karel Klíma

The Phenomenon of the European Court of Human Rights' Influence on the Constitutional Systems of the Council of Europe Member States

Key words:
Council of Europe |
European Court of
Human Rights |
Convention on Human
Rights and Fundamental
Freedoms | constitutional
judiciary | right to life |
right to privacy | right to
possessions (ownership) |
political freedoms | right
to a fair trial

Abstract | *The case law of the European Court of Human Rights, as the judicial authority of the Council of Europe, influences the legal systems in the individual Member States. It is reflected in various branches of the national legal system adopted in the Council of Europe Member States, not only in the substantive provisions of constitutional law. This European 'case law' system constitutes a certain monolithic legal system founded on the categories of constitutional law, for instance in the areas of division of power, rule of law, liability of public officials and authorities, independence of the judiciary, administrative law including procedural relations, criminal law classical principles, the organization of the judiciary and implementation of specific procedural judicial principles such as equality of arms, equal standing of the parties and the right to legal assistance. It also penetrates the categories of private law – for instance, the gradual development of case law relating to the concept of privacy, freedom of thought and protection of the family. The binding force of the Council of Europe system under constitutional law and the influence of its contents on the individual legal systems justify the conclusion that the Council of Europe system is a phenomenon in the domain of international organizations.*

Prof. and Doc. JUDr. Karel Klíma, CSc., dr. hab. is a university professor specializing in constitutional law. He is the head of the Legal Specialisations and Public Administration at the Metropolitan University in Prague. He also lectures at the Faculty of Law, Komenský University in Bratislava, Slovakia and at the Siedlce University of Natural Sciences and Humanities in Poland. He is a member of the International Association of Constitutional Law and the World Jurist Association (WJA) where he holds the office of President of the Professors of Law Section.
e-mail: advokatikhklima@gmail.com

I. The Council of Europe as a European Regional International Organization for the Protection of Human Rights

10.01. Within the framework of public international law, the European regional organizations and the Council of Europe system are phenomenon which, undoubtedly, significantly distinguishes these institutions from other international organizations. The European Union system, which is parallel to the Council of Europe is also based on the enforcement of human rights and freedoms. This applies especially to the legal status of the EU system after 1 December 2009, under the Lisbon Treaties and is reflected primarily in the Charter of Rights and Freedoms of the EU.[1]

10.02. The Council of Europe, as an international organization, has made a number of decisions and adopted many normative documents, which can be classified as 'declarations', or 'charters'. The contents of these declarations or charters significantly concern substantive law, that is fundamental principles, the law of institutions such as institutions of power and procedural relationships.[2] In itself, this phenomenon would not transgress potential international regulation in the form of treaties, if the contents of many of the treaties, charters or declarations of the Council of Europe did not exhibit principal features remarkably identical to the constitutional laws of contemporary constitutional democracies all over the world, i.e. parliamentary or presidential systems which regulate fundamental rights and freedoms.[3]

10.03. Every international treaty after the Second World War which concerned rights and freedoms has become part of the international

---

[1] The special dualism of the treaty systems of the Council of Europe and of the European Union has been analysed in KAREL KLÍMA et al., EVROPSKÉ PRÁVO [*European Law*], Plzeň: Aleš Čeněk 25 (2011).

[2] For a more detailed systematic analysis, see chapter '*Mezinárodněprávní impulsy pro ochranu lidských práv*' [*Impulses for the Protection of Human Rights under International Law*] *in* ALEŠ GERLOCH & PAVEL ŠTURMA et al., OCHRANA ZÁKLADNÍCH PRÁV A SVOBOD V PROMĚNÁCH PRÁVA NA POČÁTKU 21. STOLETÍ V ČESKÉM, EVROPSKÉM A MEZINÁRODNÍM KONTEXTU. [*Protection of Fundamental Rights and Freedoms in the Transformation of Law at the Beginning of the 21ˢᵗ Century in the Czech, European and International Context*], Prague: Auditorium 293 (2011); KAREL KLÍMA, ÚSTAVNÍ PRÁVO [*Constitutional Law*], Plzeň: Aleš Čeněk 173 (4th ed. 2010).

[3] This is particularly noticeable with respect to the international and political connotations of the process whereby the Czech and Slovak Federal Republic entered the Council of Europe in 1991. The European Convention on Human Rights and Fundamental Freedoms has become a profound model text for the adoption and contents of the Charter of Fundamental Rights and Freedoms as the new component of the constitutional foundations of the then Czechoslovakia.

potential of the law regulating the status of humans; consequently, an international or common system of values of a constitutional law nature has gradually developed.[4]

10.04. In the European context, the European Convention on Human Rights and Fundamental Freedoms serves as the basis for the 'conventionalization' of the individual branches of national law because the Member States are forced to abide by the constitutional principles enshrined in the Convention. Case law of the European Court of Human Rights (ECtHR) contributes to the juridization and constitutionalisation of the Convention. This process occurs as a result of the subsequent development of this system, based on an international treaty, by the autonomous and authentic interpretation of the European Court of Human Rights in individual cases when the Court is seized with applications lodged by natural and legal persons from the Member States.

II. Judicial System *Sui Generis*

10.05. If the rules of public international law evolve into a system which procedurally binds the Member States and, on top of that, accord procedural rights to entities of private law (natural and legal persons), they become an integral part of the '*ius cogens*' system. Applications filed by natural and legal persons challenge decisions made by public authorities of the individual Member States. This, in consequence, triggers the liabilities of the Member States under international law when the European Court of Human Rights reviews the compliance of such decisions with the values enshrined in the Convention.[5] Hence, the European Court of Human Rights reviews the compliance of the decisions, usually rendered by the last national judicial authority with which the application of the right to a fair trial ends within the respective country, with constitutional law. Such review is subsidiary and subordinate to the constitutionality of the Member States.[6]

---

[4]   Regarding this issue, see Bogusław Banaszak in: BOGUSŁAW BANASZAK, PRAWO KONSTYTUCYJNE, 4. wydanie, Warsaw: C.H.Beck 146 (2nd ed. 2008).

[5]   Concerning the developments in the Council of Europe as the control system for the protection of human rights in Europe, see Bożena Gronowska in: BOŻENA GRONOWSKA, EUROPEJSKI TRYBUNAL PRAW CZLOWIEKA W POSZUKIWANIU EFEKTYWNEJ OCHRONY PRAW JEDNOSTKI, Torun 34 (2011).

[6]   From the 47 Council of Europe Member States, this will usually apply to the supreme courts of the country or to constitutional courts which are even 'higher' in the constitutional hierarchy. If the necessity to exhaust national remedies applies to all judicial procedural remedies within the framework of specialized constitutional judiciary, which is

10.06. Liability of the individual Member States under international law is based on the enforceable decisions of the European Court of Human Rights, which has the nature of satisfaction. Symbolic satisfaction consists in the declaratory order of the decision, which reads as follows: 'The Member State violated the Convention in Article... by acts consisting in court decisions...' and is therefore 'ordered to pay' by the European Court of Human Rights. Nevertheless, the regime of applications filed under the Convention has the nature of declaratory complaints. The financial satisfaction determining the obligation of the states to pay a particular sum of money is principally limited to a compensation of legal costs; in other words, it definitely does not constitute court-ordered damages.[7]

10.07. The Council of Europe system built on the European Convention on Human Rights and Fundamental Freedoms is based on the effect of serving a natural or a legal person and on immediate enforceability. If an unequivocally international system such as the Council of Europe system is based on a materially legal and procedural convention, which the system employs as its source and interprets through decisions delivered by its own tribunal, it is possible to classify the system as a 'constitutional mechanism' *sui generis.*[8]

III. Provisions of the Convention and Their Nature as Substantive Constitutional Rules

10.08. The relationship between the values of constitutional law of sovereign democratic states and the values of public international law has undergone gradual development and approximation as well as mutual enrichment.[9] From a historical perspective, the first declarations of human rights, as national constitutional documents, served as the basis for constituting substantive international conventions – such as the 1948 Universal Declaration of Human Rights.

10.09. The European Convention on Fundamental Rights and Freedoms signed on 4 November 1950 by the Council of Europe Member States has been, from the very beginning, a 'European system' of a

---

a European and continental specialty, we can refer primarily to the Federal Republic of Germany, France, Italy, Spain, Poland and the Czech Republic.

[7] For more details, see the concept of judgments and decisions of the European Court of Human Rights in: KAREL KLÍMA et al., *supra* note 1, at 483.

[8] BOŻENA GRONOWSKA, TADEUSZ JASUDOWICZ, MICHAŁ BALCERZAK, MACIEJ LUBISZEWSKI & RAFAŁ MIZERSKI, PRAWA CZLOWIEKA I ICH OCHRONA, Torun 78 (2010).

[9] This has been pointed out by Tomáš Pezl in KAREL KLÍMA et al., *supra* note 1, at 38, where the author considers the common constitutional values of the Member States as the source of the European constitutionalism.

constitutional nature which influences democratic states. Moreover, it has explicitly endorsed this principle via the European Court of Human Rights.[10] Since its effective date, the Convention has been amended, supplemented and developed by 14 additional protocols, which significantly extend the material scope of the Convention from the perspective of the concept of constitutional law.[11] This is, in turn, reflected in the intensive and extensive interpretation of the additional Protocols by the European Court of Human Rights.[12]

10.10. Rights and freedoms provided for under the Convention are the 'rights of man and of the citizen' within the meaning of the 1789 French Declaration of the Rights of Man and of the Citizen. Hence, the rights are private (natural-law) and civil (political) in nature. Economic rights within the Council of Europe system are guaranteed by the European Social Charter. The concept of the Convention is therefore aimed at fundamental human rights and reflects constitutional national concepts which accentuate, at least in continental Europe, the natural-law nature of human rights including fundamental freedoms related to the right to life.

IV. Influence of the Jurisdiction Vested in the European Court of Human Rights on the Constitutional Systems Adopted in the Member States

10.11. The case law of the European Court of Human Rights influences legal systems in the individual Member States and is reflected in various branches of the national legal system, not only in the substantive provisions of constitutional law. The case law in itself creates a certain monolithic legal system founded on the categories of constitutional law. Examples are in the areas of division of power, rule of law, liability of public officials and authorities, independence of the judiciary, administrative law and procedural relations, the interpretation of classical principles of criminal law and the organization of the judiciary and implementation of specific procedural judicial principles such as equality of arms, equal standing of the parties and the right to legal assistance. It also penetrates categories of private law, for instance, the gradual development of case law relating to the concept of privacy,

---

[10] See the ECtHR decision in *Loizidou* v *Turkey* 15318/89 (1995).

[11] We can argue more specifically with Additional Protocol 1, which confirms the conventional concept of the 'right to one's possessions' and the concept of the protection of possessions (ownership).

[12] For instance, we will endeavour to support this by the development of the concept of protection of privacy in the case law of the European Court of Human Rights.

freedom of thought, protection of the family and the right to one's possessions (ownership rights).[13]

10.12. The analytical and synthetical processes applied by constitutional law have for several years continuously enabled us to organize a textbook 'case law' system in the area of human rights, which is based on the case law of the European Court of Human Rights.[14] The overall concept of the case law allows us to summarize a certain concept of the European rule of law model[15] and, consequently, also the European dimension of constitutional and legal systems of the Member States.[16]

V. Right to Life as a Supreme European Principle of a Constitutional Nature

10.13. The right to life represents the basic axiomatic premise of the traditional concepts of fundamental human rights. It is the fundamental premise of personal rights which protects the most important values of human existence.[17] In line with the above concept, the Convention incorporates the right to life in Article 2; this means that a signatory state is bound to adopt the relevant constitutional and statutory rules regulating the guaranties of the right. The right to life cannot be derogated from even in a state of national emergency or at

---

[13] The 'reserved' legal relationship of Great Britain to the binding nature and the contents of the Convention under international and constitutional law can be considered as rather specific and conditioned by the different history and legal culture of the English common law system, cf.

ANDRZEJ BISZTYGA, ODDZIALYWANIE EUROPEJSKIEJ KONWENCJI PRAW CZLOWIEKA NA PORZADEK PRAWNY ZJEDNOCZONEGO KROLEWSTWA, Katowice (2008).

[14] Principles concerning the protection of enjoyment of one's possessions have been introduced by Article 1 of the Additional Protocol 1 to the Convention.

[15] We, naturally, do not dismiss the different history, legal system, judicial system and legal customs in countries such as Great Britain and Scandinavia, and the often unstable social concept of justice and the structure of courts in the countries of Eastern Europe, non-European countries such as Azerbaijan, Turkey, etc. For more details concerning the phenomenon of the English constitutionalism, especially the phenomenon of constitutional conventions and, primarily, the process and the concept of 'devolution', see KAREL KÍMA, O PRÁVU ÚSTAVNÍM, [About Constitutional Law]. Prague: Wolters Kluwer ČR 184 (2012).

[16] See also the treatise on the internationalisation of human rights in LADISLAV OROSZ, JÁN SVÁK, BORIS BALOG, ZÁKLADY TEÓRIE KONŠTITUCIONALIZMU [Basic Elements of the Theory of Constitutionalism], Bratislava: Eurokodex, s.r.o. 216 (2nd ed. 2012).

[17] Concerning the constitutional concept of the right to life in its constitutional application in the European concept and context in the Charter of Fundamental Rights and Freedoms of the Czech Republic, see in: KAREL KLÍMA et al., KOMENTÁŘ K ÚSTAVĚ A LISTINĚ [Commentary on the Constitution and the Charter], Plzeň: Aleš Čeněk 1971 (2nd ed. 2009).

war. Nevertheless, it is generally accepted that the law on armed conflicts under public international law provides details regarding permitted and prohibited methods of warfare, with the exception of death resulting from permitted acts of war.[18]

10.14. In this connection, the case law of the European Court of Human Rights primarily accentuates the vertical and horizontal effects of the right to life. This means that, on the one hand, public administration authorities are prohibited from causing any violation of the right. At the same time, they are obliged to pay every attention to cases in which such acts occur, whether in public-law relationships (in vertical relations between the state and the natural/legal persons subjected to the state under public law)[19] or in private-law relationships (in relations where the parties have equal procedural standing.)[20] Moreover, public administration authorities are always obliged to examine, in all procedural public-law relations regulated under the law, whether all procedural requirements were fulfilled, which are prescribed for the given proceedings designed to clarify events associated with the deprivation of life, i.e. whether the investigation was conducted properly and in a manner corresponding to the significance of the event.[21] The case law of the European Court of Human Rights has also derived responsibility of the state for the protection of life, which extends to any person in the territory and subject to the jurisdiction of the state, comprising also the responsibility of the state for a threat posed to the life of its inhabitants, including natural disasters, industrial accidents, terrorist activity, etc.

10.15. As an international regional organization, the Council of Europe has a unique constitutional law position due to the fact that it has adopted and stipulated as mandatory the principle prohibiting the death penalty. This concept has also undergone certain developments: the gradual abandonment of this absolute penalty has gradually prevailed in Europe because of the irreparability of such a decision in the case of a judicial error. These developments are reflected in the Convention

[18] Cf. MIROSLAV POTOČNÝ, JAN ONDŘEJ, MEZINÁRODNÍ PRÁVO VEŘEJNÉ, ZVLÁŠTNÍ ČÁST, [*Public International Law. Special Part*]. Prague: C. H. Beck, 444 (2006).
[19] For an illustration of this relationship of 'superiority' established by law, see the system of enforceability of taxes by financial administration authorities and, if necessary, by courts.
[20] This would include any contractual relationship of a civil law nature between private persons.
[21] For more details, see the case law interpretation of this concept in: ELIŠKA WAGNEROVÁ, VOJTĚCH ŠIMÍČEK, TOMÁŠ LANGÁŠEK, & IVO POSPÍŠIL et al., LISTINA ZÁKLADNÍCH PRÁV A SVOBOD. KOMENTÁŘ [*Charter of Fundamental Rights and Freedoms. Commentary*], Prague: Wolters Kluwer ČR, a.s. 186 (2012).

mechanism, specifically in the Additional Protocols. The death penalty was initially permitted during war or when faced with imminent threat, and subsequently eliminated entirely.[22] This has consequently resulted in elimination of the death penalty from individual national laws.[23]

10.16. The European Court of Human Rights has held that the right to life does not entail the right to death. Nonetheless, the European Court has not prohibited national laws regulating **euthanasia**. It has not, however, found any direct support for euthanasia in the Convention either. Hence, the individual Member States exhibit significant differences as concerns the legal rules regarding euthanasia. This also applies to the issue of induced termination of a pregnancy, but the European Court of Human Rights excludes the prohibition of abortions.

10.17. Article 2 of the Convention also allows the possibility of an unintended deprivation of life as a result of specific acts defined in the provision that involves the use of force, which is no more than absolutely necessary. The first element to be evaluated is the permissibility of the intervention based on the assessment of absolute necessity. The factors to be assessed include the legality of the intervention and proper investigation of the matter. The force used must be no more than absolutely necessary to fulfil its purpose. This is the test of absolute necessity. Acts aimed against life which involve the use of force include the defence of any person against unlawful violence in the area of horizontal rights, (necessary defence and extreme necessity under Czech law),[24] effecting a lawful arrest or preventing an attack by a detained person (through public authorities) in the area of vertical effects, and action lawfully taken by public administration authorities for the purpose of quelling a riot or insurrection. If the assembly of people in a public place, a demonstration, is part of the system of democracy, the public administration protects the freedom of speech exercised by the demonstrators by its passive presence and by the physical separation of groups which express contrary opinions at the same place. This is the freedom of counter-demonstration.

10.18. The concepts of the Convention which prohibit torture and inhuman or degrading treatment in Article 3 primarily ensure that the state must guarantee conditions compatible with the understanding of human

---

[22] Cf. Protocol 6 of 1983 and Protocol 13 of 2002.

[23] In the Czech and Slovak Federal Republics, it was part of the application process whereby the former Czechoslovakia wished to enter the Council of Europe in 1992, when the enforcement of decisions with already imposed death sentences was suspended and subsequently changed.

[24] For more details, see in: KAREL KLÍMA, *supra* note 2, at 282.

dignity. Acts of the state must not exceed the inevitable degree of harshness and stress inflicted on a given person. The Convention allows no restrictions of or exceptions to that right; it is therefore an absolutely un-restrainable right. The case law implementing the Convention is primarily focused on guaranties enjoyed by persons who were in good health when imprisoned and whose body showed evidence of physical injuries after they were released from prison. Any treatment or punishment is humiliating if it is aimed at degrading human dignity, if it induces fear or feelings of inferiority in the victim or their debasement or humiliation.

10.19. Bad treatment inflicted by parents on their children must attain a certain minimal degree of gravity to fall within this definition, the determination of which depends on each individual case, such as the nature of the punishment and its physical and mental effects. As concerns medical treatment, the main focus is on cases of a failure to provide adequate medical care and on the special assessment of the ability of mentally ill persons to defend themselves against humiliating treatment.

10.20. The concept of the prohibition of slavery, servitude and forced labour under Article 4 of the Convention protects men and women both in vertical and horizontal relationships. The prohibition of slavery and servitude as the Convention's absolute imperative is based on the all-encompassing principle of equality of all people. In practice, it applies to any and all forms of home slavery or labour under exploitative conditions, abuse of dependent persons in social distress, etc. Forced labour is deemed to include any labour which is involuntary or has no basis in the legal system. Both the Convention and the European Court of Human Rights principally leave any statutory exceptions for the determination of ordered labour to the individual legal systems adopted by the Member States; it must not involve any servitude, slavery or degrading labour.[25]

10.21. 'Forced or compulsory labour' does not include work required to be done in prison or during conditional release from such detention, any service of a military character or service exacted instead of compulsory military service and service exacted in case of an emergency or calamity, such as in exceptional situations of civil emergencies. Prohibited compulsory labour does not include services which form part of civic obligations such as acts relating to a failure to provide help.

---

[25] In the Czech legal system, this applies to the statutory conditions for imposing a sentence of community work and the issue of potential mandatory labour for prisoners or persons detained in custody.

VI. European Concept of Liberty and Security of Persons

10.22. The right to liberty and security of the person under Article 5 of the Convention belongs to the most frequently employed provisions in the case law of the European Court of Human Rights[26] and in the case law of those Member States[27] that have constitutional courts. Liberty is interpreted as the integrity of the person in the physical and mental context. Security of the person is interpreted as the guaranties provided by the state when interfering with the liberty of the individual, both by the state and in relations with other persons. The Convention defines the areas of permitted interference when the individual's liberty can be encroached upon. The prohibition of imprisonment for debts has been articulated as a specifically forbidden method of deprivation of liberty by a European contractual instruction directed against national legislation. This entails an obligation of the Member States to make sure that the obligation to pay debts arising from legal contractual relationships cannot be subject to imprisonment under criminal law.

10.23. With respect to permitted methods of intervention, the Convention requires mainly legality and legal application of the national law by state authorities. The legality of the deprivation of liberty consists of two requirements: (i) adherence to the applicable procedural mechanisms introduced by the particular state, but also (ii) adequate procedural quality of national law. For instance, statutes must honour the requirements of giving due reasons for an arrest. Public administration is also responsible for proper investigation of a matter, allowing for due clarification. All permissible interventions are also legitimised by the protection of values in the public interest. Measures adopted by the states against terrorism have recently necessitated increased point-blank approaches and prevention of state power in Europe. This has significantly affected the interpretation of the system of security and un-touchability of persons.[28]

---

[26] Concerning case law, see the causal orientation and analysis in KAREL KLÍMA et al. *supra* note 1, at 495.

[27] Concerning case law in the commentary to Article 8 of the Charter, see in ELIŠKA WAGNEROVÁ, VOJTĚCH ŠIMÍČEK, TOMÁŠ LANGÁŠEK, & IVO POSPÍŠIL et al., *supra* note 21, at 218.

[28] The author's view is, in this sense, concentrated in the chapter '*Constitutionality and Terrorism: A Comparative View*' in JOSEF BLAHOŽ et al., DEMOCRACY AND ISSUES OF LEGAL POLICY IN FIGHTING TERRORISM: A COMPARISON, Prague: Wolters Kluwer Czech Republic 101 (2009).

10.24. The recent concept of the Convention provides for the following permitted interventions of state power in the sphere of liberty and security of persons:

- Imprisonment is lawful after conviction by a competent court, which has substantive-law aspects such as a criminal offence defined by the law and procedural-law aspects. On the one hand, criminal procedure is governed by procedures aimed at proving the person's guilt, and on the other hand, the person has a guaranteed possibility to defend themselves and prove their innocence. The exclusivity of state power based on the protection of public interests against criminal activities guarantees that the only authority which makes decisions regarding a person's guilt is the court and that the assignment of the case to a particular judge will be free of any improper manipulations with the process.
- Any arrest is justified by fulfilment of the intentions of the law or any other fulfilment of obligations by that person. Consequently, it usually serves as a security measure because the person is suspected of having committed a criminal offence, of having expressed their intention to commit a criminal offence, or they are suspected of the intention to go into hiding after committing a criminal offence.
- A minor can also be deprived of their liberty if such arrest or detention is effected for the purpose of educational supervision. A minor cannot be held liable for a criminal offence and the detention can therefore only serve the purpose of education and supervision; the measure is also penal in nature.
- It is also possible to legally detain persons suspected of spreading infectious diseases, persons of unsound mind, alcoholics, drug addicts or vagrants. These are conventional measures of, generally, a social and protective character. The European Court of Human Rights emphasises the protective and, especially, the therapeutic purpose of these measures, which purpose must not be replaced or interchanged.[29]
- Lawful arrest of a person to prevent their entry into the country, which is related to foreigners and asylum law and is also associated with the potential extradition of persons. It also applies to the extradition or deportation custody.

10.25. Whereas an arrest as an instrument for detaining a person usually does not last very long, detention of a person in custody frequently means detention for many months, which fundamentally interferes with the person's life, despite the fact that the law considers the person innocent

---

[29] For an analysis of causal case law, see a more detailed commentary in: LADISLAV OROSZ, JÁN SVÁK, BORIS BALOG, *supra* note 16, at 234.

and not convicted. The gravity of the impact on the entire privacy of the person is comparable to a sentence of imprisonment. The European Court of Human Rights considers the policy adopted by the individual Member States in the area of custody in the criminal process as the most important factor and it also constitutes the most frequently assessed interference with personal liberty.[30] It has been undergoing continuous developments and has also been reflected in the practices of the Member States. The Court has especially emphasized that decisions on custody must be proportionate to the necessity of interfering with the person's liberty. It is necessary to honour, as much as possible, the rights of detainees and strictly adhere to the statutory requirements of custody during criminal prosecutions. It is also necessary to give precedence to any decisions regarding custody.[31]

10.26. As concerns the containment of an infectious disease, the protection of the person requires that due attention is paid to properly distinguishing situations which concern a person who has contracted, or who is suspected of having contracted, an infectious disease, or even a person capable of transmitting the disease. An active disease stage is not a requirement for a permitted intervention because the purpose is to prevent the spreading of an infectious disease.

VII. Freedom of Thought, Conscience and Religion, and the Right to Education

10.27. Despite the fact that the inner thoughts of any person are autonomous and undiscoverable without using violence and even entirely intimate, the Convention guarantees those aspects of the freedom which concern the expression of thoughts and which constitute social orientation and thereby guarantee tolerance with respect to one's philosophical convictions. This entails, primarily, the freedom of not being subordinated to the majority. The freedom of religion in the case law of the European Court of Human Rights is reflected especially in the sphere of guaranties for the expression of one's religious beliefs and in the circumstances of religious education, primarily at state schools.[32]

---

[30] A well-structured analysis and commentary is presented by Eva Hubálková *in* EVROPSKÁ ÚMLUVA O LIDSKÝCH PRÁVECH A ČESKÁ REPUBLIKA. JUDIKATURA A ŘÍZENÍ PŘED EVROPSKÝM SOUDEM PRO LIDSKÁ PRÁVA [*European Convention on Human Rights and the Czech Republic. Case Law and Proceedings at the European Court of Human Rights*], Prague: Linde 115 (2003).

[31] See an analytical treatise in: KAREL KLÍMA et al., *supra* note 1, at 496.

[32] Concerning this issue, see also the ECtHR ruling in *Lautsi* v *Italy* 30814/06 (2009), available at: http://hudoc.echr.coe.int/sites/eng/pages/search.aspx?i=001-104040#{"itemid": ["001-104040"]} (accessed on 15 November 2013) or *Kymlia and others* v *Russia* (2009).

10.28. Education is an integral part of the cultural basis of people's lives. Article 2 of Additional Protocol 1 stipulates that no one can be denied the right to an education. The rights of parents to ensure the education and teaching of their children in conformity with their religious and philosophical convictions must be observed in any functions which the state exercises in the area of education and teaching. The European Court of Human Rights is often overwhelmed with applications that involve the rights to education in situations related to ethnic issues, especially discrimination, as well as in situations when the parents demand that their children be educated in conformity with their own religious beliefs. The case law of the European Court of Human Rights in the area of education has evolved in favour of those who protect these rights against various factual obstacles which prevent their exercise.[33]

VIII. Private and Family Life and Their Contents According to the European Approach

10.29. The right to respect for one's private and family life is provided in Article 8 of the Convention. It prohibits state authorities from interfering with one's private and family life, their home and correspondence. Only those cases which concern the interests of national security, protection of health, order and morals, stipulated by law, permit interference by the state in this area. The European Court of Human Rights has held that the law or statute must be precise, specific and must provide for the circumstances, as well as the precise manner of the interference in privacy.[34] Implementing legislation is not sufficient. Another decisive aspect is the necessity of the measure and its proportionality in relation to a specific situation. Contracting States are obliged to refrain from interfering with one's privacy unless permitted to do so by the law, but they are also obliged to adopt active and positive measures which will ensure that one's privacy is actually guaranteed.[35]

---

[33] This applies especially to the situation of the Roma people in the Czech Republic, *D. H. and others* v *Czech Republic* 57325/00 (2007), available at: http://hudoc.echr.coe.int/sites/eng/pages/search.aspx?i=001-83256#{"itemid":["001-83256"]} (accessed on 15 November 2013) concerning the integration of the Roma people in the Czech system of education.

[34] Concerning this issue, cf. also the case and the ECtHR ruling in *Khan* v *United Kingdom* 35394/97 (2000), available at: http://hudoc.echr.coe.int/sites/eng/pages/search.aspx?i=001-58841#{"itemid":["001-58841"]} (accessed on 15 November 2013).

[35] See the ECtHR ruling in *Niemitz* v *Germany* 13710/88 (1992), available at: http://hudoc.echr.coe.int/sites/eng/pages/search.aspx?i=001-57887#{"itemid":["001-57887"]} (accessed on 15 November 2013).

10.30. The text of the Convention distinguishes four separate rights in connection with the protection of privacy. First and foremost, it is the definition of the concept of 'private life' which resists any all-encompassing definition. The European Court of Human Rights has held that private life includes both physical and intellectual integrity, the life of inner thoughts of men and women and their own behaviour, as well as family relationships and other outside relationships. The concept of private life is an open system, which has been constantly expanding on the basis of the ECtHR case law. Consequently, the ECtHR has held that this category also includes the right of an individual to a favourable environment, and any serious interference in this sphere jeopardizes not only the health of the individual but also their private and family wellbeing. The ECtHR has also included in this category a father's right to dispute his paternity.[36]

10.31. The right to respect for one's family life under the Convention and in the ECtHR case law means that the state has the obligation to adopt positive measures in order to make sure that individuals have the opportunity to lead normal family lives. This also includes the right of parents to see their children and the obligation of the state to enable the exercise of this right. Family life also includes relationships with more distant relatives and the right to marry and raise a family.

10.32. The right to respect for one's home and correspondence under the Convention is a specific determination of the sphere of privacy. Home includes both the physical space for living and the right to use this space. The concept of home according to the ECtHR case law has been interpreted by the Court very extensively. The Court has also included business premises or offices in which the person conducts their profession. Interference with the right to respect for one's correspondence consists primarily in the illegal interception of telephone calls unless with a legitimate objective and in compliance with the principle of proportionality.[37]

---

[36] *Guerra* v *Italy* 116/1996/735/932 (1998), available at: http://hudoc.echr.coe.int/sites/eng/pages/search.aspx?i=001-58135#{"itemid":["001-58135"]} (accessed on 15 November 2013) *and Bronda* v *Italy* 22430/93 (1998), available at: http://hudoc.echr.coe.int/sites/eng/pages/search.aspx?i=001-58194#{"itemid":["001-58194"]} (accessed on 15 November 2013).

[37] Concerning this issue, study the ECtHR rulings in *P.G. and J.H.* v *United Kingdom* 44787/98 (2001), available at: http://sim.law.uu.nl/sim/caselaw/Hof.nsf/1d4d0dd240bfee7ec12568490035df05/a65e53da8cc8fdedc1256ad300297be7?OpenDocument (accessed on 15 November 2013), *Kruslin and Huvig* v *France* (1990), available at: (accessed on 15 November 2013) and *Heglas* v *Czech Republic* (2007), available at: (accessed on 15 November 2013).

IX. Freedom of Movement and Residence According to the European Approach

10.33. Freedom of movement and residence pursuant to Article 2 of Additional Protocol 4 represents an integral part of general freedom. It especially entails the right to choose one's home country. Freedom of movement also means the right to move within the territory of the state and to cross freely the borders of the state. Freedom of residence represents the right of any person to reside and settle down freely in any place. Freedom of movement and residence result in the right to choose one's residence, freedom to leave the country and prohibitions of depriving citizens of their citizenship and of preventing nationals from returning to their home country. At the same time, there is no right to asylum and no right to maintain one's residence in a country which was previously permitted.[38]

X. Right to Possessions and Its Definition under the Convention

10.34. Additional Protocol 1 stipulates that every natural or legal person is entitled to peaceful enjoyment of their possessions and they shall not be deprived of their possessions except in the public interest and subject to the conditions provided for by law. This concept especially guarantees that taxes and fees owed to the state and prescribed by the law will be duly paid. 'Possessions' are interpreted extensively and include both existing property and property values including receivables, which the respective person can legitimately hope for and expect. However, 'possessions' do not include every claimed ownership title, especially the original title which could not be effectively exercised, nor a receivable which expired as a result of non-fulfilment of a prescribed condition.[39]

---

[38] Concerning the issue of freedom of cross border movement, refugees, asylum, extradition and deportation of foreigners, see the extensive case law of the ECtHR such as the rulings of the Court in *James and others* v *United Kingdom* 8793/79 (1986), available at: http://sim.law.uu.nl/sim/caselaw/Hof.nsf/1d4d0dd240bfee7ec12568490035df05/0ef9f8927 a96c5a5c1256640004c2410?OpenDocument (accessed on 15 November 2013), *Moustaquin* v *Belgium* 12313/86 (1991), available at: http://hudoc.echr.coe.int/sites/eng/pages/ search.aspx?i=001-57652#{"itemid":["001-57652"]} (accessed on 15 November 2013), *Cruz Varas* v *Sweden* 15576/89 (1991), available at: http://hudoc.echr.coe.int/sites/eng/pages/ search.aspx?i=001-57674#{"itemid":["001-57674"]} (accessed on 15 November 2013), *Bozano* v *France* 9990/82 (1986), available at: http://hudoc.echr.coe.int/sites/eng/pages/search. aspx?i=001-57448#{"itemid":["001-57448"]} (accessed on 15 November 2013) and others.

[39] See *Prince Hans-Adam II. of Liechtenstein* v *Germany* 42527/98 (2001), available at: http://sim.law.uu.nl/sim/caselaw/Hof.nsf/1d4d0dd240bfee7ec12568490035df05/2212a90d 7e9c9037c1256a88003af7f9?OpenDocument (accessed on 15 November 2013).

10.35. As concerns the scope of the subject matter to which the right to possess and the right to the protection of possessions relate, the range of types and forms of possessions is very broad: movable and immovable things, tangible and intangible rights, copyrights, patents, inventions and trademarks, monetary claims arising from contractual obligations, delicts, unjust enrichment and claims for damages, insurance and pension claims.

10.36. The Convention covers the protection of property possessed by private persons – natural and legal persons. It does not extend to persons of a public-law nature, such as the state and its branches or local self-government organizations and entities. But it guarantees not only the protection of possessions in vertical relationships, (relationships between the state and a private entity), but also the protection of possessions in horizontal private-law relationships.[40]

10.37. The Convention mandates that any interference in ownership rights must comply with the law and have a legitimate objective. The guarantee of ownership does not prevent the states from depriving a private person of their possessions, but allows such interference only in the public interest. At the same time, government interference in the private sphere of ownership must preserve a reasonable relation of proportionality between the requirements of public interest of the society and the need to protect the fundamental rights of the entity. It includes nationalisation, expropriation and confiscation of property. Restitutions constitute a special category of deprivation of one's possessions. The European Court of Human Rights does not restrict the possibility of Member States determining the scope of application of their restitution laws.[41]

XI. Political Rights under the Convention

10.38. The European Court of Human Rights has held that democracy is the only political model on which the Convention is based and which is compatible with the Convention's institutions and functioning.[42] Consequently, the Convention, specifically Article 3 of Protocol 1, poses the right to free elections by secret ballot as a fundamental

---

[40] Judgments in *Velosa Barreto* v *Portugal* 40/1994/487/569 (1995), available at: http://echr.ketse.com/doc/18072.91-en-19951121/view/ (accessed on 15 November 2013) and *Spadea and Scalabrino* v *Italy* 12868/87 (1995), available at: http://sim.law.uu.nl/sim/caselaw/Hof.nsf/1d4d0dd240bfee7ec12568490035df05/a1fefa80651306bdc1256640004c2c89?OpenDocument (accessed on 15 November 2013).

[41] For an exemplary decision in this regard, see *Jantner* v *Slovakia* 39050/97 (2003), available at: http://hudoc.echr.coe.int/sites/eng/pages/search.aspx?i=001-60964#{"itemid": ["001-60964"]} (accessed on 15 November 2013).

[42] For more details, see KAREL KLÍMA et al., *supra* note 1, at 534.

condition of democracy. In this connection, the Contracting States have undertaken the obligation to hold free elections at reasonable intervals by secret ballot. Hence, the context of the Convention is primarily an obligation for the Contracting States.

10.39. Freedom of expression is, above all, a subjective right of a public-law nature and the state is expected to refrain from hindering the expression of opinions. The concept of freedom of expression protects individuals from government interventions; it is not to prevent nationals from expressing their opinions.

10.40. The European Court of Human Rights accentuates the role of free media in a democratic society as the main guarantor of the imparting of information and ideas relating to the public interest, which enables an informed participation of citizens in public life.[43]

10.41. The ECtHR has expressed a rather strange opinion regarding the freedom of privacy and the right to information with respect to public political officials. The Court has ruled that the privacy of a public official enjoys a lower degree of protection because their life, behaviour and incomes must be exposed to critical assessment and civil control within the framework of a democratic discussion. As concerns employees in public administration, the permitted degree of their activity is also broader than in the case of other citizens, but not so broad as applied to elected officials.[44] But the Convention permits a restriction of the freedom of expression with respect to courts in the interest of impartiality and independence of the judiciary; similarly, the Court does not protect expressions directed against the democratic foundations of the society.

10.42. An important jurisdiction of the European Court of Human Rights is aimed at restrictions imposed on the protection of freedom of speech in favour of personal rights. The Court distinguishes between the spreading of information regarding political topics and the transmission of information and data from the private life of a person who holds no offices and takes no part in politics. As concerns the determination of the concept of information in the area of morals, the case law of the ECtHR is open to the autonomy of the Member States in determining what is necessary from the perspective of the common national moral culture.[45]

---

[43] Cf. *Bladet Tromso and Stansaas* v *Norway* 21980/93 (1999), available at: http://hudoc.echr.coe.int/sites/eng/pages/search.aspx?i=001-58369#{"itemid":["001-58369"]} (accessed on 15 November 2013).

[44] See *Lingens* v *Austria* 9815/82 (1986), available at: http://hudoc.echr.coe.int/sites/eng/pages/search.aspx?i=001-57523 (accessed on 15 November 2013).

[45] See *Bergens Tidende* v *Norway* 26132/95 (2000), available at: http://hudoc.echr.coe.int/sites/eng/pages/search.aspx?i=001-58797#{"itemid":["001-58797"]} (accessed on 15 November 2013).

10.43. Freedom of assembly pursuant to Article 11 of the Convention must be interpreted as making space for a public discussion, as well as expressing one's protest of public affairs. The protection only extends to peaceful assembly. The state is also obliged to secure protection of the assembly against potential attacks by opponents. [46] Prohibition of an assembly as a preventive measure should be adopted by the state only exceptionally and only if the assembly is aimed at inciting violence and endangering human rights for whatever reason.

10.44. The existence of the freedom of association is a necessary prerequisite for the proper functioning of a democratic pluralistic and competitive society and for exercising voting rights. This particular right is based on the freedom to set up legal persons to implement a common interest. The concept of 'assembly' is an autonomous privilege of the Member States.[47] The Convention does not provide any specific protection to political parties, but such parties can invoke protection the same as any other association. The state is also forbidden from interfering in the formation of trade unions. The Convention provides no protection to public-law associations; it focuses strictly on private-law organizations, including political parties. Any interference in the freedom of association must be legal, adequate and tied to the assessment of compatibility of the association with the concept of a democratic society; such assessment also extends to the actual activities conducted by the association, whether they comply with the democratic model, or not.[48]

XII. Procedural Guaranties of Enforceability of Rights and Freedoms

10.45. The substantive provisions of the Convention set forth human rights and freedoms as the fundamental legal rules. However, they also focus on the procedural guaranties of enforceability of these rights and freedoms. All these issues, provided for in Article 6(1) of the Convention, are concentrated on the principle of 'access to court'.

---

[46] See *Baczkowski v Poland* 1543/06 (2007), available at: http://hudoc.echr.coe.int/sites/eng/pages/search.aspx?i=001-80464#{"itemid":["001-80464"]} (accessed on 15 November 2013).

[47] *Gorzelik and others v Poland* 44158/98 (2004), available at: http://sim.law.uu.nl/sim/caselaw/Hof.nsf/1d4d0dd240bfee7ec12568490035df05/7daf288aa7ad9d42c1256b43004ad9a2?OpenDocument (accessed on 15 November 2013).

[48] *Ezelin v France* (1991), available at: http://hudoc.echr.coe.int/sites/eng/pages/search.aspx?i=001-57675#{"itemid":["001-57675"]} (accessed on 15 November 2013), *Sidiropoulos and others v Greece* 26695/95 (1998), available at: http://sim.law.uu.nl/sim/caselaw/Hof.nsf/1d4d0dd240bfee7ec12568490035df05/ca358bcc0397faf3c1256650002b2998?OpenDocument (accessed on 15 November 2013).

Hence, the Convention bases the procedural guaranties of enforceability of the rights and freedoms on the concept of a functioning system of courts. In the tradition of the English, French and Austrian development of the judiciary, this synthetises the idea of special and independent public authorities, in the form of courts.[49] The concept of the Convention then develops the model of a quality court procedure based on a meticulous implementation of certain principles typical for court proceedings (see below) and the right of every natural or legal person to an effective legal remedy.

10.46. The right to an effective legal remedy, guaranteed under Article 13 of the Convention, is a general guarantee intended for anyone whose rights and freedoms were violated.[50] Specifically, the Convention orders the Member States to provide effective legal instruments to a person at the national level, which the person could use before a national authority in order to invoke the protection of their rights which have been violated. It means that the natural or legal person who invokes the protection of their rights guaranteed by the Convention ought to have at their disposal remedies applicable before the 'national' authority so that the authority could decide on the person's claim for compensation for damages and losses. Hence, it is up to the individual constitutional systems how they organize their respective judiciary, or rather the control mechanism of legal guaranties, in order to meet this obligation.

10.47. First and foremost, the remedy must be effective. That is that it must be an instrument capable of terminating or remedying an interference or error committed by a public authority, or capable of providing an adequate compensation or satisfaction for the breach. The concept of an effective remedy can also be interpreted as a collection of various consecutive remedies. [51]

10.48. Article 6 of the Convention provides for the right to a fair trial, the essence of which is the right to a court hearing concerning both civil claims and obligations and the subject matter of criminal procedure. Gradual cultivation of this concept by the European Court of Human Rights and its practical interpretation on the basis of complaints

---

[49] Concerning the phenomenon of English constitutionalism, cf. in: KAREL KLÍMA, O PRÁVU ÚSTAVNÍM [*About Constitutional Law*], Praha: Wolters Kluwer C□eská republika (2012).

[50] See *Klas and others* v *Federal Republic of Germany* (1978), available at: (accessed on 15 November 2013).

[51] Cf. *Leander* v *Sweden* 9248/81 (1978), available at: http://hudoc.echr.coe.int/sites/eng/pages/search.aspx?i=001-57519#{"itemid":["001-57519"]} (accessed on 15 November 2013) and *Valsamis* v *Greece* 21787/93 (1996), available at: http://hudoc.echr.coe.int/sites/eng/pages/search.aspx?i=001-58011#{"itemid":["001-58011"]} (accessed on 15 November 2013).

generated by various judicial systems in the individual Member States have contributed to the development of the concept of the rule of law and especially the degree of legality of court actions and the separation of the judiciary from the legislature and executive branches of government.[52]

10.49. The concept of Article 6 of the Convention covers several principles governing court procedure. The fundamental principle is the obligation to ensure access to court as such. The purpose of the right of access to court is to make sure that every natural and legal person has the opportunity to enforce their right before an independent and impartial tribunal and become a party to the proceedings, as well as to make sure that the court proceedings take place.[53] It is also necessary to guarantee the right to a subsequent review of the decision adopted by the trial court. The concept of the Convention guarantees the possibility of appellate court proceedings and a limited reviewability of court decisions. This concept also guarantees impartial decision-making by the judge, which is based not only on the exclusion of their bias, but also on the exclusion of any outside influences which could affect the decisions made by the judge, whether influenced by undue pressure, corruption or other factors.

10.50. The main principles stipulated by Article 6 of the Convention and subsequently developed in the ECtHR case law include the principle of equality of arms, the principle of making decisions within a 'reasonable' time and the principle of a public hearing. The principle of equality of arms guarantees to each party that they will have the same rights as their opponent and that each party has the same access to information on the basis of which the court decides. Reasonability of the time within which the decision of the court is to be made is rational and reasonable, providing any circumstances and reasons are excluded which prolong the proceedings and which are caused either by the court authorities or by the parties. State power therefore assumes responsibility only for delays caused by judicial authorities. The principle of public hearings provides a twofold guaranty. First, there is a guaranty to the parties that the process will be objective, and second, a guaranty to the public that they will have access to information. This

---

[52]   *Albert and Le Compte* v *Belgium* 7299/75; 7496/76 (1982), available at: http://hudoc.echr. coe.int/sites/eng/pages/search.aspx?i=001-57422#{"itemid":["001-57422"]} (accessed on 15 November 2013).

[53]   See also *Findlay* v *United Kingdom* 22107/93 (1997), available at: http://hudoc.echr. coe.int/sites/eng/pages/search.aspx?i=001-58016#{"itemid":["001-58016"]} (accessed on 15 November 2013).

principle also comprises the principle of verbal hearings in the trial (first-instance) court.[54]

10.51. The criminal law aspects of the right to a fair trial also guarantee the right to demand that any decision of state power is duly reasoned if the decision restricts a person's liberty such as by arrest, custody, imprisonment and other types of detention measures implemented by the state. It also guarantees the right to be informed promptly, in a language or translated which they understands and in detail, of the accusation, the right to legal assistance in the pre-trial criminal proceedings, the right to have adequate time for the preparation of defence, the right to confront witnesses and the unconditional right to have one's case reviewed by a court of appeals. [55]

10.52. Article 5(5) of the Convention guarantees the right to compensation for everyone who has been the victim of unlawful custody or imprisonment or any other interference of a public authority in their fundamental human rights. However, breach of this Article must be preceded by a court-pronounced breach of any provision of Article 5 which guarantees liberty and personal security. Member States are obliged to adopt legal rules which ensure the enforceability of this right at the national level.[56]

XIII. Jurisprudence of the European Court of Human Rights and Its Application by the Constitutional Court of the Czech Republic

10.53. The example of the Czech Republic, as a Council of Europe Member State, can serve as a helpful illustration of how the case law concept of an international tribunal whose decisions are directly binding can be conceptually developed in the national constitutional system. The example summarizes a significant part of the decisions adopted by the Constitutional Court of the Czech Republic, namely the right to a fair trial in terms of the interpretation of Article 6 of the Convention.[57]

---

[54]   *Axen v Federal Republic of Germany* 8273/78 (1983), available at: http://echr.ketse.com/ doc/8273.78-en-19831208/view/ (accessed on 15 November 2013) or *Ezelin v France* 11800/85 (1994), available at: http://hudoc.echr.coe.int/sites/eng/pages/search.aspx?i =001-57675#{"itemid":["001-57675"]} (accessed on 15 November 2013).

[55]   *Van den Hurk v Holland* 16034/90 (1994), available at: http://hudoc.echr.coe. int/sites/eng/pages/search.aspx?i=001-57878#{"itemid":["001-57878"]} (accessed on 15 November 2013).

[56]   Cf. *Hornsby v Greece* 18357/91 (1996), available at: http://hudoc.echr.coe.int/sites/eng/ pages/search.aspx?i=001-58020#{"itemid":["001-58020"]} (accessed on 15 November 2013).

[57]   For the first synthetic treatise on this issue in the Czech Republic, see the approach adopted by S. Šnebergerová in: KAREL KLÍMA et al., PRAKTIKUM ČESKÉHO ÚSTAVNÍHO PRÁVA [*Practicum in Czech Constitutional Law*], Plzeň: Aleš Čeněk 384 (2005).

10.54. The Constitutional Court of the Czech Republic has elaborated on the concept of the right to a fair trial in a number of new procedural situations, which the Constitutional Court used as a basis for stipulating mandatory principles of a procedural breach of the principles of a fair trial. These include: more details regarding the conventional principle of the right to a proper reasoning underlying every decision, prohibition of the denial of justice, extreme discrepancy between the findings of fact and legal conclusions derived therefrom, principles of omitted evidence and the principle of surprising decisions.[58]

10.55. For instance, the Constitutional Court of the Czech Republic has ruled that the court of appeals acts in breach of the Constitution if it significantly deviates from the facts of the case as established by the trial court without securing evidence which would justify the opposite legal reasoning or if it upholds the decision of a trial court on the merits despite the fact that the court of appeals based its assessment of the case on a different legal opinion than the trial court. The principle of omitted evidence means that the judge is entitled to refuse evidence proposed by the defence under the judicial principle of free assessment of evidence, but they are obliged to explain why and provide reasons for doing so. The principle mandating that every decision must be supported by proper reasons means that there must exist a causal relationship between the findings of fact and the conclusions and deductions made by the court. If the reasons for the decision of the court fail to mention certain specific evidence, the decision becomes incomprehensible and unreviewable and the court is acting arbitrarily. If the decision of the court exhibits an extreme discrepancy between the findings of fact and the considerations employed during the assessment of evidence on the one hand, and the legal conclusions on the other hand, such a situation constitutes a violation of the right to a fair trial. The Constitutional Court of the Czech Republic has held that denial of justice denotes situations in which the courts fail to issue a decision but instead terminate proceedings for an obstacle which could have been eliminated by giving instructions to the party.

XIV. Conclusion

10.56. The Council of Europe system, based on a number of multilateral substantive-law pacts and primarily the Convention as the declaration of human rights and freedoms, implements the constitutional

---

[58] For an analysis of this issue, see also the case law orientation to the individual articles 36 through 40 in: ELIŠKA WAGNEROVÁ, VOJTĚCH ŠIMÍČEK, TOMÁŠ LANGÁŠEK, & IVO POSPÍŠIL et al., *supra* note 21, at 725.

principles elevated to the level of international or European regional law through the directly binding case law of the European Court of Human Rights. Hence, it uses these legal principles in order to penetrate the constitutional and legal systems of the Council of Europe Member States. These developments can be witnessed in various situations corresponding to the varying features of the constitutional systems employed in continental Europe, Great Britain and Scandinavia, which correspond to the main types of legal cultures in Europe. National application of the case law of the European Court of Human Rights is mainly influenced by whether the constitutional systems have special and specialized constitutional courts within their structure such as the Federal Republic of Germany, France, Italy, Spain, the Czech Republic, Poland, etc.. Consequently, the concept of the case law of the European Court of Human Rights significantly influences the legislation adopted by the Council of Europe Member States, especially in the European states whose legal culture is based on codes of law.

| | |

Summaries

FRA [*L'impact de la Cour européenne des droits de l'homme sur les systèmes constitutionnels des États membres du Conseil de l'Europe*]
La jurisprudence de la Cour européenne des droits de l'homme, juridiction dépendant du Conseil de l'Europe, a un impact dans différents domaines du droit des États membres du conseil de l'Europe et pas simplement dans le domaine du droit constitutionnel. Ce système de "case law" européen constitue d'une certaine manière un système juridique unifié fondé sur des catégories de droit constitutionnel (par exemple dans les domaines de la durée de travail, de l'État de droit, de la responsabilité des pouvoirs publics, de l'indépendance de la justice), de droit administratif (par exemple dans le domaine des relations procéduriales) et de droit pénal (par exemple dans l'interprétation des grands principes du droit pénal), prenant en compte l'organisation de la justice et appliquant des principes de base concrets dans la procédure (par exemple les principes d'égalité des armes, d'égalité des parties, le droit à une aide juridique). Il s'introduit également dans le droit privé, le développement progressif de la jurisprudence se rapportant aux concepts de vie privée, de liberté de pensée ou de protection de la famille en offrant un exemple. Avec son caractère contraignant en droit constitutionnel et son impact sur le droit des États membres, la Cour européenne des droits de l'homme dépendant du Conseil de l'Europe n'est pas une organisation internationale comme une autre.

CZE [*Fenomén vlivu Evropského soudu pro lidská práva na ústavní systémy členských států Rady Evropy*]
Judikatura Evropského soudu pro lidská práva jako soudního orgánu Rady Evropy ovlivňuje právní řád členských států a nachází odraz v různých oblastech vnitrostátního právního řádu členských států Rady Evropy a to nejen v oblasti hmoty ústavního práva. Tento systém evropského "case law" tvoří takto i určitý jednolitý právní systém založený na kategoriích práva ústavního (například v oblasti dělby moci, právního státu, odpovědnosti veřejné moci, nezávislosti soudnictví), práva správního (například v oblasti administrativně procesních vztahů), v oblasti práva trestního (například v interpretaci klasických trestně právních zásad), ve vztahu k organizaci soudnictví a realizaci konkrétních procesních soudních zásad (například rovnosti zbraní, rovnost účastníků, práva na právní pomoc). Vstupuje i do kategorií práva soukromého, příkladem může být postupný rozvoj judikatury týkající se pojetí soukromého života, svobody myšlení, ochrany rodiny. Svojí ústavněprávní závazností a obsahovým vlivem na právní řády je takto systém Rady Evropy fenoménem v oblasti mezinárodních organizací.

| | |

POL [*Fenomen wpływu Europejskiego Trybunału Praw Człowieka na systemy konstytucyjne państw należących do Rady Europy*]
System Rady Europy, oparty na szeregu wielostronnych paktów natury materialnoprawnej, zwłaszcza zaś Konwencji stanowiącej deklarację praw człowieka i wolności, realizuje przez bezpośrednie orzecznictwo Europejskiego Trybunału Praw Człowieka zasady prawa konstytucyjnego, wyniesione na poziom prawa międzynarodowego (europejsko-regionalnego) w systemach konstytucyjnych państw należących do Rady Europy.

DEU [*Das Phänomen der Rückwirkung des Europäischen Gerichtshofs für Menschenrechte auf die Verfassungssysteme der Mitgliedsstaaten des Europarats*]
Über die direkte Rechtsprechung des Europäischen Gerichtshofs für Menschenrechte realisiert das System des Europarats, das auf einer Reihe multilateraler Bündnisse materiell-rechtlicher Natur und insbesondere der Konvention zum Schutze der Menschenrechte und Grundfreiheiten basiert, verfassungsrechtliche, auf die Ebene internationalen (europäisch-regionalen) Rechts erhobene Grundsätze innerhalb der Verfassungssysteme der Mitgliedsstaaten des Europarats.

Czech Yearbook of International Law

RUS [*Феномен влияния Европейского суда по правам человека на конституционные системы государств-членов Совета Европы*]

Система Совета Европы, основанная на целом ряде многосторонних соглашений, обладающих материально-правовыми чертами, и, прежде всего, на Конвенции как декларации прав и свобод человека, реализует конституционные принципы, возведенные на уровень международного (европейского регионального) права в конституционных системах государств-членов Совета Европы, посредством прямых документов судебной практики Европейского суда по правам человека.

ESP [*El fenómeno de la influencia del Tribunal Europeo de Derechos Humanos en los sistemas constitucionales de los Estados miembros del Consejo de Europa*]

El sistema del Consejo de Europa, basado en toda una serie de pactos multilaterales con carácter de Derecho subjetivo y, en particular, en el Convenio como declaración de los derechos humanos y las libertades, aplica mediante la jurisprudencia directa del Tribunal Europeo de Derechos Humanos unos principios constitucionales elevados al nivel del derecho internacional (regional europeo) en los sistemas constitucionales de los Estados miembros del Consejo de Europa.

| | |

Libor Klimek

European Police Office (Europol): Past, Present and Future

Key words:
Establishment | Legal Basis of Europol | Europol Objectives | Europol Competence | Europol Tasks | Europol National Units | Liaison Officers | Europol Information System | Analysis Work Files | Possible Legal Development of Europol

Abstract | *The European Police Office (Europol) is the primary European entity that handles police co-operation at the European level. Europol's official mission is 'to support and strengthen action by the European Union Member States' police authorities and other law enforcement services and their mutual co-operation in preventing and combating crime affecting two or more Member States of the European Union'. This paper deals with Europol and is divided into seven sections. The first two sections deal with the establishment and legal basis of Europol and analyse its objectives, competence and tasks. Additional sections are focused on special issues; the third section assesses the relationship of Europol with Member States of the European Union, namely national units and liaison officers. The fourth section deals with the Europol Information System and analysis work files and the fifth section is focused on co-operation with other European Union institutions, bodies, offices and agencies, as well as co-operation with non-EU Member States. The sixth section presents some examples of successful Europol operations. Finally, the seventh section indicates possible legal development of Europol.*

JUDr. Libor Klimek, PhD. graduated from the Faculty of Law, Pan European University, Bratislava, Slovak Republic. Since 2013 he has been a research worker at the Criminology Research Centre at the Faculty of Law, Pan European University. He is the author of over fifty publications published in the United States, Russia, the Netherlands, Belgium, the Czech Republic, Poland, Latvia, and in the Slovak Republic. Among other things, he is the co-author of the first monograph on the topic of the European Union Criminal Law published in the Slovak Republic. His research is focused solely on the international and European aspects of Criminal Law.
e-mail: libor.klimek@yahoo.com

| | |

I. Introduction

11.01. The European Police Office (Europol) is the primary European entity that handles police co-operation at the European level. Its counterpart in the United States is the *Federal Bureau of Investigation* (FBI). However, as the EU is not a federal State like the United States, Europol does not have 'federal' powers. Rather, it provides support for the Member States of the European Union (EU).[1] Pursuant to the Treaty on the Functioning of the EU[2] 'Europol's mission shall be to support and strengthen action by the Member States' police authorities and other law enforcement services and their mutual co-operation in preventing and combating serious crime affecting two or more Member States, terrorism and forms of crime which affect a common interest covered by a Union policy'.[3]

11.02. Europol is a body of the EU. It is its own legal person and is based in Hague (the Netherlands). It is headed by a director. Europol began its activities with an initial team of about twenty[4] but is now composed of hundreds of people.

11.03. This paper deals with Europol. It is divided into seven sections. The first two sections deal with the establishment and legal basis of Europol and analyse its objectives, competence and tasks. Additional sections are focused on special issues; the third section assesses the relationship of Europol with Member States of the European Union, namely national units and liaison officers. The fourth section deals with the Europol Information System and analysis work files and the fifth section is focused on co-operation with other European Union institutions, bodies, offices and agencies, as well as co-operation with non-EU Member States. The sixth section presents some examples of successful Europol operations. Finally, the seventh section indicates possible legal development of Europol.

---

[1] Libor Klimek, *Europol, in* JAROSLAV IVOR, LIBOR KLIMEK & JOZEF ZÁHORA, TRESTNÉ PRÁVO EURÓPSKEJ ÚNIE A JEHO VPLYV NA PRÁVNY PORIADOK SLOVENSKEJ REPUBLIKY [*CRIMINAL LAW OF THE EUROPEAN UNION AND ITS IMPACT ON THE LEGAL ORDER OF THE SLOVAK REPUBLIC*], Žilina: Eurokódex 757 (2013).

[2] Treaty on the functioning of the European Union as amended by the Treaty of Lisbon [2010] OJ C 83/47.

[3] Article 88(1) of the Treaty on the functioning of the EU.

[4] Georges Rauchs & Daniel. J. Koenig, *Europol, in* INTERNATIONAL POLICE COOPERATION: A WORLD PERSPECTIVE, Lanham: Lexington Books 43, 43 (Daniel. J. Koenig, Dilip K. Das ed., 2001).

II. Establishment and Legal Basis

11.04. The establishment of Europol was a political matter, not requested by the police services in the Member States of the EU.[5] Support for a centralised European police force was voiced strongly in the late 1980s and early 1990s by the German Chancellor of the period, Helmut Kohl, who repeatedly argued in favour of the establishment of a 'European FBI'.[6]

11.05. The forerunner of Europol was the European Drugs Unit. Its legal basis was first the 1993 *Ministerial Agreement on the Establishment of the Europol Drugs Unit*[7] and later the Joint Action 95/73/JHA concerning the Europol Drugs Unit.[8] The Unit was dismantled by Europol in 1995.

11.06. The establishment of Europol was agreed in the 1992 Treaty on the European Union[9].[10] It was the first organisation ever established on the basis of the Treaty in its original version. Europol was established in 1995 by the *Convention on the establishment of a European Police Office*[11] (Europol Convention), which came in to force on 1 October 1998. A lengthy process for the ratification of this Convention, as well as other approval processes, delayed the real beginning of its operations until 1999. However, as pointed out by Steve Peers, while ratification of the Europol Convention may appear to have been slow, it took place more quickly than that of any other Convention concluded in the period of the Third Pillar of the EU.[12]

---

[5] Roger Vande Sompel, *Europol, the high potential EU law enforcement agency, despite the Member States...: How serious is the problem, knowing that Belgium is "a good pupil in the Europol class"?*, 3(16) JOURNAL OF POLICE STUDIES 139, 143 (2010).

[6] VALSAMIS MITSILEGAS, EU CRIMINAL LAW, Oxford – Portland: Hart Publishing 162 (2009); Monica den Boer, *Law-Enforcement Cooperation and Transnational Organized Crime in Europe, in* TRANSNATIONAL ORGANIZED CRIME AND INTERNATIONAL SECURITY: BUSINESS AS USUAL?, Boulder: Lynne Rienner Publishers 103, 104 (Mats Berdal, Mónica Serrano eds., 2002).

[7] Ministerial Agreement on the Establishment of the Europol Drugs Unit (adopted 2 June 1993 in Copenhagen, Denmark).

[8] Joint Action 95/73/JHA of 10 March 1995 adopted by the Council on the basis of Article K.3 of the Treaty on European Union concerning the Europol Drugs Unit [1995] OJ L 62/1.

[9] Treaty on European Union (original version) [1992] OJ C 191/1.

[10] Article K.1(9) of the Treaty on EU (original version).

[11] Convention based on Article K.3 of the Treaty on European Union on the establishment of a European Police Office (Europol Convention) [1995] OJ C 316.

[12] Steve Peers, *Governance and the Third Pillar: The Accountability of Europol, in* GOOD GOVERNANCE AND THE EUROPEAN UNION: REFLECTIONS ON CONCEPTS, INSTITUTIONS AND SUBSTANCE, Antwerp – Oxford – New York: Intersentia 253, 255 (Deirdre Curtin, Ramses A. Wessel eds., 2005).

11.07. Experience demonstrated that there was a recurrent need to adopt a new legal basis for Europol by means of a decision by the Council of the EU. Since the adoption of the Europol Convention in 1995, three different Protocols had been adopted to amend and supplement the Europol Convention.[13] In 2006 a *Proposal for a Council Decision establishing the European Police Office* was introduced.[14] This proposal aimed to establish Europol on the basis of a decision of the Council of the EU, and to include all the amendments already incorporated in the Protocols to the Europol Convention, as well as further improvements to address the new challenges faced by Europol.[15]

11.08. Since 2009, the new legal basis of Europol has been the *Council Decision 2009/371/JHA establishing the European Police Office*[16] (Europol Decision), which repealed the Europol Convention from 1January 2010. The Treaty on the Functioning of the EU[17] – as amended by the Treaty of Lisbon[18] – came into force one month later. Europol, as referred to in the Europol Decision, is regarded as the legal successor of Europol as established by the Europol Convention.[19]

11.09. Thanks to its new legal status as established in the Europol Decision, Europol has an improved position on the EU stage.[20] On the one hand, Europol's legal basis is more flexible. On the other, changes introduced

---

[13] Protocol drawn up on the basis of Article 43(1) of the Convention on the establishment of a European Police Office (Europol Convention) amending Article 2 and the Annex to that Convention [2002] OJ C 358/2; Protocol amending the Convention on the establishment of a European Police Office (Europol Convention) and the Protocol on the privileges and immunities of Europol, the members of its organs, the deputy directors and the employees of Europol [2002] OJ C 312/2; Protocol drawn up on the basis of Article 43(1) of the Convention on the Establishment of a European Police Office (Europol Convention), amending that Convention [2004] OJ C 2/3.

[14] Commission of the European Communities, 'Proposal for a Council Decision establishing the European Police Office (EUROPOL)' COM(2006) 817 final, 20 December 2006.

[15] Ibid., at 2; Commission of the European Communities, 'Accompanying document to the Proposal for a Council Decision establishing the European Police Office (EUROPOL): Impact Assessment' SEC(2006) 1682, 20 December 2006, at 2 and 9.

[16] Council Decision 2009/371/JHA of 6 April 2009 establishing the European Police Office (Europol) [2009] OJ L 121/37.

[17] Treaty on the functioning of the European Union as amended by the Treaty of Lisbon [2010] OJ C 83/47.

[18] The Treaty of Lisbon amending the Treaty Establishing the European Union and the Treaty Establishing the European Community [2006] OJ C 306/231.

[19] Article 1(2) of the Europol Decision.

[20] EUROPOL REVIEW: GENERAL REPORT ON EUROPOL ACTIVITIES, Luxembourg: Publications Office of the European Union 59 (A. Biegaj ed., 2011).

by the Europol Decision have not had a significant impact on Europol's ability to support Member States' law enforcement authorities.[21]

III. Objectives, Competence and Tasks

11.10. Europol's 'objectives' are clearly defined. The objective of Europol is 'to support and strengthen action by the competent authorities of the Member States of the EU and their mutual co-operation in preventing and combating organised crime, terrorism and other forms of serious crime affecting two or more Member States'.[22]

11.11. The 'competence' of Europol is defined through the forms of crime it covers. Under the core text of the Europol Decision, Europol's competence shall cover 'organised crime, terrorism and other forms of serious crime affecting two or more Member States of the EU in such a way as to require a common approach by the Member States owing to the scale, significance and consequences of the offences'.[23] As regards the term 'other forms of serious crime', its scope is listed in the Annex of the Europol Decision. However, such a brief definition requires a detailed explanation.

11.12. To clarify in detail the exact Europol's competence, taking into account the core text of the Europol Decision and its Annex, Europol's competence shall cover:

- organised crime[24]
- terrorism[25]
- unlawful drug trafficking[26]
- illegal money-laundering activities[27]
- crime connected with nuclear and radioactive substances

---

[21] EMMA DISLEY, BARRIE IRVING, WILLIAM HUGHES & BHANU PATRUNI, EVALUATION OF THE IMPLEMENTATION OF THE EUROPOL COUNCIL DECISION AND OF EUROPOL'S ACTIVITIES, Santa Monica – Arlington – Pittsburgh – Cambridge: RAND Corporation 44 (2012).

[22] Article 3 of the Europol Decision.

[23] Article 4(1) of the Europol Decision.

[24] See the Council Framework Decision 2008/841/JHA of 24 October 2008 on the fight against organised crime [2008] OJ L 300/42.

[25] See the Council Framework Decision 2002/475/JHA of 13 June 2002 on combating terrorism (as amended by the Framework Decision 2008/919/JHA) [2002] OJ L 164/3.

[26] See the Council Framework Decision 2004/757/JHA of 25 October 2004 laying down minimum provisions on the constituent elements of criminal acts and penalties in the field of illicit drug trafficking [2004] L 335/8. Directive 2005/60/EC of the European Parliament and of the Council of 26 October 2005 on the prevention of the use of the financial system for the purpose of money laundering and terrorist financing (Directive 2010/78/EU of the European Parliament and of the Council) [2005] OJ L 309/15.

[27] See the Council Framework Decision 2001/500/JHA of 26 June 2001 on money laundering, the identification, tracing, freezing, seizing and confiscation of instrumentalities and the proceeds of crime [2001] OJ L 182/1.

- illegal immigrant smuggling[28]
- trafficking in human beings[29]
- motor vehicle crime
- murder, grievous bodily injury
- illicit trade in human organs and tissue
- kidnapping, illegal restraint and hostage taking
- racism and xenophobia[30]
- organised robbery
- illicit trafficking in cultural goods, including antiquities and works of art
- swindling and fraud
- racketeering and extortion
- counterfeiting and product piracy
- forgery of administrative documents and trafficking therein
- forgery of money and means of payment[31]
- computer crime[32]
- corruption[33]
- illicit trafficking in arms, ammunition and explosives
- illicit trafficking in endangered animal species
- illicit trafficking in endangered plant species and varieties
- environmental crime[34]

---

[28] See the Council Directive 2002/90/EC of 28 November 2002 defining the facilitation of unauthorised entry, transit and residence [2002] OJ L 328/17; Council Framework Decision 2002/946/JHA of 28 November 2002 on the strengthening of the penal framework to prevent the facilitation of unauthorised entry, transit and residence [2002] L 328/1.

[29] See the Directive 2011/36/EU of the European Parliament and of the Council of 5 April 2011 on preventing and combating trafficking in human beings and protecting its victims, and replacing Council Framework Decision 2002/629/JHA [2011] OJ L 101/1.

[30] See the Council Framework Decision 2008/913/JHA of 28 November 2008 on combating certain forms and expressions of racism and xenophobia by means of criminal law [2008] OJ L 328/55.

[31] See the Council Framework Decision 2001/413/JHA of 28 May 2001 on combating fraud and counterfeiting of non-cash means of payment [2001] OJ L 149/1.

[32] See the Council Framework Decision 2001/413/JHA of 28th May 2001 on combating fraud and counterfeiting of non-cash means of payment [2001] OJ L 149/1; Council Framework Decision 2005/222/JHA of 24 February 2005 on attacks against information systems [2005] OJ L 69/67.

[33] See the Protocol drawn up on the basis of Article K.3 of the Treaty on European Union to the Convention on the protection of the European Communities' financial interests [1996] OJ C 313/2; Convention drawn up on the basis of Article K.3(2)(c) of the Treaty on European Union on the fight against corruption involving officials of the European Communities or officials of Member States of the European Union [1997] OJ C 195/2; Council Framework Decision 2003/568/JHA of 22 July 2003 on combating corruption in the private sector [2003] OJ L 192/54.

[34] See the Directive 2008/99/EC of the European Parliament and of the Council of 19 November 2008 on the protection of the environment through criminal law [2008] OJ L 328/28.

- illicit trafficking in hormonal substances and other growth promoters.

11.13. In addition to that, Europol's competence shall also cover related criminal offences, namely criminal offences committed in order to procure the means of perpetrating acts in respect of which Europol is competent, criminal offences committed in order to facilitate or carry out acts in respect of which Europol is competent, and criminal offences committed to ensure the impunity of acts in respect of which Europol is competent.[35]

11.14. It should be not overlooked that as far as the European Union's Judicial Cooperation Unit (Eurojust) is concerned, the definition of its competence follows the Europol's competence. Pursuant to the Decision 2002/187/JHA setting up Eurojust[36] (Eurojust Decision), the general competence of Eurojust[37] shall cover 'the types of crime and the offences in respect of which Europol is at all times competent to act' and other offences committed together with these types of crime and the offences.[38] The question which begs consideration is why the Eurojust's competence follows Europol's competence. As Petra Jeney argues, Eurojust was meant to complement the work of Europol in combating cross-border crime.[39]

11.15. Many of the aforementioned crimes/offences are also listed in the procedural measures of the mechanism on the mutual recognition of judicial decision in criminal matters in the EU.[40] This is considered as a cornerstone of judicial co-operation in criminal matters in the EU.[41]

---

[35] Article 4(3) of the Europol Decision.

[36] Council Decision 2002/187/JHA of 28 February 2002 setting up Eurojust with a view to reinforcing the fight against serious crime (as amended by the Council Decision 2009/426/JHA of 16 December 2008) [2002] OJ L 63/1.

[37] As Valsamis Mitsilegas argues, its name – Eurojust – appears to be a clear analogy to the use of the term 'Europol' for the European Police Office. See VALSAMIS MITSILEGAS, EU CRIMINAL LAW, Oxford – Portland : Hart Publishing 187 (2009).

[38] Article 1(a)(c) of the Eurojust Decision.

[39] PETRA JENEY, THE FUTURE OF EUROJUST, Strasbourg: European Parliament 21 (2012).

[40] For instance: Article 2(2) of the Council Framework Decision 2002/584/JHA of 13 June 2002 on the European arrest warrant and the surrender procedures between Member States (as amended by the Framework Decision 2009/299/JHA) [2002] OJ L 190/1; Article 3(2) of the Council Framework Decision 2003/577/JHA of 22 July 2003 on the execution in the European Union of orders freezing property or evidence [2003] OJ L 195/45; Article 5(1) of the Council Framework Decision 2005/214/JHA of 24 February 2005 on the application of the principle of mutual recognition to financial penalties [2005] OJ L 76/16; Article 6(1) of the Council Framework Decision 2006/783/JHA of 6 October 2006 on the application of the principle of mutual recognition to confiscation orders [2006] OJ L 328/59; Article 14(2) of the Council Framework Decision 2008/978/JHA of 18 December

11.16. Europol's objectives are carried out via its 'tasks', which are divided into three groups, namely:
  1) principal tasks
  2) additional tasks
  3) Central Office of the EU for combating euro counterfeiting.

11.17. First, as far as 'principal tasks' are concerned, under the Europol Decision the Europol shall:
  - collect, store, process, analyse and exchange information and intelligence;
  - notify the competent authorities of the relevant Member States without delay via the national unit of information, of any connections identified between criminal offences;
  - aid investigations in the Member States, in particular by forwarding all relevant information to the national units;
  - ask the competent authorities of the Member States of the EU concerned to initiate conduct or co-ordinate investigations and suggest the setting up of Joint investigation teams in specific cases (see below);
  - provide intelligence and analytical support to Member States in connection with major international events;
  - prepare threat assessments, strategic analyses and general situation reports relating to its objective, including organised crime threat assessments. [42]

11.18. Second, as far as 'additional tasks' are concerned, under the Europol Decision the Europol shall:
  - develop specialist knowledge of the investigative procedures of the competent authorities of the Member States and provide advice on investigations;
  - provide strategic intelligence to assist and promote the efficient and effective use of the resources available at national and EU level for operational activities and the support of such activities. [43]

11.19. The third task regards the protection of the single European currency[44] (the euro). Europol is the 'Central Office of the EU for combating euro

---

2008 on the European evidence warrant for the purpose of obtaining objects, documents and data for use in proceedings in criminal matters [2008] OJ L 350/72.

[41] Pursuant to the Treaty on the Functioning the EU, judicial co-operation in criminal matters in the EU shall be based on the principle of mutual recognition of judgments and judicial decisions [...] (Article 82(1) of the Treaty on the Functioning the EU).

[42] Article 5(1)(a)(b)(c)(d)(e)(f) of the Europol Decision.

[43] Article 5(3)(a)(b) of the Europol Decision.

[44] See Libor Klimek, *Counterfeiting and Protection of the Euro: From early Beginnings to Current Legislative Development*, 4(1) ISSUES OF BUSINESS AND LAW 12 (2012). Available at: http://www.ibl.ttvam.lt/index.php/ibl/article/view/35/pdf (accessed on September 24, 2013).

counterfeiting', pursuant to the Council Decision 2005/511/JHA on protecting the euro.[45] To clarify, at international level, the basic apparatus of protection for the currency is the International Convention for the Suppression of Counterfeiting Currency (also known as the Geneva Convention), adopted by the United Nations in 1929. Europol shall for instance, centralise and process all information of a nature to facilitate the investigation, prevention and combating of euro counterfeiting and shall forward this information without delay to the national central offices of the Member States.

11.20. In addition, Europol staff may participate in a supporting capacity in 'joint investigation teams'[46] in the EU, including such teams set up in accordance with the Framework Decision 2002/465/JHA on joint investigation teams.[47] They may take on this role in accordance with the Convention on mutual assistance in criminal matters between the Member States of the EU of 2000,[48] or in accordance with the Convention on mutual assistance and co-operation between customs administrations of 1997.[49] The obligatory condition is that those teams a must be investigating criminal offences in which Europol is competent. Europol formally participates in a small number of joint investigation teams, but there is a perception that it adds value where it does participate.[50] For instance, in *Operation Golf* 28 children were rescued as part of a major joint operation led by the United Kingdom Metropolitan Police and Europol. The operation, finalised in October 2010, was part of a wider investigation, which consisted of a Joint investigation team between the Metropolitan Police and the Romanian National Police. The aim of the Joint investigation team was to tackle a specific Romanian organised crime network that was trafficking and exploiting children from the Roma community. Europol was an active member of the joint investigation team, providing assistance to the

---

45 Council Decision 2005/511/JHA of 12 July 2005 on protecting the euro against counterfeiting, by designating Europol as the Central Office for combating euro counterfeiting [2005] OJ L 185/35.

46 See Libor Klimek, *Joint Investigation Teams in the European Union*, 4(1) INTERNAL SECURITY 63 (2012). Available at: http://internalsecurity.wspol.eu/free-sample/joint-investigation-teams-in-the-european-union (accessed on September 24, 2013).

47 Council Framework Decision 2002/465/JHA of 13 June 2002 on joint investigation teams [2002] OJ L 162/1.

48 Convention established by the Council in accordance with Article 34 of the Treaty on European Union, on Mutual Assistance in Criminal Matters between the Member States of the European Union [2000] OJ C 197/3.

49 Convention drawn up on the basis of Article K.3 of the Treaty on European Union on mutual assistance and cooperation between customs administrations [1998] C 24/2.

50 EMMA DISLEY, BARRIE IRVING, WILLIAM HUGHES & BHANU PATRUNI, *supra* note 21, at 76.

competent authorities. Among other assistance, Europol gave expert advice on setting up and ensuring analytical support throughout the investigation.[51]

IV. The Relationship between Europol and Member States of the EU: National Units, Liaison Officers and Initiation of Criminal Investigations

11.21. Europol does not communicate with the competent national authorities directly, but via national units and liaison officers. In addition to that, the initiation of criminal investigations forms a significant connection with Member States. As far as 'national units' are concerned, the Europol Decision stipulates that each Member State of the EU shall 'establish or designate' a national unit, with an official appointed as head in each Member State.[52] Each State decides the unit to establish or designate. For instance, in the Slovak Republic there is the Europol National Unit (*Národná ústredňa Europol*) established as a part of the Bureau of International Police Co-operation of the Police Presidium of the Slovak Republic (*Úrad medzinárodnej policajnej spolupráce Prezídia Policajného zboru Slovenskej republiky*) based in Bratislava.[53] In the Czech Republic there is the Europol National Unit (*Národní jednotka Europolu*) established as a part of the Bureau of Criminal Police and Investigation Service of the Police Presidium of the Czech Republic (*Úřad služby kriminální policie a vyšetřování Policejního prezidia České republiky*) based in Prague.[54]

11.22. The national unit is the only liaison body between Europol and the competent authorities of the Member States of the EU.[55] Europol has a live connection 24 hours per day and 7 days per week with the Europol National Units based in all Member States of the EU.[56] Pursuant to the Europol Decision the national units shall:

- supply Europol on their own initiative with the information and intelligence necessary for it to carry out its tasks;
- respond to Europol's requests for information, intelligence and advice;

---

[51] EUROPOL REVIEW: GENERAL REPORT ON EUROPOL ACTIVITIES, *supra* note 20, at 35-36.
[52] Article 8(1) of the Europol Decision.
[53] The National Europol Unit was established on 1 January 2001, even before the Slovak Republic became a Member State of the EU. See Regulation No. 66/2000 of the Slovak Minister of the Interior.
[54] See Binding Instruction of the Police President No. 124/2009.
[55] Article 8(2) of the Europol Decision.
[56] EUROPOL REVIEW: GENERAL REPORT ON EUROPOL ACTIVITIES, *supra* note 20, at 55.

- keep information and intelligence up to date;
- evaluate information and intelligence in accordance with national law for the competent authorities and transmit that material to them;
- issue requests for advice, information, intelligence and analysis to Europol;
- supply Europol with information for storage in its databases;
- ensure compliance with the law in every exchange of information between themselves and Europol. [57]

11.23. The Europol Decision stipulates an 'information obligation' of the Member Stales of the EU towards Europol in order to allow the latter to carry out its tasks of information, analysis, co-ordination and expertise with regard to those same Member States. However, this information obligation has been created half-heartedly. Non-compliance with the information obligation cannot be censured as there is no coercive instrument to execute it. This situation means that the Member States are at the same time 'client' and 'supplier' of Europol. They decide autonomously whether or not to solicit the support of Europol and, when they do so, they expect a high-quality service. Any product or service of Europol is nearly entirely based on, and dependent on, high-quality information provided by the Member Stales. In practice however, those same Member States decide autonomously whether or not to provide that information. [58]

11.24. In spite of the fact that the national unit is the only liaison body between Europol and the competent authorities of the Member States of the EU, the Member States may allow direct contact between designated competent authorities and Europol, subject to conditions determined by the Member State in question, including prior involvement of the national unit. At the same time, Europol provides the national unit with any information exchanged in the course of direct contacts between Europol and designated competent authorities. Relations between the national unit and the competent authorities are governed by national law, and in particular, the relevant national constitutional requirements. [59]

11.25. As far as 'liaison officers' are concerned, each national unit shall second (send) at least one liaison officer to Europol in The Hague. Liaison officers play an important role in everyday law enforcement activities by facilitating the exchange of information, as well as providing support and co-ordination for ongoing investigations. Under the Europol Decision they shall:

---

[57]   Article 8(4)(a)(b)(c)(d)(e)(f)(g) of the Europol Decision.
[58]   Roger Vande Sompel, *supra* note 5, at 143.
[59]   Article 8(2) of the Europol Decision.

- provide Europol with information from their national unit;
- forward information from Europol to the their national unit;
- co-operate with Europol staff by providing information and giving advice;
- assist in the exchange of information from their national units with the liaison officers of other Member States under their responsibility in accordance with national law.[60]

11.26. In addition, Europol also hosts liaison officers from several non-EU Member States and organisations who work together with Europol on the basis of co-operation agreements. This network is supported by secure channels of communication provided by Europol. Further, Europol sends two liaison officers to Washington DC and one to Interpol's headquarters in Lyon, France.[61]

11.27. Despite the fact that Europol does not carry out investigations, it may request the 'initiation of criminal investigations' by Member States of the EU. Member States shall deal with any request by Europol to initiate, conduct or co-ordinate investigations in specific cases and shall give such requests due consideration. They shall inform Europol whether the investigation requested will be initiated.[62] Thus, the Member States are not obliged to carry out each criminal investigation initiated by Europol. They are obliged only to inform Europol whether or not they do so.

V. Information Processing Systems

11.28. Taking into account Europol's tasks, 'information' can be considered a key term. In so far as it is necessary for the achievement of its objectives, Europol shall process information and intelligence, including personal data. Europol established and maintains the Europol Information System and analysis work files.

11.29. The Europol Information System is a system in which data concerning persons is collected. Its primary purpose is to detect matches amongst data contributed by different Member States and third parties.[63] It was technically ready to be used by the Member States of the EU at a national level in October 2005. However, each Member State had to sign a bilateral agreement for the interconnection of the computer networks between Europol and the competent services at a national level. The

---

[60] Article 9(3)(a)(b)(c)(d) of the Europol Decision.
[61] EUROPOL REVIEW: GENERAL REPORT ON EUROPOL ACTIVITIES, *supra* note 20, at 10.
[62] Article 7(1) of the Europol Decision.
[63] EUROPOL REVIEW: GENERAL REPORT ON EUROPOL ACTIVITIES, *supra* note 20, at 11.

deployment of the system in the Member States was progressive and was completed for all Member Sates in February 2008.[64]

11.30. The Europol Information System may be used to process only such data as are necessary for the performance of Europol's tasks. The data input shall relate to:

- persons who, in accordance with the national law of the Member State concerned, are suspected of having committed or having taken part in a criminal offence in which Europol is competent or who have been convicted of such an offence;

- persons regarding whom there are factual indications or reasonable grounds under the national law of the Member State concerned to believe that they will commit criminal offences in which Europol is competent.[65]

11.31. Information in the Europol Information System is available for all Member States of the EU. As regards the right to input data into the Europol Information System, national units, liaison officers, the director, deputy directors and duly empowered Europol staff have the right to input data directly into the system. Only the party which has input the data may modify, correct or delete such data.[66] Germany has provided the most data in the system, followed by France, Belgium, Europol (on behalf of third parties) and Spain. In 2010, 147,345 searches were run through the system.[67]

11.32. In addition to the national units and above mentioned persons, competent authorities designated as such by the Member States of the EU may also query the Europol Information System. However, the result of the query shall indicate only whether the data requested are available in the Europol Information System. Further information may then be obtained via the national unit.

11.33. Analysis work files are files in which data concerning criminal offences is collected. Analysis work files are opened for the purposes of analysis defined as the assembly, processing or use of data with the aim of assisting criminal investigations. Where this is necessary for the performance of its tasks, Europol may store, modify, and use data concerning criminal offences in which it is competent.

11.34. Pursuant to the Europol Decision, the analysis work files may contain data on:

---

[64] EUROPOL: COORDINATING THE FIGHT AGAINST SERIOUS AND ORGANISED CRIME: 29TH REPORT OF SESSION 2007–08, House of Lords papers, Paper 183. London: Great Britain Parliament, House of Lords 89 (2008).

[65] Article 12(1)(a)(b) of the Europol Decision.

[66] Article 13(1)(2) of the Europol Decision.

[67] EUROPOL REVIEW: GENERAL REPORT ON EUROPOL ACTIVITIES, *supra* note 20, at 11-12.

- persons mentioned in relation to the Europol Information System;
- persons who might be called on to testify in investigations in connection with the offences under consideration or in subsequent criminal proceedings;
- persons who have been the victims of one of the offences under consideration or with regard to whom certain facts give reason to believe that they could be the victims of such an offence;
- contacts and associates and persons who can provide information on the criminal offences under consideration.[68]

11.35. Each analysis project entails the establishment of an analysis group closely involving analysts and other Europol staff designated by the Director and liaison officers and/or experts from the Member States supplying the information. Only analysts shall be authorised to input data into the file concerned and modify such data. All participants in the analysis group may retrieve data from the file. National units communicate to Europol all the information which it may require for the purpose of a particular analysis work file. However, the Member States of the EU communicate such data only where their national law also authorises processing thereof for the purposes of preventing, analysing or combating offences.[69]

VI. Cooperation with Other EU Institutions, Bodies, Offices and Agencies and with Non-EU Member States

11.36. The Europol Decision expects the co-operation of Europol, with other EU institutions, bodies, offices and agencies. In so far as it is relevant to the performance of its tasks, Europol may establish and maintain co-operative relations with Eurojust[70], the European Anti-Fraud Office[71] (OLAF), the European Agency for the Management of Operational Cooperation at the External Borders of the Member States of the EU[72] (Frontex), the European Police College[73] (CEPOL),

---

[68] Article 14(1) of the Europol Decision.

[69] Article 14(2)(3) of the Europol Decision.

[70] See the Council Decision 2002/187/JHA of 28 February 2002 setting up Eurojust with a view to reinforcing the fight against serious crime (as amended by the Council Decision 2009/426/JHA of 16 December 2008) [2002] OJ L 63/1.

[71] See the Commission Decision 1999/352/EC, ECSC, Euratom of 28 April 1999 establishing the European Anti-fraud Office (OLAF) [1999] OJ L 136/20.

[72] See the Council Regulation (EC) No 2007/2004 of 26 October 2004 establishing a European Agency for the Management of Operational Cooperation at the External Borders of the Member States of the European Union [2004] OJ L 349/1.

the European Central Bank, and the European Monitoring Centre for Drugs and Drug Addiction[74] (EMCDDA).[75] The basis of co-operation is in principle an agreement on 'information exchange'. For instance, Europol and Frontex concluded the agreement[76] whose purpose is to enhance co-operation between Europol and Frontex, through the exchange of strategic and technical information.

11.37. As shown, Europol is a legal person. In so far as it is necessary for the performance of its tasks, Europol may also establish and maintain co-operative relations with non-EU Member States and international organisations. The basis of co-operation is in principle an agreement on information exchange. Europol has concluded an agreement for this purpose, for instance, with Interpol[77] and with the United States.[78]

VII. Operations of the Member States of the EU Carried out with Europol's Support

11.38. Operation *Shovel* focused on the activities of an extremely violent Irish-based organised crime group involved in drugs and weapons trafficking across Europe. Europol assisted Ireland, the United Kingdom, Spain and Belgium to detect the proceeds of the group's criminal activities and to help the affected Member States in dismantling their money-laundering network. The analysis provided by Europol also helped to identify additional individuals associated with the organised crime group. An operational meeting was organised at Europol headquarters to plan the launch of a massive operation across Ireland, Spain and the United Kingdom. More than 600 pieces of information were exchanged via Europol channels. Over 700 investigators were involved and 38 arrests were executed in the three countries, in addition to numerous house searches.[79]

---

[73] See the Council Decision 2005/681/JHA of 20 September 2005 establishing the European Police College (CEPOL) and repealing Decision 2000/820/JHA [2005] L 256/63.

[74] See the Regulation (EC) No 1920/2006 of the European Parliament and of the Council of 12 December 2006 on the European Monitoring Centre for Drugs and Drug Addiction [2006] OJ L 376/1.

[75] Article 22(1) of the Europol Decision.

[76] Strategic Cooperation Agreement between the European Agency for the Management of Operational Cooperation at the External Borders of the Member States of the European Union and the European Police Office (2008, Warsaw).

[77] Agreement between Interpol and Europol (2001, Brussels).

[78] Agreement between the United States of America and the European Police Office (2001, Brussels); Supplemental Agreement between the Europol Police Office and the United States of America on the exchange of personal data and related information (2002).

[79] EUROPOL REVIEW: GENERAL REPORT ON EUROPOL ACTIVITIES, *supra* note 20, at 53.

11.39. Operation *Île Fantastique* was focused on suspects who smuggled irregular migrants mainly from Vietnam into the EU. The migrants were given a full guarantee of arrival. The price for the journey was up to 40,000 € and could take anything from a few days up to many weeks. The families of the migrants would often sell their houses and property to fund the journey. With the combined support of Europol and Eurojust, English, French, German and Hungarian police officers arrested 31 suspected facilitators of illegal immigration. In total 66 migrants from Vietnam were found during house searches. Europol experts were present at the co-ordination centre to provide technical expertise and operational analysis support. During the investigation phase, Europol prepared intelligence reports and facilitated the exchange of information. New criminal links were uncovered by Europol while working in close cooperation with national experts.[80]

11.40. As regards Operation *Most*, 14 people were arrested in the city of Lublin. The suspects were members of a major Polish network distributing counterfeit 50 € and 100 € banknotes in the EU. The raid, involving more than 120 police officers, was a result of three years of investigations in Italy, Poland and Spain, which were coordinated and supported by Europol. Two Europol officials provided on-the-spot support through the use of the Europol mobile office. Europol provided Poland with several operational analysis reports, including an important and extensive social network analysis report. The investigation concerned several branches of a Polish organised crime group, operating in various EU countries. In total more than 80 criminals were arrested under Operation *Most*. Europol also co-ordinated the international co-operation between Germany, Italy, Poland and Spain as well as providing advice and training. The operation was considered a big success as it led to the dismantling of a dangerous major criminal group involved in the mass distribution of counterfeit euro banknotes.[81]

VIII. Expected Future Development: Regulation on Europol as a New Third Legal Basis

11.41. As shown, the first legal basis of the Europol was the Europol Convention of 1999. Currently, its legal basis is the Europol Decision of 2009. However, the possibility of the adoption of a third legal basis for Europol – a Regulation on Europol – has arisen. It should be

---

[80] Ibid., at 40.
[81] Ibid., at 40.

emphasised that this is not a firm decision made by top EU institutions but merely a possibility.

11.42. Pursuant to the Treaty on the Functioning of the EU[82], the European Parliament and the Council [i.e. Council of the EU], by means of regulations adopted in accordance with the ordinary legislative procedure, shall determine Europol's structure, operation, field of action and task*s*.[83] The treaty specifies that these tasks may include:

- the collection, storage, processing, analysis and exchange of information, in particular that forwarded by the authorities of the Member States of the EU or third countries or bodies;

- the co-ordination, organisation and implementation of investigative and operational action carried out jointly with the Member States' competent authorities or in the context of joint investigative teams, where appropriate in liaison with Eurojust.[84]

11.43. In addition, the Treaty on the Functioning of the EU adds that regulations shall also lay down the procedures for scrutiny of Europol's activities by the European Parliament, together with national Parliaments.[85]

11.44. The question which begs consideration is the form of the new possible legal basis of Europol – a 'regulation'. We are of the opinion that the regulation as a form of legal basis for Europol is impossible. EU regulations are directly applicable in the Member States of the EU. In the area of criminal law one doubts the willingness of the Member States to adopt such a regulation.[86]

IX. Conclusion

11.45. The European Police Office (Europol) is the first European entity which handles police co-operation at the European level.

11.46. Europol's mission is to support and strengthen action by the EU Member States' police authorities and other law enforcement services and their mutual co-operation in preventing and combating serious crime affecting two or more Member States of the EU, terrorism and forms of crime which affect a common interest covered by a Union policy.

---

[82]   Treaty on the functioning of the European Union as amended by the Treaty of Lisbon [2010] OJ C 83/47.

[83]   Article 88(2) of the Treaty on the functioning of the EU.

[84]   Article 88(2)(a)(b) of the Treaty on the functioning of the EU.

[85]   Article 88(2)(a)(b) of the Treaty on the functioning of the EU. See Commission (EU), "Communication from the Commission to the European Parliament and the Council on the procedures for the scrutiny of Europol's activities by the European Parliament, together with national Parliaments" COM (2010) 776 final, 17 December 2010.

[86]   Libor Klimek, *supra* note 1, at 774.

11.47. Europol does not communicate with the competent national authorities directly, but via national units and liaison officers.

11.48. As shown, since 2009 the legal basis of the Europol has been the Council Decision 2009/371/JHA establishing the European Police Office. However, there is a possibility that there will be a new Europol legal basis – the Regulation on Europol but it is unlikely that the Member States will adopt such a controlling mandate. However, we are the opinion that it is impossible.

| | |

Summaries

FRA [*L'Office européen de police (Europol): passé, présent & futur*]

L'Office européen de police (Europol) est la première structure européenne consacrée à une collaboration policière à un niveau européen. Sa mission est de soutenir et de renforcer les activités des organes de police et des autres organismes des États membres de l'UE chargés de l'application du droit européen, ainsi que de soutenir et de renforcer leur collaboration mutuelle pour prévenir des actes criminels graves mettant en jeu deux États membres au moins de l'UE. Europol fait l'objet du présent exposé qui comprend sept chapitres. Alors que le premier chapitre est consacré à la création d'Europol et à sa base juridique, le second se penche sur ses objectifs, ses rôles et sa compétence. La troisième partie examine les relations entre Europol et les États membres de l'UE, ou plus concrètement entre Europol et les structures nationales, les éléments de liaison. La quatrième partie s'intéresse aux systèmes de traitement de l'information (le système d'information d'Europol et les éléments analytiques de travail) et la cinquième partie à la collaboration avec les autres institutions, organismes, bureaux et agences de l'UE, ainsi qu'à la collaboration avec les États non-membres. Le sixième chapitre présente quelques exemples d'opérations réussies menées par Europol et la septième et dernière partie décrit la possible évolution juridique de cette organisation.

CZE [*Evropský policejní úřad (Europol): Minulost, současnost & budoucnost*]

Evropský policejní úřad (Europol) je první evropskou jednotkou, která je zaměřena na policejní spolupráci na evropské úrovni. Jeho úlohou je podpora a posilňování činnosti policejních orgánů a jiných orgánů členských států EU, které prosazují výkon práva, jakož i jejich vzájemnou spolupráci při prevenci závažné trestní činnosti týkající se dvou nebo více členských států EU. Článek se zabývá Europolem a je rozdělen do sedmi oddílů. Zatímco první oddíl se zabývá jeho zřízením a právním základem, druhý oddíl rozebírá jeho cíle, pravomoc a úkoly. Třetí oddíl zkoumá vztahy Europolu s členskými státy EU, konkrétní s národními jednotkami, styčnými důstojníky. Čtvrtý oddíl se zabývá systémy zpracování informací (informační systém Europolu a analytické pracovní jednotky) a pátý oddíl se zaměřuje na spolupráci s ostatními institucemi, orgány, úřady a agenturami EU, jakož i spolupráci s nečlenskými státy. Šestý oddíl prezentuje několik příkladů úspěšných operací Europolu a sedmý oddíl naznačuje možný právní vývoj.

| | |

POL   [**Europejski Urząd Policji (Europol): Przeszłość, teraźniejszość i przyszłość**]
Niniejszy artykuł zajmuje się Europolem i został podzielony na siedem części. W pierwszej części omówiono jego powstanie i podstawy prawne, drugiej - jego cele, uprawnienia i zadania. Trzecia część zawiera analizę stosunków między Europolem a państwami członkowskimi UE, konkretnie zaś - jednostkami krajowymi i oficerami kontaktowymi. Czwarta część została poświęcona systemom przetwarzania informacji, zaś piąta zajmuje się współpracą z innymi instytucjami, organami, urzędami i agencjami UE, a także współpracą z państwami spoza Unii. W szóstej części przedstawiono kilka przykładów udanych operacji Europolu, zaś w siódmej nakreślono możliwe zmiany prawa.

DEU   [*Das Europäische Polizeiamt (Europol): Vergangenheit, Gegenwart und Zukunft*]
Der in sieben Abschnitte gegliederte Artikel befasst sich mit Europol. Der erste Abschnitt ist der Gründung und Rechtsgrundlage von Europol gewidmet, der zweite setzt sich mit seinen Zielen, Kompetenzen und Aufgaben auseinander. Der dritte Abschnitt untersucht die Beziehungen zwischen Europol und den EU-Mitgliedsstaaten – konkret also den nationalen Polizeieinheiten und Verbindungsoffizieren. Der vierte Abschnitt befasst sich mit Informationssystemen, der fünfte mit der Zusammenarbeit zwischen Europol und anderen Institutionen, Stellen, Ämtern und Agenturen der EU, sowie der Zusammenarbeit mit Drittländern. Der sechste Abschnitt stellt einige Beispiele erfolgreicher Europol-Operationen vor, und der siebte Abschnitt deutet die mögliche künftige rechtliche Entwicklung an.

RUS [*Полицейская служба Европейского Союза (Европол): Прошлое, настоящее и будущее*]

Статья разбита на семь разделов и в ней рассматривается Европол. В то время как первый раздел посвящен созданию данной организации и ее правовой основе, во втором разделе рассматриваются ее основные цели, полномочия и задачи. В третьем разделе исследуются отношения Европола с государствами-членами ЕС, в частности, с национальными подразделениями, связными офицерами. Четвертый раздел посвящен системам обработки информации, в пятом разделе рассматривается сотрудничество с другими учреждениями, организациями, комитетами и агентствами ЕС, а также сотрудничество с государствами, не входящими в состав ЕС. В шестом разделе приводятся примеры успешных операций Европола, а в седьмом разделе намечено возможное правовое развитие.

ESP [*Oficina Europea de Policía (Europol): pasado, presente y futuro*]

Este artículo, dividido en siete secciones, se refiere a Europol. Mientras que la primera sección hace referencia a su creación y a su base jurídica, la segunda analiza sus objetivos, competencias y tareas. La tercera sección examina las relaciones de Europol con los Estados miembros de la UE, en particular, con las unidades nacionales y los funcionarios de enlace. La cuarta sección trata los sistemas de procesamiento de la información y la quinta se centra en la colaboración con las demás instituciones, organismos, oficinas y agencias de la UE, así como en la cooperación con los Estados no miembros. La sexta sección presenta varios ejemplos de operaciones de éxito de Europol y la séptima sugiere el posible desarrollo jurídico.

|||

Czech Yearbook of International Law

Oskar Krejčí

The European Union and NATO: Cooperation, Competition or Conjunction?

Key words:
International organisation | European Union | NATO | geopolitics | foreign and security policy | post-modern state | political realism | liberal institutionalism | constructivism

Abstract | *The European Union is almost unanimously regarded as a new – sometimes even a post-modern – type of international organization. The concept of the post-modern state is connected with the idea of governance at several levels. One can only understand the true meaning of the European Union if it is perceived as an organic part of a few integration processes taking place in the Western world.*

But the EU is not the only Western integration organization – there is also NATO. Integration of EU and NATO was managed essentially by the same people from the very beginning. In spite of a certain organisational overlap between the Union and the Alliance, a functional division of labour is in place. The European Union, if looked at in isolation, may seem to be a new type of international organisation. Nevertheless, foreign and security policy of the Union indicates a classic role of powers and interconnections with the traditional military-political organisation. This paper discusses the nature of these two organizations and analyses whether their interaction is in the form of competition, cooperation or conjunction. Finally the issue of the impact of this interaction on the individual states is discussed.

Professor PhDr. Oskar Krejčí, CSc. (1948) is a vice-rector at the Vysoká škola mezinárodních a veřejných vztahů (University of International and public Relations) in Prague as well as the director of its Bratislava branch. He teaches at the Faculty of Political Sciences and International Relations at the Matej Bel University in Banská Bystrica. He has published around twenty-five books and more than a thousand different studies and articles. He was an adviser to two prime ministers of the Czechoslovak Federal Government.
e-mail: politicus@upcmail.cz

I. Introduction

12.01. The fundamental nature of the European Union may be presented in quite simple terms. As John Ruggie wrote, 'the institutional, juridical, and spatial complexes associated with the community may constitute nothing less than the emergence of the first truly postmodern international political form.'[1]

12.02. The perception of the European Union as a qualitatively new international organisation inherently recalls the most serious debates in the theory of international politics. The axis of debate is around the concept of 'time' – at least since 1939 when '*The Twenty Years' Crisis, 1919-1939*' was published by Edward H. Carr. Carr profiled two main conceptual lines on the nature of the world politics: the 'realistic' line arguing that the nature of world politics does not change, and the 'utopian' line advocating a constantly evolving fundamental nature of the world politics, particularly thanks to the establishment of international institutions. For the realists, such as Robert Gilpin, 'the fundamental nature of international relations has not changed over the millennia. International relations continue to be a recurring struggle for wealth and power among independent actors in a state of anarchy.'[2] Or as Martin Wight wrote, 'international politics is the realm of recurrence and repetition; it is the field in which political action is most regularly necessitous.'[3] For the utopians, however, nearly every single event in international politics is a proof of qualitative changes – or at least of the possibility for such changes to take place.

12.03. In theory of internationals politics, contemporary ideas of how 'times change' are highly varied. For instance, the English school, liberal institutionalism and constructivism, are repeatedly juxtaposed in textbooks as the antipode of realism. Likewise, there is an increasingly common view that the European Union, as an international organisation, has overcome the traditional perception of international politics and cut itself loose from the use of power instruments, first of all military force. Historians, economists, and political sociologists emphasize that radical decisions made by several statesmen structured the form of the Union from its infancy. Václav Šmejkal, for instance, points out that

---

[1] John G. Ruggie, *Territoriality and Beyond: Problematizing Modernity in International Relations*, 47(1) INTERNATIONAL ORGANIZATION 140 (1993).

[2] ROBERT GILPIN, WAR AND CHANGE IN WORLD POLITICS, Cambridge, New York: Cambridge University Press 7 (1981).

[3] Martin Wight, *Why is there no International Theory?* 2(35) INTERNATIONAL RELATIONS 43 (1960).

12.04. The existing form of the European integration is the product of a unique vision of European unification and a unique historical situation. The presumed exceptionality consists in the fact that the European integration did not originate from the linear or logical continuation of the previous economic, political and ideological development, but that it has the historical anomaly of the post-war situation in Europe and the extraordinary drive with will and imagination by several individuals to thank for its genesis.[4]

12.05. With this 'revolution of old structures', as Šmejkal puts it, the conversant group of politicians particularly in France and Germany sought a way to prevent the repeating of the horrors of the world wars they personally experienced. For example, amongst these politicians were Jean Monnet or Robert Schuman representing France and Konrad Adenauer representing the Federal Republic of Germany.

12.06. The work initiated by the aforesaid politicians was recognized in 2012 by the Norwegian Nobel Committee, in the awarding of the Nobel Prize for Peace to the European Union. The justification for the Nobel Peace Prize being awarded states *inter alia* that, in the inter-war years, the Norwegian Nobel Peace Committee made several awards to persons who were seeking reconciliation between Germany and France. 'Since 1945, that reconciliation has become a reality', and 'today war between Germany and France is unthinkable'. But the committee even went further, saying:

12.07. The Norwegian Nobel Committee wishes to focus on what it sees as the EU's most important result: the successful struggle for peace and reconciliation and for democracy and human rights. The stabilising part played by the EU has helped to transform most of Europe from a continent of war to a continent of peace.[5]

12.08. When focussing our attention on the European Union (leaving aside certain links to some countries or other European integration blocks), all of the recognitions specified above can be accepted. The European Union is without question a unique international organisation. Through integration, it has reduced the number of interstate disputes. It has done this in some cases by eliminating their root causes and in other cases by transferring them into new institutions. In certain occasions, the tasks of international diplomacy were even turned into

---

[4] Václav Šmejkal, *Poválečná evropská integrace jako revoluce starých struktur* (*Post-war European Integration as a Revolution of Old Structures*), in Geneze a Současnost Evropské Integrace (*Genesis and Presence of European Integration*), Prague: VŠE (University of Economics) 69 (Zdeněk Veselý ed., 2000).

[5] *General Report on the Activities of the European Union — 2012*. Brussels: European Commission, 2013, at 9.

the subject-matter of a democratic decision-making process. Although it has not been able to eliminate all disputes between member states, it has institutionalised suitable procedures to resolve these disputes without wars.

II. The Absence of a Common EU Policy

12.09. The nature and degree of integration of the European Union can be assessed as a whole, as can its function. The same is true for the different Union policies. Such an assessment will reveal that there is a significant difference between economic and political integration within the Union. This is particularly true of the institutional framework of the EU, but it also applies to the practices of EU foreign and security policies, which have numerous specificities. The outset of this policy can be traced back to the *Single European Act* (signed in 1986; ratified in 1987), which defined the scope of European political cooperation. The Maastricht *Treaty on European Union* (signed in 1992; ratified in 1993) subsequently underpinned the deepening integration with several pillars, with the Common Foreign and Security Policy becoming one of the main supports for the 'Maastricht cathedral'. The *Treaty of Lisbon* (signed in 2007; ratified in 2009) provided for the currently applicable concept of integration in foreign and security policy, namely in Article 24 (formerly Article 11 of the *Treaty on European Union*). This Article, specifically paragraph 1 thereof, provides *inter alia* the following:

12.10. The common foreign and security policy is subject to specific rules and procedures. It shall be defined and implemented by the European Council and the Council acting unanimously, except where the Treaties provide otherwise. The adoption of legislative acts shall be excluded. The common foreign and security policy shall be put into effect by the High Representative of the Union for Foreign Affairs and Security Policy and by Member States, in accordance with the Treaties. The specific role of the European Parliament and of the Commission in this area is defined by the Treaties. The Court of Justice of the European Union shall not have jurisdiction...[6]

12.11. The text of the *Treaty of Lisbon* quoted above shows that the domain of foreign and security policy raises the interests of the member states

---

[6] Council of The European Union (6655/08), Consolidated versions of the Treaty on European Union and the Treaty on the functioning of the European Union, at 40, available at: http://register.consilium.europa.eu/pdf/en/08/st06/st06655.en08.pdf (accesed on 11 September 2013).

above those of the Union as a whole. A technical manifestation of this principle is the fact that, apart from consensus, the Union does not have any other procedure to seek a common interest in the case of foreign and security policy. The decisions in the Council cannot be taken on the basis of any majority – relative, absolute or qualified. At the same time, a compromise-seeking mechanism is fully absent because the *Treaty of Lisbon* does not require an agreement between the member states in this area. Consequently, the EU foreign and security policy exists only as a frequently accidental common denominator of policies pursued by the individual member states.

12.12. While the current British prime minister has commented that the actions of the Union in the field of foreign and security policy are a manifestation of commendable plurality of opinions, he is not exactly right. That disunity does not show itself in the discussions, but in different practical actions. This was clear, for instance, during the intervention in Iraq in 2003, as well as when seeking a uniform position on the Russian-Georgian war of 2008. Also the independence of Kosovo has so far been recognized by 22 out of the 27 members of the European Union. Further, in May 2013, the Union was not able to collectively extend the embargo for arms supplies to Syrian rebels and their allies. This was a signal of resignation in the face of a situation where some member states would supply these arms, while others, such as Germany, Sweden, Austria, and the Czech Republic, were in favour of extending the embargo. The European Union once again proved that when it comes to escalated international conflicts, it has no foreign policy – its activities fall apart into the often contradictory actions of the individual member states.

III. The Structure and a Common Policy

12.13. This absence of unity in relation to foreign and security policy also translates, in interesting ways, into the architecture of the European Union. This becomes very clear when one compares the European Council and the Council of ministers with the Commission and the European Parliament. The former provide a forum for the presentation of the member states' independent policies, while the latter represent the element of joint policy in the Union. In decision-making, the Commission and the European Parliament apply a variously conceived principle of majority, with some elements of democracy. Compared to the European Council and the Council of Ministers, however, the Commission and the European Parliament have significantly limited powers in foreign and security policy. But the Commission has a wide prerogative, and often makes use of it. The European Parliament focuses primarily on resolutions of recommendation and promotional relevance in foreign and security policy. The case of Kosovo as previously mentioned is an example of this practice.

12.14. The European Council has not adopted any decision stipulating that the Union should jointly pursue the policy of this Serbian province becoming independent and of the subsequent recognition of the separated Kosovo. However, Javier Solana in his function as the EU High Representative for the Common Foreign and Security Policy initiated a number of secret and public activities which gradually resulted in the separation of Kosovo. A similar approach is being applied by the current EU Commissioner for Enlargement, Štefan Füle. In the negotiations on the accession of Serbia to the Union, Füle has pursued the principle of the territorial integrity of Kosovo, which has not been defined as a prerequisite at the level of the European Council or Council of Minister.

12.15. By analogy, this is also the case of the *European Parliament resolution of 18 April 2013 on the European integration process of Kosovo*. In Article 8 of this *Resolution*, the European Parliament 'reiterates that ideas of partitioning Kosovo or any other country of the West Balkan run counter to the spirit of European integration; reiterates its support for the territorial integrity of Kosovo and for commonly agreed solutions to outstanding disputes'.[7] This principle would be very difficult to accept even if its formulation was not preceded by a violation of the UN Security Council Resolution 1244 from June 1999. This begs the question of when the 'spirit of the European integration' appeared, giving the Kosovars the right to establish their own state – while, at the same time, denying the same right to Serbs in Kosovo or in Bosnia and Herzegovina, for instance.

12.16. However, the essential fact is that these issues are not discussed at the level of the Union bodies, which have the decision-making power pursuant to Article 24 of the *Treaty of Lisbon* – i.e. primarily at the European Council. A simple difference in the member states' opinions blocks the decision, which in turn opens the way for autonomous actions by the member states and for arbitrariness of the Commission. At the same time, the subsequent actions of the Commission and the resolutions adopted by the European Parliament fully and systematically avoid the only foreign policy doctrine which ever was

---

[7] European Parliament, European Parliament resolution of 18 April 2013 on the European integration process of Kosovo, available at: http://www.europarl.europa.eu/sides/getDoc.do?type=TA&reference=P7-TA-2013-0187&language=EN&ring=B7-2013-0089 (accesed on 11 September 2013).

adopted by the Union – entitled *Secure Europe in a Better World* (2003). This document, in a Chapter titled *An International Order Based on Effective Multilateralism*, provides for principles to be followed by all European Union bodies:

12.17.   In a world of global threats, global markets and global media, our security and prosperity increasingly depend on an effective multilateral system... We are committed to upholding and developing International Law. The fundamental framework for international relations is the United Nations Charter. ... We want international organisations, regimes and treaties to be effective in confronting threats to international peace and security, and must therefore be ready to act when their rules are broken.[8]

IV. Geo-functional Cooperation EU/NATO

12.18.   With such an approach to the foreign and security policy, the European Union cannot be considered to be a universal organisation embracing all sectors. This fact is apparent in the concept of the EU Common Security and Defence Policy. The following bodies have been established under CSDP: EU Military Staff (2001), the European Defence Agency (2004), and the internet-based European Security and Defence College (2005). The very first occasion when the European Union sent its armed forces to secure peace dates back to 2003 – a mission in Macedonia. Since then, the Union has organized 34 military or security operations as of May 2013.[9] But there are questions as to whether the aforesaid activities of the European Union do not duplicate or perhaps even contradict the work of the North Atlantic Alliance. The difficulties in defining the relationship between the European Union and NATO are particularly important in the sense that NATO and the European Union are 'Geopolitical Burden-Sharing' institutions, which reportedly require a 'geo-functional' division of roles and cooperation.[10]

---

[8]   European Council, A Secure Europe in a Better World. European security strategy, Brussels, 12 December 2003, at 9, available at: http://www.consilium.europa.eu/uedocs/cmsUpload/78367.pdf (accesed on 11 September 2013).

[9]   See International Security Information Service, europe, CSDP Note – CSDP and EU Mission Update, May 2013, available at: http://www.isis-europe.eu/sites/default/files/publications-downloads/CSDP%20Note%20Mission%20Update%20May%202013_2.pdf (accesed on 11 September 2013).

[10]   PAUL CORNISH, EU AND NATO: CO-OPERATION OR COMPETITION? Brussels: European Parliament 7, 12 (2006), available at: http://www.europarl.europa.eu/meetdocs/2004_2009/documents/dv/eunatorelations_/eunatorelations_en.pdf (accesed on 11 September 2013).

12.19. One of the major problems when interpreting the role and nature of the European Union concerns its separation from history. It is an undeniable truth that Robert Schuman and Konrad Adenauer were present at the origin of the Union. They were holding their state offices at the time when the treaty establishing the European Coal and Steel Community was signed (1952). In addition, Schuman was the French minister for foreign affairs at the time when France co-founded NATO (1949), just like Adenauer was the German federal chancellor when the Federal Republic of Germany was accepted to join the Alliance (1955). Schuman was a member of the government, partly as the prime minister, during the colonial war conducted by France in Indochina. Their perception of the world can by no means be considered to be utopian.

12.20. The current definition of relations between the European Union and NATO is based on the *Berlin Plus* agreement of 2002 and its subsequent additions. These agreements concern a series of arrangements governing the cooperation between these organisations in the use of resources, information sharing and planning. An essential element in the design of such relationships is the accepted principle that NATO will lend its means and planning resources to the European Union only for operations where the Alliance itself decides not to intervene. Consequently, Turkey as a NATO member state was able to block the above-mentioned Union's operation EUFOR Concordia (2003) in the Republic of Macedonia for five months. The operations of the European Union in the Balkan, Iraq or Libya illustrate very aptly that the activities of the Union in military matters are designed to complement the activities of the Alliance.

12.21. For statesmen like Schuman and Adenauer, the integration processes within the Union and the Alliance were complementary, mutually supportive activities. In general terms, it is possible to conclude that the EU and NATO were formed and managed essentially by the same people since the very beginning. The same is the case today. While both these international organisations may partially overlap in terms of their institutional configuration, they are mutually complementary in the political point of view. The organisational imperfection in ensuring cooperation between the EU and NATO does not mean that there is no common political interest. On contrary, it seems that even this organisational imperfection might have its functional advantages.

12.22. When the North Atlantic Council as the supreme decision-making and consultative body within NATO decided to bomb Yugoslavia, and the European Council as the supreme body within the European Union decided to provide humanitarian aid for the Balkans. It is important to remember that these decisions were not adopted by abstract institutions. Rather, they were made by specific statesmen who, in case of the Alliance and the Union, happen to be the same persons in the Western European powers. Furthermore, the symmetry or asymmetry of the relations and the importance of the particular policies are evidenced by the fact that it is easier to start a career in NATO and continue in the European Union – as was the case with the two European Commissioners mentioned above – than vice-versa. The Alliance and the Union are like twins; sometimes they even seem to be like Siamese twins.

V. Values and Socialization

12.23. Probably the most valuable input from the political theories of the English school, particularly from constructivism, is the idea that international institutions operating on the basis of certain values are able to translate these values into the policies of their member states and the political culture of the power elites in these countries. If this would be the case, the policies of the European Union member states could indeed experience a qualitative transformation, for instance, as a result of the adoption of the *Charter of Fundamental Rights of the European Union* (initially 2000; in force only together with the *Treaty of Lisbon*).

12.24. The Alliance's documents currently in force seem to imply its commitment to the idea of human rights. However, the actual function of NATO is to provide collective military defence. Its original understanding is embodied in Article 5 of the *North Atlantic Treaty* (1949):

12.25. [T]he Parties agree that an armed attack against one or more of them in Europe or North America shall be considered an attack against them all and consequently they agree that, if such an armed attack occurs, each of them, in exercise of the right of individual or collective self-defence recognised by Article 51 of the Charter of the United Nations, will assist the Party or Parties so attacked by taking forthwith, individually and in concert with the other Parties, such action as it deems necessary, including the use of armed force, to restore and maintain the security of the North Atlantic area.

12.26. Pursuant to Article 6, the Alliance's area of defence interests consists of the territory of the Parties (initially including the so-called Algerian Departments of France), the territory under their jurisdiction and their armed forces and occupation forces in the Mediterranean Sea and in the Euro-Atlantic area north of the Tropic of Cancer.[11]

---

[11]   NATO, The North Atlantic Treaty, available at: http://www.nato.int/cps/en/natolive/official_texts_17120.htm (accesed on 11 September 2013).

12.27. The original interpretation of the purpose and aim of NATO corresponded to the containment (Georg Kennan) or rollback (James Burnham) of communism. Following the dissolution of the Soviet Union at the end of the Cold War, the Alliance began to seek a new concept as its reason for being. The nature of NATO's transformation was probably most aptly expressed in *The Alliance's Strategic Concept* (1999)[12]. In several places, this document emphasizes the determination to conduct non-Article 5 crisis response operations in the Euro-Atlantic area, while the Euro-Atlantic area is no longer spatially concretized. While the new strategy on *Active Engagement, Modern Defence* (2010) as written pays deference to the idea of its return to the principles of international law[13], the bombing in Libya (2011) took place only after its adoption.

12.28. The NATO-centric understanding of global security is apparent from a number of both public and off-the-record statements of some Alliance officers as well as from the practical steps taken by the Brussels headquarters. Their understanding is by far closer to the concept of the clash of civilizations (coined by Samuel Huntington) than to the ideals of human rights and democracy. These were the same ideals mentioned by the Norwegian Committee when awarding the Nobel Prize to the Union. This is also confirmed by the military actions carried out by NATO or its member countries, as well as by some member states of the European Union, such as those in Yugoslavia (1999), Iraq (2002), Libya (2011) and Syria (2011-to date). These actions cast doubt upon – or at least significantly modify – the idea that the role of countries as military units has shifted in the course of increasing economic interdependence. Rosecrance's vision that, in the current international system, the 'trading state' becomes dominant at the expense of the 'military state'[14] needs to be transformed into the concept of possible control over a territory through a local elite selected by force and through transnational monopolies.

---

[12] See NATO: The Alliance's Strategic Concept, available at: http://www.nato.int/cps/en/natolive/official_texts_27433.htm (accesed on 11 September 2013).

[13] See NATO: Active Engagement, Modern Defence, available at: http://www.nato.int/cps/en/natolive/official_texts_68580.htm (accesed on 11 September 2013). For a more detailed comparison of the European Union and NATO strategies, see *Doktríny mocností a nejdůležitějších aliancí na počátku 21. Století* (*Doctrines of power and the most important alliances at the beginning of the 21st century*), Conference publication, Vysoká Škola Mezinárodních a Veřejných Vztahů Praha, Prague: Professional Publishing (2011).

[14] See Richard Rosecrance, The Rise of the Trading State: Commerce and Conquest in the Modern World, New York: Basic Books (1986).

12.29. Therefore, at first sight, Samuel Huntington and his vision of the clash of civilizations offers a better explanation for the current shape of Western integration than that articulated by the Norwegian Nobel Peace Prize Committee. However, the perception of the EU/NATO conjunction as a 'Fort West' protecting the Euro-Atlantic civilization based on Judeo-Christian values is only one of the possible options for how the division of humankind into civilization spheres can be perceived. In his essay *On Peaceful Unity of Faith* (*De pace fidei;* 1453), Cardinal Nicholas of Kues, a renaissance philosopher, described the conclusion of the imaginary dispute among the representatives of various Churches as information to God. According to the wise men participating in the discussions, 'to various nations you sent various prophets and teachers – some at one time, others at another. But the earthly human condition has this characteristic: viz., that longstanding custom, which is regarded as having passed over into nature, is defended as the truth.' However, the discussion has proved that 'in the loftiest domain of reason a harmony among the religions was reached, in the aforeshown manner.' And the King of kings commanded that the wise men return to their nations in the name of the Creator of all, who 'may be praised in peace'.[15] This is how the European humanism was born, leading towards the enlightenment rationalism which gave birth to the idea of human rights. However, this approach is fundamentally different from the social Darwinist geopolitics forming the foundations for the Huntington's understanding of the clash of civilizations.

12.30. This raises the question of whether the security-related values of the European Union and of NATO should be seen as contradictory or complementary. In any case, there is an apparent difference between cooperation-based summits between the Union and Russia and China, and NATO's transformation towards the geostrategic visions of the clash of civilizations, which are associated with permanently high military expenditures and encirclement of the core of the Euro-Asian 'Grand Chessboard'.

12.31. From the point of view of comparing the Union and Alliance policies, it is not relevant which of these values are ethical or whether or not the policies are efficient; the essential aspect is that they are different. They are indeed different although they are – in most cases – pursued and followed by the same countries and the same politicians. This is the case, *inter alia*, because of the existence of the double security concept: security as a social guarantee for citizens versus military and physical

---

security of the country. This also corresponds to the functioning of the state as such:

12.32. 1)   The ministries in charge of trade and the business elites think relatively pragmatically. They do so based on the current calculations of economic efficiency, which they use to adapt their global policy for all azimuths. However, every trade topic can be securitized or de-securitized, or prioritized to a vitally important and, thus, existential state interest. As Jana Lasicová and Jaroslav Ušiak put it, this happens 'according to the countries' own preferences, which do not necessarily have to be equally acceptable for all members and non-members' of an organisation, from the point of view of both security and ethics.[16] This reality has become very clear in the recent years, particularly in the energy sector.

12.33. 2)   The ministry of defence and the military elites think on a 'regional basis' with relatively constant front lines defined by geopolitics. The 'regional basis' in this concept has a broad scale. It ranges from global and space perception of security in the case of superpowers such as the U.S., to a full loss of the understanding of territoriality itself as is the case with small countries. In small countries like the Czech Republic, the army has been reduced below the level traditionally required for national defence. Small countries subordinate their security to the Alliance understanding and actions. Their assistance in NATO's foreign missions is only of a minor military importance; it is primarily intended as a diplomatic expression of support for the allied powers.

VI. False Promise and Future

12.34. The concept of the post-modern state is connected with idea of multi-level governance, existing at supra-national, governmental and sub-national levels.[17] But the findings in this article can lead to the conclusion that the integration of the European countries within the European Union has not penetrated into the core of sovereignty of the different national states, into the 'high politics' – their foreign, security and defence policies. This raises the most significant of all questions: Can the type of integration represented by the Union in its ideal form exist without NATO in the current world? The realist school, having

---

[16]   See JANA LASICOVÁ & JAROSLAV UŠIAK, BEZPEČNOSŤ AKO KATEGÓRIA (*Security as a Category*), Bratislava: Veda 192 (2012).

[17]   See e.g. GEORG SØRENSEN, CHANGES IN STATEHOOD. THE TRANSFORMATION OF INTERNATIONAL RELATIONS, New York: Palgrave (2001).

Edward Carr as one of its founding fathers, dramatizes this question even further.[18] It claims that:

- International organisations are established to ensure the 'small policy'.
- International organisations are established as an expression of interest by the powers. In other words, they exist as long as they suit the needs of these powers.

12.35. Essential tasks of foreign and security policy of large powers are not dealt with even at the level of institutions such as NATO: nuclear weapons remain under the sole command of the states having them in their possession, rather than under joint command of the Alliance. Individual members continue to station troops in member countries such as the U.S. troops in Germany. In crucial situations, the functioning of the Alliance is beyond democratic control. Recently, the Czech Republic was requested by NATO to give its consent to the bombing in Libya, but consent was not put to the public or the parliament for deliberation. It is actually not fully clear whom the question was directed to. Was it the prime minister, the government as a whole, or a minister? The prime minister did not give an answer even after the interpellation in the Parliament of the Czech Republic to find out who gave the consent. Given that the bombing was preceded by a publicly declared disapproval with the use of force from the minister of foreign affairs, one can only assume that the small country subordinated itself to the interests of the allied powers.

12.36. Also in the European Union, the ideals of peace and democracy are practically applied mainly inwards within the organisation. Any search for an agreement to solve major problems, such as the Euro crisis, requires an agreement between Germany and France first. A general consensus is only sought on the basis of their agreement. This approach shows a hidden bilateralism policy. The geopolitical axis of the European Union going from Berlin to Paris was also demonstrated in 2013 when looking for a solution for the debt crisis in Cyprus. It is worth noting that the final decision to impose a levy on high deposits, which was adopted by the Council of Ministers, was accompanied by an announcement that the decision does not need to be approved by the Cypriot parliament. If such a decision would be imposed on Germany or France, certainly there would be someone to remind us that the beginning of European parliamentarianism was the result of the nobility's fight for the right to express opinions on tax issues. But the

---

[18] See Arthur A. Stein, *Neoliberal Institutionalism*, *in* OXFORD HANDBOOK OF INTERNATIONAL RELATIONS, Oxford, New York: Oxford University Press 206 (Ch. Reus-Smit and D. Snidal eds., 2008).

position of Germany and France are tolerated because their exit would have catastrophic consequences for the Union.

12.37. In this respect, even the European Union is not built on the principles of justice or solidarity, but on the traditional principle of relative advantages for the member states. Integration in foreign and security policy constitutes only a 'false promise', as John Mearsheimer puts it.[19] Autonomy in international organisations is truly becoming more relevant than sovereignty (Robert O. Keohane), but only for small countries. The Czech Republic can be used as an example of the 'socialisation' of a small country within an international organisation, i.e. of the use of templates offered to choose a policy. This process does not take place through the learning of elites, or at least not only through such learning. This is to say nothing of the learning of the public. In the situation of increasing interdependence, the countries in transition seem to shift from the position of semi-periphery to the position of regional periphery within the Alliance and the Union. At the same time, jointly shared assets become so important in the organisation that they are able to suppress sovereign foreign policy. The 'socialisation' of small countries takes place in circumstances where the internal arrangements of the respective organisations are determined not only by the nature of the formal agreements, but also by the informal structure of the organisation developed based on the power potential ratios between the member states.

12.38. However, the historic processes in the European Union and Alliance are not yet over. It is not necessary to jump to 'realistic' scepticism— that nothing will ever change. If for no other reason than that 'the characteristic vice of the utopian is naivety; of the realist, sterility', to use the words of Edward Carr. To conclude with another quote from Carr: 'all healthy human action, and therefore all healthy thought, must establish a balance between utopia and reality, between free will and determinism'.[20]

| | |

Summaries

FRA [*L'Union Européenne et l'OTAN: Collaboration, rivalité ou unité ?*]
Presque tout le monde 's'accorde à considérer l'Union européenne comme un nouveau type 'd'organisation internationale – parfois

---

[19] John J. Mearsheimer, *The False Promise of International Institutions*, 19(3) INTERNATIONAL SECURITY 5 (Winter 1994/1995).

[20] EDWARD HALLETT CARR, THE TWENTY YEARS' CRISIS, 1919-1939. AN INTRODUCTION TO THE STUDY OF INTERNATIONAL RELATIONS, New York: Perennial 11–12 (2001).

carrément désignée comme postmoderne. On associe le concept d'état postmoderne à l'idée d'une gouvernance à plusieurs niveaux. Pour comprendre cependant entièrement le sens de l'Union européenne, il faut la percevoir comme une partie organique d'un certain nombre de processus d'intégration en cours dans le monde occidental.

L'UE n'est pas la seule organisation d'"intégration européenne – il ne faut pas oublier 'l'OTAN. Ce sont essentiellement les mêmes qui sont depuis l'origine derrière l'intégration dans l'UE et dans l'OTAN. Bien que les fonctions de l'UE et celles de l'OTAN se recouvrent dans certains cas, on peut parler d'une relative division du travail. Si l'on observe l'Union européenne isolément, on peut la concevoir comme un nouveau type d'organisation internationale. En tous les cas, c'est à la fois le rôle classique de grande puissance de l'Union européenne et sa relation avec une organisation politico-militaire comme l'OTAN qui caractérisent sa politique étrangère et de sécurité. On examine dans le présent article l'essence de ces deux organisations et on se demande lesquelles de leurs interactions correspondent à des collaborations, des rivalités ou des formes d'union. La question de l'impact de ces différentes interactions sur les États membres de ces organisations est abordée en conclusion.

CZE [*Evropská unie a NATO: spolupráce, konkurence, nebo jednota?*]

Evropská unie je téměř jednoznačně chápána jako nový – někdy přímo postmoderní – typ mezinárodní organizace. Pojem postmoderního státu je spojen s ideou vládnutí na více úrovních. Porozumět ale významu Evropská unie lze jen tehdy, je-li vnímána jako organická část několika integračních presesů probíhajících na Západě.

EU není jedinou západní integrační organizací – je zde též NATO. Integrace   EU a NATO byla od počátku řízena v zásadě stejnými lidmi. Přestože existuje určité organizační překrývání mezi Unií a Aliancí, je zde funkční dělba práce. Když je Evropská unie nahlížena izolovaně, může být vnímána jako nový typ mezinárodní organizace. Nicméně zahraniční a bezpečnostní politika Unie naznačuje klasickou roli mocností a propojení s tradiční vojensko-politickou organizací. Tato stať pojednává o podstatě těchto dvou organizací a rozebírá, které jejich interakce mají podobu konkurence, spolupráce nebo jednoty. V závěru je diskutována otázka, jaký vliv mají tyto interakce na jednotlivé státy.

| | |

POL [*Unia Europejska i NATO: Współpraca, konkurencja czy jedność?*]

Rzeczywiste znaczenie UE i NATO można zrozumieć jedynie wówczas, kiedy wyobrazimy je sobie jako żywe organizmy, będące częścią procesów integracyjnych w zachodnim świecie. Ponieważ organizacyjnie UE i NATO w pewnych kwestiach pokrywają się, stwarza to dobre warunki do ich współpracy w pewnych obszarach. Patrząc na Unię Europejską odrębnie od pozostałych ugrupowań, należy uznać ją za nowy typ organizacji międzynarodowej; z drugiej strony, jej polityka międzynarodowa i polityka bezpieczeństwa sugeruje klasyczną mocarstwową rolę UE i powiązania z tradycyjnymi organizacjami wojskowo-politycznymi.

DEU [*Die Europäische Union und die NATO: Zusammenarbeit, Konkurrenz oder Einheit?*]

Die wahre Bedeutung von EU und NATO lässt sich nur erfassen, wenn wir sie als lebende Organismen und als Bestandteil der in der westlichen Welt stattgefundenen und stattfindenden Integrationsprozesse begreifen. Im Hinblick auf gewisse organisatorische Überlappungen zwischen EU und NATO ist in einigen Bereichen Raum für eine Zusammenarbeit zwischen den beiden gegeben. Die Europäische Union, gesondert von anderen Gruppierungen betrachtet, darf als neuer Typ einer internationalen Organisation betrachtet werden; auf der anderen Seite verweist ihre internationale Politik und Sicherheitspolitik auf die klassische Machtrolle der EU und ihre Verflechtung mit traditionellen militärisch-politischen Organisationen.

RUS [*Европейский Союз и НАТО: сотрудничество, конкуренция или единство?*]

Реальное значение ЕС и НАТО можно понять, представив их как живые организмы и как составную часть процесса интеграции в западном мире. Учитывая, что некоторые функции ЕС и НАТО перекрываются, существуют определенные возможности для их сотрудничества в некоторых областях. Если рассматривать Европейский Союз отдельно от других групп, то его можно считать международной организацией нового типа. С другой стороны, международная политика и политика в области безопасности подразумевает классическую роль ЕС и связь с традиционными военно-политическими организациями.

244

ESP   [*¿La Unión Europea y la OTAN: cooperación, competencia o unidad?*]

La verdadera importancia de la UE y la OTAN puede ser entendida si las vemos como organismos vivos y como parte de los procesos de integración en el mundo occidental. Considerando algunos solapamientos de índole organizacional entre la UE y la OTAN, es evidente que en algunas áreas existe espacio para la cooperación mutua. Si miramos la Unión Europea fuera del contexto de otras agrupaciones, podemos observar un nuevo tipo de organización internacional; por otro lado, su política internacional y de seguridad dejan entrever el papel de poder tradicional de la UE y su interconexión con las organizaciones político-militares tradicionales.

| | |

Czech Yearbook of International Law

Davorin Lapaš | Robert Mrljić

International Non-governmental Organizations (INGOs) as Participants in the International Lawmaking Process: Examples in Environmental and Space Law

Key words:
international non-governmental organizations (INGOs) |
'soft law' | *environmental law* | *space law* |
lawmaking process

Abstract | *The article deals with the role the international non-governmental organizations (INGOs) play in the international lawmaking process. Starting from the definition of INGOs, the article analyzes their lawmaking capacity in contemporary international law through the so-called phases of imagination, standard-setting and implementation. In many fields of international law today, the INGOs participate in the lawmaking process mostly through their influence on the negotiation process at international conferences, but also through the creation of so-called 'soft law' instruments introducing some general principles which, although not legally binding, may influence the states' behaviour. The article mostly concentrates on the INGOs' role in the fields of international environmental law and space law.*

Davorin Lapaš LL.M, Ph.D, Professor of Public International Law, Department of Public International Law, University of Zagreb, Faculty of Law, Croatia.
e-mail: dlapas@pravo.hr

Robert Mrljić LL.M, Ph.D. Candidate, Assistant at the Department of Public International Law, University of Zagreb, Faculty of Law, Croatia.
e-mail: rob_mr2@yahoo.com

| | |

'We theorists have to take heed to build our doctrines on tendencies rather than on "facts"; otherwise, when we have finished constructing our systems it may happen that the facts are no longer what they were when we began building, and the system is out of date before it is established.'

F. Williams[1]

| | |

I. Introductory Remarks

13.01. International non-governmental organizations (INGOs), more than 60 years after their role within the United Nations was recognized in article 71 of the UN Charter, have not found their place among the unanimously accepted subjects of international law. In spite of their increasing significance in contemporary international relations, international legal doctrine still hesitates to accept them as participants in international legal relations. However, some of these organizations, due to their knowledge, competence and active participation in international relations, significantly influence the international lawmaking process in many fields, particularly through the negotiation process at international conferences. Sometimes these organizations appear as an organized means of public participation in international decision-making directed at the identification of problems that require legal regulation, but sometimes they participate through the drafting, promotion and implementation of 'soft-law' or even legally binding documents. There is no doubt that such roles of INGOs, not only within the UN system, but in the contemporary international lawmaking process in general could be analyzed in many fields. In this paper we have decided to focus on two specific branches of international law – environmental law and space law.

II. The Notion of INGOs

13.02. There are numerous definitions of INGOs in international law doctrine, since international lawyers are not unanimous in understanding their constitutive elements. Certain authors focus on only one element of INGOs – their non-governmental character. Thus, Rodley defines an NGO as 'any group of individuals who have come together voluntarily to work for a particular objective, other than by

---

[1]   Quoted from: JOSEF J. LADOR-LEDERER, INTERNATIONAL NON-GOVERNMENTAL ORGANIZATIONS AND ECONOMIC ENTITIES, Leiden: A.W. Sythoff 12 (1963).

Czech Yearbook of International Law

means of governmental action.'[2] The private, non-governmental element of INGOs is also stressed by Charlotte Ku, who defines them as 'voluntary organizations of individuals'.[3] Some authors require that such organizations 'are not established by a government or by intergovernmental agreement'.[4] A similar provision can be found in UN ECOSOC resolution 288B(X) granting consultative status to certain INGOs within ECOSOC,[5] while later ECOSOC resolutions on the same topic broaden the notion of the non-governmental character of an organization. These resolutions even consider as non-governmental the organizations 'which accept members designated by governmental authorities, provided that such membership does not interfere with the free expression of views of the organization'.[6]

13.03. The above-mentioned definitions of INGOs actually indicate two different understandings of their non-governmental character: the non-governmental structure of an organization and the functioning of the organization independent of the governmental sector. In our view, the non-governmental character of INGOs should be accepted as a basic element of their definition, but understood in both its aspects. Consequently, even an organization that accepts both categories of membership (private, as well as those designated by governmental authorities) should be considered non-governmental as long as all

---

[2] Nigel S. Rodley, *Human Rights NGOs: Rights and Obligations (Present Status and Perspectives), in* THE LEGITIMACY OF THE UNITED NATIONS: TOWARDS AN ENHANCED LEGAL STATUS OF NON-STATE ACTORS, Utrecht: Netherlands Institute of Human Rights 41, 44 (Th. C. van Boven, C. Flinterman, F. Grünfeld, & R. Hut eds., 1997). Similarly, Hart and Thetaz-Bergman determine the entire non-governmental sector in this way: 'The nongovernmental sector is best defined by exclusion; it includes all those persons, individually and collectively, who are not formally within the government.' Stuart N. Hart, Laura Thetaz-Bergman, *The Role of Nongovernmental Organizations in Implementing the Convention on the Rights of the Child*, 6(2) TRANSNATIONAL LAW AND CONTEMPORARY PROBLEMS 373, 376 (1996).

[3] Charlotte Ku, *The Developing Role of Non-governmental Organizations in Global Policy and Law Making*, 13 CHINESE YEARBOOK OF INTERNATIONAL LAW AND AFFAIRS 140, 142 (1994-95).

[4] Hermann H.-K. Rechenberg, *Non-governmental Organizations, in* 3 EPIL, Amsterdam, New York, Oxford: North-Holland 612, 612 (R. Bernhardt ed., 1997). Cf. also Stephan Hobe, *Non-Governmental Organizations, in* 7 THE MAX PLANCK EPIL, Oxford: Oxford University Press 716, 716-717 (R. Wolfrum ed., 2012).

[5] 'Any international organization which is not established by inter-governmental agreement shall be considered as a non-governmental organization (...) UN Doc. ECOSOC Res. 288B(X), of 27 February 1950, Part I, para. 8. Cf. also: LYMAN C. WHITE, INTERNATIONAL NON-GOVERNMENTAL ORGANIZATIONS, New Brunswick: Rutgers University Press 3 (1951).

[6] See: UN Doc. ECOSOC Res. 1296(XLIV), of 23 May 1968, Part I, para. 7; UN Doc. ECOSOC Res. 1996/31, of 25 July 1996, Part I, para. 12.

members have equal rights and influence with regard to the work of the organization. For example, it is worth mentioning here the so-called quasi non-governmental organizations (QUANGOs). These organizations accept single-country NGOs in their membership, as well as individuals from various states, but at the same time open their membership to governmental or intergovernmental entities such as states and intergovernmental organizations. Therefore, QUANGOs should be understood as a kind of 'symbiosis' of the governmental and non-governmental sectors where both categories of members accept one another as equal participants in the decision-making process within the organization. Such mixed participation is usually determined by the very nature of an organization whose functioning is dependent on such co-operation.

13.04. Furthermore, there are many authors who, besides the non-governmental character of INGOs, emphasise their international character as well. Although it may seem that there is a consensus in international law concerning this element, it is sometimes understood in two different ways. Some authors (probably a majority) require that an organization, in order to be *international*, should have members from two or more countries.[7] Similarly, Willetts determines an INGO as an 'organized group of individuals or organizations from more than one country.'[8] Sometimes, such requirements go even further and consider a non-governmental organization to be international if it has members from three countries,[9] six countries,[10] or even from different continents.[11]

---

[7] See e.g.: LYMAN C. WHITE, *supra* note 5, at 7. Thus, for example, Cavaré states: *'Les Membres de ces groupements sont des categories d'individus ressortissants aux différents Etats."* 1 LOUIS CAVARE, LE DROIT INTERNATIONAL PUBLIC POSITIF, Paris: Éditions A. Pedone 488-489 (1951). Cf. 1 OPPENHEIM'S INTERNATIONAL LAW, London: Longman 21 (R. Jennings & A. Watts eds., 1995).

[8] Peter Willetts, *Introduction,* in 'THE CONSCIENCE OF THE WORLD' THE INFLUENCE OF NON-GOVERNMENTAL ORGANIZATIONS IN THE UN SYSTEM, Washington D.C.: The Brookings Institution 5 (P. Willetts ed., 1996).

[9] See: Neri Sybesma-Knol, *Non-State Actors in International Organizations: An Attempt at Classification, in* THE LEGITIMACY OF THE UNITED NATIONS: TOWARDS AN ENHANCED LEGAL STATUS OF NON-STATE ACTORS, Utrecht: Netherlands Institute of Human Rights 21, 29 (Th.C. van Boven, C. Flinterman, F. Grünfeld, & R. Hut eds., 1997).

[10] See: Draft Convention aiming at facilitating the work of international non-governmental organizations, submitted to UNESCO by the Union of International Associations (UIA); for the text see in:, 1 *International Association Statutes Series,* München, New York, London, Paris: K.G. Saur Verlag, Appendix 4.10 (Union of International Associations ed., 1988).

[11] See: BORKO D. STOSIC, LES ORGANISATIONS NON GOUVERNEMENTALES ET LES NATIONS UNIES, Genève: Librairie Droz 77 (1964).

13.05. In contrast, some other definitions of INGOs do not require an international character in the structure of the organization, but an international character in terms of its aims and activities. Such a definition of INGOs as 'international associations' was proposed by the *Institut de Droit International* in its Resolution of 1950: '*Les associations internationales (...) sont des groupements de personnes ou de collectivités (...) qui exercent (...) une activité internationale d'intérêt général, en dehors de toute préoccupation d'ordre exclusivement national*'[12]

13.06. In addition, there is also a cumulative approach which combines both the requirement concerning the international structure of an organization and the international character of its aims and work.[13] However, it seems that the international character of the structure of an organization necessarily determines the international character of its aims and activities, since the mere fact that an organization's membership consists of individuals and/or associations from various states that should guarantee the international character of the aims and activities which bind its members across state borders.

13.07. Probably the most disputable element in defining the notion of INGOs is their non-profit-making character. For example, Lador-Lederer defines non-governmental organizations as non-profit-making.[14] The requirement concerning the non-profit-making character of INGOs is also emphasised by Willetts[15] and Stosic,[16] and is found in the above-mentioned Resolution of the *Institut de Droit* International,[17] in the European Convention on the Recognition of the Legal Personality of International Non-Governmental Organizations of 1986,[18] as well as in the UIA Draft Convention aiming at facilitating the work of international non-governmental organizations.[19]

13.08. However, there are other opinions. Rechenberg differentiates between two kinds of non-governmental organizations, 'those with non-profit,

---

[12]   43 *Annuaire de l'Institut de Droit International*, Session de Bath, II at 384 (1950).

[13]   Such an approach is proposed in the Draft Convention aiming at facilitating the work of international non-governmental organizations, *supra* note 10.

[14]   See: JOSEF J. LADOR-LEDERER, *supra* note 1, at 60.

[15]   See: Peter Willetts (ed.), *supra* note 8, at 5.

[16]   See: BORKO D. STOSIC, *supra* note 11, at 77 et 311.

[17]   '*Les associations internationales (...) sont des groupements de personnes ou de collectivités, librement crées (...) qui exercent, sans esprit de lucre, une activité internationale (...)*'; *supra* note 12, at 384.

[18]   For the text of the Convention see: Council of Europe, *Explanatory Report on the European Convention on the Recognition of the Legal Personality of International Non-Governmental Organizations*, Strasbourg 13-17 (1986). See also: *ETS* 124.

[19]   See: *supra* note 10.

i.e. idealistic objectives, and those with economic aims. (...) NGOs with economic aims include mainly so-called multinational or transnational corporations.'[20]

13.09. It would seem that the distinction between profit-making and non-profit-making organizations goes beyond the question of their field of activities. However, such an element is the main criterion for distinguishing multinational corporations, companies and other subjects of international trade law from public international law and its subjects. At least they can be differentiated from other participants in international relations regulated by the norms of public international law.

13.10. Having discussed the above definitions, we determined the definition of INGOs, at least for the purpose of this article. INGOs are organizations that are international in their membership, non-governmental in their activities and non-profit-making in their objectives.

III. INGOs and Lawmaking Capacity in International Law

13.11. The participation of INGOs in the creation of international law can be analyzed through the same three phases of the general international lawmaking process. So despite their strong connection, it is possible to sort out:

a) the phase of imagination;
b) the phase of standard-setting; and
c) the phase of implementation.[21]

13.12. In the imagination phase, INGOs appear as an organized means of public participation in international decision-making. Their activities here can be described as some kind of pre-legal initiative: they point out the necessity of international legal regulations of certain issues at the same time usually offering some general ideas for such regulation. In this phase, INGOs use a combination of campaigns, from educational activities, the publication of results of scientific research, propaganda, lobbying and other extralegal means in order to influence public opinion, as well as international legislation.

13.13. In the phase of standard-setting, we usually find the active legal participation of INGOs in the international legislative process.

---

[20] Hermann H.-K. Rechenberg, *supra* note 4, at 612.

[21] Cf. Antonio Cassese, *How Could Nongovernmental Organizations Use U.N. Bodies More Effectively?*, 1(4) UNIVERSAL HUMAN RIGHTS 73, 76 (1979); Davorin Lapaš, *International Non-Governmental Organizations and the Protection of the Environment*, 31 THESAURUS ACROASIUM 665, 670 (2002).

Generally, such participation may be initiated whether by INGOs themselves, upon the invitation of states, or more often, by intergovernmental organizations. Thus, INGOs usually organize so-called NGO forums, i.e. unofficial NGO conferences organized, if possible, alongside official diplomatic conferences in order to enable diplomats to hear INGOs proposals.[22] On the other hand, when the initiative comes from intergovernmental organizations, INGOs are allowed to participate at the conference, and usually they are invited to officially submit their statements and proposals.

13.14. The phase of implementation is the last, but very important stage in the international lawmaking process. If it fails, all the achievements of previous phases will be nothing more than a 'dead letter'. The role of INGOs in this phase of the lawmaking process in some international law branches like environmental law, as well as in human rights law, includes INGOs visits to different areas, taking samples and photographs, and other fact-finding activities in order to control the implementation of the standards adopted in the previous phase.[23]

IV. INGOs and International Environmental Law

13.15. Among some of the new actors who have appeared on the international lawmaking stage, INGOs started to play a significant role in international environmental law almost from its beginning. What is more, it would be possible to follow the history of international environmental law through the activities of some of the most influential INGOs. However, the turning point happened in the beginning of the 1970s, in the moment when INGOs started to play a more visible role in environmental matters on the global stage.[24] In

---

[22] Cf. Ibid., at 671.

[23] Ibid., at 674-675.

[24] The above mentioned activities of environmental INGOs can be traced back to the beginning of the 20th century, with creation of the International Association of Academics in 1899 and the International Research Council in 1919. Based on the activities of these two organizations, the International Council of Scientific Unions (ICSU) was established in 1931, today known as the International Council of Science; available at: http://www.icsu.org/about-icsu/about-us/a-brief-history (accessed on 3 November 2012). This organization is an example of so-called QUANGO (Quasi non-governmental organization) as representatives of governments, governmental agencies but also other INGOs participate in its membership. Also, the International Union for Conservation of Nature (IUCN), which in 1956 changed its name from the International Union for the Protection of Nature, belongs to the same type of organization; available at: http://www.iucn.org/ (accessed on 3 November 2012). For a historical overview of the environmental INGOs see: DAVORIN LAPAŠ, MEĐUNARODNE NEVLADINE ORGANIZACIJE KAO SUBJEKTI MEĐUNARODNOG PRAVA, Zagreb: Pravni fakultet u Zagrebu 66-71 (1999).

1972, the United Nations Conference on the Human Environment (Stockholm Conference) took place which resulted in the Stockholm Declaration. Also, at the same time the United Nations Environmental Programme (UNEP) was established.[25] Some of today's most influential environmental INGOs such as Greenpeace,[26] World Watch Institute (WWI),[27] World Wide Fund for Nature (WWF),[28] Friends of the Earth,[29] International Institute for Environment and Development (IIED),[30] etc. started their activities at that time. During that period INGOs began to organize INGOs conferences, usually taking place along-side the official, governmental environmental conferences.[31] The following decades witnessed the proliferation of global environmental concerns in many fields: the creation of treaties, conferences, the increasing interest of the media and NGO activities. One of the best known soft-law instruments from that period is the Report of the World Commission on Environment and Development (WCED)[32] of 1987: Our Common Future (Brundtland Report).[33] It is interesting to compare the number of 400 NGOs that attended the Stockholm Conference in 1972 to some 10000 NGOs participating in the UN Conference on Environment and Development (Rio Conference) in 1992,[34] where many of these organizations have already been organized within large NGOs networks.[35]

13.16. The Rio Conference resulted in the famous Rio Declaration and Agenda 21. While the first document elaborated further the principles confirmed at the Stockholm Conference, the second presented an

---

[25] UNEP was created by UN General Assembly Resolution A/Res./2997 on 15 December 1972.

[26] Available at: http://www.greenpeace.org/international/en/about/history (accessed on 3 November 2012).

[27] Available at: http://www.worldwatch.org/mission (accessed on 3 November 2012).

[28] Available at: http://wwf.panda.org (accessed on 3 November 2012).

[29] Available at: http://www.foei.org (accessed on 3 November 2012).

[30] Available at: http://www.iied.org/ (accessed on 3 November 2012).

[31] Periodically, and especially in the beginning of 1990s, this trend turned to organizing of counter-summits which clearly oppose the official, governmental summits. See: Farhana Yamin, *NGOs and International Environmental Law: A Critical Evaluation of their Roles and Responsibilities*, 10(2) REVIEW OF EUROPEAN COMMUNITY AND INTERNATIONAL ENVIRONMENTAL LAW 149, 150-152 (2001).

[32] UN General Assembly Resolution A/Res./38/161 of 19 December 1983.

[33] Gro Harlem Brundtland was the Chairman of the Commission.

[34] Ibid.

[35] Ibid., As the examples of such networks Yamin mentions the Climate Action Network (CAN), Pesticide Action Network (PAN), Regional Environmental Centre for Central and Eastern Europe (REC), Global Legislators for a Balanced Environment (GLOBE); see: Farhana Yamin, *supra* note 31, at 152.

action programme for the creation and implementation of sustainable development, the term clearly defined in the Brundtland Report and was enormously used and discussed by different actors on the international stage in the following years.[36] Another result of the Rio Conference is the UN Framework Convention on Climate Change (UNFCCC).[37] Some authors see the period of the 1980s and 1990s as an era of populist approaches to environmental problems but at the same time they remark on the significant progress in certain environmental fields.[38] The activities of environmental INGOs continued in the beginning of 2000s, although in a different atmosphere and circumstances compared to those which prevailed at the time of the Rio Summit.[39] Some of the environmental INGOs today enjoy very broad public support and significant financial resources. In 2010, Greenpeace raised over 226 million EUR and had more than 2.8 million donors.[40] The income of the WWF was 525 million EUR,[41] and Friends of the Earth gathered more than 2 million members and supporters.[42] These numbers are important by themselves but if we compare them to the same categories in 2000, a very significant increase will be visible in all

---

[36]   For an overview on the meaning and concept of sustainable development see: Stathis N. Palassis, *Beyond the Global Summits: Reflecting on the Environmental Principles of Sustainable Development*, 22(1) COLORADO JOURNAL OF INTERNATIONAL ENVIRONMENTAL LAW AND POLICY 41, 42-57 (2011).

[37]   Available at: http://unfccc.int/essential_background/items/6031.php (accessed on November 4, 2011). The Convention entered into force in 1994. The subsequent Kyoto Protocol was adopted in 1997 and entered into force in 2005; available at: http://unfccc.int/essential_background/kyoto_protocol/items/6034.php (accessed on 4 November 2011).

[38]   Thus, Palassis has remarked the following achievements in that period: '1) the significant reduction of vessel-source environmental pollution; 2) the international regulation of the trade in hazardous waste; and 3) the successful avoidance of the narrowly-averted disaster of irreversible ozone depletion.' Also, the same author mentions the 'greening of the European Union (EU) treaty-system' as an environmental success of the time. See: Stathis N. Palassis, *supra* note 36, at 46.

[39]   The Rio Conference was held at the time of significant changes such as the end of the Cold War, expansion of communication technologies and rapid globalization. In general, the optimism has prevailed that the environmental problems are solvable. The period after 2000 was characterized by a limited progress in major environmental problems, increased terrorist activities and global dissemination of economic and financial instability. As a result, the general atmosphere for solving global environmental problems now seems more pessimistic than it was at the time of Rio Conference.

[40]   Available at: http://www.greenpeace.org/international/Global/international/publications/greenpeace/2011/GPI_Annual_Report_2010.pdf (accessed on 6 November 2011).

[41]   The data is from WWF Annual Review 2010; available at: http://wwf.panda.org/ (accessed on 6 November 2011).

[42]   Available at: http://www.foei.org/en/who-we-are (accessed on 6 November 2011).

of them.[43] This being so, one can conclude that some important conditions for the increasing participation of INGOs in the environmental field have been improved, as well as the support of the public for their work.

IV.1. Pluralism of Environmental INGOs

13.17. When speaking about environmental INGOs one should bear in mind that numerous differences among them exist and various methods of classification can be applied.[44] For the purpose of this paper, we will try to distinguish three main groups of INGOs:[45]
1) activist INGOs,
2) scientific INGOs,
3) business INGOs.

13.18. The first group of INGOs relates to those organizations whose activities and programmes are recognized world-wide and whose actions are organized in accordance with clearly expressed goals about particular environmental problems. Some examples of the biggest INGOs belonging to this group are the previously mentioned Greenpeace, WWF and Friends of the Earth, whose range of activities, budget and influence can easily stand comparison with some of intergovernmental organizations and programmes.[46] The second group of 'scientific INGOs' consists of research-based INGOs, whose activities and scientific research provide very significant contribution to the environmental regimes and different fields of environmental sciences. The WWF, IIED, Union of Concerned Scientists,[47] World Resources Institute,[48] Institute for European Environmental Policy,[49] Foundation for International Environmental Law and Development (FIELD),[50] are some of the best known INGOs in this group. Thus,

---

[43] F. Yamin quoted the following data for the year 2000: The World Wide Fund for Nature had around 5 million supporters and income of around SFr 470 million; Greenpeace International had more than 2.5 million members in 158 countries with an annual budget in the region of 30 million USD and Friends of the Earth had over 1 million members in 58 countries. See: Farhana Yamin, *supra* note 31, at 151.

[44] See: Davorin Lapaš, *supra* note 24, at 68-69.

[45] However, we are fully aware that in practice some INGOs could belong to more than one of these categories, as the activities of many of them often include some distinctive features of another group.

[46] Cf. http://www.unep.org/rms/en/Financing of UNEP/index.asp (accessed on 7 November 2011).

[47] Available at: http://www.ucsusa.org/about/ (accessed on 7 November 2011).

[48] Available at: http://www.wri.org/ (accessed on 7 November 2011).

[49] Available at: http://www.ieep.eu/about-us/about-ieep/ (accessed on 7 November 2011).

[50] See: http://www.field.org.uk/ (accessed on 7 November 2011).

some authors refer to these organizations as 'epistemic communities'[51] describing them as 'conscience keepers.'[52] However, the most controversial group of environmental INGOs is undoubtedly the third one – 'business INGOs.' The first doubt in relation to this group arises with the question as to whether the entities having the profit-making objectives can be regarded as NGOs at all. The attitudes toward this problem are not unanimous. If we consider strictly that the non-profit character is one of the key elements of an NGO, it will be possible to exclude (theoretically) business NGOs from the NGO world. On the other hand, what seems more plausible is the position of authors who propose a softer understanding of environmental non-state actors concerning their profit-making character.[53] Actually, their exclusion would be possible only in theory since the business community has always been very much involved in the process of environmental lawmaking, especially in some environmental fields such as climate change.[54] The influence and diversity of this group of INGOs in the negotiations directed to the establishment and implementation of the UNFCCC have led some authors to distinguish those business INGOs representing 'gray industry groups' whose primary concern is the impact of the climate change treaties on economies, from those that are

---

[51]   One of the explanations of this term is offered by P.M. Haas: 'An epistemic community is a network of professionals with recognized expertise and competence in a particular domain and an authoritative claim to policy relevant knowledge within that domain or issue-area. Although an epistemic community may consist of professionals from a variety of disciplines and backgrounds, they have (1) a shared set of normative and principle beliefs, which provide a value based rationale for the social action of community members; 2) shared casual beliefs, which are derived from their analysis of practices leading to or contributing to a central set of problems (...); 3) shared notions of validity – that is intersubjective, internally defined criteria for weighing and validating knowledge in the domain of their expertise and 4) a common policy enterprise – that is a set of common practices associated with a set of problems to which their professional competence is directed...' Peter M. Haas, *Introduction: Epistemic Communities and International Policy Coordination*, 46(1) INTERNATIONAL ORGANIZATION 1, 3 (1992). On epistemic communities, NGOs and climate changes see: Clair Gough & Simon Shackley, *The Respectable Politics of Climate Change: The Epistemic Communities and NGOs*, 77(2) INTERNATIONAL AFFAIRS 329, 329-346 (2001).

[52]   Cf. Farhana Yamin, *supra* note 31, at 154-155.

[53]   See: Asher Alkoby, *Non-state Actors and the legitimacy of international environmental law*, 3(1) NON-STATE ACTORS AND INTERNATIONAL LAW 23, 48-50 (2003).

[54]   Different proposals were made for the improvement of the role of the business community in the climate change treaty system within the framework of UNFCCC. One of them was the establishment of the Business Consultative Mechanism between business representatives and UNFCCC system. The last proposal of this kind was submitted by the International Chamber of Commerce in 2010. See: http://unfccc.int/resource/docs/2010/smsn/ngo/200. pdf (accessed on 8 November 2012).

members of the 'light green groups' representing some energy-efficient industries such as the ones that relied on renewable energy resources, natural gas, cogeneration etc.[55] The example of this group of INGOs was the Global Climate Coalition (GCC) whose findings, often in clear collision with those of Intergovernmental Panel of Climate Change (IPCC), were highly controversial.[56] Equally, the World Business Council for Sustainable Development (WBCSD) can be mentioned here, being one of the major members of the so-called 'Carbon Club'.[57]

IV.2. 'Soft Law' and Environmental INGOs in the Climate Change Regime and in the Concept of Sustainable Development

13.19. Two environmental subsystems, the international climate change regime and the concept of sustainable development, are chosen here for a short analysis of the diversity of 'soft law' and the role INGOs play in each of them.

IV.2.1. International Climate Change Regime

13.20. The influence of INGOs on the climate change regime had already been visible during the negotiation phase and before the treaty was concluded. Some authors even claim that their informal influence and lobbying were the key factors contributing to the success of the UNFCCC.[58] This treaty is also significant as it defines in detail the role of the INGOs within the treaty system. The treaty provisions describing the role of the INGOs have formalized their position in the treaty system and made them almost unavoidable partners for the states,

---

[55] Asher Alkoby, *supra* note 53, at 38.

[56] The GCC ceased its activities in 2002. See: http://www.nytimes.com/2009/04/24/science/earth/24deny.html (accessed on 8 November 2012). An extreme example of how sensitive the relation between business society and NGOs can be was the latest verdict of the French court, which fined multinational energy company EDF Group for spying on Greenpeace nuclear campaign, while four persons are to be imprisoned. See: http://www.bbc.co.uk/news/science-environment-15683090 (accessed on 10 November 2012).

[57] Available at: http://www.wbcsd.org/home.aspx (accessed on 8 November 2012). According to Giorgetti, another major member of this group is the American Petroleum Institute (API), representing the positions of American oil companies.. See: Chiara Giorgetti, *From Rio to Kyoto: A Study of the Involvement ol Non-Governmental Organizations in the Negotiations on Climate Change*, 7 NEW YORK UNIVERSITY ENVIRONMENTAL LAW JOURNAL, 201, 222 (1999).

[58] See: Asher Alkoby, *supra* note 53, at 36.

requiring for the concerned INGOs only to be 'competent enough'.[59] If an INGO possesses such competence, no state alone can object to its participation but it has to secure the votes of at least one third of the parties participating at the conference.[60] Such an observer status led some authors to the conclusion that INGOs and non-governmental sectors in general have played the leading role in the climate change negotiation process through such actions as the identification of the problems and the application of knowledge relevant to policy development.[61] On the other hand, these 'soft entities', representatives of NGOs at the 1992 Conference, were at the same time the main opponents to the 'softness' of the states' obligations according to the UNFCCC.[62]

13.21. The influence of the INGOs rose further at conferences and in documents created after the UNFCCC and particularly in the most important document related to it - the Kyoto Protocol.[63] At the same time, the attendance of representatives of civil society at key environmental conferences gradually has become more visible. Thus, some 533 INGOs attended the second official meeting of the

---

[59] Art 4.1. defines the role of the NGOs in the treaty system in general terms: 'All parties, taking into account their common but differentiated responsibilities and their specific national and regional priorities, objectives and circumstances shall: (...) (i) Promote and cooperate in education, training and public awareness related to the climate change and encourage the widest participation in this process, including that of non-governmental organizations (...).' Art. 7.2. mentioned the first condition for the participation of the NGOs in treaty system – their competence: 'The Conference of the parties, as the supreme body of this Convention, shall keep under regular review the implementation of the Convention, and any related legal instrument that the Conference of the Parties may adopt (...). To this end, it shall: (l) seek and utilize, where appropriate, the services and cooperation of, and information provided by, competent international organizations and inter-governmental and non-governmental bodies (...)' The second criterion for the participation of NGOs in UNFCCC concerns states' consent for such participation. Art. 7.6 states as follows: '(...) Any body or the agency, whether national or international, governmental or non-governmental, which is qualified in matters covered by the Convention, and which has informed the Secretariat of its wish to be represented at a session of the Conference of the parties as an observer, may be so admitted, unless at least one third of the parties present object (...).'

[60] Ibid. On the formal participation of NGOs in similar treaties see: Asher Alkoby, *supra* note 53, at 36-38.

[61] See: Robyn Eckersley, *Soft Law, Hard Politics and the Climate Change Treaty*, in POLITICS OF INTERNATIONAL LAW, Cambridge: Cambridge University Press 80, 102-104 (C. Reus Smit ed., 2004).

[62] See: Ibid., 81-86. The author explains the role of the NGOs from the point of critical constructivism which allows a more prominent role of the NGOs in the lawmaking process as compared with the neoliberal and neorealist theories.

[63] For the text of the Kyoto Protocol see: http://unfccc.int/resource/docs/convkp/kpeng.pdf (accessed on 11 November 2012).

Conference of the Parties (COP) of the UNFCCC in Berlin in 1995.[64] In 2009, more than 1300 INGOs were admitted to the Copenhagen meeting including representatives from all the three major groups of INGOs (activist, scientific and business INGOs) mentioned in the previous section.[65] At the last COP meeting in Durban in December 2011, almost 1400 INGOs were registered as observers.[66] However, it is worth noting that a huge majority of the INGOs attending the Conference were Western hemisphere INGOs.[67]

13.22. Additionally, INGOs have continued to play a very significant role in all key documents adopted after the Kyoto Protocol among which the most important are: the Bali Roadmap of 2007,[68] the Cancun Agreements of 2010,[69] and the Durban Package of 2011.[70] All these documents represent a set of different kinds of predominantly 'soft law' instruments which include action plans, recommendations and decisions. The general aim of these documents is an endeavour for the development and implementation of goals defined in the UNFCCC and the Kyoto Protocol on the one hand and for the creation of a new obligatory multilateral instrument for the period after the expiration of the Kyoto Protocol at the end of 2012, on the other.

IV.2.2. Sustainable Development Concept

13.23. In the context of the 'soft law' phenomenon it is hard to find a more controversial environmental issue than the concept of sustainable development. The concept appeared fully in international legal discourse in 1987 with the Brundtland Report. In this Report sustainable development has been defined as 'the concept that meets

---

[64] Data quoted from: Anna Spain, *Who is going to Copenhagen – The Rise of Civil Society in International Treaty Making*, 23(35) AMERICAN SOCIETY OF INTERNATIONAL LAW INSIGHTS 1, 2 (2009).

[65] Ibid.

[66] Data quoted from: Melanie Müller, *The Myth of a Global Civil Society*, available at: http://www.dandc.eu/articles/197598/index.en.shtml (accessed on 11 January 2013).

[67] Müller states, for example, that from populous and ecologically threatened Bangladesh only 8 civil society organizations were presented in comparison to some 120 German or 50 French. Other interesting data she states is that some large western INGOs as Oxfam or Germanwatch endeavoured to represent the voices of NGOs from developing countries. Ibid.

[68] For the text of the Bali Roadmap see: http://unfccc.int/meetings/bali_dec_2007/meeting/6319.php (accessed on 11 November 2011).

[69] For the text of the Cancun Agreements see: http://unfccc.int/meetings/cancun_nov_2010/items/6005.php (accessed on 11 November 2011).

[70] For the results of the Durban Conference see: http://unfccc.int/meetings/durban_nov_2011/meeting/6245.php (accessed on 10 June 2012).

the needs of the present without compromising abilities of future generations to meet their own needs...'[71]

13.24. The concept itself has linked global environmental and economic problems in a persuasive way, emphasizing at the same time the dramatic increase in world population and the scarcity of natural resources. In 1992, the UN General Assembly established the Commission on Sustainable Development (CSD),[72] charged with reviewing progress in the implementation of the Agenda 21 and the Rio Declaration – documents which broadened the concept of sustainable development. The UN sponsored World Summit on Sustainable Development[73] in Johannesburg in 2002 resulted in new plans and documents: The Johannesburg Declaration on Sustainable Development, the Plan of Implementation of the World Summit on Sustainable Development and the Statement Regarding the Use of Renewable Energy Resources.[74] All the three documents from 2002 are entirely 'soft law' instruments, declaratory by their wording and characterized by very general provisions. After all, it has been clear from the history of negotiations at the Johannesburg Conference that even when it seemed that some precise legal obligations would be accepted, in the final result only the declaratory documents appeared.[75] If we try to reach the answer to the question of why the concept of sustainable development looks so hard to achieve, it will lead us to the conclusion that from its beginning the lack of clarity and the ambiguity of the concept have contributed to its low implementation.[76] It seems that all the problems which followed from this initial vagueness had turned the sustainable development into a highly hortatory concept in its nature

---

[71] For the full text see: http://www.un-documents.net/ocf-02.htm#I (accessed on 11 November 2011).The process of the creating of the concept of sustainable development was initiated at the Stockholm Conference, but in the Bruntdland Report it was expressed for the first time in an explicit way.

[72] UN Doc. A/Res./47/191 of 22 December 1992.

[73] See: http://www.johannesburgsummit.org/html/basic_info/basicinfo.html (accessed on 11 November 2011).

[74] Ibid.

[75] Palassis describes how the intended adoption of the planned treaty on the use of renewable energy resources was transformed into the non-binding energy plan which calls states to develop cleaner and more 'green' energy instead of complete reliance on fossil fuels energy. See: Stathis N. Palassis, *supra* note 36, at 54 – 55.

[76] In this regard Palassis asked a question about the meaning of the concept of 'sustainable development': 'Does it mean development that is economically sustainable or this is a contradiction in terms as nothing physical can grow indefinitely or that indeed that 'development' can never be 'sustained'? What about sustainable use of renewable resources at rates within the capacity for renewal? What about non-renewable resources?' Ibid., at 58.

and was insufficient in achieving its goals.[77] Concerning the role of the INGOs in this system it is worth noting that numerous INGOs have been involved in all stages of the creation of previously mentioned documents related to sustainable development. Their formal influence on the system of sustainable development is recognized by the creation of the initiative Partnership for Sustainable Development by the UN Department of Economic and Social Affairs, Division for Sustainable Development in which many INGO networks have taken part.[78] However, the criteria for the INGOs participation have become much softened when compared to those in the climate change regime.[79] This softening has helped some INGOs to significantly influence the concept of sustainable development by creating the particular treaty models in that field. The IUCN and International Council of Environmental Law (ICEL) made the Draft International Covenant on Environment and Development as an attempt to offer a model for multilateral negotiations which would eventually lead to the adoption of a binding instrument.[80] Whether such INGO activity will lead one day to the adoption of a legally binding instrument on sustainable development or will simply be marked as a brave but not very influential attempt remains to be seen.

V. INGOs' Lawmaking Capacity in Space Law

13.25. Some authors point out that the very beginning of space law is related to the role of certain INGOs, like the International Astronautical Federation (IAF), the *Institut de Droit International*, and the International Law Association (ILA).[81] The role of scientific INGOs is

---

[77] For the discussion on the existence of the customary rule of sustainable development see: Ibid., at 70-73. A very interesting view on sustainable development as an 'ideal' is presented by J. Verschuuren. He recognizes that the ideal of sustainable development has influenced many international, regional (European) and national binding and non-binding documents, but first of all, he sees its influence on the principles of environmental law. He defines that 'ideal' as 'a value that is explicit, implicit, or latent in the law or the public and moral culture of a society or group that usually cannot be fully realized, and that partly transcends contingent, historical formulations, and implementations in terms of rules and principles and policies.' JONATHAN VERSCHUUREN, PRINCIPLES OF INTERNATIONAL ENVIRONMENTAL LAW, Baden-Baden: Nomos Verlagsgesellschaft; Umweltrechtliche Studien 49-50 (2003).

[78] Available at: http://www.un.org/esa/dsd/dsd_aofw_par/par_about.shtml (accessed on 12 June 2012).

[79] Ibid.

[80] Available at: http://www.i-c-e-l.org/indexen.html (accessed on 12 November 2011). The first version of this document was already made in 1995, but both the second version from 1999 and the third one form 2003 were presented to the UN member states. See: Stathis N. Palassis, *supra* note 36, at 75-76.

[81] See: NANDASIRI JASENTULIYANA, INTERNATIONAL SPACE LAW AND THE UNITED NATIONS, The Hague, London, Boston: Kluwer Law International 9 (1999).

extremely valuable in the phase of imagination here, since only knowledge about space and space activities can be the starting point in the process of their legal regulation. There is no doubt that the role of INGOs like the International Academy of Astronautics (IAA), the International Astronomical Union (IAU), the IAF, the International Space University (ISU), and the Space Generation Advisory Council (SGAC), can be of great significance. After all, the simultaneous creation of the Legal, and the Scientific and Technical Sub-committee of the Committee on the Peaceful Uses of Outer Space (COPUOS) proves the close connection between law, science and technology in the uses of outer space.[82] Recognising such a connection, the IAF established the International Institute of Space Law (IISL) in 1959. Meanwhile, a number of INGOs have obtained permanent observer status with COPUOS.[83] Observer status is usually granted by international organizations to those entities that are able and willing to contribute to the work of the organization so that it may profit from their services or spread knowledge about its activities. Thus, observers are usually admitted to the meetings of the organization and their organs, but also to conferences organised by the organization. This being so, the role of INGOs in this phase is recognised by the United Nations in general, particularly in organising international conferences

---

[82] Ibid., at 24-25.

[83] The following INGOs have obtained permanent observer status in COPUOS: the African Organization of Cartography and Remote Sensing (AOCRS), the Association of Space Explorers (ASE), the Committee on Earth Observation Satellites (CEOS), the Committee on Space Research (COSPAR), the European Space Policy Institute (ESPI), the European Association for the International Space Year (EURISY), the International Academy of Astronautics (IAA), the International Astronautical Federation (IAF), the International Astronomical Union (IAU), the International Institute for Applied Systems Analysis (IIASA), the International Institute of Space Law (IISL), the International Law Association (ILA), the International Society for Photogrammetry and Remote Sensing (ISPRS), the International Space University (ISU), the National Space Society (NSS), the Prince Sultan Bin Abdulaziz International Prize for Water (PSIPW), the Secure World Foundation (SWF), the Space Generation Advisory Council (SGAC), The Planetary Society (TPS) and the World Space Week Association (WSWA). See: COPUOS, A/AC.105/2009/CRP.11. Also, the same status was granted to the Scientific Committee on Solar-Terrestrial Physics (SCOSTEP). Exceptionally, at its 660th meeting, the COPUOS decided to invite the Inter-Islamic Network on Space Sciences and Technology (ISNET) to attend the 56th session of the Committee. See: Report of the Committee on the Peaceful Uses of Outer Space, Fifty-sixth session (12-21 June 2013), General Assembly Official Records, Sixty-eight Session, Supplement No. 20, A/68/20. For more details on INGOs' permanent observer status with COPUOS see: Davorin Lapaš, *The Role of International Non-Governmental Organizations (INGOs) in Space Activities and Space Law*, in INTERNATIONAL LAW: NEW ACTORS, NEW CONCEPTS – CONTINUING DILEMMAS, The Hague: Brill 125, 129-139 (B. Vukas & T.M. Šošić eds., 2010).

and symposia on space issues. Thus, INGOs had a significant role with COPUOS in preparation for UNISPACE III.[84] Equally, the UN General Assembly in resolution A/59/2, of 3 December 2004 encourages space-related non-governmental entities to contribute to the Trust Fund for the United Nations Programme on Space Applications (para. 17). It should also be mentioned here that the UN General Assembly in resolution A/59/116 invited the Committee on Space Research (COSPAR) and the IAF to arrange a symposium on high-resolution and hyperspectral satellite data integration for precision farming, environmental monitoring and other possible new applications (para 15). In addition, it is worth noting that some of the earlier mentioned INGOs also have consultative status with the UN Economic and Social Council (ECOSOC), for example the SGAC and the International Institute for Applied Systems Analysis (IIASA).

13.26. It cannot be doubted that there are many fields of space law open to INGO initiatives and participation in order to make the international lawmaking process more effective. For instance, the role of the International Society for Photogrammetry and Remote Sensing (ISPRS) and the Committee on Earth Observation Satellites (CEOS) in the regulation of remote sensing, or the role of the IAA, ISPRS, and the CEOS in the creation of an international regulatory regime for satellite communications or regulation of geostationary satellite orbits would be very useful. In addition, some of these organizations could provide fruitful co-operation with states and intergovernmental organizations in the field of the sustainability of human development. In fact, such a role for INGOs has already been recognised in The Space Millennium: Vienna Declaration on Space and Human Development, adopted by UNISPACE III in 1999.

13.27. In the standard-setting phase, as previously mentioned, we usually find the active legal participation of INGOs in the international legislative process. Thus, INGOs that had observer status with COPUOS were invited by the UNISPACE III Preparatory Committee to submit their statements in writing to the plenary and their papers to the executive secretariat. They were also invited to identify agenda items and conference activities, including workshops, through which they could participate in the work of the conference. In particular, pursuant to the request by the Preparatory Committee, the executive secretariat of the conference invited the ISPRS, IAU, COSPAR and IISL to participate at

---

[84] See: Preparations for The Third United Nations Conference on the Exploration and Peaceful Uses of Outer Space (UNISPACE III) by the Advisory Committee for UNISPACE III; UN Doc. A/AC.105/685, of 6 January 1998.

the Conference which dealt with various topics: the environment and remote sensing (ISPRS), science and education including astronomy, the preservation of the space environment (IAU), the contribution of space techniques in exploring the universe, recent progress in future plans for the exploration of the solar system (COSPAR), and space law (IISL).[85] The importance of space science and consequently the role of scientific INGOs for the fundamental knowledge of space and for its peaceful uses is visible in the final UNISPACE III document, The Space Millennium: Vienna Declaration on Space and Human Development.[86] Some scientific INGOs also enjoy the support of UNESCO in their space science programmes (e.g. the IAF and IISL).

13.28. Finally, the role of INGOs in the creation of space law is sometimes emphasised in doctrine as well. Jasentuliyana states: 'Several non-governmental international organizations also play a prominent and significant role in the formation and development of space law. These include the *Institut de Droit International*, the International Law Association and the International Institute of Space Law.'[87]

13.29. In fact, there are a number of INGOs that participate in this phase of the space lawmaking process, usually by making resolutions, declarations and other proposals on the legal regulation of space issues. For example, the Inter-American Bar Association adopted the 'Magna Carta of Space' in 1961 at Bogota. It was one of the first documents aimed at the legal regulation of outer space.[88] Similarly, as early as 1963 the *Institut de Droit International* started to deal with the international legal regulation of outer space.[89] However, there is no doubt that the most important INGO in the development of space law is the ILA.

---

[85] See: UN Doc. A/AC.105/685, of 6 January 1998, at 6-8, et 10. The standard-setting role is sometimes provided by the statutes of these organizations. Thus, for example, provision IV of the ISPRS Statutes includes the development of standards in photogrammetry, remote sensing and spatial information sciences in the activities of the organization. Similarly, the preparation of scientific and technical standards related to space research is one of the most important COSPAR activities; see: *supra* note 83. There is no doubt that these scientific standards are going to become legal standards as well, serving as a basis for the international legal regulation of these activities. On the INGOs' role in international standard-setting see also: INGRID ROSSI, LEGAL STATUS OF NON-GOVERNMENTAL ORGANIZATIONS IN INTERNATIONAL LAW, Antwerp, Oxford, Portland: Intersentia 16-21 (2010).

[86] See: The Space Millennium: Vienna Declaration on Space and Human Development, of 30 July 1999. For the text see: http://www.un.org/events/unispace3/pressrel/e30pm.htm (accessed on 11 September 2013).

[87] NANDASIRI JASENTULIYANA, *supra* note 81, at 9.

[88] For the text see: 1 YEARBOOK OF AIR AND SPACE LAW, 645 (1965).

[89] See: *Le droit international des espaces célestes*, 50 ANNUAIRE DE L'INSTITUT DE DROIT INTERNATIONAL I at 128-496 et II at 60-187 (1963).

Since the mid-fifties, it has been dealing with space law, particularly through the work of its Space Law Committee. In recent decades, the ILA has been working on various topics of space law: for example the problem of the protection of the environment from damage caused by space debris, dispute settlement related to space activities and a review of UN space law instruments in view of commercial space activities.[90] The ILA's work on a particular topic results, in principle, with the adoption of a resolution. These resolutions, although not legally binding, are of great importance, as they present the progressive development of international law concerning space issues rather than its codification. Therefore, their main purpose is to serve as a basis for the future development of space law, usually through treaty-making processes within the United Nations system.[91]

13.30. Finally, with regards to the implementation phase, the very nature of space activities, the inaccessibility of outer space and the ever-present financial difficulties for non-governmental organizations seem to make their role here quite modest. On the other hand, implementation is much more than mere monitoring. It is primarily the broad co-operation of all entities, governmental or non-governmental, states and intergovernmental organizations, as well as INGOs and other private entities, which are all included, in one way or another, in space activities.

13.31. The Space Millennium: Vienna Declaration on Space and Human Development emphasises the need for co-operation between states, intergovernmental organizations and private sector and civil society around the world to promote the exploration and peaceful uses of outer space.[92] Consequently, the UN General Assembly in resolution A/57/116, of 26 February 2003,

'...urges all Governments, entities of the United Nations system and intergovernmental and non-governmental entities conducting

---

[90] See e.g.: *The ILA Report of the Sixty-sixth Conference*, Buenos Aires at 9 et seq.(1994); *The ILA Report of the Sixty-eighth Conference*, Taipei at 239 et seq. (1998).; *The ILA Report of the Sixty-ninth Conference*, London (2000), (Resolution 13/2000); *The ILA Report of the Seventieth Conference*, New Delhi (2002).

[91] For more details on the lawmaking process in space law in general see e.g.: MANFRED LACHS, THE LAW OF OUTER SPACE – AN EXPERIENCE IN CONTEMPORARY LAWMAKING, Leiden: Sijthoff 135-147 (1972). However, it should not be forgotten that in spite of the increasing influence of INGOs in this process, the consent of states to be bound by any legal instrument remains of major importance here. See in this context: Božidar Bakotić, *Some Questions (Without Answers) Concerning the Consent of States to be Bound by Treaties Governing Activities in Outer Space*, INTERNATIONAL ASTRONAUTICAL FEDERATION, XXX Congress held in München, September 17-22, 1979.

[92] See: *supra* note 86, Chap. I, para. 1,e, iii), and Chap. II.

space-related activities to take the necessary action for the effective implementation of the recommendations of UNISPACE III, in particular its resolution entitled 'The Space Millennium: Vienna Declaration on Space and Human Development' (para. 25).

13.32. What is more, the General Assembly expressly recognised,

'...that responsibility for implementing the recommendations of UNISPACE III rests with Member States, the Office for the Outer Space Affairs of the Secretariat, under the guidance of the Committee on the Peaceful Uses of Outer Space and its subsidiary bodies, intergovernmental organizations for multilateral cooperation and other entities with space-related activities, including non-governmental entities.'[93]

13.33. In addition, in resolution A/59/116, of 25 January 2005, the General Assembly requests COPUOS to consider ways to improve participation in its work not only by member states, but also by entities with observer status in order to ensure the implementation of the recommendations of UNISPACE III (para. 45). Such a request for co-operation between member states and observers in COPUOS has been repeated in subsequent General Assembly resolutions, including the most recent resolution A/63/90 (para. 37) and there is no doubt that it will be found in future resolutions as well. This confirms the earlier thesis that the implementation of a legal norm is in fact the co-operation of its addressees.

13.34. However, it seems that within the United Nations such an idea was recognised almost half a century ago, at the very beginning of the space era. In resolution 1721(XVI)B (para. 3a), of 20 December 1961, the UN General Assembly requested COPUOS 'to maintain close contact with governmental and non-governmental organizations concerned with outer space matters'.

VI. Concluding Remarks

13.35. Evaluating the place and role of INGOs in the contemporary international lawmaking system, particularly through their participation in the international lawmaking process in environmental and space law, it is inevitable to recall, probably the most frequently mentioned objection to all international legislation. That objection is to the too strong state sovereignty followed by often equally strong conflicts of states' interests. Such a situation sometimes makes any progress impossible. Usually, the INGOs are not directly bound by

---

93   See: UN Doc. A/Res./59/2, of 3 December 2005; Preamble.

these interests. On the other hand, some of them have knowledge and are much more competent in the fields they deal with than states and their diplomats. This being so, some INGOs today by their knowledge, competence and flexibility in international relations significantly influence the international lawmaking process, particularly through the drafting and promoting of 'soft-law' documents in the field.

| | |

Summaries

DEU [*Internationale nichtstaatliche Organisationen (INGOs) als Teilnehmer am internationalen gesetzgeberischen Prozess: Beispiele aus dem Umweltrecht und Weltraumrecht*]
Der Artikel befasst sich mit der Rolle internationaler nichtstaatlicher Organisationen bei der Rechtsbildung. Er definiert zunächst den Begriff internationaler nichtstaatlicher Organisationen und analysiert deren Befugnis, an der Rechtsbildung im heutigen internationalen Recht vermittels der sog. Imaginationsphase und vermittels der Vorlage und Implementierung von Standards mitzuwirken. Heute sind internationale nichtstaatliche Organisationen in vielen Fällen am Vorbereitungsprozess des internationalen Rechts beteiligt, über ihren Einfluss auf die Verhandlungen auf internationalen Konferenzen, sowie über die Schaffung von Instrumenten, die dem Bereich des sog. 'soft law' zuzurechnen sind, d. h. die Einführung bestimmter allgemeiner 'Spielregeln'. Diese Regeln sind zwar nicht rechtsverbindlich, aber haben dennoch im Einzelfall Einfluss auf das Verhalten von Staaten. Der Beitrag befasst sich v. a. mit der Rolle internationaler nichtstaatlicher Organisationen im Bereich des internationalen Umweltrechts und Weltraumrechts.

CZE [*Mezinárodní nevládní organizace (INGOs) jako účastník mezinárodního legislativního procesu: příklady z oblasti životního prostředí a práva kosmického prostoru*]
Článek se zabývá úlohou mezinárodních nevládních organizací při tvorbě práva. Nejprve článek definuje mezinárodní nevládní organizace, rozebírá jejich způsobilost působit při tvorbě práva v současném mezinárodním právu prostřednictvím tzv. imaginační fáze, navrhování standardů a jejich implementace. V mnoha případech mezinárodní nevládní organizace v současnosti působí v rámci procesu přípravy mezinárodního práva svým vlivem na vyjednávání na mezinárodních konferencích, jakož i tvorbou nástrojů spadajících do oblasti tzv. 'soft law', zaváděním některých obecných pravidel. Ačkoliv tato pravidla

nejsou právně závazná, mají někdy vliv na chování států. Článek se zabývá především úlohou mezinárodních nevládních organizací v oblasti mezinárodního práva životního prostředí a kosmického práva.

| | |

POL [*Międzynarodowe organizacje pozarządowe (INGOs) jako strona w międzynarodowym procesie legislacyjnym: Przykłady z dziedziny ochrony środowiska i prawa przestrzeni kosmicznej*]

Niniejszy artykuł analizuje rolę międzynarodowych organizacji pozarządowych w procesie tworzenia prawa międzynarodowego, dotyczącego międzynarodowej ochrony środowiska i prawa kosmicznego. Międzynarodowe organizacje pozarządowe są obecnie aktywne w wielu obszarach prawa międzynarodowego w procesie prawodawczym głównie ze względu na ich wpływ na przebieg konferencji międzynarodowych oraz tworzenie tzw. „soft law". W artykule przedstawiono niektóre ogólne problemy odnoszące się do takich reguł, które co prawda nie są ogólnie wiążące, jednak mogą wpływać na postępowanie państw.

FRA [*Les organisations internationales non-gouvernementales (OING) en tant que contributeurs à la législation internationale : exemples choisis dans les domaines de l'environnement et du droit de l'espace*]

L'article examine le rôle des organisations internationales non-gouvernementales dans le processus législatif international particulièrement dans les domaines du droit de l'environnement international et du droit de l'espace. Dans de nombreux domaines du droit international aujourd'hui, les ONG participent au processus législatif principalement à travers leur influence sur le processus de négociation dans les conférences internationales, mais aussi par la création de "soft law." L'article analyse quelques problèmes caractéristique de cette normes qui, bien que n'étant pas juridiquement obligatoires en générale, peuvent influencer le comportement des Etats.

RUS [*Международные неправительственные организации (МНПО) как участник международного законодательного процесса: примеры из области права охраны окружающей среды и космического права*]

В статье рассматривается роль международных неправительственных организаций в процессе создания международного права в области международной охраны окружающей среды и космического права. Настоящее время международные неправительственные организации во многих областях международного права принимают активное участие в законодательном процессе, прежде всего, благодаря их влиянию на ход международных конференций, а также путем создания так называемого «мягкого права». В статье представлены некоторые общие вопросы, связанные с такими правилами, которые, хотя и не являются общеобязательными, но могут оказывать влияние на политику государств.

ESP   [***Organizaciones internacionales no gubernamentales (OINGs) como participantes en el proceso legislativo internacional: ejemplos del sector del medio ambiente y del derecho del espacio ultraterrestre***]

El artículo examina el papel de las organizaciones internacionales no gubernamentales en el proceso de creación del derecho internacional relativo a la protección internacional del medio ambiente y del derecho del espacio ultraterrestre. En cuanto al proceso legislativo, las organizaciones internacionales no gubernamentales están activas en una serie de campos del derecho internacional, principalmente, gracias a su impacto sobre el desarrollo de las conferencias internacionales y mediante la creación del denominado "soft law". El artículo presenta algunas cuestiones generales relativas a tales normas, que generalmente no son vinculantes, pero pueden influir en el comportamiento de los estados.

| | |

Czech Yearbook of International Law

Jan Lhotský

The UN Mechanisms for Human Rights Protection: Strengthening Treaty Bodies in Light of a Proposal to Create a World Court of Human Rights

Key words:
Human rights | universal level | treaty bodies | Human Rights Committee | World Court of Human Rights

Abstract | *This article discusses the universal level of human rights protection, in particular the work of the treaty bodies in relation to their efficiency and contribution to the improvement of the human rights situation. The treaty bodies on the one hand examine state reports and recommend changes in the states' policy. On the other hand they operate as quasi-judicial bodies, but without the authority to render legally binding decisions. After providing a short background, the most critical deficiencies of the system are analyzed. The most significant of these is the lack of cooperation on the part of the states. Furthermore, there are other shortcomings regarding a significant backlog on the part of the treaty bodies, as well as inadequate qualifications and guaranties of independence of the treaty body members, mainly in relation to their competence to consider individual complaints. The paper further explains the reaction of the UN High Commissioner for Human Rights and her proposed measures. Moreover, with regard to the reform, a proposal of creating a World Court of Human Rights is discussed that could gradually take over the competencies of the treaty bodies in relation to considering individual complaints.*

JUDr. Ing. Jan Lhotský is a PhD candidate in international law at the Masaryk University, Faculty of Law. His research and publications primarily cover two areas. Firstly, he writes on international criminal law with focus on the functioning of the International Criminal Court. Secondly, he also focuses on international human rights law in terms of its institutional frameworks and their influence on the enforceability of human rights.
e-mail: jan.m.lhotsky@ gmail.com

| | |

I. Introduction

14.01. With regard to international human rights protection, both scholars and law practitioners working in the field of international law primarily focus on regional mechanisms, such as the European system of human rights protection with the European Court of Human Rights in Strasbourg.[1] It was the first international system of human rights protection, but it is certainly not the only one. In order to find out what other options an individual has at the international level and how efficient those measures are, it is appropriate to have a closer look at the other mechanisms that are not as widely used as the above-mentioned system.

14.02. Just as the European Court of Human Rights provides protection under the European Convention on Human Rights, the American Convention on Human Rights later established an Inter-American Court of Human Rights which provides similar international protection within the American states that have become parties.[2] There is an important difference, however. Unlike the current European Convention after Protocol no. 11,[3] the American Convention does not allow direct access of the individual to the court. Individuals thus can bring the case to the court only through another body, a commission. Subsequent to both of these, another regional human rights system was established in Africa with the African Court on Human and Peoples' Rights at its centre.[4] It combines the two models, being in reality closer to the Inter-American system. There are thus three more or less analogous regional systems of human rights protection in Europe, America and Africa.

14.03. Apart from the regional level, there are also mechanisms intended for all states in the world, at the universal level. On the one hand, there are organs directly integrated within the UN structures, such as the Human Rights Council or the High Commissioner for Human Rights. On the other hand, there are mechanisms for human rights protection that have been created by particular human rights treaties on the universal level. Those bodies are also connected to the UN in many ways, but

---

[1] *Convention for the Protection of Human Rights and Fundamental Freedoms*, adopted in 1950 and entering into force in 1953.

[2] *American Convention on Human Rights*, adopted in 1969 and entering into force in 1978.

[3] *Protocol No. 11 to the Convention for the Protection of Human Rights and Fundamental Freedoms, restructuring the control machinery established thereby*, adopted in 1994 and entering into force in 1998.

[4] *Protocol to the African Charter on Human and Peoples' Rights on the Establishment of an African Court on Human and Peoples' Rights*, adopted in 1998 and entering into force in 2004.

they are legally based on those treaties, which is why they can provide protection only towards the states that have voluntarily became parties to them.

14.04. This text aims to analyse the operation of these latter treaty bodies and assess their possible contribution to human rights protection. Furthermore, based on the analysis and enforceability of rights, views will be expressed regarding the institutional set up of human rights mechanisms on the universal level.

II. Treaty-based Mechanisms on the Universal Level

14.05. When the Universal Declaration of Human Rights was adopted in 1948, it was in the form of a UN General Assembly resolution,[5] which is not of a legally binding nature. However, from the initial discussions during the preparation of the document, some delegates supported the idea that it should be a legally binding international treaty. Because of the wish to have the wide support of the states, it was decided that it would be in the form of a declaration and that binding treaties would follow later.[6] However, it should be stressed that it took almost another twenty years until the adoption of such treaties on the universal level that cover the content of the Universal Declaration.

II.1. Role of the Treaty Bodies

14.06. The treaties transforming the values enshrined in the Universal Declaration of Human Rights into international law were primarily the International Covenant on Civil and Political Rights and the International Covenant on Economic, Social and Cultural Rights. Together with the Optional Protocol to the first mentioned covenant, they were adopted in 1966 and came into force in 1977. Since that time, a number of other treaties on the universal level also came into being which focus on a specific area of human rights protection (e.g. Convention against Torture, Convention on the Rights of the Child). Those treaties create committees (treaty bodies) that function as control mechanisms in respect to the particular rights contained in the treaties.

---

[5] *General Assembly resolution 217 A (III)*, adopted on 10 December 1948.
[6] JOHANNES MORSINK, THE UNIVERSAL DECLARATION OF HUMAN RIGHTS: ORIGINS, DRAFTING AND INTENT, Philadelphia: University of Pennsylvania Press 9-11 (1999).

14.07. At this time, there are the following nine treaty bodies with similar competences:[7]

- Human Rights Committee;
- Committee on Economic, Social and Cultural Rights;
- Committee on the Elimination of Racial Discrimination;
- Committee on the Elimination of Discrimination against Women;
- Committee against Torture (plus Subcommittee on Prevention of Torture);
- Committee on the Rights of the Child;
- Committee on Migrant Workers;
- Committee on the Rights of Persons with Disabilities;
- Committee on Enforced Disappearances.

14.08. In general, it can be said that the treaty bodies have two primary roles.[8] Firstly, they receive and examine state reports. If a state becomes a party to a particular treaty, the human rights language contained in the treaty becomes binding for it and it has to submit reports to the committee, usually once in four years. The report should explain the relevant human rights situation and measures taken by the state to improve it. The committee composed of human rights experts then examines the report and meets with a state delegation to discuss the most important issues. Subsequently it publishes its own report (*Concluding Observations*) that contains concrete recommendations for the state to implement in the subsequent period.

14.09. Secondly, if a state party also ratifies an optional protocol or issues a relevant declaration, it additionally allows the committee to consider individual complaints (*communications*). In that case, after exhausting all available domestic remedies,[9] an individual can submit a complaint to the committee claiming that their rights have been violated. The treaty body considers the individual complaint in a closed meeting and it passes a decision (*view*) on the violation of the right in that particular case. The decision, however, lacks a legally binding nature and is thus considered a recommendation.

14.10. In short, through the first role, the treaty bodies address the human rights situation in the states and help them to improve the situation.

---

[7] For more on the individual treaty bodies, see JULIE A. MERTUS, THE UNITED NATIONS AND HUMAN RIGHTS: A GUIDE FOR A NEW ERA, London: Routledge 82-94 (2nd ed. 2009).

[8] In addition to that some of them can conduct inquiries. Treaty bodies can also accept inter-state complaints, although this has never been used by the states. JAVAID REHMAN, INTERNATIONAL HUMAN RIGHTS LAW, Essex: Pearson Education Limited 119-120 (2nd ed. 2010).

[9] An exception represents cases in which domestic remedies were in reality not available to the victim. Ibid., at 134-136.

However, through the second role they work as quasi-judicial bodies, but without the possibility of issuing a legally binding decision.

II.2. Inefficiencies of the Mechanism

14.11. It has to be acknowledged that there are several important virtues of the treaty-based human rights mechanisms on the universal level. They are intended for all states in the world, which can voluntarily join the particular treaties. Because the system was created primarily in the 1960s when the world was politically divided over the Cold War, it is no wonder that its enforcement authority is not very strong. Nevertheless, at present 167 states have already become parties to the covenant that created the Human Rights Committee and 114 have joined its Optional Protocol which allows them to file individual complaints.[10]

14.12. There are at least two advantages of the mechanism to be mentioned. Firstly, the assessment of the human rights situation in the particular state is performed by experts in the field of human rights, which is why the conclusions are mostly very objective and of a high quality. Secondly, within the examination the committees lead a direct dialogue with the representatives of the particular state. This results in a better understanding of the situation on the part of the committee and of the required standard of human rights on the part of the state representatives, leading to better implementation of the committee's recommendations.

14.13. However, it is also necessary to admit that the system lacks significant efficiency and the potential to help improve the human rights situation in the relevant states parties. There are several important deficiencies of the treaty bodies' functioning.[11]

14.14. First, there is a significant lack of cooperation by the states in submitting the state reports. To be precise, only 16 % of states submit their reports on time.[12] Additionally, approximately two thirds of reports are submitted later than one year after the deadline, that is to say, with several years' delay. Furthermore, several states have joined

---

[10] UN Multilateral Treaties (United Nations Treaty Collection), available at: http://treaties.un.org/pages/ParticipationStatus.aspx (accessed on 24 August 2013).
[11] These and other arguments were discussed within the monograph Human Rights Protection in International Law (in Czech language). See JAN LHOTSKÝ, OCHRANA LIDSKÝCH PRÁV V MEZINÁRODNÍM PRÁVU: KONTROLNÍ MECHANISMY NA REGIONÁLNÍ A UNIVERZÁLNÍ ÚROVNI A MOŽNOST VZNIKU SVĚTOVÉHO SOUDU PRO LIDSKÁ PRÁVA, Brno: Masarykova univerzita 139-250 (2012).
[12] Report of the UN High Commissioner for Human Rights A/66/860 of 22 June 2012, at 21-22.

particular treaties, but do not report at all. That is why, for example, the Human Rights Committee started to examine states even in the absence of a report.[13] However, the Committee proceeds to this measure only after many years, in some cases as much as twenty years after the submission date. Nevertheless, it should also be said that elaboration of a state report is a very complex process and given the fact that states have to submit these reports regularly to several separate treaty bodies, it is a relatively heavy burden, especially for smaller states.

14.15. Second, there is also a significant rate of states' non-compliance with the decision of treaty bodies regarding individual complaints. These decisions are actually not legally binding judgments, but rather recommendations from a legal point of view. That is why the states very often simply ignore them. For example, within the work of the Human Rights Committee the overall satisfactory response rate on the part of the states in this regard amounts only to 12%.[14] That is to say, the impact of the quasi-judicial activity of the treaty bodies can in no way be compared to the regional human rights mechanisms such as the one represented by the European Court of Human Rights, where enforcement of such decisions is much stronger. In the event of non-compliance of the state with the decision of the treaty body, this information can only be included in the committee's annual report.[15]

14.16. Third, despite the fact that states do not cooperate adequately, the treaty bodies are overloaded with work and have too many pending state reports and individual complaints. The reason for this is that they are not full-time bodies. Their sessions are held only a few times a year for several weeks. Unfortunately, the UN General Assembly is unwilling to finance longer sessions. So if we take into account the average time from submitting a state report to its examination, the whole process takes between two and four years. Similarly regarding the individual complaints, within the Human Rights Committee the waiting time usually amounts to three and a half years.[16] This shows that in relation to time efficiency, the system has significant weaknesses.

---

[13] The provision is contained in Rule 70 of the Rules of Procedure of the Human Rights Committee.

[14] DAVID C. BALUARTE & CHRISTIAN M. DE VOS, FROM JUDGEMENT TO JUSTICE: IMPLEMENTING INTERNATIONAL AND REGIONAL HUMAN RIGHTS DECISIONS, New York: Open Society Foundations 27 (2010).

[15] WALTER KÄLIN – JÖRG KÜNZLI, THE LAW OF INTERNATIONAL HUMAN RIGHTS PROTECTION, Oxford: Oxford University Press 226 (2009).

[16] Report of the UN High Commissioner for Human Rights A/66/860 of 22 June 2012, at 19-20.

14.17. Fourth, within their competence to consider individual complaints, the treaty body members have similarities to judges, but they do not have to possess the qualifications for such a position. In fact, the treaties do not even require them to be lawyers, although within their decision-making activity they decide on the violation of rights. Thus the professional background of committee members varies and apart from lawyers like judges or academics includes also a number of government representatives.[17]

14.18. Fifth, the system does not provide for satisfactory guarantees of independence for the treaty body members. On the one hand, as was already mentioned, twenty per cent of them are active as diplomats, government officials or within national parliaments.[18] On the other hand, an important independence issue is connected with the remuneration of experts. In 2001, the General Assembly reduced the annual payment of members to $1.00.[19] Essentially, the treaty body members exercise their demanding work in a voluntary and unpaid capacity, so they need to have another job which allows them to take part in the proceedings of the committee. They only receive daily subsistence allowances to cover costs during the treaty body sessions.

14.19. Sixth, as the treaty body system has grown, so have its costs. A High Commissioner's report states that whereas in 2000, the overall meeting time of the treaty bodies was 51 weeks and there were 97 committee members, in 2011, it was 72 weeks and there were 172 committee members.[20] Similarly, the costs of travel and expenses of the experts amounted to $4.3 mil. in the biennium 2000-2001 and rose to $13.8 mil. in 2012-2013.[21] Thus the growth of the system, in which treaty bodies carry out their competence of examining both state reports, as well as considering individual complaints, seems to be very demanding on the budgetary requirements. In reality, however, because they still have significant backlogs, it must be said that if the system wants to

---

[17] HENRY J. STEINER, PHILIP ALSTON & RYAN GOODMAN, INTERNATIONAL HUMAN RIGHTS IN CONTEXT: LAW, POLITICS, MORALS, Oxford: Oxford University Press 846 (3rd ed. 2007).

[18] Report of the UN High Commissioner for Human Rights A/66/860 of 22 June 2012, at 76-77.

[19] Nigel Rodley, *Civil and Political Rights, in* INTERNATIONAL PROTECTION OF HUMAN RIGHTS: A TEXTBOOK, Turku: Institute for Human Rights, Åbo Akademi University 105, 122 (Catarina Krause and Martin Scheinin eds., 2009).

[20] Requirements and implications of the ongoing growth of the treaty body system on the periodic reporting procedures, documentation and meeting time (Office of the High Commissioner for Human Rights), available at: http://www2.ohchr.org/english/bodies/HRTD/docs/ReportingUnderTtreatyBodies.pdf, at 1-2 (accessed on 24 August 2013).

[21] Report of the UN High Commissioner for Human Rights A/66/860 of 22 June 2012, at 26-27.

provide an efficient contribution to the human rights situation on the ground, the political will to provide the necessary resources will have to be found.

14.20. Seventh, it is appropriate to say that the system of treaty bodies remains mostly unknown, not only to the general public, but also within the general legal community. One reason for this is that it is a very complicated system of different bodies with different competencies towards different states. Moreover, it does not have any effective enforcement tools, leading many states to join due to international pressure, but not cooperate afterwards. Because of the lack of awareness of the system and its complexity, the media mostly do not report on the examinations of states. Regarding the individual complaints, because the committee's decisions are not legally binding, states mostly do not comply with them. Given that, there is no rational motivation for an individual whose rights have been violated to file a complaint to a treaty body.

14.21. In conclusion, it has to be said that the deficiencies of the functioning of the treaty bodies are substantial and thus there is a need for appropriate measures to be taken.

II.3. Proposals for the Strengthening of Treaty Bodies

14.22. It has already been more than a decade since potential reforms of the treaty body system started to be seriously discussed. In the second half of 2009, the High Commissioner for Human Rights launched a Treaty Body Strengthening Process by inviting states, treaty body members and stakeholders to negotiate various reform proposals. Based on a number of expert meetings, taking place over two and a half years, in June 2012, she introduced a comprehensive report entitled "Strengthening the United Nations Treaty Body System",[22] in which she presents the principal ideas discussed during the process.

14.23. The High Commissioner's June 2012 report criticises some of the system's shortcomings and presents a set of proposals, the most significant of which is the 'comprehensive reporting calendar'. This is the main tool that should be introduced in order to make the states cooperate with the committees. Today, the treaty bodies arrange a dialogue with the state delegation after receiving the state report. That is why, in the case of a considerable delay, the committee may not examine a state party for ten or even twenty years. After the implementation of

---

[22] For more information, see Treaty Body Strengthening (Office of the High Commissioner for Human Rights), available at: http://www.ohchr.org/EN/HRBodies/HRTD/Pages/TBStrengthening.aspx (accessed on 24 August 2013).

the comprehensive reporting calendar, however, all states would have a fixed timetable well in advance. If they did not submit a report, they would be examined in the particular amount of time anyway.

14.24. It will be interesting to see whether the implementation of this measure results in more states parties being examined in the absence of a report, or if it stimulates the states to cooperate with the treaty bodies more fully. Both would be an improvement over the present situation, although the latter result is more preferable. An important factor regarding the implementation of this proposal, however, is that it requires significant additional meeting time and the costs of the system would rise from an annual $56.4 mil. to $108 mil.[23] The report also includes a proposal to use a simplified reporting procedure and several other important recommendations. But for the goal of enhancing the cooperation of the states, the proposal of introducing a fixed calendar is of the highest importance.

14.25. The proposals of the High Commissioner are, without a doubt, a significant move in the right direction. After her report was published, an intergovernmental process was launched in order to put the necessary changes into practice.

14.26. The proposal reacts to one of the most important deficiencies of the functioning of treaty bodies, namely the lack of cooperation of states parties regarding submitting the reports. It also presents several other useful recommendations, whose implementation should be supported. On the other hand, it is appropriate to ask whether the changes could or should be stronger.[24]

14.27. In fact, many of the deficiencies of the system mentioned above would remain, even if all the proposals were to be implemented. The issues remaining to be addressed would include the states' non-compliance regarding the decisions on violation of rights, public lack of awareness, the amount of pending cases or lack of competence and guaranties of

---

[23] Report of the UN High Commissioner for Human Rights A/66/860 of 22 June 2012, p. 34-46 and 95-96.

[24] Regarding the system of examining state reports, there are two stronger proposals to be mentioned. Firstly, there is the 'consolidated treaty body system' proposed by Martin Scheinin which aims at transforming the treaty bodies into more integrated organs with the Human Rights Committee at its centre. See Martin Scheinin, *The Proposed Optional Protocol to the Covenant on Economic, Social and Cultural Rights: A Blueprint for UN Human Rights Treaty Body Reform-Without Amending the Existing Treaties*, 6(1) HUMAN RIGHTS LAW REVIEW 131-142 (2006). Another, even stronger reform proposal was presented by the High Commissioner for Human Rights already in 2006, where she supported the idea of merging all treaty bodies into one body, whose members would work full-time in it. See the *Concept Paper on the High Commissioner's Proposal for a Unified Standing Treaty Body*, HRI/MC/2006/2 of 22 March 2006.

independence regarding the quasi-judicial decision-making of treaty body members. After the possible implementation of the comprehensive reporting calendar, the shortcomings analyzed above will relate mainly to the competence of the treaty bodies to receive and consider individual complaints. However, the High Commissioner's report of June 2012 does not offer any effective measures to streamline the individual complaints procedure.

14.28. The treaty bodies, from their very nature, cannot render a legally binding decision. That is why parties do not comply with them, because in their view they are mere recommendations. Therefore, with regard to the competence of treaty bodies to consider individual complaints, it is appropriate to look at the possible creation of a new institution which could enrich the system by being able to render binding decisions and finally provide individuals with an efficient mechanism to enforce the rights contained in the treaties on a universal level.

III. Possible Establishment of a World Court of Human Rights

14.29. The idea of creating an international court on the universal level, whose purpose would be to protect human rights according to a particular treaty, is not a completely new idea. Actually, it was proposed by Australia in 1947 during the work on the wording of the Universal Declaration of Human Rights.[25] However, it did not obtain sufficient support.

14.30. Much later, on the occasion of the 60th anniversary of the adoption of the Universal Declaration, a 'Swiss Initiative' was launched.[26] Within this research project, two statute proposals were created for a potential new court. They were proposed by leading experts on international law and human rights protection, namely Manfred Nowak, Julia Kozma and Martin Scheinin. Afterwards, this expert group consolidated the proposals into one and published a draft statute of the World Court of Human Rights.[27]

---

[25] JOHANNES MORSINK, *supra* note 6, at 15-16. Furthermore, MARY ANN GLENDON, A WORLD MADE NEW: ELEANOR ROOSEVELT AND THE DECLARATION OF HUMAN RIGHTS, New York: Random House 38, 84 (2001).

[26] This has been preceded by some scholarly discussion on the topic of the possible creation of a new human rights court on the universal level. See Manfred Nowak, *The Need for a World Court of Human Rights*, 7(1) HUMAN RIGHTS LAW REVIEW 251-259 (2007). Before this also Stefan Trechsel, *A World Court of Human Rights?* 1(3) NORTHWESTERN UNIVERSITY JOURNAL OF INTERNATIONAL HUMAN RIGHTS 1-18 (2003).

[27] JULIA KOZMA, MANFRED NOWAK & MARTIN SCHEININ, A WORLD COURT OF HUMAN RIGHTS - CONSOLIDATED STATUTE AND COMMENTARY, Wien: Neuer Wissenschaftlicher

14.31. According to the proposal, the Court would be created by a new international treaty (statute) which individual states could ratify, and this act would be treated as notification of the suspension of the operation of the relevant complaint procedures.[28] In other words, by ratifying the statute, states would automatically transfer the competence for considering individual complaints from treaty bodies to the Court. This competence would thus gradually move to the new court and the treaty bodies could devote more time and attention to the examination of state reports. Thus, the creation of this new judicial institution would not only enhance the enforceability of human rights on the universal level, but also strengthen the primary role of the treaty bodies.

14.32. The new court would not serve as an appeals court to regional human rights courts. Regarding the criteria for admissibility, all domestic remedies would have to be exhausted before filing an individual complaint. That means that the individual would get direct access to the international court, similarly to the European Court of Human Rights after Protocol no. 11.

14.33. The jurisdiction of the prospective court plays a central role in the proposal. In Article 5 para. 1 the statute lists UN human rights treaties over which the Court would have jurisdiction. This list not only contains the treaties that created the discussed treaty bodies, but also several other human rights treaties. However, it does not mean that after ratification of the statute by a particular state the Court would be able to apply all those treaties towards the state. It would be able to receive and examine individual complaints only if the alleged violation of the right is covered by a treaty to which the respective state is a party.[29]

14.34. States can declare at ratification that they do not recognize the jurisdiction of the Court in relation to certain human rights treaties. They can also declare that they recognize its jurisdiction towards more treaties than those listed in Article 5 para. 1.[30] According to the draft statute, states are thus given a wide scope for influencing which treaties and provisions the Court will be able to use towards them.

14.35. It is important to mention that in practice there could be states which do not have a lot of interest in protecting human rights on the ground, but because of international pressure they would want to join the Court. In this case they would be able to limit the possible use of jurisdiction to a specific treaty or set of treaties covering issues with

---

Verlag 113 (2010). For the research activities see Swiss Initiative (Agenda for Human Rights), available at: http://www.udhr60.ch (accessed on 24 August 2013).

[28] Art. 7 para. 3 of the draft statute.
[29] Art. 7 para. 1 of the draft statute.
[30] Art. 50 para. 1 and para. 4.

which they do not have many problems. However, accession to such an institution should show a real interest in human rights protection. That is why, in my opinion, there should be a common base or core of the Court's jurisdiction. This could be represented by the International Covenant on Civil and Political Rights and the Convention against Torture. By introducing this rule into the statute, all states wishing to accept the jurisdiction of the Court would have to agree that these treaties can be applied towards all states parties. The implementation of this proposal could thus prevent using acceptance of a part of the Court's jurisdiction only for political purposes.

14.36. The possibility for non-state actors to accept the Court's jurisdiction, presented in the draft statute, represents a major development in international human rights protection. The statute categorizes them as Entities, which includes inter-governmental organizations or business corporations, and they can recognize the jurisdiction of the Court by lodging a relevant declaration. While making such a declaration, they can also specify which treaties will be subject to the jurisdiction of the Court.[31] The widening of the subjects of human rights treaties from states to non-state actors would represent a very significant development in the international protection of human rights. This is especially true since the influence of inter-governmental organizations and transnational corporations is growing and today, many of them carry much more power than several of the smaller states.[32] By allowing them to voluntarily accept the jurisdiction of the potential new court, the proposal provides for a competent solution to decrease the problem of the lack of accountability on the part of non-state actors.

14.37. In the event of finding a violation of rights, the Court would have a wider scope of reparation methods to use than, for example, the European Court of Human Rights. The statute states that in such a case, the Court should afford the victim adequate reparation for the harm suffered, including restitution, rehabilitation, compensation, guaranties of non-repetition, or any other form of satisfaction.[33] The execution of judgments should then be supervised by the High Commissioner for Human Rights, who could, in a case of non-compliance by a state, call upon the Human Rights Council or potentially even the Security Council with a request to take measures to enforce the judgment.[34] Due to the political influence in these last two

---

[31] Art. 4 para. 1 and Art. 51.

[32] Andrew Clapham, *Non-State Actors*, in INTERNATIONAL HUMAN RIGHTS LAW, Oxford: Oxford University Press 561-582 (Daniel Moeckli et al. eds., 2010).

[33] Art. 17, para. 2 of the draft statute.

[34] Art. 18 para. 4 and 5.

mentioned organs, it is right that the supervision should be primarily performed by the High Commissioner.

14.38. A legally precise draft is available and further development will depend on whether it gains sufficient support. In this regard it is appropriate to mention that after four years of work on a COST Action research project *The Role of the EU in UN Human Rights Reform* which focused on any gaps in human rights policy and their elimination, a set of proposals was presented in 2013 to the relevant policy-makers. On the one hand the recommendations support the implementation of the measures contained in the High Commissioner's June 2012 report. On the other hand the recommendations also support the creation of the World Court of Human Rights.[35] Since the release of the draft statute, this idea has been supported by several other important stakeholders.[36]

14.39. In relation to the further development of the proposal, much will depend on how strong the arguments of supporters will be. In the first place, it is necessary to fully implement the current proposals from the June 2012 report regarding the treaty bodies to enhance their efficiency towards examining state reports. Afterwards, the proposal to make the individual complaints procedures more efficient by means of creating a new judicial institution on a universal level should be seriously discussed.

IV. Conclusion

14.40. The system of the treaty-based human rights protection on the universal level is very complex. There are nine treaty bodies which function in a similar way. They examine state reports regarding the human rights situation, while they also consider individual complaints as quasi-judicial bodies. In reality, the performance of both activities

---

[35] The Role of the EU in UN Human Rights Reform: A Policy Debate (COST), available at: http://www.cost.eu/media/newsroom/humanrights (accessed on 24 August 2013).

[36] In this regard, a Declaration on Access to Justice and Right to a Remedy by the International Commission of Jurists supports the creation of the new court. See ICJ adopts Declaration on Access to Justice and Right to a Remedy (International Commission of Jurists), available at: http://www.icj.org/icj-world-congress-adopts-landmark-declaration-on-access-to-justice-and-right-to-a-remedy (accessed on 24 August 2013). Furthermore, in June 2013 a conference titled Vienna+20 was held to commemorate the 20 years since the important Second World Conference on Human Rights in Vienna. The final Declaration of the conference, among other things, calls for acceleration of discussions with a view to the establishment of a World Court of Human Rights. See Vienna+20 CSO Declaration: Reclaiming the Primacy of Human Rights (Vienna+20), available at: http://viennaplus20.wordpress.com (accessed on 24 August 2013).

shows a significant amount of inefficiency and non-cooperation on the part of the states. After initiating a process of strengthening the treaty bodies, the High Commissioner for Human Rights presented a report with proposals to tackle the system's deficiencies. Those measures are to be fully implemented. However, they are aimed above all at improving the competence of treaty bodies towards examination of state reports.

14.41. Regarding the competence of the committees to consider individual complaints, the treaty bodies are in their very nature unable to render legally binding decisions. That is why the level of state compliance with those decisions is extremely low. Therefore, it is necessary to admit that a more courageous reform is needed in order to achieve an efficient system of protecting the rights covered by treaties on the universal level. Within the Swiss Initiative, leading experts on international human rights law prepared a draft statute of the World Court of Human Rights that could, in the event of its creation, take over the competencies of current treaty bodies and move towards considering individual complaints.

14.42. In brief, three important virtues of such a reform should be mentioned. Firstly, the Court would be able to render a legally binding decision, i.e. a judgment. That would be a significant change compared to the current situation in which states perceive the treaty body decisions as mere recommendations. Therefore, the authority of the decision-making body and the pressure to comply with the judgment would be much stronger.

14.43. Secondly, in addition to the system providing for wider protection in areas where regional systems of human rights protection exist (Europe, America, Africa), it would be of very high importance that also states from Asia could join, where an analogical regional system of human rights protection does not exist. It is necessary to bear in mind that more than four billion people live in Asia itself (which amounts to approximately sixty per cent of the world population). In the absence of a relevant regional system they could join an efficient system on the universal level in the future. This argument should not be underestimated.

14.44. Thirdly, the statute allows non-state actors to voluntarily accept the jurisdiction of the court. The proposal thus reacts to the long-term lack of accountability of these subjects of international law regarding human rights protection. In the event of the establishment of the new court, inter-governmental organisations and transnational corporations or other relevant actors could also be subject to the jurisdiction of the new human rights court.

14.45. In general, the proposal should be supported. However, many particular issues regarding the jurisdiction of the potential new court and many other areas would firstly have to be properly discussed. It is, nevertheless, important to say that the Court would not actually bring any new rights. It would only provide stronger protection for those that the states have already accepted. In the long-term, the current treaty bodies could thus pay more attention to examining the state reports and the World Court of Human Rights would provide for an efficient mechanism for individuals to attain their rights. As such, those two reforms should be viewed as two sides of the same coin.

| | |

Summaries

FRA   [*Les mécanismes de l'ONU pour la protection des droits de l'homme : le renforcement des organes de traités sur les droits de l'homme qui surveillent la mise en oeuvre des principaux traités internationaux à la lumière de la proposition de création d'une Cour internationale des droits de l'homme*]

C'est le niveau général de la protection des droits de l'homme et plus concrètement le fonctionnement desdits organes de traités, leur efficacité et leur contribution à l'amélioration de la situation des droits de l'homme, qui fait l'objet de cet exposé. Les organes de traités récoltent les informations que lui fournissent les États et émettent des recommandations en matière de respect des droits de l'homme. Ils fonctionnent également comme des organismes quasi judiciaires, mais sans compétence pour délivrer des décisions contraignantes sur un plan juridique. Après une brève introduction, les principaux écueils du présent système sont analysés. L'insuffisance de la collaboration des États avec les organes de traités constitue une des principales faiblesses de ce système, ses autres déficiences étant principalement liées au volume consistant des travaux en cours des comités, au manque de qualification et de garanties d'indépendance de ses membres, en particulier lorsqu'il s'agit de juger des plaintes individuelles pour infraction aux droits de l'homme. On explique la réaction du Haut-Commissariat aux droits de l'homme des Nations Unies et les mesures qu'il a proposées. On discute ensuite de la question en lien avec la réforme de la proposition de création d'une Cour internationale des droits de l'homme qui pourrait progressivement récupérer les compétences des organes de traités pour juger les plaintes individuelles.

CZE [*Mechanismy OSN na ochranu lidských práv: posílení smluvních výborů ve světle návrhu na vytvoření Světového soudu pro lidská práva*]
Příspěvek se zaměřuje na univerzální úroveň ochrany lidských práv, a to konkrétně na fungování tzv. smluvních výborů s ohledem na jejich účinnost a míru přispívání ke zlepšování situace lidských práv. Smluvní výbory na jedné straně přijímají zprávy států a doporučují jim změny v přístupu k dodržování lidských práv, na druhou stranu také fungují jako kvazijudiciální orgány, ale bez pravomoci vydat z právního hlediska závazné rozhodnutí. Po krátkém úvodu jsou v textu analyzovány nejvýznamnější nedostatky současného systému. Mezi tyto slabiny patří zejména velmi nízká míra spolupráce s výbory ze strany států, přičemž další nedostatky se vztahují zejména k závažnému objemu nevyřízené práce výborů a nedostatečné míře kvalifikace a garancí nezávislosti členů smluvních výborů, a to zejména ve spojitosti s pravomocí posuzovat individuální stížnosti na porušení práv. Článek dále vysvětluje reakci Vysoké komisařky OSN pro lidská práva a jí navrhovaná opatření. V souvislosti s reformou je poté diskutován návrh na vytvoření Světového soudu pro lidská práva, který by případně mohl postupně převzít pravomoci smluvních výborů k posuzování individuálních stížností.

||||

POL [*Mechanizmy ONZ w zakresie ochrony praw człowieka: Wzmocnienie komitetów traktatowych w świetle planu stworzenia Światowego Trybunału Praw Człowieka*]
Artykuł poświęcony uniwersalnemu wymiarowi ochrony praw człowieka, a mianowicie funkcjonowaniu tzw. komitetów traktatowych pod kątem ich skuteczności i przyczyniania się do powszechniejszego przestrzegania praw człowieka. Tekst analizuje najważniejsze braki w aktualnym systemie komitetów traktatowych i w tym kontekście wyjaśnia rozwiązania zgłaszane przez Wysoką Komisarz Narodów Zjednoczonych ds. Praw Człowieka. W związku z reformą omówiono tu również propozycję utworzenia Światowego Trybunału Praw Człowieka, który mógłby zacząć stopniowo przejmować uprawnienia komitetów traktatowych w zakresie rozpatrywania poszczególnych skarg.

DEU [*Mechanismen der Vereinten Nationen zum Schutz der Menschenrechte: die Stärkung der Vertragsausschüsse im Lichte des Vorschlags zur Schaffung eines Weltgerichtshofs für Menschenrechte*]

Der Beitrag konzentriert sich auf die universale Ebene des Schutzes der Menschenrechte, konkret die Arbeitsweise der sog. Vertragsausschüsse, unter dem Aspekt ihrer Wirksamkeit und des Grads ihres tatsächlichen Beitrags zur Besserung der Menschenrechtslage. Der Text analysiert die dringlichsten Mängel des bestehenden Systems der Vertragsausschüsse und erläutert vor diesem Hintergrund die von der UN-Hochkommissarin für Menschenrechte vorgeschlagenen Lösungen. Im Zusammenhang mit der Reform wird außerdem der Vorschlag zur Schaffung eines Weltgerichtshofs für Menschenrechte diskutiert, der womöglich schrittweise die Kompetenzen der Vertragsausschüsse übernehmen könnte, was die Beurteilung individueller Beschwerden anbelangt.

RUS [*Механизмы ООН в области защиты прав человека: укрепление договорных комитетов в связи с предложением о создании Международного суда по правам человека*]

В статье рассматривается универсальный уровень защиты прав человека, а именно функционирование договорных комитетов с учетом их эффективности и степени вклада в улучшение ситуации в области прав человека. В тексте анализируются наиболее существенные недостатки существующей системы договорных комитетов, и в данном контексте поясняются решения, внесенные Верховным комиссаром ООН по правам человека. В связи с реформой также обсуждается предложение по созданию Международного суда по правам человека, который, в случае необходимости, постепенно принял бы полномочия договорных комитетов по рассмотрению индивидуальных жалоб.

ESP [*Los mecanismos de las Naciones Unidas para la protección de los derechos humanos: fortalecimiento de los comités de contratación a la luz de la propuesta de crear un Tribunal Mundial de los Derechos Humanos*]

El artículo se centra en el nivel universal de protección de los derechos humanos y, específicamente, en el funcionamiento de los denominados comités de contratación, con respecto a su eficacia y a la medida de su contribución para mejorar la situación de los derechos humanos. En el texto se analizan las deficiencias más importantes del sistema actual de los comités de contratación y, dado el contexto, se explican las soluciones propuestas por la Alta Comisaria para los Derechos Humanos de la ONU. En cuanto a la reforma, se debate también la propuesta de crear un Tribunal Mundial de los Derechos Humanos que podría asumir gradualmente las responsabilidades de los comités de contratación con el fin de atender denuncias individuales.

| | |

Hana Marková | Nicole Grmelová

Institutional Framework of Combating Money Laundering in the European Union

Key words:
EU law | *Money laundering* | *Financial Intelligence Units* | *Financial Analytical Unit* | *OLAF* | *Europol* | *FATF*

Abstract | *Money laundering is associated with efforts to obtain property from illicit actions. The need to use proceeds of criminal activities generates the need to get rid of this gain of illegal origin – money needs to be laundered. The international community has gradually become aware of the necessity of adopting a common and coordinated approach in tackling money laundering and that is why international treaties started to be adopted to fight these activities. Different countries have established organizations and institutions that deal with combating money laundering. In this respect, a key role has been played by the Action Task Force on Money Laundering (FATF). Individual states have set up their Financial Intelligence Units (FIUs), which should actively contribute to preventing the misuse of financial systems within their territories. Also, the European Union has adopted measures which help incorporate the FATF standards into the legislation of its Member States. Some European Union bodies also actively participate in preventing and prosecuting money laundering, yet the powers to suppress this illegal activity still lie largely in the hands of the Member States.*

| | |

Hana Marková is a Professor of Financial Law at Charles University Law School, Prague and the University of Economics, Prague. She is a Member of the Legislative Council of the Czech Government from 2008, a Member of the Information and Research Center of the Public Finance and Tax Law of Central and Eastern European Countries and a mentor of PhD students. She is the author of numerous articles in the field of Financial Law and Financial Policy published worldwide. e-mail: markova@ prf.cuni.cz

Nicole Grmelová graduated from Charles University Law School, Prague and the Law Faculty of Universidad de Sevilla. She defended her Ph.D. thesis at the Faculty of International Relations, University of Economics, Prague,

I. Historical and Legal Background of Combating Money Laundering

where she teaches courses on EU Institutions and EU Law as a Senior Lecturer. Between 2004 and 2008 she worked as a lawyer-linguist for the European Parliament in Brussels and later cooperated with the Court of Justice of the European Union.
e-mail:
nicole.grmelova@vse.cz

15.01. The term "money laundering" is believed to have been coined during the Watergate affair in the1970s;[1] however, its origins go back to the 1920s and 1930s in the United States.[2] The first significant response addressing money laundering in the U.S., however, did not come until 1970 when the Bank Secrecy Act (BSA) was passed. In 1986, the U.S. Congress adopted the Money Laundering Control Act, which considered money laundering a criminal offence.

15.02. After 1985, the trend launched by the U.S. was extended to other countries such as Great Britain, Japan, Australia and Canada. Also, the United Nations actively joined this process in 1988 by adopting the Convention against Illicit Traffic in Narcotic Drugs and Psychotropic Substances. The Council of Europe followed in 1990 by adopting the Convention on Laundering, Search, Seizure and Confiscation of the Proceeds from Crime, which was amended by the Convention on the Laundering, Search, Seizure and Confiscation of the Proceeds from Crime and on the Financing of Terrorism in 2005.

15.03. Another initiative aimed at combating money laundering stems from the G7 Group Paris summit in 1989, which established an intergovernmental body to combat money laundering, called "Financial Action Task Force on Money Laundering" (FATF). The objective of FATF was to create rules governing this field and to support an efficient implementation of both repressive and preventive measures with respect to jeopardizing the integrity of the international financial system.[3]

15.04. In 1990, this body adopted the so-called 40 FATF Recommendations, which set the international standard for combating money laundering and constitute a basic pillar for drafting individual national laws

---

[1]   Jeffrey Robinson. *Pánové z prádelny špinavých peněz (The Laundrymen)*, Praha: BIVŠ 12 (1st. ed. 2009).

[2]   In the 1920s and 1930s American gangsters managed to obtain significant sums of money in cash from importing and selling alcohol and from other illegal activities and they needed to cover up the origins of the money. It was quite common to merge this income with that coming from public laundries, which is probably how the term "money laundering" came into being. For more details on the etymology of this term see Jonathan E. Turner, Money Laundering Prevention: Deterring, Detecting, and Resolving Financial Fraud, Hoboken: Wiley 2 (1st ed. 2011).

[3]   Available at: www.fatf-gafi.org (accessed on 10 July 2013).

worldwide. Following the terrorist attacks in the U.S. in September 2001, FATF added another recommendation to the existing set, the so-called 'Special Recommendation', targeted at combating the financing of terrorism, which continued to be amended in the years to come.

15.05. In 2012, FATF responded to the global development of combating money laundering by further updating its recommendations and by extending its scope of application to the proliferation of weapons of mass destruction.[4]

II. The European Union's Legal Framework for Fighting Money Laundering

15.06. The internal market of the European Union (EU) enables free movement of capital and makes money transfers from one Member State to another very straightforward. This could easily be misused by criminals trying to launder the proceeds of their illicit activities. That is why regulating measures against money laundering at the EU level is essential to a smooth and efficient functioning of the internal market in a transparent way.

15.07. As a response to the adoption of international standards, the European Community (nowadays the European Union) in 1991 adopted Council Directive 91/308/EEC on the prevention of the use of the financial system for the purpose of money laundering, referred to as the AML (Anti-Money Laundering) Directive.[5] This directive called on the Member States to take measures to ban money laundering and to involve the financial sector in terms of verifying the identity of its clients, keeping the necessary records, introducing national procedures for preventing money laundering and reporting any suspicion of money laundering to the designated authorities.

15.08. This directive underwent a thorough review in the European Union. Its second version was replaced in 2005 by adopting the European Parliament and Council Directive 2005/60/EC on prevention of the use of the financial system for the purpose of money laundering, referred to as the third AML Directive.[6] This directive reinforces cooperation among the different national Financial Intelligence Units (FIUs).

15.09. The third AML Directive is currently under review. The wording of the draft directive, which is to replace the existing one, was published by

---

[4]   Czech Ministry of Finance, International Institutions combating money laundering: available   at: http://www.mfcr.cz/cs/verejny-sektor/regulace/boj-proti-prani-penez-a-financovani-tero/mezinarodni-instituce (accessed on 10 July 2013).

[5]   [1991] OJ L 91/308.

[6]   [2005] OJ L 309/15.

the European Commission under File No. (COM(2013)0045)[7] in February 2013, and is being discussed in the legislative processes. The wording of the proposal for the fourth AML Directive should particularly respond to the amendments of the FATF standards adopted in 2012. The draft directive provides for the possibility to include in its scope of application all persons trading in goods (such as car dealers) or providing services in exchange for a cash payment of no less than 7,500 EUR. Member States may further reduce this limit. At present, the limit is 15,000 EUR, which the European Commission considers insufficient. The draft directive further enhances cooperation among the national FIUs.

15.10. This legal framework of regulating measures against money laundering in the European Union is based on directives which are only binding on its Member States in terms of the objectives to be achieved. Member States have to transpose the directive into their national legislations within an implementation period and notify the European Commission of the measures taken to comply with the objectives of the directive. Should a Member State fail to implement a directive or miss its target in the implementing measures, the European Commission may initiate an infringement procedure in which the Court of Justice of the European Union can fine the Member State concerned for having failed to meet its obligations under the Treaty on the Functioning of the European Union.

15.11. Hence, the legal regulation of measures on the EU level is not based on a unified approach, which could only be achieved by means of regulations (directly applicable in all Member States to the full extent without the need for their incorporation into national laws), but only on harmonization, i.e. by providing a common denominator for all Member States, yet granting them a certain level playing field in terms of the manner of implementing the corresponding directives into their national legislations.

III. Scope of the Application of the Third AML Directive of the EU

15.12. The third AML Directive based on the international standards set by the FATF concentrates on harmonizing preventive measures against these illicit practices. However, it leaves aside the regulation of repressive measures, which are also crucial, if the fight against money

---

[7] European Commission. Proposal for a Directive of the European Parliament and the Council on the prevention of the use of the financial system for the purpose of money laundering and terrorist financing. Available at: http://eur-lex.europa.eu/LexUriServ/LexUriServ.do?uri=COM:2013:0045:FIN:EN:PDF (accessed on 10 July 2013).

laundering is to be efficient on the internal market. At present, the legal regulation of repression with respect to money laundering lies entirely in the hands of EU Member States, which all have their national (hence not unified) definitions of what money laundering is. The disparity existing among the different national definitions of money laundering is not ideal since a certain action may be considered criminal in one Member State but not in another. The European Commission, which is in charge of drafting new proposals of legislation and of drafting amendments to the existing EU measures, is certainly aware of the shortcomings of the current EU action concentrating on prevention only, but lagging behind on the repression side. Some Member States are opposed to the idea of the EU taking action in the field of repressive measures associated with money laundering. That is why the required qualified majority to adopt these measures cannot be reached in the Council of EU, where national interests are represented.

IV. Application of the Third AML Directive

15.13. The European Commission hired an external expert company, Deloitte, to carry out an evaluation of the application of the third AML Directive. This study is available online on the webpage of the European Commission.[8] It constitutes the basis for the Commission's report on the application of the third AML Directive published in April 2012.[9]

15.14. One of the key topics addressed in the Commission's report on the application of the third AML Directive is the use of the risk-based approach (RBA) by individual Member States. The Commission believes that

[a] risk-based approach enables a more targeted and focussed approach to assessing risks and applying resources to where they are most needed. [...] The Deloitte study reported that a wide diversity of national measures can complicate cross-border compliance, and that there is a lack of practical guidance available. The new FATF standards broaden the application of the RBA. [...] Countries need to ensure that higher risks are identified and mitigated, but may permit simplified measures for certain requirements when lower risk has been identified.[10]

---

[8]   European Commission: DG Internal Market, available at: http://ec.europa.eu/internal_ market/company/docs/financial-crime/20110124_study_amld_en.pdf (accessed on 10 July 2013).

[9]   COM(2012)0168 final.

[10]   Ibid.

15.15. The fourth AML Directive should therefore concentrate on harmonizing the risk-based approach so as to align it with the new FATF requirements.

15.16. In its above mentioned report, the Commission identified another inconsistency with the new FATF standards in the field of exemptions which may be granted under the current regime to those "who engage in a financial activity on an occasional or very limited basis and where there is little risk of money laundering or terrorist financing." However, "[t]he revised FATF standards stipulate that transferring of money or value cannot benefit from such an exemption".[11] This issue will thus be addressed in the proposed fourth AML Directive.

15.17. Last but not least, the Deloitte study addresses a wide variety of national sanctions applied across Member States for non-compliance with the reporting duties to the obliged entities. It says that "the variety in national penalty regimes is so large that it is not possible to compare penalties through all Member States".[12] Regulating this issue in the fourth AML Directive is thus another challenge for the European Union.

V. EU Institutions Dealing with Money Laundering

15.18. As outlined above, the EU does not have any specialized bodies which could take EU-wide repressive measures with respect to money laundering activities. Taking repressive action lies fully in the powers of the individual Member States. However, there are two bodies within the institutional framework of the EU which play a key role in the field of combating money laundering and fighting financing terrorism: OLAF and Europol.

15.19. OLAF is the French acronym of the European Anti-Fraud Office.[13] It is an independent investigation service within the European Commission established in 1999 to prevent fraud to the EU budget.[14] Its role in preventing money laundering is crucial, especially in the area of EU structural funds which have been misused for money laundering purposes on a number of occasions. It investigates reports of suspected fraud in the EU budget. If there is evidence that fraud has been committed, OLAF forwards the case to the competent national police

---

[11] Ibid.
[12] Ibid.
[13] Office européen de lutte antifraude.
[14] Chris Lewis, *International Structures and Transnational Crimes*, in HANDBOOK OF CRIMINAL INVESTIGATION, London: Routledge 175, 187 (Tim Newburn, Tom Williamson & Alan Wright eds., 2012).

and judiciary authorities to pursue criminal sanctions but cannot impose any sanctions of its own. In order to strengthen the prosecution powers on the EU level, "[t]ogether with the Directorate-General for Justice, OLAF prepared a legislative proposal concerning the establishment of a European Public Prosecutor's Office. The proposal is planned for adoption in 2013. It seeks to strengthen the investigation and prosecution of fraud against the EU budget."[15]

15.20.   Europol is an abbreviation for the European Police Office. It started limited operations in 1994, but did not become fully operational until 1999.[16] The current legal framework of Europol's functioning can be found in the Council Decision of 6 April 2009 establishing the European Police Office (Europol). Its mission statement is in Article 3: "The objective of Europol shall be to support and strengthen action by competent authorities of the Member States and their mutual cooperation in preventing and combating organized crime, terrorism and other forms of serious crime affecting two or more Member States". Europol's mandate includes action against money laundering in so far as it "provides support to Member States in the areas of preventing and combating money laundering as well as tracing criminal assets. Operation Spectre II was one such operation supported by Europol and features in the Europol Review 2011."[17]

15.21.   The Spectre II operation detected a multinational cash courier in Great Britain in November 2011 where a Europol team was deployed. Cash couriers are commonly used in the money laundering process to escape risks of detection involved in bank transfers. "Over the course of this operation, GBP 418 136 was seized and a further GBP 1 412 722 in cash was detected alongside silver, jewellery and khat [a plant whose leaves are chewed for an amphetamine-like stimulant effect, derived from its active ingredients of cathine and cathinone. It is a banned substance in most EU countries]."[18]

15.22.   The Europol Review 2011 also recalls that "Real estate investments, commercial activities and luxury goods still remain some of the most apparent investments for organized crime groups. [...] The Europol

---

[15]   OLAF Report 2012. Available at: http://europa.eu/rapid/press-release_OLAF-13-2_en.htm (accessed on 10 July 2013).

[16]   Mario Matassa & Tim Newburn, *Social context of criminal investigation, in* HANDBOOK OF CRIMINAL INVESTIGATION, London: Routledge 41, 51 (Tim Newburn, Tom Williamson & Alan Wright eds., 2012).

[17]   Europol: Mandate, available at: www.europol.europa.eu/content/page/mandate-119 (accessed on 10 July 2013).

[18]   Europol Review 2011, available at: https://www.europol.europa.eu/sites/default/files/publications/europolreview2011.pdf (accessed on 10 July 2013).

Criminal Assets Bureau (ECAB) assists Member States´ financial investigators to trace worldwide the proceeds of crime, when assets have been concealed outside their jurisdictional boundaries. The ECAB exists primarily to trace the criminal proceeds in investigations supported by Europol."[19]

VI. Case Study – Bodies in Charge of Combating the Legalization of Crime Proceeds in the Czech Republic

15.23. In 1995, the Czech Republic signed the Council of Europe Convention on Laundering, Search, Seizure and Confiscation of Proceeds from Crime (hereinafter referred to as the "Strasbourg Convention"), which became effective for this country on 1 March 1997. Based on this Convention, the first national act dealing with this issue was passed in 1996 – Act No. 61/1996 Collection, on Selected Measures against Legitimization of Proceeds of Crime. This Act became effective as of 1 July 1996. It delegated to the Finance Ministry the power to issue a decree to determine the name of a specialized unit which should deal with combating money laundering on behalf of the Ministry. The Finance Ministry Decree No. 186/1996 Coll., on the Implementation of Reporting by Finance Institutions, established a specialized department of the Finance Ministry – a "Finance Intelligence Unit" in compliance with the requirements of International Law. This unit became operational as of January 1996.

15.24. As the above Act was amended several times (one of the amendments was linked to the Czech Republic's joining of the European Union and constituted a harmonization with EU law), the legal regulation stopped being intelligible. That is why in 2008, a new act was adopted, Act No. 253/2008 Coll., on Selected Measures against Legitimization of Proceeds of Crime and Financing of Terrorism, which incorporates the third AML Directive as well as Commission Directive 2006/70/EC. It is often referred to as the AML Act.

15.25. A crucial condition for a successful fight against the legitimization of proceeds of crime consists in an active cooperation of bodies, which are in charge of it to a greater or lesser extent. Among the bodies operational in the Czech Republic, a prominent position is held by the Financial Analytical Unit of the Ministry of Finance of the Czech Republic (hereinafter referred to as "FAU"), which is conceived as a "central body for collecting and analyzing reports of suspicious

[19] Ibid.

transactions" and at the same time fulfils the mission of "the Czech Finance Intelligence Unit". This corresponds to the position of the FAU with respect to foreign countries.[20]

15.26. The law empowers the FAU to exchange information with bodies having the same scope of activity, i.e. with Financial Intelligence Units. The International Law Framework for this exchange of information has been laid down particularly by the multilateral Strasbourg Convention of 1990, amended in 2005 by the Warsaw Convention, as well as by bilateral intergovernmental treaties which provide for cooperation in combating money laundering. The individual FIUs often conclude a Memorandum of Understanding with their counterparts, however, such a Memorandum is not a condition for establishing cooperation with foreign bodies.

15.27. The legal basis for establishing international cooperation by the Czech FAU in contained in the above mentioned international treaties. The term "Financial Intelligence Unit" is international, often referred to by its acronym as "FIU".[21] The FIU can be defined as a national central unit in charge of receiving communicated and reported financial information concerning a possible case of money laundering or financing terrorism, of analyzing it and forwarding it to the competent bodies.

15.28. To reinforce mutual cooperation the national FIUs joined the so-called Egmont group, which was set up in 1995 in Brussels.[22] This organization now has more than 100 members. The directors of the member FIUs decide on the membership of new applicants in a plenary session which takes place once a year. Also, an Egmont working group meets twice a year. Even though the individual FIUs are members of the Egmont group and thus follow some uniform rules for their operation, they still display numerous differences. The wide range of different

---

[20] The first FIUs started being set up in the early 1990s following an increasing demand for a central body which would receive, analyze and forward financial information in order to combat money laundering. In the subsequent ten years the number of FIUs increased substantially and in 2004 the informal international association, the so-called Egmont group, registered 94 members. In 2003, the Financial Action Task Force (FATF) adopted a revised recommendation on money laundering which included an explicit instruction to set up FIUs. In 2012, the number of FIUs associated in the Egmont group amounted to 127.

[21] The definition of FIUs has been incorporated into the basic documents and rules governing money laundering and financing terrorism, such as the Egmont Group standards, FATF Recommendation No. 8, Article 21 of the third AML Directive, and Article 2 of the Council Decision concerning arrangements for cooperation between financial intelligence units of the Member States in respect of exchanging information.

[22] Czech Ministry of Finance, Financial and Analytical Unit: available at http://www.mfcr.cz/cs/verejny-sektor/regulace/boj-proti-prani-penez-a-financovani-tero/financni-analyticky-utvar (accessed on 10 July 2013).

modes of operation within this association may be summarized on the basis of information provided by the Egmont group and the report on FIUs by the International Monetary Fund in 2004. This report distinguishes four basic types of FIUs: the administrative type, the prosecutorial type, the judicial type and the "hybrid" type.

15.29. The Czech Republic has the administrative type of FIU. FIUs of this type are usually part of another body or they are subject to supervision. Most frequently, such a unit is established within the Finance Ministry or the Central Bank. In either case the FIU is not part of the police or the judiciary. The reason for establishing this type of FIU lies particularly in an effort to set up a relatively independent or autonomous body to serve as an intermediary between persons who are obliged to report suspicious transactions and the bodies involved in criminal proceedings. A strong advantage of this type of FIU lies in its intermediary role between the financial sector, which may detect possible money laundering, and the police, which investigates and eliminates the direct or indirect relations that may exist between these two sectors that could compromise the final case investigation.

15.30. An administrative FIU, being largely a neutral and a specialized body, may thoroughly assess whether a received report made by the financial sector really corresponds to money laundering or whether it constitutes other activity, e.g. tax evasion. Such a FIU only forwards to the police authorities a report with a well-grounded suspicion of money laundering, which spares the police an excessive workload and also provides for a better protection of sensitive data forwarded by the financial sector. Last but not least, this type of FIU offers a simpler manner of forwarding and generally exchanging information with all types of FIUs and given its position, it is more likely to gain the trust of the financial sector.

15.31. Nevertheless, this type of FIU also features some disadvantages. It does not have the same statutory powers as other types of FIUs, which may delay freezing money or arresting a person, since the FIU is not a body involved in criminal proceedings.[23] Also, this type of FIU is the most predisposed to be misused politically. Countries which have this type of FIUs include France, Canada, the Netherlands, Poland, the U.S. and Spain.[24]

---

[23] The Czech AML Act, for example, does not grant the Ministry of Finance the power to withdraw the Banking License to a Credit Institution which has continuously and repeatedly breached its reporting duties, but it must refer the case to the competent body (Article 36 of the Czech AML Act). This can produce delays in preventing further money laundering.

[24] The characteristics of the other types of FIUs include the following: the prosecutorial type unit is part of the bodies involved in criminal proceedings and, given its position, it

15.32. The FAU is part of the Finance Ministry of the Czech Republic. Even though it is a field unit, its budget is part of the budget of the Ministry of Finance. It does not fall within the powers of the police or judiciary. It is an intermediary between the financial sector and the bodies involved in criminal proceedings and hence constitutes a typical administrative type of a FIU. The organizational structure of the FAU is similar to that of other departments of the Finance Ministry. It is a rather small unit, subdivided into four sections: international and legal section, analytical section, control section and a section of data collection and processing. The main pillar of the FAU is its analytical department, which analyzes reports on suspicious transactions[25] and subsequently investigates them.

15.33. The aim of the measures taken against money laundering and financing terrorism is establishing conditions that hinder misusing the financial system to pursue these activities and enable at the same time the financial system to keep exploitable traces of all transfers of property.

15.34. The primary role of the FAU is preventive. It provides a bonus in the form of an analytical activity while processing reports on suspicious transactions delivered by credit and financial institutions and from other duty bound parties. The system of measures hindering money laundering in the Czech Republic is able to trace both an effort to legitimize financial proceeds of criminal activity within the territory of this country and to detect efforts to pursue "money laundering" with respect to funds stemming from criminal activities abroad.[26]

---

may closely cooperate with units specialized in financial criminality. Countries featuring this type of FIU include Estonia, Ireland, Iceland, Hungary, Germany, Austria, Slovakia, Sweden and Great Britain. The judicial type of FIU is part of the judiciary and often falls within the powers of the public prosecutor. This type of FIU is common in countries where the public prosecutor has investigatory powers or oversees criminal investigation. Detections of suspected money laundering are forwarded directly to the public prosecutor in this case. The public prosecutor may, once the suspicion has been confirmed, subsequently launch investigations and proceed to freeze money without undue delay. This type of FIU is found in Cyprus and Luxembourg. The hybrid type features different combinations of the above models. In Europe, this type of FIU is used in Denmark and Norway. For a detailed discussion on the different types of FIUs see LOUISE FORGET, FINANCIAL INTELLIGENCE UNITS: AN OVERVIEW, International Monetary Fund (2004).

[25] The definition of a suspicious transaction has been incorporated into Article 6 (1) of the Czech AML Act: "For the purpose of this Act, a suspicious transaction amounts to a transaction carried out under circumstances raising suspicion as to the effort to legitimize proceeds of criminal activities or a suspicion that the funds used in the transaction are aimed at financing terrorism, or a different fact which may give rise to such a suspicion."

[26] Czech Ministry of Finance: Annual Report on the Activities of the Financial Analytical Unit for 2012, available at: http://www.mfcr.cz/cs/verejny-sektor/regulace (accessed on 10 July 2013).

15.35. The FAU takes an active part in the work of an informal Platform of FIUs of the European Union, which is organized by the European Commission, and takes place twice a year. Also, it participates in the European Commission's Committee for prevention of money laundering and financing terrorism in Brussels and in other international activities, such as the evaluation of Member States in terms of money laundering within the framework of the ECOLEF project.[27] Its aim is to provide for the implementation of international sanctions[28] adopted to maintain international peace and security, the protection of human rights and fight against terrorism.

VII. Conclusion

15.36. At its plenary session in April 2013, the European Union's supervisory body, the European Economic and Social Committee, declared that it considers necessary the adoption of such measures by the individual FIUs, so as to prevent criminal activities as efficiently as possible. It emphasized the need to apply dissuasive sanctions to professionals failing to meet their duties with respect to money laundering and financing terrorism. These sanctions shall be proportionate to the sums of money corresponding to the value of money laundering.

15.37. The FATF has launched a new round of mutual evaluation of its members as of 2014. It will concentrate particularly on the efficiency of implementing its new recommendations, which specify in greater detail the approach based on risk assessment to be applied by countries and duty bound entities so as to better recognize the risks of money laundering and financing terrorism in their daily transactions and to adjust their supervisory systems accordingly to enable an optimal use of their financial resources depending on the nature of the detected risks.

| | |

---

[27] ECOLEF is a research project funded by the European Commission and conducted under the auspices of the University of Utrecht in the Netherlands, associating experts of all EU Member States to perform research of the economic and legal effectiveness of the anti-money laundering and combating terrorist financing policy in the European Union. For more information on this project, consult the webpage of the University available at: www.uu.nl (accessed on 10 July 2013).

[28] At present, the European Union has been applying sanctions with respect to more than twenty countries and terrorist organizations. These measures are adopted by the Council of the European Union or by the European Commission in the form of regulations, which are directly applicable in the Czech Republic.

Summaries

DEU [*Institutioneller Rahmen der Bekämpfung der Geldwäsche in der Europäischen Union*]

Die Geldwäsche hängt mit der Bestrebung zusammen, Geld aus illegaler Aktivität zu gewinnen. Der Bedarf an dem Gebrauch der Erlöse aus Straftaten generiert einen Bedarf an Reinigung dieser Gelder – das Geld muss gewaschen werden. Die Internationale Gemeinschaft ist der Meinung gewesen, dass nur ein koordinierter Ansatz im Kampf gegen Geldwäsche effektiv sein kann. Folglich wurden verschiedene internationale Verträge in diesem Bereich unterschrieben. Auf der institutionellen Ebene gehört eine prominente Stelle im Kampf gegen Geldwäsche der Action Task Force on Money Laundering (FATF). Einzelne Staaten haben zentrale Meldestellen (FIU) gegründet, welche in Bereich der Prävention der Geldwäsche tätig sind. Die Europäische Union hat Instrumente erlassen, welche die Inkorporation der FATF Standards in den Mitgliedstaaten verpflichtend machen. Einige Organe der Europäischen Union sind für die Prävention und Detektion der Geldwäsche zuständig, verfügen aber über keine repressiven Kompetenzen, die weiterhin in den Händen der einzelnen Mitgliedstaaten liegen.

CZE [*Institucionální rámec boje proti praní špinavých peněz v Evropské unii*]

Praní špinavých peněz je fenomén, který je spojen se snahou získat z určitého, nezákonného jednání majetkový prospěch. Potřeba využít zisku z nelegální činnosti vede k potřebě zbavit tento zisk dřívějšího původu – peníze je třeba vyprat. Mezinárodní společenství si postupně a stále více uvědomovalo potřebnost společného a koordinovaného postupu v boji proti praní špinavých peněz a proto byly na mezinárodním poli přijímány úmluvy upravující postupy při potírání této činnosti. Státy iniciovaly zakládání organizací a institucí, které se zabývají bojem proti praní špinavých peněz. Klíčovou úlohu v tomto směru sehrál a hraje Finanční akční výbor proti praní peněz - zkráceně FATF. Jednotlivé státy si zřizují FIU – finančně zpravodajské jednotky, které mají aktivně přispívat k postupu proti zneužívání finančního systému v rámci jednotlivých států. Také Evropská unie přijala opatření, která napomáhají inkorporaci standardů FATF do právních řádů členských států. Také některé orgány Evropské unie se aktivně podílejí na prevenci a vyšetřování praní špinavých peněz, avšak pravomoci v oblasti represe zůstávají do značné míry nadále v rukou členských států.

| | |

POL [*Ramy instytucjonalne walki z praniem brudnych pieniędzy w Unii Europejskiej*]

Niniejszy artykuł został poświęcony problematyce efektywności narzędzi Unii Europejskiej w walce z praniem brudnych pieniędzy. W związku z wyborem narzędzia prawnego, mającego formę dyrektyw, jest materia ta dziedziną bardziej zharmonizowaną niż unifikowaną. W obecnym czasie Unia Europejska w zakresie prania brudnych pieniędzy dysponuje kompetencjami prewencyjnymi, więc stosowanie instrumentów represyjnych zostaje nadal w rękach państw członkowskich, których praktyka w tej dziedzinie wykazuje znaczą cerozbieżności.

FRA [*Le cadre institutionnel de la lutte contre le blanchiment de l'argent sale dans l'Union européenne*]

Le présent article se préoccupe de l'efficacité des instruments légaux de l´Union Européenne (UE) dans le domaine de la lutte contra le blanchiment de capitaux. Car le choix d´instrument légal a été la directive, la lutte contra le blanchiment de capitaux représente plutôt une matière harmonisé que une matière unifiée. Au présent, l´UE dispose de pouvoirs dans le domaine de prévention, pendent que l´application diversifiée de mesures répressives reste toujours dans les mains des Etats Membres.

RUS [*Институциональные основы для борьбы с отмыванием денег в Европейском Союзе*]

В данной статье толкуется эффективность правовых документов Европейского Союза, направленных на борьбу с незаконным отмыванием грязной валюты. С учётом выбора правового инструмента ввиде директивы, то для регионов данный документ намеревается больше к согласованию, чем к унификации. В настоящее время распоряжпет Евросоюз полномочиями в сфере предупредительных мер по отмыванию грязной валюты и применение репрессивных мер остаётся за государствами-членами. Решение ими данного вопроса на практике резко различается.

ESP [*El marco institucional para combatir el blanqueo de capitales en la Unión Europea*]

El presente artículo trata de la eficacia de los instrumentos legales de la Unión Europea en el campo de la lucha contra el blanqueo de dinero. Puesto que el instrumento elegido es la directiva, la lucha contra el blanqueo de dinero representa más bien un campo harmonizado que un campo unificado. Hoy día, la Unión Europea sólo dispone de poderes a nivel preventivo, mientras que la aplicación muy diversa de medidas represivas sigue en las manos de los Estados Miembros.

Pavel Mates | Jan Šmíd

Can the Welfare State Be Lean?

Key words:
public interest | welfare state | regulation | security/safety | communication | environment | financial markets | competition | taxes | employment | liberalism | conservatism | socialism

Abstract | There are various basic ideas that justify the necessity for a welfare state, which are joined together by the idea of social consensus and solidarity in the interest of preserving peace in society. The only entity capable of exercising all these functions is the state.

This holds true for the state's traditional roles, internal order and external security. Modern states must secure communication both among its individual authorities and among citizens. This requires the implementation of technologies that enhance the quality of services provided by the state. Market failures affect the stability of the state, and consequently, states are forced to enter this domain, but also protect themselves against monopolization and secure the functioning of the market economy. A substantial portion of the funds that the state has at its disposal is spent on various social expenditures. All developed countries are faced with the necessity to protect the environment, which is, again, a global requirement. Last, but not least, the state must collect taxes to finance the activities of the welfare state. All of the above must be distributed and implemented by competent authorities established by the state. Despite the critics of the welfare state who argue that it is expensive, demotivating and bureaucratic, it is a reality without any adequate alternative, and its role will definitely increase in the near future.

Doc. JUDr. Pavel Mates CSc. lectures on administrative law at the University of Finance and Administration in Prague and the theory of law at the Faculty of Social and Economic Studies, Jan Evangelista Purkyně University in Ústí nad Labem. He specializes in criminal administrative law and the legal issues of e-government. These topics are covered in several of his monographs and articles published in academic magazines. He has also participated in the drafting of a number of laws regulating the above issues. He is a member of the legislative bodies of the government.
e-mail: mate@ksp.zcu.cz, pavel.mates@ujep.cz

PhDr. Mgr. Jan Šmíd, Ph.D. teaches theory of law, constitutional law and political science at the University of Finance and

| | |

16.01. Starting with a hypothesis is a scientific method that currently holds favour in more than the social sciences. The answer to the question formulated in the title, i.e. our premise, is that it is a contradiction in terms, either a *contradictio in se* or a *contradictio in adiecto*.

I. Definition of Welfare State – Basic Ideas

16.02. It is necessary to start with a brief analyse of the reasons for the very existence of the welfare state. Even though the concept has relatively deep roots, its actual development started during the second half of the twentieth century, when it became the standard in most western democracies.

> Administration in Prague, political philosophy and philosophy of law at Jan Evangelista Purkyně University in Ústí nad Labem, and political ideologies at the University of Economics in Prague. He specializes in the above topics, which he has elaborated on in his contributions to several collections of papers and articles published in academic magazines.
> e-mail:
> john_smid@yahoo.com
> , jan.smid@vsfs.cz

16.03. After 1945, left-wing, right-wing and centrist parties reached consensus on the establishment of the welfare state (welfare consensus). All parties acknowledged its necessity, but differed with respect to the means by which the state ought to secure the individual services and the extent thereof.[1] Sweden is an illustration of these developments. Their welfare state was established by the social democratic party, and the governments ruling the country from 1975 to 1981, which were composed of exclusively centrist and right-wing parties, not only respected the established welfare state system, but also actually implemented the largest increase in social expenditures.[2]

16.04. Individual countries differ in the depth and intensity with which they implemented the idea, but none of them are indifferent to the ideas of the welfare state. All of them have introduced, albeit to a varying extent, systems of social security, healthcare and public education.

16.05. The welfare state can be developed by positive instruments – i.e. the provision of specific services by the government, or by negative instruments – by regulating market behaviour. Three fundamental models have evolved over time:

1) Liberal or limited welfare state (U.S., Canada and Australia), endeavouring to secure a safety net for the needy;

---

[1] ANDREW HEYWOOD, POLITICKÁ TEORIE [*Political Theory*], Prague: Eurolex Bohèmia 262 (2005).

[2] ĽUBOŠ BLAHA, SPÄŤ K MARXOVI?: (SOCIÁLNY ŠTÁT, EKONOMICKÁ DEMOKRACIA A TEÓRIE SPRAVODLIVOSTI) [*Back to Marx?: (Welfare State, Economic Democracy And Theory of Justice)*], Bratislava: Veda 87 (2009).

2) Conservative (corporate) model (Germany), which only provides certain services in return for payment, and specific benefits and services are connected with jobs; and

3) Social democratic (Sweden), which is based on universally distributed benefits and services and the maintenance of full employment.[3]

16.06. There are multiple reasons why the welfare state has become the political standard in western democracies. The reasons inhere in the psychology of voters, as well as in individual ideologies and the theory of democracy.[4]

16.07. The welfare state is no doubt one of the crucial policy issues of left-wing parties. But the concept has undergone significant changes. Until the 1970s, the welfare state was perceived as an intermediate stage between capitalism and socialism. It was even rejected by many as allegedly being a compromise that diverts the oppressed from their struggle against capitalism. Socialism was then faced with the crucial question: Is the welfare state only an intermediate stage, or is it a final form of society, i.e. the final cause of their left-wing policy?[5] In other words, have we reached the 'historical end', in that the welfare state can only be improved, but principally have we nothing better to offer?

16.08. Moreover, the political left must face new challenges. First there is the crisis of Keynesianism. There is also the fact that the achievements of the welfare state have benefited the third, or even the fourth generation, and these generations take them for granted. These developments are countered by the tendency adopted by many, even left-wing parties to reform the welfare state because it is so expensive.[6] They hope to create a new, modernized version of the welfare state, which would be viable and competitive in global economic and political competition. There are strong tendencies to replace the classical left-wing model of radical politics by a 'third way', a consensus. This would be achieved by left-wing parties moderating their ideas and moving closer to the centre, 'trying to understand, not fight, the market mechanisms'.[7]

---

[3] ANDREW HEYWOOD, POLITOLOGIE [*Political Science*], Prague: Eurolex Bohemia 260-261 (2008).

[4] ARISTOTLE, POLITIKA [*Politics*], Bratislava: Pravda 144, 213 (1988).

[5] Michael Hauser, *Dilemata sociálního státu* [*Welfare State Dilemmas*], *in* 2 SOCIÁLNÍ STÁT A KAPITALISMUS [*Welfare State and Capitalism*], Svoboda Servis 6-14 (Michael Hauser ed., 2007).

[6] Ibid, at 16-77.

[7] ANTHONY GIDDENS, TŘETÍ CESTA A JEJÍ KRITICI [*The Third Way and Its Critics*], Prague: Mladá fronta 39 (2004).

16.09. The political left certainly deserves high praise for their enormous success. At least the fundamental standards of the welfare state have been accepted by most currents of competing political ideologies. Both conservatism and liberalism,[8] are reconciled with, or even help to actively establish the welfare state, whether in the area of practical politics or political theory.

16.10. One of the oldest, but still active premises of the welfare state includes conservatism. The practical politics involves several essential groups some rather important ones accept the welfare state. Andrew Heywood finds them primarily in paternalistic conservatism, which he divides into two trends:

- one-nation conservatism and
- Christian democracy.[9]

16.11. One-nation conservatism was inspired by Benjamin Disraeli, who tried to highlight social responsibility in contrast with the then-prevailing extreme individualism. He feared that the nation would split into two nations – the rich and the poor. He was not so concerned with the values of equality (preferred by socialists) or positive freedom (preferred by the modern left and modern liberalism).[10] He focused on conservative reasoning, which realizes the destructive revolutionary, potential of huge social inequalities. The privileged status of the rich ought to be balanced by the acceptance of social responsibility.[11] Hence, Disraeli organically developed the ideas of Edmund Burke. Burke believed that the French nobility's loss of interest in positive social functions and their focus on individual enjoyment of benefits and privileges, enabled by their status, was one of the causes of the French Revolution.[12]

16.12. In the twentieth century, one-nation conservatism appeared in the politics of many conservative governments (not only the British), while accepting the Keynesian economic policy aimed at full employment and a certain standard of social security. It was an attempt to steer

---

[8] Concepts from political ideologies are used in compliance with their established usage on the European continent.

[9] ANDREW HEYWOOD, POLITICKÉ IDEOLOGIE [*Political Ideologies*], Pilsen: Aleš Čeněk 100 (2008).

[10] Positive and negative freedom have also been analysed in a famous essay written by Isaiah Berlin, or, as applied to practical matters, by Gerald A. Cohen. ISAIAH BERLIN, TWO CONCEPTS OF LIBERTY. FOUR ESSAYS ON LIBERTY, Oxford: Oxford University Press 118-172 (1969); Gerald Allan Cohen, *Svoboda a peníze* [*Freedom and Money*], (1) FILOSOFICKÝ ČASOPIS 89-114 (2000).

[11] ANDREW HEYWOOD, *supra* note 9, at 100-101.

[12] Christopher Olaf Blum, *On Being Conservative: Lessons from Louis de Bonald*, 41(1) THE INTERCOLLEGIATE REVIEW 23-31 (2006).

politics between the extremes of laissez-faire and the socialist centrally-planned economy. The welfare state, in itself, is not the aim; it is merely an instrument for stabilizing the society and moderating the radical inclinations of poor people. These ideas are currently employed in the U.S. and in Great Britain in the form of the concept of compassionate conservatism.[13]

16.13. After the Second World War, Europe experienced the rise of Christian democratic parties, which were democratically oriented, but which did not support an unrestricted free market. They preferred a certain measure of corporatism, supporting institutions standing between citizens and the state (churches, trade unions and entrepreneurial associations), and the idea of social partnership. This resulted in the 'social market economy', which does not deny the importance of the market and entrepreneurial activities, but at the same time, introduces social security and public services in order to cement the society. Capitalism built on these premises is sometimes called Rhine (Rhenish) or 'social' capitalism, as opposed to the 'entrepreneurial' Anglo-American (Anglo-Saxon) capitalism.[14] It is sometimes also referred to as German-Japanese capitalism. The Japanese example is an effort to combine the ethical principle of cooperation with other principles of effectiveness and justice.[15]

16.14. The two abovementioned types of conservatism are based on the principle of an organic society, which is inherent to conservatism. A society that is not individualistic.

16.15. There is also libertarian conservatism, which was fundamentally influenced by the ideas of classical liberalism. It directly invokes Edmund Burke, who supported the ideas voiced by Adam Smith about free market.[16] This facet of conservatism advocates the idea that the free market deserves protection as one of the consequences of tradition.

16.16. Many other conservatives believe that the principles of laissez-faire and a minimal state are inseparable from conservatism, but at the same time, they admit that the welfare state is a reality that cannot be denied. For instance, Robert Nisbet refers to 'assistance conservatism' and considers the assistance state to be a protection against social disaster, which, in the absence thereof, could occur at any moment. He also regretfully admits that Sir William Harcourt was right when he

---

[13] ANDREW HEYWOOD, *supra* note 9, at 102.

[14] Ibid., at 103.

[15] YUICHI SHIONOYA, ECONOMY AND MORALITY: THE PHILOSOPHY OF THE WELFARE STATE, Edward Elgar, North Hampton, MA: Edward Elgar 176 (2005).

[16] ANDREW HEYWOOD, *supra* note 9, at 104.

proclaimed, at the beginning of the twentieth century, that: 'We are all socialists now.' The welfare state has already absorbed the middle class, which has become the main recipient of such welfare, and at that moment, 'any actual opposition against the assistance state is a matter of history'.[17]

16.17. In the past, liberalism represented an unappeasable opponent to any endeavour to redistribute and transfer competences to the state. However, this only applies to classical liberalism, which used to be strongly individualistic. Liberalism has undergone further developments and branched out into various currents. One of the basic divisions is the division into classical and modern liberalism. The most significant representatives of classical liberalism in the twentieth century were Friedrich August von Hayek, Robert Nozick and Milton Friedman. For instance, Robert Nozick considered any redistribution as morally unacceptable, because it represented an involuntary and forced act restricting the individual's freedom.[18]

16.18. Classical liberalism has evolved side by side with another tradition, the egalitarian liberalism which has strived to revise liberal ideas and unite them with the ideas of social justice and the welfare state.[19] Hence, our current liberalism involves both the individualistic and the egalitarian approaches, the most famous proponents of the latter being Ronald Dworkin and John Rawls.

16.19. Dworkin's aim is to justify ownership. If rich people do not legitimately own all of their property, redistribution does not interfere with their freedom. From this perspective, freedom is not considered identical to arbitrariness, but to autonomy.[20] Liberal defence of redistribution is usually conducted in the name of freedom, not in the name of equality. Even if we admit that redistribution from the rich to the poor curtails the freedom of the rich, we can argue that it increases the freedom of the poor, because the overall quantity of effective freedom[21] in society

---

[17] ROBERT A. NISBET, KONZERVATISMUS: SEN A REALITA [*Conservatism: Dream and Reality*], Prague: Občanský institut [*Civic Institute*] 116, 130-131 (1993).

[18] ROBERT NOZICK, ANARCHY, STATE AND UTOPIA, Oxford: Basil Blackwell 26-33, 149-164 (1990).

[19] JOHN GRAY, LIBERALISMUS [*Liberalism*], Prague: Občanský institut [Civic Institute] 49 (1999).

[20] ADAM SWIFT, POLITICKÁ FILOZOFIE: ZÁKLADNÍ OTÁZKY MODERNÍ POLITOLOGIE [*Political Philosophy: A Beginner's Guide for Students and Politicians*], Prague: Portál 73-74 (2005).

[21] Adam Swift defines effective freedom in contrast with formal freedom as the difference between mere non-intervention and 'our power or ability to act in a certain way'. He therefore essentially adopts Berlin's division into negative and positive freedom (Ibid., at 61).

thereby increases. These utilitarian arguments have been opposed by John Rawls, whose theory offers an alternative to this utilitarian concept.

16.20. Rawls stipulates two principles that should underlie a fair society:
- Each person should have an equal right to the broadest possible elementary freedom compatible with a similar freedom enjoyed by others; and
- Social and economic inequalities must be arranged in such a manner as to permit their connection with:
  a) the reasonable expectation that they will benefit everybody (primarily the most disadvantaged members of the society); and
  b) status and offices that are equally accessible to everyone.

16.21. The principles of justice as articulated by Rawls clearly indicate that, whereas the first principle is a defence of individual freedom, the second principle is a defence of certain aspects of the welfare state. The reason is that Rawls started with methodological individualism, but finished with conclusions that are, in certain respects, close to socialism.[22] Another of Rawls' arguments in favour of the welfare state is the need for cooperation in society. A lack of cooperation means a lack of a satisfactory life, and the distribution of advantages should therefore be executed in such a manner as to facilitate the voluntary cooperation of all, including those whose situations are less fortunate.[23]

16.22. In connection with liberalism, Ronald Dworkin speaks of the value of equality, appreciated more by the liberal than by the conservative, although not as much as by the socialist (radical). He promotes the primary principle of equality, which requires that 'the government considers all those subject to it equal, i.e. equally worthy of its interest and esteem'. But liberals also acknowledge the derivative principle of equality, i.e. equality in the distribution of certain sources of opportunities.[24]

16.23. In his essay *Why Liberals Should Care about Equality*, Dworkin distinguishes liberalism based on neutrality, which requires the government's impartiality in moral issues, from liberalism based on equality, which treats citizens as equal to one another. He tries to prove why he believes in liberalism based on equality. However, he does not strive to attain equality of result (typical of socialism), but equality of opportunities and conditions, which are different for everybody. He

---

[22] ĽUBOŠ BLAHA, *supra* note 2, at 137-138.

[23] JOHN RAWLS, TEORIE SPRAVEDLNOSTI [*Theory of Justice*], Prague: Victoria Publishing 23 (1995).

[24] Ronald Dworkin, *Liberalism, in* LIBERALISM AND ITS CRITICS, New York: New York University Press 60-79 (Michael J. Sandel ed., 1984).

advocates a system in which no member of the society has less than an equal share of the community's resources. This does not, however, rule out the possibility that, for instance, different people will have different assets in different stages of their lives.[25] He respects the existence of the free market, but does not share the enthusiasm of many liberals of the past, who appreciated its role in the allocation of resources. The reason is that in the real world, the market does not provide an equal share in the community's resources. Moreover, people differ in the abilities that the market appreciates, irrespective of their effort and good will. Consequently, the alleged equality of opportunities does not provide sufficiently 'fair' results either. The results of market allocation must therefore be corrected by access to resources in connection with differences in initial advantages, luck and abilities.[26] Hence, it is necessary to distinguish Rawls' fair society and fair distribution performed by Gerald Allan Cohen. The aim of distributive justice ought to be the correction of 'innumerable forms of lucky or unlucky circumstances'.[27]

16.24. By broadening the principles of equality, both Dworkin's and Rawls' approaches endeavour to address the objections raised by the critics of liberalism: liberalism insists on legal, political and moral equality of citizens, but classical liberals strictly refuse material equality. Egalitarian liberalism considers equality and freedom to merely be formal, unless they are backed up by material assets. They have thereby essentially become the proponents of a 'third way' between socialists and libertarians. Contrary to socialists, they do not reject capitalism and consider it the most effective economic model; however, they refuse to respect the consequences of capitalism consisting in unfair distribution, and rely on correction by the state.[28]

II. Reality of Ideas

16.25. The proclaimed ideal of (possibly) all politicians and governments is *schlange Staat*, a trim state with a minimum of offices. But the reality is that the functions of each modern state have been expanding, and the welfare state is, in this respect, the most demanding of all. The reasons are multiple. First of all, once the society reaches a certain level, it

---

[25] RONALD DWORKIN, A MATTER OF PRINCIPLE, Oxford: Clarendon Press 206 (1986).
[26] Ibid., at 207.
[27] Gerald Allan Cohen, *Justice, Incentives, and Selfishness, in* GERALD ALLAN COHEN, IF YOU'RE AN EGALITARIAN, HOW COME YOU'RE SO RICH?, Cambridge, Mass.: Harvard University Press 117 (2000).
[28] ĽUBOŠ BLAHA, *supra* note 2, at 137-139.

demands the satisfaction of various needs of its members, which, at a certain point, can no longer be secured by civil society and must be taken over by the state, especially because it is a rather expensive enterprise.[29] Moreover, the situation is also influenced, or complicated, by the fact that our modern welfare state is necessarily also a democratic state honouring the principles of the rule of law.

16.26. It appears that the core of the problem revolves around the concept of public interest, of which the state should take care. But the definition of public interest is rather difficult. As Professor G. Hardin already noted in 1968, public interest cannot be perceived as the sum of individual interests, because individual interests can be selfish and totally devastating in their consequences.[30] It is much more advisable to define public interest as those issues that are supported by the majority of the society. We shall not analyse in any greater detail the associated subtle questions, such as which percentage means the majority, or at which moment sectoral interests become public interests? At this point, let us assume content ourselves with the conclusion that public interest in current democracies is mostly articulated by the assembly of representatives or by the citizens, using the instruments of direct democracy.[31] In any case, the scope of issues that comprise the public interest and become public domain has been expanding. This, in turn, increases the number of authorities and their employees who are supposed to take care of them.[32]

III. New Traditions

16.27. The traditional tasks entrusted to the state are the establishment of internal order and external security. These functions are performed by a number of authorities, beginning with the police (state and municipal) and customs authorities, and ending with the fire fighters. This applies to the Czech Republic, and *mutatis mutandis* to other European countries and the U.S.

16.28. This would be quite unremarkable, but combined with the requirements of the rule of law, the applicable laws become more and

---

[29] MILOŠ VEČEŘA, SOCIÁLNÍ STÁT-VÝCHODISKA A PŘÍSTUPY [*Welfare State – Premises and Approaches*], Prague: Sociologické nakladatelství 11 (1996).

[30] Garrett Hardin, *The Tragedy of Commons*, 162(3859) SCIENCE, NEW SERIES 1243-1248 (December 13, 1968).

[31] ANDREW HEYWOOD, *supra* note 1, at 207-211; KAREL KLÍMA and others, STÁTOVĚDA [*Science of Politics*], Pilsen: Vydavatelství a nakladatelství Aleš Čeněk 156 (2006).

[32] STEPHAN LEIBFRIED and ELMAR RIEGER have responded by saying that the welfare state has become so oversized that it hardly moves (GRUNDLAGEN DER GLOBALISIERUNG. PERSPEKTIVE DES WOHLFAHRTSSTAATES, Frankfurt am Main: Suhrkamp 46 (2001).

more detailed, especially as concerns the application of, necessarily, increasingly sophisticated methods and means of protecting safety. Moreover, the requirement that the individual forces and corps be subject to supervision is voiced with increasing emphasis. For example, the Czech Republic has set up the General Inspectorate of Security Forces, a special armed security corps charged with the task of detecting, discovering and investigating circumstances indicating that a criminal offence has been committed by a member or a civil employee of the Police, Prison Service or Customs Administration.[33] Considering the political significance of the entity, it is anticipated that a special Parliamentary committee will be set up to participate in the appointment of the Director of the Inspectorate, and indirectly in supervising the functioning thereof.

16.29. Many European countries have introduced the demerit points system (*Vormerksystem*), *which is intended to contribute to better discipline of drivers.* The specific systems in the individual countries vary. For instance, in France and Italy, points are deducted. In the Czech Republic, conversely, points are added. But the principle remains the same: after the driver attains or loses a certain number of points, their driving licence is automatically withdrawn.[34] In this connection, it is irrelevant whether the system is effective, i.e. whether it has helped to reduce the number of traffic accidents and contributed to better compliance with the laws and regulations by the drivers, and the results vary in this respect. But the introduction of the system has, in any case, resulted in an increase in the agenda administered by the police forces and other administrative authorities, and consequently, the number of their employees.

16.30. Internal security also involves the isolation of dangerous individuals based on judicial decisions. Pressures for humanisation and preservation of the rights of persons detained have become more intensive, and consequently, the apparatus required to secure their administration has increased proportionately. For instance, Czech Act No. 169/1999 Coll., on Imprisonment and Amending Selected Associated Legislation, as subsequently amended, envisages five types of prisons differentiated according to the seriousness of the offence for which the prisoner was sentenced and also facilities for juvenile offenders and women with children under the age of three. The latter institutions also anticipate the participation of authorities for the social

---

[33] Act No. 341/2011 Coll., on General Inspection of Security Forces and Amending Associated Legislation.

[34] For instance, the 1998 judgment of the European Court of Human Rights in *Malige v France*, No. 27812/95.

and legal protection of children. Prisoners enjoy a significant range of social rights including the possibility to communicate with the outside world, the right to spiritual services, etc.[35] The director of each prison must set up an advisory committee for the application of the expertise, forms and methods of treating prisoners that facilitate the achievement of the purpose of imprisonment. This is certainly not intended to criticise the prison system (which is even more prisoner-friendly in other countries, such as the Scandinavian states). We only point out that the list of tasks to be secured by the state is expanding in this particular area too, as concerns the necessary organization, material resources and funds.

16.31. Internal security also involves the handling of emergency situations that transgress the national level and become global, at least in the European Union.[36] At the beginning of the 1990s, emergency situations were still resolved using a rather random set of measures necessitated by the actual situation. A few years later, after several disastrous floods, the set of measures has evolved into a system of crisis management subject to a detailed statutory regulation (Act No. 240/2000 Coll.). This is undoubtedly better than the situation before, but, naturally, more expensive.

16.32. But the reasons for adopting security measures are also rather prosaic: investors do not venture into, or even leave, countries that do not guarantee safety and security.[37]

IV. Better Communication Equals More Expense

16.33. Our modern welfare state is sometimes compared to the brontosaurus. The brontosaurus had such a huge body that its brain failed to manage all of its functions; hence, the animal was allegedly forced to have two brains. This is the reason why there are efforts to simplify the communication between the brain, i.e. the central authorities, and the individual body parts at the local and regional level, as well as the

---

[35] VĚRA KALVODOVÁ, POSTAVENÍ TRESTU ODNĚTÍ SVOBODY V SYSTÉMU TRESTNĚPRÁVNÍCH SANKCÍ [*The Status of Imprisonment in the System of Punishment for Criminal Offences*], Brno: Masaryk University (2002); LUBOMÍR BAJCURA, PRÁVA VĚZNĚ [PRISONER'S RIGHTS], Prague: Grada Publishing (1999).

[36] See also Council Directive 2008/114/EC of 8 December 2008 on the identification and designation of European critical infrastructures and the assessment of the need to improve their protection. Czech law on cybernetic security is at the drafting stage.

[37] This is one of the vicious cycles of the welfare state, because the requirements for the organisational, technical, personal and other measures necessary to ensure safety are increasing (see HORST AFHELDT, WIRTSCHAFT, DIE ARM MACHT. VOM SOCZIALSTAAT ZUR GESPALTENEN GESELLSCHAFT, Munich: Verlag Antje Kunstmann 111 (2003)).

citizens themselves. Private entities may participate in these processes (for instance, by supplying technologies), but the procedures themselves can only be implemented by the state in a welfare state.

16.34. Again, the objective is being implemented using a number of instruments. In the Czech Republic, this primarily involves the basic registers whose function it is to collect permanently updated and verified information about natural and legal persons, spatial identification and agendas of public authorities, and to provide this information to all or selected entities.[38] It is expected that the registers will generate savings, especially as concerns the number of work tasks. The register of inhabitants introduced in Austria, for example, reduced the number of administrative operations by three million. The costs associated with the registers are, however, a different story. At the moment, we know the establishment costs, but nobody has supplied any figures indicating whether the entire system has become cheaper. In any event, it has necessitated the setting up of another authority, namely the Basic Registers Administration under the Ministry of the Interior.

16.35. Analogous conclusions apply to the introduction of data mailboxes, electronic storage facilities used for the exchange of data messages between individual public authorities, for communication between public authorities and natural and legal persons and for communication between natural and legal persons themselves.[39] This method of communication will undoubtedly expedite and increase the quality of service and the filing of various documents, but it is not free of charge. The introduction of the data mailboxes themselves cost almost CZK 1.5 billion, and the state must, naturally, also pay for the running of the system arranged by the state-owned Czech Post. Moreover, the state was not released from its duty to supervise the functioning of the system, which means that it has only generated further bureaucracy for the state.

16.36. There is another factor that must be taken into consideration: almost all experts familiar with these issues repeatedly emphasize that only a

---

[38] Act No. 111/2009 Coll., on Basic Registers, as subsequently amended; Pavel Rieger & Pavel Mates, *Zákon o základních registrech-přínos k rozvoji e-governmentu* [*Act on Basic Registers – Contribution to the Development of E-Government*], 43(5) SPRÁVNÍ PRÁVO (2010). Basic registers can be found in a number of states, the most progressive being the countries of northern Europe.

[39] Act No. 300/2008 Coll., on Electronic Acts and Authorized Conversion of Documents, as subsequently amended; see PAVEL MATES & VLADIMÍR SMEJKAL, E-GOVERNMENT V ČESKÉ REPUBLICE. PRÁVNÍ A TECHNOLOGICKÉ ASPEKTY [*E-Government in the Czech Republic. Legal and Technological Aspects*], Prague: Leges 162 (2012).

transformation of the competent authorities would bring about the real effect – but this procedure has not been initiated yet, and if so, then only formally and (at best) very slowly.[40]

V. Market Regulation

16.37. The welfare state also requires partial regulation of the economy. The reason provided to justify such regulation is the necessity to correct market failures that could have an adverse effect on the society and its stability. The satisfactory existence of certain groups of people could be jeopardized by the efforts of others to generate high profits and their freedom could result in unilateral dependency, while the regulation is intended to prevent such consequences. Such aberrations occur where, for instance, there is a natural monopoly on the side of supply or demand, information asymmetry between buyer and seller and the necessity to protect the public domain.[41]

16.38. Due to the ever-increasing importance of information and the migration of information, the provision of electronic services is very often subject to detailed regulation in order to eliminate the risk of abusing the monopolist status enjoyed by providers supplying these services. Considering the global nature of information, the national legislation of EU Member States is based on the applicable Community laws.

16.39. The European regulatory framework for electronic communications encompasses several directives. These include Directive 2009/140/EC of the European Parliament and of the Council of 25 November 2009 amending Directive 2002/21/EC on a common regulatory framework for electronic communications networks and services, Directive 2002/19/EC on access to, and interconnection of, electronic communications networks and associated facilities and Directive 2002/20/EC on the authorisation of electronic communications networks and services. The above legislation requires, inter alia, the establishment of a national regulatory authority independent of business interests and endowed with sufficient powers, as prescribed by law.

---

[40] For instance, Andrew Atkeson & Patrick J. Kehoe, *Modeling the Transition to a New Economy: Lessons from Two Technological Revolutions*, 97(1) THE AMERICAN ECONOMIC REVIEW 66 (2007).

[41] MARTIN POTŮČEK, NEJEN TRH [*Not Only the Market*], Prague: Sociologické nakladatelství 25 (1997); JAN KELLER, SOUMRAK SOCIÁLNÍHO STÁTU [*The Dusk of the Welfare State*], Prague: Sociologické nakladatelství 14 (2009); HANNO DRECHSLER, WOLFGANG HILLIGEN & FRANZ NEUMANN, GESELLSCHAFT UND STAAT. LEXIKON DER POLITIK, Munich: Verlag Franz Vahlen 761-762 (1995), key word Socialstaat.

16.40. In the Czech Republic, these functions have been performed by the Czech Telecommunications Office, an administrative authority for the exercise of state administration in matters prescribed by the Electronic Communications Act, including market regulation and the formulation of conditions for doing business in electronic communications and postal services. The legislature obviously presumed that regulation should only be a transitional measure, required to replace competition wherever the latter fails to have the desired effects, to create conditions for the proper functioning of competition and for the protection of users and other market participants until competition is fully functional and effective and the regulation becomes unnecessary.[42] If we accept the premise, though, that the market can never be fully sufficient in this respect, especially from the perspective of consumer protection and the supply of generally accessible services, it appears that this particular function will hardly become obsolete in the near future. But the regulation is introduced *ex ante* in all EU countries, for instance, by the regulation of prices where the EU considers them to be excessively high, or, conversely, to constitute dumping.

16.41. Regulation is also applied to the supply of energy and heating. The reason is that it is necessary to eliminate the dominance of one contracting party, the suppliers, and to make sure that these socially very sensitive services are supplied under any circumstances. Moreover, the situation is complicated by very serious potential security risks, represented by natural and other disasters or terrorist attacks, which require special qualifications possessed by those who operate the systems. National laws are, again, based on the Community legislation,[43] which envisages the establishment of an independent regulatory body, such as the Energy Regulatory Office (ERO) in the Czech Republic. Pursuant to Section 17 of the Energy Act (Act No. 458/2000 Coll.), the ERO is supposed to protect legitimate interests of customers and consumers in energy sectors. In order to attain this objective, the ERO regulates prices, promotes competition in energy sectors and supervises the markets in the energy sectors. Regulation is primarily exercised by granting licences, which are the necessary prerequisite for doing business in these sectors, by regulating the prices

---

[42]   Section 4 of the Electronic Communications Act (Act No. 127/2005 Coll.), cf. also Section 112 et seq. of the Austrian Telekommunikationsgesetz of 2003, or Section 116 et seq. of the German Telekomunikationgesetz of 2004, or 2012, as applicable.

[43]   Regulation (EC) No. 714/2009 of the European Parliament and of the Council of 13 July 2009 on conditions for access to the network for cross-border exchanges in electricity, or No. 715/2009 of 13 July 2009 on conditions for access to the natural gas transmission networks, and others.

of electricity transmission, gas transmission, electricity and gas distribution.[44]

16.42. However, there are also many other regulators, for instance, with respect to radio and TV broadcasting. These regulators also make sure that the prohibition of endangering the moral welfare of children and young people is duly observed. Other regulators supervise postal services and railroad transport.[45] Apart from these specialized authorities, there are also many special inspectorates and agencies. We must also add the supervisory powers of various general administrative authorities, which, for instance, protect consumers and supervise the quality of food and education.[46] The welfare state supports the idea that the best regulation is little regulation, only the necessary minimum, and as much competition as possible. However, the reality is that the expanding agenda and functions of the welfare state go hand in hand with the tendency to permanently (sometimes insidiously) increase the volume of regulation; this is accompanied by ever-expanding detailed legislation, the purpose of which is often highly dubious.

16.43. The struggle against the adverse effects of capital concentration on social welfare is much older. In the U.S., for instance, it dates back to 1890 when the Sherman Antitrust Act was adopted, and to 1914, when the Clayton Act was passed. Both of these documents sought to protect competition and keep it free and open. The on-going globalization of the economy after the Second World War further reinforced the tendencies to regulate various forms of monopolies that could gain a dominant position and curtail one of the pillars of a democratic country, the free market. These prohibitions have been closely monitored by the European Union, which is founded on the principle of the free market, and whose legislation is implemented in national laws.[47]

---

[44] Concerning this topic, see JAKUB HANDRLICA, JADERNÉ PRÁVO [*Nuclear Law*], Prague: Auditorium (2012).

[45] OLIVIER GOHIN, INSTITUTIONS ADMINISTRATIVES, Paris: L. G. D. J. 255-257 (2002); in the Federal Republic of Germany, for instance, the regulation is concentrated in the common Bundesnetzagentur für Elektrizität, Gas, Telekommunikation, Post und Eisenbahnen. This model will probably also inspire the Czech Republic, which should regulate competition in railroad transport.

[46] Several years ago, the Czech Republic witnessed strenuous efforts to promote the establishment of an administrative authority for equal opportunities without executive powers; proposals to set up a special authority for the free access to information have been lodged repeatedly.

[47] For instance, Council Regulation (EC) No. 1/2003 of 16 December 2002 on the implementation of the rules on competition laid down in Articles 81 and 82 of the Treaty, or Council Regulation (EC) No. 139/2004 on the control of concentrations between undertakings.

These laws indirectly protect the consumer by keeping competition and thus not leaving the consumer to be taken advantage of.

16.44. Naturally, market regulation must be institutionalized in the prescribed manner, because a mere prohibition would lack the effect of promoting social welfare. In the Czech Republic, the institutionalization is implemented by the Office for the Protection of Competition, whose duties include the promotion and protection of competition against unlawful impairments. Similar tasks are performed by the French Conseil de la concurrence, established in 1986, which watches over the preservation of natural economic activities and intervenes if any entity should achieve a dominant economic status.[48] We could paraphrase the situation, somewhat paradoxically, by saying that the free market is restricted in the interests of the free market. The only entity that could effectively secure these functions is, again, the state. However, this naturally necessitates the establishment of offices with the respective competences, and generates costs associated therewith.

16.45. On the other hand, it is generally accepted for the welfare state to be successful, the state or other public-owned or public-controlled corporations must monopolize certain domains in order to protect public interests. This primarily applies to domains relating to public services, the energy sector, or other matters of significant general interest (see also Article 43 of the Constitution of the Italian Republic, Article 15 of the Basic Law for the Federal Republic of Germany or Article 18 of the Constitution of the Hellenic Republic). A perfect example is that the Czech Republic has monopolized reserved mineral deposits, which means that only the state has the right to dispose with such deposits. Pursuant to Article 7 of the Constitution, the state must concern itself with the prudent use of its natural resources and the protection of its natural wealth. It may stipulate which assets are necessary for securing the needs of the entire society, for the development of the national economy and the public welfare, which may be owned exclusively by the state, a municipality or by designated legal persons (Article 11(2) of the Charter of Fundamental Rights and Freedoms). In practice, this primarily includes minerals important for the production of energy, such as coal and uranium. Naturally, the use itself of the minerals is licensed to private entities. The granting of the licence is *de facto* an act of control exercised *ex ante*. The subsequent use of the licence is also supervised by the state and a number of

---

[48] Section 1 of Act No. 273/1996 Coll., on the Scope of Competence of the Office for the Protection of Competition, as subsequently amended; OLIVIER GOHIN, *supra* note 45, at 258-261.

professional and other authorities (e.g. Czech Mining Office, Ministry of Environment, Ministry of Industry and Trade and others).

16.46. But such traditional monopolies may also appear in other areas, such as railroad transport or postal services.[49]

VI. Financial Markets

16.47. The defining criteria of a modern state include easy access to financial markets for the general public. This, in most cases, means lay people who are easily tempted by various, ostensibly safe and profitable, products, which, however, can cause serious economic turmoil. The English, Irish, American and other mortgage crises of the past decade persuasively prove the need for governmental intervention. Again, the state must step in to mitigate the consequences and then attempt to limit such negative consequences in the future. Where the affluent should have access to financial advisors, the poor often struggle to make sense of the complex world they must navigate in order to secure housing and other basic needs. Providing supervision of the financial market is a benefit that has become essential in the welfare state.

16.48. The central banks play a major role in this procedure, which is, again, based on the policy of the European Union and EU laws.[50] For instance, Section 2 of the Czech National Bank Act (Act No. 6/1993 Coll.) stipulates that the Bank's primary duties include supervision over individuals and entities on the financial market. The Bank is also part of the European System of Financial Supervision. Its supervisory powers extend to banks, insurance companies, securities brokers/dealers, pension funds, investment companies, savings and credit cooperatives, etc. Supervision is exercised both *ex ante* (for instance, by granting licences) and *ex post*, in the form of repeated and one-off inspections

---

[49] Concerning this topic, see also Rolf Adlung, *Public Services and the GATS*, 9(2) JOURNAL OF INTERNATIONAL ECONOMIC LAW 455-485 (2006).

[50] ZBYNĚK REVENDA, CENTRÁLNÍ BANKOVNICTVÍ [*Central Banking*], Prague: Nakladatelství Management Press [*Management Press Publishing*] (2011); see also Regulation (EU) No. 1092/2010 of the European Parliament and of the Council of 24 November 2010 on European Union macro-prudential oversight of the financial system and establishing a European Systemic Risk Board, Regulation (EU) No. 1093/2010 of the European Parliament and of the Council of 24 November 2010 establishing European Supervisory Authority / European Banking Authority, Regulation (EU) No. 1094/2010 of the European Parliament and of the Council of 24 November 2010 establishing a European Supervisory Authority (European Insurance and Occupational Pensions Authority), amending Decision No. 716/2009/EC, and Regulation (EU) No. 1095/2010 of the European Parliament and of the Council of 24 November 2010 establishing a European Supervisory Authority (European Securities and Markets Authority), amending Decision No. 716/2009/EC and repealing Commission Decision 2009/77/EC.

monitoring the observance of the applicable laws and regulations. The main objective is the safe functioning, stability and development of the financial market. Any disturbance can have far-reaching social consequences and affect financial, as well as economic and social stability. Such disturbances can be ascribed to commercial banks and other entities providing money services, which are often able to do anything to generate profit, but also to the introduction of modern technologies and other factors. For instance, high-frequency trading (HFT) caused a flash crash on U.S. stock exchanges in the summer of 2008 – the setup of the programme resulted in a sharp drop in share prices by up to 99% within minutes, only to return to their original value a few minutes later. This is the reason why Germany has subjected these types of transactions with shares to special supervision exercised by the regulatory body, Die Bundesanstalt für Finanzdienstleistungsausicht (BaFin).

VII. Social Welfare

16.49. The welfare state, per definitionem, implies that the majority of the finances that the state has at its disposal are spent on various social expenditures in the narrower sense of the word. At the turn of the nineteenth and twentieth centuries, the distribution of funds was predominantly executed by various public-owned or public-controlled corporations, such as municipalities, brotherhood cash offices or funds. Today, these duties are primarily performed by the state, and the state has established various offices to execute the agenda on its behalf.[51] This applies, for instance, to the French *Ministère des affaires sociales et de la santé*, which has a broad agenda ranging from the distribution of funds for social and healthcare, to special education and family care. In the Czech Republic, this agenda has been divided among a number of offices, from the Ministry of Labour and Social Affairs and the Czech Social Security Administration and its district branches, to the Employment Office and its regional branches. The general trend is to transfer these duties to private entities, such as consultants, nursing and retirement homes. Naturally, the costs of running such facilities are paid by the state, and the state must also supervise their activities – which again requires the existence of one or more administrative authorities.[52] The problem is that the worse the economic situation, the

---

[51] Again based on EU legislation, for instance, Regulations (EC) No. 883/2004 and 987/2009 of the European Parliament and of the Council concerning the coordination of social security of migrating persons within the EU.

[52] We can certainly presume that people will take care of themselves by contracting private supplementary insurance. In the welfare state, however, this only holds true for a

higher the demand for such services, without the possibility to reduce the resources, especially funds and personnel, required for the provision of these services.

16.50. For example in the 1960s, employment was still only a marginal issue. Ten years later, however, it became a major issue and has remained a crucial problem ever since. We again encounter the role of the state, which sets out to resolve the situation. It can do so using its own offices (such as the Czech Employment Office subordinated to the Ministry of Labour and Social Affairs, and the German Bundesagentur für Arbeit and its local departments), or it can employ private job centres, or do both. It goes without saying that even if the entire agenda were entrusted to the private sector, the state would at least have to arrange for the necessary supervision.

16.51. Apart from that, more and more rigorous requirements are imposed on the observance of work conditions, safety at work and the safety of technical facilities, etc.[53] As repeatedly mentioned above, actual compliance with the applicable laws and regulations and the performance of the obligations arising can only be secured by the state. In the Czech Republic, these duties are primarily performed by the State Labour Inspection Office and its local inspectorates, whose competence usually covers several regions.

VIII. Expensive Ecology

16.52. Ecology is also covered by the 'wide wings' of the welfare state. We would be taking sand to the beach, or as the French say, "transporter l' eau dans la rivière", if we overloaded our article with a voluminous chapter advocating the need to protect nature and its resources, and then argued that such protection is very expensive. Just like in the examples provided above, and perhaps even more so, ecology is an issue with more than European connotations. It is a global phenomenon, and plenty of mandatory obligations are laid down in international treaties and Community law, which the individual states must project into their national legislation.

16.53. All developed countries establish ministries of environmental protection (see, for instance, the German Bundesministeriums für Umwelt, Naturschutz und Reaktorsicherheit), special administrative

---

minority of people. The decisive majority, primarily the majority of middle and lower-middle classes, i.e. including voters, will always prefer to rely on assistance provided by the state (CHRISTOPH BUTTERWEGGE, WOHHLFARRTSTAAT IM WANDEL. PROBLEME UND PERSPEKTIVEN SOZIALPOLITIK, Opladen: Leske+Budrich 200 (2001)).

[53] See Section 3 of Act No. 251/2005 Coll., on Labour Inspection, as subsequently amended.

authorities (such as the French Agence des aires marines protégées), and public funds (the Czech Fund for the Creation and Protection of Environment). They are charged with policy management in this particular area,[54] and with supervision over the performance of obligations, by granting permits for exceptions (see, for instance, the integrated permit under Czech law authorizing its holder to operate a facility which could be harmful to the environment, Section 3 et seq. of the Integrated Prevention Act No. 76/2002 Coll.), and with the prevention of environmental damage, etc.

16.54. We ought to add that the measures adopted in this field are (probably) not motivated only by the regard paid by polluters to the environment and by the pressure exerted by various activists, but also by purely political circumstances. As the Czech sociologist J. Keller has remarked, the consequences of environmental damage most affect the middle classes, i.e. the main reservoir of voters who, contrary to the rich, only have the possibility to escape to a better place during their few weeks of holiday.[55]

IX. Collection of Taxes

16.55. In the preceding paragraphs, we have focused on some of the functions exercised by the welfare state, primarily those that are most expensive and require a complicated organizational structure. It is not possible to enumerate each and every item on the agenda anyway.

16.56. But we must not overlook one important fact: expenses of the welfare state. These expenses are paid primarily from taxes, and partly also from other sources, such as the structural funds of the European Union. The tax system is gradually getting more and more complicated. It is a convolution of direct and indirect taxes, which often change depending on the currently ruling cabinet. This causes one of the many paradoxes of the welfare state: in order to properly collect taxes and supervise their due payment, the state must again set up another system of administrative authorities.

16.57. Despite the many references to a crisis of the welfare state, manifested in the reduction of all possible expenditures, primarily social expenses, it is practically impossible to imagine that the welfare state would cease to exist. Perhaps the best reason why the welfare state must continue is to apply the logic of Winston Churchill, when he said, 'who said that

---

[54] This involves the protection of water, atmosphere, fishery, landscape, waste management and many others (see also MILAN DAMOHORSKÝ, PRÁVO ŽIVOTNÍHO PROSTŘEDÍ [*Environmental Law*], Prague: C. H. Beck (2010)).

[55] JAN KELLER, *supra* note 41, at 88.

liberal democracy is the worst imaginable form of government, except that there is no better one.' Consequently, if we call the welfare state bureaucratic, expensive and demotivating, we ought to bear in mind that we have not yet managed to find any adequate substitute. Hence, if we ask about the role of governmental authorities in the welfare state of the twenty-first century, the answer is inevitable: their functions will be preserved, and most probably expanded further still.

| | |

Summaries

DEU [*Kann es den schlanken Sozialstaat geben?*]

Es gibt eine ganze Reihe verschiedenster ideeller Ausgangspunkte, die für die Notwendigkeit des Sozialstaates sprechen; das Bindeglied, unter dem sie alle zusammengeführt sind, ist der Gedanke des sozialen Konsenses und der Solidarität im Interesse der Erhaltung der gesamtgesellschaftlichen Aussöhnung. Das alles kann eben nur der Staat leisten.

Das gilt zum einen, wenn es um die Erfüllung seiner traditionellen Rollen geht: innere Ordnung und äußere Sicherheit. Sodann müssen moderne Staaten dafür sorgen, dass die Kommunikation sowohl zwischen staatlichen Stellen untereinander als auch in Richtung Bürger funktioniert. Zu diesem Zweck müssen Technologien implementiert werden, die die staatlichen Serviceleistungen aufwerten. Weil Märkte von Zeit zu Zeit auch einmal versagen können, mit Folgen für deren Stabilität, muss der Staat auch hier eingreifen - aber zugleich muss er sich gegen Monopolisierungsbestrebungen wehren und für eine funktionierende Marktwirtschaft sorgen. Ein wesentlicher Teil der Mittel, über die der Staat verfügt, entfällt auf Sozialausgaben verschiedenster Art. Alle entwickelten Staaten stehen vor der Notwendigkeit, die Umwelt zu schützen - das ist wiederum ein globales Erfordernis. Keineswegs an letzter Stelle steht die Beitreibung der Steuereinnahmen, aus denen die Aktivitäten des Sozialstaats finanziert werden. Das alles lässt sich nicht anders verteilen und umsetzen als durch die Schaffung entsprechender Behörden und Stellen. Der Sozialstaat mag heutzutage als teuer, demotivierend, bürokratisch usw. in der Kritik stehen - aber er ist eine Realität, für die bis dato keine adäquate Alternative gefunden werden konnte, und seine Rolle wird in absehbarer Zukunft sicherlich eher noch zunehmen.

CZE [*Může být sociální stát štíhlý?*]

Existují nejrůznější ideová východiska odůvodňující nezbytnost sociálního státu a jakýmsi svorníkem nad nimi je myšlenka sociálního konsensu a solidarity v zájmu zachování smíru ve společnosti. To vše může zajistit právě jen stát. Platí to o zajišťování jeho tradičních rolí, jakými je vnitřní pořádek a vnější bezpečnost. Moderní státy musí zajišťovat komunikaci jak mezi svými orgány, tak i občany. Za tím účelem je třeba, aby byly implementovány technologie, které jeho služby zkvalitní. Protože dochází k selhávání trhu s dopady na jeho stabilitu, musí státy vstupovat i do této sféry, ale také se bránit proti monopolizaci a zajišťovat fungování tržní ekonomiky. Podstatná část prostředků, jimiž disponuje, padne na nejrůznější sociální výdaje. Všechny vyspělé státy stojí před nutností chránit životní prostředí, což je opět požadavek globálního rázu. Na místě nikoli posledním stojí vybírání daní, z nichž jsou aktivity sociálního státu zajišťovány. To vše lze distribuovat a realizovat vytvářením příslušných orgánů. Jakkoli je dnes sociální stát kritizován jakožto drahý, demotivující, byrokratický atd., jde o realitu, k níž se zatím nepodařilo nalézt adekvátní variantu a jeho role bude určitě v dohledné době spíše vzrůstat.

| | |

POL [*Czy państwo opiekuńcze może być szczupłe?*]

Problematyka państwa opiekuńczego (socjalnego) jest nieustannie w centrum zainteresowania różnych dyscyplin społeczno-naukowych. Wydaje się, że społeczeństwo postmodernistyczne znalazło się w zaklętym kręgu, z którego nie ma wyjścia. Współczesne państwo musi pełnić coraz to nowe funkcje, co powoduje wzrost liczby odpowiedzialnych za nie organów. Perspektywy losów państwa socjalnego są raczej pesymistyczne, jednak jak dotąd nie udało się jeszcze znaleźć dla niego satysfakcjonującej alternatywy.

FRA [*L'État providence est-il voué à être un État pléthorique ?*]

La problématique de l'État-providence est au centre des préoccupations de nombreuses sciences sociales. On a l'impression que la société postmoderne tourne en rond sans trouver d'issue. L'État moderne est tenu de remplir de plus en plus de fonctions et le nombre de ses administrations ne fait qu'augmenter. Les perspectives d'avenir de l'État-providence sont plutôt sombres, mais l'on n'a pas encore réussi à lui trouver d'alternative adéquate.

RUS [*Может ли быть социальное государство бедным?*]

Вопрос социального государства постоянно находится в центре внимания различных обществоведческих наук. Очевидно, что постмодернистское общество находится в заколдованном круге, из которого нет выхода. Современное государство вынуждено выполнять все новые и новые функции, в результате чего увеличивается количество гарантирующих их органов. Перспективы судьбы социального государства достаточно пессимистичны, тем не менее, до сих пор не удалось найти альтернативное решение.

ESP [*¿Puede existir un Estado del bienestar escuálido?*]

La problemática del Estado del bienestar continúa siendo el centro de atención de las más diversas disciplinas científico-sociales. Parece ser que la sociedad postmoderna se encuentra en un círculo vicioso del que no logra hallar la salida. El Estado moderno está obligado a garantizar continuamente nuevas funciones, con lo que aumenta el número de autoridades garantes de las mismas. Las perspectivas con respecto al destino del Estado del bienestar son más bien pesimistas, no obstante hasta el momento no parece existir una alternativa adecuada.

|||

Czech Yearbook of International Law

Daniela Nováčková

The Legal Instruments of EU Fiscal and Monetary Stability

Key words:
monetary stability | euro
area | international
financial institution |
fiscal treaty

Abstract | *This article analyses the legal instruments enhancing the coordination of monetary stability in the eurozone. In order to meet the aims set in its main treaties, the European Union has been adopting legal instruments in a concerted action with its Member States since 2010, to foster the coordination of their economic policies and improve the functioning of the euro area (eurozone). By introducing these measures, the European Union has been eliminating potential risks associated with weakening the stability of the euro area and committing the Member States to a higher responsibility for abiding by jointly agreed-upon rules. As the legal instruments of monetary policy coordination did not meet requested expectations the international treaties have also become the legal instruments for the coordination of monetary and fiscal relations among the euro area Member States and the EU Member States.*

Daniela Nováčková is an associate professor at the Faculty of Management of Comenius University in Bratislava and a Coordinator of the German Programme. In her academic work she has focused on European Economic Integration and Bilateral Investment Treaties. She has experience in approximation of European Law as a former expert of the Ministry of Finance of the Slovak Republic (1994-2004). She has published numerous articles in professional journals.
e-mail:
daniela.novackova
@fm.uniba.sk

| | |

I. Economic and Monetary Union in the Context of the EU Primary Law

17.01. The European Union (EU) is a union of 28 sovereign states within an international community based on an international multilateral treaty. Membership in any international organisation requires fulfilling the commitments ensuing from such membership. The EU differs from other international organisations in its aims and tasks. Primarily, it requires from its Member States that they delegate part of the execution of their sovereign rights to the institutions of the EU. In turn, these institutions act in accordance with the principles of subsidiarity and proportionality. The Member States voluntarily delegate part of the execution of their sovereign rights to the EU institutions for an unlimited period, while at the same time they limit their own competence. This fact is regulated in the provision of Article 2 of the Treaty on the Functioning of the European Union (TFEU), which stipulates explicitly that if

> the Treaties confer on the Union exclusive competence in a specific area, only the Union may legislate and adopt legally binding acts, the Member States being able to do so themselves only if so empowered by the Union or for the implementation of Union acts.[1]

17.02. This primary law is complemented by a Declaration in relation to the delimitation of competences. It states that: 'The Member States retain all competence they have not delegated to the EU institutions via the treaties.'[2] In other words, the Member States perform their activities to the extent stipulated in the EU treaties or in the EU secondary law.

17.03. Competence conferred by the Member States allows the EU to carry out monetary policy under Article 3 of the TFEU as monetary policy is an exclusive competence of the European Union.[3]

17.04. Article 121 of the TFEU states that the European Union requires its Member States to subordinate their national economic policies to common European interests and to collaborate when the ECOFIN Council coordinates this policy.[4] A Monetary Union is stipulated in Articles 3,119-144, 219 and 282-284 of the TFEU. Protocol No 12 on the excessive deficit procedure is *inter alia* an integral part of this Treaty. The Treaty of Lisbon has introduced the Protocol on the Euro Group requesting closer coordination among economic policies of the

---

[1] Art. 2 TFEU, OJ EU C 83 of 30.3.2010 ISSN 1725-5236, at 50.
[2] 18. Declaration in relation to the delimitation of competences, OJ EU C 83 30.3.2010, ISSN 1725-5236, at 344.
[3] Art. 3 TFEU, OJ EU C 83, 30.3.2010 ISSN1725-5236, at 51.
[4] Art. 121TFEU, OJ EU C, 83 30.3.2010 ISSN1725-5236, at 97.

states belonging to the euro area with the aim of creating conditions for higher economic growth within the EU as a whole.[5] This Protocol, acknowledges the Euro Group as an informal advisory body. The Protocol creates legal prerequisites for discussion by the ministers of finance of the euro area states. The aim of this discussion is meeting compliance with rules of economic and financial stability.

17.05. Besides primary law, the European Union also adopts other legal instruments enhancing its members' macroeconomic surveillance and financial discipline. These consist of secondary acts in the form of regulations and decisions, as well as international treaties. International treaties are legal instruments most frequently used as the basis for cooperation between the entities of international law. An international treaty regulates relations between contracting parties and defines their rights and obligations. The international treaties regulating legal relations among the Member States and the European Union make up some of the sources of European Union law. In order for the European Union to meet the aims to which it has committed itself, it also concludes international treaties in the areas of monetary and financial relations. Conclusion of such treaties has an impact on the Member States. The aim of any given legal instrument is to introduce preventive measures for strengthening budgetary responsibility of the euro area Member States and to extend the mechanism of economic surveillance so that fiscal policy can be guided over the entire economic cycle. As for the process of adoption of these legal instruments they may be considered as measures of political coordination of economic and monetary union. So far, the activity of the European Union has not only been focused on the development of the economic, social, political and cultural relations between the Member States and third countries. It has also focused on strengthening its influence in the area of international financial and monetary relations. International treaties are becoming the instruments of geopolitical influence on political and economic systems of the Member States of the euro area and weakening their sovereignty in certain areas. The harmonisation of legal, financial and monetary relations is necessary for securing the proper functioning of the monetary union and the EU internal market. Due to the internal market the economy of the Member States is mutually interconnected.

---

[5] Protocol on the Euro Group, OJ EU C 83, C 83 30.3.2010 ISSN1725-5236, at 283.

II. The Legal Basis for the Adoption of Fiscal and Monetary Policy Legal Instruments

17.06. The Treaty of Lisbon, amending the Treaty on European Union and the Treaty establishing the European Community, (signed in Lisbon, 13 December 2007) amended original provisions on the economic and monetary union adopted by the Treaty on European Union (TEU). Under the new provision adopted on the basis on the Treaty of Lisbon – Article 136 par. 1 of the TFEU the Member States of the euro area may also adopt measures to strengthen coordination and surveillance over their budgetary discipline and set directions for economic policy with the aim to secure proper functioning of the economic and monetary union.[6] The given provision obliges the Member States to carry out their economic and budgetary policies in such a way that they would not put the financial stability of the euro area at risk.[7] Amending international treaties is a familiar instrument in the current theory and practice of international contract law. For the amendment of an international treaty, approval of the contracting parties is necessary and relevant constitutional rules have to be observed. The Provision of the Article 48 par.1 of the TEU stipulates the way of modifying and amending the TEU itself, as well as the TFEU and the Treaty establishing the European Atomic Energy Community. This can be done through either an ordinary revision procedure or through a simplified revision procedure.[8] In its Article 48 par. 6 TEU introduces the so-called simplified revision procedure. After consultation with the European Parliament and the European Commission and where the issues of monetary union are concerned with the European Central Bank, the European Council has the mandate to make decisions requiring unanimous approval.[9] The decision adopted based on the given article may not extend competences of the European Union and comes into effect once approved by the Member States in compliance with their constitutional rules. In 2010, the European Council used this instrument and initiated the adoption of a decision amending Article 136 of the TFEU with regard to a stability mechanism for Member

---

[6]   Art.136 (1) TEU OJ EU C 83, 30.3.2010 ISSN 1725-5236, at 106.

[7]   Financial stability can be defined as a condition in which the financial system – comprising of financial intermediaries, markets and market infrastructures – is capable of withstanding shocks, thereby reducing the likelihood of disruptions in the financial intermediation process which are severe enough to significantly impair the allocation of savings to profitable investment opportunities. Available at: http://www.ecb.europa.eu/pub/fsr/html/index.en.html (accessed on 30 September 2013).

[8]   Art.48 (1) TEU OJ EU C 83, 30.3.2010 ISSN 1725-5236, at 41.

[9]   Art.48(6) TEU OJ EU C 83, 30.3.2010 ISSN1725-5236, at 42.

States whose currency is the Euro. As this European Council decision came into effect (a non-legislative act), amending Article 136 of the TFEU with regard to a stability mechanism for Member States whose currency is the euro, the TFEU itself was likewise amended. The reasons for the amendment of the given Treaty pertained to differences in competitiveness and macroeconomic imbalance among Member States of the euro area put the functioning of the economic and monetary union at risk.

17.07. The new provision of Article 136 par. 3 of the TFEU says that: 'The Member States whose currency is the Euro may establish a stability mechanism to be activated if indispensable to safeguard the stability of the Euro area as a whole. The granting of any required financial assistance under the mechanism will be made subject to strict conditionality.'[10] In March 2011, the European Parliament adopted a resolution on the amended provision of article 136 of the TFEU.[11] The given provision enables the adoption of measures for securing stability and for providing funds to Member States of the euro area. This process has been preceded by an approval process in the Member States.

17.08. The draft European Council decision amending Article 136 of the TFEU was discussed by the government of the Slovak Republic at its session on 17 August 2011.[12] The given draft decision was subsequently submitted to the Parliament of the Slovak Republic for approval on 15 May 2012, although the Constitution of the Slovak Republic does not explicitly require European Council decisions amending primary European Union law to be discussed in the Parliament of the Slovak Republic.[13] From a legal point of view the reason for submitting the draft decision to the Parliament of the Slovak Republic was the fact that the decision amended an international treaty to which the Slovak Republic was a party, the TFEU. Because of that, the usual process, as when concluding presidential international treaties was applied. However the given decision in its substantive scope may neither be considered an international treaty under the Vienna Convention on the Law of Treaties (UN)[14] nor under the standard practice of international

---

[10] European council decision of 25 March 2011 amending Article 136 of the Treaty on the Functioning of the European Union with regard to a stability mechanism for Member States whose currency is the Euro, 199/2011/EU,OJ EU L 91, 6 April 2011.

[11] Available at: http://www.europarl.europa.eu/webnp/cms/pid/1833 (accessed on 4 June 2013).

[12] Slovak Government resolution No.543 of 17 August 2011, available at: www.rokovanie.sk/ Rokovanie.aspx/GetUznesenia/?idRokovanie=591 (accessed on 30 September 2013).

[13] Slovak Parliament resolution No. 25 of 25 May 2012.

[14] Vienna Convention on the Law of Treaties, Coll. of Laws No. 53/1994.

contract.[15] The above mentioned facts suggest that the international treaty (EU primary law) has been amended by the European Council decision and the Slovak Republic has applied the regular procedure in compliance with constitutional rules as in the case of amending an international treaty. With regard to those facts and the provision of Article 7 par.5 of the Constitution of the Slovak Republic, it is not necessary to adopt the act for the execution of the decision (if it is considered an international treaty).[16] This brings up a question as to why the amendment of the international treaty has been done in this way, which could be described as flexible. Based on the experience of ratifying treaties amending basic treaties (Nice, Lisbon) where the process itself was accompanied by certain problems, it may be assumed that if the amendment of the TFEU was carried out in compliance with the principles of international contract law, there could be a possibility of some Member States rejecting the amendment. For example, such a negative position was expressed by the Irish nation in its referendum on the Treaty of Nice in the year 2002. The procedure that the European Council has chosen is thus not a traditional one from the point of international contract theory or practice. Likewise, the Vienna Convention on the Law of Treaties specifies procedures that entities of international law should follow when amending international treaties.

III. The European Stability Mechanism

17.09. The European Stability Mechanism (ESM) was established by international treaty as an institution with legal personality and legal capacity.[17] The legal basis for the establishment of this entity is the provision of Article 122 of the TFEU.[18] From the point of view of international contract theory the given treaty is a multilateral financial treaty regulating rights and obligations of states whose common currency is the Euro.[19] Basically it is an international document with the character of a framework treaty that has enabled the establishment of the ESM organization with regard to the new Article 136 par. 3 of the TFEU. Under the provision of Article 1 of the Treaty establishing the European Stability Mechanism, the ESM is considered an international financial institution. There are two financial institutions

---

[15] The instrument of ratification to the decision of the European Council was ratified by the President of the Slovak Republic 30 May 2012.

[16] Constitution of the Slovak Republic, 460/1992 Coll of 1 September 1992.

[17] Communication of the Ministry of Foreign Affairs SR: Treaty establishing the European Stability Mechanism Col. of Laws No. 295/2012.

[18] Art. 122 TFEU, OJ EU C 83, 30.3.2010, ISSN 1725-5236.

[19] Entered into force on 27 September 2012.

with legal personality already operating within the European Union: the European Central Bank (ECB) and the European Investment Bank. This new financial entity also cooperates with the International Monetary Fund. The ESM as an institution of the European Union cooperates with the European Commission and the European Central Bank. The Treaty *inter alia* on one hand defines obligations for the Member States to contribute financially into the common system of the 'guarantee fund', and on the other hand defines the rights for Member States whose currency is the Euro to draw on the ESM should these states have difficulties. Under the provision of Article 32 of the Treaty establishing the European Stability Mechanism, the ESM has the right to 'acquire and dispose of movable and immovable property; contract, be a party to legal proceedings and enter into a headquarter agreement and/or protocols as necessary for ensuring that its legal status and its privileges and immunities are recognised and enforced.'[20] The ESM has its own structure of bodies including the Board of Directors, Board of Governors and the Board of Auditors. Just like several international organisations the ESM also has immunity. To be more specific, the property, funding and assets of the ESM shall, wherever located and by whomsoever held, be immune from search, requisition, confiscation, expropriation or any other form of seizure, taking or foreclosure by executive, judicial, administrative or legislative action. Personal immunity applies to the ESM staff.[21] Tax immunity (from direct taxes) applies to the ESM and to the assets, revenues and property as well as to its operations and transactions performed within this treaty. Bonds or securities issued by the ESM, including relevant interests and dividends irrespective of who is their holder, are taxed under certain conditions. Disputes on interpretation of this framework treaty are adjudicated by the European Court of Justice.

17.10. The given Treaty is also open for the accession of other EU Member States after meeting required procedures.[22] The ECB Governing Board has a mandate to approve the application for an accession of a new member of the ESM. The ESM has its own system of financing based on a set of parameters. The contracting parties contribute to the capital, which is at the level of EUR 700 bn. Of that, EUR 80 bn are in the form of shares payable on application and the remaining EUR 620 bn of guarantees are in the form of shares payable on demand.

---

[20] Available at: http://europa.eu/rapid/press-release DOC-12-3 en.htm (accessed on 5 July 2013).

[21] The ESM Treaty (Art. 32) http://ec.europa.eu/economy finance/articles/financial operations/2011-07-11-esm-treaty en.htm (accessed on 8 July 2013).

[22] The ESM Treaty was signed by 17 Member States of the euro area.

17.11. As an example, the Slovak Republic must repay its share at the level of EUR 659.2 m in five equal instalments. The total level of shares underwritten by the Slovak Republic is EUR 5.768 bn.[23] Funds from this capital are provided to those Member States whose macroeconomic equilibrium is at risk. This financial assistance is accorded under certain loan conditions. The decision whether a Member State should receive such financial assistance is taken by a mutual agreement of 85% of a majority of the ESM contracting parties. The Slovak Republic is represented in this intergovernmental organisation by representatives of the Ministry of Finance of the Slovak Republic.

17.12. The framework treaty is considered a presidential international treaty under Slovak international contract practice and has been passed by the Parliament of the Slovak Republic prior to its ratification.[24] Certain significant financial commitments ensue from this international treaty for Slovakia. The most prominent is the participation of Slovakia in the ESM but there is also a possibility of getting financial assistance in case financial stability is broken. The Act No 296/2012 Col. of Laws on the European Stability Mechanism is the legal instrument regulating execution of commitments ensuing from the international Treaty on the establishment of the European Stability Mechanism under Article 9 par. 5 of the Constitution of the Slovak Republic. Participation of Slovakia via financial commitment has a negative impact on its public finance. Funds from the issue of government securities belonging to state financial assets will be used for the repayment of the ESM capital payment instalments.[25]

IV. The Treaty on Enhancing Budgetary Discipline

17.13. The contracting parties to the *Treaty on Stability, Coordination and Governance in the Economic and Monetary Union,*[26] sometimes also

---

[23] The explanatory report on the draft law on the European Stabilisation Mechanism, www.nrsr.sk/rokovania, on 6 July 2013.

[24] The instrument of ratification to the Treaty establishing the European Stability Mechanism was signed by the President of the Slovak Republic 23 June 2012.

[25] Under the Article No. 41 (1) of the Treaty the members are obliged to pay their first and second instalments at the latest by 15 days from the Treaty coming into force (15-day deadline is the maximum period by which the ESM members are obliged to pay these instalments). The Treaty came into force 28 September 2012.

[26] *Treaty on Stability, Coordination and Governance in the Economic and Monetary Union* between the Kingdom of Belgium, the Republic of Bulgaria, the Kingdom of Denmark, the Federal Republic of Germany, the Republic of Estonia, Ireland, the Hellenic Republic, The Kingdom of Spain, The French Republic, The Italian Republic, the Republic of Cyprus, the Republic of Latvia, Malta, the Kingdom of the Netherlands, the Republic of Austria, the Republic of Poland, the Portuguese Republic, Romania, the Republic of

called the 'fiscal treaty', are the Member States of the euro area and the Member States not belonging to the euro area for whom only some provisions are binding such as coordination of economic policies and convergence. In practice this means that the Member States not belonging to the euro area acceded to the Treaty with reservations. The primary commitment of the contracting parties has been that the general government budget of the euro area Member States be balanced or in surplus. Here the political function of the fiscal treaty is expressed as the budgetary policy of the Member States and this should be discussed in their national parliaments. This obligation should also be regulated by national legislation within one year from the date of the fiscal treaty coming into force. With regard to this the competence of the European Court of Justice (ECJ) has also been extended. In compliance with Article 260 of the TFEU the ECJ has a mandate to evaluate compliance of the contracting parties with transposing the 'balanced budget rule' into their national legislation.[27] In case of not meeting the commitments and not adopting recommended measures the ECJ has a mandate to impose a sanction or a penalty on the given Member State adequate to the circumstances but not higher than 0.1% of its gross domestic product.

17.14. In its Article 6 the fiscal treaty obliges the Member States to inform the European Council and the European Union on their plans to issue government bonds.

17.15. A provision of Article 16 of the fiscal treaty creates a legal framework for its content to be included into the European Union framework by five years from the date of the treaty coming into force, at the latest. The fiscal treaty is not part of EU law. It is a legal instrument that is coordinated with and to a large extent depending on primary law of the EU.

17.16. There is a considerable body of legal theory, as well as practical exploration of the provisions on conditions for international treaty denunciation. The Vienna Convention of the Law of Treaties Art. 56 (1) defines conditions for denunciation of an international treaty as well. There are no such provisions in the fiscal treaty, which I consider non-standard from the point of theory and practice of international contract law.[28]

17.17. Contractual documents of the European Union usually come into force if ratified by all contracting parties in compliance with constitutional

---

Slovenia, the Slovak Republic, the Republic of Finland and the Kingdom of Sweden, available at: www.consilium.europa.eu/media/.../07_-_tscg.en12 (accessed on 4 June 2013).

[27] Art. 273 TFEU, OJ EU C 83, 30.3.2010, ISSN 1725-5236, at 165.

[28] Vienna Convention on the Law of Treaties, Coll. of Laws No. 53/1994.

rules. The fiscal treaty came into force when it was ratified by the twelfth state of the euro area (Finland, in 2012), although there are 17 Member States of the euro area.[29]

17.18. It is important to mention here that the Czech Republic and the United Kingdom are not contracting parties to the so-called fiscal treaty. The fiscal treaty is not a treaty of all the European Union Member States but an intergovernmental agreement of some EU Member States. Disunity of Member States in pursuing common European interests was also seen in the case of the Pact Euro Plus when the United Kingdom, Czech Republic, Hungary and Sweden refused to participate in the Pact. In Ireland a referendum on participation in the fiscal treaty was organised on 31 May 2012 with a positive result – it was accepted. Additionally, the Constitutional Court of France had to rule on the complaint with regard to the amendment of the Constitution of France due to the participation of France in the fiscal treaty. It made a decision that it was not necessary to amend the Constitution of France should France become the contracting party to the given treaty. The Federal Constitutional Court of Germany dealt with the complaint on the participation of Germany in the 'permanent' euro area rescue mechanism and in the above-mentioned fiscal treaty. It ruled that the complaint against the participation of Germany in the permanent euro area rescue mechanism and in the fiscal treaty was ungrounded. The Court further ruled that the commitments of Germany within the EU mechanism could not exceed EUR 190 bn without prior approval of its parliament. Thus misgivings of complainants have not been confirmed. The legal grounds for filing the complaint before the Federal Constitutional Court of Germany came from the fact that participation of Germany in the ESM would weaken competences of the German Parliament regarding the spending of tax money.[30]

17.19. In Slovakia, the fiscal treaty was approved in compliance with the constitutional rules and was ratified by the President of the Slovak Republic on 11 January 2013. It means that the Slovak Republic is one of the contracting parties to the treaty. To this end Slovakia passed the Act No. 36/2013 Col. of Laws on the competence of the Slovak Republic authorities in securing budgetary responsibility in the European Union, as well as amendments of related legislation. This national legislation stipulates the obligations of the Prime-Minister of the Slovak Government, and the competence of the Ministry of Finance

---

[29] Art. 14 (2) TSCG (ratification by twelve Contracting Parties whose currency is the Euro).
[30] Available at: http://www.bundesverfassungsgericht.de/pressemitteilungen/bvg12-067. html (accessed on 6 May 2013).

SR and the Ministry of Justice SR with regard to the implementation of the treaty. The national fiscal framework includes provisions creating the basis for national public finance management in order to insure complementarities between the EU fiscal framework and the Slovak Republic fiscal framework. Enhanced public finance management includes tax policy, as well as financial sector and broader political interventions aimed at the recovery of macroeconomic stability. A constitutional Act No 493/2011 Col. of Laws on budgetary responsibility has been passed, to aid in the sound execution of the budgetary policy. The given act outlines the framework whereby the general government debt would not exceed the upper threshold of 50%. At the same time the act defines rules for local self-government budgets that feed into the general government budget. Based on this act an independent body for evaluation and monitoring of financial development has been created: the Council for Budget Responsibility. The European Central Bank expressed its opinion on the above mentioned national act. In its opinion on 5 December 2011 the ECB commented on the financing of the Council for Budget Responsibility and on its institutional inclusion into the National Bank of Slovakia. The ECB opinion further mentioned the discrepancy of the draft act with the Council directive 2011/85/EU of 8 November 2011 on requirements for budgetary frameworks of the Member States.[31]

17.20. The T*reaty on Stability, Coordination and Governance in the Economic and Monetary Union* contains certain provisions that were already present in the existing EU legal instruments. First, there are the Council regulations of general application, which are binding in their entirety and directly applicable in all Member States (Article 288 TFEU and Article 161 TEURATOM). Secondly, there are aspects of primary law for example in the TFEU that has precedence over the national legislation. Finally, there is Protocol No. 12 which is part of the EU primary law. Member States have also participated in the drafting of the-above mentioned legal acts. Member States obviously fail to meet the expectations of the European Union and that is why it has adopted new legal instruments for securing monetary stability. Commitments ensuing from the euro area membership are clearly of economic character. Specifically, contracting parties are obliged to transpose the 'balanced budget rule' and to prefer the budgetary consolidation strategy focused in particular on limiting general government expenditures.

---

[31] Opinion of the European Central Bank of 5 December 2011 on fiscal responsibility (CON/2011/96).

V. Conclusion

17.21. This paper deals with a topic highly pertinent to matters associated to the stability of currency and finance. It presents the consequences of the legal instruments of the European Union for the Slovak Republic. The introduction of new legal instruments to secure euro stability does not only have legal consequences but also financial ones. Commitments ensuing from these legal instruments in the form of international treaties limit the competence of the Member States of the euro area in the fiscal arena which increases centralisation and deepens integration. Mandatory financial participation in the stability mechanism can be characterised as a financial rescue mechanism, and is clearly reflected in the fiscal policy of the given state.

| | |

Summaries

DEU [*Rechtliche Instrumente der Fiskal- und Währungsstabilität der EU*]
In der Gegenwart nimmt der Einfluss der Europäischen Union in den internationalen Organisationen immer mehr zu, wobei die EU im Hinblick auf die Realisierung ihrer gemeinsamen Politik besondere Rechtsinstrumente einsetzt. Die Verpflichtungen, die aus diesen Rechtsinstrumenten in Form von internationalen Verträgen folgen, beschränken die Kompetenzen der Mitgliedsstaaten der Eurozone im Fiskalbereich, was zu einer Zentralisierung und Vertiefung der Integration beiträgt. Die Zukunft des Euro und die Erhaltung der Finanzstabilität hängt von den einzelnen Mitgliedsstaaten und der internationalen Rechtsverantwortung ab, wobei die Verpflichtungen im guten Willen eingehalten werden müssen. Auch trotz der Tatsache, dass die Wirtschaftspolitik der Mitgliedsstaaten eine Angelegenheit des gemeinsamen Interesses sein sollte, kommen in den Mitgliedsstaaten unterschiedliche Meinungen zur künftigen Orientierung der gemeinsamen Währungspolitik zum Vorschein.

CZE [*Právní nástroje fiskální a měnové stability EU*]
V současnosti neustále narůstá vliv Evropské unie mezi mezinárodními organizacemi. Evropská unie přitom v zájmu realizace svých společných politik zavádí zvláštní právní nástroje. Závazky vyplývající z těchto právních nástrojů v podobě mezinárodních smluv omezují pravomoce členských států eurozóny ve fiskální oblasti, čímž dochází k centralizaci a k prohlubování integrace. Budoucnost eura a zachování finanční stability závisí na samotných členských státech a na mezinárodněprávní

odpovědnosti plnit závazky v dobré víře. I přesto, že hospodářské politiky členských států by měly být věcí společného zájmu, objevují se mezi členskými státy rozdílné názory na budoucí směřování společné měnové politiky.

| | |

POL [*Instrumenty prawne zapewniające stabilność fiskalną i walutową UE*]

Obecnie istnieje coraz większy wpływ Unii Europejskiej wśród organizacji międzynarodowych, która w celu realizacji swych wspólnych polityk wprowadza szczególne instrumenty prawne. Zobowiązania wynikające z tych instrumentów prawnych w formie umów międzynarodowych ograniczają kompetencje państw członkowskich strefy euro w zakresie fiskalnym, wynikiem czego jest centralizacja i pogłębianie integracji. Przyszłość euro i utrzymanie stabilności finansowej zależy od pojedyńczych państw członkowskich oraz od międzynarodowoprawnej odpowiedzialności spełnienia swych zobowiązań w dobrej wierze. Mimo, że polityki gospodarcze państw członkowskich powinni być przedmiotem wspólnego zainteresowania państw członkowskich, pojawiają się różne poglądy na temat przyszłego kierunku wspólnej polityki pieniężnej.

FRA [*Les instruments juridiques fiscaux et de stabilité monétaire de l'UE*]

De nos jours, l'influence et l'importance de l'Europe unie parmi d'autres organisations internationales ne cesse de grandir, qui dans l'intérêt de la réalisation de ses politiques communes, introduit ses instruments juridiques particuliers. Les engagements résultant de ces instruments en question , en forme de contrats internationaux limitent les compétences des pays de la zone euro dans le domaine fiscal ce qui mène à la centralisation et l'approfondissement de l'intégration. L'avenir de l'euro et le maintien de la stabilité financière dépend des pays membres et de la responsabilité juridico-internationale de tenir ces engagements dans la bonne foi. Mais malgré le fait que les politiques économiques des pays membres devraient faire partie de l'intérêt commun, il y a des pays membres chez lesquels on voit apparaitre des opinions diverses concernant l'orientation de la politique monétaire commune.

RUS [*Правовые инструменты фискальной и монетарной стабильности ЕС*]

В настоящее время непрерывно усиливается влияние Европейского Союза на международные организации. В рамках реализации своей политики Евросоюз вводит особые правовые нормы (правовой порядок).. Обязательства, вытекающие из этого правопорядка в форме международных договоров, ограничивают правомочия членов Евросоюза в фискальной области. Это приводит к централизации и к усилению интеграции. Будущее совместной валюты евро и сохранение финансовой стабильности зависит только от самих членов Евросоюза и от его международно-правовой ответственности выполнять свои обязательства. Несмотря на хозяйственную политику отдельных членов Евросоюза, которые должны защищать совместные интересы, существуют разногласия о будущем совместной валютной политики.

ESP [***Instrumentos jurídicos de la estabilidad fiscal y monetaria de la UE***]

En la época actual, sigue creciendo la influencia que la Unión Europea ejerce sobre las organizaciones internacionales y en el benificio de sus políticas comunes aplica instrumentos jurídicos particulares. Las obligaciones que representan estos instrumentos jurídicos bajo la forma de los convenios internacionales limitan las competencias de los Estados miembros de la eurozona en la esfera fiscal lo que facilita la centralización y conduce hacia la profundización de la integración.

El futuro del EURO y el mantenimiento de la estabilidad financiera depende de los Estados miembros mismos tanto como de su responsabilidad legal en la escala internacional de cumplir sus compromisos de buena fe. Aunque las políticas económicas de los Estados miembros han de ser el asunto del interés común, aparecen entre los Estados miembros opiniones diferentes sobre la futura orientación de la política monetaria común.

| | |

Zdeněk Nový

The Role of the UNIDROIT in the Unification of International Commercial Law with a Specific Focus on the Principles of International Commercial Contracts

Key words:
Comparative law |
Contract | Efficiency |
Harmonization |
Humanity |
International commerce
| International
organizations |
International convention
| Non-state law | the
UNIDROIT | Unification

Abstract | *The UNIDROIT Institute has played a prominent and indispensable role amongst international inter-governmental organizations in the field of the unification of private law. It has thus been a perfect example of the creation of private law beyond national states.*

This paper has two parts. The first part focuses upon the analysis of the UNIDROIT institutional structure, its powers as an international organization and the lawmaking process leading to the adoption of a unifying instrument. Afterwards, it identifies two kinds of these instruments, referred to as legally binding and non-binding. Whilst binding instruments are international conventions, those which are non-binding may have a form of model law, principles or guidelines. It is then emphasised that non-binding instruments have gained more success than binding ones.

The second part of the paper offers an insight into the legal nature, purpose and main ideological tenets of the UNIDROIT Principles for International Commercial Contracts as the most successful non – binding instrument of the unification. The Paper concludes with the statement that there are two main goals of unification: efficiency and humanity.

Zdeněk Nový is a senior lecturer in international law at Faculty of Law, Masaryk University, Brno, Czech Republic. He also acts as a legal counsel in international business and economic law and arbitration in Brno, Czech Republic. He holds a master of law and Ph.D. in private international law from Faculty of Law, Masaryk University, Brno, Czech Republic and LL.M. from European University Institute, Florence, Italy; He also obtained the Scholarship for the Summer Session in Private International law by The Hague Academy of International Law, The Hague, Netherlands. He enjoyed a status of Independent Researcher at the UNIDROIT, Rome, Italy. He is Fellow of the European Law Institute, Vienna, Austria.
e-mail: zdenek.novy@law.muni.cz

I. When in Rome Do as the Romans Do

18.01. The imprint of the Roman Empire has certainly survived in architecture and art, but even more so Roman law survives in contemporary legal thinking. Unlike architecture or art, however, Roman law was not intended for all humanity. In short, it was intended solely for Roman citizens.

18.02. Nevertheless, as the Roman Empire was very expansive, both in terms of war and trade, it became clear that it would be useful to take into account the relations between Roman citizens and aliens. As a result, two sets of legal rules came into existence: one for internal relations among Roman citizens (*ius civile*) and another for the relations between Romans and aliens (*ius gentium*).[1]

18.03. Yet, by the medieval period, the increasingly international character of commerce, as well as the alterations in its nature, revealed that Roman law, including the distinction and relation between the two sets of rules, was no longer feasible for merchant transactions.[2] Moreover, the need arose for common rules,[3] the obedience and enforcement of which would be expected whichever market the medieval merchant was to enter.

18.04. In the 21th century, the old dilemmas have persisted. Is it still necessary and feasible to unify private law? Is there any need for separate sets of legal rules for internal and international commercial relations?

18.05. Various international organizations have undertaken the task of providing answers to these questions by pursuing the unification of private law. The most prominent of these is the International Institute for the Unification of Private Law ('UNIDROIT').

18.06. It would take a voluminous book to describe all activities of the UNIDROIT. Hence, I shall confine myself to its most important aspects. I shall describe the institutional structure, the purpose(s) of the UNIDROIT, its legislative process and instruments used for the unification.

18.07. Furthermore, I shall devote close attention to the UNIDROIT Principles for International Commercial Contracts ('UPICC') that have become the most recognised UNIDROIT instrument in recent years.

---

[1]　See e.g. *Comparative Law before the Code Napoléon in* THE OXFORD HANDBOOK OF COMPARATIVE LAW, Oxford: Oxford University Press, 5-6 (Mathias Reimann & Reinhard Zimmermann eds., 2006).

[2]　See e.g. RUDOLF B. SCHLESINGER, HANS W. BAADE, MIRJAN R. DAMASKA AND PETER E. HERZOG, COMPARATIVE LAW CASES-TEXT-MATERIALS, Mineola, NY: The Foundation Press, Inc. 302-303 (1988).

[3]　In those times, of course, one may speak at best of the 'approximation' of trade usages at markets in medieval cities, namely in Northern Italy.

II. The Institutional Aspects

18.08. The UNIDROIT is an international intergovernmental organization which was set up as an auxiliary organ of the League of Nations in 1926. The city of Rome was chosen as the UNIDROIT seat.[4]

18.09. The UNIDROIT has 63 members.[5] The continuing functioning of the UNIDROIT is ensured by the contribution of Member States, with a specific role for the Italian government.

18.10. The official languages of the UNIDROIT are Italian, English, French, German and Spanish[6], while working languages of the UNIDROIT are English and French. The instruments adopted by the UNIDROIT are available in more languages either as official versions or translations.

18.11. The Institutional structure of the UNIDROIT does not deviate from the structure common to international organizations:

1) a General Assembly;
2) a President;
3) a Governing Council;
4) a Permanent Committee;
5) an Administrative Tribunal;
6) a Secretariat.[7]

18.12. The General Assembly is the decision-making organ of UNIDROIT consisting of one representative from each member Government.[8] The Presidency of the General Assembly is held by the Ambassador of one of the Organisation's member States, on a rotating basis and for one year.[9] The General Assembly has the following powers:

- it decides on the UNIDROIT budget every year;
- it approves the Work Programme every three years;
- it elects the Governing Council every five years.

18.13. The Governing Council exerts supervision over all policy aspects related to the UNIDROIT statutory objectives, and in particular over

---

[4]   As intimated above, the choice of Rome as the UNIDROIT seat has had its symbolic value due to the heritage of Roman law that is still alive in contemporary private law. See thereto the quote from the speech given at the occasion of the opening of the UNIDROIT in Roy Goode, Herbert Kronke, Ewan Mckendrick And Jeffrey Wool, Trasnational Commercial Law Text Cases, And Materials, Oxford: Oxford University Press, 203, 204 (2007): '...*le plus important c'est d'avoir son siège a Rome; lorsqu'on parle du droit, on ne peut penser qu'à Rome....*'

[5]   Information accurate as of 20 July 2013.

[6]   Art. 10 of the Statute.

[7]   Art. 4 of the Statute.

[8]   Art. 5 of the Statute.

[9]   Ibid.

whether and how the Work Programme is attained.[10] It is composed of one *ex officio* member, the President of the Institute, and 25 elected members, mostly eminent judges, practitioners, academics and civil servants.[11]

18.14. A unique feature of the Governing Council is that once the person suggested for a candidature to this organ is elected, he becomes independent from his government and therefore may rely exclusively on his expertise, not on political motives. The Governing Council is thus a scientific organ of the UNIDROIT, the existence of which may be seen as a distinguishing feature in comparison to other international organizations.[12]

18.15. The Secretariat is the executive organ of UNIDROIT. It is headed by a Secretary-General appointed by the Governing Council on the nomination of the President.[13]

III. Sources of Information on the UNIDROIT

18.16. There are several sources of information about the UNIDROIT. There is, first of all, a very useful UNIDROIT website[14] where one can find most information about the UNIDROIT, including founding documents of the UNIDROIT, texts of all instruments and Reports produced by the Working Group which is established for the preparation of individual instruments.[15]

18.17. A mention should also be made of the UNILEX database[16] in which one can find the vast majority of available court decisions and arbitration awards on the UPICC and also the UN Convention on Contracts for the International Sale of Goods ('CISG'). The vast majority of them are in English or translated, and hence access to them is fairly easy. Furthermore, there has been a published journal entitled the *Uniform Law Review* that was originally published by the UNIDROIT and more recently has been published by Oxford University Press. Its content

---

[10] Art. 6 of the Statute.

[11] Ibid.

[12] It was rightly observed that this reflects the original spirit of 1920s when the UNIDROIT was set up, in that it was to be composed of pre-eminent jurists. See ROY GOODE, HERBERT KRONKE, EWAN MCKENDRICK AND JEFFREY WOOL, *supra* note 4, at 205.

[13] Art. 8 of the Statute.

[14] Available at: www.unidroit.org (accessed on 20 July 2013).

[15] The working (study) groups are a distinguishing feature in which the UNIDROIT differs from most international organizations. They consist of experts sitting in their personal capacity, thus not as a representative of any particular state. This ensures that the main rationale behind the adopted instrument is expertise, rather than any national or administrative interests.

[16] Available at: www.unilex.info (accessed on 20 July 2013).

includes bilingual articles and notes on the UNIDROIT work as well as more general information on harmonization and unification in an international context.

18.18. Last but not least, there has been a widely recognised UNIDROIT library where one may find various materials related to the work of the UNIDROIT, as well as on unification in general. There is also a wide array of useful sources in many languages for all fields of private law.

IV. The Scope of the UNIDROIT

18.19. The scope of the UNIDROIT, similarly to other international organizations, is defined in the *Statute Organique d'UNIDROIT*[17] ('Statute') as its founding international treaty. The founding fathers are Member States, while Italy possesses a specific position among them.[18]

18.20. The Statute defines the scope of the UNIDROIT as follows:

'The purposes of the International Institute for the Unification of Private Law are to examine ways of harmonising and coordinating the private law of States and of groups of States, and to prepare gradually for the adoption by the various States of uniform rules of private law. To this end the Institute shall:

(a) prepare drafts of laws and conventions with the object of establishing uniform internal law;

(b) prepare drafts of agreements with a view to facilitating international relations in the field of private law;

(c) undertake studies in comparative private law;

(d) take an interest in projects already undertaken in any of these fields by other institutions with which it may maintain relations as necessary;

(e) organise conferences and publish works which the Institute considers worthy of wide circulation.'[19]

18.21. The abbreviation UNIDROIT derives etymologically from two French words: *l'unification* and *le droit*. Accordingly, it is the key task of this

---

[17] The original version of the Statute was adopted only in French, with the following official translation to English approved by the General Assembly at its 45th Session in 1991, and the unofficial translation into Arabic. Available at: http://www.unidroit.org/english/presentation/statute.pdf (accessed on 20 July 2013). In the following, I will be working only with the official English translation of the Statute.

[18] For instance, the Italian government provides the premises to the UNIDROIT. On the other hand, the Italian Government has had a privilege to nominate the President of the UNIDROIT.

[19] Art. 1 of the Statute.

international organization to unify private, primarily commercial, law. The UNIDROIT is therefore the perfect example of the creation of private law beyond -state.

18.22. One may frequently find in various official documents of the UNIDROIT, including the Statute, both the words 'harmonization' and 'unification', without there being any explanation of the difference between the two. From a theoretical standpoint, there is certainly a conceptual difference between unification and harmonization. Whilst the former implies uniformity of law, the latter refers to approximation between laws. In other words, harmonization does not go as far as unification. Just to avoid confusion, no matter whether the UNIDROIT instrument actually pursues harmonization or unification, I shall speak in the following of unification as covering both concepts.

18.23. There is a consciousness in the UNIDROIT of the importance of sensitivity regarding cultural differences when undertaking the unification of private law among the countries of the world.[20] Therefore, the unification pursued by the UNIDROIT has been focused on the fields of law that are of a rather technical and/or commercial nature where the national sentiment would not be endangered.[21] This may however, be easier said than done for there are fields of law that at a first sight appear 'technical', but in fact have important policy choices lurking beneath their surface.[22]

V. The Unification Process

18.24. The UNIDROIT lawmaking process may be broken down into three stages:

1) the Preliminary Stage
2) the Intergovernmental Stage
3) the adoption of the UNIDROIT instrument.[23]

---

[20]   See e.g. *Comparative Law and the Europeanization of Private Law*, in THE OXFORD HANDBOOK OF COMPARATIVE LAW, Oxford: Oxford University Press, 541 (Mathias Reimann and Reinhard Zimmermann eds., 2006).

[21]   Available at: http://www.unidroit.org/dynasite.cfm?dsmid=103284 (accessed on 20 July 2013).

[22]   One may recall the strong reaction against good faith as a 'legal irritant' in UK contract law as a result of the implementation of the *Council Directive 93/13/EEC of 5 April 1993 on Unfair Terms in Consumer Contracts*. See Günter Teubner, *Legal Irritants: Good Faith in British Law or How Unifying Law Ends Up in New Divergencies*, 61 (1) MODERN LAW REVIEW 11-32 (1998).

[23]   See: http://www.unidroit.org/dynasite.cfm?dsmid=103284 (accessed on 20 July 2013).

V.1. Preliminary Stage

18.25. Once a subject has been put on the Work Programme, the Secretariat will draw up a feasibility study and/or a preliminary comparative law report. The report may include a tentative draft of the principles or uniform rules. It will thereafter be assessed by the Governing Council which, if satisfied with the report, will ask the Secretariat to convene a study group, chaired normally by a member of the Council, to prepare a preliminary draft instrument for the unification.[24]

V.2. Intergovernmental Negotiation Stage

18.26. A preliminary draft instrument prepared by the study group will be laid before the Governing Council for approval.[25]

18.27. In the case where a preliminary draft convention is used as a binding instrument, the Council will usually ask the Secretariat to convene a committee of governmental experts to finalise a draft convention, so that it will be suitable for adoption by a diplomatic conference.[26] In the case of non-binding instruments, the Council will be asked to authorise its publication and dissemination by the UNIDROIT in the circles for which it was intended.[27]

18.28. All member States are represented in committees of governmental experts, based upon their interest in the subject-matter. Also other states and stakeholders may participate in the process of the adoption of the preliminary convention upon invitation by the Secretariat.[28]

V.3. The Adoption of the Instrument

18.29. A final draft will then be submitted to the Governing Council for approval. If the Governing Council recognizes that the draft convention reflects a consensus between the States represented in the committee of governmental experts, it will authorise the transmission of the draft convention to a diplomatic conference for adoption as an international convention.[29]

---

[24] Ibid.; The study groups are a distinguishing feature in which the UNIDROIT differs from most international organizations. They consist of experts sitting in their personal capacity, thus not as a representative of any particular state. This ensures that the main rationale behind the adopted instrument is expertise, rather than any national or administrative interests.

[25] Ibid.

[26] Ibid.

[27] Ibid.

[28] Ibid.

[29] Ibid.

VI. Lawmaking Policy Considerations in Pursuing Unification

18.30. The lawmaking policy considerations encompass three important aspects regarding the legislative policy of the UNIDROIT:

- the nature of the instrument chosen and the factors decisive for this choice;
- technical rather than political questions;
- the suitability and feasibility of the subject-matter for unification.

18.31. The first aspect concerns the nature of the rules unified by the UNIDROIT. These are primarily rules of private law. Nonetheless, as the distinction between private and public law is nowadays often blurred – and even more so at transnational level – from time to time the UNIDROIT needs to unify rules that might also be characterised as pertaining to public law.[30]

18.32. Next, the willingness of member States to adapt domestic law to the prepared UNIDROIT instrument is taken into account. Accordingly, the choice is made between rules that are intended for purely cross-border situations and internal ones.[31]

18.33. According to the UNIDROIT lawmaking policy, the choice between a binding or non-binding instrument depends upon whether there are interests that go beyond the pure contractual relationship, like the rights of third parties or the protection of public interests.[32] If this is the case, the traditional choice is an international convention as a binding instrument. By the same token, if the issue falls under the remit of the private autonomy of the contracting parties, the non-binding instrument is likely to be opted for.

VI.1. Means of Unification

18.34. There are two means whereby the UNIDROIT pursues unification:[33]

- formal and legally binding – by an international convention as a source of international law and
- informal and non-binding *per se* – by a model law, principles or guidelines.

---

[30] Available at: http://www.unidroit.org/dynasite.cfm?dsmid=103284 (accessed on 20 July 2013).

[31] Ibid.

[32] Available at: http://www.unidroit.org/dynasite.cfm?dsmid=103284 (accessed on 19 July 2013).

[33] See also Hans Van Houtte, *La Modelisation Substantielle, in* LA MONDIALISATION DU DROIT, Paris: Litec 221 (*sous la direction* de E. Loquin and Catherine Kessedijan, 2000).

18.35. It is striking that although unification via international conventions has had some popularity, non-binding principles have attracted much more attention and have been popular not only with academic circles, but also with decision-makers in disputes arising from international commercial transactions.[34] This is particularly true with regards to the UPICC (as discussed in section VII). This may be a signal that those involved in the practice of international commercial law have a more favourable attitude towards spontaneous unification via non-binding instruments than by international treaties.[35]

VI.1.1. Binding Instruments

18.36. This paper examines only the UPICC in more detail, leaving aside binding international conventions. This is because the majority of them have not been particularly successful, a fact revealed by the low number of ratifications.[36]

18.37. Nonetheless, these conventions deserve to be addressed at least briefly. They contain mostly substantive rules. In total there are 10 conventions and 2 protocols, as follows (in descending chronological order):

- The Protocol to the Convention on International Interests in Mobile Equipment on Matters Specific to Space Assets (Berlin, 2012);
- The UNIDROIT Convention on Substantive Rules for Intermediated Securities (Geneva, 2009);
- The Luxembourg Protocol to the Convention on International Interests in Mobile Equipment on Matters specific to Railway Rolling Stock (Luxembourg, 2007);
- The Convention on International Interests in Mobile Equipment (Cape Town, 2001);
- The Protocol to the Convention on International Interests in Mobile Equipment on Matters Specific to Aircraft Equipment (Cape Town, 2001);
- The UNIDROIT Convention on Stolen or Illegally Exported Cultural Objects (Rome, 1995);
- The UNIDROIT Convention on International Factoring (Ottawa, 1988);

---

[34] See also JAN KLABBERS, AN INTRODUCTION TO INTERNATIONAL INSTITUTIONAL LAW, Cambridge: Cambridge University Press 202 *et seq.* (2002).

[35] For the preference of a non-binding harmonizing instrument to a binding one in the field of contract law see Roy Goode, *International Restatement of Contract and English Contract Law*, 2 UNIFORM LAW REVIEW 232-233 (1997).

[36] See Status of UNIDROIT Conventions, available at: http://www.unidroit.org/dynasite.cfm?dsmid=84211 (accessed on 22 September 2013).

- The UNIDROIT Convention on International Financial Leasing (Ottawa, 1988);
- The Convention on Agency in the International Sale of Goods (Geneva, 1983);
- The Convention providing a Uniform Law on the Form of an International Will (Washington, D.C., 1973);
- The International Convention on Travel Contracts (Brussels, 1970);
- The Convention relating to a Uniform Law on the Formation of Contracts for the International Sale of Goods (The Hague, 1964);
- The Convention relating to a Uniform Law on the International Sale of Goods (The Hague, 1964). [37]

VI.1.2. Non-binding Instruments

18.38. There are three forms of non-binding instruments that have been adopted by the UNIDROIT:
- model laws;
- guides for contracting;
- principles.

18.39. A good example of a model law can be found in the UNESCO – UNIDROIT Model Legislative Provisions on State Ownership of Undiscovered Cultural Objects (2011) as it addresses an acute problem in international practice.[38] Likewise, guidelines serve as a good practice for contracting parties regarding a certain type of contract, for example franchising which was set out in the UNIDROIT Guide to Master Franchise Agreements.[39]

18.40. Last, there are two sets of principles, one related to substantive rules for international commercial contracts as in the UPICC and the other related to rules for international civil procedures, entitled the Principles of Transnational Civil Procedure (PTCP).[40] The PTCP are the outcome of the cooperation between the UNIDROIT and the American Law Institute.[41] The reason behind the cooperation with the American Law Institute is clear. Such a project requires there to be cooperation between experts from both Civil and Common law jurisdictions.

---

[37] See: http://www.unidroit.org/dynasite.cfm?dsmid=84211 (accessed on 20 July 2013).

[38] Available at: http://www.unidroit.org/english/modellaws/main.htm (accessed on 19 July 2013).

[39] See: http://www.unidroit.org/english/guides/2007franchising/franchising2007-guide-2nd-e.pdf (accessed on 19 July 2013)

[40] Available at: http://www.unidroit.org/english/principles/civilprocedure/main.htm (accessed on 19 July 2013).

[41] Ibid.

18.41. The aim of this cooperation was to establish certain principles of civil procedure that would be useful for national courts dealing with transnational cases.[42] It should be borne in mind that national procedural laws around the globe differ in a variety of areas. For example, there are great differences in the language of the proceedings and costs.[43]

VII. The UPICC

18.42. Differences among legal systems would make the effort to set contract principles in a binding way (by an international convention) futile. Thus, the only viable way to unify contract law was to create a set of non-binding principles, the intellectual authority of which would prompt private parties to incorporate them into their international commercial contracts. This authority would likewise spur decision-makers to take them into account when deciding the disputes arising out of international commercial contracts.

18.43. The UPICC are the result of the long-term activity of a considerable number of scholars and practitioners specialised in contract law. The first effort towards the preparation of principles of international commercial contracts dates back to 1971 when the Governing Council of UNIDROIT gave its *imprimatur* to commencement of work on the *Progressive Codification of International Trade Law*.[44] This document was thereafter re-named the *Preparation of the Principles of International Commercial Contracts*.[45] In 1980, a Working Group was established so as to elaborate on individual chapters of these principles.[46]

18.44. As was mentioned above, there have been three editions of the UPICC. In 1994, the first edition of the UPICC came into existence. The second edition of the UPICC was issued in 2004. The last one was adopted at the 90th session of the Governing Council of UNIDROIT in 2010.[47] In

---

[42] For instance, the PTCP offer a rule for those national civil procedural codes that contain no regulation of *cautio judicatum solvi*. See art. 3.

[43] Art. 6 and 25 of the PTCP.

[44] See MICHAEL JOACHIM BONELL, AN INTERNATIONAL RESTATEMENT OF CONTRACT LAW. THE UNIDROIT PRINCIPLES OF INTERNATIONAL COMMERCIAL CONTRACTS, Ardsley, NY: Transnational Publishers 28 (3rd ed. 2005).

[45] Ibid., at 29.

[46] Ibid., at 29.

[47] The UPICC 2010 edition. Available in English, French and Italian at: http://www.unidroit.org/english/principles/contracts/main.htm (accessed on 19 July 2013). As the numbering in the three editions differs, in the following the numbering of the UPICC 2010 will be used. The structure of the UPICC 2010 edition consists of 211

the same year, the United Nations Commission on International Trade Law ('UNCITRAL') has underscored the importance of the UPICC by officially endorsing its text.[48]

VII.1. The Nature, Scope and Purpose of the UPICC

18.45. The nature and purposes of the UPICC may be seen in its Preamble:

'These Principles set forth general rules for international commercial contracts.

They shall be applied when the parties have agreed that their contract be governed by them. They may be applied when the parties have agreed that their contract be governed by general principles of law, the lex mercatoria, or the like.

They may be applied when the parties have not chosen any law to govern their contract.

They may be used to interpret or supplement international uniform law instruments.

They may be used to interpret or supplement domestic law.

They may serve as a model for national and international legislators.'

18.46. Of course, the analysis of the role of the UPICC cannot rely solely on the self-perception of their nature and purpose as expressed in the Preamble. It is also necessary to consider the perceptions of national legislators and decision-makers such as judges and arbitrators.

18.47. Along the same lines, the list contained in the Preamble may present a 'restatement' and 'pre-statement' of international commercial law. [49] This means that the UPICC express both how these they may already be applied under the applicable laws (*lex lata*) and how they may work in the future if certain alterations in international and national lawmaking are made (*lex ferenda*).[50]

18.48. However, doubts were expressed as to whether the proper procedure set forth in the Statute regarding the adoption of unifying instruments

---

Articles, 11 chapters, while each chapter includes Sections. As far as the substance of the UPICC is concerned, these contain black-letter rules and the commentary that explains their use, including the model examples of the application of a concrete black-letter rule.

[48] Report of the United Nations Commission on International Trade Law Fourty-fifth Session (25 June – 6 July 2012), at 33. Available at: http://unctad.org/meetings/en/SessionalDocuments/a67d17_en.pdf (accessed on September 25, 2013).

[49] Ralf Michaels, *Preamble I: Purposes of the UPICC, in COMMENTARY ON THE UNIDROIT PRINCIPLES OF INTERNATIONAL COMMERCIAL CONTRACTS*, Oxford: Oxford University Press 25 (Stefan Vogenauer & Jan Kleinheisterkamp eds, 2009).

[50] Ibid.

was complied with in the case of the UPICC.[51] Strictly speaking, therefore, the UPICC seem to be best considered as a study in comparative private law as per Art. 1(c) of the Statute or a publication of a work the UNIDROIT considers 'worthy of wide circulation' under the Art. 1(e) of the Statute.

18.49. This reading of the Statute would contradict the declared purposes of the UPICC laid down in the Preamble indicating that these go far beyond a mere comparative-law publication. It is even more important that there seems to be no opposition from Member States to this 'informal unification'. This may be evidenced both by the use of the UPICC as a model for new legislation in Member States and by the growing use of the UPICC by their national courts (see VII.3.).

18.50. There is no denying that the UPICC are based on comparative studies. Yet, in contrast to other comparative enterprises, like the Common Core of European Private Law[52] project, the UPICC are intended to be actively used in contracting practice. Moreover, the UPICC certainly reflect the common stock of most developed national contract laws, international conventions, business customs and standard terms.[53]

18.51. As far as the use of comparative methodology in preparing the UPICC is concerned, if a national rule is shared by multiple legal systems, but appears to be inappropriate for the purpose of international commerce, it would not be adopted into the text of the UPICC. In contrast, a minority solution[54] may find its way into the UPICC, if it is suitable for international commercial contracts, as well as a legal solution unknown to national legal orders. Furthermore, the very appearance of the UPICC resembles civil law codifications to a certain extent. This, however, does not mean that it would contain legal solutions coming exclusively from Civil law. Accordingly, one may find black-letter rules in the UPICC that adopt legal solutions existing in Common law, but lacking in civil codes, like the regulation of merger clauses.[55]

---

[51] Catherine Kessedijan, *Un Exercice de Rénovation des Sources du Droit des Contrats du Commerce International: Les Principes Proposés par l'UNIDROIT*, 84 (4) REV. CRIT. DR. INTERNAT. PRIVÉ 648 (1995).

[52] More information is available at: http://www.common-core.org/ (accessed on 20 July 2013).

[53] MICHAEL JOACHIM BONELL, *supra* note 44, at 48.

[54] As a traditional rule one may consider, for instance, Art.4. 1 of the UPICC, which stipulates that a contract is interpreted in accordance with the intention of the parties. On the other hand, there are innovative rules, like Art.1.12(3) of the UPICC that deals with the question of 'relevant time zone'.

[55] Art. 2.1.17 UPICC; To be precise, merger clauses are the reaction of contracting practice to the so-called Parole Evidence Rule existing only in Common law jurisdictions.

VII.1.1. Principles and Rules

18.52. The Preamble lays down general rules for international commercial contracts. By the same token, there has so far been no regulation of specific types of contracts by the UPICC. Put differently, the UPICC contain what has been known in the continental tradition as the general part of contract law. This, inter alia, distinguishes the UPICC from Common European Sales Law[56] or the CISG.

18.53. Furthermore, the UPICC abbreviate, inter alia, 'Principles'. Yet, it would be a mistake to think that the word 'principles' reflects meticulously a distinction made by legal theory between 'principles' and 'rules'.[57] As a matter of fact, the UPICC contain both rules and principles. On the one hand, general notions, like 'good faith and fair dealing' or 'reasonableness', may be found in the text, being closer to legal principles, while on the other hand there are fairly detailed rules, like those setting forth the length of limitation periods.[58]

VII.1.2. International and Commercial

18.54. In a nutshell, the reason for the creation of the UPICC is that national laws cannot provide a sufficient legal framework for transnational transactions. While the UPICC were created with international transactions in mind, this cannot be said of most of national contract laws.[59]

18.55. The Preamble states that the UPICC covers only international contracts. There is, however, no explanation of what 'international' refers to. Although the sole incorporation of the UPICC into the contract makes it in no way international,[60] there seems to be no legal obstacle that would prevent parties from validly incorporating certain provisions from the UPICC into their contract (see VIII.1.3.).

18.56. The Preamble also stipulates that the UPICC regulate commercial contracts. Nowhere in the UPICC can criteria be found under which

---

For the critical analysis on merger clauses see GIORGIO DE NOVA, IL CONTRATTO ALIENO, Torino: G. Giapichelli 95-101 (2008).

[56] *Proposal for a Regulation of the European Parliament and of the Council on a Common European Sales Law* COM (2011) 635 final (11.10. 2011).

[57] Interestingly, according to *Ralf Michaels* the term 'principles' is an indirect heritage of the general principles of law as per Art. 38 of the ICJ Statute. See Ralf Michaels, *supra* note 49, at 30.

[58] See Section 11 of the UPICC.

[59] Michael Joachim Bonell, *The UNIDROIT Principles of International Commercial Contracts: Why? What? How?*, 69 (5) TULANE LAW REVIEW 1123 (1995).

[60] See Art. 3(3) of the *Regulation (EC) no 593/2008 of the European Parliament and of the Council of 17 June 2008 on the Law Applicable to Contractual Obligations* (Rome I).

one would draw a borderline between 'commercial' from 'non-commercial' contracts. It appears nonetheless reasonable to interpret 'commercial' in an extensive manner, while excluding only consumer contracts.[61]

VII.1.3. May the UPICC Be a Law Applicable to a Contract?

18.57.   The Preamble gives a straightforward and seemingly clear answer to this question. However, as intimated above, the UPICC are, as such, non-binding for decision-makers. Thus, the self-proclamation of the UPICC regarding the situations in which these should apply to a contract is one thing, but it is quite another thing to make courts and arbitrators obliged to apply the UPICC to it. There are therefore two necessary conditions to make the UPICC binding between the parties: their consent and the permissibility of using the UPICC under applicable national law.[62]

18.58.   The traditional private-international-law approach, which has been employed by state courts, rests on the premise that only law of a state may govern a contract.[63] Therefore, if parties to a contract wish to incorporate the UPICC by inserting the UPICC model clause,[64] this will mean no more, but no less, than derogating from default rules of the otherwise applicable national law.[65] Thus, as non-state rules governing a contract, the UPICC is as welcome as ants at a picnic in the classical choice-of-law scheme. It is precisely one of the reasons for the adoption of non-state rules (like the UPICC) to obviate the need to turn to a private-international-law analysis.

---

[61]   See also Thomas Wilhelmsson, *International Lex Mercatoria and Local Consumer Law: An Impossible Combination?*, 8(1-2) UNIFORM LAW REVIEW 141-144 (2003).

[62]   See e.g. Luis Olavo Baptista, *The UNIDROIT Principles for International Commercial Law Project: Aspects of International Private Law*, 69 (5) TULANE LAW REVIEW 1217 (1995).

[63]   See para (13) of the Preamble of the *Regulation (EC) no 593/2008 of the European Parliament and of the Council of 17 June 2008 on the Law Applicable to Contractual Obligations (Rome I)*. See e.g. Gralf Peter Callies, *Article 3 Freedom of Choice, in* ROME REGULATIONS. COMMENTARY ON THE EUROPEAN RULES OF THE CONFLICT OF LAWS, Alphen aan den Rijn: Wolters Kluwer 66-68 (Gralf Peter Callies *ed.* 2011).

[64]   'This contract shall be governed by the UNIDROIT Principles (2010) [except as to Articles...]' or 'This contract shall be governed by the UNIDROIT Principles (2010) [except as to Articles...], supplemented when necessary by the law of [jurisdiction X].' See the footnote to the Preamble.

[65]   In other words, the UPICC substitute default rules, whereas mandatory rules of applicable national law continue to be applied. See thereto e.g. Franco Ferrari, *Defining the Sphere of Application of the 1994 'UNIDROIT Principles of International Commercial Contracts'*, 69(5) TULANE LAW REVIEW 1229 (1995).

18.59. Nonetheless, in recent times, national courts seem to have had a favourable attitude towards the UPICC, while they have found that the latter would be at variance with applicable national law only in a rather limited number of cases.[66] This may indicate that the time is ripe to reconsider putting non-state rules like the UPICC on equal footing with national laws within the conflict-of-laws theory and practice.[67]

18.60. Moreover, the situation regarding the legal status of the UPICC may be different for arbitrators as they have wider leeway in the application of non-state rules for international commercial contracts. Accordingly, many national arbitration laws, as well as the rules of major arbitration institutions, allow arbitrators to apply 'rules of law' to merits of a dispute, as opposed to 'law'.[68] The UPICC falls within the former category. In addition, an arbitration award will not be refused recognition and enforcement under the New York Convention on the Recognition and Enforcement of Arbitration Awards of 1958 ('NY Convention') for the sole reason that it is based on the UPICC.[69]

VII.1.4. The UPICC and Lex Mercatoria

18.61. The Preamble suggests that if parties refer in their contract to *lex mercatoria* or transnational commercial law, this may be understood as a reference to the UPICC. Hence, there is a link between the UPICC and *lex mercatoria*. The former may be perceived to give 'substance and content'[70] to the concept of *lex mercatoria* or to be the 'attempt to codify transnational principles' of contract law.[71]

---

[66] Luca Radicati Di Brozolo, *Non-National Rules and Conflicts of Laws,* 3 Rivista di Diritto Internazionale Privato e Processuale 5 (2012). Available at: www.ssrn.com (accessed on 19 July 2013).

[67] See the recent initiative of the Hague Conference on Private International Law *'Choice of Law in International Contracts'*, which indicates that the UPICC would govern a contract as a full-fledged alternative to national law. Available at: *Hague Conference on Private International Law:* http://www.hcch.net/upload/wop/genaff2010pd06e.pdf (accessed on July 20, 2012).

[68] The distinction between 'law' and 'rules of law' is thus not an accidental slip of the tongue. See Art. 1511 *Code de procédure civile* (France);§ 1051 (1) *Zivilprozessordnung* (Germany); Art. 187 (1) *Loi fédérale sur le droit international privé* (Switzerland); see also Art. 22 (3) *the London Court of International Arbitration Rules* (1998); Art. 28 *the Arbitration Rules of the American Arbitration Association* (1997); Art. 35 (1) *UNCITRAL Arbitration Rules* (2010).

[69] Luca Radicati di Brozolo, *supra* note 66, at 5.

[70] Jean-Baptiste Racine And Fabrice Siiriainen, Droit Du Commerce International, Paris: Dalloz 71 (2007).

[71] Giorgio De Nova, *supra* note 55, at 8.

18.62. It was, however, rightly observed by *Catherine Kessedijan* that it may do more harm than good to mention the UPICC and *lex mercatoria* together as the latter notion is rather controversial due to its inherent murkiness.[72]

18.63. Moreover, the fact that there have been only a handful of references to *lex mercatoria* in international commercial contracts, which would otherwise allow the UPICC to come into play, limits the practical usefulness of the connection between the UPICC and *lex mercatoria*.

VII.2. Ideas Underpinning the UPICC

18.64. A considerable quantity of ink has already been used on writing about particular rules contained in the UPICC. Hence, the following will focus solely on the UPICC ideological tenets. To define them is important not least because the UPICC state that '(i)ssues within the scope of these Principles but not expressly settled by them are as far as possible to be settled in accordance with their underlying general principles.'[73]

18.65. It seems to be even more significant for explaining the general attitude of the UPICC towards international business, and in particular its view on how a contractual relationship ought to look like between international merchants.

18.66. It appears that the UPICC are based at least on the following tenets:
- freedom of contract;
- keeping a contract alive;
- fairness in the marketplace;
- contractual equilibrium.[74]

VII.2.1. Freedom of Contract

18.67. The freedom of contract is a *condition sine qua non* for the functioning of the international commerce as such.

18.68. In this respect, the parties contracting under the UPICC enjoy the widest possible autonomy, regarding for instance the form of a contract,[75] unless the UPICC mandatory rules are breached.[76]

---

[72] Catherine Kessedijan, *supra* note 51, at 654.

[73] Art. 1.6 (2) UPICC.

[74] See a comprehensive examination of the ideas underlying UPICC in MICHAEL JOACHIM BONELL *supra* note 44, at 87-172.

[75] Art. 1.2 UPICC.

[76] THE UNIDROIT, THE UNIDROIT PRINCIPLES OF INTERNATIONAL COMMERCIAL CONTRACTS, Rome: UNIDROIT 8-9 (2010).

Mandatory rules may then be of 'national, international or supra-national origin'.[77]

18.69. To be sure, the term 'mandatory rules' in a non-binding instrument might seem to be a contradiction in terms. Yet, it informs the users of the UPICC about the values they are based upon. Disregarding these values would diminish the sense of applying the UPICC to a contract as such. It may be argued, therefore, that the parties' freedom of contract expressed by choosing the UPICC as a set of rules governing it leads, paradoxically, to the binding nature of the rules set forth as mandatory in the UPICC.

VII.2.2. Keeping a Contract Alive

18.70. The traditional maxim *ut res magis valeat quam pereat* has also been adopted to the UPICC. The basic idea is that in cases of doubt as to whether a contract is valid or not, the preference is to be given to its validity.[78] The rationale behind this idea may be seen as twofold. First, all contractual conditions may not be known at the time of contracting, but parties nevertheless wish to conclude a contract. Second, favouring the validity of a contract over its invalidity increases legal security, which is of vital importance in international commerce.

18.71. The specific expression of 'keeping the contract alive' are then rules on a battle of forms[79] or conflict of individually and non-individually negotiated terms[80] since both aim to maintain the contract validity despite the doubts as to the content of the contract.

VII.2.3. Fairness in the Marketplace

18.72. One of the significant contributions by the UPICC to international commercial law lies in taking a normative stance on how contracting parties ought to behave during the life of their contractual relationship.[81]

18.73. Accordingly, the UPICC require that parties act in accordance with the principle of good faith and fair dealing[82] or cannot act inconsistently with their previous conduct.[83] The UPICC also regulate the issue of

---

[77] See Ibid. and art. 1.4 UPICC.
[78] See arts. 3.1. 2 a 3.1.3 UPICC.
[79] 2.1. 12 UPICC.
[80] 2.1. 21 UPICC.
[81] This includes also the pre-contract stage. See 2. 1.15 UPICC.
[82] Art. 1.7 UPICC.
[83] Art. 1. 8 UPICC.

fraud that links the freedom of contract with fairness.[84] Last but not least, the contract party which proffers standard terms cannot profit from surprising conditions contained therein.[85]

18.74. Therefore, the UPICC provide a certain yardstick to measure whether a contracting party is acting in a fair and reasonable manner. The model of business morality promoted by the UPICC is not deprived of its individualistic character (utilitarian morality), but at the same time it requires taking the interest of the other party into account (cooperative morality).[86]

VII.2.4. Contractual Equilibrium

18.75. A sharp dividing line is often drawn between B2B and B2C contracts. In the latter case there is usually disequilibrium of powers between the parties. However, in some cases the disparity between businesses may be even greater than between a business and consumer.[87]

18.76. It is thus praiseworthy that the authors of the UPICC were aware of a potential 'gross disparity'[88] between contracting parties, and therefore offered a guideline to arbitrators and judges for situations where treating the parties as equal is clearly unjust.

18.77. In this situation the UPICC provide that the aggrieved party may avoid the contract or ask for its modification.[89] Yet, this is possible only in exceptional circumstances, where one party takes an 'unfair advantage'[90] over the other because of the latter's 'dependence, economic distress or urgent needs, or of its improvidence, ignorance, inexperience and lack of bargaining skill', while having regard to 'the nature of purpose of the contract'.[91]

18.78. Additionally, the UPICC are based on the idea that contract ought not to be a mere hazard. Hence, it lays down the rule of 'Hardship' reacting to situations in which the equilibrium between contracting parties existing at the time of contracting is disturbed due to unexpected

---

[84]   Art. 3.2. 5 UPICC.

[85]   Art. 2.1. 20 UPICC.

[86]   For the interplay between these two types of morality as being typical for almost any marketplace see Boris Kozolczyk, *On the State of Commercial Law at the End of the 20th Century*, 8(1) ARIZ. J. INT'L & COMP. L. 16 (1991).

[87]   This may be due to various reasons, e.g. the weaker party has much less financial resources or market dominance than the stronger one.

[88]   See art. 3.2.7 UPICC.

[89]   Ibid.

[90]   Ibid.

[91]   Ibid.

circumstances beyond the control of the 'disadvantaged party'.[92] In such a case, the disadvantaged party has the right to renegotiate the contract.[93] If this is not possible, the contract shall be adapted or terminated by a court or arbitrator.[94]

VII.3. The UPICC in Practice

18.79. It seems useful at the outset to recall the users of the UPICC in practice:

- arbitrators or judges in a dispute;
- contracting Parties and their counsels;
- legislators.

18.80. Since the first edition, the available data has shown a sharp increase in the use of the UPICC mainly by arbitrators, but also by national courts.[95] There are an abundance of cases where the UPICC have been used as an interpretative tool or support for a solution reached by arbitrators or courts.[96]

18.81. The growth in the use of the UPICC by national courts may indicate an attempt to demonstrate that their decisions based on national law are not parochial, and therefore reflect the developments in current international commercial law.[97]

18.82. Furthermore, as indicated already by the Preamble, the UPICC may also serve as a gap-filler both in national and international adjudication. The UPICC have gained success namely in filling *lacunae* in the CISG.[98]

18.83. There is, however, one important caveat: the very fact that the UPICC are mentioned in a court decision or arbitration award does not mean that they are actually applied and that they are part of *ratio decidendi*. In this respect, it was rightly stated by *Christophe Seraglini* that the success of the UPICC hinges largely on whether they would be properly

---

[92]   Art. 6.2. 2 UPICC.

[93]   Art. 6.2. 3 UPICC.

[94]   Ibid.

[95]   See the cases contained in the UNILEX database; further see DAVID OSER, THE UNIDROIT PRINCIPLES OF INTERNATIONAL COMMERCIAL CONTRACTS: A GOVERNING LAW? Leiden:Martinus Nijhoff Publishers 27, 71 *et seq.*, (2008).

[96]   Luca Radicati Di Brozolo, *supra* note 66, at 2.

[97]   See e.g. the decision by the *US District Court, S. D. California* of 7 December 1998 in the case of *Ministry of Defence of the Islamic Republic of Iran v. Cubic Defense Systems.* The information on the decision is contained in FABIO BORTOLOTTI, MANUALE DI DIRITTO COMMERCIALE INTERNAZIONALE. DIRITTO DEI CONTRATTI INTERNAZIONALI.TERZA EDIZIONE, Padova: CEDAM 73 (2009).

[98]   See e.g. MICHAEL JOACHIM BONELL *supra* note 44, at 228.

used by decision-makers, namely arbitrators.[99] Accordingly, arbitrators and judges always ought to make clear in which way they use the UPICC and introduce the reasons for their use. It is rather harmful to the UPICC if a decision-maker only mentions them *en passant.*

18.84. Next, the parties and their counsels should not hesitate to justify or support their legal position using the UPICC. This may be helpful in particular where none of potentially applicable laws provides an unambiguous or satisfactory answer to the issue at hand.[100]

18.85. It is also recommended that parties consult the principles before drafting international commercial contracts. They may contain a particular solution sought for the contract or contain certain rules that may be used to formulate a particular contract clause, such as a merger clause.[101]

18.86. Finally, some national law-makers have used the UPICC as a model for the reform of their civil contract law. This is the case, inter alia, of the new Czech civil code.[102]

VII.4. Shortcomings Related to the UPICC

18.87. Like anything made by humans, the UPICC have both advantages and disadvantages. Although, in my view, the pros prevail, it is also fair to mention the cons. There are basically two disadvantages of the UPICC.

18.88. First, the UPICC contain only a body of rules of contract law. The general part of contract law is, however, just one part of the entire puzzle of legal regulation for international business transactions. Thus, for instance, the UPICC lack rules on the transfer of ownership which are inherent to most international sale contracts.[103] Second, there is no international body that would ensure the unified interpretation of the UPICC, comparable for example to the Court of Justice of the EU.[104] As a consequence, there is a peril of the diverging interpretation of the UPICC by decision-makers which would indeed undermine uniformity, hence increasing uncertainty in international business transactions.

---

[99] See Christophe Seraglini, *Du bon usage des Principes UNIDROIT dans l'arbitrage international,* 4 REVUE DE L'ARBITRAGE 1101-1166 (2003).

[100] Luca Radicati di Brozolo, *supra* note 66, at 5.

[101] See *supra* note 47.

[102] See e.g. sec. 1765-1766 of the new Czech civil code adopting the UNIDROIT rule on hardship. See also KAREL ELIÁŠ *ET AL.,* NOVÝ OBČANSKÝ ZÁKONÍK, Ostrava: Sagit 720 (2012).

[103] HANS VAN HOUTTE, *supra* note 33, at 231.

[104] See Bénédicte Fauvarque-Cosson, *Les contrats du commerce international, une approche nouvelle : Les Principes d'UNIDROIT relatifs aux contrats du commerce international,* 2 REVUE INTERNATIONALE DE DROIT COMPARE 464 (1998).

VIII. Conclusion

The ethos of unification lies in facilitating cross-border commerce. The criterion of effectiveness requires there be a certain common framework for international commercial transactions which enhances predictability and decreases the costs that international businesses would have to invest in coping with varying legal orders.

18.89. One of the key roles of the UNIDROIT in the field of unification hearkens back to what was once common to all laws in Europe. This consists of adding to the 'common stock' of legal systems having their roots in Roman law, and partly adapting them to the new conditions of the contemporary society and trade.

18.90. However, it is worth recalling the speech held on the occasion of founding of the UNIDROIT in 1926. In that speech, little was said about efficiency. Rather the emphasis was put on unification as a matter of humanity.[105] Unification is not just a purposeful plan, but it contributes to the development of closer ties between nations, not only international business contracts across borders.

18.91. The UPICC present a vivid illustration of the balanced interconnection between the pursuit of efficiency on one hand and the promotion of humanity on the other. In addition, they provide a bridge between the worlds of Civil and Common law. The UPICC also create a good equilibrium between individualistic and cooperative attitudes towards international commercial contracts, which seems to be one of the hardest tasks of any regulatory framework of contract law.

18.92. In summary, the role of the UNIDROIT has proven to be indispensable in the field of the unification of international commercial law, thereby contributing substantially to the development of both efficiency and humanity in international trade.

| | |

Summaries

FRA [*Le rôle d'UNIDROIT dans l'unification du droit commercial international en accordant une attention toute particulière aux Principes des contrats commerciaux internationaux*]

L'institut UNIDROIT joue un rôle irremplaçable et de premier plan parmi les organisations intergouvernementales internationales dans le domaine de l'unification du droit privé. Il apporte la démonstration

---

[105] '(N)ous voyons, au premier plan, le droit, dont les nombreuses er varies dispositions actuellement en vigueur présentaient une possibilité d'unification du plus grand intérêt pour l'humanité.' Cited according to ROY GOODE, HERBERT KRONKE, EWAN MCKENDRICK AND JEFFREY WOOL, *supra* note 4, at 203.

parfaite qu'il est possible de créer un droit privé indépendamment des États.

Dans une première partie, on s'intéresse à la structure institutionnelle d'UNIDROIT, à la compétence de cette organisation internationale et au processus de formation de ses instruments d'unification. Deux types d'instruments sont identifiés : des instruments juridiquement contraignants et des instruments non contraignants. Alors que les instruments contraignants prennent la forme de traités internationaux, les instruments non contraignants constituent en lois types, principes ou instructions. Il est souligné que les instruments non contraignants sont plus fréquemment utilisés.

La deuxième partie constitue une étude critique des Principes des contrats commerciaux internationaux, instruments d'unification non contraignants les plus remarquables d'UNIDROIT. Elle s'intéresse à leur caractère et à leur objet juridique ainsi qu'aux idées qui les sous-tendent. Deux principaux buts d'unification sont en définitive identifiés – l'efficacité et l'altruisme.

CZE [*Úloha UNIDROIT při unifikaci mezinárodního obchodního práva se zvláštním zřetelem k Principům mezinárodních obchodních smluv*]

Institut UNIDROIT sehrává prvořadou a nezastupitelnou úlohu mezi mezinárodními mezivládními organizacemi v oblasti unifikace soukromého práva. Jedná se přitom dokonalý příklad, že tvorba soukromého práva může probíhat mimo národní státy.

Článek má dvě části. První část se zaměřuje na institucionální strukturu UNIDROIT, kompetence této mezinárodní organizace a proces tvorby unifikačních instrument. Dále jsou identifikovány dva druhy těchto instrument: právně závazné a nezávazné. Jestliže závazné instrumenty mají podobu mezinárodních úmluv, ty nezávazné jsou ve formě modelového zákona, principů nebo návodů. Příspěvek následně zdůrazňuje, že se nezávazné instrumenty setkaly obecně s větším úspěchem, než ty závazné.

Druhá část předkládá kritický vhled do Principů mezinárodních obchodních smluv jakožto nejúspěšnějšího nezávazného unifikačního instrumentu UNIDROIT. Zabývá se jejich právní povahou a účelem a jejich ideovými základy. Nakonec příspěvek identifikuje dva základní cíle unifikace efektivitu a humanitu.

| | |

POL [*Rola UNIDROIT w unifikacji międzynarodowego prawa handlowego, ze szczególnym uwzględnieniem Zasad międzynarodowych umów handlowych*]

Artykuł zawiera analizę pozycji i zadań Instytutu UNIDROIT jako międzynarodowej organizacji międzyrządowej, zajmującej się unifikacją prawa (prywatnego). W pierwszej części artykułu znajduje się omówienie aspektów instytucjonalnych, uprawnień oraz procedur i instrumentów legislacyjnych, stosowanych przez tę organizację międzynarodową w celu unifikacji. W drugiej części przedstawiono analizę krytyczną Zasad międzynarodowych umów handlowych jako najlepszego dzieła unifikacyjnego UNIDROIT. Wreszcie artykuł określa dwa podstawowe cele unifikacji, a mianowicie efektywność i humanitaryzm.

DEU [*Die Rolle des UNIDROIT bei der Vereinheitlichung des internationalen Handelsrechts, unter besonderer Berücksichtigung der Grundregeln für Internationale Handelsverträge*]

Dieser Beitrag ist einer Analyse der Stellung und des Zwecks des UNIDROIT-Instituts als internationaler, mit der Harmonisierung des (Privat-)Rechts befasster Organisation gewidmet. Der erste Teil des Beitrags enthält eine Auseinandersetzung mit den institutionellen Aspekten, Kompetenzen, gesetzgeberischen Ansätzen und Instrumenten, auf die diese internationale Organisation bei der Rechtsvereinheitlichung zurückgreift. Der zweite Teil legt eine kritische Analyse der Grundregeln für Internationale Handelsverträge (also der erfolgreichsten Harmonisierungsleistung von UNIDROIT) vor. Abschließend identifiziert der Beitrag die zwei Grundziele der Rechtsvereinheitlichung: Effektivität und Humanität.

RUS [*Роль УНИДРУА в унификации международного коммерческого права с особым акцентом на «Принципы международных коммерческих договоров»*]

Статья посвящена анализу роли и цели Института УНИДРУА как международной межправительственной организации, деятельность которой посвящена унификации (частного) права. Первая часть статьи содержит анализ институциональных аспектов, полномочий, а также законодательных процедур и инструментов, используемых данной международной организацией для унификации. Во второй части – проводится критический анализ документа «Принципы международных коммерческих договоров» как самой успешной инициативы УНИДРУА в области унификации. Наконец, в статье определены две основные цели унификации – эффективность и гуманизм.

ESP   [*El papel de UNIDROIT en la unificación del derecho comercial internacional con especial referencia a los Principios de contratos comerciales internacionales*]

El artículo se centra en el análisis de la situación y la finalidad del Instituto UNIDROIT en su condición de organización internacional intergubernamental para la unificación del derecho (privado). La primera parte del artículo contiene un análisis de los aspectos institucionales y las competencias, así como de los procedimientos e instrumentos legislativos que esta organización internacional aplica en la unificación. La segunda parte presenta un análisis crítico de los principios de contratos comerciales internacionales como el paso de mayor éxito en materia de unificación de UNIDROIT. Por último, el artículo identifica dos objetivos básicos de la unificación: la eficiencia y la humanidad.

| | |

Katarzyna Sękowska-Kozłowska

The Role of Non-governmental Organisations in Individual Communication Procedures before the UN Human Rights Treaty Bodies

Key words:
human rights | United Nations | treaty body | non-governmental organization | individual complaint | Human Rights Committee | Committee on the Elimination of Racial Discrimination | Committee on the Elimination of Discrimination against Women

Abstract | *The aim of this article is to analyse different modes of Non-governmental organisations (NGOs) participation in individual communication procedures before the United Nations (UN) human rights treaty bodies. Although treaties laying down provisions on communication procedures remain silent as to the role of NGOs, in practice treaty bodies allow for some forms of their participation. In the light of jurisprudence of three bodies with the most extensive record in this matter, namely the Human Rights Committee, the Committee on the Elimination of Racial Discrimination and the Committee on the Elimination of Discrimination against Women, the article will discuss the role of NGOs acting as representatives of the petitioner, in their capacity as entities submitting communication on behalf of the victim, entities submitting individual complaints and as third parties (authors of amicus curiae briefs). The article will show that the jurisprudence of certain bodies has evolved as regards NGO participation, which proves that their position in individual communication procedures has become stronger.*

Katarzyna Sękowska-Kozłowska, Ph.D. is a senior researcher at the Poznań Human Rights Centre of the Institute of Legal Studies of the Polish Academy of Sciences. Her Ph.D. thesis on the *UN Committee on the Elimination of Discrimination against Women (CEDAW) was published in Polish (Komitet ONZ ds. Likwidacji Dyskryminacji Kobiet - ustrój, kompetencje, funkcjonowanie,* Toruń 2011). Her main fields of research are discrimination issues with special focus on gender discrimination and the UN human rights mechanisms.
e-mail: k.sekowska-kozlowska@inp.pan.pl

| | |

I. Preliminary Remarks

19.01. It is hard to deny the immense influence of Non-Government Organizations (NGOs) on today's human rights. Both large, multinational NGOs and small local organisations are active on many levels. Their work focuses mainly on activities aimed at the creation of legal standards (both on national and international levels) and participation in human rights monitoring.

19.02. Of course, one should not lose sight of the fact that today's interaction of NGOs and international human rights bodies is a phenomenon of merely the last decades. Before, and especially during the Cold War, the NGOs involvement in the human rights monitoring mechanism was controversial.[1] One can easily illustrate the evolution of NGOs relations with international control bodies by looking at their cooperation with the United Nations (UN) human rights treaty bodies,[2] which is particularly highlighted by their ever growing role in the state reports examination procedure. Even though the third sector is still an informal participant to this procedure, in practice it is hard to imagine its effective functioning without the possibility of NGOs submitting information, which for the members of control bodies constitute an

---

[1]　See, for example, Ida Lintel, Cedric Ryngaert, *The Interface between Non-governmental Organisations and the Human Rights Committee*, 15 INTERNATIONAL COMMUNITY LAW REVIEW 359, 362 (2013).

[2]　'Treaty bodies' are bodies set up under the most important UN human rights treaties to monitor States Parties' compliance with treaty obligations. These are: the Human Rights Committee established under the International Covenant on Civil and Political Rights (ICCPR) of 1966; the Committee on Social, Economic and Cultural Rights (CESCR) established under the International Covenant on Economic, Social and Cultural Rights (ICESCR) of 1966; the Committee on the Elimination of Racial Discrimination (CERD) established under the International Convention on the Elimination of All Forms of Racial Discrimination (ICERD) of 1965; the Committee on the Elimination of Discrimination against Women (CEDAW) established under the Convention on the Elimination of All Forms of Discrimination against Women (CEDAW Convention) of 1979; the Committee against Torture (CAT) established under the Convention against Torture and Other Cruel, Inhuman or Degrading Treatment or Punishment (CAT Convention) of 1984; the Subcommittee on Prevention of Torture (SPT) established under the Optional Protocol to the Convention against Torture and Other Cruel, Inhuman or Degrading Treatment or Punishment (OP CAT) of 2002; the Committee on the Rights of the Child (CRC) established under the Convention on the Rights of the Child (CRC Convention) of 1989; the Committee on Migrant Workers (CMW) established under the International Convention on the Protection of the Rights of All Migrant Workers and Members of Their Families (ICRMW) of 1990; the Committee on the Rights of Persons with Disabilities (CRPD) established under the Convention on the Rights of Persons with Disabilities (CRPD Convention) of 2006; and the Committee on Enforced Disappearances (CED) established under the International Convention for the Protection of All Persons from Enforced Disappearance (CPED) of 2006.

important, alternative source of knowledge, alongside reports submitted by governments.

19.03.	The individual communication procedure is the second most important instrument of control, next to the state reporting system, used by almost all treaty bodies.[3] Yet, unlike regional control mechanisms, such as the system of individual complaints to the European Court of Human Rights, treaty provisions governing communication procedures before UN committees do not provide for any form of NGOs participation. Nevertheless some treaty bodies allow to a certain extent for NGOs to participate in these procedures. This article will try to provide an overall picture of their practice by defining and examining different modes of NGOs participation in individual communication procedures before the UN human rights treaty bodies. The analysis will primarily focus on the jurisprudence of those committees, whose record in this matter is most extensive. This is namely the Human Rights Committee (HRC), which is competent to consider individual communications under Article 1 of the Optional Protocol to the International Covenant on Civil and Political Rights (OP ICCPR), the Committee on the Elimination of Racial Discrimination (CERD), which is competent to consider individual communications under Article 14 of the International Convention on the Elimination of All Forms of Racial Discrimination (ICERD), and the Committee on the Elimination of Discrimination against Women (CEDAW), whose competence to consider individual complaints is provided for in Article 1 of the Optional Protocol to the Convention on the Elimination of Discrimination against Women (OP CEDAW).

II. Modes of NGO Participation in Communication Procedures

19.04.	Although several dozen years have passed between the adoption of first provisions governing communication procedures, such as the Optional Protocol to the International Covenant on Civil and Political Rights of 1966, and the adoption of the latest measures, such as the Optional Protocol to the Covenant on Economic, Social and Cultural Rights of 2008, each committee has similar regulations in this respect. This means that no treaty contains provisions on NGOs participation in communication procedures. This fact may be surprising, given that

---

[3]	With the exception of the Committee on the Rights of the Child, whose competence to consider individual complaints will become operative when 10 state parties have ratified the Optional Protocol on a communications procedure of 2011 to the Convention on the Rights of the Child.

during that time the role of the third sector has greatly increased. This is best explained by the fact that even though no one should question the presence of NGOs in today's 'human rights universe', the fact remains that NGOs stand in natural opposition to the states which create international law. This is also why the idea of granting NGOs specific powers with regard to individual communications brings opposition from certain states,[4] especially since reaching consensus on an international level is far more difficult than under the regional system. All in all, certain committees do allow for some degree of NGO participation. There are four different modes, which will be looked at closely:

- An NGO acting in its capacity as a representative of the petitioner;
- An NGO acting in its capacity as an entity submitting communication on behalf of the victim;
- An NGO acting in its capacity as an entity submitting communication on its own behalf;
- An NGO acting in its capacity as a third party.

II.1. An NGO Acting as a Representative of the Petitioner

19.05. Acting as a representative of the petitioner is the most common form of NGOs participation in the communication procedures before treaty bodies. It is also the only form uncontested and admitted by all the committees. Despite the fact that treaties governing communication procedures contain no specific provisions on the possibility of submitting communications by representatives, it is foreseen by the rules of procedures of individual committees.[5] That being said, committees do not specify who can act as a representative, for example by restricting the circle of those entitled to professional representatives.[6] In practice, all committees accept that petitioners may be represented by NGOs,[7] as well as by other legal entities, e.g. trade

---

[4] See, for example, discussions surrounding the adoption of the OP CEDAW, Report of the Secretary General submitted to the Commission on the Status of Women at its 40th session, 11-22 of March 1996, E/CN.6/1996/10, paras. 66-70.

[5] See, for example, Rule 96(b) of the Rules of procedure of the HRC, or Rule 68 of the Rules of procedure of the CEDAW.

[6] The tone of discussions around the adoption of the Rules of procedure of the HRC suggests that this measure was destined mostly for professional representatives, MANFRED NOWAK, U.N. COVENANT ON CIVIL AND POLITICAL RIGHTS, Kehl am Rhein: Engel 834 (2nd. rev. ed., 2005).

[7] See, for example: views of HRC in *Llantoy Huaman* v *Peru*, No. 1153/2003, 24 October 2005; views of CERD in *Adan* v *Denmark*, No. 43/2008, 13 August 2010; views of CAT in

unions or religious associations.[8] The only requirement is the submission of the authorisation signed by the petitioner. Still, despite being assisted by a representative, the alleged victim remains the petitioner, i.e. the author of the communication. As a result, it is hard to agree with the opinion expressed in relation to the HRC's practice by Y. Tyagi, who maintains that the fact that this body does not oppose NGOs assisting individuals in submitting their communications, it proves its willingness 'to grant an appropriate but unofficial *locus standi* to NGOs without violating the letter of the [Optional] *Protocol)*',[9] since NGOs do not have separate procedural standing, and their role is restricted to classic procedural representation.

II.2. An NGO Acting as an Entity Submitting Communication on Behalf of the Victim

19.06. The situation described above needs to be contrasted with a case where the communication is submitted on behalf of a victim who is unable to submit it personally. This means that in the course of the procedure the alleged victim does not act before the committee him/herself, which usually is the case, but is substituted by a different person. Such possibility is foreseen by most treaties laying down individual communication procedures, and where the treaties are silent in that regard – as in the case of the OP ICCPR – that solution is available as a result of the control body's practice.[10]

19.07. Circumstances that prevent the victim of an alleged human rights violation to submit a communication (usually his/her death or disappearance) are usually the very same circumstances that prevent the victim from giving the petitioner his/her consent to act on his/her behalf. Thus, the petitioner must bring to the attention of the control body circumstances that prevented the alleged victim from giving authorisation and justify standing to bring the communication. The practice of the HRC, which dealt with most cases of this type, shows that the petitioner must provide evidence that he/she has personal links with the victim, in particular that he/she is a member of the victim's family. The HRC also allows for communications to be brought by

---

Ristic v *Yugoslavia*, No. 113/1998, 11 May 2011; views of CEDAW in *A.S.* v *Hungary*, No. 4/2004, 14 August 2006.

[8] MANFRED NOWAK, *supra* note 7, at 835.

[9] YOGESH TYAGI, THE UN HUMAN RIGHTS COMMITTEE: PRACTICE AND PROCEDURE, Cambridge: Cambridge University Press 403 (2011).

[10] See, for example, HRC jurisprudence concerning a series of communications submitted on behalf of Uruguayan political prisoners, in particular *Lopez* v *Uruguay*, No. 52/1979, 29 July 1981.

Czech Yearbook of International Law

distant relatives, e.g. cousins.[11] Failure to justify by the petitioner that he/she has a sufficiently close relationship with the victim would render the communication inadmissible.[12]

19.08. Such an approach is difficult to follow with regard to NGOs, whose relations with the victim are naturally different from family ties. A good example of this problem is the Decision of the HRC of 2007 in the case *Humanitarian Law Center v Serbia*.[13] The communication was brought on behalf of X, a minor boy, who became a victim of sexual abuse. According to the organisation, a number of irregularities that occurred during the investigation of the case by domestic authorities resulted in violation of the boy's rights protected by the ICCPR, including the prohibition of torture and inhuman treatment, right to privacy and rights of the child. The organisation had the consent of the boy's parents to represent him in domestic proceedings. This was extended by a social worker, who became the boy's legal guardian after the parents had been stripped of parental authority. The consent was subsequently revoked and restored a number of times, until it was finally withdrawn. At the time of bringing the communication to the HRC, the organisation had no knowledge about X's faith or his legal situation. Justifying its standing to represent the boy before the HRC, the organisation argued that based on the 'best interest of the child' test, referred to in HRC's jurisprudence, their communication should be declared admissible, as neither the Centre for Social Work, nor the boy's parents were interested in claiming his rights and did not act in his best interest, resulting in domestic proceedings against those responsible for the abuse being dropped. Moreover, the organisation was representing X in domestic proceedings until the power of attorney granted to it was revoked.

19.09. Deciding on the communication's admissibility, the HRC recalled that Children must generally rely on other persons to present their claims and represent their interests, and may not be of an age or capacity to authorise any steps to be taken on their behalf. A restrictive approach should thus be avoided. Indeed, it has been the constant practice of the Committee to consider that a parent has standing to act on behalf of his or her children without explicit authorisation from them. While a parent is the most appropriate

---

[11] More in MANFRED NOWAK, *supra* note 7, at 836.
[12] For example the HRC declared inadmissible a communication submitted by a Swedish Amnesty International activist on behalf of a Uruguayan political prisoner, as the author of the communication was unable to justify its standing, *U.R v Uruguay*, No. 128/1982, 6 April 1983.
[13] *Humanitarian Law Center v Serbia*, No. 1355/2005, 26 March 2007.

person to act on behalf of a child, the Committee does not exclude that the counsel of the child in the domestic proceedings may continue to present the child's claims to the Committee. Nonetheless, the Committee must still examine [...] whether counsel has authorisation from the child (or his or her immediate family) to act on his or her behalf, whether there are circumstances which prevented counsel from receiving such authorisation, or that given the close relationship in the past between counsel and the child it is fair to assume that the child did indeed authorise counsel to proceed with a communication to the Committee.[14]

19.10. Thus, the HRC did not *a priori* reject the possibility of submitting a communication by an NGO and the existence of a 'close relationship' between such an organisation and the alleged victim. The key problem was, however, the lack of authorisation from the child or his legal guardians. The HRC noted the organisation's argument that consent from his parents or the Centre for Social Work could not be obtained, since they were under the influence of the alleged perpetrators and refused to act in the best interest of the child. Yet, it seems that the decisive element in that case was the fact that at the time of bringing the communication to the HRC the organisation was not in contact with the boy and could not provide evidence that it had sought to obtain consent from the child to proceed with the communication. Therefore, it is hard to maintain that it had a sufficiently close relationship with the alleged victim, and 'the Committee [could] not even assume that the child [did] not object, let alone consent, to the author proceeding with a communication to the Committee'.[15]

19.11. This decision must be met with approval, as the declaration of inadmissibility was made with the view to protect the interests of the victim. The decision lends itself to the assumption that if the organisation which lodged the complaint had been able to provide better evidence of its relationship with the victim and its attempts to contact him, the HRC might have accepted it as petitioner, despite it lacking formal consent to proceed with the communication.

19.12. The analysis of the CEDAW's jurisprudence also shows that this body is open to permitting NGOs to submit complaints on behalf of alleged victims, who are unable to lodge complaints themselves. This statement could be illustrated by two 2007 views issued in twin domestic violence cases − *Goecke* v *Austria*[16] and *Yildirim* v *Austria*.[17]

---

[14] Ibid., para. 6.4.
[15] Ibid., para. 6.7.
[16] *Goecke* v *Austria*, No. 5/2005, 6 August 2007.
[17] *Yildirim* v *Austria*, No. 6/2005, 6 August 2007.

Both cases concerned a violation of the CEDAW Convention by Austria in that the State Party failed to provide appropriate protection to victims of domestic violence, who were killed by their husbands. In both cases the communications were submitted by two NGOs on behalf of the victims' children. The NGOs supported the victims, while they were still alive, in particular by assisting them during the court proceedings and informing the Police about the danger the victims faced. Nevertheless, it must be emphasised that in the proceedings before CEDAW both NGOs not only acted as representatives, but were also granted the status of 'the authors of the communication'. So, the status of petitioner was granted not to the relatives of the victims, but to the organisations acting on their behalf. Justifying their *locus standi* before the CEDAW, the organisations argued that

> It is justified and appropriate for them to submit the complaint on behalf of [the victim] — who cannot give consent because she is dead. [The petitioners] consider it appropriate to represent her before the Committee because she was a client of theirs and had a personal relationship with them and because they are special protection and support organisations for women victims of domestic violence [...]. They are seeking justice for [the victim] and to improve the protection of women in Austria from domestic violence so that her death would not be in vain.[18]

19.13. Moreover, the authors obtained written consent from the victims' children and/or their legal guardians. The CEDAW did not question these statements. The fact that in these cases the NGOs were given the status of authors leads to the presumption that even in situations where victims left no relatives, who could authorise the organisations to proceed with submitting the communication to the CEDAW, there is a good chance that their communications would stand. Unlike in *Humanitarian Law Center* v *Serbia*, referred to above, the organisations were able to prove their close relationships with the victims. It seems, however, that the mere fact that such a relationship existed should not be sufficient in situations where the victims had relatives or left any heirs, and the organisations did not receive their consent to submit the communication, or at least did not prove that they had sought to receive it. In such cases the communication should be declared inadmissible.

---

[18] *Goecke* v *Austria*, No. 5/2005, 6 August 2007, para. 3.13; *Yildirim* v *Austria*, No. 6/2005, 6 August 2007, para. 3.13.

II.3. An NGO Acting as an Entity Submitting Communication on Its Own Behalf

19.14. Without doubt the method of giving NGOs full competence in communication procedures before treaty bodies would be to allow them to submit individual communications on their own behalf. Unfortunately, unlike the European Convention on Human Rights or the Inter-American Convention on Human Rights, no treaty providing for the mechanism of individual communication to treaty bodies mentions organisations, or, more broadly, legal entities among the entities entitled to submit such communications. There are two approaches in that regard: some treaties allow communications to be lodged only by 'individuals',[19] and some by 'individuals or groups of individuals'.[20] As the subsequent analysis of the jurisprudence of the HRC and the CERD will show, the above determination is decisive as to whether an NGO will be granted standing before treaty bodies or not.

19.15. Provisions of the OP ICCPR on individual communications to the HRC allow the complaints to be submitted only by 'individuals'. As Manfred Nowak, a UN human rights system expert points out, restricting the circle of those competent to come forward with communications to individuals only was evidently intended. Indeed, the first draft of the treaty proposed by the Netherlands extended the possibility to submit communications to 'groups of individuals'. Nevertheless, the proposal was rejected, as concerns were raised that it would open the door to communications pouring from NGOs and the measure will turn into a sort of *actio popularis*. Thus, there is a gap between the substantive aspect of the rights enshrined in ICCPR, and procedural measures of protecting them laid down in the OP ICCPR, as a number of rights contained in the ICCPR (*inter alia* in Article 1, 18, 21, 22, 23, 25, 27) have also been extended to groups of individuals and legal entities.[21]

19.16. The current record of the HRC does not fill one with optimism that this gap could be bridged in its jurisprudence, as recommended by some academics,[22] since the body interprets the term 'an individual' literally, meaning natural persons only. Therefore communications concerning violations of rights of such legal persons as political parties[23] or different types of companies[24] have all been declared

---

[19]   These are: OP ICCPR (Art. 1), CAT Convention (Art. 22), ICRMW (Art. 77), CPED (Art. 31).

[20]   These are: ICERD (Art. 14), OP CEDAW (Art. 2), OP ICESCR (Art. 2), OP CRPD (Art. 1), OP CRC (Art. 5).

[21]   MANFRED NOWAK, *supra* note 7, at 829-830.

[22]   Ibid., at 830, footnote 7.

[23]   For example, *J. R. T.* v *Canada*, No. 104/1981, 6 April 1983.

inadmissible. Communications brought by NGOs are also dismissed as inadmissible. For instance, the HRC declared inadmissible a communication submitted by an Italian organisation for the protection of the rights of persons with disabilities.[25] The communication, concerning measures on access of persons with disabilities to employment, was submitted by the representatives of the association acting on behalf of the organisation and on their own – them being persons with disabilities or parents of such persons. The communication was declared inadmissible, as the NGO lacked personal standing. In the words of the HRC: 'according to Article 1 of the Optional Protocol, only individuals have the right to submit a communication. To the extent, therefore, that the communication originates from the [association], it has to be declared inadmissible because of lack of personal standing'.[26]

19.17. In its views of 1987 expressed in *Lubicon Lake Band* v *Canada*, which concerned a communication submitted on behalf of an Indian tribe by its chief, the HRC declared:

> The Optional Protocol provides a procedure under which individuals can claim that their individual rights have been violated [...]. There is, however, no objection to a group of individuals, who claim to be similarly affected [by the violation], collectively to submit a communication about alleged breaches of their rights.[27]

19.18. The HRC's practice shows, however, that its interpretation of the term 'group of individuals' is restricted to individual natural persons, who submit a communication collectively, and does not extend to organisations. The views expressed in *Beydon and others* v *France*[28] in 2005 show that attempts from NGOs to bypass this obstacle by means of, 'attacking' the HRC through the backdoor by submitting a communication individually by members of an association, not by the organisation itself, will most probably fail. The communication in question was submitted by 20 members of an association for the creation of the International Criminal Court. In their communication to the HRC they claimed that France violated their right to access to court and the right to take part in the conduct of public affairs by not

---

[24] For example, *A Newspaper Publishing Company* v *Trinidad and Tobago*, No. 360/1989, 14 July 1989; *S.M.* v *Barbados*, no. 502/1992, 31 March 1994; *Lamanga* v *Australia*, No. 737/1997, 7 April 1999.

[25] *A group of associations for the defence of the rights of disabled and handicapped persons in Italy* v *Italy*, No. 163/1984, 10 April 1994.

[26] Ibid., para. 5.

[27] *Lubicon Lake Band* v *Canada*, No. 167/1984, 26 March 1990, para. 32.1.

[28] *Beydon and others* v *France*, No. 1400/2005, 31 October 2005.

letting a public debate on the conditions of France's accession to the Rome Statute. As regards the petitioners' claim that their right to access to court was violated in domestic proceedings, the communication was declared inadmissible, since it was not the petitioners, but the association that was party to the domestic proceedings. As to the claim that the complainants were deprived of an effective judicial remedy, the HRC concluded that they did not prove that they were victims. Lastly, the HRC declared that the authors failed to substantiate the claim that their right to take part in the conduct of public affairs had been violated. The views are too general to hypothesise that if the complaint had been sufficiently substantiated, it would have been declared admissible, and that a communication concerning an alleged violation of NGO's rights would *de facto* have been considered as a communication submitted by its representatives. One of the issues that might arise here is whether the HRC would consider that all domestic remedies had been exhausted, if the party to domestic proceedings was the organisation and not individual complainants – members of this organisation. Nevertheless, so far the HRC seems to be very resistant to any attempts by NGOs to gain individual standing and there is nothing to indicate that its practice in that regard might change.

19.19. The practice of CERD is somehow different. Its interpretation of the term 'group of individuals' has evolved, which resulted in granting NGOs standing in the communication procedure before it. This evolution could be illustrated by four communications submitted by NGOs which the CERD considered over the time of just a few years. All the NGOs concerned claimed violations of ICERD provisions prohibiting the support and promotion of racial hatred. With regard to two Danish cases considered in 2003, the CERD found the communications inadmissible. First communication, *P.O.E.M and F.A.S.M v Denmark*,[29] was lodged by two NGOs acting for the rights of ethnic minorities. The case concerned a statement made by a Member of Parliament and the leader of one of the political parties, in which she said that the rise of multiculturalism in Denmark brings trouble such as gang formation and mass rape. The petitioners argued that discontinuation of criminal proceedings amounts to the violation of Denmark's obligations under ICERD. The CERD found the communication inadmissible, as the complainants failed to exhaust all domestic remedies. Indeed, no action on the domestic level was taken by the petitioners, and the alleged offence was reported to the Police by

---

[29] *P.O.E.M and F.A.S.M v Denmark*, No. 22/2002, 19 March 2003.

another NGO. By declaring the communication inadmissible, the CERD made no comments on the petitioner's standing and restricted itself to stating that domestic remedies have to be exhausted by the petitioners themselves and not by other organizations or individuals.[30] It is hard to disagree with this decision, unlike the second one, namely the decision in *Documentation and Advisory Centre on Racial Discrimination* v *Denmark*.[31] The case concerned a job advertisement published in a nationwide newspaper by a construction company seeking 'a Danish foreman' to work in Latvia. The Documentation and Advisory Centre on Racial Discrimination, who considered that such wording amounted to discrimination on grounds of national or ethnic origin, reported this incident to the Police. The complaint was dismissed. It is clear that, unlike in *P.O.E.M and F.A.S.M*, the author of the petition to the CEDR exhausted all domestic remedies. However, the treaty body questioned its standing. The petitioners used a twofold argument to justify its *locus standi*. First, they claimed that the head of the organisation herself was the victim of the alleged violation, because, since she was lacking Danish origin, it would have been futile for her to apply for the post. Second, the organisation itself was also a victim, as it represented a large group of persons of non-Danish origin discriminated against by the job advertisement in question. Although the CERD admitted that it had not excluded the possibility that a group of persons representing the interests of an ethnic group might submit an individual communication, it stated that in the case at hand the communication was inadmissible, since no member of the organisation or any other identifiable person, whom the petitioner would be authorized to represent, applied or showed the necessary qualifications for the advertised post. The CERD relied on the concept of *identifiable victim*,[32] stating that where no such victim exists, the communication cannot be considered. Such an approach practically prevented NGOs from submitting communications alleging breaches of the ICERD, in particular related to statements present in the public domain addressed to a wide range of unspecified recipients.

19.20. A real breakthrough came in 2005 with the views in *Jewish Community of Oslo e.a.* v *Norway*.[33] The communication was submitted by two Jewish Communities, three individuals and an antiracist NGO. The communication concerned a speech made during a march organised by

---

[30]   Ibid., para. 6.3.
[31]   *Documentation and Advisory Centre on Racial Discrimination* v *Denmark*, No. 28/2003, 19 August 2003.
[32]   Ibid., para. 6.7.
[33]   *Jewish Community of Oslo e.a.* v *Norway*, No. 30/2003, 15 August 2005.

a Nazi organisation in commemoration of Adolf Hitler and Rudolf Hess, in which immigrants and people of Jewish origin were *inter alia* accused of committing robberies, rapes and killings. The author of the speech was charged with a violation of the criminal code provisions which prohibit racial hatred. The case reached the Supreme Court, which acquitted the accused. The Court held that the statements in the speech were simply 'Nazi rhetoric' and that the conviction of the accused would be incompatible with his right to freedom of speech. In their communication to the CERD the complainants argued that Norway had violated the ICERD provisions in that the Supreme Court's judgment would serve as a precedent, which would hinder prosecution of Nazi propaganda. The petitioners claimed to be victims of the violation, as due to the judgment they would no longer be able to rely on the protection of the law in conducting their work against the dissemination of racial hatred and incitement to acts of violence. They also claimed that they lacked effective remedies to prevent such situations. The CERD agreed with the petitioners and declared their communication admissible. This decision must be regarded as progressive. The CERD relied on the concept of the 'potential victim', arguing that because the authors belonged to a particular ethnic group, the very existence of a certain legal standard affected them personally in that they faced an imminent risk of suffering racial violence, and therefore they were entitled to submit the communication. The CERD referred in that regard to the jurisprudence of the Human Rights Committee[34] and the European Court of Human Rights.[35] As to the

---

[34] See *Toonen v Australia*, No. 488/1992, 30 March 1994. The communication was submitted by a homosexual, an activist of the movement for the protection of the rights of homosexual persons, who challenged the provisions of the Tasmanian Criminal Code, claiming that they violated his rights contained in the ICCPR, including his right to privacy and non-discrimination. This code criminalised all forms of sexual contacts between consenting adult homosexual men. Even though the claimant had not been convicted based on these provisions, the HRC granted him victim status and considered that his rights under the ICCPR had been violated.

[35] See *Open Door and Dublin Well Woman v Ireland*, No. 14234/88&14235/88, 29 October 1992. The case originated in two applications brought by two NGOs engaged in counselling pregnant women, including providing them certain information concerning abortion facilities outside the Irish jurisdiction. The Irish Supreme Court ruled that the organisations' activities violated the constitutionally guaranteed right to life of unborn children, which, according to applicants, violated their right to freedom of speech. The application was joined by two Irish citizens, who argued that by its judgment the Supreme Court violated their right to receive information. The ECHR declared the application admissible in respect of the two women, holding that even though they had not been pregnant, they were in a child-bearing age so the Supreme Court's judgment affected them personally.

standing of legal entities, including NGOs, the CERD did not consider the fact that three of the authors are organizations posed any problem to admissibility. As has been noted, article 14 of the Convention refers specifically to the Committee's competence to receive complaints from 'groups of individuals'. The Committee considered that to interpret this provision in the way suggested by the State party, namely to require that each individual within the group be an individual victim of an alleged violation, would be to render meaningless the reference to 'groups of individuals'. The Committee had not hitherto adopted such a strict approach to these words. The Committee considered that, bearing in mind the nature of the organisations' activities and the classes of person they represent, they too satisfied the 'victim' requirement in article 14.[36]

19.21. Indeed, in its previous decisions, in particular in *Documentation and Advisory Centre on Racial Discrimination* v *Denmark*, the CERD did not directly challenge the *locus standi* of an NGO by saying that it could not be considered as victim because of its status. However, in practice its restrictive interpretation of the term 'victim' prevented it from considering the NGO's communication, as the CERD required that the 'identifiable vic*tim*' of the alleged violation be named. In the Norwegian case the more progressive interpretation of the admissibility requirements made it possible to consider the communication brought by the NGO.

19.22. The above interpretation found confirmation in the 2008 views in *Zentralrat Deutscher Sinti und Roma e.a.* v *Germany*.[37] The case concerned an article published in a Police journal, whose author claimed that criminality, as well as 'social parasitism', were the key characteristics of the Roma community. According to the petitioners, two of which were NGOs, the publication contributed to the dissemination of negative stereotypes against the Roma and fuelled hatred against the community. The criminal proceedings started by the organisations were discontinued. Referring to the *Jewish Community of Oslo e.a.* v *Norway* case, the CERD confirmed the NGOs' standing to bring the communication, and stated that bearing in mind the nature of the organisations' activities and the groups of individuals they represented, they satisfied the requirements to bring a communication. In the light of the foregoing, one can therefore argue that CERD has developed a settled practice of allowing NGOs to bring individual communications, provided that they individually exhaust domestic

[36] *Jewish Community of Oslo e.a.* v *Norway*, No. 30/2003, 15 August 2005, para. 7.4.

[37] *Zentralrat Deutscher Sinti und Roma e.a.* v *Germany*, No. 38/2006, 22 Febuary 2008.

remedies and that their activities be connected to the subject of communication.

II.4. An NGO Acting as a Third Party

19.23. Submission of *'amicus curiae* briefs' in the proceedings before international human rights bodies is an important element of NGO activities.[38] For instance, such a possibility is provided under the European Convention on Human Rights in its Article 36, which allows third party intervention – an instrument that NGOs use to a considerable extent.

19.24. Provisions governing the submission of communications to UN treaty bodies do not provide for the *amicus curiae* mechanism. Nevertheless, even though NGOs do sometimes submit such briefs,[39] there is no official information on this topic, because treaty bodies generally do not accept such interventions. This practice is slowly changing, as shown by the latest jurisprudence of the CEDAW. In its views on two cases considered in 2011[40] the CEDAW included information (albeit in a footnote) on *amicus curiae* briefs it received. The content of the briefs was not quoted in the views, nor did the CEDAW refer to them in any other way. However, the information on *amicus curiae* briefs suggests that in fact they had been admitted by this treaty body. This is an important step in the process of treaty bodies opening up to the idea of NGOs participating in the individual communications procedure.

19.25. The lack of possibility to submit *amicus curiae* briefs effectively limits NGOs' potential to influence treaty bodies' decisions. For this reason NGOs engaged in lobbying activities for admitting *amicus curiae* briefs in committee communication procedures. In 2011 a group of the largest human rights NGOs issued a statement on the strengthening of the treaty body individual communications procedures.[41] The statement should be seen as part of the long debate on the reform of

---

[38] More in: Lloyd Hitoshi Mayer, *NGO Standing and Influence in Regional Human Rights Courts and Commissions*, 36 BROOK. J. INT'L L. 911 (2010-2011).

[39] I. Lintel and C. Ryngaert note in relation to the Human Rights Committee's practice that 'There are instances where they [NGO's submissions] have been informally circulated to Committee members, or where they are submitted by the petitioners, as legal memoranda or opinions of third parties, as part of the petitioner's file', Ida Lintel &Cedric Ryngaert, *supra* note 2, at 372, footnote 76.

[40] *Teixeira* v *Brazil*, No. 17/2008, 25 July 2011; *L. C. v Peru*, No. 22/2009, 17 October 2011.

[41] NGO Statement: Strengthening the Treaty Body Individual Communications Procedures, available at: http://www2.ohchr.org/english/bodies/HRTD/docs/NGO Joint_statement_IC.pdf (accessed on 12 September 2013).

the UN human rights treaty body system. The statement includes the following recommendation: 'Where appropriate and relevant, Treaty Bodies should solicit and accept amicus curiae briefs submitted by NGOs regarding Individual Communications. Measures to inform the public of the submission of communications and to call for the submission of amicus curiae briefs should be implemented'.[42] Undoubtedly, in order to facilitate NGOs or other entities intervening as *amici curiae*, an Internet database should be created, which would contain information about the cases communicated to governments, similar to the ECHR database. Unfortunately, no such information source currently exists, as the data available on UN websites are restricted to committee views. This means that decisions are published only after the proceedings have ended which prevents the work of the treaty bodies, as regards individual communications, to be monitored systematically. This makes the whole process less transparent.

III. Conclusion

19.26. Even though the provisions governing the submission of individual communications to treaty bodies remain silent on the role of NGOs, in practice committees allow for some participation of NGOs in procedures before them. The jurisprudence of all treaty bodies shows that the possibility of NGOs acting as representatives of the victims raises no doubts. Treaty bodies are more restrictive when it comes to allowing NGOs to submit communications on behalf of the victims who were unable to give them their consent. Also the possibility of NGOs submitting individual communications on their own behalf is greatly restricted, although one can point to some evolution in this respect, especially in the jurisprudence of the CERD. Moreover, provisions governing the submission of communications to treaty bodies do not provide for the *amicus curiae* mechanism, albeit there are cases where such briefs were considered, especially by the CEDAW.

19.27. Measures governing communication procedures, even the latest ones, are not adapted to current realities, in which the third sector is an important and influential actor of modern societies. Paradoxically, this statement finds confirmation in the practice of treaty bodies concerning the state reporting mechanism. Currently, committees use the information provided by NGOs to such an extent, that it has become a crucial and unquestionable source of information and it is hard to see how the procedure could function effectively without this element. If NGOs could participate in individual communications procedures more

[42] Ibid.

actively, they would gain an important tool to influence the process of creation of international human rights standards.

19.28. Strengthening the role of NGOs in communication procedures could happen as a result of treaty bodies' practice. Such a step would help to avoid the troublesome and, most probably, unlikely process of treaty revision. A good example of this phenomenon is the practice of the CERD, whose progressive interpretation of the term 'groups of individuals' allows NGOs to submit communications. As regards *amicus curiae* briefs, although treaties do not provide for such a mechanism, treaty bodies could introduce it to their rules of procedure, which they adopt, making it part of the complaint procedure before them. Such an approach is certainly acceptable, as confirmed by the state reports examination procedure, whereby the current participation of NGOs is the result of the changing treaty bodies practice. Securing a broad standing for NGOs in the communication procedures would be an important step to strengthen their position in international control mechanisms and make the whole process more effective.

|||

Summaries

FRA [*Le rôle des organisations non-gouvernementales dans le cadre de procédures individuelles de recours suivant la Charte internationale des droits de l'homme*]

L'objectif est d'analyser ici les différents standards de participation des organisations non-gouvernementales dans les procédures individuelles de recours suivant la Charte internationale des droits de l'homme. Bien que les traités internationaux comportant des dispositions sur les dépôts des recours ne fixent aucune règle pour les organisations non-gouvernementales, les organismes définis par ces traités permettent dans une certaine mesure à ces organisations de prendre part aux procédures. On s'intéresse ici au rôle des organisations non-gouvernementales officiant comme représentant des plaignants, comme sujets agissant au nom des victimes, comme sujets déposant des plaintes individuelles et comme tierces parties (auteurs d'un recours à l'amicus curiae) du point de vue de la jurisprudence des trois organismes que sont le Comité des droits de l'homme, le Comité pour l'élimination de la discrimination raciale et le Comité pour l'élimination de la discrimination à l'égard des femmes. On présente ici la jurisprudence d'un certain nombre d'organismes par rapport à la participation d'organisations non-gouvernementales à des procédures de recours: elle montre que leur position s'est renforcée dans le cas de recours individuel.

CZE [*Úloha nevládních organizací v rámci individuálních postupů pro podání před orgány podle Úmluvy OSN o lidských právech*] *Účelem tohoto článku je rozbor různých standardů účasti nevládních organizací v individuálních postupech pro podání před orgány podle Úmluvy OSN o lidských právech. Ačkoliv mezinárodní úmluvy obsahující ustanovení o podáních a přednesech neupravují postavení nevládních organizací, orgány určené těmito úmluvami umožňují jistou míru účasti těchto organizací. Článek se zabývá úlohou nevládních organizací jednajících jako zástupci žalobců, jako subjekty činné jménem obětí, subjekty podávající individuální stížnosti a jako třetí strany (autoři podání amicus curiae) z pohledu judikatury tří orgánů, a to Výboru pro lidská práva, Výboru pro odstraňování rasové diskriminace a Výboru pro odstraňování diskriminace žen. Článek prezentuje judikaturu některých orgánů ohledně účasti nevládních organizací, která prokazuje, že jejich postavení v případě individuálních podání posílilo.*

| | |

POL [*Rola organizacji pozarządowych w postępowaniach skargowych przed traktatowymi organami ochrony praw człowieka ONZ*] *Przedmiotem artykułu jest analiza wariantów uczestnictwa organizacji pozarządowych (NGOs) w indywidualnych postępowaniach skargowych przed traktatowymi organami ochrony praw człowieka ONZ. W szczególności omówiona zostanie rola NGOs jako pełnomocnika skarżącego, podmiotu składającego skargę w imieniu ofiary, podmiotu składającego skargę we własnym imieniu oraz jako strony trzeciej (autora amicus curiae).*

DEU [*Die Rolle von nichtstaatlichen Organisationen im Rahmen des Individualbeschwerdeverfahrens gemäß den Menschenrechtsabkommen der Vereinten Nationen*] *Dieser Artikel dient dazu, die verschiedenen Standards zu analysieren, nach denen sich die Teilnahme nichtstaatlicher Organisationen am Individualbeschwerdeverfahren gemäß den Menschenrechtsabkommen der Vereinten Nationen richtet. Konkret analysiert wird die Rolle von nichtstaatlichen Organisationen in der Stellung als Vertreter der Anklage, als Sprecher der Opfer, als Beschwerdeführer und als Verfahrensbeteiligte ohne Parteistellung (die sich als amicus curiae in Schriftsätzen - sog. briefs - äußern).*

RUS [*Роль неправительственных организаций в рамках процедур подачи индивидуальных заявлений в органы власти в соответствии с Конвенцией ООН по правам человека*]
Целью данной статьи является анализ различных стандартов участия неправительственных организаций в процедурах подачи индивидуальных заявлений в органы власти в соответствии с Конвенцией ООН по правам человека. В частности, рассматривается роль неправительственных организаций, действующих в качестве представителей истцов, в качестве субъектов, выступающих от имени потерпевшего, субъектов, направляющих жалобы, а также в качестве третьих лиц (авторы заявлений amicus curiae).

ESP [*Papel de las organizaciones no gubernamentales en el marco de los procedimientos individuales de la presentación ante las autoridades según la Convención de la ONU sobre Derechos Humanos*]
El propósito de este artículo es analizar varias normas de participación por parte de organizaciones no gubernamentales en los procedimientos individuales de presentación ante las autoridades, según la Convención de la ONU sobre los Derechos Humanos. En concreto, se analiza el papel de aquellas organizaciones no gubernamentales que actúan como representantes de los demandantes, como agentes que actúan en nombre de las víctimas o que presentan denuncias, o como terceros (autores de la presentación de amicus curiae).

|||

Book Reviews

Book Reviews

Jaroslav Ivor | Libor Klimek | Jozef Záhora
Criminal Law of the European Union and Its Impact on the Legal Order of the Slovak Republic

Jaroslav Ivor, Libor Klimek & Jozef Záhora, Trestné právo Európskej únie a jeho vplyv na právny poriadok Slovenskej republiky *[Criminal Law of the European Union and Its Impact on the Legal Order of the Slovak Republic],* Žilina: Eurokódex, 2013, 888 pp, ISBN 978-80-8155-017-1.

The Slovak and Czech legal communities have been enriched by a new research monograph entitled *Criminal Law of the European Union and Its Impact on the Legal Order of the Slovak Republic.* It was written by the team of authors of Professor Jaroslav Ivor, JUDr., DrSc., Libor Klimek, JUDr., PhD. and Professor Jozef Záhora, JUDr., PhD. Professor Záhora is also the Editor in Chief. All authors work at the Faculty of Law, Pan-European University, in the Slovak Republic. Reviewers of the work are Jiří Jelínek, JUDr., CSc., who is head of the Department of Criminal Law, Faculty of Law of Charles University in Prague, the Czech Republic and Professor Ivan Šimovček, JUDr., CSc., who is head of the Department of Criminal Law, Faculty of Law, University of Trnava, in the Slovak Republic.

It is necessary to emphasise that the monograph is a very successful pioneering scientific work of high value. Taking into account the current state of professional legal literature, the work is important not only for the development of criminal law in the Slovak Republic, but also because of its language accessibility in the Czech Republic. The work is a positive step in Slovak doctrine.

The monograph is the first of its kind in the Slovak language. Thus, it is a precedent in the Slovak Republic. The work links European Union law to

Slovakian criminal law and adds an international context. The authors process fundamental issues of European Union law in the field of criminal law and its impact on the national law of the Slovak Republic. Moreover, they introduce expected current developments. In addition, they argue about fundamental issues, resulting in a number of considerations *lex ferenda* and offer constructive criticism. In some cases, the authors express their disagreement with views of the European Union. However, the monograph is sympathetic to the subject matter. Therefore, the work can be understood as a milestone in the sense that it begins a new stage of perception of Slovak criminal law, which is influenced by the standards of the European Union. In addition, the monograph is a source of knowledge for theory and practice.

The monograph is a complex compilation of highly professional and well-founded knowledge, stemming from the current legal status of the European Union, the Council of Europe, the United Nations and the domestic law of the Slovak Republic. It also elaborates on the case law of the Court of Justice of the European Union, the European Court of Human Rights, and the national courts of the Member States of the European Union.

Some of the sources of knowledge for the book were, among others, official documents of the European Union and its political and other institutions. The work required a significantly large number of professionally demanding translations of legal texts, especially in the English language. The bibliography exceeds 70 pages of listed sources. It includes more than 1,900 footnotes. All this testifies to its sophistication. The book is spectacular and extensive at 888 pages. It is divided into four parts: Fundamental Methodological Pillars, Euro Crimes, European Procedural Criminal Law and Bodies Co-ordinating Police and Judicial Co-operation. Each part contains chapters totalling 29 in all. It is accompanied by an introduction, conclusion, summary and registry.

In the first part, Fundamental Methodological Pillars, the authors introduce definitions and the system of the European Union (EU) criminal law (Chapter 1), the Europeanization of criminal law in its historical development (Chapter 2), the impact of the Lisbon Treaty on criminal law (Chapter 3), fundamental rights and EU criminal law (Chapter 4) and fragments of general parts of criminal law (Chapter 5).

The second part, Euro Crimes, is of a substantive nature. Its title suggests that it is focused on European offences. The authors analyse precisely those offences that in the European Union have been harmonised under its standards: terrorism (Chapter 6), trafficking in human beings and sexual exploitation of women and children (Chapter 7), money laundering (Chapter 8), corruption (Chapter 9), counterfeiting of means of payment (Chapter 10), computer crimes (Chapter 11), organised crime (Chapter 12), protection of the financial interests of the EU (Chapter 13), racism and xenophobia (Chapter 14), environmental crimes (Chapter 15) and drug trafficking (Chapter 16).

Czech Yearbook of International Law

Part three, European Procedural Criminal Law, is of a procedural nature. In this chapter, the authors deal with the procedural aspects of the standards of the European Union, especially in the light of judicial co-operation in criminal matters. These are: fundamental procedural rights in the European Union (Chapter 17), standing of victims in criminal proceedings and compensation to victims of crime (Chapter 18), fundamental pillars of co-operation in criminal matters and recognition and enforcement of decisions (Chapter 19), European arrest warrants (Chapter 20), freezing property and evidence in the European Union (Chapter 21), the mutual recognition of judgments and other decisions in criminal matters (Chapter 22), joint investigation teams (Chapter 23), other forms of co-operation in criminal matters between Member States of the European Union (Chapter 24) and the Schengen area and the Schengen co-operation in the field of criminal law (Chapter 25).

The fourth part, Bodies Co-ordinating Police and Judicial Co-operation, is a complex of knowledge on institutional issues. The authors deal with: Eurojustice (Chapter 26), networks of judicial cooperation in criminal matters (Chapter 27), Europol (Chapter 28) and OLAF (Chapter 29).

In conclusion, the Slovak Republic was missing a monograph of this nature. It is an extremely sophisticated achievement of the authors, with added value that is reflected in the synthesis of theoretical and practical issues, the expected developments in the field, or in constructive criticism and its own considerations *lex ferenda*. The work is a unique source of new information, not yet existing in Slovakian publications.

[Bystrík Šramel, JUDr., PhD.]
Assistant Professor

Faculty of Social Sciences, University of Ss. Cyril and Methodius
The author of the review graduated from the Faculty of Law, Trnava University in Trnava, the Slovak Republic. During the years of 2009 - 2012 the author was an internal PhD student at the Faculty of Law, Pan-European University in Bratislava, Department of Criminal Law, Criminalistics and Criminology of the Institute of Public Law. He currently is an assistant professor at the Faculty of Social Sciences of the University of Ss. Cyril and Methodius, Trnava, Slovak Republic. His research activities are mainly focused on issues of public prosecution in the Slovak Republic and in the world.
Email: bystrik.sramel@gmail.com

|||

Zdeněk Nový
Good Faith as Principle of Contract Law in International Commerce

Zdeněk Nový, Dobrá víra jako princip smluvního práva v mezinárodním obchodu [Good Faith as Principle of Contract Law in International Commerce], Prague: C.H.Beck Publishing House, 2012, 207 pp, ISBN: 978-807-400-376-9.

In the past few years the C. H. Beck Publisher presented in its Series: "Právní instituty" ["Concepts of Law"] readers with some very motivating and interesting studies, often written by authors from among the younger generation of lawyers. One of those studies is a book that should not go unnoticed and ought to draw the attention of any lawyer specializing in international commerce, or any lawyer dealing with the theory and practice of private law. It is a monograph written by Zdeněk Nový, senior lecturer at the Faculty of Law of Masaryk University in Brno. The book represents not only a very specific and structured analysis of the topic mentioned in the title, based on a very meticulous comparative approach, but also a methodologically accomplished and robust insight into a number of principles governing private law.

Depending on the values and moral principles adhered to by an individual and the legal culture by which they were influenced, the concept of good faith is considered either a "natural" and implicit principle. This principle is applicable as a corrective, supplementary or interpretative criterion with or without any normative rule. It may also be rejected as an unidentified and uncertain notion. The most common approaches to the concept are also modified opportune and artificial approaches ranging somewhere between the two extremes. The monograph authored by Zdeněk Nový provides excellent guidance, facilitating a practical understanding of the premises enshrined in important legal systems and important sources of non-state contract law. However, it also serves as a structured guide to the theoretical understanding of the concept of good faith. Consequently, the overlap with the general theory of private law ensures that the reviewed publication contains more than its title implies.

The author's deductions are prefaced by a reference to immanent criteria of equity and ethics that appear in law, albeit by different means and ways. Despite the absence of any statutory definitions, good faith has been interpreted as a manifestation of the above criteria, as a reference to one's own honesty and faith in the honesty and credibility of others.

The author is inclined towards a more practical, non-psychologizing and objective concept of good faith as a standard of conduct adopted by individuals and entities. He employs the etymological differences as a tool demonstrating the various elements ascribed to the concept of good faith in the selected legal systems, as well as an overlap with the concept of honesty and differences from the abuse of law. There are the reservations expressed against the concept of good faith as in English law of "brazen merchants" which is entirely unfamiliar with the concept and opposite to U.S. federal law representing the perspective of preference for legal certainty and the actual wording of contracts. The author recognizes the functionality of "bona fide" as a guarantee of effective commerce, which the concept of good faith releases from the necessity to deal with each and every casuistic unethical aspect of negotiations between business partners and which therefore reduces the transaction costs in an atmosphere of legitimate expectations of decency, honesty and reasonability, significantly limiting the elements of "hazardous games". This may also have direct economic effects and boost the willingness to invest. The penalty for a lack of good faith is construed as a kind of legal penalty for unlawful, uncooperative conduct, even if it is not specified in any particular detail. The importance of the corrective criterion of good faith increases with the duration of commercial connections. The vague concept of good faith also facilitates the economically effective and predictable filling of "gaps" in contracts and legal rules can be interpreted in the respective context, while oscillating between individualistic and cooperative contractual ethics. The former emphasizes the merchant's own economic interests, while the latter prioritizes the prevalent social values and the benefit of the other party.

The author has analysed the topic of his choice with impeccable methodological diligence and according to *lex artis*. He postulated a hypothesis that contract law in international commerce involves the standard of good faith, the elements of which are the same whether the applied law is of a state or non-state origin (p. 27). When examining the standard, the author does not settle for vague generalities, but breaks good faith down into three fundamental functions: supplementary, corrective and interpretative. The second hypothesis has been articulated as a presumption that good faith constitutes an autonomous principle in international arbitration. Again this is irrespective of the state or non-state origin of the source of contract law referring to good faith. The two hypotheses have been examined from the standpoint adopted by important European legal systems (Germany, France and Great Britain) and U.S. law. The functions of good faith constituted *tertium comparationis* of the above legal systems. The author applies this criterion to the examined legal systems most thoroughly, yet avoiding any excessive explications.

One of the most valuable assets of the book is that it is not a crabbed and useless compilation of tens and hundreds of boring pages deprived of any essence, but a very concise, clear and precise explication of the substance. The author has successfully avoided any information that would be redundant and purposeless from the perspective of his topic. The result is an extraordinarily valuable and compact study, which, despite its relative brevity, is very persuasive and informative. It can also serve as a practical tool with which lawyers practicing in the area of international commerce can orient themselves.

Reading the chapter on the German concept of good faith (*Treu und Glauben*, p. 37 et seq.), one realizes how its emphasis on "immanent social-ethical limits of the law" influenced our "natural-law" perception of the concept of good faith and our expectations regarding its practical influence. The contrast becomes clear when compared to the more reserved French approach (p. 53 et seq.), which is based on economic and political liberalism and often denies any significance of "good faith". Nonetheless, even the French concept invokes the "spirit of the contract", which no reference to the simple wording of the contract can override.

Of all the examined legal systems, English law has adopted the most reserved approach to good faith (see p. 64) Here the author refers to a statement made by an English professor of business law, who says that "it may come as a surprise, but we are fairly unclear on the concept of good faith".

There is a rigorous adherence by English law to individual contract terms as expressed, for instance, in the belief that if the contract explicitly provided for a particular situation in any individual provision and the situation occurs, the parties ought to know for certain that the terms of the contract will simply be enforced – p. 66. This is also reflected in the current, and much more rigorous approach of English courts to the binding force of the contract, and to the detriment of the principle of protecting the weaker party (cf. the recent conflicting verdicts passed by the German and by the British Supreme Courts regarding the lawfulness of bank account fees – see Právní rozhledy 13-14/2013, p. 144 et seq.). The author mentions that, under English law, each party is entitled to principally advance his or her interests (individualistic concept), short of misleading the other party. He notes that despite the above, and notwithstanding the reserved approach to the corrective function of good faith, the consideration for reasonable expectations of honest people ("good faith" – p. 69) is gaining ground.

The concept of good faith under U.S. contract law is obviously influenced by German legal thinking. Nevertheless, contrary to German law, it does not recognize pre-contractual liability based on good faith. U.S. law is specific on the combination and mutual supplementation of the individual approaches to good faith as a moral and economically utilitarian concept.

Following an analysis of four legal systems and jurisprudences, the author concludes with a persuasive summary that German law is the closest to the extreme pole of cooperative ethics. French and U.S. law are nearer to the pole of individualistic ethics. The law of Great Britain contains no explicit concept of good faith at all. The author has employed a matrix table to communicate the finding that good faith has different functions in each of the examined national legal systems and that a breach of good faith entails different consequences. Hence, good faith does not represent a standard with uniform elements. The author's first hypothesis is thereby disproven. However, all of the examined legal systems share one principle, namely that parties do not possess the autonomy to eliminate good faith from their contract.

The author continues with an analysis of the concept of good faith in selected non-state sources, again employing the *tertium comparationis* criterion – the functions of good faith. The author has again concluded that the sources of contract law of non-state origin, similar to state legal systems in the examined countries, do not represent any uniform standard of good faith as concerning the possibility of the parties to make dispositions with the standard of good faith. The parties are free to exclude good faith under Article 7(1) CISG (United Nations Convention on Contracts for International Sale of Goods). The UPICC (Unidroit Principles of International Commercial Contracts) and the DCFR (Draft Common Frame of Reference) stipulate, where they become the governing law, that the incorporation of good faith is mandatory.

Concerning the elements (the function) of the standard of good faith, all non-state sources incorporate the corrective, interpretative and supplementary function thereof; hence, it is possible to conclude, in this context, that a uniform standard exists. The same applies to the consequences of breaching good faith, which are in all of the above cases limited to the reduced possibility to insist on rights arising from the contract and on legal defence or remedy. They do not include compensation for damage or losses, the possibility to cancel (withdraw from) a contract or the correction of the contract or the rule in a non-state source (p. 150). State sources allow a broader spectrum of consequences punishing the breach of good faith.

The book also examines empirical data regarding the application of good faith in international arbitration. It is an empirical probe into the decision-making practice, which, naturally, is limited with respect to how telling it can be, but it suitably illustrates the presented hypotheses. The author is aware of the limited number of examined cases and the inevitable limited statistical conclusiveness and validity of his conclusions. The author has analysed 18 publicly available awards within the jurisdiction of the International Arbitration Court of the International Chamber of Commerce that relate to the application of good faith. These more or less illustrative examples confirmed, or rather illustrated, the author's findings and his conclusions.

The examined cases indicated that the arbitrators applied the concept of good faith mostly in terms of contract law of state origin, although they were ready to apply a somewhat different interpretation compared to an interpretation pursuant to national legal systems. But even the divergent interpretations were based either on different national legal systems, or on sources of contract law of non-state origin (such as the UPICC) The author has explained this phenomenon as the arbitrators endeavour to persuade the parties that they do not apply national law to international commercial contracts mechanically. This explanation is not entirely uncontroversial. Naturally, the arbitrators could have been guided by these artificial "meta-reasons", but the modification of national rules and the discretion of the arbitrators might simply have been better suited to the nature of the agreement, or the requirement of a just resolution of the dispute.

The hypothesis has been persuasively disproven that good faith constitutes an autonomous principle in international arbitration, which would be independent of the concepts of good faith in sources of contract law, whether of state or of non-state origin.

From the overall perspective, the book is a most valuable contribution to the discussion on the essence and function of good faith, both generally and in relation to international commerce and international arbitration. The years of systematic effort on the part of the author, concentrated in a consistent, representative and apposite treatise, enable the Czech reader to become familiar, in a very comfortable manner, with the discussion on the essence of good faith and its application in several influential legal systems. The author's expertise and proficiency in foreign literature is above the usual Czech standard and can easily be compared to similar works published in countries with an uninterrupted continuity of historical development. The author's methodological austerity and systematic approach in theoretical and comparative chapters also stand out as exceptional, together with the conservatism and poignancy of his proven conclusions and his concise and succinct style. The book will no doubt attract the attention of academics and students alike, together with practitioners, businessmen, judges, attorneys and arbitrators.

[**Prof. JUDr. Josef Bejček, CSc.**]
Faculty of Law, MU, Brno

Formerly the Dean of the Faculty of Law of Masaryk University in Brno, he currently chairs the Commercial Law Department of the same faculty. He has been called upon as an expert witness in important international arbitrations. He has been a member of the Remonstrance Commission of the Czech Antitrust Office. He works as an arbitrator and as an attorney. He is a member of several scientific councils and international scientific organizations. He has authored a number of articles, studies, and textbooks.
Email: Josef.Bejcek@law.muni.cz

| | |

News & Reports

News & Reports

Current Events,
Past and Ongoing CYIL and CYArb® Presentations

I. Current Events
I.1. Selected Scientific Conferences, Seminars, Academic Lectures and Other Professional Events in the Czech Republic[1]

OLOMOUC [CZE] 9 – 10 May 2013 – VIIth International Research Conference "**Olomoucké právnické dny 2013**" [**Olomouc Days Of Law**] held jointly by the Faculty of Law Palacký University Olomouc.[2]
Special attention to be paid to:
➤ Section EU Law – "**Application of EU law by national Constitutional Courts in Visegrad countries**" – chaired by Václav Stehlík and Ondrej Hamuľák;
➤ Section of Public International Law – "**International Aspects of the Creation or Extinction of a State or 20th Anniversary of the Independent Czech Republic**" – Chaired by Pavel Bureš;

---

[1] Contributions mentioned herein represent a selection from papers related to issues with an international element. CYIL editors hereby apologize to the lecturers for omitting some of them and their topics due to the limited space provided for this section. Editors referred especially to published and other accessible information. Readers are specifically warned that the information about papers presented at the individual conferences and other academic and scientific events is only a selection and definitely does not provide a full report on the entire proceedings and the academic scope of each particular event.

[2] Further information available on http://www.opdny.upol.cz/?page_id=169 [Last visit May 1st 2013].

> Section Financial Law and Economy – **"Current Issues of Financial Law in Central European Territory"** – chaired by Zdenka Papoušková;
> Section Private International Law (Conflict-of-Laws) – **"International Court Jurisdiction"** – chaired by Renáta Šánová and Michal Malacka.

PRAGUE [CZE] 13 – 14 June 2013 – Seminar of DRI International (The Voice of the Defense Bar) [USA][3] **"Hot Topics in International Dispute Resolution"**

PRAGUE [CZE] 22 October 2013 – International Researchers´ Conference **"Rights and Duties Related to EU-Citizenship"**. Organized by the Faculty of Law Charles University in Prague jointly with the Office of the Government Czech Republic.

PRAGUE [CZE] 31 October 2013 "3rd Investment Treaty Arbitration Conference 2013". Organized by the Ministry of Finance of the Czech Republic.

PLZEŇ / PILSEN [CZE] 1 November 2013 – Third International Researchers´ Conference **"Current Issues of Arbitration"**. Organized by the Dept. of International Law, Faculty of Law, University of West Bohemia in Pilsen, Czech Republic.[4]

BRNO [CZE] 14-15 November 2013 – VIIth International Conference **Days-of-Law 2013**. Organized by the Faculty of Law, Masaryk University Brno, Czech Republic.[5]

Section – Trade in Goods – Its Regulation in International Law and Common Commercial Policy of the EU
> Mgr. et Mgr. **Helena BONČKOVÁ**, LL.M., Czech Republic – *Trade in Goods: Supreme Courts' Preliminary References*
> **Krzysztof DOBIEŻYŃSKI**, PhD, Poland – *Protection of Freedom of Description of Goods and Grounds for Refusal of Trade Marks*
> Mgr. **Jakub HARAŠTA**, Czech Republic – *Cybersecurity and Dual-use Goods*
> Mgr. **Eva HLADKÁ**, Czech Republic – *State v. International Trade Regulation: Economic Sanctions of the USA*
> Mgr. **Anna CHURSHINA**, LL.M., Russian Federation – *Legal regulation of the non-conventional trademarks in the EU and Russia*

---

[3]   Further information available on www.dri.org.
[4]   Further details see http://fpr.zcu.cz/research/Rozhodci/ [Last visit 20 November 2013]. The Yearbooks CYIL and CYArb® were General Partner of the Conference.
[5]   Further details see http://www.dnyprava.cz [Last visit 23 November 2013].

➢ **Filip KŘEPELKA**, Czech Republic – *Czech Republic Methanol Poisonings 2012 a Free Movement of Goods in the European Union*
➢ Mgr. **Peter PAVLOVIČ**, Czech Republic – *The Kimberley Process Certification Scheme for Prevention of Trade in Conflict Diamonds Revisited*
➢ **Jan PETROV**, Czech Republic; Mgr. **Roman ŘÍČKA**, Czech Republic – *The "Recycling Conflict" of the EU and the Russian Federation in the Context of the WTO*
➢ JUDr., PhDr. **Miroslav SLAŠŤAN**, PhD., Slovak Republic – *Free movement of goods vs. fundamental rights*
➢ **Mariia SOLOVEVA**, Russian Federation – *The correlation between the EU and the WTO legislations on international trade of goods: problem aspects*
➢ **Dušan SULITKA**, Czech Republic – *Judicial Review in EU Law: Challenging the Common Commercial Policy Measures (Not Only) after the Lisbon Treaty*
➢ Mgr. **Kateřina UHLÍŘOVÁ**, Ph.D., LL.M., Czech Republic; Ph D **MARIUS VACARELU**, Ph D , Romania – *Shale gas and its legal dimensions*

Section – The New Czech Civil Code from the Perspective of International Commercial Transactions
➢ JUDr. **Filip ČERNÝ**, Czech Republic – *Polemics on absence of material norms of international private law in international trade*
➢ JUDr. **Petr DOBIÁŠ**, Ph.D., Czech Republic – *Insurance of the Complete Industrial Plants in International Trade*
➢ JUDr. **Klára DRLIČKOVÁ**, Ph.D., Czech Republic – *Application of the New Civil Code on the International Sale of Goods*
➢ RNDr. Mgr. **Hana FUNKOVÁ**, Czech Republic – *Conflict of Laws Rules for an Insurance Contract under Old and New Private International Law Act*
➢ Mgr. **Slavomír HALLA**, Czech Republic – *Assignment of contract and its impacts on the subjective scope of arbitration clause*
➢ JUDr. **Jan HAVLÍČEK** , Czech Republic
➢ **Ivo HEGER**, Czech Republic – *Standard Terms & Conditions in International Trade*
➢ JUDr. **Miluše HRNČIŘÍKOVÁ**, Ph.D., Czech Republic
➢ **Pavlína JANEČKOVÁ**, Czech Republic – *Usages in the International Trade*
➢ Mgr. **Tomáš KOZÁREK**, Czech Republic – *Pre-contract liability – comparation existing regulations and the new Civil Code*
➢ Mgr. **Jaroslav KRÁLÍČEK**, Czech Republic – *Formation of the contract under the new Czech Civil Code as an alternative to CISG*

➢ JUDr. **Tereza KYSELOVSKÁ**, Ph.D., Czech Republic – *Selected Issues of Electronic Contracting in the view of CISG, the New Civil Code and CESL*
➢ **Radvan NOVÁČEK**, Czech Republic; **Mária PASTORKOVÁ**, Czech Republic – *Liquidated damages under the New Civil Code with the connection to CISG*
➢ JUDr. Mgr. **Magdalena PFEIFFER**, Ph.D., Czech Republic; Mgr. **Kateřina REMSOVÁ**, Czech Republic – *Factual defect in the view of new Czech Civil Code and CISG*
➢ Mgr. **Iveta ROHOVÁ**, Czech Republic – *Standard terms as part of international sales contract with a view to the New Civil Code (in comparison with CISG and UNIDROIT Principles)*
➢ Bc. **Irena RYŠÁNKOVÁ**, Czech Republic; Mgr. **Iva ŠIMKOVÁ**, Czech Republic – *Damages under the new Civil Code – comparison with the CISG*
➢ **Josef ZICH**, Czech Republic

PRAGUE [CZE] 21 – 22 November 2013 – International Researchers' Conference "**Current Problems of Law in Entrepreneurship of Czech Republic and European Union**". Organized by the Dept. of Enterprise and EU Law, Faculty of International Relations, University of Economics in Prague on the occasion of the 60th Anniversary of Est. the University.

II. Past and Ongoing CYIL and CYArb® Presentations
II.1. Past Presentations in 2013

➢ The *Ninth Annual Leading Arbitrators' Symposium on the Conduct of International Arbitration*, Vienna [Austria], 25 March 2013
➢ The *Seventh Annual Investment Treaty Arbitration Conference*, Washington D.C. [USA], 22 April 2013
➢ The *VIIth International Conference "Days-of-Law-2013"*, Brno [CZE], 14 – 15 November 2013, organized by the Faculty of Law, Masaryk University, Brno, Czech Republic.
➢ University of International and Public Relations, Prague *Conference on Democratic Peace* under the auspices of Deputy Prime Minister and Minister of Interior Czech Republic, within the program *Prague Legal Autumn*, Prague [CZE], 21 November 2013
➢ *Conference on Court Litigation and ADR* under the auspices of the President of the Czech Bar Association, Deputy Mayor of the City of Prague and the CYArb®, within the series of events Prague "Prague Judicial Autumn."

II.2   Selected Ongoing Presentations in 2014

The CYIL and the CYArb® Will Hold Presentations (among Other Projects) in the Following 2014 Events:[6]

> ➤ The *Tenth Annual Leading Arbitrators' Symposium on the Conduct of International Arbitration*, Vienna [Austria]
> ➤ The *Eighth Annual Investment Treaty Arbitration Conference*, Washington D.C. [USA]
> ➤ The *Congress of the International Academy of Comparative Law*, Vienna [Austria]

Selected Bibliography for 2013

Compiled by:
Alexander J. Bělohlávek, Prague (Czech Republic)

Opening Remarks:
This overview lists only works published in 2013. The individual chapters into which this overview is divided always cover both substantive and procedural issues.

Titles in translations are indicative.

I. (Public) International Law, including Constitutional Issues and Other Public-law Areas with Transnational Dimensions and Including the Legal Issues of International Business Relations, International Relationships.[7]

I.1. [CZE] – [CZECH REPUBLIC] – Titles Published within the Czech Republic

Monographs and Collections

Michal Bobek; Jiří Kmec; David Kosař; Jan Kratochvíl et al. *Dvacet Let Evropské úmluvy v České republice a na Slovensku* [title in translation – *Twentieth Anniversary of the European Convention in the Czech Republic and in Slovakia*]. Prague, C. H. Beck, 2013.

---

[7] This sub-chapter includes some publications on selected EU law topics if they cross-boarding another areas of public [international] law and / or constitutional law. Predominantly EU law publications see the separate sub-chapter below.

Simona Stočesová. *Omyl v českém a zahraničním trestním právu* [title in translation – *Error in Czech and Foreign Criminal Law*]. Plzeň [Czech Republic]: Vydavatelství a nakladatelství Aleš Čeněk, s.r.o., 2013.

Bulletin advokacie [*Bulletin of the Czech Bar*], **Prague: Česká advokátní komora** [*Czech Bar Association*], **2012, ISSN: 1210-6348**[8]
Dominika Barnetová. *K otázce nepřiměřené délky trestního řízení a prostředkům nápravy zejména s přihlédnutím k judikatuře ESLP* [title in translation – *The Issue of Inadequate Length of Criminal Proceedings and Legal Remedies, Taking in Particular Account of Judicial Decisions of the ECHR*]. No. 5, p. 31-34.

Mezinárodní politika [Title in translation – *International Politics*], **Prague: Ústav mezinárodních vztahů** [Institute of International Relations], **2013, Vol. 37, ISSN: 0543-7692.**
Veronika Bílková. *Arabské jaro a uznání povstalců – za co vlastně* [title in translation – *Arab Spring and Recognition of Rebels – Recognized as What, Actually?*]. No. 1.
Samuel Bozek. *Brazilia: soft power mocnost a jej geopoliticky vplyv* [title in translation – *Brazilia: Soft Power and Its Geopolitical Influence*]. No. 9.
Marie Bydžovská. *Analýza problémů irských bank* [title in translation – *Analysis of the Problems Troubling Irish Banks*]. No. 2.
Marek Čejka. *Kdo jsou vlastně islamisté v Arabském jaru?* [title in translation – *Who Are the Islamists in the Arab Spring?*]. No. 1.
Tomáš Ehler. *Německo-ruské energetické vztahy* [title in translation – *German-Russian Energy Relations*]. No. 3.
Linda Flanderová. *Kung-fu, pandy a Konfucius, ale co dál?* [title in translation – *Kung-Fu, Pandas and Confucius, But What Next?*]. No. 5.
Linda Flanderová. *Soft power: mít či nemít?* [title in translation – *Soft Power: To Have or Not to Have?*]. No. 9.
Petr Fojtík. *Budoucnost transformačního nástroje a západní Balkán* [title in translation – *The Future of the Transformation Instrument and the Western Balkans*]. No. 7.
Olga Francová. *Vrátí se keltský tygr* [title in translation – *The Celtic Tiger Will Return*]. No. 2.
Rudolf Fürst. *Plíživá kuomintangizace Komunistické strany Číny* [title in translation – *Insidious Kuomintangisation of the Chinese Communist Party*]. No. 5.

---

[8]   Papers published in Czech with abstracts in a foreign language. Abstracts in English and in German.

Adam Gazda. *Řecko-makedonský spor o název. Jaký má vliv na integraci do EU?* [title in translation – *Greek-Macedonian Name Dispute. How Does it Influence Integration in the EU?*]. No. 7.

Vladimír Handl; Daniel Helwig. *Německé volby a česko-německé vztahy* [title in translation – *German Elections and Czech-German Relations*]. No. 3.

Roman Joch. *Soft power coby doplněk hard power, nikoli však její náhrada* [title in translation – *Soft Power as an Appendix to, Not a Substitute for Hard Power*]. No. 9.

Petr Kalinič. *Fetih 1453. Redefinice sekularismu* [title in translation – *Fetih 1453. Redefinition of Secularism*]. No. 1.

Petr Kalinič. *Red Dawn – militarizace USA a "tatarská invaze"* [title in translation – *Red Dawn – Militarization of the United States and the "Tatar Invasion"*]. No. 5.

Petr Kalinič. *5 Days of War – propaganda v rusko-gruzínském konfliktu* [title in translation – *5 Days of War – Propaganda in the Russian-Georgian Conflict*]. No. 8.

Petr Kaniok. *Post-lisabonské předsednictví: vliv, který není vidět* [title in translation – *Post-Lisbon Chairmanship: Invisible Influence*]. No. 2.

Jakub Kulhánek. *Rusko a Východní partnerství: geopolitické soupeření prozatím nehrozí* [title in translation – *Russia and Eastern Partnership: No Geopolitical Competition Imminent Yet*]. No. 4.

Jan Kužvart. *Al-Džazíra: televize v osidlech zahraniční politiky Kataru* [title in translation – *Al Jazeera: Television Ensnared by Qatar Foreign Policy*]. No. 8.

Rostislav Moric. *Klimatické politiky EU a konkurenceschopnost* [title in translation – *EU Climatic Policies and Competitiveness*]. No. 6.

Břetislav Panák. *Čínský film "Back to 1942"* [title in translation – *Chinese Film "Back to 1942"*]. No. 5.

Břetislav Panák. *Admirál Čeng Che. Může být historie použita jako soft power?* [title in translation – *Admiral Zheng He. Can History Serve as Soft Power?*]. No. 9.

Petr Patočka. *Kam bude směřovat energetická politika EU po roce 2020?* [title in translation – *Where Will Be the EU Energy Policy Heading after 2020?*]. No. 6.

Jana Peterková. *Česká veřejná diplomacie v odrazu změn* [title in translation – *Czech Public Diplomacy in the Reflection of Changes*]. No. 9.

Mariana Pítrová. *Berlusconi: manuál na propojení politiky a médií* [title in translation – *Berlusconi: Manual for Interconnecting Politics and Media*]. No. 8.

Marino Radačič. *Chorvatsko v Evropské unii: pragmatik bez iluzí* [title in translation – *Croatia in the European Union: Pragmatist without Illusions*]. No. 7.

Tomáš Rezek. *Kybernetická bezpečnost a irské předsednictví* [title in translation – *Cybernetic Security and Irish Presidency*]. No. 2.

Michael Romancov. *Rusko a Evropa. Úvaha o sousedství* [title in translation – *Russia and Europe. Essay on Neighbor Relations*]. No. 4.

Lucie Uhlířová. *Konflikt v Sýrii ohrožuje Jordánsko* [title in translation – *The Conflict in Syria Threatens Jordan*]. No. 1.

Klára Sutlovičová. *Pomůžou Irové krachujícímu emisnímu obchodování z bryndy?* [title in translation – *Will the Irish Help the Crashing Emission Trading Clear the Hurdle?*]. No. 2.

Josef Šmída. *Přehrada Belo Monte: katastrofa v přímém přenosu* [title in translation – *The Belo Monte Dam: Disaster Live*]. No. 6.

Josef Šmída. *Koncept Buen vivir: Ochrana lidskosti i životního prostředí* [title in translation – *The Concept of Buen Vivir: Protection of Humanity and Environment*]. No. 6.

Lukáš Tichý. *Elektřina a plyn ve vztazích EU-Rusko* [title in translation – *Electricity and Gas in EU-Russia Relations*]. No. 4.

Filip Tuček. *Středomoří: vysoká hra o plyn* [title in translation – *The Mediterranean: Great Game for Gas*]. No. 1.

Věra Veselá. *Svět očima Tálibánu* [title in translation – *The World through the Eyes of the Taliban*]. No. 10.

Michal Vít. *Německo zachraňuje euro – mnoho povyku pro nic?* [title in translation – *Germany Saves the Euro – Much Ado about Nothing?*]. No. 3.

Jakub Záhora. *Přinesou předčasné volby v Izraeli opět vítězství pravice?* [title in translation – *Will the Right Wing Parties Again Succeed in the Early Elections in Israel?*]. No. 1.

Mezinárodní vztahy [Title in translation – *International Relations*], **Prague: Institute of International Relations Prague, 2013, Vol. 48, ISSN: 0323-1844.**[9]

Filip Fuxa. **Džihádistický diskurz teroristické propagandy na internetu** [title in translation – *The Jihadi Discourse of the Terrorist Propaganda on the Internet*]. No. 2, p. 5-26

Jaroslava Gahurová. *Vnější migrační vládnutí Evropské unie* [title in translation – *External Migration Governance of the European Union*]. No. 2, p. 91-115.

---

[9] Contributions published in Czech. Abstracts regarding the core articles of the individual issues in English. Information on the periodical and abstracts of the papers available in electronic version at http://www.iir.cz/display.asp?ida=155&idi=401.

Michal Hrušík. *Kauza pašovania orgánov v Kosove: Iniciatívy, zlyhania a nové možnosti medzinárodného spoločenstva* [title in translation – *Organ Smuggling in Kosovo: Initiatives, Failures and New Opportunities for the International Community*]. No. 2, p. 51-71.

Lukáš Kantor. *Bezpečnostní dilema americké protiraketové obrany* [title in translation – *Security Dilemma of the American Ballistic Missile Defense*]. No. 2, p. 27-50.

Jiří Malenovský. *300 let Utrechtské smlouvy a nevyřešený rébus mezinárodněprávního postavení Gibraltaru* [title in translation – *300 Years of the Treaty of Utrecht and the Unsolved Puzzle of the Status of Gibraltar under International Law*]. No. 1, p. 5-26.

Arnošt Novák. *Česká environmentální přímá akce v mezinárodním kontextu* [title in translation – *Czech Environmental Direct Action in an International Context*]. No. 3, p. 81-103.

Miroslav Nožina. *Barma: Na cestě k "asijské demokracii"?* [title in translation – *Burma: On the Road to "Asian Democracy"?*]. No. 2, p. 72-90.

Michal Smetana. *Role jaderných zbraní v bezpečnostní strategii Spojených států ve 21. století* [title in translation – *The Role of Nuclear Weapons in the US Security Strategy for the 21ˢᵗ Century*]. No. 1, p. 27-49.

Robert Stojanov; Barbora Duží. *Migrace jako adaptace na změnu klimatu* [title in translation – *Migration as an Adaptation to Climate Change*]. No. 3, p. 9-31.

Zuzana Trávníčková; Vladimíra Knotková. *Ochrana životního prostředí v Arktidě jako mezinárodní režim* [title in translation – *Environmental Protection in the Arctic as an International Regime*]. No. 3, p. 62-80.

Šárka Waisová. *Od hrozby k příležitosti: Vede nedostatek environmentálních zdrojů ke spolupráci?* [title in translation – *From Threat to Opportunity: Does the Lack of Environmental Resources Lead to Cooperation?*]. No. 3, p. 32-61.

Obchodněprávní revue [Commercial Law Review], Prague: C. H. Beck, 2013, Vol. 5, ISSN: 1803-6554[10]

Pavel Šturma. *Nová společná politika Evropské unie v oblasti mezinárodních investic (uzavírání smluv a rozdělení odpovědnosti mezi EU a členskými státy)* [title in translation – *New Common Policy of the European Union regarding International Investments (Conclusion of Treaties and Allocation of Responsibility between the EU and the Member States)*]. No. 5, p. 120-133.

---

[10] Papers published in Czech. Abstracts regarding the core articles of the individual issues in English, exceptionally in German.

Právník [Title in translation – *The Lawyer*], Prague: Ústav státu a práva Akademie věd České republiky [Institute of State and Law of the Academy of Sciences of the Czech Republic], 2013, Vol. 152, ISSN: 0231-6625[11]
Michal. Davala. *Pozitívne záväzky amerických štátov vo vzťahu k mučeniu* [title in translation – *Positive Obligations of American States in Relation to Torture*]. No. 6, p. 589-610.
Milan Dubovský. *Konanie o pilotnom rozsudku ako zvláštny procesný postup Európskeho súdu pre ľudské práva* [title in translation – *Pilot Judgment Procedure as Special Procedural Approach of the European Court of Human Rights*]. No 10, p. 1013-1028.
Jaroslav Větrovský. *Čl. 31 a 32 Vídeňské úmluvy o smluvním právu: pravidla výkladu mezinárodních smluv v judikatuře Mezinárodního soudního dvora* [title in translation – *Articles 31 and 32 of the Vienna Convention on the Law of Treaties: the International Treaties; Rules of Interpretation in the International Court of Justice's Case Law*]. No. 8, p. 809-825.

Soudní rozhledy [Title in translation – *Court Review*], Prague: C. H. Beck, 2013, Vol. 19, ISSN: 1211-4405[12]
Markéta Lehká. *Zajišťování cizinců správními orgány. Glosa.* [title in translation – *Apprehension of Foreigners by Administrative Authorities. Note*]. No. 9, p. 309-310.

The Lawyer Quarterly, Prague: Ústav státu a práva Akademie věd České republiky] Institute of State and Law of the Academy of Sciences of the Czech Republic], 2013, Vol. III, ISSN: 0231-6625[13]
Josef Blahož. *The Theory of Global Governance, Constitutionalization and Comparative Constitutional Law.* No. 3, p. 195-207.
Jan Malíř. *Judicialization of International Relations: Do International Courts Matter?* No. 3, p. 208-224.
Valentin Alekseevich Ovchinnikov; Jaroslav Valerievich Antonov. *Perceptions of the European Concept of Sovereignty of the Russian Judicial Community: Problems of Implementation of ECHR Decisions in the Russian Federation.* Discussion. No. 3, p. 159-163.

---

[11] Papers published in Czech with abstracts in a foreign language. The abstract is most often in English (exceptionally in German or French).
[12] Papers published in Czech. The contents of the individual issues always provided in German as well. The annotation of the major article of each issue is usually also translated into German.
[13] As subsidiary title to the monthly periodical Právník [in translation – *The Lawyer*], which will be published by the Institute of State and Law of the Academy of Science of the Czech Republic in Czech. Papers published in *The Lawyer Quarterly* are in English, exceptionally in other languages (German for instance); abstracts are in English. For papers published in the monthly periodical "*Právník*" [in translation – *The Lawyer*], see a separate selection of papers listed under the particular periodical.

Other Titles Published in the Czech Republic

Jan Čapek. *Vztah mezi Evropskou úmluvou o lidských právech a jinými mezinárodními smlouvami.* Judikatura a kasuistika [title in translation – *Relation between the European Convention on Human Rights and Other International Treaties. Case Law and Casuistics*]. Soudce [title in translation – The Judge], 2013, Vol. XV, No. 5, p. 29-40, ISSN: 1211-5347.

I.2. [CZE] – [CZECH REPUBLIC] – Selected Titles of Czech Authors Published outside the Czech Republic

Alexander J. Bělohlávek. *Energy Security and Energy Sovereignty from the Investment Protection Perspective: International Law, EU Law and National Policies.* Journal of International Trade and Arbitration Law / Uluslararasi Ticeret ve Tahkim Hukuku Dergisi. 2013, Vol. II, Issue No. 1, p. 3-47.

I.3. [SVK] – [SLOVAK REPUBLIC] – Selected Titles Published in the Slovak Republic

Bulletin slovenskej advokacie [*Bulletin of the Slovak Bar*]**, Bratislava: Slovenská advokátska komora** [*Slovak Bar Association*]**, 2010, Vol. 16, ISSN: 1335-1079.**[14]

Lenka Špiriaková. *Všeobecne k obchodovaniu s ľudmi podľa výsledkov UNODC.* [title in translation – *General Note regarding Human Trafficking According to the UNODC Outcomes*]. No. 5, p. 38-45.

Právny obzor: časopis Ústavu štátu a práva Slovenskej akademie vied, [*Legal Horizon: The Review of the Institute of State and Law of the Slovak Academy of Science*] **Bratislava, 2013, Vol. 96, ISSN: 0032-6984**

J. Handrlica. *Medzinárodná energetická agentúra a jej význam pri harmonizácii administratívnych opatrení vo vzťahu k energetickej bezpečnosti štátu* [title in translation – *International Energy Agency and Its Role in the Harmonisation of Administrative Measures concerning the National Energy Security*]. No. 2, p. 149-164.

M. Hodás. *Vzťah slobody, bezpečnosti a právneho štátu (inter arma silent leges* [title in translation – *Relationship of liberty, security and rule of law (inter arma silent leges)*]. No. 3, p. 201-221.

---

[14] Papers published in Slovak with abstracts in a foreign language. Abstracts in English and in German.

O. Hamuľák. *Suvorenita štátu včera a dnes – k dynamicepojmu a hermeneutickým posunům v jeho chápání* [title in translation – *State Sovereignty Then and Now – On the Dynamics of the Concept and Hermeneutical Shifts in Its Understanding*]. No. 3, p. 222-239.

Ľ. Kukliš. *Test proporcionality a štrukturálne aspekty kolízie základných práv* [title in translation – *The proportionality test and structural aspects of fundamental rights collisions*]. No. 1, p. 50-66.

Justičná revue [*Judicial Revue*], Bratislava: Ministry of Justice Slovak Republic, 2013, Vol. 65, ISSN: 1335-6461[15]

M. Dubovský; *K implementácii rozsudkov Európskeho súdu pre ľudské práva in meritum* [title in translation – *Regarding the Implementation of the Merits of Judgments Rendered by the European Court of Human Rights*]. Justičná revue, 2013, Vol. 65, No. 1, p. 91-106. ISSN: 1335-6461.

Bulletin slovenskej advokacie [*Bulletin of the Slovak Bar*], Bratislava: Slovenská advokátska komora [*Slovak Bar Association*], 2010, Vol. 16, ISSN: 1335-1079.[16]

Marta Halajová. *Problematika žločinov podľa medzinárodného práva* [title in translation – *The Issue of Crimes under International Law*]. Bulletin slovenskej advokácie. Bratislava: Slovenská advokátska komora [Slovak Bar Association], 2013, Vol XIX, No. 1-2, p. 10-18. ISSN: 1335-1079.

II. (Private) International Law, European Private International Law and Legal Relations in Foreign Trade Relations, Including International Arbitration and Other Private-law Areas with Transnational Dimensions

II.1. [CZE] – [CZECH REPUBLIC] – Titles Published within the Czech Republic

Monographs, Collections and Conference Proceedings

Monika Pauknerová. *Evropské mezinárodní právo soukromé* [title in translation – *European Private International Law*]. 2nd edition. Prague : C. H. Beck, 2013.

---

[15] Papers published in Czech. Abstracts in English.
[16] Papers published in Slovak with abstracts in a foreign language. Abstracts in English and in German.

Monika Pauknerová; Naděžda Rozehnalová; M. Zavadilová et al. *Zákon o mezinárodním právu soukromém. Komentář* [title in translation – *Act on Private International Law. Commentary*]. Prague : Wolters Kluwer, 2013.

Naděžda Rozehnalová; Jiří Valdhans; Klára Drličková; Tereza Kyselovská. *Mezinárodní právo soukromé Evropské unie* [title in translation – *Conflict-of-Laws of the European Union*]. Praha [Prague / Czech Republic] : Wolters Kluwer ČR, 2013. ISBN: 978-80-7478-016-5 (Hardcopy) / 978-80-7478-003-5 (ePublication).

Obchodněprávní revue [Commercial Law Review], Prague: C. H. Beck, 2013, Vol. 5, ISSN: 1803-6554[17]

Jiří Lojda. *Nákladní list a elektronický nákladní list podle Úmluvy CMR* [title in translation – *Consignment Note and Electronic Consignment Note under the CMR Convention*]. No. 5, p. 157-159.

Filip Plašil; Luboš Kliment. *Spory z mezinárodní přepravy zboží a místní příslušnost vnitrostátních soudů* [title in translation – *Disputes from International Carriage of Goods and Territorial Jurisdiction of National Courts*]. No. 11-12, p. 311-313.

Obchodní právo [Commercial Law], Prague: Prospektrum, 2013, Vol. 21, ISSN: 1210-8278[18]

Alexander J. Bělohlávek; Vít Horáček. *Nová pravidla o rozhodčím řízení Mezinárodního rozhodčího soudu ICC* [title in translation – *New Rules of the ICC International Court of Arbitration*]. No. 1, p. 10-19.

Daniel Dressler. Vstup na čínský trh prostřednictvím podniku plně vlastněného zahraničním subjektem [Chinese Market Entry Via WFOE]. No. 6, p. 221-227.

Zdeněk Kučera. *Rekodifikace českého mezinárodního práva soukromého* [title in translation – *Czech Recodification of Private International Law*]. No. 4, p. 122-131.

Právní rozhledy [Law Review], Prague: C. H. Beck, 2013, Vol. 23, ISSN: 1210-6410[19]

Petr Bříza. *Nový český zákon o mezinárodním právu soukromém v kontextu práva EU a mezinárodních smluv* [title in translation – *New Czech Code on Private International Law in the Context of EU Law and International Treaties*]. No. 17, p. 580-589.

---

[17] Papers published in Czech. Abstracts in English, exceptionally in German.
[18] Papers published in Czech. Abstracts in English.
[19] Papers published in Czech.

Tomáš Břicháček. *Změny v obecném režimu uznávání a výkonu soudních rozhodnutí v civilních věcech v EU* [title in translation – *Changes in the General System of Recognition and Enforcement of Court Decisions in Civil Matters in the EU*]. No. 5, p. 165-171.

Monika Pauknerová; M. *Pfeiffer. Mezinárodní mediace a české právo* [title in translation – *International Mediation and Czech Law*]. No. 1, p. 21-25.

Právník [Title in translation – *The Lawyer*], Prague: Ústav státu a práva Akademie věd České republiky] Institute of State and Law of the Academy of Sciences of the Czech Republic], 2013, Vol. 152, ISSN: 0231-6625[20]

Martin Štefko. Právo vyslat cizince na pracovní cestu v rámci České republiky? [title in translation – *The Right to Send an Employee on a Business Trip within the Czech Republic?*]. No 10, p. 1045-1050.

Soudní rozhledy [Title in translation – *Court Review*], Prague: C. H. Beck, 2013, Vol. 19, ISSN: 1211-4405[21]

František Balák. *"Obvyklé bydliště" podle čl. 8 odst. 1 nařízení Rady ES č. 2201/2003 : usnesení NS z 27. 9. 2011, sp. zn. 30 Cdo 2244/2011* [Titul v překladu – *"Habitual Residence" pursuant to Article 8(1) of Regulation EC No. 2201/2003: Resolution of the Supreme Court of 27 September 2011, docket 30 Cdo 2244/2011*] No. 3, sp 96-98.

Magdalena Pfeiffer. *Obvyklý pobyt v evropském rodinném právu* [Titul v překladu – *Habitual Residence in the European Family Law*] No. 3, sp 87-89.

The Lawyer Quarterly, Prague: Ústav státu a práva Akademie věd České republiky] Institute of State and Law of the Academy of Sciences of the Czech Republic], 2012, Vol. II, ISSN: 0231-6625[22]

Lukáš Klee. *Delivery Methods under FIDIC Forms of Contract.* No. 2, p. 164-168.

---

[20] Papers published in Czech with abstracts in a foreign language. The abstract is most often in English (exceptionally in German or French).

[21] Papers published in Czech. The contents of the individual issues always provided in German as well. The annotation of the major article of each issue is usually also translated into German.

[22] As subsidiary title to the monthly periodical Právník [in translation – *The Lawyer*], which will be published by the Institute of State and Law of the Academy of Science of the Czech Republic in Czech. Papers published in *The Lawyer Quarterly* are in English, exceptionally in other languages (German for instance); abstracts are in English. For papers published in the monthly periodical "*Právník*" [in translation – *The Lawyer*], see a separate selection of papers listed under the particular periodical.

Czech Yearbook of International Law

Other Publications

Sjev van Erp. *Nové nařízení o dědictví – je zapotřebí přehodnotit pravidlo lex rei sitae?* [title in translation – *New Regulation on Inheritance – Is It Necessary to Review the Lex Rei Sitae Rule?*] *Ad Notam.* Prague: Chamber of Public Notaries Czech Republic, 2013, No. 2, p. 7-8, ISSN: 1211-0558.

Martina Kondrová. *Osvědčení vydávaná notářem při přeshraničních přeměnách* [title in translation – *Notary Certificates in Cross-Border Company Transformations*]. *Ad Notam.* Prague: Chamber of Public Notaries Czech Republic, 2013, No. 2, p. 14-19, ISSN: 1211-0558.

Petr Trebatický. *Určení pravomoci (příslušnosti) soudů České republiky ve sporech o zaplacení směnky s mezinárodním prvkem a některé jeho důsledky* [title in translation – *Determination of the Jurisdiction of Czech Courts in Disputes over the Payment of Promissory Notes and Bills of Exchange with an International Dimension and Selected Consequences Thereof*]. Soudce [title in translation – The Judge]: Union of Judges. 5, p. 6-16, ISSN: 1211-5347.

II.2. [CZE] – [CZECH REPUBLIC] – Selected Titles of Czech Authors Published outside the Czech Republic

Alexander J. Bělohlávek. *Arbitration Law of Czech Republic: Practice & Procedure.* Hungtington, New York : JurisNet LLC, 2013, 2270 p. ISBN: 978-1-937518-18-9.

Alexander J. Bělohlávek. *Szwajcarska regulacja wszkazania prawa właściwego dla zobowiązań umownych i jej znaczenie dla prawa Unii Europejskiej* [title in translation – *The Swiss Regulation on the Law Applicable to Contractual Obligations and Its Significancy for the EU Law*]. **Kwartalnik prawa prywatnego** [title in translation – **The Private Law Quarterly**]. Kraków [Poland], 2013, Vol. XXII, Issue No. 2, p. 349-378, ISSN: 1230-7173.[23]

Petr Dobiáš. *Die Neuregelung des Versicherungsrechts im reformierten tschechischen ZGB* [title in translation – *New Rules on Insurance Law in the Recodified Czech Civil Code*]. VersRAI. 2013, No. 1, p. 5-11.[24]

Monika Pauknerová; Jan Brodec; M. Pfeiffer. **Mediation in the Czech Republic**, In: J. L. Igleias; G. Palao (eds.) **Civil and Commercial Mediation in Europe**. Intersentia, 2012, p. 97-130.

414

[23] Original language: Polish, summary in English.
[24] Published in German language.

Monika Pauknerová. **EU Regulations and International Conventions – Shifts in Time**. In: **Between Brussels and The Hague. Essays on the International and Regional Unification of Private International Law**. Barcelona, 2013, p. 671-684.

Monika Pauknerová. **Defendants with Unknown Address**. In: **Festschrift Michael Bogdan**. Lund, 2013, p. 411-424.

II.3. [SVK] – [SLOVAK REPUBLIC] – Selected Titles Published in the Slovak Republic

Monika Jurčová. Jozef Štefanko (eds.) *Proposal for a Regulation on a Common European Sales Law: A New Legal Regime for Domestic and Cross-Border Trade*. Trnava: Trnava University, Law Faculty, Department of Civil and Commercial Law, 2013 ISBN: 978-80-8082-618-5.[25]

Bulletin slovenskej advokacie [*Bulletin of the Slovak Bar*], **Bratislava: Slovenská advokátska komora** [*Slovak Bar Association*], **2010, Vol. 16, ISSN: 1335-1079.**[26]

    Martin Husár. *Cenová doložka* [title in translation – *Price Clause*]. No. 4.

Justičná revue [*Judicial Revue*], **Bratislava : Ministry of Justice Slovak Republic, 2013, Vol. 65, ISSN: 1335-6461**[27]

Katarína Chovancová; *Res iudicata medzinárodného rozhodcovského rozsudku* [title in translation – *Res Judicata with Respect to an International Arbitral Award*]. Justičná revue, 2013, Vol. 65, No. 1, p. 1-16. ISSN: 1335-6461.

Ľ. Jakubíková. Problematika kontradiktórnosti konania z pohľadu rôznych právnych systémov [title in translation – *The Issue of Adversary Proceedings from the Perspective of Various Legal Systems*]. Justičná revue, 2013, Vol. 65, No. 1, p. 44-53. ISSN: 1335-6461.

---

[25]   Published in English.
[26]   Papers published in Slovak with abstracts in a foreign language. Abstracts in English and in German.
[27]   Papers published in Czech. Abstracts in English.

III. EU Law (general, not classified under Chapter I.1 or I.2 above)

III.1. [CZE] – [CZECH REPUBLIC] – Titles Published within the Czech Republic

Monographs, Collections and Conference Proceedings

Rastislav Funta; Štefan Nebeský. Filip Juriš. *Európske právo – Otázky a odpovede / European Law – Questions and Answers*. Brno : Tribun EU, 2013, 221 p. ISBN: 978-80-263-0371-8.

Naděžda Rozehnalová; Jiří Valdhans; Klára Drličková; Tereza Kyselovská. *Mezinárodní právo soukromé Evropské unie* [title in translation – *Conflict-of-Laws of the European Union*]. Praha [Prague / Czech Republic] : Wolters Kluwer ČR, 2013. ISBN: 978-80-7478-016-5 (Hardcopy) / 978-80-7478-003-5 (ePublication).

Markéta Selucká et al. *Koupě a prodej. Nový občanský zákoník. Společná evropská právní úprava prodeje* [title in translation – *Purchase and Sale. The New Civil Code. Common European Sales Law*]. Praha: C. H. Beck, 2013.

The Lawyer Quarterly, Prague: Ústav státu a práva Akademie věd České republiky [Institute of State and Law of the Academy of Sciences of the Czech Republic], 2012, Vol. II, ISSN: 0231-6625[28]
Eva Indruchová. *European Union Member States outside the Euro Area: Their Legal Status and Approach towards the Euro*. No. 3, p. 225-234.

Obchodněprávní revue [Commercial Law Review], Prague: C. H. Beck, 2013 Vol. 5 ISSN: 1803-6554[29]
Tomáš Břicháček. *K návrhu směrnice o zastoupení žen ve vedení společností* [title in translation – *About the Proposal for a Directive regarding the Representation of Women on Boards*]. No. 5, p. 133-140.
Radek Jurčík. *Nové zadávací směrnice v Evropské unii – vývoj, očekávané přijetí a hlavní změny* [title in translation – *New Procurement Directives in the European Union – Developments, Expected Adoption and Crucial Changes*]. No. 6, p. 164-168.

---

[28] As subsidiary title to the monthly periodical Právník [in translation – *The Lawyer*], which will be published by the Institute of State and Law of the Academy of Science of the Czech Republic in Czech. Papers published in *The Lawyer Quarterly* are in English, exceptionally in other languages (German for instance); abstracts are in English. For papers published in the monthly periodical "*Právník*" [in translation – *The Lawyer*], see a separate selection of papers listed under the particular periodical.
[29] Papers published in Czech. Abstracts in English, exceptionally in German.

Peter Mišúr. Evropská komise předložila přezkum směrnice o nekalých obchodních praktikách [title in translation – *The European Commission Submitted a Review of the Unfair Commercial Practices Directive*]. No. 5, p. 148-.

Obchodní právo [Commercial Law], Prague: Prospektrum, 2013, Vol. 21, ISSN: 1210-8278[30]
Miluše Hrnčiříková; Filip Černý; Jan Havlíček. *Několik zamyšlení nad společnou evropskou úpravou prodeje* [title in translation – *Few Thourghts on the New Common European Sales Law*]. No. 2, p. 54-63.

Právník [Title in translation – *The Lawyer*], Prague: Ústav státu a práva Akademie věd České republiky [Institute of State and Law of the Academy of Sciences of the Czech Republic], 2013, Vol. 152, ISSN: 0231-6625[31]
Jan Exner. Sportovní národnost ve světle práva Evropské unie [title in translation – Nationality in Sport in the Light of the EU Law]. No. 10, p. 1029-1044.
Jakub Handrlica. *55 let evropské integrace v oblasti mírového využívání jaderné energie: vývoj, současnost a perspektivy právního řádu z Euroatomu* [title in translation – *55 years of European Integration in the Area of Peaceful Use of Nuclear Energy: Developments, Current Status and Perspectives of the Euratom Legal Rules*]. No 9, p. 895-913.
Pavel Svoboda. *Přidružení k Evropské unii po Lisabonské smlouvě* [title in translation – *Accession to the European Union after the Lisbon Treaty*]. No. 7, p. 641-663

Právní rozhledy [*Law Review*], Prague: C. H. Beck, 2012, Vol. 20, ISSN: 1210-6410[32]
Michal Bobek. Kam až sahá právo EU? K věcnému aplikačnímu rámci unijního práva v členských státech [title in translation – *How Far Does the EU Law Reach? Regarding the Substantive Framework of Application of the EU Law in the Member States*]. No. 18, p. 611-618.
Martin Lyčka. *Právní ochrana zaměstnanců v případě převodu podniků – pohled Soudního dvora EU* [title in translation – *Legal Protection of Employees in the Transfer of Undertakings – from the Perspective of the EU Court of Justice*]. No. 10, p. 354-361.
Jindřich Neubauer. Historicky první sankce vůči České republice za nerespektování rozsudku Soudního dvora EU [title in translation –

---

[30] Papers published in Czech. Abstracts in English.
[31] Papers published in Czech with abstracts in a foreign language. The abstract is most often in English (exceptionally in German or French).
[32] Papers published in Czech.

First Penalties in History Imposed on the Czech Republic for Failure to Honour a Judgment of the EU Court of Justice]. No. 18, p. 626-630.

The Lawyer Quarterly, Prague: Ústav státu a práva Akademie věd České republiky [Institute of State and Law of the Academy of Sciences of the Czech Republic], Supplement to Journal Právník [The Lawyer], 2012, Vol. 151, ISSN: 0231-6625[33]

Jan Durica. *Directive on the Retention of Data on Electronic Communication in the Rulings of the Constitutional Courts of EU Member States and Efforts for Its Renewed Implementation*. No. 3, p. 143-158.

David Elischer. *Age Discrimination in the Czech and European Context – Compensation of Non-pecuniary Damage*. No. 3, p. 128-142.

Martin Kusák; Lenka Pítrová; Hana Bambasová; Jan Durica; David Elischer; Olga Francová. *Legal Aspects of the Treaty on Stability, Coordination and Legal Governance in the Economic and Monetary Union*. No. 2, p. 102-127.

Právník [Title in translation – *The Lawyer*], Prague: Ústav státu a práva Akademie věd České republiky] [Institute of State and Law of the Academy of Sciences of the Czech Republic], 2013, Vol. 152, ISSN: 0231-6625[34]

Jan Malíř. *Unijní právo veřejných podpor ve finanční krizi: od existenční krize k modernizaci?* [title in translation – *EU State Aid Law in the Financial Crisis: from an Existential Crisis to Modernization?*]. No. 8, p. 773-789.

Other Publications

Jan Čapek. *Adopce z pohledu Evropy* [title in translation – *Adoption from the European Perspective*]. Rodinné listy, 2013, Vol. II, No. 5, p. 12-17, ISSN: 1805-0824.

III.2. [SVK] – [SLOVAK REPUBLIC]

Justičná revue [*Judicial Revue*], Bratislava: Ministry of Justice Slovak Republic, 2013, Vol. 65, ISSN: 1335-6461[35]

M. Jánošíková; *A čo keď (ne)predloží? (Možnosti obrany proti predloženiu, prípadne nepredloženiu prejudiciálnej otázky Súdnemu dvoru*

---

[33] Papers published in English.

[34] Papers published in Czech with abstracts in a foreign language. The abstract is most often in English (exceptionally in German or French).

[35] Papers published in Czech. Abstracts in English.

Európskej únie) [title in translation – *And What if They Do (Not) Refer? (Potential Defence against Reference or Failure to Make a Reference for a Preliminary Ruling to the Court of Justice of the European Union)*]. Justičná revue, No. 1, p. 17-30.

P. Kotira. *Smerovanie vývoja pracovných práv nelegálne pracujúcich migrantov z tretích krajín v rámci politiky EÚ* [title in translation – *Trends in the Development of Employment Rights of Illegally Working Migrants from Third Countries under the EU Policy*]. Justičná revue, No. 1, p. 91-106.

Právny obzor: časopis Ústavu štátu a práva Slovenskej akademie vied, *[Legal Horizon: The Review of the Institute of State and Law of the Slovak Academy of Science]* **Bratislava, 2013, Vol. 96, ISSN: 0032-6984**

M. Hodás. *Problematika názvov právnych predpisov a názvov právnych aktov Európskej únie* [title in translation – *The issue of titles of the bills and of the legal acts of the European Union*]. NO. 2, p. 137-148.

L. Klimek; R. Klimek. *Genéza vzájomného uznávania justičných rozhodnutí v trestných veciach v EU* [title in translation – *Genesis of the mutual recognition of judicial decisions in criminal matters in the EU*]. No. 3, p. 271-292.

Important Web Sites

http://www.czechyearbook.org.

Czech Yearbook of International Law® and Czech (& Central European) Yearbook of Arbitration®

The web site is currently available in sixteen languages: English, Bulgarian, Czech, Chinese, Japanese, Korean, Hungarian, German, Polish, Romanian, Russian, Portuguese, Slovenian, Spanish, Ukrainian, Vietnamese. This web site allows access to the annotations of all core articles and to information about the authors of these articles as well as to the entire remaining contents (except core articles) of both yearbooks (CYIL and CYArb®).

I. [CZE] – [CZECH REPUBLIC]

- http://www.cnb.cz.
  Česká národní banka (Czech National Bank as the Central bank of the Czech Republic).[36]

- http://www.compet.cz.
  Office for the protection of competition.[37]

- http://www.concourt.cz.
  The Constitutional Court of the Czech Republic.[38]

- http://www.csesp.cz.
  Czech Society for European and Comparative Law.[39]

- http://www.csmp-csil.org.
  The Czech Society of International Law.[40]

- http://www.czech.cz.
  Portal "Hello Czech Republic". Basic information about the Czech Republic and news interesting for foreigners. Rather a promotional portal.[41]

- http://www.czso.cz.
  Czech Statistical Office.[42]

- http://dtjvcnsp.org.
  Česko-německý spolek právníků. [Czech-German Lawyers Association]. Deutsch-Tschechische Juristenvereinigung e.V.[43]

- http:// ekf.vsb.cz.
  Faculty of Economics, VŠB Technical University of Ostrava.[44]

---

[36] Web site available in English and Czech.
[37] Web site available in English and Czech. Basic laws and regulations on the protection of competition in the Czech Republic are also available at the web site, both in Czech and in English (unofficial translation).
[38] Web site available in English and Czech. Part of the (significant) case law also available in English.
[39] Web site available in English and Czech.
[40] Web site available in Czech. In English only a brief summary of the webpages.
[41] Web site available in English, Czech, French, German, Russian and Spanish.
[42] Web site available in English and Czech.
[43] Web site available in German.
[44] Web site available in English and Czech. Some information (regarding post-graduate studies) also available in German. Department of Law see http://en.ekf.vsb.cz/information-about/departments/structure/departments/dept-119 (in English).

- http://www.hrad.cz.[45]
  Web site of the Office of the President of the Czech Republic.

- http://www.icc-cr.cz.
  ICC National Committee Czech Republic

- http://www.iir.cz.
  Institute of International Relations Prague.[46]

- http://www.ilaw.cas.cz.
  Ústav státu a práva Akademie věd ČR, v.v.i. [Institute of State and Law of the Academy of Sciences of the Czech Republic][47]

- http://www.jednotaceskychpravniku.cz.
  Jednota českých právníků [Czech Lawyers Union]

- http://justice.cz.
  Czech justice portal including both courts and the Ministry of Justice, prosecution departments, Judicial Academy, Institute of Criminology and Social Prevention, as well as the Probation and Mediation Service and the Prison Service. [48]

- http://www.law.muni.cz.
  Faculty of Law, Masaryk University, Brno.[49]

- http://www.mzv.cz.
  Ministry of Foreign Affairs of the Czech Republic.[50]

- http://www.nsoud.cz.
  The Supreme Court of the Czech Republic.[51]

- http://www.nssoud.cz.
  The Supreme Administrative Court of the Czech Republic.[52]

- http://www.ochrance.cz.
  Public Defender of Rights (Ombudsman).[53]

---

[45] Web site available in English and Czech. This web site also allows access to the personal webpage of the President of the Czech Republic.
[46] Web site available in English and Czech. This Institute was founded by the Ministry of Foreign Affairs of the Czech Republic.
[47] Web site available in English and Czech.
[48] Web site available in Czech. The individual web sites of the institutions covered by this portal also contain pages or summary information in English.
[49] Web site available in English and Czech.
[50] Web site available in Czech. Important information from this portal also available in English.
[51] Web site available in Czech. Some basic information also in English and French.
[52] Web site available in English and Czech.
[53] Web site available in English and Czech.

- http://www.ok.cz/iksp/en/aboutus.html.
  Institute of Criminology and Social Prevention.[54]

- http://portal.gov.cz.
  Portal of the Public Administration.[55] This web site allows access to the web sites of most supreme public administration authorities (including ministries).

- http://www.prf.cuni.cz.
  Faculty of Law, Charles University in Prague.[56]

- http://www.psp.cz.
  Parliament of the Czech Republic. Chamber of Deputies.[57]

- http://www.senat.cz.
  Parliament of the Czech Republic. Senate.[58]

- http://www.society.cz/wordpress/#awp.
  Common Law Society.[59]

- http://www.soud.cz.
  Arbitration Court attached to the Economic Chamber of the Czech Republic and Agricultural Chamber of the Czech Republic.[60]

- http://www.umpod.cz.
  Office for International Legal Protection of Children.[61]

- http://www.upol.cz/fakulty/pf/.
  Faculty of Law. Palacký University, Olomouc.

- http://www.vse.cz.
  The University of Economics, Prague.[62]

- http://www.zcu.cz/fpr/.
  Faculty of Law, Western Bohemia University in Pilsen.[63]

---

[54] Web site available in English and Czech.
[55] Web site available in English and Czech.
[56] Web site available in Czech. Basic information available in English.
[57] Web site available in English and Czech.
[58] Web site available in English and Czech.
[59] Web site available in Czech.
[60] Web site available in English, Czech, German and Russian.
[61] The Office is the Central authority responsible for protection of children in civil matters having cross-border implications. Web site available in English and Czech.
[62] Web site available in English and Czech.

Czech Yearbook of International Law

II.   [SVK] – [SLOVAK REPUBLIC]

- http://www.concourt.sk.
  Constitutional Court of the Slovak Republic.[64]

- http://www.flaw.uniba.sk.
  Faculty of Law, Comenius University in Bratislava (SVK).[65]

- http://iuridica.truni.sk.
  Faculty of Law. Trnava University in Trnava (SVK).[66]

- http://www.justice.gov.sk.
  Ministry of Justice of the Slovak Republic.[67]

- http://www.nbs.sk.
  Národná banka Slovenska (National Bank of Slovakia as the Central bank of Slovak Republic).[68]

- http://www.nrsr.sk.
  National Council of the Slovak Republic (*Slovak Parliament*).[69]

- http://www.prf.umb.sk.
  Faculty of Law. Matej Bel University, Banská Bystrica (SVK).

- http://www.prezident.sk.
  President of the Slovak Republic and Office of the President (SVK).[70]

- http://www.uninova.sk/pf_bvsp/src_angl/index.php.
  Faculty of Law, Pan European University (SVK).[71]

- http://www.upjs.sk/pravnicka-fakulta.
  Faculty of Law, Pavol Jozef Šafárik University in Košice (SVK).[72]

- http://www.usap.sav.sk.
  Institute of State and Law, Slovak Academy of Science.[73]

---

[63]   Web site available in Czech.
[64]   Web site available in English and Slovak.
[65]   Web site available in English and Slovak.
[66]   Web site available in English and Slovak.
[67]   Web site available in English and Slovak. This web site also allows access to the following portals: Courts, Slovak Agent before the European Court for Human Rights, Slovak Agent before the Court of Justice of the European Union, The Judicial Academy.
[68]   Web site available in English and Slovak.
[69]   Web site available in English, French, German and Slovak.
[70]   Web site available in English and Slovak.
[71]   Web site available in English, German and Slovak.
[72]   Web site available in English and Slovak.
[73]   Web site available in Slovak.

Index

CALL FOR PAPERS FOR VOLUMES 2015/2016/2017

Did you find the articles in the fifth volume of CYIL interesting?
Would you like to react to a current article
or contribute to future volumes?

We are seeking authors for both
the Czech Yearbook on International Law® and the
Czech (& Central European) Yearbook of Arbitration®.

The general topics for the 2015/2016/2017 volumes are the following:

CYIL 2015

International Transportation

CYArb® 2015

*Interaction of Arbitration
(Arbitrators) and Courts*

CYIL 2016

International Dispute Resolution

CYArb® 2016

*Rights and Duties of Parties in
Arbitration*

CYIL 2017

*Application and Interpretation of
International Treaties*

CYArb® 2017

Conduct of Arbitration

More general and contact information available at:

www.czechyearbook.org

CYIL – Czech Yearbook of International Law®, 2015
International Transportation

International transportation lies at the heart of international business, because no business or even country is self-sufficient. Therefore, this topic is all encompassing and covers as much issues of local or domestic importance as it does of global importance. From this point of view, the difficulties – to name just a few – associated with transportation of freight or passengers, of import/export customs or of free trade unions and international organizations, fall under the scope of the topic. However, we don't want to limit the breadth of authors' possible interpretation of the theme. Therefore, articles covering the topic from comparative domestic/international perspectives are also very welcome.

CYArb® – Czech (& Central European) Yearbook of Arbitration®, 2015
Interaction of Arbitration (Arbitrators) and Courts

Arbitration proceedings are not self-sustaining. Even if the arbitration lies outside the national court system at the place of arbitration, the local courts play an important role as much during the arbitral proceedings, as they do after the proceedings end. Therefore, this topic invites authors to undertake a full spectrum analysis of the interaction of arbitral tribunals and local courts during enforcement or annulment arbitral proceedings, when the local courts execute their supportive and controlling functions as well as after the arbitral proceedings have come to an end. Again, comparative analyses are very much welcomed, whether they are of the interaction between national arbitration laws with international applicable standards or between international rules. Because this is a general topic, any type of arbitral proceedings (commercial, consumer, investment, sport...) may be covered.

CYIL – Czech Yearbook of International Law®, 2016
International Dispute Resolution

Papers published in the previous editions of the CYIL focused primarily on issues of substantive law. The 2016 volume aims to concentrate on proceedings with an international dimension and the specific features thereof in terms of private law and public law. Hence, our attention will be devoted to purely private disputes, disputes involving states and state agencies, as well as disputes which are the exclusive domain of public law, primarily public international law. Papers should deal with procedural issues, despite the fact that this edition of our yearbook will not be limited to procedural matters. We therefore aim to focus also on the specifics of the application of substantive law in proceedings with an international dimension, the issue of personal status (personal law), etc. We intend to identify and analyse the specific features of proceedings regarding international disputes as well as the current trends in conflict resolution.

CYArb® – Czech (& Central European) Yearbook of Arbitration®, 2016
Rights and Duties of Parties in Arbitration

The 2016 volume of the CYArb® yearbook will concentrate on the status of parties in arbitration, together with the status of the other individuals and entities involved in the proceedings (except arbitrators), such as third parties in the proceedings (intervenor, *amicus curiae*). Papers dealing with the special status of expert witnesses and witnesses among others, primarily as regards their connection to the parties and the rights and duties of the parties, will also be appreciated. However, our editorial team is also expecting essays from academicians as well as practitioners regarding parties' counsels, including their special status in arbitration as opposed to litigation (court proceedings) and as opposed to proceedings conducted by other public authorities.

CYIL – Czech Yearbook of International Law®, 2017
Application and Interpretation of International Treaties

The editorial team and the publisher have intentionally chosen a very broad topic. The application and interpretation of international treaties is dealt with in many publications and within the voluminous international and national case law. Nonetheless, since the topic continues to generate much controversy, an open discussion is indispensable. Our objective is to analyse the day-to-day application of international treaties from the procedural perspective (in various private- and public-law proceedings), in contractual practice and elsewhere. We also welcome articles focusing on international treaties in connection with the rules applied in regional integration organizations, including the European Union, in connection with the interpretation practice employed by international organizations and others.

CYArb® – Czech (& Central European) Yearbook of Arbitration®, 2017
Conduct of Arbitration

This volume of the CYArb® will be devoted to the methods and procedures of hearing disputes, including the examination of evidence. Our aim is to focus primarily but not exclusively on procedural differences between arbitration and litigation. The nature and, above all, the effects of arbitral awards bring arbitration closer to decisions rendered by courts and other public authorities. However, the contractual autonomy of the parties and arbitrators and the variability of the standards used in arbitration offer a great potential that is not always fully exploited. The team of authors therefore wishes to analyse this autonomy and the flexibility of arbitration and include this potential in the broader discussion introduced in the seventh volume of the CYArb®.